D0132059

MySQL 5 Certification Study Guide

Paul DuBois, Stefan Hinz, and Carsten Pedersen

MySQL Press

800 East 96th Street, Indianapolis, Indiana 46240 USA

MySQL 5 Certification Study Guide

Copyright © 2006 by Pearson Education

All rights reserved. No part of this book shall be reproduced, stored in a retrieval system, or transmitted by any means, electronic, mechanical, photocopying, recording, or otherwise, without written permission from the publisher. No patent liability is assumed with respect to the use of the information contained herein. Although every precaution has been taken in the preparation of this book, the publisher and author assume no responsibility for errors or omissions. Nor is any liability assumed for damages resulting from the use of the information contained herein.

International Standard Book Number: 0-672-32812-7

Library of Congress Catalog Card Number: 2005902140

Printed in the United States of America

First Printing: August 2005

08 07 06 05   4 3 2 1

Trademarks

All terms mentioned in this book that are known to be trademarks or service marks have been appropriately capitalized. Pearson Education cannot attest to the accuracy of this information. Use of a term in this book should not be regarded as affecting the validity of any trademark or service mark.

Warning and Disclaimer

Every effort has been made to make this book as complete and as accurate as possible, but no warranty or fitness is implied. The information provided is on an "as is" basis.

Bulk Sales

Pearson Education offers excellent discounts on this book when ordered in quantity for bulk purchases or special sales. For more information, please contact

U.S. Corporate and Government Sales
1-800-382-3419
corpsales@pearsontechgroup.com

For sales outside of the U.S., please contact

International Sales
international@pearsoned.com

MySQL® 5
Certification
Study Guide

ASSOCIATE PUBLISHER	MANAGING EDITOR	INDEXER	DESIGNER
Mark Taber	Charlotte Clapp	Ken Johnson	Gary Adair
ACQUISITIONS EDITOR	**PROJECT EDITOR**	**TECHNICAL EDITOR**	**PAGE LAYOUT**
Shelley Johnston	George E. Nedeff	MySQL AB	Brad Chinn
DEVELOPMENT EDITOR	**COPY EDITOR**	**PUBLISHING COORDINATOR**	Toi Davis
Damon Jordan	Mike Henry	Vanessa Evans	

MySQL® **Press** is the exclusive publisher of technology books and materials that have been authorized by MySQL AB. MySQL Press books are written and reviewed by the world's leading authorities on MySQL technologies, and are edited, produced, and distributed by the Que/Sams Publishing group of Pearson Education, the worldwide leader in integrated education and computer technology publishing. For more information on MySQL Press and MySQL Press books, please go to **www.mysqlpress.com**.

MYSQL HQ
MySQL AB
Bangårdsgatan 8
S-753 20 Uppsala
Sweden

UNITED STATES
MySQL Inc.
2510 Fairview Avenue East
Seattle, WA 98102
USA

GERMANY, AUSTRIA AND SWITZERLAND
MySQL GmbH
Schlosserstraße 4
D-72622 Nürtingen
Germany

FINLAND
MySQL Finland Oy
Tekniikantie 21
FIN-02150 Espoo
Finland

FRANCE
MySQL AB (France)
123, rue du Faubourg St. Antoine
75011, Paris
France

MySQL® **AB** develops, markets, and supports a family of high-performance, affordable database servers and tools. MySQL AB is the sole owner of the MySQL server source code, the MySQL trademark, and the mysql.com domain. For information on MySQL AB and MySQL AB products, please go to **www.mysql.com** or the following areas of the MySQL Web site:

- Training information: **www.mysql.com/training**

- Support services: **www.mysql.com/support**

- Consulting services: **www.mysql.com/consulting**

Contents at a Glance

MySQL DBA Exams

Table of Contents

MySQL Developer Exams

MySQL Developer I Exam

MySQL Developer II Exam

MySQL DBA Exams

MySQL DBA I Exam

Foreword

For the past many years, the MySQL® Relational Database Management System has been the most widely adopted Open Source database system in the world. With the release of MySQL version 5.0, adoption of MySQL into the enterprise sector of companies is certain to grow even faster than ever before. When the first edition of the *MySQL Certification Study Guide* was published in April 2004, we noted how MySQL adoption had grown to an estimated 4 million installations. At the time of writing, that estimate has risen to more than 6 million—and by the time you read this, who knows?

With that kind of adoption rate, the need for qualified personnel to write applications for, and to manage, MySQL installations increases dramatically. Not only will many more companies be moving to MySQL; many companies that already employ MySQL will be using it in larger and larger parts of their organizations, perhaps to support new functionality, perhaps to replace legacy systems.

Whether you are new to MySQL certification, know a little bit about it, or already hold the Core or Professional certification titles, you should know that many changes are taking place in the transition from the version 4.0/4.1 exams to the version 5.0 exams.

When we launched the MySQL Certification program in late 2002, two exams gave us ample opportunity to test on most, if not all, of the important bits of the MySQL universe. When MySQL 4.1 came out, a small—but significant—set of features was added: prepared statements, better character set support, subqueries, and more. The additional feature list of MySQL version 5.0 is much too long to mention here. Suffice to say, there is no way we could pack all of this into just two exams, and so we have had to revisit and revise the structure of the certification and the exams.

Another reason to revisit the exam structure are the changes that have evolved among MySQL users in the last few years. When the certification program was launched, a common situation in a company using MySQL was that those who wrote application programs were also the ones doing the database administration. This is of course still the case in many places, but as MySQL adoption grows, a trend of increasing specialization is becoming apparent. Today, there is often a more clear-cut split between those who do application development, and those who do database administration. All in all, this gave us another reason to look into the existing certification exam structure and consider whether it meets the needs of our users.

Finally, there was a small, but to many certification candidates very annoying, thing about the MySQL Certification program: The titles of "Core" and "Professional" do not really convey what the certified user *does* as part of his or her workday. Moreover, what do you *call* someone that is Core certified? It's not exactly easy to come up with a snappy title to go along with that. Those issues, too, have been addressed by the new exam layout.

So here is what all of those changes amount to for the MySQL version 5.0 exams:

- There are still two levels of certification to pass, but they are now called *Developer* and *Database Administrator* (DBA) certifications.

- The titles that belong with the two certification levels will be *Certified MySQL Developer* (CMDEV) and *Certified MySQL Database Administrator* (CMDBA), respectively.

- For the 4.x exams, having the Core certification was a prerequisite to attaining the Professional certification. There is no longer such a prerequisite requirement.

- There will be two exams per certification level. If you wish to attain both titles, you will need to pass four exams.

The *MySQL Developer* Certification ensures that the candidate knows and is able to make use of all the features of MySQL that are needed to develop and maintain applications that use MySQL for back-end storage.

The *MySQL Database Administrator* Certification attests that the person holding the certification knows how to maintain and optimize an installation of one or more MySQL servers, and perform administrative tasks such as monitoring the server, making backups, and so forth.

Passing a MySQL certification exam is no easy feat. That's not just me saying so; the statistics tell the story: 40 to 50 percent will fail an exam the first time they take it. So how do you better your chances of passing? This study guide gives you the basis for doing just that: By reading the main text, you get the needed background *knowledge*; by following the examples and doing the exercises, you get the *understanding* of what is going on inside MySQL whenever you perform a given action.

There is of course something that no amount of reading and exercise solving can give you, and that is the *experience* that allows you to extrapolate from knowledge and understanding and tackling situations that might at first seem unfamiliar. This you can get only by hands-on work with MySQL. To this end, MySQL AB (the company that develops MySQL and related products and services) offers several training programs that could be beneficial to you. More information on the MySQL training and certification programs may be found on the MySQL AB Web site (see `http://www.mysql.com/training`).

Thanks go to Lisa Scothern, Trudy Pelzer and Peter Gulutzan, each of whom made extensive reviews on the book's contents and provided a lot of valuable feedback.

Working with people like Stefan and Paul is always a great source of inspiration. And when the result is something like this book, the sense of enjoyment is certainly not lessened. As for you, dear reader, I hope you will feel some of the same enjoyment when you get to frame your new MySQL 5.0 certificate and hang it on the wall.

Good luck on your exams!

— Carsten Pedersen, Certification Manager, MySQL AB

About the Authors

Paul DuBois is a member of the MySQL documentation team, a database administrator, and a leader in the Open Source and MySQL communities. He contributed to the online documentation for the MySQL and is the author of *MySQL* (Developer's Library), *MySQL and Perl for the Web* (New Riders Publishing), and *MySQL Cookbook*, *Using csh and tcsh*, and *Software Portability with imake* (O'Reilly and Associates).

Stefan Hinz is the MySQL documentation team lead, a former MySQL trainer, and the German translator of the *MySQL Reference Manual*. He is also the translator of Paul's *MySQL Cookbook* (O'Reilly and Associates) and translator and author of MySQL-related German books. Stefan passed the MySQL Certification exam before he joined MySQL AB.

Carsten Pedersen is the MySQL AB certification manager who has led the development of the MySQL certification program since its inception in 2002. He has lectured at conferences and taught MySQL courses in many countries, from Silicon Valley, USA in the west, across Europe, to Beijing, China, in the East. Before joining MySQL AB, he administered databases in several production systems and maintained a very popular "MySQL FAQ and Tools" Internet site.

Acknowledgments

We would like to thank all of our colleagues at MySQL who have helped build the certification program over the past 3 years, and without whom this book wouldn't have come into existence. A special thank you to Kaj Arnö, who was the person to conceive and initiate the and initiate the MySQL certification program and to Ulf Sandberg, for his continued support of the program.

References

The MySQL Reference Manual is the primary source of information on MySQL. It is available in book form and online in several formats and languages from the MySQL AB Web site (`http://dev.mysql.com`).

The MySQL Developer's Zone at `http://dev.mysql.com` is constantly updated with technical articles, many of which refer to subjects covered in this book.

We Want to Hear from You!

As the reader of this book, *you* are our most important critic and commentator. We value your opinion and want to know what we're doing right, what we could do better, what areas you'd like to see us publish in, and any other words of wisdom you're willing to pass our way.

You can email or write me directly to let me know what you did or didn't like about this book—as well as what we can do to make our books stronger.

Please note that I cannot help you with technical problems related to the topic of this book, and that due to the high volume of mail I receive, I might not be able to reply to every message.

When you write, please be sure to include this book's title and author as well as your name and phone number or email address. I will carefully review your comments and share them with the author and editors who worked on the book.

E-mail: mysqlpress@pearsoned.com

Mail: Mark Taber
            Associate Publisher
            Pearson Education/MySQL Press
            800 East 96th Street
            Indianapolis, IN 46240 USA

Introduction

About This Book

This is a study guide for the *MySQL Developer Certification* and the *MySQL Database Administrator Certification*. As such, it is a primer for the MySQL certification exams, but not a replacement for the *MySQL Reference Manual* or any other MySQL documentation. As part of your preparation for an exam, make sure that you are thoroughly familiar with the *MySQL Reference Manual*, the *MySQL Query Browser Manual* (for the Developer exams) and the *MySQL Administrator Manual* (for the Database Administrator exams). All of these manuals are available on-line from the MySQL Developer Zone Web site at `http://dev.mysql.com`.

This introduction provides some general hints on what to expect from the exam, what to do in order to take the exam, what happens on the day of the exam, and what happens after you have passed the exam.

The remainder of this study guide covers each section of the exams, as defined in the *MySQL 5.0 Certification Candidate Guide*. The book is divided into two main parts, each corresponding to one of the two certifications:

- Chapter 1, "Client/Server Concepts," through Chapter 22, "Basic Optimizations," pertain to the Developer certification.
- Chapter 23, "MySQL Architecture," through Chapter 42, "Scaling MySQL," pertain to the Database Administrator certification.

Each of the sections is further subdivided into Parts I and II, as follows:

- Chapter 1, "Client/Server Concepts," through Chapter 11, "Updating Data," pertain to the Developer-I exam.
- Chapter 12, "Joins," through Chapter 22, "Basic Optimizations," pertain to the Developer-II exam.
- Chapter 23, "MySQL Architecture," through Chapter 32, "Data Backup and Recovery Methods," pertain to the DBA-I exam.
- Chapter 33, "Using Stored Routines and Triggers for Administration," through Chapter 42, "Scaling MySQL," pertain to the DBA-II exam.

However, the split between parts I and II within a certification title may not always be as clear-cut as is suggested by the chapter divisions. Therefore, you should be familiar with all of the material presented for a certification level before going to any particular exam.

There are many cross-references within this book that go across the "boundary" between the two certifications. For example, Chapter 22, "Basic Optimizations," which is in the Developer part of the book, contains a cross reference to Chapter 37, "Optimizing Queries," which is in the DBA part of the book. In cases like this, you are not expected to read the chapter outside the exam for which you're studying. However, doing so will obviously increase your understanding of the subject area.

You might find that the wording of a topic covered in this guide corresponds exactly to the wording of a question on an exam. However, that is the exception. Rote memorization of the material in this guide will not be very effective in helping you pass the exam. You need to *understand* the principles discussed so that you can apply them to the exam questions. Working through the exercises will be very beneficial in this respect. If you find that you are still having difficulties with some of the materials, you might want to consider the training classes offered by MySQL AB. These classes are presented in a format that facilitates greater understanding through interaction with the instructor.

Because the study guide is targeted to MySQL 5.0, it doesn't normally point out when features are unavailable in earlier versions (nor are you expected to know about this on the exams). This differs from what you might be used to in the *MySQL Reference Manual*.

Sample Exercises

The CD-ROM that accompanies this book has a number of sample exercises. It's essential that you work through the exercises to test your knowledge. Doing so will prepare you to take the exam far better than just reading the text. Another reason to read the exercises is that occasionally they augment a topic with more detail than is given in the body of the chapter.

Note that the exercises are not always in the same format as the exam questions. The exam questions are in a format that is suited for *testing* your knowledge. The exercises are designed to help you get a better *understanding* of the contents of this book, and to help you prove to yourself that you really grasp the topics covered.

Other Required Reading

This book will give you a good overall insight into everything you need to know for MySQL certification. It will not tell you every little detail about how things work in MySQL; nor does it tell you every detail you need to know about actually attending the exam. Other material that you can take advantage of is listed in the following sections.

Manuals

- Before going to any of the exams, make sure you have familiarized yourself with the *MySQL Reference Manual*. Familiarizing yourself with the manual is not the same as knowing every word in it, but you should at least skim through it and look more closely at those parts that pertain to the particular exam which you are going to attend.

- Before taking either of the Developer exams, you should read the *MySQL Query Browser Manual*.

- Before taking either of the DBA exams, you should read the *MySQL Administrator Manual*.

Each of the manuals just listed is available on the MySQL developer Web site, `http://dev.mysql.com`. You will also find many good technical articles on that Web site. These articles do not make up part of the exam curriculum per se, but they explain many of the concepts presented in this book in a different way and may enable you to get a better perspective on some details.

Sample Data

Almost all examples and exercises in this study guide use the *world database* as the sample data set. The accompanying CD-ROM contains the data for this database and instructions that describe how to create and populate the database for use with your own MySQL installation.

Study Guide Errata

Although this book was thoroughly checked for correctness prior to publication, errors might remain. Any errors found after publication are noted at `http://www.mysql.com/certification/studyguides`.

Certification Information at `www.mysql.com`

The Certification pages at `http://www.mysql.com/certification` contain the overview of the current state of all things you need to know about the MySQL certification program. It is recommended that you read through this information as you start planning your certification, as well as when you plan to go to exams to ensure that you are aware of any last-minute updates.

The Certification area of the MySQL Web site provides comprehensive information on the certifications offered, upcoming certifications and betas, training offers, and so forth. After you've taken a certification exam, the Web site is also where you will be able to check the status of your certification.

The MySQL Certification Candidate Guide

Of particular interest on the MySQL certification Web pages is the *MySQL Certification Candidate Guide*. It contains the overall description of the MySQL Certification program, as well all the practical information you will need in order to write an exam. The latest version of the Candidate Guide can be found at `http://www.mysql.com/certification/candguide`.

The Candidate Guide contains a list of items providing practical advice to you as the candidate, an overview of the entire certification program, prices, policies, practical details regarding going to the exam, and so forth.

The Candidate Guide includes the *MySQL Certification Non-Disclosure and Logo Usage Agreement* (NDA/LUA). You'll be asked to agree to the agreement when you go to take the exam. At that point, legal agreements will probably be the last thing on your mind, so reading the agreement *before* you go will save you some distraction and also some exam time.

The Certification Mailing List

Anyone considering pursuing MySQL certification should subscribe to the MySQL Certification mailing list. This is a low-volume list (messages go out once every two months or so), to which MySQL AB posts news related to the certification program. The subscription address for the mailing list is `certification-subscribe@lists.mysql.com`. To subscribe, send an empty message to that address.

Conventions Used in This Book

This section explains the conventions used in this study guide.

`Text in this style` is used for program and shell script names, SQL keywords, and command output.

`Text in this style` represents input that you would type while entering a command or statement.

`Text in this style` represents variable input for which you're expected to enter a value of your own choosing. Some examples show commands or statements that aren't meant to be entered exactly as shown. Thus, in an example such as the following, you would substitute the name of some particular table for *`table_name`*:

```
SELECT * FROM table_name;
```

In syntax descriptions, square brackets indicate optional information. For example, the following syntax for the `DROP TABLE` statement indicates that you can invoke the statement with or without an `IF EXISTS` clause:

```
DROP TABLE [IF EXISTS] table_name;
```

Lists of items are shown with items separated by vertical bars. If choosing an item is optional, the list is enclosed within square brackets. If choosing an item is mandatory, the list is enclosed within curly braces:

```
[ item1 | item2 | item3 ]
{ item1 | item2 | item3 }
```

In most cases, SQL statements are shown with a trailing semicolon character (';'). The semicolon indicates where the statement ends and is useful particularly in reading multiple-statement examples. However, the semicolon is not part of the statement itself.

If a statement is shown together with the output that it produces, it's shown preceded by a `mysql>` prompt. An example shown in this manner is meant to illustrate the output you would see were you to issue the statement using the `mysql` client program. For example, a section that discusses the use of the VERSION() function might contain an example like this:

```
mysql> SELECT VERSION();
+-----------------+
| VERSION()       |
+-----------------+
| 5.0.10-beta-log |
+-----------------+
```

Some commands are intended to be invoked from the command line, such as from a Windows console window prompt or from a Unix shell prompt. In this guide, these commands are shown preceded by a `shell>` prompt. Some Windows-specific examples use a prompt that begins with `C:`. The prompt you will actually see on your own system depends on your command interpreter and the prompt settings you use. (The prompt is likely to be `C:\>` for a Windows console and `%` or `$` for a Unix shell.)

SQL keywords such as SELECT or ORDER BY aren't case sensitive in MySQL and may be specified in any lettercase when you issue queries. However, for this guide, keywords are written in uppercase letters to help make it clear when they're being used as keywords and not in a merely descriptive sense. For example, "UPDATE statement" refers to a particular kind of SQL statement (one that begins with the keyword UPDATE), whereas "update statement" is a descriptive term that refers more generally to any kind of statement that updates or modifies data. The latter term includes UPDATE statements, but also other statements such as INSERT, REPLACE, and DELETE.

Sample commands generally omit options for specifying connection parameters, such as `--host` or `--user` to specify the server host or your MySQL username. It's assumed that you'll supply such options as necessary. Chapter 1, "Client/Server Concepts," discusses connection parameter options.

In answers to exercises that involve invocation of client programs, you might also have to provide options for connection parameters. Those options generally are not shown in the answers.

Running MySQL on Microsoft Windows

Windows-specific material in this Guide (and the certification exams) assumes a version of Windows that is based on Windows NT. This includes Windows NT, 2000, XP, and 2003. It does not include Windows 95, 98, or Me.

About the Exams

To take a MySQL certification exam, you must go to a Pearson VUE testing center. MySQL AB creates the exams and defines the content, the passing score, and so forth. Pearson VUE is responsible for delivering the exams to candidates worldwide.

Registering for an Exam

There are three ways to register for an exam:

- You can use the Pearson VUE Web site, `http://www.vue.com/mysql`. Note that you must pre-register on the Web site to set up an account with VUE. VUE processes your application and notifies you when your account is ready. This process usually takes about 24 hours. After your account has been set up, you can register for the exam you want to take.

- You can call one of the VUE call centers. The telephone numbers are listed in on the Pearson VUE Web site: `http://www.vue.com/contact/mysql`.

- You can register directly at your local VUE test center on the day of the exam. A complete list of the test centers can be found on the Web at `http://www.vue.com/mysql`. Click on the Test Centers link about halfway down the page to find a testing center near you. Note that many test centers have limited hours of operation, so it's always a good idea to call ahead to ensure that you can be accommodated at the time you want to take the exam.

MySQL AB recommends that you use the VUE Web site for exam registration and payment, but you're welcome to use any method you choose.

If you register through the Web or a call center, a receipt will be sent to you as soon as the registration process is completed. If you register directly at the test center, please ask for your receipt when you submit payment.

Going to the Exam

On the day of your exam, you should ensure that you arrive at the test center well ahead of the appointed time (at least 15 minutes early is recommended). When you arrive at the testing center, you will be asked by the test administrator to:

1. Sign the test log.

2. Provide two forms of identification. One must contain your address, and one must be a photo ID.

3. Sign a page explaining the test center rules and procedures.

After you've completed these steps, you'll be taken to your testing station. You'll be furnished with a pen and scratch paper, or an erasable plastic board. During the exam, the test administrator will be monitoring the testing room, usually through a glass partition in the wall. As you come to the testing station, your exam will be called up on the screen and the exam will start when you are ready. Remember to make any adjustments to your chair, desk, screen, and so forth before the exam begins. Once the exam has begun, the clock will not be stopped.

The first thing you will be asked on the exam is to accept the *MySQL AB Certification Non-Disclosure and Logo Usage Agreement.* As mentioned earlier, it's a good idea to have read the copy found in the *MySQL Certification Candidate Guide* before going to the exam, so you do not have to spend exam time reading and understanding what it says.

FIGURE IN.1   The Certification Non-Disclosure and Logo Usage Agreement as it will be presented at the testing station.

Taking the Exam

Each MySQL Certification Exam lasts 90 minutes. In that time, you must answer approximately 70 questions. Beta exams contain more questions, but also allow you more time to answer them. For more information on Beta exams and their availability, see the certification pages on http://www.mysql.com.

The questions and answers in any particular exam are drawn from a large question pool. Each section of the exam will have a different number of questions, approximately proportional to the percentages shown in the following tables. These were the percentages as planned at the time this book went to press; although they are unlikely to change, you should consult the *MySQL Certification Candidate Guide* for the exact details.

TABLE IN.1   Division of Questions on Exam Sections for the Developer Exams

MySQL Developer I Exam		MySQL Developer II Exam	
Client/Server Concepts	5%	Joins	15%
The mysql Client Program	5%	Subqueries	10%
MySQL Query Browser	5%	Views	10%
MySQL Connectors	5%	Importing and Exporting Data	10%
Data Types	15%	User Variables	5%
Identifiers	5%	Prepared Statements	5%
Databases	5%	Stored Procedures and Functions	15%
Tables and Indexes	15%	Triggers	5%
Querying for Data	15%	Obtaining Database Metadata	5%
SQL Expressions	15%	Debugging MySQL Applications	5%
Updating Data	10%	Basic Optimizations	15%

TABLE IN.2   Division of Questions on Exam Sections for the DBA Exams

MySQL DBA I Exam		MySQL DBA II Exam	
MySQL Architecture	10%	Using Stored Routines and Triggers for Administration	5%
Starting, Stopping, and Configuring MySQL	15%	User Management	15%
Client Programs for DBA Work	5%	Securing the MySQL Installation	10%
MySQL Administrator	10%	Upgrade-Related Security Issues	5%
Character Set Support	5%	Optimizing Queries	15%
Locking	10%	Optimizing Databases	15%
Storage Engines	15%	Optimizing the Server	15%

MySQL DBA I Exam		MySQL DBA II Exam	
Table Maintenance	5%	Interpreting Diagnostic Messages	5%
The INFORMATION_SCHEMA Database	10%	Optimizing the Environment	5%
Data Backup and Recovery Methods	15%	Scaling MySQL	10%

This study guide organizes topic material into the sections shown in the Candidate Guide, but you shouldn't expect the exam to follow the same format. While you're taking the exam, questions may occur in any order. For example, on the Developer-I exam, you might be presented with a question about indexing, followed by a question pertaining to data types.

Some features in MySQL are version specific. The current exam and this book cover MySQL 5.0, and you should consider a feature available if it's available as of MySQL 5.0. For example, stored procedures and views were implemented for MySQL 5.0, so for purposes of the exam, you should consider them to be topics upon which you might be tested.

Reading Questions

The single most important factor in answering any exam question is first to *understand* what the question is asking. The questions are written in very concise language and are thoroughly checked for readability. But you also need to know how to interpret any additional information presented with the question.

On the exam, you will see some SQL statements followed by a semicolon, and some not. This occasionally confuses people. What you need to keep in mind is that SQL statements need only be terminated with a semicolon when used in the context of the mysql command-line client, not in any other contexts. So only when shown in the context of the command-line client should you expect to see a terminator.

One type of information that's often provided is a display of the structure of a table. Instructions for interpreting this information are given later in this introduction (see "Interpreting DESCRIBE Output").

Answering Questions

You should attempt to answer all exam questions, because an unanswered question counts as an incorrect answer. When taking the exam, you'll be able to move back and forth between questions. This enables you to initially skip questions you're unsure of and return to them as time permits. You'll also be able to mark a question "for review," if you want to spend more time on it later. When you've gone through all questions, a review screen will be presented that contains any questions that you've marked for review, as well as all unanswered questions.

All questions are multiple-choice questions, only varying in whether you need to choose single or multiple correct answers among those presented to you.

You select an answer to a question either by clicking with the mouse on the field to the left of the answer, or by pressing the corresponding letter on the keyboard.

For a single-answer question, only one response is correct and you must identify the correct answer from among the possible responses. Some of the responses provided might be partially correct, but only one will be completely correct. In a single-answer question, the fields that you can select are circles ("radio buttons") and the text in the status bar below the question says "select the best response."

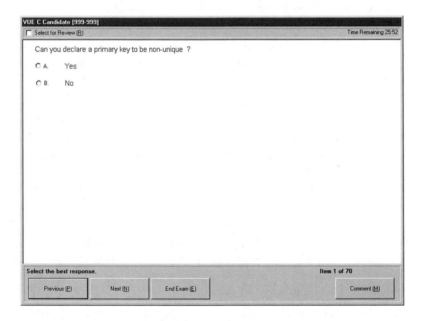

FIGURE IN.2   A multiple-choice/single-answer question. Note that each answer key has a circle ("radio button") beside it, and the status bar says "select the best response.

For a multiple-answer question, you must choose *all* correct answers to get credit for your response. As with single-answer questions, there might be subtle differences between correct and incorrect answers; take your time to read each possible answer carefully before deciding whether it is correct. In multiple-answer questions, the fields that you can select are square ("check boxes") and the status line says "Select between 1 and *n* answers," where *n* is the total number of possible answers.

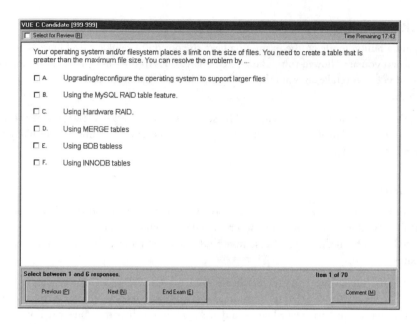

FIGURE IN.3 A multiple-choice/multiple-answer question. Note that each answer key has a square ("check box") beside it, and the status bar says "select between 1 and 6 answers.

After the Exam

Unless you're taking part in a Beta exam, you'll receive your grade as soon as you complete the exam. The test center will provide you with a score report.

If you pass, MySQL AB will mail your certificate four to six weeks after receiving your exam results from the test center.

Whether you pass or fail, after you've taken any MySQL certification exam, you'll receive a letter from MySQL AB telling you how to gain access to extra information at http://www.mysql.com. There are two main entry points into this area:

- The candidate area: http://www.mysql.com/certification/candidate

  Here, you will find information specially set aside for MySQL certification candidates. For example, there might be special offers, information on pre-releases of new certifications, and so on.

- The results area: http://www.mysql.com/certification/results

  In this area, potential clients and employers can confirm that your certificate is valid. Access for others to this area is controlled by you, using the candidate area.

Retaking Exams

If you get a failing grade on the exam, you have the option of retaking it. There is no limit set on when you are allowed to retake an exam. MySQL AB does not place restrictions on how soon you can retake an exam, but doing so is not advised until you've done some further study.

This isn't just a commonsense warning. The statistics show with great clarity that those who attempt to retake a failed exam within five days of the first exam are much more likely to fail once again rather than passing.

Warning

For every popular certification exam, there are always enterprising individuals who set up so-called "braindump" Internet sites, where people anonymously post questions and answers purported to be from the exam. Please note these cautions about using or contributing to these sites:

- If you use such a site, you are very likely to be misled. We've seen these sites, and trust us: The answers they provide are more often wrong than correct. Worse, most of the questions shown have never been—and are so ludicrous that they never will be—on an exam; they exist only in the submitter's head. As a result, instead of being helpful, such sites lead to confusion.

- If you contribute to such a site by posting your own exam questions and answers, you risk forfeiting not only the certification for the exam about which you have posted details, but your involvement in the entire MySQL Certification program. You might thus never be able to regain MySQL certification credentials.

Interpreting DESCRIBE Output

You should understand how to interpret the output of the DESCRIBE *table_name* statement. This is of particular importance both for this study guide and for taking certification exams. In both cases, when it's necessary that you know the structure of a table, it will be shown as the output of a DESCRIBE statement in the same format as that displayed by the mysql program. For example, assume that a question requires you to know about a table named City. The table's structure will be presented as follows:

```
mysql> DESCRIBE City;
+-------------+----------+------+-----+---------+----------------+
| Field       | Type     | Null | Key | Default | Extra          |
+-------------+----------+------+-----+---------+----------------+
| ID          | int(11)  | NO   | PRI | NULL    | auto_increment |
| Name        | char(35) | NO   |     |         |                |
| CountryCode | char(3)  | NO   |     |         |                |
```

```
| District   | char(20) | NO  |     |          |                |
| Population | int(11)  | NO  |     | 0        |                |
+------------+----------+-----+-----+----------+----------------+
```

The output of the DESCRIBE statement contains one row for each column in the table. The most important features of the output are as follows:

- The Field value indicates the column name.

- The Type value shows the column data type.

- The Null indicator is the word YES if the column can contain NULL values and NO if it cannot. In the example shown, Null is NO for all columns of the City table. This indicates that none of that table's columns can contain NULL values.

- The Key indicator may be empty or contain one of three non-empty values:

  - An empty Key value indicates that the column in question either isn't indexed or is indexed only as a secondary column in a multiple-column, non-unique index. For purposes of the exam, you should assume that if Key is empty, it's because the column is not indexed at all.

  - If the Key value is the keyword PRI (as in the output shown for the ID column), this indicates that the column is a PRIMARY KEY or is one of the columns in a multiple-column PRIMARY KEY.

  - If the Key value is the keyword UNI, this indicates that the column is the first column of a unique-valued index that cannot contain NULL values.

  - If the Key value is the keyword MUL, this indicates that the column is the first column of a non-unique index or a unique-valued index that can contain NULL values.

  It's possible that more than one of the Key values may apply to a given column of a table. For example, a column that is a PRIMARY KEY might also be part of other indexes. When it's possible for more than one of the Key values to describe an index, DESCRIBE displays the one with the highest priority, in the order PRI, UNI, MUL.

  Because a column can be part of several indexes, the Key values do not necessarily provide an exhaustive description of a table's indexes. However, for purposes of the exam, you should assume that the table descriptions given provide all the information needed to correctly answer the question.

- Default shows the column's default value. This is the value that MySQL assigns to the column when a statement that creates a new record does not provide an explicit value for the column. (For example, this can happen with the INSERT, REPLACE, and LOAD DATA INFILE statements.)

- The Extra value displays other details about the column. The only Extra detail about which you need be concerned for the exam is the value auto_increment. This value indicates that the column has the AUTO_INCREMENT attribute. The ID column shown in the example is such an instance.

You can read more about data types, default values, and the AUTO_INCREMENT column attribute in Chapter 5, "Data Types." Indexing is covered in Chapter 8, "Tables and Indexes." The DESCRIBE statement and other methods of obtaining table metadata are covered in more detail in Chapter 20, "Obtaining Database Metadata."

Sample Tables

This study guide uses several different database and table names in examples. However, one set of tables occurs repeatedly: the tables in a database named world. This section discusses the structure of these tables. Throughout this study guide, you're assumed to be familiar with them. To make it easier for you to try the examples, the accompanying CD-ROM includes the world database. MySQL AB also provides a downloadable copy of the world database that you can obtain at http://dev.mysql.com/doc.

The world database contains three tables, Country, City, and CountryLanguage:

- The Country table contains a row of information for each country in the database:

```
mysql> DESCRIBE Country;
```

Field	Type	Null	Key	Default	Extra
Code	char(3)	NO	PRI		
Name	char(52)	NO			
Continent	enum('Asia', ...)	NO		Asia	
Region	char(26)	NO			
SurfaceArea	float(10,2)	NO		0.00	
IndepYear	smallint(6)	YES		NULL	
Population	int(11)	NO		0	
LifeExpectancy	float(3,1)	YES		NULL	
GNP	float(10,2)	YES		NULL	
GNPOld	float(10,2)	YES		NULL	
LocalName	char(45)	NO			
GovernmentForm	char(45)	NO			
HeadOfState	char(60)	YES		NULL	
Capital	int(11)	YES		NULL	
Code2	char(2)	NO			

The entire output of the DESCRIBE statement is too wide to display on the page, so the Type value for the Continent line has been shortened. The value enum('Asia', ...) as shown actually stands for enum('Asia', 'Europe', 'North America', 'Africa', 'Oceania', 'Antarctica', 'South America').

- The City table contains rows about cities located in countries listed in the Country table:

```
mysql> DESCRIBE City;
```

```
+-------------+----------+------+-----+---------+----------------+
| Field       | Type     | Null | Key | Default | Extra          |
+-------------+----------+------+-----+---------+----------------+
| ID          | int(11)  | NO   | PRI | NULL    | auto_increment |
| Name        | char(35) | NO   |     |         |                |
| CountryCode | char(3)  | NO   |     |         |                |
| District    | char(20) | NO   |     |         |                |
| Population  | int(11)  | NO   |     | 0       |                |
+-------------+----------+------+-----+---------+----------------+
```

- The CountryLanguage table describes languages spoken in countries listed in the Country table:

```
mysql> DESCRIBE CountryLanguage;
+-------------+---------------+------+-----+---------+-------+
| Field       | Type          | Null | Key | Default | Extra |
+-------------+---------------+------+-----+---------+-------+
| CountryCode | char(3)       | NO   | PRI |         |       |
| Language    | char(30)      | NO   | PRI |         |       |
| IsOfficial  | enum('T','F') | NO   |     | F       |       |
| Percentage  | float(4,1)    | NO   |     | 0.0     |       |
+-------------+---------------+------+-----+---------+-------+
```

The Name column in the Country table contains full country names. Each country also has a three-letter country code stored in the Code column. The City and CountryLanguage tables each have a column that contains country codes as well, though the column is named CountryCode in those tables.

In the CountryLanguage table, note that each country may have multiple languages. For example, Finnish, Swedish, and several other languages are spoken in Finland. For this reason, CountryLanguage has a composite (multiple-column) index consisting of both the Country and Language columns.

MySQL Developer Exams

MySQL Developer I Exam

Client/Server Concepts

This chapter discusses the client/server architecture of the MySQL database system and basic concepts of how to invoke client programs. The chapter covers the following exam topics:

- General MySQL architecture
- Syntax for command-line options
- Parameters for connecting to the server with client programs
- Using option files
- Using the SQL mode to control server operation

1.1 General MySQL Architecture

MySQL operates in a networked environment using a client/server architecture. In other words, a central program acts as a server, and various client programs connect to the server to make requests. A MySQL installation has the following major components:

- *MySQL Server*, or mysqld, is the database server program. The server manages access to the actual databases on disk and in memory. MySQL Server is multi-threaded and supports many simultaneous client connections. Clients can connect via several connection protocols. For managing database contents, MySQL Server features a modular architecture that supports multiple storage engines that handle different types of tables (for example, it provides both transactional and non-transactional tables).

  mysqld comes in several configurations. MySQL Max distributions contain a server named mysqld-max that includes features that are not built into the non-Max version, such as support for additional storage engines. On Windows, the mysqld-nt and mysql-max-nt servers provide support for named-pipe connections on Windows NT, 2000, XP, and 2003. If a given installation includes multiple server programs, you pick one to run from among those available.

The exact feature configuration of MySQL Server may change over time, so whenever you download a new version, it's wise to check the documentation. For the purposes of the exam, the preceding information suffices.

As you read this guide, please keep in mind the difference between a *server* and a *host*. The server is software (the MySQL server program mysqld). Server characteristics include its version number, whether certain features are included or excluded, and so forth. The host is the physical machine on which the server program runs. Host characteristics include its hardware configuration, the operating system running on the machine, its network addresses, and so forth.

- *Client programs.* These are programs that you use for communicating with the server to manipulate the information in the databases that the server manages. MySQL AB provides several client programs. The following list describes a few of them:

  - MySQL Query Browser and MySQL Administrator are graphical front ends to the server.

  - mysql is a command-line program that acts as a text-based front end for the server. It's used for issuing queries and viewing the results interactively from a terminal window.

  - Other command-line clients include mysqlimport for importing data files, mysqldump for making backups, mysqladmin for server administration, and mysqlcheck for checking the integrity of the database files.

- *MySQL non-client utilities.* These are programs that act independently of the server. They do not operate by first establishing a connection to the server. myisamchk is an example. It performs table checking and repair operations. Another program in this category is myisampack, which creates compressed read-only versions of MyISAM tables. Both utilities operate by accessing MyISAM table files directly, independent of the mysqld database server.

MySQL runs on many varieties of Windows, Unix, and Linux, but client/server communication is not limited to environments where all computers run the same operating system. Client programs can connect to a server running on the same host or a different host, and the client and server host need not have the same operating system. For example, client programs can be used on Windows to connect to a server that is running on Linux.

Most of the concepts discussed here apply universally to any system on which MySQL runs. Platform-specific information is so indicated. Unless otherwise specified, "Unix" as used here includes Linux and other Unix-like operating systems.

1.2 Invoking Client Programs

MySQL client programs can be invoked from the command line, such as from a Windows console prompt or a Unix shell prompt. When you invoke a client program, you can specify options following the program name to control its behavior. Options also can be given in option files. Some options tell the client how to connect to the MySQL server. Other options tell the program what actions to perform.

You also specify connection parameters for graphical client programs such as MySQL Query Browser and MySQL Administrator. However, graphical clients provide an interactive interface by which you enter those parameters. See Section 1.2.5, "Establishing a Connection with a GUI Client." The graphical clients store connection parameters in their own files, in XML format. See Section 3.5, "Connection Management."

This section discusses the following option-related topics:

- The general syntax for specifying options
- Specifying connection parameter options
- Specifying options in an option file

Most examples in this section use the `mysql` program, but the general principles apply to other MySQL client command-line programs as well.

To determine the options supported by a MySQL program, invoke it with the `--help` option. For example, to find out how to use `mysql`, use this command:

```
shell> mysql --help
```

To determine the version of a program, use the `--version` option. For example, the following output from the `mysql` client indicates that the client is from MySQL 5.0.10:

```
shell> mysql --version
mysql  Ver 14.12 Distrib 5.0.10-beta, for apple-darwin8.2.0 (powerpc)
```

It is not necessary to run client programs that have the same version as the server. In most cases, clients that are older or newer than the server can connect to it successfully.

1.2.1 General Command Option Syntax

Options to MySQL programs have two general forms:

- Long options consist of a word preceded by double dashes.
- Short options consist of a single letter preceded by a single dash.

In many cases, a given option has both a long and a short form. For example, to display a program's version number, you can use the long `--version` option or the short `-V` option. These two commands are equivalent:

```
shell> mysql --version
shell> mysql -V
```

Options are case sensitive. `--version` is recognized by MySQL programs, but lettercase variations such as `--Version` or `--VERSION` are not. This applies to short options as well: `-V` and `-v` are both legal options, but mean different things.

Some options are followed by values. For example, when you specify the `--host` or `-h` option to indicate the host machine where the MySQL server is running, you must follow the option with the machine's hostname. For a long option, separate the option and the value by an equal sign (=). For short options, the option and the value can but need not be separated by a space. The option formats in the following three commands are equivalent. Each one specifies `myhost.example.com` as the host machine where the MySQL server is running:

```
shell> mysql --host=myhost.example.com
shell> mysql -h myhost.example.com
shell> mysql -hmyhost.example.com
```

In most cases, if you don't specify an option explicitly, a program uses a default value. This makes it easier to invoke MySQL client programs because you need specify only those options for which the defaults are unsuitable. For example, the default server hostname is `localhost`, so if the MySQL server to which you want to connect is running on the local host, you need not specify any `--host` or `-h` option.

Exceptions to these option syntax rules are noted in the following discussion wherever relevant. The most important exception is that password options have a slightly different behavior than other options.

1.2.2 Connection Parameter Options

To connect to a server using a client program, the client must know upon which host the server is running. A connection may be established locally to a server running on the same host as the client program, or remotely to a server running on a different host. To connect, you also must identify yourself to the server with a username and password.

Each MySQL client has its own program-specific options, but all command-line clients support a common set of options for making a connection to the MySQL server. This section describes the options that specify connection parameters, and how to use them if the default values aren't appropriate. The discussion lists each option's long form and short form, as well as its default value.

The primary options for connecting to the server specify the type of connection to make and identify the MySQL account that you want to use. The following tables summarize these two sets of options.

Table 1.1   Options for Establishing a Connection

Option	Meaning
`--protocol`	The protocol to use for the connection
`--host`	The host where the server is running

Table 1.1   Continued

Option	Meaning
`--port`	The port number for TCP/IP connections
`--shared-memory-base-name`	The shared-memory name for shared-memory connections
`--socket`	The Unix socket filename or named-pipe name

Table 1.2   Options for MySQL User Identification

Option	Meaning
`--user`	The MySQL account username
`--password`	The MySQL account password

The `--protocol` option, if given, explicitly selects the communication protocol that the client program should use for connecting to the server. (In the absence of a `--protocol` option, the protocol used for the connection is determined implicitly based on the server hostname value and the client operating system, as discussed later.) The allowable values for the `--protocol` option are given in the following table.

`--protocol` Value	Connection Protocol	Allowable Operating Systems
`tcp`	TCP/IP connection to local or remote server	All
`socket`	Unix socket file connection to local server	Unix only
`pipe`	Named-pipe connection to local server	Windows only
`memory`	Shared-memory connection to local server	Windows only

As shown by the table, TCP/IP is the most general protocol. It can be used for connecting to local or remote servers, and is supported on all operating systems. The other protocols can be used only for connecting to a local server running on the same host as the client program. They also are operating system-specific, and might not be enabled by default.

Named-pipe connections can be used only for connections to the local server on Windows. However, for the named-pipe connection protocol to be operative, you must use the `mysqld-nt` or `mysqld-max-nt` server, and the server must be started with the `--enable-named-pipe` option.

Shared-memory connections can be used only for connections to the local server on Windows. The server must be started with the `--shared-memory` option. Specifying this option has the additional effect that shared memory becomes the default connection protocol for local clients.

The following list describes the other connection parameters. The descriptions indicate how parameter values may affect which connection protocol to use, but note that the values have this effect only if the --protocol option is not given.

- --host=*host_name* or -h *host_name*

   This option specifies the machine where the MySQL server is running. The value can be a hostname or an IP number. The hostname localhost means the local host (that is, the computer on which you're running the client program). On Unix, localhost is treated in a special manner. On Windows, the value . (period) also means the local host and is treated in a special manner as well. For a description of this special treatment, refer to the discussion of the --socket option.

   The default host value is localhost.

- --port=*port_number* or -P *port_number*

   This option indicates the port number to which to connect on the server host. It applies only to TCP/IP connections.

   The default MySQL port number is 3306.

- --shared-memory-base-name=*memory_name*

   This option can be used on Windows to specify the name of shared memory to use for a shared-memory connection to a local server.

   The default shared-memory name is MYSQL (case sensitive).

- --socket=*socket_name* or -S *socket_name*

   This option's name comes from its original use for specifying a Unix domain socket file. On Unix, for a connection to the host localhost, a client connects to the server using a Unix socket file. This option specifies the pathname of that file.

   On Windows, the --socket option is used for specifying a named pipe. For Windows NT-based systems that support named pipes, a client can connect using a pipe by specifying . as the hostname. In this case, --socket specifies the name of the pipe. Pipe names aren't case sensitive.

   If this option is omitted, the default Unix socket file pathname is /tmp/mysql.sock. The default Windows pipe name is MySQL.

As mentioned earlier, if the --protocol option is not given, the connection protocol is determined implicitly based on the server hostname and the client operating system:

- On Windows, a client can establish a named-pipe connection to the local server by specifying . (period) as the hostname.

- On Unix, the hostname localhost is special for MySQL: It indicates that the client should connect to the server using a Unix socket file. In this case, any port number specified with the --port option is ignored.

- To explicitly establish a TCP/IP connection to a local server, use `--protocol=tcp` or else specify a host of `127.0.0.1` (the address of the TCP/IP loopback interface) or the server's actual hostname or IP number.

Two options provide identification information. They indicate the username and password of the account that you want to use for accessing the server. The server rejects a connection attempt unless you provide values for these parameters that correspond to a MySQL account that is listed in the server's grant tables.

- `--user=user_name` or `-u user_name`

  This option specifies the username for your MySQL account. To determine which account applies, the server uses the username value in conjunction with the name of the host from which you connect. This means that there can be different accounts with the same username, which can be used for connections from different hosts.

  On Windows, the default MySQL account name is `ODBC`. On Unix, client programs use your system login name as your default MySQL account username.

- `--password=pass_value` or `-ppass_value`

  This option specifies the password for your MySQL account. There is no default password. If you omit this option, your MySQL account must be set up to allow you to connect without a password.

MySQL accounts are set up using statements such as `CREATE USER` and `GRANT`, which are discussed in Chapter 34, "User Management."

Password options are special in two ways, compared to the other connection parameter options:

- You can omit the password value after the option name. This differs from the other connection parameter options, each of which requires a value after the option name. If you omit the password value, the client program prompts you interactively for a password, as shown here:

```
shell> mysql -p
Enter password:
```

  When you see the `Enter password:` prompt, type in your password and press Enter. The password isn't echoed as you type, to prevent other people from seeing it.

- If you use the short form of the password option (`-p`) and give the password value on the command line, there must be no space between the `-p` and the value. That is, `-ppass_val` is correct, but `-p pass_val` is not. This differs from the short form for other connection parameter options, where a space is allowed between the option and its value. (For example, `-hhost_name` and `-h host_name` are both valid.) This exceptional requirement that there be no space between `-p` and the password value is a logical necessity of allowing the option parameter to be omitted.

If you have a password specified in an option file but you want to connect using an account that has no password, specify -p or --password on the command line without a password value, and then press Enter at the Enter password: prompt.

Another option that affects the connection between the client and the server is --compress (or -C). This option causes data sent between the client and the server to be compressed before transmission and uncompressed upon receipt. The result is a reduction in the number of bytes sent over the connection, which can be helpful on slow networks. The cost is additional computational overhead for both the client and server to perform compression and uncompression. --compress and -C take no value after the option name.

Here are some examples that show how to specify connection parameters:

- Connect to the server using the default hostname and username values with no password:

```
shell> mysql
```

- Connect to the local server via shared memory (this works only on Windows). Use the default username and no password:

```
shell> mysql --protocol=memory
```

- Connect to the server on the local host with a username of myname, asking mysql to prompt you for a password:

```
shell> mysql --host=localhost --password --user=myname
```

- Connect with the same options as the previous example, but using the corresponding short option forms:

```
shell> mysql -h localhost -p -u myname
```

- Connect to the server at a specific IP address, with a username of myname and password of mypass:

```
shell> mysql --host=192.168.1.33 --user=myname --password=mypass
```

- Connect to the server on the local host, using the default username and password and compressing client/server traffic:

```
shell> mysql --host=localhost --compress
```

1.2.3 Using Option Files

As an alternative to specifying options on the command line, you can place them in an option file. The standard MySQL client programs look for option files at startup time and use any appropriate options they find there. Putting an option in a file saves you time and effort because you need not specify the option on the command line each time you invoke a program.

Options in option files are organized into groups, with each group preceded by a
[*group-name*] line that names the group. Typically, the group name is the name of the program to which the group of options applies. For example, the [mysql] and [mysqldump]
groups are for options to be used by mysql and mysqldump, respectively. The special group
named [client] can be used for specifying options that you want all client programs to use.
A common use for the [client] group is to specify connection parameters because typically
you connect to the same server no matter which client program you use.

To write an option in an option file, use the long option format that you would use on the
command line, but omit the leading dashes. If an option takes a value, spaces are allowed
around the = sign, something that isn't true for options specified on the command line.
Here's a sample option file:

```
[client]
host = myhost.example.com
compress

[mysql]
safe-updates
```

In this example, the [client] group specifies the server hostname and indicates that the
client/server protocol should use compression for traffic sent over the network. Options in
this group apply to all standard clients. The [mysql] group applies only to the mysql program. The group shown indicates that mysql should use the --safe-updates option. (mysql
uses options from both the [client] and [mysql] groups, so it would use all three options
shown.)

Where an option file should be located depends on your operating system. The standard
option files are as follows:

- On Windows, programs look for option files in the following order: my.ini and my.cnf
  in the Windows directory (for example, the C:\Windows or C:\WinNT directory), and then
  C:\my.ini and C:\my.cnf.

- On Unix, the file /etc/my.cnf serves as a global option file used by all users. Also, you
  can set up your own user-specific option file by creating a file named .my.cnf in your
  home directory. If both exist, the global file is read first.

Programs look for each of the standard option files and read any that exist. No error occurs
if a given file is not found. MySQL programs can access options from multiple option files.

To use an option file, create it as a plain text file using an editor.

To create or modify an option file, you must have write permission for it. Client programs
need only read access.

To tell a program to read a single specific option file instead of the standard option files, use the `--defaults-file=file_name` option as the first option on the command line. For example, to use only the file `C:\my-opts` for `mysql` and ignore the standard option files, invoke the program like this:

```
shell> mysql --defaults-file=C:\my-opts
```

To tell a program to read a single specific option file in addition to the standard option files, use the `--defaults-extra-file=file_name` option as the first option on the command line. To tell a program to ignore all option files, specify `--no-defaults` as the first option on the command line.

Option files can reference other files to be read for options by using `!include` and `!includedir` directives:

- A line that says `!include file_name` suspends processing of the current option file. The file `file_name` is read for additional options, and then processing of the suspended file resumes.

- A line that says `!includedir dir_name` is similar except that the directory `dir_name` is searched for files that end with a `.cnf` extension (`.cnf` and `.ini` on Windows). Any such files are read for options, and then processing of the suspended file resumes.

If an option is specified multiple times, either in the same option file or in multiple option files, the option value that occurs last takes precedence. Options specified on the command line take precedence over options found in option files.

1.2.4 Selecting a Default Database

For most client programs, you must specify a database so that the program knows where to find the tables that you want to use. The conventional way to do this is to name the database on the command line following any options. For example, to dump the contents of the `world` database to an output file named `world.sql`, you might run `mysqldump` like this:

```
shell> mysqldump --password --user=user_name world > world.sql
```

For the `mysql` client, a database name can be given on the command line, but is optional because you can explicitly indicate the database name for any table when you issue queries. For example, the following statement selects rows from the table `Country` in the `world` database:

```
mysql> SELECT * FROM world.Country;
```

To select or change the default database while running `mysql`, issue a `USE db_name` statement, where `db_name` is the name of the database you'd like to use. The following statement makes `world` the default database:

```
mysql> USE world;
```

The advantage of selecting a default database with USE is that in subsequent queries you can refer to tables in that database without having to specify the database name. For example, with world selected as the default database, the following SELECT statements are equivalent, but the second is easier to enter because the table name doesn't need to be qualified with the database name:

```
mysql> SELECT * FROM world.Country;
mysql> SELECT * FROM Country;
```

The default database sometimes is called the current database.

1.2.5 Establishing a Connection with a GUI Client

When you use a graphical client such as MySQL Query Browser or MySQL Administrator, the parameters used to connect to the server are similar to those used for command-line clients, but you specify them differently. Instead of reading options from the command line, the graphical clients present a dialog containing fields that you fill in. These programs also have the capability of saving sets of parameters as named connection profiles so that you can select profiles by name later. Section 3.5, "Connection Management," describes the connection process for the graphical clients.

1.3 Server SQL Modes

Many operational characteristics of MySQL Server can be configured by setting the SQL mode. This mode consists of optional values that each control some aspect of query processing. By setting the SQL mode appropriately, a client program can instruct the server how strict or forgiving to be about accepting input data, enable or disable behaviors relating to standard SQL conformance, or provide better compatibility with other database systems. This section discusses how to set the SQL mode. It's necessary to understand how to do this because references to the SQL mode occur throughout this study guide.

The SQL mode is controlled by means of the sql_mode system variable. To assign a value to this variable, use a SET statement. The value should be an empty string, or one or more mode names separated by commas. If the value is empty or contains more than one mode name, it must be quoted. If the value contains a single mode name, quoting is optional. SQL mode values are not case sensitive, although this study guide always writes them in uppercase. Here are some examples:

- Clear the SQL mode:

  ```
  SET sql_mode = '';
  ```

- Set the SQL mode using a single mode value:

  ```
  SET sql_mode = ANSI_QUOTES;
  SET sql_mode = 'TRADITIONAL';
  ```

- Set the SQL mode using multiple mode names:

```
SET sql_mode = 'IGNORE_SPACE,ANSI_QUOTES';
SET sql_mode = 'STRICT_ALL_TABLES,ERROR_FOR_DIVISION_BY_ZERO';
```

To check the current sql_mode setting, select its value like this:

```
mysql> SELECT @@sql_mode;
+-----------------------------------------------+
| @@sql_mode                                    |
+-----------------------------------------------+
| STRICT_ALL_TABLES,ERROR_FOR_DIVISION_BY_ZERO  |
+-----------------------------------------------+
```

Some SQL mode values are composite modes that actually enable a set of modes. Values in this category include ANSI and TRADITIONAL. To see which mode values a composite mode consists of, retrieve the value after setting it:

```
mysql> SET sql_mode='TRADITIONAL";
Query OK, 0 rows affected (0.07 sec)

mysql> SELECT @@sql_mode\G
*************************** 1. row ***************************
@@sql_mode: STRICT_TRANS_TABLES,STRICT_ALL_TABLES,NO_ZERO_IN_DATE,
            NO_ZERO_DATE,ERROR_FOR_DIVISION_BY_ZERO,TRADITIONAL,
            NO_AUTO_CREATE_USER
1 row in set (0.03 sec)
```

The *MySQL Reference Manual* lists all available SQL mode values. The following list briefly describes some of the values referred to elsewhere in this study guide:

- ANSI_QUOTES

  This mode causes the double quote character ('"') to be interpreted as an identifier-quoting character rather than as a string-quoting character.

- IGNORE_SPACE

  By default, functions must be written with no space between the function name and the following parenthesis. Enabling this mode causes the server to ignore spaces after function names. This allows spaces to appear between the name and the parenthesis, but also causes function names to be reserved words.

- ERROR_FOR_DIVISION_BY_ZERO

  By default, division by zero produces a result of NULL and is not treated specially. Enabling this mode causes division by zero in the context of inserting data into tables to produce a warning, or an error in strict mode.

- STRICT_TRANS_TABLES, STRICT_ALL_TABLES

  These values enable "strict mode," which imposes certain restrictions on what values are acceptable as database input. By default, MySQL is forgiving about accepting values that are missing, out of range, or malformed. Enabling strict mode causes bad values to be treated as erroneous. STRICT_TRANS_TABLES enables strict mode for transactional tables, and STRICT_ALL_TABLES enables strict mode for all tables.

- TRADITIONAL

  This is a composite mode that enables both strict modes plus several additional restrictions on acceptance of input data.

- ANSI

  This is a composite mode that causes MySQL Server to be more "ANSI-like." That is, it enables behaviors that are more like standard SQL, such as ANSI_QUOTES (described earlier) and PIPES_AS_CONCAT, which causes || to be treated as the string concatenation operator rather than as logical OR.

Section 5.8, "Handling Missing or Invalid Data Values," provides additional detail about the use of strict and traditional SQL modes for controlling how restrictive the server is about accepting input data.

2

The `mysql` Client Program

This chapter discusses `mysql`, a general-purpose client program for issuing queries and retrieving their results. It can be used interactively or in batch mode to read queries from a file. The chapter covers the following exam topics:

- Using `mysql` interactively and in batch mode
- `mysql` statement terminators and prompts
- Using the `mysql` input line-editing capability
- `mysql` output formats
- `mysql` internal commands
- Using server-side help
- Using the `--safe-updates` option to prevent dangerous data changes

2.1 Using `mysql` Interactively

The `mysql` client program enables you to send queries to the MySQL server and receive their results. It can be used interactively or it can read query input from a file in batch mode:

- Interactive mode is useful for day-to-day usage, for quick one-time queries, and for testing how queries work.
- Batch mode is useful for running queries that have been prewritten and stored in a file. It's especially valuable for issuing a complex series of queries that's difficult to enter manually, or queries that need to be run automatically by a job scheduler without user intervention.

This section describes how to use `mysql` interactively. Batch mode is covered in Section 2.5, "Using Script Files with `mysql`."

To invoke mysql interactively from the command line, specify any necessary connection parameters after the command name:

```
shell> mysql -u user_name -p -h host_name
```

You can also provide a database name to select that database as the default database:

```
shell> mysql -u user_name -p -h host_name db_name
```

mysql understands the standard command-line options for specifying connection parameters. It also reads options from option files. Connection parameters and option files are discussed in Section 1.2, "Invoking Client Programs."

After mysql connects to the MySQL server, it prints a mysql> prompt to indicate that it's ready to accept queries. To issue a query, enter it at the prompt. Complete the query with a statement terminator (typically a semicolon). The terminator tells mysql that the statement has been entered completely and should be executed. When mysql sees the terminator, it sends the query to the server and then retrieves and displays the result. For example:

```
mysql> SELECT DATABASE();
+------------+
| DATABASE() |
+------------+
| world      |
+------------+
```

A terminator is necessary after each statement because mysql allows several queries to be entered on a single input line. mysql uses the terminators to distinguish where each query ends, and then sends each one to the server in turn and displays its results:

```
mysql> SELECT DATABASE(); SELECT VERSION();
+------------+
| DATABASE() |
+------------+
| world      |
+------------+
+----------------+
| VERSION()      |
+----------------+
| 5.0.10-beta-log |
+----------------+
```

Statement terminators are necessary for another reason as well: mysql allows a single query to be entered using multiple input lines. This makes it easier to issue a long query because you can enter it over the course of several lines. mysql will wait until it sees the statement terminator before sending the query to the server to be executed. For example:

```
mysql> SELECT Name, Population FROM City
    -> WHERE CountryCode = 'IND'
```

```
    -> AND Population > 3000000;
+--------------------+------------+
| Name               | Population |
+--------------------+------------+
| Mumbai (Bombay)    |   10500000 |
| Delhi              |    7206704 |
| Calcutta [Kolkata] |    4399819 |
| Chennai (Madras)   |    3841396 |
+--------------------+------------+
```

Further information about statement terminators can be found in Section 2.2, "Statement Terminators."

In the preceding example, notice what happens when you don't complete the statement on a single input line: mysql changes the prompt from mysql> to -> to give you feedback that it's still waiting to see the end of the statement. The full set of mysql prompts is discussed in Section 2.3, "The mysql Prompts."

If a statement results in an error, mysql displays the error message returned by the server:

```
mysql> This is an invalid statement;
ERROR 1064 (42000): You have an error in your SQL syntax.
```

If you change your mind about a statement that you're composing, enter \c and mysql will cancel the statement and return you to a new mysql> prompt:

```
mysql> SELECT Name, Population FROM City
    -> WHERE \c
mysql>
```

To quit mysql, use \q, QUIT, or EXIT:

```
mysql> \q
```

You can execute a statement directly from the command line by using the -e or --execute option:

```
shell> mysql -e "SELECT VERSION()"
+-----------------+
| VERSION()       |
+-----------------+
| 5.0.10-beta-log |
+--------------- -+
```

No statement terminator is necessary unless the string following -e consists of multiple statements. In that case, separate the statements by semicolon characters.

2.2 Statement Terminators

You may use any of several terminators to end a statement. Two terminators are the semicolon character (';') and the \g sequence. They're equivalent and may be used interchangeably:

```
mysql> SELECT VERSION(), DATABASE();
+----------------+------------+
| VERSION()      | DATABASE() |
+----------------+------------+
| 5.0.10-beta-log | world     |
+----------------+------------+
mysql> SELECT VERSION(), DATABASE()\g
+----------------+------------+
| VERSION()      | DATABASE() |
+----------------+------------+
| 5.0.10-beta-log | world     |
+----------------+------------+
```

The \G sequence also terminates queries, but causes mysql to display query results in a vertical style that shows each output row with each column value on a separate line:

```
mysql> SELECT VERSION(), DATABASE()\G
*************************** 1. row ***************************
  VERSION(): 5.0.10-beta-log
DATABASE(): world
```

The \G terminator is especially useful if a query produces very wide output lines because vertical format can make the result much easier to read.

If you are using mysql to define a stored routine or a trigger that uses compound statement syntax and consists of multiple statements, the definition will contain semicolons internally. In this case, it is necessary to redefine the ';' terminator to cause mysql to pass semicolons in the definition to the server rather than interpreting them itself. Terminator redefinition is covered in Section 18.4, "Defining Stored Routines."

2.3 The mysql Prompts

The mysql> prompt displayed by mysql is just one of several different prompts that you might see when entering queries. Each type of prompt has a functional significance because mysql varies the prompt to provide information about the status of the statement you're entering. The following table shows each of these prompts.

Prompt	Meaning of Prompt
mysql>	Ready for new statement
->	Waiting for next line of statement
'>	Waiting for end of single-quoted string
">	Waiting for end of double-quoted string or identifier
`>	Waiting for end of backtick-quoted identifier
/*>	Waiting for end of C-style comment

The mysql> prompt is the main (or primary) prompt. It signifies that mysql is ready for you to begin entering a new statement.

The other prompts are continuation (or secondary) prompts. mysql displays them to indicate that it's waiting for you to finish entering the current statement. The -> prompt is the most generic continuation prompt. It indicates that you have not yet completed the current state-ment, for example, by entering ';' or \G. The '>, ">, and `> prompts are more specific. They indicate not only that you're in the middle of entering a statement, but that you're in the middle of entering a single-quoted string, a double-quoted string, or a backtick-quoted identifier, respectively. When you see one of these prompts, you'll often find that you have entered an opening quote on the previous line without also entering the proper closing quote.

If in fact you have mistyped the current statement by forgetting to close a quote, you can cancel the statement by entering the closing quote followed by the \c clear-statement command.

The /*> prompt indicates that you're in the middle of entering a multiple-line C-style com-ment (in /* ... */ format).

2.4 Using Editing Keys in mysql

mysql supports input-line editing, which enables you to recall and edit input lines. For exam-ple, you can use the up-arrow and down-arrow keys to move up and down through previous input lines, and the left-arrow and right-arrow keys to move back and forth within a line. Other keys, such as Backspace and Delete, erase characters from the line, and you can type in new characters at the cursor position. To submit an edited line, press Enter.

mysql also supports tab-completion to make it easier to enter queries. With tab-completion, you can enter part of a keyword or identifier and complete it using the Tab key. This feature is supported on Unix only.

2.5 Using Script Files with `mysql`

When used interactively, `mysql` reads queries entered at the keyboard. `mysql` can also accept input from a file. An input file containing SQL statements to be executed is known as a "script file" or a "batch file." A script file should be a plain text file containing statements in the same format that you would use to enter the statements interactively. In particular, each statement must end with a terminator.

One way to process a script file is by executing it with a `SOURCE` command from within `mysql`:

```
mysql> SOURCE input_file;
```

Notice that there are no quotes around the name of the file.

`mysql` executes the queries in the file and displays any output produced.

The file must be located on the client host where you're running `mysql`. The filename must either be an absolute pathname listing the full name of the file, or a pathname that's specified relative to the directory in which you invoked `mysql`. For example, if you started `mysql` on a Windows machine in the `C:\mysql` directory and your script file is `my_commands.sql` in the `C:\scripts` directory, both of the following `SOURCE` commands tell `mysql` to execute the SQL statements in the file:

```
mysql> SOURCE C:\scripts\my_commands.sql;
mysql> SOURCE ..\scripts\my_commands.sql;
```

The other way to execute a script file is by naming it on the `mysql` command line. Invoke `mysql` and use the `<` input redirection operator to specify the file from which to read query input:

```
shell> mysql db_name < input_file
```

If a statement in a script file fails with an error, `mysql` ignores the rest of the file. To execute the entire file regardless of whether errors occur, invoke `mysql` with the `--force` or `-f` option.

A script file can contain `SOURCE` commands to execute other files, but be careful not to create a `SOURCE` loop. For example, if `file1` contains a `SOURCE file2` command, `file2` should not contain a `SOURCE file1` command.

2.6 `mysql` Output Formats

By default, `mysql` produces output in one of two formats, depending on whether you use it in interactive or batch mode:

- When invoked interactively, `mysql` displays query output in a tabular format that uses bars and dashes to display values lined up in boxed columns.
- When you invoke `mysql` with a file as its input source on the command line, `mysql` runs in batch mode with query output displayed using tab characters between data values.

To override the default output format, use these options:

- --batch or -B

  Produce batch mode (tab-delimited) output, even when running interactively.

- --table or -t

  Produce tabular output format, even when running in batch mode.

In batch mode, you can use the --raw or -r option to suppress conversion of characters such as newline and carriage return to escape-sequences such as \n or \r. In raw mode, the characters are printed literally.

To select an output format different from either of the default formats, use these options:

- --html or -H

  Produce output in HTML format.

- --xml or -X

  Produce output in XML format.

2.7 Client Commands and SQL Statements

When you issue an SQL statement while running mysql, the program sends the statement to the MySQL server to be executed. SELECT, INSERT, UPDATE, and DELETE are examples of this type of input. mysql also understands a number of its own commands that aren't SQL statements. The QUIT and SOURCE commands that have already been discussed are examples of mysql commands. Another example is STATUS, which displays information about the current connection to the server, as well as status information about the server itself. Here is what a status display might look like:

```
mysql> STATUS;
mysql  Ver 14.12 Distrib 5.0.10-beta, for pc-linux-gnu (i686)

Connection id:          14498
Current database:       world
Current user:           myname@localhost
SSL:                    Not in use
Current pager:          stdout
Using outfile:          ''
Using delimiter:        ;
Server version:         5.0.10-beta-log
Protocol version:       10
Connection:             Localhost via UNIX socket
Server characterset:    latin1
Db      characterset:   latin1
Client characterset:    latin1
```

```
Conn. characterset:      latin1
UNIX socket:             /tmp/mysql.sock
Uptime:                  37 days 16 hours 50 min 3 sec

Threads: 4  Questions: 2439360  Slow queries: 854  Opens: 2523
Flush tables: 3  Open tables: 64  Queries per second avg: 0.749
--------------
```

A full list of mysql commands can be obtained using the HELP command.

mysql commands have both a long form and a short form. The long form is a full word (such as SOURCE, STATUS, or HELP). The short form consists of a backslash followed by a single character (such as \., \s, or \h). The long forms may be given in any lettercase. The short forms are case sensitive.

Unlike SQL statements, mysql commands cannot be entered over multiple lines. For example, if you issue a SOURCE *input_file* command to execute statements stored in a file, *input_file* must be given on the same line as SOURCE. It cannot be entered on the next line.

By default, the short command forms are recognized on any input line, except within quoted strings. The long command forms aren't recognized except at the mysql> primary prompt. For example, CLEAR and \c both clear (cancel) the current command, which is useful if you change your mind about issuing the statement that you're currently entering. But CLEAR isn't recognized after the first line of a multiple-line statement, so you should use \c instead. To have mysql recognize the long command names on any input line, invoke it with the --named-commands option.

2.8 Using Server-Side Help

The mysql program can access server-side help. That is, you can perform lookups in the *MySQL Reference Manual* for a particular topic, right from the mysql> prompt. The general syntax for accessing server-side help is HELP *keyword*. To display the topmost entries of the help system, use the contents keyword:

```
mysql> HELP contents;
You asked for help about help category: "Contents"
For more information, type 'help <item>', where <item> is one of
the following categories:
    Administration
    Column Types
    Data Definition
    Data Manipulation
    Functions
    Geographic features
    Transactions
```

You need not step through the items listed in the contents list to get help on a specific subject. Suppose that you need to know how to get status information from the server, but can't remember the command. Typing in the following command yields some hints:

```
mysql> HELP STATUS;
Many help items for your request exist
To make a more specific request, please type 'help <item>',
where <item> is one of the following
topics:
    SHOW
    SHOW MASTER STATUS
    SHOW SLAVE STATUS
```

To get the more specific information offered, use the HELP command with the SHOW keyword:

```
mysql> HELP SHOW;
Name: 'SHOW'
Description:

SHOW has many forms that provide information about databases,
tables, columns, or status information about the server.
This section describes those following:

SHOW [FULL] COLUMNS FROM tbl_name [FROM db_name] [LIKE 'pattern']
SHOW CREATE DATABASE db_name
SHOW CREATE TABLE tbl_name
SHOW DATABASES [LIKE 'pattern']
SHOW [STORAGE] ENGINES
SHOW ERRORS [LIMIT [offset,] row_count]
SHOW GRANTS FOR user
SHOW INDEX FROM tbl_name [FROM db_name]
SHOW INNODB STATUS
SHOW [BDB] LOGS
SHOW PRIVILEGES
SHOW [FULL] PROCESSLIST
SHOW STATUS [LIKE 'pattern']
SHOW TABLE STATUS [FROM db_name] [LIKE 'pattern']
SHOW [OPEN] TABLES [FROM db_name] [LIKE 'pattern']
SHOW [GLOBAL | SESSION] VARIABLES [LIKE 'pattern']
SHOW WARNINGS [LIMIT [offset,] row_count]

The SHOW statement also has forms that provide information about
replication master and slave servers and are described in [Replication
SQL]:

SHOW BINLOG EVENTS
SHOW MASTER LOGS
SHOW MASTER STATUS
```

```
SHOW SLAVE HOSTS
SHOW SLAVE STATUS
```

```
If the syntax for a given SHOW statement includes a LIKE 'pattern' part,
'pattern' is a string that can contain the SQL '%' and '_' wildcard
characters.  The pattern is useful for restricting statement output to
matching values.
```

Server-side help requires the help tables in the mysql database to be loaded, but normally these files will be loaded by default unless you install MySQL by compiling it yourself.

2.9 Using the --safe-updates Option

It's possible to inadvertently issue statements that modify many rows in a table or that return extremely large result sets. The --safe-updates option helps prevent these problems. The option is particularly useful for people who are just learning to use MySQL. --safe-updates has the following effects:

- UPDATE and DELETE statements are allowed only if they include a WHERE clause that specifically identifies which records to update or delete by means of a key value, or if they include a LIMIT clause.
- Output from single-table SELECT statements is restricted to no more than 1,000 rows unless the statement includes a LIMIT clause.
- Multiple-table SELECT statements are allowed only if MySQL will examine no more than 1,000,000 rows to process the query.

The --i-am-a-dummy option is a synonym for --safe-updates.

MySQL Query Browser

This chapter discusses MySQL Query Browser, a client program that provides a graphical interface to the MySQL server for querying and analyzing data. The chapter covers the following exam topics:

- An overview of MySQL Query Browser features
- Launching MySQL Query Browser
- Query construction and execution capabilities
- The MySQL Table Editor
- Connection management capabilities
- The Options dialog

3.1 MySQL Query Browser Capabilities

MySQL Query Browser is a cross-platform GUI client program that's intuitive and easy to use. It provides a graphical interface to the MySQL server for querying and analyzing data. It's similar in style of use to MySQL Administrator but is oriented toward accessing database contents rather than server administration.

The following list describes some of the ways that you can use MySQL Query Browser:

- Interactively enter, edit, and execute queries.
- Navigate result sets with scrolling. Multiple result sets are tabbed so that you can switch between them easily by selecting the appropriate tab.
- Browse the databases available on the server, the tables and stored routines in databases, and the columns in tables.
- Browse your query history to see what queries you've issued, or recall and re-execute previous queries.
- Bookmark queries for easy recall.
- Create or drop databases and tables, and modify the structure of existing tables.

- Create and edit SQL scripts, with debugging.
- Edit connection profiles that can be used to connect to servers more easily.
- Access information from the MySQL Reference Manual, such as statement syntax and function descriptions.

MySQL Query Browser supports multiple server connections and opens a separate window for each connection that you establish.

3.2 Using MySQL Query Browser

MySQL Query Browser is not included with MySQL distributions but can be obtained from the MySQL AB Web site. It's available in precompiled form for Windows and Linux, or it can be compiled from source.

MySQL Query Browser requires a graphical environment such as Windows or the X Window System. On Linux, MySQL Query Browser is designed for Gnome, but can be run under KDE if GTK2 is installed. If a MySQL server is running on a host with no graphical environment, you can connect to it remotely by running MySQL Query Browser on a client host that does have a graphical environment.

On Windows, the installer creates a desktop icon and an entry in the Start Menu, so you can start MySQL Query Browser using either of those. The program itself is located in the installation directory, `C:\Program Files\MySQL\MySQL Query Browser 1.1`, so you can also start MySQL Query Browser from the command line by invoking it directly after changing location into that directory:

```
C:\> cd "C:\Program Files\MySQL\MySQL Query Browser 1.1"
C:\Program Files\MySQL\MySQL Query Browser 1.1> MySQLQueryBrowser.exe
```

RPM installations on Linux place MySQL Query Browser in `/usr/bin`. Assuming that this directory is in your search path, you can invoke the program as follows:

```
shell> mysql-query-browser
```

For `tar` file distributions, MySQL Query Browser is installed wherever you unpacked the distribution, and the program is located in the `bin` directory under the installation directory. To invoke the program, change location to that `bin` directory. For example, if you installed the distribution at `/opt/mysql-query-browser`, start MySQL Query Browser like this:

```
shell> cd /opt/mysql-query-browser/bin
shell> ./mysql-query-browser
```

On all platforms, after you start MySQL Query Browser, it displays a Connection dialog. To connect to a MySQL server, fill in the required connection parameters in the dialog or select from among any connection profiles that may already have been defined. The Connection dialog is described in Section 3.5, "Connection Management."

After you connect to the MySQL server, MySQL Query Browser displays a window that you can use for issuing queries. (See Figure 3.1.)

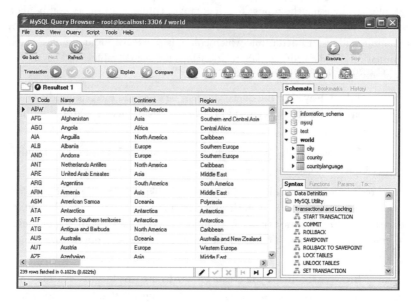

FIGURE 3.1   MySQL Query Browser main window.

To open connections to additional servers, select New Instance Connection ... from the File menu. MySQL Query Browser opens a separate query window for each connection.

As shown in the figure, a query window has several major areas:

- The top part of the window contains an area for entering queries and has several sets of buttons that aid in query construction and execution.

- At the lower left, a result area displays results from queries. There can be multiple results, each accessible as a tab so that you can easily switch from one to another.

- At the right, there are two browser areas. The Object Browser allows you to navigate databases, bookmarked queries, and your query history. The Information Browser provides access to statement syntax and function documentation and to query parameters.

The query window also contains several menus from which you can access additional features. For example, you can access the Script Editor from the File menu.

3.3 Using the Query Window

This section describes how to use the different areas of the MySQL Query Browser query window.

3.3.1 Entering Queries

You can enter queries manually by typing them into the query area, or you can construct queries graphically by using the mouse to select tables, columns, or query components such as joins or WHERE clauses. If you drag multiple tables into a query, MySQL Query Browser constructs a join and tries to determine which columns to use for joining tables. It makes this determination based on foreign key relationships for InnoDB tables, and based on identical column names for other types of tables.

The query currently displayed in the query area can be executed by clicking the Execute button, by entering Ctrl-E at the keyboard, or by selecting a query execution option from the Query menu.

MySQL Query Browser provides syntax highlighting, which helps you see and understand the structure of queries more readily.

Queries are saved in your query history, and you can bookmark specific queries by dragging them to the bookmark browser. Previously executed queries can be recalled by using the bookmark browser or history browser. To use a previous query from one of these browsers, drag it from the browser area to the query area. Recalled queries are subject to further editing.

MySQL Query Browser also helps you create views. To use this feature, execute a SELECT statement and click the Create View button. This brings up a dialog for you to enter the view name. MySQL Query Browser creates a view with the given name, defined using the current SELECT statement. (You can also enter a CREATE VIEW statement directly.)

3.3.2 The Result Area

When you execute a query, its results appear in the query window result area. This area provides flexible result display and has the following characteristics:

- For results that do not fit within the display area, scroll bars appear that allow you to navigate the result by scrolling. It's also possible to toggle the result set display to use the entire query window.

- If a result set is selected from a single table that has a primary key, the result set can be edited to modify the original table. (There is an Edit button in the result area that enables editing.) You can modify individual values within rows to update them, enter new rows, or delete rows.

- The contents of a result are searchable. The result area has a Search button that provides access to Search and Replace dialogs. You can look for a given value in the entire result or within specific columns. Searches can be case sensitive or not, and they can be based on whole word or partial word matching.

- A result is placed within the current tab of the result area, and each successive query overwrites the tab contents. To prevent this, you can create additional tabs for displaying multiple results and then switch between then.

- You can split a result area tab horizontally or vertically to customize its display or to take advantage of additional features. For example, you can split a tab vertically, load two results into the left and right halves, and then click the Compare button to compare the results. MySQL Query Browser matches up the rows in the two halves to make visual comparison easier. You can also perform master-detail analysis using a split result tab. This type of analysis displays the relationship between master records in one table and the corresponding detail records in another table.

3.3.3 The Script Editor

The query area is designed for entry and execution of single SQL statements. To extend this capability, MySQL Query Browser includes a Script Editor that allows you to edit, execute, and debug scripts that consist of multiple statements.

The Script Editor presents an interface that is displayed as a tab in the result area. To activate it, select either New Script Tab or Open Script … from the File menu, depending on whether you want to create a new script or edit one that is stored in a file.

The Script Editor offers these features:

- Syntax highlighting
- Line numbering
- Script execution
- Debugging options such as single-stepping and breakpoints

3.3.4 Stored Routine Management

MySQL Query Browser assists you in managing stored procedures several ways:

- It helps you create new routines by prompting for a routine name and taking you to the Script Editor and providing a template for the routine definition.
- You can edit existing routines.
- The database browser shows stored routines in a database when you expand the display for the database. If you expand the display for a routine, the browser shows the routine's parameters.

3.3.5 The Object and Information Browsers

The right side of the query window contains two browsers: the Object Browser and the Information Browser. The area for each browser contains several sub-browsers.

The area for the Object Browser provides access to databases and queries:

- The database browser (schemata browser) displays a hierarchical view of your databases. It lists each database, with the default database name highlighted so that you can tell at a glance which one is current. The default database is the one used for references to tables and routines that are not qualified with a database name.

The display for any database can be expanded to show the tables and stored routines within the database. Likewise, expanding a table display shows its columns and expanding a routine's display shows its parameters.

Double-clicking a database name selects it as the default database. Double-clicking a table name enters a `SELECT * FROM` *table_name* statement in the query area.

Right-clicking in the database browser brings up a menu for additional capabilities:

- Right-click in the browser to create a new database or table.
- Right-click on a database name to drop the database.
- Right-click on a table name to drop the table or edit it with the MySQL Table Editor.

- The bookmark browser lists those queries that you have bookmarked. You can organize bookmarks hierarchically by creating folders and moving, removing, or renaming bookmarks.
- The history browser contains previously issued queries, hierarchically organized by day.
- You can drag queries from the bookmark or history browser to the query area for re-execution. Double-clicking a query also enters it into the query area.

The area for the Information Browser provides access to documentation, query parameters, and current-transaction information:

- The syntax browser lists SQL statements. Double-clicking on a statement displays syntax information for it from the *MySQL Reference Manual*. The information appears in a tab in the result area.
- The function browser lists the built-in functions that you can use in SQL statements. Double-clicking on a function displays the description for it from the *MySQL Reference Manual*. The information appears in a tab in the result area.
- The parameter browser displays query parameters.
- The transaction browser shows the statements that are part of the current transaction.

3.4 The MySQL Table Editor

MySQL Query Browser has a table editor facility that enables you to create tables or edit the definitions of existing tables. To access the MySQL Table Editor, right-click on a table name in the database browser and select Edit Table. The MySQL Table Editor also can be accessed from the MySQL Administrator program: Select the Catalogs section of the main window, select a database, and then right-click on a table name and select Edit Table.

The MySQL Table Editor provides a graphic interface for manipulation of table definitions, as shown in Figure 3.2.

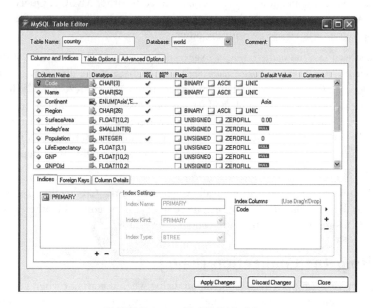

FIGURE 3.2   MySQL Table Editor.

The MySQL Table Editor enables you to perform the following tasks:

- Create new tables or edit the structure of existing tables
- Rename tables or move tables to a different database
- Change table options, such as the storage engine, character set and collation, or table comment
- Specify column definitions (name, data type, and attributes)
- Define indexes and foreign keys

The Options dialog has an Editors section that enables you to set MySQL Table Editor preferences. See Section 3.6, "The Options Dialog."

3.5 Connection Management

MySQL Query Browser provides a Connection dialog that enables you to connect to a MySQL server, and a connection editor that you can use to create profiles that store connection parameters for later use. This section describes how to use the Connection dialog and the connection editor. The discussion also applies to MySQL Administrator, which has the same connection management facilities.

A connection profile is a set of connection parameters to which you assign a name. You can recall profiles by name later. The use of profiles makes it easy to set up and use connections for multiple servers. Connection profiles can be created in either MySQL Query Browser or MySQL Administrator, and are shared by the two programs. That is, a profile created within one program can be used within the other.

Profiles are stored in a file named `mysqlx_user_connections.xml`. The location of this file is the `C:\Documents and Settings\`*user_name*`\Application Data\MySQL` directory on Windows and the `~/.mysqlgui` directory on Unix. Profiles are stored as plain text in XML format, which means that profiles are portable and have good cross-platform compatibility. A file containing connection profiles can be given to other users on the same or different machines. This makes it easy to set up standard profiles and distribute them, a feature that can be useful in a classroom or training setting, or if you want to distribute standard profiles along with an application.

The connections file is updated automatically when you use the Connection dialog or connection editor. Because the file is plain text, its contents can be edited by other programs as well, and the changes will be visible to the connection editor.

3.5.1 Using the Connection Dialog

MySQL Query Browser presents a Connection dialog when it starts or when you select New Instance Connection … from the File menu. (See Figure 3.3.) This dialog enables you to connect to a MySQL server. You can either fill in its fields with the parameters required to connect to a server or select from among any predefined connection profiles. The Connection dialog also provides access to the connection editor, which enables you to create, edit, and delete connection profiles.

FIGURE 3.3   Connection dialog.

To connect to a MySQL server by specifying connection parameters directly, fill in the appropriate fields beginning with the `Username` field and click the `OK` button. To connect using the parameters stored in a connection profile, select the profile from the Connection drop-down list and click the OK button. To access the connection editor, click the ... button next to the Connection drop-down list.

3.5.2 Editing Connection Profiles

The connection editor enables you to create, edit, and delete connection profiles. The connection editor also maintains a history of recent connections. You can access this editor from the Connection dialog or by selecting Options ... from the Tools menu and selecting the Connections section of the Options dialog. In either case, the connection editor window is displayed, as shown in Figure 3.4.

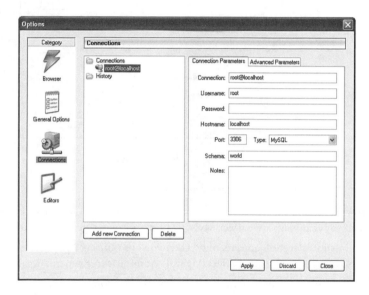

FIGURE 3.4   Connection Editor.

The Connections section has a browser for existing connection profiles. It also displays a history of previous connections that were made without using a connection profile. The other part of the Connections section has a tab for specifying general connection parameters and another for other options. To edit a profile, select it in the browser and then modify the fields displayed by the two tabs. You can also use the Add New Connection and Delete buttons to create and delete profiles.

3.6 The Options Dialog

The Options dialog allows you to configure several aspects of MySQL Query Browser behavior. The settings configured via this dialog are read by MySQL Administrator, so they affect that program, too.

To access the Options dialog, select the Options … item from the Tools menu. The dialog has several sections, as shown in Figure 3.5.

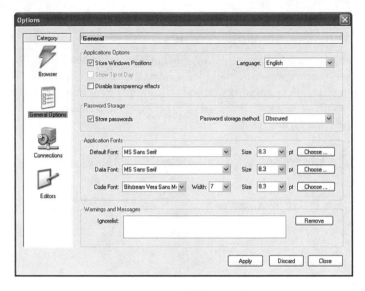

FIGURE 3.5   Options dialog.

The sections in the Options dialog are used as follows:

- The Browser section appears only when you are running MySQL Query Browser. It allows you to set options that affect MySQL Query Browser general defaults.

- The Administrator section appears only when you are running MySQL Administrator. It allows you to set options that affect MySQL Administrator general defaults.

- The General Options section customizes program behavior. It controls settings such as font, language selection, and whether to save passwords in connection profiles. Passwords can be saved as plain text or in "obscured" format. The latter is weak encryption that is unsophisticated and will not defeat a determined attack, but it does make stored passwords not directly visible via simple inspection.

- The Connections section allows you to create, edit, and delete connection profiles. It also has a browser that provides information about recent connections. The connection editor is discussed in Section 3.5, "Connection Management."

- The Editors section configures defaults for the MySQL Table Editor for creating tables, such as the default storage engine and data type, whether to define columns as NOT NULL by default, and whether integer columns should be UNSIGNED by default. It also gives you control over the conventions used when naming indexes and foreign keys.

4

MySQL Connectors

This chapter discusses the family of MySQL Connectors that provide connectivity to MySQL Server for client programs. It covers the following exam topics:

- An overview of the programming interfaces available for MySQL client programs
- The MySQL Connector/ODBC driver for programs that use the ODBC (Open Database Connectivity) interface
- The MySQL Connector/J driver that provides JDBC connectivity to Java programs
- The MySQL Connector/NET driver for programs that use the .NET Framework

4.1 MySQL Client Interfaces

MySQL AB provides several application programming interfaces (APIs) for accessing the MySQL server. The interface included with distributions of MySQL itself is libmysqlclient, the C client library. This API may be used for writing MySQL-based C programs. It is also the basis for most higher-level APIs written for other languages (the Java and .NET interfaces are notable exceptions).

MySQL AB also provides drivers that aren't programs in themselves, but act as bridges to the MySQL server for client programs that communicate using a particular protocol. These drivers comprise the family of MySQL Connectors. They are available as separate packages.

- MySQL Connector/ODBC provides a MySQL-specific driver for ODBC. It allows ODBC-compliant programs to access MySQL.
- MySQL Connector/J is a JDBC driver for use in Java programs. It allows JDBC-compliant programs to access MySQL.
- MySQL Connector/NET is a driver written in C# that supports the ADO.NET interfaces required to run .NET applications that access MySQL.

The MySQL connectors are available for Windows and Unix. To use a connector, you must install it on the client host. It isn't necessary for the server to be running on the same machine or for the server to be running the same operating system as the client. This means that MySQL connectors are very useful for providing MySQL connectivity in heterogeneous environments. For example, people who use Windows machines can run client applications that access MySQL databases located on a Linux server host.

Each of the preceding APIs is officially supported by MySQL AB. In addition, many third-party client interfaces are available. Most of them are based on the C client library and provide a binding for some other language. These include the mysql and mysqli extensions for PHP, the DBD::mysql driver for the Perl DBI module, and interfaces for other languages such as Python, Ruby, Pascal, and Tcl. Although you can download these client APIs from the MySQL Web site and members of the MySQL AB development team often work closely with the developers of these products, the APIs do not receive official support from MySQL AB. If you're embarking on a project that involves these APIs, you should contact the developers to determine whether future support will be available.

4.2 MySQL Connector/ODBC

MySQL Connector/ODBC acts as a bridge between the MySQL server and client programs that use the ODBC standard. It provides a MySQL-specific driver for ODBC so that ODBC-based clients can access MySQL databases.

MySQL Connector/ODBC uses the C client library to implement the client/server communication protocol. It converts ODBC calls made by the client program into C API operations that communicate with the server. Connections can be established using TCP/IP, Unix socket files, or named pipes.

MySQL Connector/ODBC is available for Windows and Unix.

4.3 MySQL Connector/J

MySQL Connector/J is similar in spirit to Connector/ODBC, but is used by JDBC-based Java programs. It is not based on the C client library. Instead, it is written in Java and implements the client/server communication protocol directly. Connections can be established using TCP/IP or named pipes. MySQL Connector/J converts JDBC calls made by the client program into the appropriate protocol operations.

MySQL Connector/J is a Type 4 (pure Java) driver that implements version 3.0 of the JDBC specification.

MySQL Connector/J includes support for MySQL capabilities such as server-side prepared statements, stored routines, and Unicode.

MySQL Connector/J is available for Windows and Unix.

4.4 MySQL Connector/NET

MySQL Connector/NET enables .NET applications to use MySQL. It is not based on the C client library. Instead, it is written in C# and implements the client/server communication protocol directly. Connections can be established using TCP/IP, Unix socket files, named pipes, or shared memory.

MySQL Connector/NET includes support for MySQL capabilities such as server-side prepared statements, stored routines, and Unicode.

MySQL Connector/NET is available for Windows. If you use Mono, the Open Source implementation of .NET developed by Novell, it is also available on Linux.

5

Data Types

This chapter discusses data types for representing information in MySQL. It covers the following exam topics:

- An overview of available data types
- Numeric data types
- The BIT data type
- String data types
- Temporal (date and time) data types
- Attributes that modify how columns are handled
- The AUTO_INCREMENT attribute for sequence generation
- Controlling how MySQL handles missing or invalid input data values

5.1 Data Type Overview

MySQL enables you to store several different types of data, and it's important to understand what data types are available so that you can define your tables appropriately for the information they'll contain. Generally speaking, data values can be grouped into the following categories:

- Numeric values. Numbers may or may not have a fractional part and may have a leading sign. For example, 14, -428.948, and +739 all are legal numbers. Integer values have no fractional part; columns for values with a fractional part can be declared to have either a fixed or variable number of decimal places. Numeric columns can be declared to be unsigned to prevent negative values from being accepted in the column. A BIT data type holds bit-field values, and a b'nnnn' notation is available for writing literal bit values.

- String values. Strings may be non-binary or binary, to store characters or raw bytes, respectively. Strings that store characters have a character set and collation; they can be case sensitive or case insensitive. Strings are written within quotes (for example, 'I am a `string`'). String columns can be declared as either fixed length or variable length. `BLOB` values (binary large objects) are treated as strings in MySQL.

- Temporal values. Temporal values include dates (such as `'2005-11-03'`), times (such as `'14:23:00'`), and values that have both a date and a time part (`'2005-11-03 14:23:00'`). MySQL also supports a special temporal type that represents year-only values efficiently. Date and time values can be written as quoted strings and may sometimes be written as numbers in contexts where numeric temporal values are understood.

MySQL also supports manipulation of spatial values using a set of spatial data types. Spatial types are not covered in this study guide or on the exam. See the *MySQL Reference Manual* for details.

When you create a table, the declaration for each of its columns includes the column name, a data type that indicates what kind of values the column may hold, and possibly some attributes (options) that more specifically define how MySQL should handle the column. For example, the following statement creates a table named `people`, which contains an integer-valued numeric column named `id` and two 30-character string columns named `first_name` and `last_name`:

```
CREATE TABLE people
(
    id         INT,
    first_name CHAR(30),
    last_name  CHAR(30)
);
```

The column definitions in that `CREATE TABLE` statement contain only names and data types. To more specifically control how MySQL handles a column, add attributes to the column definition. For example, to disallow negative values in the `id` column, add the `UNSIGNED` attribute. To disallow missing or unknown values in the columns, add `NOT NULL` to each column definition so that `NULL` values cannot be stored. The modified `CREATE TABLE` statement looks like this:

```
CREATE TABLE people
(
    id         INT UNSIGNED NOT NULL,
    first_name CHAR(30) NOT NULL,
    last_name  CHAR(30) NOT NULL
);
```

For additional control over input data handing, you can set the SQL mode to determine how forgiving or strict MySQL Server is about accepting invalid values.

For each of the general data categories (number, string, and temporal), MySQL has several specific data types from which to choose. It's important to properly understand what data types are available for representing data, to avoid choosing a type that isn't appropriate. The following sections describe these data types and their properties. For additional details, see the *MySQL Reference Manual*.

5.2 Numeric Data Types

For storing numeric data, MySQL provides integer data types, floating-point types that store approximate-value numbers, a fixed-point type that stores exact-value numbers, and a BIT type for bit-field values. When you choose a numeric data type, consider the following factors:

- The range of values the data type represents
- The amount of storage space that column values require
- The display width indicating the maximum number of characters to use when presenting column values in query output
- The column precision and scale for floating-point and fixed-point values

Precision and scale are terms that apply to floating-point and fixed-point values, which can have both an integer part and a fractional part. Precision is the number of significant digits. Scale is the number of digits to the right of the decimal point.

5.2.1 Integer Data Types

Integer data types include TINYINT, SMALLINT, MEDIUMINT, INT, and BIGINT. Smaller integer types require less storage space, but are more limited in the range of values they represent. For example, TINYINT column values take only one byte each to store, but the type has a small range (–128 to 127). INT column values require four bytes each, but the type has a much larger range (–2,147,483,648 to 2,147,483,647). The integer data types are summarized in the following table, which indicates the amount of storage per value that each type requires as well as its range. For integer values declared with the UNSIGNED attribute, negative values are not allowed, and the high end of the range shifts upward to approximately double the maximum positive value of the signed range.

Type	Storage Required	Signed Range	Unsigned Range
TINYINT	1 byte	–128 to 127	0 to 255
SMALLINT	2 bytes	–32,768 to 32,767	0 to 65,535
MEDIUMINT	3 bytes	–8,388,608 to 8,388,607	0 to 16,777,215
INT	4 bytes	–2,147,683,648 to 2,147,483,647	0 to 4,294,967,295
BIGINT	8 bytes	–9,223,372,036,854,775,808 to 9,223,372,036,854,775,807	0 to 18,446,744,073, 709,551,615

Integer data types may be declared with a display width, which affects the number of digits used to display column values in query output. For example, assume that you declare an INT column with a display width of 4 like this:

```
century INT(4)
```

The result is that values in the century column usually are displayed four digits wide. However, it's important to understand that the display width is unrelated to the range of the data type. The display width specified for a column affects only the maximum number of digits MySQL uses to display column values. Values shorter than the display width are padded with spaces as necessary. Note also that the display width is not a hard limit; it won't cause output truncation of a value that's too long to fit within the width. Instead, the full value is shown. For example, assume that you've inserted the number 57622 into the century column. When you SELECT the column in a query, MySQL displays the entire value (57622), not just the first four digits of the value.

The display width for integer types also is unrelated to storage requirements. For example, an INT(4) column does not require half as much storage per value as INT(8). All values for the INT data type require four bytes.

If you specify no display width for an integer type, MySQL chooses a default based on the number of characters needed to display the full range of values for the type (including the minus sign, for signed types). For example, SMALLINT has a default display width of 6 because the widest possible value is -32768.

5.2.2 Floating-Point Data Types

The floating-point data types include FLOAT and DOUBLE. Each of these types may be used to represent approximate-value numbers that have an integer part, a fractional part, or both. FLOAT and DOUBLE data types represent values in the native binary floating-point format used by the server host's CPU. This is a very efficient type for storage and computation, but values are subject to rounding error.

FLOAT represents single-precision floating-point values that require four bytes each for storage. DOUBLE represents double-precision floating-point values that require eight bytes each for storage.

You can specify explicit precision and scale values in the column definition to indicate the number of significant digits and the number of decimal places to the right of the decimal point. The following definitions specify a single-precision column with a precision of 10 digits and scale of 3 decimals, and a double-precision column with a precision of 20 digits and scale of 7 decimals:

```
weight FLOAT(10,3)
avg_score DOUBLE(20,7)
```

If you specify no precision or scale, MySQL represents values stored in FLOAT and DOUBLE columns to the maximum accuracy allowed by the hardware of the MySQL server host. The following definitions include no explicit precision or scale:

```
float_col FLOAT
double_col DOUBLE
```

Floating-point values are stored using mantissa/exponent representation, which means that the precision is defined by the width of the mantissa and the scale varies depending on the exponent value. The result of these factors is that stored values are approximate.

5.2.3 Fixed-Point Data Types

The fixed-point data type is DECIMAL. It is used to represent exact-value numbers that have an integer part, a fractional part, or both.

DECIMAL uses a fixed-decimal storage format: All values in a DECIMAL column have the same number of decimal places and are stored exactly as given when possible. DECIMAL values are not processed quite as efficiently as FLOAT or DOUBLE values (which use the processor's native binary format), but DECIMAL values are not subject to rounding error, so they are more accurate. In other words, there is an accuracy versus speed tradeoff in choosing which type to use. For example, the DECIMAL data type is a popular choice for financial applications involving currency calculations, because accuracy is most important.

DECIMAL columns may be declared with a precision and scale to indicate the number of significant digits and the number of decimal places to the right of the decimal point. For example, if you want to represent values such as dollar-and-cents currency figures, you can do so using a two-digit scale:

```
cost DECIMAL(10,2)
```

The precision and scale can be omitted, or just the scale. The defaults for omitted precision and scale are 10 and 0, respectively, so the following declarations are equivalent:

```
total DECIMAL
total DECIMAL(10)
total DECIMAL(10,0)
```

The amount of storage required for DECIMAL column values depends on the precision and scale. Approximately four bytes are required per nine digits on each side of the decimal point.

The NUMERIC data type in MySQL is a synonym for DECIMAL. (If you declare a column as NUMERIC, MySQL uses DECIMAL in the definition.) Standard SQL allows for a difference between the two types, but in MySQL they are the same. In standard SQL, the precision for NUMERIC must be exactly the number of digits given in the column definition. The precision for DECIMAL must be at least that many digits but is allowed to be more. In MySQL, the precision is exactly as given, for both types.

5.3 The BIT Data Type

The BIT data type represents bit-field values. BIT column specifications take a width indicating the number of bits per value, from 1 to 64 bits. The following columns store 4 and 20 bits per value, respectively:

```
bit_col1 BIT(4)
bit_col2 BIT(20)
```

For a BIT(n) column, the range of values is 0 to $2^n - 1$, and the storage requirement is approximately INT((n+7)/8) bytes per value.

BIT columns can be assigned values using numeric expressions. To write literal bit values in binary format, the literal-value notation b'val' can be used, where val indicates a value consisting of the binary digits 0 and 1. For example, b'1111' equals 15 and b'1000000' equals 64.

5.4 String Data Types

The following table lists the string data types provided in MySQL.

Type	Description
CHAR	Fixed-length non-binary string
VARCHAR	Variable-length non-binary string
TEXT	Variable-length non-binary string
BINARY	Fixed-length binary string
VARBINARY	Variable-length binary string
BLOB	Variable-length binary string
ENUM	Enumeration consisting of a fixed set of legal values
SET	Set consisting of a fixed set of legal values

When you choose a string data type, consider the following factors:

- Whether you need to store non-binary or binary strings; are character set and collation important?
- The maximum length of values you need to store.
- Whether to use a fixed or variable amount of storage.
- How trailing spaces are handled for comparison, storage, and retrieval.
- The number of distinct values required; ENUM or SET may be useful if the set of values is fixed.

The following discussion first describes the general differences between non-binary and binary strings, and then the specific characteristics of each of the string data types.

5.4.1 Character Set Support

Strings in MySQL may be treated as non-binary or binary. The differences between these types of strings make them suited to different purposes. The most general difference is that non-binary strings have a character set and consist of characters in that character set, whereas binary strings consist simply of bytes that are distinguished only by their numeric values. This section explores the implications of this difference.

Non-binary strings have the following characteristics:

- A non-binary string is a sequence of characters that belong to a specific character set. Characters may consist of a single byte, or multiple bytes if the character set allows it. For example, MySQL's default character set is latin1 (also known as ISO-8859-1). The latin1 character set uses one byte per character. In contrast, sjis (the Japanese SJIS character set), contains so many characters that they cannot all be represented in a single byte, so each character requires multiple bytes to store.

- Multi-byte character sets may require a fixed or variable number of bytes per character. The ucs2 Unicode character set uses two bytes per character, whereas the utf8 Unicode character set uses from one to three bytes per character.

- Non-binary string comparisons are based on the collation (sorting order) of the character set associated with the string. A given character set may have one or more collations, but a given string has only one of those collations.

- Multi-byte character comparisons are performed in character units, not in byte units.

- The collation determines whether uppercase and lowercase versions of a given character are equivalent. If the collation is not case sensitive, strings such as 'ABC', 'Abc', and 'abc' are all considered equal. If the collation is case sensitive, the strings are all considered different.

- The collation also determines whether to treat instances of a given character with different accent marks as equivalent. The result is that comparisons of non-binary strings may not be accent sensitive. For example, an 'a' with no accent may be considered the same as the 'á' and 'à' characters. A given collation may be case or accent sensitive, or both.

- A collation can be a binary collation. In this case, comparisons are based on numeric character values. One effect of this is that for character sets with uppercase and lowercase characters or accented characters, the collation is case sensitive and accent sensitive because each of these characters has a different numeric value. Comparison based on a binary collation differs from comparison of binary strings: A binary collation is performed per character, and characters might consist of multiple bytes. Comparisons for binary strings are always byte-based.

A given character set may have several collations to choose from. This enables you to select different sort orders for the same character set. For example, with the latin1 character set, you can choose from any of the following collations, many of which correspond to the sorting order rules of specific languages:

```
mysql> SHOW COLLATION LIKE 'latin1%';
+------------------+---------+----+---------+----------+---------+
| Collation        | Charset | Id | Default | Compiled | Sortlen |
+------------------+---------+----+---------+----------+---------+
| latin1_german1_ci | latin1 |  5 |         |          |       0 |
| latin1_swedish_ci | latin1 |  8 | Yes     | Yes      |       1 |
| latin1_danish_ci  | latin1 | 15 |         |          |       0 |
| latin1_german2_ci | latin1 | 31 |         | Yes      |       2 |
| latin1_bin        | latin1 | 47 |         | Yes      |       1 |
| latin1_general_ci | latin1 | 48 |         |          |       0 |
| latin1_general_cs | latin1 | 49 |         |          |       0 |
| latin1_spanish_ci | latin1 | 94 |         |          |       0 |
+------------------+---------+----+---------+----------+---------+
```

Each collation name ends with _ci, _cs, or _bin, signifying that the collation is case insensitive, case sensitive, or binary.

Binary strings have the following characteristics:

- A binary string is treated as a sequence of byte values. It might appear to contain characters, because you can write a binary string value as a quoted string, but it "really" contains binary data as far as MySQL is concerned.

- Because binary strings contain bytes, not characters, comparisons of binary strings are performed on the basis of the byte values in the string. This has the implication that the concept of lettercase does not apply the same way as for non-binary strings. Binary strings may appear to be case sensitive, but that is because uppercase and lowercase versions of a given character have different numeric byte values. A binary string also may appear to be accent sensitive, but that is because versions of a character with different accents have different byte values.

  The following example shows the difference in how non-binary and binary strings are treated with respect to lettercase. The non-binary string is converted to uppercase by UPPER() because it contains characters for which lettercase applies. The binary string remains unchanged because it consists of byte values that have no lettercase.

```
mysql> SELECT UPPER('AaBb'), UPPER(BINARY 'AaBb');
+---------------+----------------------+
| UPPER('AaBb') | UPPER(BINARY 'AaBb') |
+---------------+----------------------+
| AABB          | AaBb                 |
+---------------+----------------------+
```

- A multi-byte character, if stored in a binary string, is treated simply as multiple individual bytes. Character boundaries of the original data no longer apply.

String comparison rules are addressed in more detail in Section 10.3.1, "Case Sensitivity in String Comparisons."

The different treatment of non-binary and binary strings in MySQL is important when it comes to choosing data types for table columns. You normally base the decision on whether you want to treat column values as containing characters or raw bytes. Thus, non-binary columns are more suitable for character strings such as textual descriptions, and binary columns are more suitable for raw data such as images or compressed data.

Three data types store non-binary strings: CHAR, VARCHAR, and TEXT. Three data types store binary strings: BINARY, VARBINARY, and BLOB. They're each described further in the following sections.

You can mix non-binary and binary string columns within a single table. Also, for non-binary string columns, different columns can use different character sets and collations. For example, assume that you want to create a table named auth_info, to store login name and password authorization information for users of an application, as well as a picture to associate with each user. You want login names to match in any lettercase, passwords to be case sensitive, and the picture column must store binary image data. The following table definition satisfies these requirements:

```
CREATE TABLE auth_info
(
    login    CHAR(32) CHARACTER SET latin1,
    password CHAR(32) CHARACTER SET latin1 COLLATE latin1_general_cs,
    picture  MEDIUMBLOB
);
```

5.4.2 Non–Binary String Data Types: CHAR, VARCHAR, TEXT

The CHAR, VARCHAR, and TEXT data types store non-binary strings (that is, strings of characters that have a character set and collation). The types differ in terms of their maximum allowable length and in how trailing spaces are handled.

The CHAR data type is a fixed-length type. To define a CHAR column, provide the column name, the keyword CHAR, and the maximum length of acceptable values in parentheses. The length should be a number from 0 to 255.

The CHAR data type holds strings up to the length specified in the column definition. Values in a CHAR column always take the same amount of storage. For example, a column defined as CHAR(30) requires 30 characters for each value, even empty values. Values shorter than the designated length are padded with spaces to that length when they are stored. Trailing spaces are removed from CHAR values when they are retrieved, so retrieved values might not be the same length as when stored.

VARCHAR is a variable-length data type. VARCHAR columns are defined similarly to CHAR columns, but the maximum length can be a number up to 65,535. (The actual allowable maximum length is a few characters less due to internal restrictions imposed by storage engines.) A string stored into a VARCHAR column takes only the number of characters required to store it, plus one or two bytes to record the string's length. (One byte for columns declared with a length less than 256, two bytes otherwise.)

Values in a VARCHAR column are stored as given. Trailing spaces are not removed or added for storage or retrieval.

The TEXT data type comes in four different sizes, differing in the maximum length of values they can store. All are variable-length types, so an individual value requires storage equal to the length (in characters) of the value, plus 1 to 4 bytes to record the length of the value. Trailing spaces are not removed or added for storage or retrieval.

The following table summarizes the non-binary string data types. For the storage requirement values, M represents the maximum length of a column. L represents the actual length of a given value, which may be 0 to M.

Type	Storage Required	Maximum Length
CHAR(M)	M characters	255 characters
VARCHAR(M)	L characters plus 1 or 2 bytes	65,535 characters (subject to limitations)
TINYTEXT	L characters + 1 byte	255 characters
TEXT	L characters + 2 bytes	65,535 characters
MEDIUMTEXT	L characters + 3 bytes	16,777,215 characters
LONGTEXT	L characters + 4 bytes	4,294,967,295 characters

For fixed-length (CHAR) columns, MySQL must allocate enough space to store any value containing up to as many characters allowed by the column declaration. For CHAR(10), 10 bytes are required if the column has a single-byte character set. If the column has a multi-byte character set, MySQL must allocate 10 times the width of the widest allowed character. For utf8, each character takes from one to three bytes, so MySQL must allocate three bytes per character, or 30 bytes per column value. This amount of storage is required even for storing an empty string.

For variable-length (VARCHAR, TEXT) columns, MySQL allocates only the required amount of space for each stored value. A 10-character utf8 VARCHAR column requires 10 bytes (plus a length byte) for a value that contains only single-byte characters, but 30 bytes (plus a length byte) if it contains only triple-byte characters.

Non-binary strings have a character set and collation, and non-binary string columns by default are assigned the character set and collation of the table that contains them. The CHARACTER SET and COLLATE attributes can be used to designate specific values for a column, as described in Section 5.6, "Column Attributes."

5.4.3 Binary String Data Types: BINARY, VARBINARY, BLOB

The BINARY, VARBINARY, and BLOB data types are the binary string equivalents of the non-binary CHAR, VARCHAR, and TEXT data types. That is, they store strings that consist of bytes rather than characters, and they have no character set or collation. Like the corresponding non-binary types, binary string types differ in terms of their maximum allowable length and in how trailing spaces are handled.

BINARY is a fixed-length data type. The length should be a number from 0 to 255. Values shorter than the designated length are padded with spaces to that length when they are stored. Trailing spaces are removed from BINARY values when they are retrieved, so retrieved values might not be the same length as when stored. For this reason, BINARY may not be suited for applications that store binary data if stored values can have trailing spaces. For example, if an encrypted value happens to end with spaces, the retrieved value will be different from the value that was stored.

VARBINARY is a variable-length data type. The maximum length can be a number up to 65,535. (The actual allowable maximum length is a few bytes less due to internal restrictions imposed by storage engines.) Values in a VARBINARY column are stored as given. Trailing spaces are not removed or added for storage or retrieval.

The BLOB data type comes in four different sizes, differing in the maximum length of values they can store. All are variable-length types, so an individual value requires storage equal to the length (in bytes) of the value, plus 1 to 4 bytes to record the length of the value.

The following table summarizes the binary string data types. For the storage requirement values, M represents the maximum length of a column. L represents the actual length of a given value, which may be 0 to M.

Type	Storage Required	Maximum Length
BINARY(M)	M bytes	255 bytes
VARBINARY(M)	L bytes plus 1 or 2 bytes	65,535 bytes (subject to limitations)
TINYBLOB	L + 1 bytes	255 bytes
BLOB	L + 2 bytes	65,535 bytes
MEDIUMBLOB	L + 3 bytes	16,777,215 bytes
LONGBLOB	L + 4 bytes	4,294,967,295 bytes

5.4.4 The ENUM and SET Data Types

The ENUM and SET string data types are used when the values to be stored in a column are chosen from a fixed set of values. You define columns for both types in terms of string values, but MySQL represents them internally as integers. This leads to very efficient storage, but can have some results that are unintuitive unless you keep this string/integer duality in mind.

ENUM is an enumeration type. An ENUM column definition includes a list of allowable values; each value in the list is called a "member" of the list. Every value stored in the column must equal one of the values in the list. A simple (and very common) use for ENUM is to create a two-element list for columns that store yes/no or true/false choices. The following table shows how to declare such columns:

```
CREATE TABLE booleans
(
    yesno      ENUM('Y','N'),
    truefalse ENUM('T','F')
);
```

Enumeration values aren't limited to being single letters or uppercase. The columns could also be defined like this:

```
CREATE TABLE booleans
(
    yesno      ENUM('yes','no'),
    truefalse ENUM('true','false')
);
```

An ENUM column definition may list up to 65,535 members. Enumerations with up to 255 members require one byte of storage per value. Enumerations with 256 to 65,535 members require two bytes per value. The following table contains an enumeration column continent that lists continent names as valid enumeration members:

```
CREATE TABLE Countries
(
    name char(30),
    continent ENUM ('Asia','Europe','North America','Africa',
                    'Oceania','Antarctica','South America')
);
```

The values in an ENUM column definition are given as a comma-separated list of quoted strings. Internally, MySQL stores the strings as integers, using the values 1 through n for a column with n enumeration members. The following statement assigns the enumeration value 'Africa' to the continent column; MySQL actually stores the value 4 because 'Africa' is the fourth continent name listed in the enumeration definition:

```
INSERT INTO Countries (name,continent) VALUES('Kenya','Africa');
```

MySQL reserves the internal value 0 as an implicit member of all ENUM columns. It's used to represent illegal values assigned to an enumeration column. For example, if you assign 'USA' to the continent column, MySQL will store the value 0, rather than any of the values 1 through 7, because 'USA' is not a valid enumeration member. If you select the column later, MySQL displays 0 values as the empty string ''. (In strict SQL mode, an error occurs if you try to store an illegal ENUM value.)

The SET data type, like ENUM, is declared using a comma-separated list of quoted strings that define its valid members. But unlike ENUM, a given SET column may be assigned a value consisting of any combination of those members. The following definition contains a list of symptoms exhibited by allergy sufferers:

```
CREATE TABLE allergy
(
    symptom SET('sneezing','runny nose','stuffy head','red eyes')
);
```

A patient may have any or all (or none) of these symptoms, and symptom values therefore might contain zero to four individual SET members, separated by commas. The following statements set the symptom column to the empty string (no SET members), a single SET member, and multiple SET members, respectively:

```
INSERT INTO allergy (symptom) VALUES('');
INSERT INTO allergy (symptom) VALUES('stuffy head');
INSERT INTO allergy (symptom) VALUES('sneezing,red eyes');
```

MySQL represents SET columns as a bitmap using one bit per member, so the elements in the symptom definition have internal values of 1, 2, 4, and 8 (that is, they have the values of bits 0 through 3 in a byte). Internally, MySQL stores the values shown in the preceding INSERT statements as 0 (no bits set), 4 (bit 2 set), and 9 (bits 0 and 3 set; that is, 1 plus 8).

A SET definition may contain up to 64 members. The internal storage required for set values varies depending on the number of SET elements (1, 2, 3, 4, or 8 bytes for sets of up to 8, 16, 24, 32, or 64 members).

If you try to store an invalid list member into a SET column, it's ignored because it does not correspond to any bit in the column definition. For example, setting a symptom value to 'coughing,sneezing,wheezing' results in an internal value of 1 ('sneezing'). The 'coughing' and 'wheezing' elements are ignored because they aren't listed in the column definition as legal set members. (In strict SQL mode, an error occurs if you try to store an illegal SET value.)

As mentioned earlier in this section, the conversion between string and numeric representations of ENUM and SET values can have unintuitive results. For example, although you would normally refer to an enumeration column using the string forms of its values, you can also use the internal numeric values. The effect of this can be very subtle if the string values look like numbers. Suppose that you define a table t like this:

```
CREATE TABLE t (age INT, siblings ENUM('0','1','2','3','>3'));
```

In this case, the enumeration values are the strings '0', '1', '2', '3', and '>3', and the matching internal numeric values are 1, 2, 3, 4, and 5, respectively. Now suppose that you issue the following statement:

```
INSERT INTO t (age,siblings) VALUES(14,'3');
```

The siblings value is specified here as the string '3', and that is the value assigned to the column in the new record. However, you can also specify the siblings value as a number, as follows:

```
INSERT INTO t (age,siblings) VALUES(14,3);
```

But in this case, 3 is interpreted as the internal value, which corresponds to the enumeration value '2'! The same principle applies to retrievals. Consider the following two statements:

```
SELECT * FROM t WHERE siblings = '3';
SELECT * FROM t WHERE siblings = 3;
```

In the first case, you get records that have an enumeration value of '3'. In the second case, you get records where the internal value is 3; that is, records with an enumeration value of '2'.

5.5 Temporal Data Types

MySQL provides data types for storing different kinds of temporal information. In the following descriptions, the terms *YYYY*, *MM*, *DD*, *hh*, *mm*, and *ss* stand for a year, month, day of month, hour, minute, and second value, respectively.

The following table summarizes the storage requirements and ranges for the date and time data types.

Type	Storage Required	Range
DATE	3 bytes	'1000-01-01' to '9999-12-31'
TIME	3 bytes	'-838:59:59' to '838:59:59'
DATETIME	8 bytes	'1000-01-01 00:00:00' to '9999-12-31 23:59:59'
TIMESTAMP	4 bytes	'1970-01-01 00:00:00' to mid-year 2037
YEAR	1 byte	1901 to 2155 (for YEAR(4)), 1970 to 2069 (for YEAR(2))

Each temporal data type also has a "zero" value that's used when you attempt to store an illegal value. The "zero" value is represented in a format appropriate for the type (such as '0000-00-00' for DATE values and '00:00:00' for TIME) values.

MySQL represents date values in '*YYYY-MM-DD*' format when it displays them. This representation corresponds to the ANSI SQL date format, also known as ISO 8601 format. If necessary, you can reformat date values into other display formats using the DATE_FORMAT() function.

For date entry, MySQL also expects to receive dates in ISO format, or at least close to ISO format. That is, date values must be given in year-month-day order, although some deviation from strict ISO format is allowed:

- Leading zeros on month and day values may be omitted. For example, both '2000-1-1' and '2000-01-01' are accepted as legal.

- The delimiter between date parts need not be '-'; you can use other punctuation characters, such as '/'.

- Two-digit years are converted to four-digit years. You should be aware that this conversion is done based on the rule that year values from 70 to 99 represent the years 1970 to 1999, whereas values from 00 to 69 represent the years 2000 to 2069. It's better to provide values with four-digit years to avoid problems with conversion of values for which the rule does not apply.

If you need to load values that aren't in an acceptable format into a DATE column, you should convert them into ISO format before loading them. An alternative approach that's useful in some circumstances is to load the values into a string column and perform reformatting operations using SQL string functions to produce ISO format values that can be assigned to a DATE column.

MySQL represents time values in 'hh:mm:ss' format. For TIME value entry, some variation on this format is allowed. For example, leading zeros on TIME parts may be omitted.

MySQL represents time values in 'hh:mm:ss' format when displaying them. If necessary, you can reformat time values into other display formats using the TIME_FORMAT() function.

For time value entry, some variation on this format is allowed. For example, leading zeros on TIME parts may be omitted.

5.5.1 The DATE, TIME, DATETIME, and YEAR Data Types

The DATE data type represents date values in 'YYYY-MM-DD' format. The supported range of DATE values is '1000-01-01' to '9999-12-31'. You might be able to use earlier dates than that, but it's better to stay within the supported range to avoid unexpected behavior.

The TIME data type represents time values in 'hh:mm:ss' format. The range of TIME columns is '-838:59:59' to '838:59:59'. This is outside the time-of-day range of '00:00:00' to '23:59:59' because TIME columns can be used to represent elapsed time. Thus, values might be larger than time-of-day values, or even negative.

The DATETIME data type stores date-and-time values in 'YYYY-MM-DD hh:mm:ss' format. It's similar to a combination of DATE and TIME values, but the TIME part represents time of day rather than elapsed time and has a range limited to '00:00:00' to '23:59:59'. The date part of DATETIME columns has the same range as DATE columns; combined with the TIME part, this results in a DATETIME range from '1000-01-01 00:00:00' to '9999-12-31 23:59:59'.

The YEAR data type represents year-only values. You can declare such columns as YEAR(4) or YEAR(2) to obtain a four-digit or two-digit display format. If you don't specify any display width, the default is four digits.

If you don't need a full date and the range of values you need to store falls into the YEAR range, consider using YEAR to store temporal values. It's a very space-efficient data type because values require only one byte of storage each.

5.5.2 The TIMESTAMP Data Type

The TIMESTAMP type, like DATETIME, stores date-and-time values, but has a different range and some special properties that make it especially suitable for tracking data modification times.

MySQL displays TIMESTAMP values using the same format as DATETIME values; that is, 'YYYY-MM-DD hh:mm:ss'.

The range of TIMESTAMP values begins at 1970-01-01 00:00:00 (UTC) and extends partway into the year 2037. TIMESTAMP values actually represent the number of seconds elapsed since the beginning of 1970 and are stored using four bytes. This provides room for sufficient seconds to represent a date in the year 2037. MySQL Server stores TIMESTAMP values internally in UTC. It converts TIMESTAMP values from the server's current time zone for storage, and converts back to the current time zone for retrieval. It is possible for individual clients to use connection-specific time zone settings, as described in Section 5.5.3, "Per-Connection Time Zone Support."

The TIMESTAMP data type in MySQL is special in that you can cause a TIMESTAMP column to be initialized or updated automatically to the current date and time without explicitly assigning it a value. That is, you can specify that any single TIMESTAMP column in a table should be initialized with the current timestamp when the record is created with INSERT or REPLACE, updated with the current timestamp when the record is changed with UPDATE, or both. (Setting a column to its current value doesn't count as updating it.)

It's important to know about the automatic initialization and update properties of TIMESTAMP. These properties make TIMESTAMP columns useful for tracking record modification times, but can be a source of confusion if you're not aware of them. Do not choose TIMESTAMP for a column on the basis of the fact that it stores date-and-time values unless you also understand the circumstances under which the column will update automatically when other columns in a record change.

To control the initialization and update behavior of a TIMESTAMP column, you add either or both of the DEFAULT CURRENT_TIMESTAMP and ON UPDATE CURRENT_TIMESTAMP attributes to the column definition when creating the table with CREATE TABLE or changing it with ALTER TABLE.

The DEFAULT CURRENT_TIMESTAMP attribute causes the column to be initialized with the current timestamp at the time the record is created. The ON UPDATE CURRENT_TIMESTAMP attribute causes the column to be updated with the current timestamp when the value of another column in the record is changed from its current value.

For backward compatibility with older versions of MySQL (before 4.1), if you do not specify either of the DEFAULT CURRENT_TIMESTAMP or ON UPDATE CURRENT_TIMESTAMP attributes when creating a table, the MySQL server automatically assigns both attributes to the first TIMESTAMP column:

```
mysql> CREATE TABLE ts_test1 (
    ->    ts1 TIMESTAMP,
    ->    ts2 TIMESTAMP,
    ->    data CHAR(30)
    -> );
Query OK, 0 rows affected (0.00 sec)


mysql> DESCRIBE ts_test1;
+-------+-----------+------+-----+---------------------+-------+
| Field | Type      | Null | Key | Default             | Extra |
+-------+-----------+------+-----+---------------------+-------+
| ts1   | timestamp | YES  |     | CURRENT_TIMESTAMP   |       |
| ts2   | timestamp | YES  |     | 0000-00-00 00:00:00 |       |
| data  | char(30)  | YES  |     | NULL                |       |
+-------+-----------+------+-----+---------------------+-------+
3 rows in set (0.01 sec)


mysql> INSERT INTO ts_test1 (data) VALUES ('original_value');
Query OK, 1 row affected (0.00 sec)


mysql> SELECT * FROM ts_test1;
+---------------------+---------------------+----------------+
| ts1                 | ts2                 | data           |
+---------------------+---------------------+----------------+
| 2005-01-04 14:45:51 | 0000-00-00 00:00:00 | original_value |
+---------------------+---------------------+----------------+
1 row in set (0.00 sec)


mysql> . . . time passes . . .


mysql> UPDATE ts_test1 SET data='updated_value';
Query OK, 1 row affected (0.00 sec)
Rows matched: 1  Changed: 1  Warnings: 0
```

```
mysql> SELECT * FROM ts_test1;
+---------------------+---------------------+---------------+
| ts1                 | ts2                 | data          |
+---------------------+---------------------+---------------+
| 2005-01-04 14:46:17 | 0000-00-00 00:00:00 | updated_value |
+---------------------+---------------------+---------------+
1 row in set (0.00 sec)
```

The same behavior occurs if you specify both DEFAULT CURRENT_TIMESTAMP and ON UPDATE
CURRENT_TIMESTAMP explicitly for the first TIMESTAMP column. It is also possible to use just one
of the attributes. The following example uses DEFAULT CURRENT_TIMESTAMP, but omits ON
UPDATE CURRENT_TIMESTAMP. The result is that the column is initialized automatically, but not
updated when the record is updated:

```
mysql> CREATE TABLE ts_test2 (
    ->   created_time TIMESTAMP DEFAULT CURRENT_TIMESTAMP,
    ->   data CHAR(30)
    -> );
Query OK, 0 rows affected (0.00 sec)

mysql> INSERT INTO ts_test2 (data) VALUES ('original_value');
Query OK, 1 row affected (0.01 sec)

mysql> SELECT * FROM ts_test2;
+---------------------+----------------+
| created_time        | data           |
+---------------------+----------------+
| 2005-01-04 14:46:39 | original_value |
+---------------------+----------------+
1 row in set (0.00 sec)

mysql> . . . time passes . . .

mysql> UPDATE ts_test2 SET data='updated_value';
Query OK, 1 row affected (0.00 sec)
Rows matched: 1  Changed: 1  Warnings: 0

mysql> SELECT * FROM ts_test2;
+---------------------+----------------+
| created_time        | data           |
+---------------------+----------------+
| 2005-01-04 14:46:39 | updated_value  |
+---------------------+----------------+
1 row in set (0.00 sec)
```

Note that even though the record is updated, the created_time column is not. In versions of MySQL Server before 4.1, the UPDATE statement would have caused the created_time column to be updated as well.

The next example demonstrates how to create a TIMESTAMP column that is not set to the current timestamp when the record is created, but only when it is updated. In this case, the column definition includes ON UPDATE CURRENT_TIMESTAMP but omits DEFAULT CURRENT_TIMESTAMP:

```
mysql> CREATE TABLE ts_test3 (
    ->    updated_time TIMESTAMP ON UPDATE CURRENT_TIMESTAMP,
    ->    data CHAR(30)
    -> );
Query OK, 0 rows affected (0.01 sec)

mysql> INSERT INTO ts_test3 (data) VALUES ('original_value');
Query OK, 1 row affected (0.00 sec)

mysql> SELECT * FROM ts_test3;
+---------------------+----------------+
| updated_time        | data           |
+---------------------+----------------+
| 0000-00-00 00:00:00 | original_value |
+---------------------+----------------+
1 row in set (0.00 sec)

mysql> UPDATE ts_test3 SET data='updated_value';
Query OK, 1 row affected (0.00 sec)
Rows matched: 1  Changed: 1  Warnings: 0

mysql> SELECT * FROM ts_test3;
+---------------------+---------------+
| updated_time        | data          |
+---------------------+---------------+
| 2005-01-04 14:47:10 | updated_value |
+---------------------+---------------+
1 row in set (0.00 sec)
```

Note that you can choose to use CURRENT_TIMESTAMP with neither, either, or both of the attributes for a single TIMESTAMP column, but you cannot use DEFAULT CURRENT_TIMESTAMP with one column and ON UPDATE CURRENT_TIMESTAMP with another:

```
mysql> CREATE TABLE ts_test4 (
    ->    created TIMESTAMP DEFAULT CURRENT_TIMESTAMP,
    ->    updated TIMESTAMP ON UPDATE CURRENT_TIMESTAMP,
    ->    data CHAR(30)
    -> );
```

```
ERROR 1293 (HY000): Incorrect table definition; there can be
only one TIMESTAMP column with CURRENT_TIMESTAMP in DEFAULT
or ON UPDATE clause
```

Nevertheless, you can achieve the effect of having one column with the creation time and another with the time of the last update. To do this, create two TIMESTAMP columns. Define the column that should hold the creation time with DEFAULT 0 and explicitly set it to NULL whenever you INSERT a new record. Define the column that should hold the updated time with DEFAULT CURRENT_TIMESTAMP:

```
mysql> CREATE TABLE ts_test5 (
    ->    created TIMESTAMP DEFAULT 0,
    ->    updated TIMESTAMP ON UPDATE CURRENT_TIMESTAMP,
    ->    data CHAR(30)
    -> );
Query OK, 0 rows affected (0.01 sec)

mysql> INSERT INTO ts_test5 (created, data)
    -> VALUES (NULL, 'original_value');
Query OK, 1 row affected (0.00 sec)

mysql> SELECT * FROM ts_test5;
+---------------------+---------------------+----------------+
| created             | updated             | data           |
+---------------------+---------------------+----------------+
| 2005-01-04 14:47:39 | 0000-00-00 00:00:00 | original_value |
+---------------------+---------------------+----------------+
1 row in set (0.00 sec)

mysql> . . . time passes . . .

mysql> UPDATE ts_test5 SET data='updated_value';
Query OK, 1 row affected (0.00 sec)
Rows matched: 1  Changed: 1  Warnings: 0

mysql> SELECT * FROM ts_test5;
+---------------------+---------------------+---------------+
| created             | updated             | data          |
+---------------------+---------------------+---------------+
| 2005-01-04 14:47:39 | 2005-01-04 14:47:52 | updated_value |
+---------------------+---------------------+---------------+
1 row in set (0.00 sec)
```

By default, MySQL defines TIMESTAMP columns as NOT NULL and stores the current timestamp in the column if you assign it a value of NULL. If you want to be able to store NULL in a TIMESTAMP column, you must explicitly write the column definition to allow NULL when creating or altering the column:

```
mysql> CREATE TABLE ts_null (ts TIMESTAMP NULL);
Query OK, 0 rows affected (0.04 sec)

mysql> DESCRIBE ts_null;
+-------+-----------+------+-----+---------+-------+
| Field | Type      | Null | Key | Default | Extra |
+-------+-----------+------+-----+---------+-------+
| ts    | timestamp | YES  |     | NULL    |       |
+-------+-----------+------+-----+---------+-------+
1 row in set (0.10 sec)
```

Note that specifying NULL for a TIMESTAMP column implicitly changes its default value from CURRENT_TIMESTAMP to NULL if no explicit default value is given.

5.5.3 Per-Connection Time Zone Support

In MySQL Server, it is possible to set the current time zone on a per-connection basis.

To discuss time zones, we must first introduce a number of concepts:

- *UTC* is "Coordinated Universal Time" and is the common reference point for time measurement. For purposes of this discussion, UTC is the same as Greenwich Mean Time (GMT), although time zone aficionados get into long discussions about astronomical observations, atomic clocks, "Universal Time" versus "Greenwich Mean Time" versus "Coordinated Universal Time," and much else.

- There are three *time zone formats* available to use with MySQL:

  - The *signed hour/minute offset* of a time zone is expressed as '+hh:mm' or '-hh:mm', where *hh* and *mm* stand for two-digit hours and minutes, respectively. UTC is, in this format, commonly expressed as '+00:00'. Each time zone bases its offset according to the distance between it and the UTC time zone. Berlin, Germany, is one hour ahead of Greenwich, England (for example, the sun rises in Berlin approximately one hour before it does in Greenwich), so the hour/minute offset for Berlin is expressed as '+01:00'. In New York, where the sun rises some five hours after it does in Greenwich, the hour/minute offset is expressed as '-05:00'.

  - The *named time zone* for a given location is defined by a string such as 'US/Eastern', which is translated into the correct time zone by the server. MySQL supports named time zones through a set of time zone tables in the mysql database. (For named time zones to work, these tables must be properly populated by the MySQL administrator. See Section 24.6, "Loading Time Zone Tables.")

  - The third format is the SYSTEM time zone. This stands for the time zone value that the MySQL server retrieves from the server host. The server uses this value as its default time zone setting when it begins executing.

The exact details of support for named time zones differ slightly from one operating system to the next, and are not covered in any detail on the Developer certification exam. However, knowing how to use time zone support using signed offsets *is* mandatory.

Time zone settings are determined by the time_zone system variable. The server maintains a global time_zone value, as well as a session time_zone value for each client that connects. The session value is initialized for a given client, from the current value of the global time_zone variable, when the client connects.

The default setting for the global value is SYSTEM, which thus also becomes each client's initial session time_zone value. The global and session time zone settings can be retrieved with the following statement:

```
mysql> SELECT @@global.time_zone, @@session.time_zone;
+--------------------+---------------------+
| @@global.time_zone | @@session.time_zone |
+--------------------+---------------------+
| SYSTEM             | SYSTEM              |
+--------------------+---------------------+
1 row in set (0.00 sec)
```

MySQL Server stores TIMESTAMP values internally in UTC. It converts TIMESTAMP values from the server's current time zone for storage, and converts back to the current time zone for retrieval. The standard setting for both the server and the per-client connection is to use the SYSTEM setting, which the server retrieves from the host at startup.

If the time zone setting is the same for both storage and retrieval, you will get back the same value you store. If you store a TIMESTAMP value, and then change the time zone to a different value, the returned TIMESTAMP value will be different from the one you stored.

The following examples demonstrate how to change the session time zone settings to store and retrieve TIMESTAMP data. First, we set the session time zone to UTC, that is, '+00:00':

```
mysql> SET time_zone = '+00:00';
Query OK, 0 rows affected (0.00 sec)

mysql> SELECT @@session.time_zone;
+---------------------+
| @@session.time_zone |
+---------------------+
| +00:00              |
+---------------------+
1 row in set (0.00 sec)
```

Next, we create a simple table containing just a TIMESTAMP column named ts and insert one record that assigns the current time to ts. Then we retrieve the record:

```
mysql> CREATE TABLE ts_test (ts TIMESTAMP);
Query OK, 0 rows affected (0.01 sec)
```

```
mysql> INSERT INTO ts_test (ts) VALUES (NULL);
Query OK, 1 row affected (0.00 sec)

mysql> SELECT * FROM ts_test;
+---------------------+
| ts                  |
+---------------------+
| 2005-01-04 20:50:18 |
+---------------------+
1 row in set (0.00 sec)
```

Finally, we change the session time zone twice, each time retrieving the value after the change. This demonstrates that, even though we're retrieving the same TIMESTAMP value, the change in time zone setting causes the "localized" display value to be different each time:

```
mysql> SET time_zone = '+02:00';
Query OK, 0 rows affected (0.00 sec)

mysql> SELECT * FROM ts_test;
+---------------------+
| ts                  |
+---------------------+
| 2005-01-04 22:50:18 |
+---------------------+
1 row in set (0.00 sec)

mysql> SET time_zone = '-05:00';
Query OK, 0 rows affected (0.00 sec)

mysql> SELECT * FROM ts_test;
+---------------------+
| ts                  |
+---------------------+
| 2005-01-04 15:50:18 |
+---------------------+
1 row in set (0.00 sec)
```

The per-connection time zone settings also influence other aspects of the MySQL server that depend on the current time, most notably the function NOW().

MySQL Server also supports the CONVERT_TZ() function, which performs time zone conversions of datetime values:

```
mysql> SELECT CONVERT_TZ('2005-01-27 13:30:00', '+01:00', '+03:00');
+------------------------------------------------------+
| CONVERT_TZ('2005-01-27 13:30:00', '+01:00', '+03:00') |
+------------------------------------------------------+
```

```
| 2005-01-27 15:30:00                                     |
+---------------------------------------------------------+
1 row in set (0.00 sec)
```

CONVERT_TZ() assumes that the given datetime value has the time zone represented by the first hour/minute offset argument, and converts it to a value in the time zone represented by the second offset argument. The result is that you get the same datetime value, from the point of view of a different time zone.

5.6 Column Attributes

The final part of a column definition (following the data type) can include optional attributes that modify how MySQL handles the column. The following table contains an integer column that is UNSIGNED and cannot contain NULL values, a string column that has a character set of utf8, and a date column that has a default value of '1999-12-31':

```
CREATE TABLE t
(
    i INT UNSIGNED NOT NULL,
    c CHAR(10) CHARACTER SET utf8,
    d DATE DEFAULT '1999-12-31'
);
```

The following sections describe the allowable column attributes.

5.6.1 Numeric Column Attributes

Numeric data types other than BIT may have the following attributes:

- UNSIGNED causes negative values to be disallowed.
- ZEROFILL causes retrieved values to be left-padded with leading zeros up to the column's display width. For example, if you store the values 0, 14, and 1234 in a column that's defined as INT(5) ZEROFILL, MySQL displays them as 00000, 00014, and 01234 when you retrieve them.

  Using the ZEROFILL attribute for a column causes it to be UNSIGNED as well.
- AUTO_INCREMENT applies to integer data types. It's used to generate sequences of successive unique values. Defining a column with AUTO_INCREMENT causes a special behavior: When you insert NULL into the column, MySQL generates the next value in the sequence automatically and stores that in the column instead. Use of AUTO_INCREMENT carries with it other requirements: There may be only one AUTO_INCREMENT column per table, the column must be indexed, and the column must be defined as NOT NULL. Section 5.7, "Using the AUTO_INCREMENT Column Attribute," provides further details on AUTO_INCREMENT columns.

5.6.2 String Column Attributes

The following attributes apply to the non-binary string data types (CHAR, VARCHAR, and TEXT):

- CHARACTER SET specifies the character set to use for the column. CHARSET is a synonym for CHARACTER SET.

- COLLATE specifies the character set collation.

- BINARY is shorthand for specifying the binary collation of the column's character set. Note that the BINARY attribute differs from the BINARY data type. The former sets the collation for a non-binary string column. The latter creates a binary string column.

If both CHARACTER SET and COLLATE are given, the collation must be legal for the character set. Specifying CHARACTER SET without COLLATE sets the collation to the default collation for the character set. Specifying COLLATE without CHARACTER SET sets the character set to the collation's character set. (Each collation is unique to a specific character set.)

If both the CHARACTER SET and COLLATE attributes are omitted, the table defaults are used.

The character set binary is special and modifies the column's data type: It causes columns declared using the CHAR, VARCHAR, and TEXT non-binary string types to be created using the BINARY, VARBINARY, and BLOB binary string types, respectively.

5.6.3 General Column Attributes

The following attributes can be used with all data types, subject to the exceptions noted:

- NULL and NOT NULL apply to all types of columns. They indicate whether a column can contain NULL values. If you specify neither attribute, the default is to allow NULL values in the column. The exceptions are that NULL cannot be stored in AUTO_INCREMENT columns (the next sequence number is stored instead), or in TIMESTAMP columns that are defined to update automatically with the current timestamp when set to NULL.

- DEFAULT *value* provides a column with a default value to be used when you create a new record but don't explicitly specify a value for the column. For example, default values are used when you execute an INSERT statement that doesn't provide values for all columns in the table.

  There are certain limitations on when DEFAULT can be given and on the values that you can specify:

  - DEFAULT can be used with all data types with the exception of TEXT and BLOB columns, or integer columns that have the AUTO_INCREMENT attribute.

  - A default value must be a constant, not an expression whose value is calculated at record-creation time. The exception is that DEFAULT for a single TIMESTAMP column in a table can be given as the CURRENT_TIMESTAMP function to specify a default of "the current date and time." The rules for declaring TIMESTAMP columns are discussed in Section 5.5.2, "The TIMESTAMP Data Type."

- It is an error to specify a default value of NULL for a NOT NULL column.
- It is an error to specify a default value that is out of range for the data type, such as a negative number for an UNSIGNED numeric column.

If you specify no DEFAULT value for a column, MySQL determines whether to add a DEFAULT clause to the column definition based on whether the column allows NULL values. If the column allows NULL, MySQL adds DEFAULT NULL to the column definition. If the column does not allow NULL, MySQL adds no DEFAULT clause to the definition. In this case, the default value is implicit and may or may not be used when the column is missing from an INSERT statement, depending on whether the server is operating in strict SQL mode. Treatment of missing values is described in Section 5.8, "Handling Missing or Invalid Data Values."

Implicit default values are defined as follows:

- For numeric columns, the default is zero.
- For string columns other than ENUM, the default is the empty string. For ENUM columns, the default is the first enumeration member.
- For temporal columns, the default value is the "zero" value for the data type, represented in whatever format is appropriate to the type (for example, '0000-00-00' for DATE and '00:00:00' for TIME). For TIMESTAMP, the implicit default is the current timestamp if the column is defined to be automatically initialized, or the "zero" value otherwise.

For all data types except BLOB and TEXT, it's also possible to specify a PRIMARY KEY or UNIQUE clause at the end of a column definition, although these aren't really column attributes as such. They cause the creation of a PRIMARY KEY or UNIQUE index for the column. Adding either of these clauses to a column definition is the same as defining the index in a separate clause. For example, the following table definitions are equivalent:

```
CREATE TABLE t (i INT NOT NULL PRIMARY KEY);

CREATE TABLE t (i INT NOT NULL, PRIMARY KEY (i));
```

5.7 Using the AUTO_INCREMENT Column Attribute

The AUTO_INCREMENT attribute may be added to an integer column definition to create a column for which MySQL automatically generates a new sequence number each time you create a new row. There may be only one AUTO_INCREMENT column per table, the column must be indexed, and the column must be defined as NOT NULL.

The AUTO_INCREMENT attribute is used in conjunction with an index (usually a primary key) and provides a mechanism whereby each value is a unique identifier that can be used to refer unambiguously to the row in which it occurs. MySQL also provides a LAST_INSERT_ID()

function that returns the most recently generated AUTO_INCREMENT value. The value returned by LAST_INSERT_ID() is specific to the client that generates the AUTO_INCREMENT value. It cannot be affected by other clients. The LAST_INSERT_ID() function is useful for determining the identifier when you need to look up the record just created, or when you need to know the identifier to create related records in other tables.

The following scenario illustrates how you can set up and use an AUTO_INCREMENT column. Assume that you're organizing a conference and need to keep track of attendees and the seminars for which each attendee registers. (When someone submits a registration form for the conference, the form must indicate which of the available seminars the person wants to attend.)

Your task is to record seminar registrations and associate them with the appropriate attendee. Unique ID numbers provide a way to keep track of attendees and an AUTO_INCREMENT column makes the implementation for the task relatively easy:

1. Set up an attendee table to record information about each person attending the conference. The table shown here includes columns for ID number, name, and job title:

```
mysql> CREATE TABLE attendee
    -> (
    ->     att_id      INT UNSIGNED NOT NULL AUTO_INCREMENT,
    ->     att_name    CHAR(100),
    ->     att_title   CHAR(40),
    ->     PRIMARY KEY (att_id)
    -> );
```

The att_id column is created as a PRIMARY KEY because it must contain unique values, and as an AUTO_INCREMENT column because it's necessary for MySQL to generate values for the column automatically.

2. Set up a seminar table to record the seminars for which each attendee registers. Assume that there are four seminars: Database Design, Query Optimization, SQL Standards, and Using Replication. There are various ways in which these seminars can be represented; an ENUM column is one that works well because the seminar titles form a small fixed list of values. The table also must record the ID of each attendee taking part in the seminar. The table can be created with this statement:

```
mysql> CREATE TABLE seminar
    -> (
    ->     att_id      INT UNSIGNED NOT NULL,
    ->     sem_title   ENUM('Database Design','Query Optimization',
    ->                      'SQL Standards','Using Replication'),
    ->     INDEX (att_id)
    -> );
```

Note both the differences and similarities of the att_id column declarations in the two tables. In attendee, att_id is an AUTO_INCREMENT column and is indexed as a PRIMARY KEY to ensure that each value in the column is unique. In seminar, att_id is indexed for faster lookups, but it isn't indexed as a PRIMARY KEY. (There might be multiple records for a given attendee and a PRIMARY KEY does not allow duplicates.) Nor is the column declared in the seminar table with the AUTO_INCREMENT attribute because ID values should be tied to existing IDs in the attendee table, not generated automatically. Aside from these differences, the column is declared using the same data type (INT) and attributes (UNSIGNED, NOT NULL) as the att_id column in the attendee table.

3. Each time a conference registration form is received, enter the attendee information into the attendee table. For example:

```
mysql> INSERT INTO attendee (att_name,att_title)
    -> VALUES('Charles Loviness','IT Manager');
```

Note that the INSERT statement doesn't include a value for the att_id column. Because att_id is an AUTO_INCREMENT column, MySQL generates the next sequence number (beginning with 1) and sets the att_id column in the new row to that value. You can use the new att_id value to look up the record just inserted, but how do you know what value to use? The answer is that you don't need to know the exact value. Instead, you can get the ID by invoking the LAST_INSERT_ID() function, which returns the most recent AUTO_INCREMENT value generated during your current connection with the server. Thus, the record for Charles Loviness can be retrieved like this:

```
mysql> SELECT * FROM attendee WHERE att_id = LAST_INSERT_ID();
+--------+------------------+------------+
| att_id | att_name         | att_title  |
+--------+------------------+------------+
|      3 | Charles Loviness | IT Manager |
+--------+------------------+------------+
```

This output indicates that the Loviness form was the third one entered.

4. Next, enter new records into the seminar table for each seminar marked on the entry form. The att_id value in each of these records must match the att_id value in the newly created attendee record. Here again, the LAST_INSERT_ID() value can be used. If Loviness will participate in Database Design, SQL Standards, and Using Replication, create records for those seminars as follows:

```
mysql> INSERT INTO seminar (att_id,sem_title)
    -> VALUES(LAST_INSERT_ID(),'Database Design');
mysql> INSERT INTO seminar (att_id,sem_title)
    -> VALUES(LAST_INSERT_ID(),'SQL Standards');
mysql> INSERT INTO seminar (att_id,sem_title)
    -> VALUES(LAST_INSERT_ID(),'Using Replication');
```

To see what the new seminar records look like, use the LAST_INSERT_ID() value to retrieve them:

```
mysql> SELECT * FROM seminar WHERE att_id = LAST_INSERT_ID();
```

```
+--------+-------------------+
| att_id | sem_title         |
+--------+-------------------+
|      3 | Database Design   |
|      3 | SQL Standards     |
|      3 | Using Replication |
+--------+-------------------+
```

5. When you receive the next registration form, repeat the process just described. For every new attendee record, the value of LAST_INSERT_ID() will change to reflect the new value in the att_id column.

The preceding description shows how to use an AUTO_INCREMENT column: how to declare the column, how to generate new ID values when inserting new records, and how to use the ID values to tie together related tables. However, the description glosses over some of the details. These are presented in the following discussion, beginning with declaration syntax and then providing further information about how AUTO_INCREMENT columns work.

The att_id-related declarations in the attendee table look like this:

```
att_id INT UNSIGNED NOT NULL AUTO_INCREMENT,
PRIMARY KEY (att_id)
```

These declarations involve the following factors, which you should consider when creating an AUTO_INCREMENT column:

- The column must have an integer data type. Choose the specific type based on the number of values the column must be able to hold. For the largest range, use BIGINT. However, BIGINT requires 8 bytes per value. If you want to use less storage, INT requires only 4 bytes per value and provides a range that's adequate for many applications. You can use integer types smaller than INT as well, but it's a common error to choose one that's *too* small. For example, TINYINT has a range that allows very few unique numbers, so you'll almost certainly run into problems using it as an AUTO_INCREMENT column for identification purposes.

- An AUTO_INCREMENT sequence contains only positive values. For this reason, it's best to declare the column to be UNSIGNED. Syntactically, it isn't strictly required that you declare the column this way, but doing so doubles the range of the sequence because an UNSIGNED integer column has a larger maximum value. Defining the column as UNSIGNED also serves as a reminder that you should never store negative values in an AUTO_INCREMENT column.

- The most common way to use an AUTO_INCREMENT column is as a primary key, which ensures unique values and prevents duplicates. The column should thus be defined to contain unique values, either as a PRIMARY KEY or a UNIQUE index. (MySQL allows you to declare an AUTO_INCREMENT column with a non-unique index, but this is less common.)

- An AUTO_INCREMENT column must be NOT NULL.

After setting up an AUTO_INCREMENT column, use it as follows:

- Inserting NULL into an AUTO_INCREMENT column causes MySQL to generate the next sequence value and store it in the column. Omitting the AUTO_INCREMENT column from an INSERT statement is the same as inserting NULL explicitly. In other words, an INSERT statement that does not provide an explicit value for an AUTO_INCREMENT column also generates the next sequence value for the column. For example, if id is an AUTO_INCREMENT column in the table t, the following two statements are equivalent:

```
INSERT INTO t (id,name) VALUES(NULL,'Hans');
INSERT INTO t (name) VALUES('Hans');
```

- A positive value can be inserted explicitly into an AUTO_INCREMENT column if the value isn't already present in the column. If this value is larger than the current sequence counter, subsequent automatically generated values begin with the value plus one:

```
mysql> CREATE TABLE t (id INT AUTO_INCREMENT, PRIMARY KEY (id));
mysql> INSERT INTO t (id) VALUES(NULL),(NULL),(17),(NULL),(NULL);
mysql> SELECT id FROM t;
+----+
| id |
+----+
|  1 |
|  2 |
| 17 |
| 18 |
| 19 |
+----+
```

- After an AUTO_INCREMENT value has been generated, the LAST_INSERT_ID() function returns the generated value. LAST_INSERT_ID() will continue to return the same value, regardless of the number of times it's invoked, until another AUTO_INCREMENT value is generated.

- The value returned by LAST_INSERT_ID() is specific to the client that generates the AUTO_INCREMENT value. That is, it's connection-specific, so the LAST_INSERT_ID() value is always correct for the current connection, even if other clients also generate AUTO_INCREMENT values of their own. One client cannot change the value that LAST_INSERT_ID() returns to another, nor can one client use LAST_INSERT_ID() to determine the AUTO_INCREMENT value generated by another.

- If you update an AUTO_INCREMENT column to NULL or 0 in an UPDATE statement, the column is set to 0.

- By default, inserting 0 into an AUTO_INCREMENT column has the same effect as inserting NULL: The next sequence value is generated. However, if the NO_AUTO_VALUE_ON_ZERO SQL mode is enabled, inserting 0 causes 0 to be stored instead of the next sequence number.

- AUTO_INCREMENT behavior is the same for REPLACE as it is for INSERT. Any existing record is deleted, and then the new record is inserted. Consequently, replacing an AUTO_INCREMENT column with NULL causes it to be set to the next sequence value. This also occurs if you replace the column with 0 unless the NO_AUTO_VALUE_ON_ZERO SQL mode is enabled.

- When you reach the upper limit of an AUTO_INCREMENT column, an attempt to generate the next sequence value results in a duplicate-key error. This is a manifestation of MySQL's general out-of-range value clipping behavior. For example, assume that you have a TINYINT UNSIGNED column as an AUTO_INCREMENT column and that it currently contains 254 as the maximum sequence value. The upper limit for this data type is 255, so the next insert generates a sequence value of 255 and successfully stores it in the new record. However, the insert after that fails because MySQL generates the next sequence value, which is 256. Because 256 is higher than the column's upper limit of 255, MySQL clips 256 down to 255 and attempts to insert that value. But because 255 is already present in the table, a duplicate-key error occurs.

- If you delete rows containing values at the high end of a sequence, those values are not reused for MyISAM or InnoDB tables when you insert new records. For example, if an AUTO_INCREMENT column contains the values from 1 to 10 and you delete the record containing 10, the next sequence value is 11, not 10.

The MyISAM storage engine supports composite indexes that include an AUTO_INCREMENT column. This allows creation of independent sequences within a single table. Consider the following table definition:

```
CREATE TABLE multisequence
(
    name     CHAR(10) NOT NULL,
    name_id  INT UNSIGNED NOT NULL AUTO_INCREMENT,
    PRIMARY KEY (name, name_id)
);
```

Inserting name values into the multisequence table generates separate sequences for each distinct name:

```
mysql> INSERT INTO multisequence (name)
    -> VALUES('Petr'),('Ilya'),('Ilya'),('Yuri'),('Ilya'),('Petr');
mysql> SELECT * FROM multisequence ORDER BY name, name_id;
+------+---------+
| name | name_id |
+------+---------+
| Ilya |       1 |
| Ilya |       2 |
| Ilya |       3 |
| Petr |       1 |
| Petr |       2 |
```

```
| Yuri |        1 |
+------+---------+
```

Note that for this kind of AUTO_INCREMENT column, values deleted from the high end of any sequence are reused. This differs from MyISAM behavior for single-column AUTO_INCREMENT sequences.

5.8 Handling Missing or Invalid Data Values

Many database servers perform a great deal of value checking for data inserted into tables and generate errors for invalid input values that don't match column data types. MySQL, on the other hand, historically has been non-traditional and more "forgiving" in its data handling: The MySQL server converts erroneous input values to the closest legal values (as determined from column definitions) and continues on its way. For example, if you attempt to store a negative value into an UNSIGNED column, MySQL converts it to zero, which is the nearest legal value for the column. This forgiving behavior stems from MySQL's origins, which did not include transactional storage engines. Because a failed or erroneous transaction could not be rolled back, it was deemed preferable to convert the input values as well as possible and continue on, rather than perform a partial insert or update operation that processes only some of the rows specified in a data-modifying statement.

MySQL now includes transactional storage engines and in MySQL 5 you can tell the server to check input values more restrictively and to reject invalid values. The following discussion describes how to control whether rejection of invalid input values should occur, and the circumstances under which conversions take place if you allow them. The discussion is framed in terms of INSERT statements, but REPLACE and UPDATE are handled similarly.

The choice of how strict to be is up to individual applications. If the default forgiving behavior is suitable, you can continue to use that behavior. An application that requires more restrictive checking and needs to see errors for invalid input data can select that behavior instead. The behavior is configurable for each client by setting the SQL mode through use of the sql_mode system variable. In this way, MySQL Server accommodates a broad range of application requirements. General information about setting the SQL mode is given in Section 1.3, "Server SQL Modes." The following discussion focuses on using the SQL mode to control input data handling.

By default, the server uses a sql_mode value of '' (the empty string), which enables no restrictions. Thus, the server operates in forgiving mode by default. To set the mode this way explicitly, use the following statement:

```
SET sql_mode = '';
```

The most general means of enabling input value restrictions is by using the STRICT_TRANS_TABLES or STRICT_ALL_TABLES modes:

```
SET sql_mode = 'STRICT_TRANS_TABLES';
SET sql_mode = 'STRICT_ALL_TABLES';
```

The term "strict mode" refers collectively to both of these modes. They prevent entry of invalid values such as those that are out of range, or NULL specified for NOT NULL columns.

Another SQL mode, TRADITIONAL, enables strict mode plus other restrictions on date checking and division by zero. Setting the sql_mode system variable to TRADITIONAL causes MySQL to act like more traditional database servers in its input data handling:

```
SET sql_mode = 'TRADITIONAL';
```

The differences between the two strict modes are discussed later, as are the additional restrictions turned on by TRADITIONAL mode.

In many cases, type conversion affords you the flexibility to write a statement different ways and get the same result. For example, if i is an integer column, the following statements both insert 43 into it, even though the value is specified as a number in one statement and as a string in the other. MySQL performs automatic string-to-number conversion for the second statement:

```
INSERT INTO t (i) VALUES(43);
INSERT INTO t (i) VALUES('43');
```

MySQL also performs a conversion to 43 for the following statement, but it generates a warning as well because the conversion changes the value:

```
INSERT INTO t (i) VALUES('43x');
```

In this case, the string '43x' is not completely numeric, so you may want it to be rejected as invalid with an error rather than a warning. You can do this by enabling strict SQL mode.

When MySQL performs type conversions that change values, it generates warnings that can be displayed with the SHOW WARNINGS statement.

5.8.1 Handling Missing Values

In MySQL, INSERT statements may be incomplete in the sense of not specifying a value for every column in a table. Consider the following table definition:

```
CREATE TABLE t
(
    i INT NULL,
    j INT NOT NULL,
    k INT DEFAULT -1
);
```

For this table, an INSERT statement is incomplete unless it specifies values for all three columns in the table. Each of the following statements is an example of a statement that is missing column values:

```
INSERT INTO t (i) VALUES(0);
INSERT INTO t (i,k) VALUES(1,2);
INSERT INTO t (i,k) VALUES(1,2),(3,4);
INSERT INTO t VALUES();
```

In the last statement, the empty VALUES list means "use the default value for all columns."

MySQL handles missing values as follows:

- If the column definition contains a DEFAULT clause, MySQL inserts the value specified by that clause. Note that MySQL adds a DEFAULT NULL clause to the definition if it has no explicit DEFAULT clause and the column can take NULL values. Thus, the definition of column i actually has DEFAULT NULL in its definition:

```
mysql> SHOW CREATE TABLE t\G
*************************** 1. row ***************************
       Table: t
Create Table: CREATE TABLE `t` (
  `i` int(11) default NULL,
  `j` int(11) NOT NULL,
  `k` int(11) default '-1'
) ENGINE=MyISAM DEFAULT CHARSET=latin1
```

- If a column definition has no DEFAULT clause, missing-value handling depends on whether strict SQL mode is in effect and whether the table is transactional:

  - If strict mode is not in effect, MySQL inserts the implicit default value for the column data type and generates a warning.
  - If strict mode is in effect, an error occurs for transactional tables (and the statement rolls back). An error occurs for non-transactional tables as well, but a partial update might result: If the error occurs for the second or later row of a multiple-row insert, the earlier rows will already have been inserted.

  The definition of column j has no DEFAULT clause, so INSERT statements that provide no value for j are handled according to these rules.

DEFAULT clause specification and implicit default values are discussed in Section 5.6, "Column Attributes."

5.8.2 Handling Invalid Values in Non-Strict Mode

In general, when operating in non-strict mode, MySQL performs type conversion based on the constraints implied by a column's definition. These constraints apply in several contexts:

- When you insert or update column values with statements such as INSERT, REPLACE, UPDATE, or LOAD DATA INFILE.
- When you change a column definition with ALTER TABLE.

- When you specify a default value using a DEFAULT *value* clause in a column definition. (For example, if you specify a default value of '43' for a numeric column, that string is converted to 43 when the default value is used.)

If MySQL is not operating in strict mode, it adjusts invalid input values to legal values when possible and generates warning messages. These messages can be displayed with the SHOW WARNINGS statement.

The following list discusses some of the conversions that MySQL performs. It isn't exhaustive, but is sufficiently representative to provide you with a good idea of how MySQL treats input values and what you'll be tested on for the exam.

- *Conversion of out-of-range values to in-range values.* If you attempt to store a value that's smaller than the minimum value allowed by the range of a column's data type, MySQL stores the minimum value in the range. If you attempt to store a value that's larger than the maximum value in the range, MySQL stores the range's maximum value. For example, TINYINT has a range of –128 to 127. If you attempt to store values less than –128 in a TINYINT column, MySQL stores –128 instead. Similarly, MySQL stores values greater than 127 as 127. If you insert a negative value into an UNSIGNED numeric column, MySQL converts the value to 0.

- *String truncation.* String values that are too long are truncated to fit in the column. If you attempt to store 'Sakila' into a CHAR(4) column, MySQL stores it as 'Saki' and discards the remaining characters. (It is not considered an error to trim trailing spaces, so MySQL will insert 'Saki   ' into the column as 'Saki' without generating a warning.)

- *Enumeration and set value conversion.* If a value that's assigned to an ENUM column isn't listed in the ENUM definition, MySQL converts it to '' (the empty string). If a value that's assigned to a SET column contains elements that aren't listed in the SET definition, MySQL discards those elements, retaining only the legal elements.

- *Conversion to data type default.* If you attempt to store a value that cannot be converted to the column data type, MySQL stores the implicit default value for the type. For example, if you try to store the value 'Sakila' in an INT column, MySQL stores the value 0. The "zero" value is '0000-00-00' for date columns and '00:00:00' for time columns. The implicit default value for each data type is given in Section 5.6, "Column Attributes."

- *Handling assignment of NULL to NOT NULL columns.* The effect of assigning NULL to a NOT NULL column depends on whether the assignment occurs in a single-row or multiple-row INSERT statement. For a single-row INSERT, an error occurs and the statement fails. For a multiple-row INSERT, MySQL assigns the column the implicit default value for its data type.

Using ALTER TABLE to change a column's data type maps existing values to new values according to the constraints imposed by the new data type. This might result in some values being changed. For example, if you change a TINYINT to an INT, no values are changed because all

TINYINT values fit within the INT range. However, if you change an INT to a TINYINT, any values that lie outside the range of TINYINT are clipped to the nearest endpoint of the TINYINT range. Similar effects occur for other types of conversions, such as TINYINT to TINYINT UNSIGNED (negative values are converted to zero), and converting a long string column to a shorter one (values that are too long are truncated to fit the new size).

If a column is changed to NOT NULL using ALTER TABLE, MySQL converts NULL values to the implicit default value for the data type.

The following table shows how several types of string values are handled when converted to DATE or INT data types. It demonstrates several of the points just discussed. Note that only string values that look like dates or numbers convert properly without loss of information.

String Value	Converted to DATE	Converted to INT
'2010-03-12'	'2010-03-12'	2010
'03-12-2010'	'0000-00-00'	3
'0017'	'0000-00-00'	17
'500 hats'	'0000-00-00'	500
'bartholomew'	'0000-00-00'	0

5.8.3 Handling Invalid Values in Strict Mode

Input values may be invalid for a number of reasons:

- For a numeric or temporal column, a value might be out of range.
- For a string column, a string might be too long.
- For an ENUM column, a value might be specified that is not a legal enumeration value or as part of a value For a SET column, a value might contain an element that is not a set member.
- For a column that is defined as NOT NULL, a value of NULL might have been given.

Enabling strict mode turns on general input value restrictions. In strict mode, the server rejects values that are out of range, have an incorrect data type, or are missing for columns that have no default. Strict mode is enabled using the STRICT_TRANS_TABLES and STRICT_ALL_TABLES mode values.

STRICT_TRANS_TABLES enables strict behavior for errors that can be rolled back or canceled without changing the table into which data is being entered. If an error occurs for a transactional table, the statement aborts and rolls back. For a non-transactional table, the statement can be aborted without changing the table if an invalid value occurs in a single-row insert or the first row of a multiple-row insert. Otherwise, to avoid a partial update for a non-transactional table, MySQL adjusts any invalid value to a legal value, inserts it, and generates a warning. (Adjustment of NULL inserted into a NOT NULL column is done by inserting the implicit default value for the column data type.)

STRICT_ALL_TABLES is similar to STRICT_TRANS_TABLES but causes statements for non-transactional tables to abort even for errors in the second or later rows of a multiple-row insert. This means that a partial update might occur, because rows earlier in the statement will already have been inserted.

5.8.4 Enabling Additional Input Data Restrictions

Strict mode turns on general input value restrictions, but it is not as strict as you can tell the MySQL server to be. When strict mode is in effect, certain SQL mode values enable additional restrictions on input data values:

- Division by zero can be treated as an error for data entry by enabling the ERROR_FOR_DIVISION_BY_ZERO mode value and strict mode. In this case, attempts to enter data via INSERT or UPDATE statements produce an error if an expression includes division by zero. (With ERROR_FOR_DIVISION_BY_ZERO but not strict mode, division by zero results in a value of NULL and a warning, not an error.)

  SET sql_mode = 'STRICT_ALL_TABLES,ERROR_FOR_DIVISION_BY_ZERO';

- By default, MySQL allows "zero" dates ('0000-00-00') and dates that have zero parts ('2009-12-00', '2009-00-01'). Such dates are allowed even if you enable strict mode, but if you want to prohibit them, you can enable the NO_ZERO_DATE and NO_ZERO_IN_DATE mode values:

  SET sql_mode = 'STRICT_ALL_TABLES,NO_ZERO_DATE,NO_ZERO_IN_DATE';

The TRADITIONAL mode value is a composite mode that enables strict mode as well as the other restrictions just described. If you want your MySQL server to be as restrictive as possible about input data checking (and thus to act like other "traditional" database servers), the simplest way to achieve this is to enable TRADITIONAL mode rather than a list of individual more-specific modes:

SET sql_mode = 'TRADITIONAL';

Setting the SQL mode by using TRADITIONAL has the additional advantage that if future versions of MySQL implement other input data restrictions that become part of TRADITIONAL mode, you won't have to explicitly enable those modes to take advantage of them.

5.8.5 Overriding Input Data Restrictions

To override input data restrictions that may be enabled, use INSERT IGNORE or UPDATE IGNORE rather than just INSERT or UPDATE (without IGNORE). The IGNORE keyword causes MySQL to use non-strict behavior for the statement (for example, to produce warnings rather than errors).

Before MySQL 5, date values were required only to have month and day values in the range from 1 to 12 and 1 to 31, respectively. This means that MySQL accepted dates such as

'2009-02-31'. MySQL 5 requires that month and day values correspond to an actual legal date, so '2009-02-31' is not considered a valid date. MySQL converts it to '0000-00-00' and generates a warning. In strict mode, '2009-02-31' results in an error.

If you want relaxed date checking that requires only that month and day values be in the respective ranges of 1 to 12 and 1 to 31, enable the ALLOW_INVALID_DATES SQL mode value:

```
SET sql_mode = 'ALLOW_INVALID_DATES';
```

You can use ALLOW_INVALID_DATES for relaxed date checking even in strict mode:

```
SET sql_mode = 'STRICT_ALL_TABLES,ALLOW_INVALID_DATES';
```

6

Identifiers

When you write SQL statements, you use names to refer to databases and objects contained in databases such as tables, stored routines, and triggers. Some of these objects have components with their own names. For example, tables have columns and indexes. It's also possible to create aliases, which act as synonyms for table and column names.

This chapter discusses the use of identifiers in SQL statements. It covers the following exam topics:

- Identifier syntax
- Identifier case sensitivity
- Using qualified names
- Using reserved words as identifiers

6.1 Identifier Syntax

Identifiers may be unquoted or quoted. If unquoted, an identifier must follow these rules:

- An identifier may contain all alphanumeric characters, the underline character ('_'), and the dollar sign ('$').
- An identifier may begin with any of the legal characters, even a digit. However, it's best to avoid identifiers that might be misinterpreted as constants. For example, 1e3 might be taken as a number in scientific notation, and 0x1 might be interpreted as a hex constant. Therefore, neither is a good choice for an identifier.
- An identifier cannot consist entirely of digits.

An identifier may be quoted, in which case it can contain characters such as spaces or dashes that aren't otherwise legal. To quote an identifier, you may enclose it within backtick ('`') characters. If the ANSI_QUOTES SQL mode is enabled, you may also quote an identifier by enclosing it within double quotes ('"'). Quoting causes the identifier syntax rules to be relaxed as follows:

- In general, any character may be used in a quoted identifier. Exceptions are that an identifier cannot contain a byte with a numeric value of 0 or 255, and database and table names cannot contain '.', '/', or '\'.
- A quoted identifier may consist entirely of digits.

An alias identifier can include any character, but should be quoted if it's a reserved word (such as SELECT or DESC), contains special characters, or consists entirely of digits. Aliases may be quoted within single quotes (' '), double quotes, or backticks. Within a quoted identifier, to include the quote character, double it.

If you aren't sure whether an identifier is legal, quote it. It's harmless to put quotes around an identifier that's legal without them.

6.2 Case Sensitivity of Identifiers

A property that affects how you use identifiers is whether they're case sensitive; some identifiers are case sensitive and others are not. You should understand which is which and use them accordingly.

The rules that determine whether an identifier is case sensitive depend on what kind of identifier it is:

- For database and table identifiers, case sensitivity depends on the operating system and filesystem of the server host, and on the setting of the lower_case_table_names system variable. Databases and tables are represented by directories and files, so if the operating system has case-sensitive filenames, MySQL treats database and table identifiers as case sensitive. If filenames aren't case sensitive, these identifiers are not either. Windows systems do not have case-sensitive filenames, but most Unix systems do. However, if the lower_case_table_names system variable is set to 1 or 2, database and table identifiers and table aliases are used in case-insensitive fashion in SQL statements. If you plan to use this variable, you should set it *before* creating any databases and tables.

  Regardless of the case-sensitive properties of your filesystem, database and table identifiers must be written consistently with the same lettercase throughout a given statement.

- Column, index, stored routine, and trigger identifiers are not case sensitive.
- Column aliases are not case sensitive.

6.3 Using Qualified Names

Column and table identifiers can be written in qualified form—that is, together with the identifier of a higher-level element, with a period ('.') separator. Sometimes qualifiers are necessary to resolve ambiguity. Other times you may elect to use them simply to make a statement clearer or more precise.

A table name may be qualified with the name of the database to which it belongs. For example, the Country table in the world database may be referred to as world.Country, where a '.' character is placed between the two identifiers in the name. If world is the default database, these statements are equivalent:

```
SELECT * FROM Country;
SELECT * FROM world.Country;
```

A column name may be qualified with the name of the table to which it belongs. For example, the Name column in the Country table may be referred to as Country.Name.

A further level of column qualification is possible because a table name may be qualified with a database name. So, another way to refer to the Name column is world.Country.Name. If world is the default database, the following statements are equivalent. They differ only in having successively more specific levels of name qualification:

```
SELECT Name FROM Country;
SELECT Country.Name FROM Country;
SELECT world.Country.Name FROM world.Country;
```

Stored routines and triggers also may be referred to in qualified form. Qualify a stored routine with the name of the database that it belongs to (*db_name.routine_name*). A trigger is associated with a table, so a trigger identifier should be qualified with a table identifier (*table_name.trigger_name*).

To use quoted identifiers in a qualified name, quote them separately. For example, quote world.Country as `world`.`Country`, not as `world.Country`.

6.4 Using Reserved Words as Identifiers

Reserved words are special. For example, function names cannot be used as identifiers such as table or column names, and an error occurs if you try to do so. The following statement fails because it attempts to create a column named order, which is erroneous because order is a reserved word (it's used in ORDER BY clauses):

```
mysql> CREATE TABLE t (order INT NOT NULL UNIQUE, d DATE NOT NULL);
ERROR 1064 (42000): You have an error in your SQL syntax.  Check
the manual that corresponds to your MySQL server version for the
right syntax to use near 'order INT NOT NULL UNIQUE, d DATE
NOT NULL)' at line 1
```

Similarly, the following statement fails because it uses a reserved word as an alias:

```
mysql> SELECT 1 AS INTEGER;
ERROR 1064 (42000): You have an error in your SQL syntax.  Check
```

```
the manual that corresponds to your MySQL server version for the
right syntax to use near 'INTEGER' at line 1
```

The solution to these problems is to quote the identifiers properly. The rules depend on the type of identifier you're quoting:

- To use a reserved word as a database, table, column, or index identifier, there are either one or two allowable quoting styles, depending on the server SQL mode. By default, quoting a reserved word within backtick ('`') characters allows it to be used as an identifier:

  ```
  mysql> CREATE TABLE t (`order` INT NOT NULL UNIQUE, d DATE NOT NULL);
  Query OK, 0 rows affected (0.00 sec)
  ```

  If the ANSI_QUOTES SQL mode is enabled, it's also allowable to quote using double quotes:

  ```
  mysql> CREATE TABLE t ("order" INT NOT NULL UNIQUE, d DATE NOT NULL);
  Query OK, 0 rows affected (0.00 sec)
  ```

  If an identifier must be quoted in a CREATE TABLE statement, it's also necessary to quote it in any subsequent statements that refer to the identifier.

- To use a reserved word as an alias, quote it using either single quotes, double quotes, or backticks. The SQL mode makes no difference; it's legal to use any of the three quoting characters regardless. Thus, to use INTEGER as an alias, you can write it any of these ways:

  ```
  SELECT 1 AS 'INTEGER';
  SELECT 1 AS "INTEGER";
  SELECT 1 AS `INTEGER`;
  ```

It's a good idea to avoid using function names as identifiers. Normally, they aren't reserved, but there are circumstances under which this isn't true:

- Some functions have names that are also keywords and thus are reserved. CHAR() is one example.
- By default, a function name and the opening parenthesis that follows it must be written with no intervening space. This allows the statement parser to distinguish a name in a function invocation from the same name used for another purpose, such as an identifier. However, if the IGNORE_SPACE SQL mode is enabled, the server allows spaces between a function name and the following parenthesis. A side effect of running the server with this mode enabled is that all function names become ambiguous in certain contexts because the statement parser no longer can distinguish reliably whether a function name represents a function invocation or an identifier. Consider the following statement:

  ```
  INSERT INTO COUNT (id) VALUES(43);
  ```

In ignore-spaces mode, this statement might mean "create a new row in the COUNT table, setting the id column to 43," or it might simply be a malformed INSERT statement that has an invocation of the COUNT function where a table name ought to be. The parser cannot tell.

Reserved words are not case sensitive. They can be given in uppercase, lowercase, or even mixed case, and need not be written the same way throughout a query. The same is true for function names.

7

Databases

Databases contain tables, which are used for storing data. Databases also contain related data-manipulation objects such as stored routines or triggers. This chapter discusses each of the SQL statements that are used in MySQL to define the structural characteristics of your databases. It covers the following exam topics:

- General database properties
- Creating, modifying, and dropping databases
- Obtaining database metadata

7.1 Database Properties

MySQL Server manages data by performing storage, retrieval, and manipulation of data records. Records are organized into tables, and tables are organized into databases. In MySQL, databases are stored in a common location called the "data directory." Each MySQL server has a data directory under which it manages the contents of its databases. With respect to databases, the data directory has the following structure:

- The server represents each database using a subdirectory of the data directory. This subdirectory is called a "database directory." The data directory therefore is the parent of all database directories.

- A database directory has the same name as the database that it represents. For example, a database named world corresponds to a database directory named world under the data directory.

- MySQL uses the database directory to manage the components of the database such as its tables. A database may be empty or have one or more tables. A database directory may also contain files for other database objects such as triggers.

- Each database directory has a default character set and collation. You can specify these properties for a database when you create it. The properties are stored in a file named db.opt in the database directory.

- Databases cannot be nested; one database cannot contain another.

The preceding description of data directory organization indicates that MySQL Server can manage multiple databases, each of which may contain multiple tables. MySQL does not place any limits on the number of databases, although your operating system or filesystem might: If the filesystem on which the data directory resides has a limit on the number of subdirectories a directory may contain, MySQL can create no more than that number of database directories with which to represent databases.

Another word for "database" is "schema." In MySQL 5, statements that use the DATABASE keyword can be written with SCHEMA instead. The same is true for DATABASES and SCHEMAS. For example, CREATE SCHEMA is the same as CREATE DATABASE, and SHOW SCHEMAS is the same as SHOW DATABASES. This study guide generally uses DATABASE and DATABASES, but you should recognize that statements may use either pair of keywords. Also, GUI tools such as MySQL Query Browser and MySQL Administrator use the term "schema." You should recognize when using those programs that the two terms mean the same thing.

The structure of database directories in relation to table storage is discussed in Chapter 8, "Tables and Indexes," and Chapter 29, "Storage Engines." The structure of the database directory is discussed further in Chapter 23, "MySQL Architecture."

7.2 Creating Databases

To create a new database, use the CREATE DATABASE statement. The following statement creates a database named mydb:

```
CREATE DATABASE mydb;
```

If you try to create a database that already exists, an error occurs. If you simply want to ensure that the database exists, add an IF NOT EXISTS clause to the statement:

```
CREATE DATABASE IF NOT EXISTS mydb;
```

With the additional clause, the statement creates the database only if it does not already exist. Otherwise, the statement does nothing and no error occurs. This can be useful in applications that need to ensure that a given database is available, without disrupting any existing database with the same name.

The CREATE DATABASE statement has two optional clauses, CHARACTER SET and COLLATE, that assign a default character set and collation for the database. If given, they appear at the end of the statement following the database name. The following statement specifies that the mydb database has a default character set of utf8 and collation of utf8_danish_ci:

```
CREATE DATABASE mydb CHARACTER SET utf8 COLLATE utf8_danish_ci;
```

The default character set and collation for the database are used as the defaults for tables created in the database for which no explicit character set or collation of their own are specified. The database defaults are stored in the db.opt file in the database directory.

Creating a database has no effect on which database currently is selected as the default database. To make the new database the default database, issue a USE statement:

```
USE mydb;
```

After a database has been created, you can populate it with objects such as tables or stored routines. The CREATE statements for these objects are discussed in later chapters.

7.3 Altering Databases

The ALTER DATABASE statement changes options for an existing database. The allowable options are the same as for CREATE DATABASE; that is, CHARACTER SET and COLLATE. The following statement changes the default collation of the mydb database to utf8_polish_ci:

```
ALTER DATABASE mydb COLLATE utf8_polish_ci;
```

This statement changes both the default character set and collation:

```
ALTER DATABASE mydb CHARACTER SET latin1 COLLATE latin1_swedish_ci;
```

Changing the default character set or collation affects only creation of new tables in the database. It does not affect existing tables.

The database name is optional for ALTER DATABASE. If no database is named, the statement changes the options for the default database. This requires that there be a currently selected database. Otherwise, an error occurs.

You cannot use ALTER DATABASE to rename a database. One way to accomplish this is to dump the database, create a database with the new name, reload the data into the new database, and drop the old database.

7.4 Dropping Databases

When you no longer need a database, you can remove it with DROP DATABASE:

```
DROP DATABASE mydb;
```

It is an error if the database does not exist. To cause a warning instead, include an IF EXISTS clause:

```
DROP DATABASE IF EXISTS mydb;
```

Any warning generated when IF EXISTS is used can be displayed with SHOW WARNINGS.

DROP DATABASE does not require the database to be empty. Before dropping the database, MySQL removes any objects that it contains, such as tables, stored routines, and triggers.

DROP DATABASE is a dangerous statement and you should use it with care. There is no statement to "undo" DROP DATABASE. If you drop a database by mistake, your only option is to recover the database and its contents from your backups.

7.5 Obtaining Database Metadata

The INFORMATION_SCHEMA database has a SCHEMATA table that contains database metadata (information about databases). For example, to display information about the world database, use this statement:

```
mysql> SELECT * FROM INFORMATION_SCHEMA.SCHEMATA
    -> WHERE SCHEMA_NAME = 'world'\G
*************************** 1. row ***************************
              CATALOG_NAME: NULL
               SCHEMA_NAME: world
DEFAULT_CHARACTER_SET_NAME: latin1
    DEFAULT_COLLATION_NAME: latin1_swedish_ci
                  SQL_PATH: NULL
```

For further information about INFORMATION_SCHEMA, see Chapter 20, "Obtaining Database Metadata."

MySQL also supports a family of SHOW statements that display metadata. The statement that lists database names is SHOW DATABASES:

```
mysql> SHOW DATABASES;
+--------------------+
| Database           |
+--------------------+
| information_schema |
| menagerie          |
| mysql              |
| test               |
| world              |
+--------------------+
```

The information_schema database should always be listed by SHOW DATABASES. The mysql and test databases are created during MySQL installation, so you're likely to see both of them in the output from the statement as well. The mysql database contains the grant tables and should always be present because the grant tables contain user account information that the server uses to control access to the databases. The test database will be present unless someone has removed it.

SHOW DATABASES can take a LIKE 'pattern' clause. With LIKE, the statement performs a pattern-matching operation and displays information only about databases with names that match the pattern. Patterns are discussed in Section 10.3.2, "Using LIKE for Pattern Matching."

```
mysql> SHOW DATABASES LIKE 'm%';
+---------------+
| Database (m%) |
+---------------+
| menagerie     |
| mysql         |
+---------------+
```

The output of the SHOW DATABASES statement depends on whether you have the SHOW DATABASES privilege. If you have the privilege, the statement shows the names of all existing databases. Otherwise, it shows only those databases to which you have access.

SHOW CREATE DATABASE shows the CREATE DATABASE statement that creates a database:

```
mysql> SHOW CREATE DATABASE world\G
*************************** 1. row ***************************
       Database: world
Create Database: CREATE DATABASE `world`
                 /*!40100 DEFAULT CHARACTER SET latin1 */
```

8

Tables and Indexes

Tables are used for storing data and tables can be indexed to speed up access to their contents. This chapter discusses each of the SQL statements that are used in MySQL to define the structural characteristics of your tables. It covers the following exam topics:

- General table properties
- Creating, altering, and dropping tables
- Emptying table contents
- Creating and dropping indexes
- Obtaining table and index metadata

The term "table" can mean either "base table" (a table that contains data) or "view" (a virtual table). In this chapter, views do not enter the discussion, so "table" means "base table." Views are covered in Chapter 14, "Views."

8.1 Table Properties

Each MySQL server has a directory called the "data directory" under which it stores its databases. The data directory contains one subdirectory for each database managed by the server. Each of these is called a "database directory" and has the same name as the database that it represents. The server uses a given database directory to manage the tables in that database. Tables have both a logical and physical structure.

Logically, each table in a database consists of rows and columns. A table can be empty (it can have zero rows of data), but it must have at least one column. A table may also be indexed to improve query performance. Indexes enable MySQL to look up data values quickly rather than searching through the entire table. Indexes become increasingly important the larger a table becomes.

Physically, each table is associated with one or more files on disk. Every table has a format file in its database directory. The format file is created by the server and contains the definition, or structure, of the table. The format filename is the same as the table name, plus an

.frm suffix. For example, the format file for a table named Country in the world database is named Country.frm and is located in the world database directory under the server's data directory.

MySQL manages tables using storage engines, each of which handles tables that have a given set of characteristics. Different storage engines have differing performance characteristics, and you can choose which engine most closely matches the characteristics that you need. For example, you might require transactional capabilities and guaranteed data integrity even if a crash occurs, or you might want a very fast lookup table stored in memory for which the contents can be lost in a crash and reloaded at the next server startup. With MySQL, you can make this choice on a per-table basis. Any given table is managed by a particular storage engine. In addition to the .frm file that the server creates, a table may be associated with one or more other files that the storage engine creates in which to store the table's contents. The number and types of files vary per storage engine, because each engine manages table storage differently. Here are some examples:

- The MyISAM engine creates a data file and index file for each table. If Country is a MyISAM table, the MyISAM storage engine creates data and index files named Country.MYD and Country.MYI to store data rows and indexes (respectively) for the table.

- By default, the InnoDB engine shares files for multiple tables. If Country is an InnoDB table, there will be a Country.frm format file created by the in the database directory, but the InnoDB storage engine itself stores the table data and index information elsewhere, in the InnoDB shared tablespace. The tablespace is used by multiple tables. That is, files for storing table contents are not per-table as for MyISAM but are shared among tables.

- The MEMORY engine does not use any disk storage at all for table contents. It manages table contents in memory.

Additional detail on storage management for these engines is given in Chapter 29, "Storage Engines."

The MySQL server places no limits on the number of tables in a database, although individual storage engines might have their own limits. For example, the InnoDB storage engine allows a maximum of two billion tables to exist within the InnoDB shared tablespace. This places a limit (albeit a rather high one) on the number of InnoDB tables that can be created among all databases combined. (The limit isn't enforced on a per-database basis because the InnoDB tablespace is shared among all databases.)

A limit on the maximum number of tables allowed might also be imposed by your operating system or filesystem. For example, the MyISAM storage engine places no limits on the number of tables in a database. However, MyISAM tables are represented by data and index files in database directories, so a limit on the number of tables in a database might arise from factors external to MySQL:

- If the operating system or filesystem places a limit on the number of files in a directory, MySQL is bound by that constraint.

- The efficiency of the operating system in handling large numbers of files in a directory can place a practical limit on the number of tables in a database. If the time required to open a file in the directory increases significantly as the number of files increases, database performance can be adversely affected.

- The amount of available disk space limits the number of tables. If you run out of space, you cannot create more tables.

MySQL storage engines do place limits on the allowable maximum size of individual tables. These limits vary per storage engine, but they tend to be rather high. Another factor that limits table size is the maximum file size allowed by your operating system or filesystem. An operating system may support different types of filesystems, each of which may have a different maximum file size.

For large tables, you might find that you run up against operating system or filesystem limits on file sizes before you reach MySQL's internal table size limits. Several strategies can be used for working around file size limits:

- Exploit any features allowed by a given table storage manager for increasing table size. For example, the contents of a MyISAM table can sometimes be distributed into several smaller tables, which then can be treated as a single logical unit by combining them into a MERGE table. This effectively multiplies the maximum table size by the number of component MyISAM tables in the MERGE table.

- Convert the table for use with a storage engine that allows larger tables. For example, convert a MyISAM table to an InnoDB table. The InnoDB storage engine manages tables within a tablespace that can be configured to be much larger than the size of a single file, and InnoDB tables can grow as large as the available storage within the tablespace.

- Modify your operating system. A factor external to MySQL that can be used to allow larger tables is to modify your operating system to support larger files. This might be possible by using a different filesystem type, or by using a newer version of the operating system that relaxes the limits on file sizes compared to an older version. You might also consider switching to an operating system that supports larger files than does your current operating system.

8.2 Creating Tables

MySQL provides several ways to create tables:

- You can create an empty table, either by specifying its definition explicitly or by using the definition of an existing table.

- You can create a table populated from the result of a SELECT statement.

- You can create temporary tables.

The following discussion describes each of these table-creation methods. All of them use the CREATE TABLE statement in one form or another.

8.2.1 Creating Tables Using an Explicit Definition

A new table can be created from an explicit definition by using a CREATE TABLE statement that includes the table name and a list of columns. Each column has its own name and definition. The table definition may also include index definitions.

This section describes basic CREATE TABLE syntax using columns that have relatively simple definitions. For more information on the available data types and attributes for column definitions, see Chapter 5, "Data Types."

To create a table, give its name followed by a list of column definitions within parentheses:

```
CREATE TABLE table_name (column_definitions);
```

In the simplest case, a table contains only one column. The following statement creates a table named t with a single column named id that will contain INT (integer) values:

```
CREATE TABLE t (id INT);
```

A column definition may include attributes that define the column data more precisely. For example, to disallow NULL values in the column, include NOT NULL in the definition:

```
CREATE TABLE t (id INT NOT NULL);
```

If you try to create a table that already exists, an error occurs. If you simply want to ensure that the table exists, add an IF NOT EXISTS clause to the statement:

```
CREATE TABLE IF NOT EXISTS t (i INT);
```

However, MySQL does not perform any check on the table structure when you add the IF NOT EXISTS clause. If a table with the given name exists but has a structure different from the one you've defined in the CREATE TABLE statement, MySQL will issue no warning.

More complex tables have multiple columns, with the column definitions separated by commas. The following table definition includes, in addition to an id column, two 30-character columns for storing last names and first names, and a column for storing date values. All columns are declared NOT NULL to indicate that they require non-NULL values.

```
CREATE TABLE t
(
    id          INT NOT NULL,
    last_name   CHAR(30) NOT NULL,
    first_name  CHAR(30) NOT NULL,
    d           DATE NOT NULL
);
```

Every table must belong to a database. That is, you cannot create a table that is not located within some database. If the table named in the CREATE TABLE statement is not qualified with a database name, the table is created in the default database. To indicate explicitly where to create the table, you can qualify the table name with the name of the desired database, using *db_name.table_name* syntax. For example, if you want to create a table called mytable in the test database, write the CREATE TABLE statement like this:

```
CREATE TABLE test.mytable (column_definitions);
```

Use of a database qualifier for the table name is helpful when there's no default database or when some other database is currently selected as the default. If test happens to be the default database, the statement still works. In that case, the database name is unnecessary but harmless.

When you create a table, you can provide index definitions in addition to the column definitions. Indexes are useful for speeding up queries by reducing record lookup time. Here's a simple table that includes two index definitions. The first creates an index on the id column and requires each id value to be unique. The second index definition creates a two-column index on the last_name and first_name columns of the table:

```
CREATE TABLE t
(
    id         INT NOT NULL,
    last_name  CHAR(30) NOT NULL,
    first_name CHAR(30) NOT NULL,
    UNIQUE (id),
    INDEX (last_name, first_name)
);
```

Section 8.6.2, "Creating Indexes," discusses index creation further.

8.2.2 Specifying the Storage Engine for a Table

Every table is created using one of the storage engines supported by the server. The set of storage engines available depends both on how the server was compiled when it was built and on the options used at startup:

- The MyISAM, MERGE, and MEMORY storage engines are always available.
- The InnoDB storage engine is included in all binary distributions.
- Additional storage engines are included in MySQL Max binary distributions.

To see which storage engines your server supports, use the SHOW ENGINES statement.

To specify a storage engine when you create a table, include an ENGINE = *engine_name* option in the CREATE TABLE statement. The following statement creates t as an InnoDB table:

```
CREATE TABLE t (i INT) ENGINE = InnoDB;
```

The ALTER TABLE statement also understands the ENGINE option. This allows you convert a table from one storage engine to another. The following statement changes t to use the MyISAM storage engine:

```
ALTER TABLE t ENGINE = MyISAM;
```

If a CREATE TABLE statement includes no ENGINE option, MySQL creates the table using the default storage engine, which is determined from the value of the storage_engine system variable. The built-in default value of storage_engine is MyISAM. However, depending on how MySQL was installed or configured, storage_engine might be set to a different storage engine. Make sure to double-check the setting to ensure that it is really what you expect.

The default storage engine can be changed at server startup or at runtime:

- The default storage engine can be specified at server startup with the --default-storage-engine option.
- For a running server, an administrator who has the SUPER privilege can change the default storage engine globally for all clients by setting the global storage_engine system
  variable:

  ```
  SET GLOBAL storage_engine = engine_name;
  ```

  Setting the storage engine this way affects any client that connects after the statement executes. Clients that are connected at the time of statement execution are unaffected.
- Any client can change its own default storage engine by issuing either of these statements:

  ```
  SET SESSION storage_engine = engine_name;
  SET storage_engine = engine_name;
  ```

If an ENGINE clause names a storage engine that is legal but not available, the server uses the storage_engine system variable to determine which engine to use. (A storage engine might be unavailable if it was not compiled in or was disabled at startup time.) If the server uses the default storage engine rather than the one specified in the CREATE TABLE statement, it issues a warning. For example, ISAM is a legal storage engine name, but is no longer supported in MySQL 5. (ISAM was the predecessor to MyISAM.) The following example shows what happens if the default storage engine is InnoDB and you issue a request to create an ISAM table:

```
mysql> SET storage_engine = InnoDB;
mysql> CREATE TABLE t (i INT) ENGINE = ISAM;
Query OK, 0 rows affected, 1 warning (0.01 sec)
mysql> SHOW WARNINGS\G
*************************** 1. row ***************************
  Level: Warning
   Code: 1266
Message: Using storage engine InnoDB for table 't'
```

8.2.3 Creating Tables Based on Existing Tables

MySQL provides two ways to create a table based on another table:

- CREATE TABLE ... SELECT creates a table and populates it from the result set returned by an arbitrary SELECT statement. In this case, the "other table" is the set of rows and columns retrieved by the SELECT.

- CREATE TABLE ... LIKE creates an empty table using the definition of another existing table.

CREATE TABLE ... SELECT can create a table that is empty or non-empty, depending on what is returned by the SELECT part. The following statements create a table that contains the entire content of the City table, a table that contains partial content from City, and an empty copy of City:

```
CREATE TABLE CityCopy1 SELECT * FROM City;
CREATE TABLE CityCopy2 SELECT * FROM City WHERE Population > 2000000;
CREATE TABLE CityCopy3 SELECT * FROM City WHERE 0;
```

Using the LIKE keyword with CREATE TABLE creates an empty table based on the definition of another table. The result is a new table with a definition that includes all column attributes and indexes of the original table. Suppose that table t looks like this:

```
mysql> CREATE TABLE t
    -> (i INT NOT NULL AUTO_INCREMENT,
    -> PRIMARY KEY (i))
    -> ENGINE = InnoDB;
```

The result of CREATE TABLE ... LIKE differs from the result of using CREATE TABLE ... SELECT to create an empty table. Either of the following statements will create an empty copy of the table t:

```
mysql> CREATE TABLE copy1 SELECT * FROM t WHERE 0;
mysql> CREATE TABLE copy2 LIKE t;
```

However, the resulting copies differ in the amount of information retained from the original table structure:

```
mysql> SHOW CREATE TABLE copy1\G;
*************************** 1. row ***************************
       Table: copy1
Create Table: CREATE TABLE `copy1` (
  `i` int(11) NOT NULL default '0'
) ENGINE=MyISAM DEFAULT CHARSET=latin1
mysql> SHOW CREATE TABLE copy2\G;
*************************** 1. row ***************************
       Table: copy2
Create Table: CREATE TABLE `copy2` (
```

```
  `i` int(11) NOT NULL auto_increment,
  PRIMARY KEY  (`i`)
) ENGINE=InnoDB DEFAULT CHARSET=latin1
```

The CREATE TABLE ... SELECT statement copies the column name and data type from the original table, but does not retain the PRIMARY KEY index information or the AUTO_INCREMENT column attribute information. The new table also uses the default storage engine, rather than the storage engine utilized by table t. The copy created with CREATE TABLE ... LIKE has none of these problems.

Some table attributes are not copied, even when issuing CREATE TABLE ... LIKE. The most notable examples are:

- If the original table is a MyISAM table for which the DATA DIRECTORY or INDEX DIRECTORY table options are specified, those options are not copied to the new table. The data and index files for the new table will reside in the database directory for the chosen database.

- Foreign key definitions in the original table are not copied to the new table. If you wish to retain the foreign key definitions, they must be re-specified with ALTER TABLE after creating the copy.

8.2.4 Using TEMPORARY Tables

Each storage engine in MySQL implements tables with a particular set of characteristics. One characteristic held in common by all storage engines is that by default they create tables that exist until they are removed with DROP TABLE. This behavior may be changed by using CREATE TEMPORARY TABLE rather than CREATE TABLE. A TEMPORARY table differs from a non-TEMPORARY table in the following ways:

- It's visible only to the client that created it and may be used only by that client. This means that different clients can create TEMPORARY tables that have the same name and no conflict occurs.

- A TEMPORARY table exists only for the duration of the connection in which it was created. The server drops a TEMPORARY table automatically when the client connection ends if the client has not already dropped it. This is convenient because you need not remember to remove the table yourself.

- A TEMPORARY table may have the same name as a non-TEMPORARY table. The non-TEMPORARY table becomes hidden to the client that created the TEMPORARY table as long as the TEMPORARY table exists.

- A TEMPORARY table can be renamed only with ALTER TABLE. You cannot use RENAME TABLE.

A table created with TEMPORARY is not the same thing as a MEMORY table. A MEMORY table is temporary in the sense that its contents are lost if you restart the server, but the table definition continues to exist in its database. A TEMPORARY table exists only while the client that created it remains connected, and then disappears completely. Given that a server restart necessarily involves termination of all client connections, it also results in removal of all TEMPORARY tables. Another difference is that a MEMORY table is available to any client that has permission to access it, not just to the client that created it.

8.3 Altering Tables

After creating a table, you might discover that its structure is not quite suited to its intended use. If that happens, you can change the table's structure. One way to do this is to remove the table with DROP TABLE and then issue another CREATE TABLE statement that defines the table correctly. However, that can be a drastic method: If the table already contains data, dropping and re-creating the table destroys its contents unless you first make a backup. To change a table "in place," use the ALTER TABLE statement. The following list describes some of the modifications to a table's structure that ALTER TABLE makes possible:

- Adding or dropping columns
- Changing the name or definition of a column
- Adding or dropping indexes
- Renaming the table

This section describes how to perform each of these changes except for adding and dropping indexes, topics that are covered later in the chapter. (See Section 8.6.2, "Creating Indexes.")

Most of the examples shown in this section use a table named HeadOfState, designed to keep track of world leaders. Assume that the table initially has the following structure:

```
CREATE TABLE HeadOfState
(
    ID          INT NOT NULL,
    LastName    CHAR(30) NOT NULL,
    FirstName   CHAR(30) NOT NULL
);
```

The initial DESCRIBE output for the table looks like this:

```
mysql> DESCRIBE HeadOfState;
+-----------+----------+------+-----+---------+-------+
| Field     | Type     | Null | Key | Default | Extra |
+-----------+----------+------+-----+---------+-------+
| ID        | int(11)  | NO   |     |         |       |
| LastName  | char(30) | NO   |     |         |       |
| FirstName | char(30) | NO   |     |         |       |
+-----------+----------+------+-----+---------+-------+
```

8.3.1 Adding and Dropping Columns

To add a new column to a table, use ALTER TABLE with an ADD clause that specifies the column's definition. A column definition uses the same syntax for ALTER TABLE as for CREATE TABLE. For example, to add a DATE column named Inauguration for recording the dates that the leaders listed in the table assumed office, you can issue this statement:

```
ALTER TABLE HeadOfState ADD Inauguration DATE NOT NULL;
```

That ALTER TABLE statement changes the table structure as follows:

```
mysql> DESCRIBE HeadOfState;
+--------------+----------+------+-----+---------+-------+
| Field        | Type     | Null | Key | Default | Extra |
+--------------+----------+------+-----+---------+-------+
| ID           | int(11)  | NO   |     |         |       |
| LastName     | char(30) | NO   |     |         |       |
| FirstName    | char(30) | NO   |     |         |       |
| Inauguration | date     | NO   |     |         |       |
+--------------+----------+------+-----+---------+-------+
```

As shown by the DESCRIBE output, when you add a new column to a table, MySQL places it after all existing columns. This is the default placement unless you specify otherwise. To indicate that MySQL should place the new column in a specific position within the table, append either the keyword FIRST or the keyword-identifier combination AFTER *column_name* to the column definition. For example, assume that you had executed this ALTER TABLE statement instead of the previous one:

```
ALTER TABLE HeadOfState ADD Inauguration DATE NOT NULL FIRST;
```

The FIRST keyword tells ALTER TABLE to place the new column before all existing columns (in the "first" position), resulting in the following table structure:

```
mysql> DESCRIBE HeadOfState;
+--------------+----------+------+-----+---------+-------+
| Field        | Type     | Null | Key | Default | Extra |
+--------------+----------+------+-----+---------+-------+
| Inauguration | date     | NO   |     |         |       |
| ID           | int(11)  | NO   |     |         |       |
| LastName     | char(30) | NO   |     |         |       |
| FirstName    | char(30) | NO   |     |         |       |
+--------------+----------+------+-----+---------+-------+
```

Using AFTER *column_name* tells ALTER TABLE to place the new column after a specific existing column. For example, to place the new Inauguration column after the existing FirstName column, you would issue this statement:

```
ALTER TABLE HeadOfState ADD Inauguration DATE NOT NULL AFTER FirstName;
```

That ALTER TABLE statement results in a table structure that looks like this:

```
mysql> DESCRIBE HeadOfState;
+--------------+----------+------+-----+---------+-------+
| Field        | Type     | Null | Key | Default | Extra |
+--------------+----------+------+-----+---------+-------+
| ID           | int(11)  | NO   |     |         |       |
| LastName     | char(30) | NO   |     |         |       |
| FirstName    | char(30) | NO   |     |         |       |
| Inauguration | date     | NO   |     |         |       |
+--------------+----------+------+-----+---------+-------+
```

Column names within a table must be unique, so you cannot add a column with the same name as one that already exists in the table. Also, column names are not case sensitive, so if the table already contains a column named ID, you cannot add a new column using any of these names: ID, id, Id, or iD. They all are considered to be the same name.

To drop a column, use a DROP clause that names the column to be removed:

```
ALTER TABLE table_name DROP column_name;
```

8.3.2 Modifying Existing Columns

There are two ways to change the definition of an existing column within a table. One of these also enables you to rename the column.

The first way to alter a column definition is to use a MODIFY clause. You must specify the name of the column that you want to change, followed by its new definition. Assume that you want to change the ID column's data type from INT to BIGINT, to allow the table to accommodate larger identification numbers. You also want to make the column UNSIGNED to disallow negative values. The following statement accomplishes this task:

```
ALTER TABLE HeadOfState MODIFY ID BIGINT UNSIGNED NOT NULL;
```

DESCRIBE now shows the table structure to be as follows::

```
mysql> DESCRIBE HeadOfState;
+--------------+--------------------+------+-----+---------+-------+
| Field        | Type               | Null | Key | Default | Extra |
+--------------+--------------------+------+-----+---------+-------+
| ID           | bigint(20) unsigned | NO   |     |         |       |
| LastName     | char(30)           | NO   |     |         |       |
| FirstName    | char(30)           | NO   |     |         |       |
| Inauguration | date               | NO   |     |         |       |
+--------------+--------------------+------+-----+---------+-------+
```

Note that if you want to disallow NULL in the column, the column definition provided for MODIFY must include the NOT NULL attribute, even if the column was originally defined with

NOT NULL. This is true for other column attributes as well. If you don't specify them explicitly, the new definition won't carry them over from the old definition.

The second way to alter a column definition is to use a CHANGE clause. CHANGE enables you to modify both the column's definition and its name. To use this clause, specify the CHANGE keyword, followed by the column's existing name, its new name, and its new definition, in that order. Note that this means you must specify the existing name twice if you want to change only the column definition (and not the name). For example, to change the LastName column from CHAR(30) to CHAR(40) without renaming the column, you'd do this:

```
ALTER TABLE HeadOfState CHANGE LastName LastName CHAR(40) NOT NULL;
```

To change the name as well (for example, to Surname), provide the new name following the existing name:

```
ALTER TABLE HeadOfState CHANGE LastName Surname CHAR(40) NOT NULL;
```

8.3.3 Renaming a Table

Renaming a table changes neither a table's structure nor its contents. The following statement renames table t1 to t2:

```
ALTER TABLE t1 RENAME TO t2;
```

Another way to rename a table is by using the RENAME TABLE statement:

```
RENAME TABLE t1 TO t2;
```

RENAME TABLE has an advantage over ALTER TABLE in that it can perform multiple table renames in a single operation. One use for this feature is to swap the names of two tables:

```
RENAME TABLE t1 TO tmp, t2 TO t1, tmp TO t2;
```

For TEMPORARY tables, RENAME TABLE does not work. You must use ALTER TABLE instead.

8.3.4 Specifying Multiple Table Alterations

You can specify multiple alterations for a table with a single ALTER TABLE statement. Just separate the actions by commas. For example:

```
ALTER TABLE HeadOfState RENAME TO CountryLeader,
    MODIFY ID BIGINT UNSIGNED NOT NULL,
    ADD Salutation CHAR(30) NULL AFTER FirstName;
```

8.4 Dropping Tables

To remove a table when you no longer need it, use the DROP TABLE statement:

```
DROP TABLE t;
```

In MySQL, a single DROP TABLE statement can name several tables to be dropped simultaneously:

```
DROP TABLE t1, t2, t3;
```

Normally, an error occurs if you attempt to drop a table that does not exist:

```
mysql> DROP TABLE no_such_table;
ERROR 1051 (42S02): Unknown table 'no_such_table'
```

To prevent an error from occurring if a table does not exist when you attempt to drop it, add an IF EXISTS clause to the statement. In this case, a warning occurs if the table does not exist, which can be displayed with SHOW WARNINGS:

```
mysql> DROP TABLE IF EXISTS no_such_table;
Query OK, 0 rows affected, 1 warning (0.00 sec)

mysql> SHOW WARNINGS;
+-------+------+-----------------------------+
| Level | Code | Message                     |
+-------+------+-----------------------------+
| Note  | 1051 | Unknown table 'no_such_table' |
+-------+------+-----------------------------+
1 row in set (0.00 sec)
```

If you drop a table by mistake, you must recover it from backups, so be careful.

8.5 Emptying Tables

To remove records from a table without removing the table itself, use the DELETE or TRUNCATE TABLE statement. Either of the following statements completely empties the named table:

```
DELETE FROM t;
TRUNCATE TABLE t;
```

DELETE takes an optional WHERE clause that identifies which records to remove. This is useful when you want to delete only a given subset of records from a table. The following statement removes only those records from t that have a status column value of 'expired':

```
DELETE FROM t WHERE status = 'expired';
```

DELETE and TRUNCATE TABLE are discussed further in Section 11.5, "The DELETE and TRUNCATE TABLE Statements," where you can find a comparative breakdown of their operational characteristics.

8.6 Indexes

Tables in MySQL can grow very large, but as a table gets bigger, retrievals from it become slower. To keep your queries performing well, it's essential to index your tables. Indexes allow column values to be found more efficiently, so retrievals based on indexes are faster than those that are not. For large tables, the presence of an index can make the difference between a query that executes quickly and one that is unacceptably slow.

Another reason to use indexes is that they can enforce uniqueness constraints to ensure that duplicate values do not occur and that each row in a table can be distinguished from every other row.

This section discusses the following index-related topics:

- Types of indexes
- Defining indexes at table creation time with CREATE TABLE
- Using primary keys
- Adding indexes to existing tables with ALTER TABLE or CREATE INDEX
- Dropping indexes from tables with ALTER TABLE or DROP INDEX
- Choosing an indexing algorithm

8.6.1 Types of Indexes

MySQL supports three general types of indexes:

- A primary key is an index for which each index value differs from every other and uniquely identifies a single row in the table. A primary key cannot contain NULL values.
- A unique index is similar to a primary key, except that it can be allowed to contain NULL values. Each non-NULL value uniquely identifies a single row in the table.
- A non-unique index is an index in which any key value may occur multiple times.

There are also more specialized types of indexes:

- A FULLTEXT index is specially designed for text searching.
- A SPATIAL index applies only to columns that have spatial data types.

FULLTEXT indexes are covered in Section 38.3.3, "FULLTEXT Indexes." SPATIAL indexes are not covered in this study guide or on the exam.

8.6.2 Creating Indexes

You can create indexes at the same time that you create a table by including index definitions in the CREATE TABLE along with the column definitions. It is also possible to add indexes to an existing table with ALTER TABLE or CREATE INDEX.

8.6.2.1 Defining Indexes at Table Creation Time

To define indexes for a table at the time you create it, include the index definitions in the CREATE TABLE statement along with the column definitions. An index definition consists of the appropriate index-type keyword or keywords, followed by a list in parentheses that names the column or columns to be indexed. Suppose that the definition of a table HeadOfState without any indexes looks like this:

```
CREATE TABLE HeadOfState
(
    ID           INT NOT NULL,
    LastName     CHAR(30) NOT NULL,
    FirstName    CHAR(30) NOT NULL,
    CountryCode  CHAR(3) NOT NULL,
    Inauguration DATE NOT NULL
);
```

To create the table with the same columns but with a non-unique index on the date-valued column Inauguration, include an INDEX clause in the CREATE TABLE statement as follows:

```
CREATE TABLE HeadOfState
(
    ID           INT NOT NULL,
    LastName     CHAR(30) NOT NULL,
    FirstName    CHAR(30) NOT NULL,
    CountryCode  CHAR(3) NOT NULL,
    Inauguration DATE NOT NULL,
    INDEX (Inauguration)
);
```

The keyword KEY may be used instead of INDEX.

To include multiple columns in an index (that is, to create a composite index), list all the column names within the parentheses, separated by commas. For example, a composite index that includes both the LastName and FirstName columns can be defined as follows:

```
CREATE TABLE HeadOfState
(
    ID           INT NOT NULL,
    LastName     CHAR(30) NOT NULL,
    FirstName    CHAR(30) NOT NULL,
    CountryCode  CHAR(3) NOT NULL,
    Inauguration DATE NOT NULL,
    INDEX (LastName, FirstName)
);
```

Composite indexes can be created for any type of index.

The preceding indexing examples each include just one index in the table definition, but a table can have multiple indexes. The following table definition includes two indexes:

```
CREATE TABLE HeadOfState
(
    ID              INT NOT NULL,
    LastName        CHAR(30) NOT NULL,
    FirstName       CHAR(30) NOT NULL,
    CountryCode     CHAR(3) NOT NULL,
    Inauguration DATE NOT NULL,
    INDEX (LastName, FirstName),
    INDEX (Inauguration)
);
```

To create a unique-valued index, use the UNIQUE keyword instead of INDEX. For example, if you want to prevent duplicate values in the ID column, create a UNIQUE index for it like this:

```
CREATE TABLE HeadOfState
(
    ID              INT NOT NULL,
    LastName        CHAR(30) NOT NULL,
    FirstName       CHAR(30) NOT NULL,
    CountryCode     CHAR(3) NOT NULL,
    Inauguration DATE NOT NULL,
    UNIQUE (ID)
);
```

There's one exception to the uniqueness of values in a UNIQUE index: If a column in the index may contain NULL values, multiple NULL values are allowed. This differs from the behavior for non-NULL values.

A PRIMARY KEY is similar to a UNIQUE index. The differences between the two are as follows:

- A PRIMARY KEY cannot contain NULL values; a UNIQUE index can. If a unique-valued index must be allowed to contain NULL values, you must use a UNIQUE index, not a PRIMARY KEY.
- Each table may have only one index defined as a PRIMARY KEY. (The internal name for a PRIMARY KEY is always PRIMARY, and there can be only one index with a given name.) It's possible to have multiple UNIQUE indexes for a table.

It follows from the preceding description that a PRIMARY KEY is a type of unique-valued index, but a UNIQUE index isn't necessarily a primary key unless it disallows NULL values. If it does, a UNIQUE index that cannot contain NULL is functionally equivalent to a PRIMARY KEY.

To index a column as a PRIMARY KEY, use the keywords PRIMARY KEY rather than UNIQUE and declare the column NOT NULL to make sure that it cannot contain NULL values.

The use of PRIMARY KEY and UNIQUE to create indexes that ensure unique identification for any row in a table is discussed in the next section.

8.6.2.2 Creating and Using Primary Keys

The most common reason for creating an index is that it decreases lookup time for operations that search the indexed columns, especially for large tables. Another important use for indexing is to create a constraint that requires each index value to be unique.

An index with unique values allows you to identify each record in a table as distinct from any other. This kind of index provides a primary key for a table. Without a primary key, there might be no way to identify a record that does not also identify other records at the same time. That is a problem when you need to retrieve, update, or delete a specific record in a table. A unique ID number is a common type of primary key.

Two kinds of indexes can be used to implement the concept of a primary key:

- An index created with the PRIMARY KEY keywords
- An index created with the UNIQUE keyword

In both cases, the column or columns in the index should be declared as NOT NULL. For a PRIMARY KEY, this is a requirement; MySQL won't create a PRIMARY KEY from any column that may be NULL. (If you omit NOT NULL from the definition of any PRIMARY KEY column, MySQL adds it implicitly to enforce the NOT NULL requirement.) For a UNIQUE index, declaring columns as NOT NULL is a logical requirement if the index is to serve as a primary key. If a UNIQUE index is allowed to contain NULL values, it may contain multiple NULL values. As a result, some rows might not be distinguishable from others and the index cannot be used as a primary key.

The following definition creates a table t that contains an id column that's NOT NULL and declared as a primary key by means of a PRIMARY KEY clause:

```
CREATE TABLE t
(
    id   INT NOT NULL,
    name CHAR(30) NOT NULL,
    PRIMARY KEY (id)
);
```

A primary key on a column also can be created by replacing PRIMARY KEY with UNIQUE in the table definition, provided that the column is declared NOT NULL:

```
CREATE TABLE t
(
    id   INT NOT NULL,
    name CHAR(30) NOT NULL,
    UNIQUE (id)
);
```

An alternative syntax is allowed for the preceding two statements. For a single-column primary key, you can add the keywords PRIMARY KEY or UNIQUE directly to the end of the column definition. The following CREATE TABLE statements are equivalent to those just shown:

```
CREATE TABLE t
(
    id   INT NOT NULL PRIMARY KEY,
    name CHAR(30) NOT NULL
);

CREATE TABLE t
(
    id   INT NOT NULL UNIQUE,
    name CHAR(30) NOT NULL
);
```

Like other indexes, you can declare a PRIMARY KEY or UNIQUE index as a composite index that spans multiple columns. In this case, the index must be declared using a separate clause. (You cannot add the PRIMARY KEY or UNIQUE keywords to the end of a column definition because the index would apply only to that column.) The following definition creates a primary key on the last_name and first_name columns using a PRIMARY KEY clause:

```
CREATE TABLE people
(
    last_name  CHAR(30) NOT NULL,
    first_name CHAR(30) NOT NULL,
    PRIMARY KEY (last_name, first_name)
);
```

This primary key definition allows any given last name or first name to appear multiple times in the table, but no combination of last and first name can occur more than once.

If the columns are declared NOT NULL, you can also create a multiple-column primary key using UNIQUE:

```
CREATE TABLE people
(
    last_name  CHAR(30) NOT NULL,
    first_name CHAR(30) NOT NULL,
    UNIQUE (last_name, first_name)
);
```

Primary keys are an important general database design concept because they allow unique identification of each row in a table. For MySQL in particular, primary keys are frequently defined as columns that are declared with the AUTO_INCREMENT attribute. AUTO_INCREMENT columns provide a convenient way to automatically generate a unique sequence number for each row in a table and are described in Section 5.7, "Using the AUTO_INCREMENT Column Attribute."

8.6.2.3 Naming Indexes

For all index types other than PRIMARY KEY, you can name an index by including the name just before the column list. For example, the following definition uses names of NameIndex and IDIndex for the two indexes in the table:

```
CREATE TABLE HeadOfState
(
    ID           INT NOT NULL,
    LastName     CHAR(30) NOT NULL,
    FirstName    CHAR(30) NOT NULL,
    CountryCode  CHAR(3) NOT NULL,
    Inauguration DATE NOT NULL,
    INDEX NameIndex (LastName, FirstName),
    UNIQUE IDIndex (ID)
);
```

If you don't provide a name for an index, MySQL assigns a name for you based on the name of the first column in the index.

For a PRIMARY KEY, you provide no name because the name is always PRIMARY. A consequence of this fact is that you cannot define more than one PRIMARY KEY per table because indexes, like columns, must have unique names.

Index names are displayed by the SHOW CREATE TABLE or SHOW INDEX statement.

8.6.2.4 Adding Indexes to Existing Tables

To add an index to a table, you can use ALTER TABLE or CREATE INDEX. Of these statements, ALTER TABLE is the most flexible, as will become clear in the following discussion.

To add an index to a table with ALTER TABLE, use ADD followed by the appropriate index-type keywords and a parenthesized list naming the columns to be indexed. For example, assume that the HeadOfState table used earlier in this chapter is defined without indexes as follows:

```
CREATE TABLE HeadOfState
(
    ID           INT NOT NULL,
    LastName     CHAR(30) NOT NULL,
    FirstName    CHAR(30) NOT NULL,
    CountryCode  CHAR(3) NOT NULL,
    Inauguration DATE NOT NULL
);
```

To create a PRIMARY KEY on the ID column and a composite index on the LastName and FirstName columns, you could issue these statements:

```
ALTER TABLE HeadOfState ADD PRIMARY KEY (ID);
ALTER TABLE HeadOfState ADD INDEX (LastName,FirstName);
```

However, MySQL allows multiple actions to be performed with a single ALTER TABLE statement. One common use for multiple actions is to add several indexes to a table at the same time, which is more efficient than adding each one separately. Thus, the preceding two ALTER TABLE statements can be combined as follows:

```
ALTER TABLE HeadOfState ADD PRIMARY KEY (ID), ADD INDEX (LastName,FirstName);
```

The syntax for CREATE INDEX is as follows, where the statements shown create a single-column UNIQUE index and a multiple-column non-unique index, respectively:

```
CREATE UNIQUE INDEX IDIndex ON HeadOfState (ID);
CREATE INDEX NameIndex ON HeadOfState (LastName,FirstName);
```

Note that with CREATE INDEX, it's necessary to provide a name for the index. With ALTER TABLE, MySQL creates an index name automatically if you don't provide one.

Unlike ALTER TABLE, the CREATE INDEX statement can create only a single index per statement. In addition, only ALTER TABLE supports the use of PRIMARY KEY. For these reasons, ALTER TABLE is more flexible.

8.6.3 Choosing an Indexing Algorithm

When you create an index, it is possible to specify the indexing algorithm to be used. The only engine for which this feature is currently applicable is the MEMORY engine that manages in-memory tables. For other engines, the syntax is recognized but ignored.

MEMORY tables use hash indexes by default. This index algorithm provides very fast lookups for all operations that use a unique index. However, hash indexes are usable only for comparisons that use the = or <=> operator. Also, for non-unique indexes, operations that change the indexed values (including DELETE statements) can become relatively slow when there are many duplicate index values.

If you will have only unique indexes on a MEMORY table, you should create them as HASH indexes. Because HASH indexes are the default for MEMORY tables, you can do so when defining an index either by specifying an explicit USING HASH clause or by omitting the index algorithm specification entirely. The following two statements are equivalent:

```
CREATE TABLE lookup
(
    id INT,
    INDEX USING HASH (id)
) ENGINE = MEMORY;

CREATE TABLE lookup
(
    id INT,
    INDEX (id)
) ENGINE = MEMORY;
```

On the other hand, if a MEMORY table contains only non-unique indexes for which you expect that there will be many duplicate values in the index key, a BTREE index is preferable. BTREE indexes also are usable if the indexed column will be used with comparison operators other than = or <=>. For example, BTREE can be used for range searches such as id < 100 or id BETWEEN 200 AND 300. To create an index that uses the BTREE algorithm, include a USING BTREE clause in the index definition:

```
CREATE TABLE lookup (
  id INT,
  INDEX USING BTREE (id)
) ENGINE = MEMORY;
```

If you have already created the table, you can add a new index using either ALTER TABLE or CREATE INDEX, making use of the USING *index_type* clause. If the lookup table had been created without the index on the id column, either of the following statements would add a BTREE index on that column:

```
ALTER TABLE lookup ADD INDEX USING BTREE (id);
```

```
CREATE INDEX id_idx USING BTREE ON lookup (id);
```

Although choosing between alternative indexing algorithms currently is limited to MEMORY tables, work is ongoing on extending this functionality to other storage engines such as MyISAM and InnoDB.

8.7 Dropping Indexes

To drop an index from a table, use ALTER TABLE or DROP INDEX.

With ALTER TABLE, use a DROP clause and name the index to be dropped. Dropping a PRIMARY KEY is easy:

```
ALTER TABLE HeadOfState DROP PRIMARY KEY;
```

To drop another kind of index, you must specify its name. If you don't know the name, you can use SHOW CREATE TABLE to see the table's structure, including any index definitions, as shown here:

```
mysql> SHOW CREATE TABLE HeadOfState\G
*************************** 1. row ***************************
       Table: HeadOfState
Create Table: CREATE TABLE `HeadOfState` (
  `ID` int(11) NOT NULL default '0',
  `LastName` char(30) NOT NULL default '',
  `FirstName` char(30) NOT NULL default '',
  `CountryCode` char(3) NOT NULL default '',
  `Inauguration` date NOT NULL default '0000-00-00',
```

```
    KEY `NameIndex` (`LastName`,`FirstName`)
) ENGINE=MyISAM DEFAULT CHARSET=latin1
```

The KEY clause of the output shows that the index name is NameIndex, so you can drop the index using the following statement:

```
ALTER TABLE HeadOfState DROP INDEX NameIndex;
```

After you've dropped an index, you can recover it merely by re-creating it:

```
ALTER TABLE HeadOfState ADD INDEX NameIndex (LastName, FirstName);
```

Dropping an index differs from dropping a database or a table, which cannot be undone except by recourse to backups. The distinction is that when you drop a database or a table, you're removing data. When you drop an index, you aren't removing table data, you're removing only a structure that's derived from the data. The act of removing an index is a reversible operation as long as the columns from which the index was constructed have not been removed. However, for a large table, dropping and recreating an index may be a time-consuming operation.

To drop an index with DROP INDEX, indicate the index name and table name:

```
DROP INDEX NameIndex ON t;
```

To drop a PRIMARY KEY with DROP INDEX, refer to the index name (PRIMARY), but use a quoted identifier because this name is a reserved word:

```
DROP INDEX `PRIMARY` ON t;
```

Unlike ALTER TABLE, the DROP INDEX statement can drop only on a single index per statement.

8.8 Obtaining Table and Index Metadata

The SELECT statement retrieves the information *contained* in your tables. You can also ask MySQL to show you table metadata; that is, information *about* your tables. Metadata includes information such as table names or column or index definitions.

The INFORMATION_SCHEMA database has a TABLES table that contains table metadata. For example, to display information about the world.City table, use this statement:

```
mysql> SELECT * FROM INFORMATION_SCHEMA.TABLES
    -> WHERE TABLE_SCHEMA = 'world'
    -> AND TABLE_NAME = 'City'\G
*************************** 1. row ***************************
  TABLE_CATALOG: NULL
   TABLE_SCHEMA: world
     TABLE_NAME: City
```

```
        TABLE_TYPE: BASE TABLE
            ENGINE: MyISAM
           VERSION: 10
        ROW_FORMAT: Fixed
        TABLE_ROWS: 4079
    AVG_ROW_LENGTH: 67
       DATA_LENGTH: 273293
   MAX_DATA_LENGTH: 18858823439613951
      INDEX_LENGTH: 43008
         DATA_FREE: 0
    AUTO_INCREMENT: 4080
       CREATE_TIME: 2005-05-28 20:20:22
       UPDATE_TIME: 2005-05-29 20:54:51
        CHECK_TIME: NULL
   TABLE_COLLATION: latin1_swedish_ci
          CHECKSUM: NULL
     CREATE_OPTIONS:
     TABLE_COMMENT:
```

Information about indexes is available from INFORMATION_SCHEMA in the STATISTICS table.

For further information about INFORMATION_SCHEMA, see Chapter 20, "Obtaining Database Metadata."

MySQL also supports a family of SHOW statements that display metadata. Some that pertain to tables are SHOW TABLES and SHOW CREATE TABLE.

To determine the tables that a particular database contains, use SHOW TABLES:

```
mysql> SHOW TABLES FROM world;
+-----------------+
| Tables_in_world |
+-----------------+
| City            |
| Country         |
| CountryLanguage |
+-----------------+
```

The FROM clause names the database whose table names you want to determine. With no FROM clause, SHOW TABLES displays the names of the tables in the default database. If there is no default database, an error occurs:

```
mysql> SHOW TABLES;
ERROR 1046 (3D000): No database selected
```

SHOW TABLES can take a LIKE 'pattern' clause. With LIKE, the statement performs a pattern-matching operation and displays information only about tables with names that match the pattern. Patterns are discussed in Section 10.3.2, "Using LIKE for Pattern Matching."

```
mysql> SHOW TABLES FROM world LIKE '%tr%';
+-----------------------+
| Tables_in_world (%tr%) |
+-----------------------+
| Country               |
| CountryLanguage       |
+-----------------------+
```

SHOW CREATE TABLE shows the CREATE TABLE statement that corresponds to a table's definition, including its columns, indexes, and any table options the table has:

```
mysql> SHOW CREATE TABLE CountryLanguage\G
*************************** 1. row ***************************
       Table: CountryLanguage
Create Table: CREATE TABLE `CountryLanguage` (
  `CountryCode` char(3) NOT NULL default '',
  `Language` char(30) NOT NULL default '',
  `IsOfficial` enum('T','F') NOT NULL default 'F',
  `Percentage` float(4,1) NOT NULL default '0.0',
  PRIMARY KEY  (`CountryCode`,`Language`)
) ENGINE=MyISAM DEFAULT CHARSET=latin1
```

DESCRIBE is another statement that displays table structure metadata. You're already familiar with DESCRIBE; its output format was discussed in the Introduction and it has been used in several examples earlier in this study guide. Here is an example of its output:

```
mysql> DESCRIBE CountryLanguage;
+------------+---------------+------+-----+---------+-------+
| Field      | Type          | Null | Key | Default | Extra |
+------------+---------------+------+-----+---------+-------+
| Country    | char(3)       | NO   | PRI |         |       |
| Language   | char(30)      | NO   | PRI |         |       |
| IsOfficial | enum('T','F') | NO   |     | F       |       |
| Percentage | float(3,1)    | NO   |     | 0.0     |       |
+------------+---------------+------+-----+---------+-------+
```

DESCRIBE *table_name* is a synonym for SHOW COLUMNS FROM *table_name* or SHOW FIELDS FROM *table_name*. These statements are equivalent:

```
DESCRIBE CountryLanguage;
SHOW COLUMNS FROM CountryLanguage;
SHOW FIELDS FROM CountryLanguage;
```

You can also use SHOW to obtain index information. To find out what indexes a table has, use SHOW CREATE TABLE to display the CREATE TABLE statement that corresponds to the table structure, including its indexes. For more detailed information about the indexes, use SHOW INDEX. For example, SHOW INDEX produces the following output for the Country table of the world database:

```
mysql> SHOW INDEX FROM Country\G
*************************** 1. row ***************************
        Table: Country
   Non_unique: 0
     Key_name: PRIMARY
  Seq_in_index: 1
  Column_name: Code
    Collation: A
  Cardinality: NULL
     Sub_part: NULL
       Packed: NULL
         Null:
   Index_type: BTREE
      Comment:
```

The output indicates that the table has a single index, a primary key on the Code column. For the CountryLanguage table, the output has two rows because the primary key includes two columns, Country and Language:

```
mysql> SHOW INDEX FROM CountryLanguage\G
*************************** 1. row ***************************
        Table: CountryLanguage
   Non_unique: 0
     Key_name: PRIMARY
  Seq_in_index: 1
  Column_name: Country
    Collation: A
  Cardinality: NULL
     Sub_part: NULL
       Packed: NULL
         Null:
   Index_type: BTREE
      Comment:
*************************** 2. row ***************************
        Table: CountryLanguage
   Non_unique: 0
     Key_name: PRIMARY
  Seq_in_index: 2
  Column_name: Language
    Collation: A
  Cardinality: NULL
     Sub_part: NULL
       Packed: NULL
         Null:
   Index_type: BTREE
      Comment:
```

The Seq_in_index values show the order of the columns within the index. They indicate that the primary key columns are Country first and Language second. That information corresponds to the following PRIMARY KEY declaration:

```
PRIMARY KEY (Country, Language)
```

9

Querying for Data

This chapter discusses how to use the SELECT statement to retrieve information from database tables. It covers the following exam topics:

- Specifying which columns to retrieve and the table from which to retrieve them
- Using WHERE to identify the characteristics that define which records to retrieve
- Using ORDER BY to sort query results
- Using LIMIT to limit the output to a specific number of the rows retrieved
- Using DISTINCT to eliminate duplicates
- Computing summary values from groups of rows
- Using UNION to combine results from multiple queries into a single result set

9.1 Using SELECT to Retrieve Data

The SELECT statement retrieves information from one or more tables. Retrievals tend to be the most common database operation, so it's important to understand how SELECT works and what you can do with it.

This chapter provides general instructions on how to write SELECT statements and how to use the various parts of its syntax to get the results you want. A representative syntax for the SELECT statement is as follows:

```
SELECT values_to_display
    FROM table_name
    WHERE expression
    GROUP BY how_to_group
    HAVING expression
    ORDER BY how_to_sort
    LIMIT row_count;
```

The syntax shown here is simplified from the full SELECT syntax, which includes additional clauses that aren't covered in this chapter.

All clauses following the output column list (*values_to_display*) are optional. For example, you don't need to include a LIMIT clause when writing a SELECT statement. However, any clauses that you do include must be specified in the order shown.

The examples in this chapter use SELECT statements for retrievals involving no more than a single table, but it's possible to retrieve records from more than one table in a single query. One way is by selecting records from one table after the other with multiple SELECT statements and concatenating the results using the UNION keyword. UNION is covered in Section 9.6, "Using UNION." Other multiple-table queries use joins and subqueries, which are covered in later chapters.

In most cases, the sample queries shown here assume that you've already selected a default database. If that isn't true, you can select a database named *db_name* by issuing a USE *db_name* statement. For example, select the world database like this:

```
mysql> USE world;
Database changed
```

9.2 Specifying Which Columns to Retrieve

To indicate what values to retrieve, name them following the SELECT keyword. In the simplest case, you specify an expression or list of expressions. MySQL evaluates each expression and returns its value. Expressions may return numbers, strings, temporal values, or NULL. The following SELECT statement retrieves a value of each of those types:

```
mysql> SELECT 2+2, REPEAT('x',5), DATE_ADD('2001-01-01',INTERVAL 7 DAY), 1/0;
+-----+---------------+---------------------------------------+------+
| 2+2 | REPEAT('x',5) | DATE_ADD('2001-01-01',INTERVAL 7 DAY) | 1/0  |
+-----+---------------+---------------------------------------+------+
|   4 | xxxxx         | 2001-01-08                            | NULL |
+-----+---------------+---------------------------------------+------+
```

The first expression is a sum of numbers and returns the number 4. The second expression returns a string ('xxxxx') consisting of the character 'x' repeated five times. The third expression returns a date value. The fourth expression returns NULL because it involves a divide-by-zero condition. In general, if MySQL finds it impossible to evaluate an expression because it involves some exceptional condition, the result is NULL or an error occurs.

SELECT can retrieve the values of expressions, as just shown, but it's more commonly used to retrieve columns from tables. To select information from a table, it's necessary to identify the table by adding a FROM *table_name* clause following the list of columns to retrieve. The names of the columns can be seen with DESCRIBE:

```
mysql> DESCRIBE City;
+-------------+----------+------+-----+---------+----------------+
| Field       | Type     | Null | Key | Default | Extra          |
```

```
+------------+----------+------+-----+---------+----------------+
| ID         | int(11)  | NO   | PRI | NULL    | auto_increment |
| Name       | char(35) | NO   |     |         |                |
| CountryCode| char(3)  | NO   |     |         |                |
| District   | char(20) | NO   |     |         |                |
| Population | int(11)  | NO   |     | 0       |                |
+------------+----------+------+-----+---------+----------------+
```

To retrieve the contents of these columns, write the SELECT statement as follows:

```
SELECT ID, Name, CountryCode, District, Population FROM City;
```

MySQL returns a result set consisting of one row of output for each row in the table. (The term "result set" refers to the set of rows resulting from a SELECT statement.) If the table is empty, the result will be empty, too. An empty result set is perfectly legal. A syntactically valid SELECT that returns no rows is not considered erroneous.

For a SELECT operation that retrieves every column from a table, the shortcut * can be used to specify the output columns. The * stands for "all columns in the table," so for the City table, the following statements are equivalent:

```
SELECT ID, Name, CountryCode, District, Population FROM City;
SELECT * FROM City;
```

The * shorthand notation is clearly more convenient to type than a list of column names. However, you should understand when it is useful and when it isn't:

- If you want to retrieve all columns from a table and you don't care about the order in which they appear from left to right, * is appropriate. If you want to ensure that the columns appear left to right in a particular order, * cannot be used because it gives you no control over the order in which columns will appear. You should name the columns explicitly in the order you want to see them.

- If you don't want to retrieve all the columns from the table, you cannot use *. Instead, name the columns in the order they should appear.

You should not issue a SELECT * query to find out the current left-to-right display order for the columns in a table and then assume that they will always be displayed in that same order for future queries. The left-to-right column order produced by SELECT * retrievals depends implicitly on the internal structure of the table, which is determined by the order of the columns in the table definition. However, the table's internal structure can be changed with ALTER TABLE, so a SELECT * statement might return different results before and after an ALTER TABLE statement.

9.2.1 Renaming Retrieved Columns

Output column names, by default, are the same as the column or expression selected. To rename a column, provide an alias following the column in the output list:

```
mysql> SELECT 1 AS One, 4*3 'Four Times Three';
+-----+------------------+
| One | Four Times Three |
+-----+------------------+
|   1 |               12 |
+-----+------------------+
```

Columns aliases are used as follows:

- The keyword AS is optional.

- An alias may be quoted. If it consists of multiple words, it must be quoted.

- You can refer to a column alias elsewhere in the query, in the GROUP BY, HAVING, or ORDER BY clause. However, you cannot refer to aliases in the WHERE clause.

9.2.2 Identifying the Database Containing a Table

When you name a table in a SELECT statement, it's normally assumed to be a table in the default database. (This is true for other statements as well.) For example, if world is the default database, the following statement selects rows from the Country table in the world database:

```
SELECT * FROM Country;
```

If there's no default database, the statement results in an error because MySQL cannot tell where to find the table:

```
mysql> SELECT * FROM Country;
ERROR 1046 (3D000): No database selected
```

To specify a database explicitly in the SELECT statement itself, qualify the table name. That is, precede the table name with the database name and a period:

```
SELECT * FROM world.Country;
```

The database name acts as a qualifier for the table name. It provides to the server a context for locating the table. Qualified table names are useful under several circumstances:

- When there's no default database. In this case, a qualifier is necessary for accessing the table.

- When you want to select information from a table that's located somewhere other than the default database. In this situation, it's possible to issue a USE statement to select the other database as the default, a SELECT that uses the unqualified table name, and then another USE to select the original database as the default. However, qualifying the table name in the SELECT allows the two USE statements to be avoided.

- When you aren't sure what the default database is. If the default isn't the database in which the table is located, the qualifier enables the server to locate the table. If the default happens to be the same as the named database, the qualifier is unnecessary, but harmless.

9.3 Specifying Which Rows to Retrieve

If you specify no criteria for selecting records from a table, a SELECT statement retrieves every record in the table. This is often more information than you need, particularly for large tables. To be more specific about which rows are of interest, include a WHERE clause that describes the characteristics of those rows.

A WHERE clause can be as simple or complex as necessary to identify the rows that are relevant for your purposes. For example, to retrieve records from the Country table for those countries that achieved independence after the year 1990, it's sufficient to use a WHERE clause that specifies a single condition:

```
SELECT * FROM Country WHERE IndepYear > 1990;
```

More complex WHERE clauses specify multiple conditions, which may be combined using logical operators such as AND and OR. The following statement returns rows with Population values in the range from 1 million to 2 million:

```
SELECT * FROM Country
WHERE Population >= 1000000 AND Population <= 2000000;
```

For testing values in a range, you can also use the BETWEEN operator:

```
SELECT * FROM Country
WHERE Population BETWEEN 1000000 AND 2000000;
```

Some operators have higher precedence than others. For example, AND has a higher precedence than OR. To control the order of evaluation of terms within a complex expression (or simply to make the evaluation order explicit), use parentheses to group expression terms. Consider the following WHERE clause:

```
WHERE GNP < 1000 AND Continent = 'Africa' OR Continent = 'Asia'
```

Because AND has a higher precedence than OR, the preceding expression is equivalent to the following one:

```
WHERE (GNP < 1000 AND Continent = 'Africa') OR Continent = 'Asia'
```

That expression finds all records with a GNP value less than 1000 that also have a Continent value of 'Africa', as well as all records with a Continent value of 'Asia' (regardless of their GNP value). However, a different placement of parentheses results in a very different meaning:

```
WHERE GNP < 1000 AND (Continent = 'Africa' OR Continent = 'Asia')
```

That expression finds records that have a GNP value less than 1000 and a Continent value of either 'Africa' or 'Asia'.

More information on writing expressions can be found in Chapter 10, "SQL Expressions." Detailed descriptions of the operators and functions that you can use in expressions are provided in the *MySQL Reference Manual*.

It's possible to prevent SELECT statements that might generate a great deal of output from returning more than 1,000 rows. The mysql client supports this feature if you invoke it with the --safe-updates option. For more information, see Section 2.9, "Using the --safe-updates Option."

9.3.1 Using ORDER BY to Sort Query Results

By default, the rows in the result set produced by a SELECT statement are returned by the server to the client in no particular order. When you issue a query, the server is free to return the rows in any convenient order. This order can be affected by factors such as the order in which rows are actually stored in the table or which indexes are used to process the query. If you require output rows to be returned in a specific order, include an ORDER BY clause that indicates how to sort the results.

The examples in this section demonstrate ORDER BY using a table t that has the following contents (id is numeric, last_name and first_name are strings, and birth contains dates):

```
mysql> SELECT id, last_name, first_name, birth FROM t;
+------+-----------+------------+------------+
| id   | last_name | first_name | birth      |
+------+-----------+------------+------------+
|    1 | Brown     | Bill       | 1972-10-14 |
|    2 | Larsson   | Sven       | 1965-01-03 |
|    3 | Brown     | Betty      | 1971-07-12 |
|    4 | Larsson   | Selma      | 1968-05-29 |
+------+-----------+------------+------------+
```

ORDER BY provides a great deal of flexibility for sorting result sets. It has the following characteristics:

- You can name one or more columns, separated by commas, to use for sorting. With a single sort column, rows are sorted based on the values in that column:

```
mysql> SELECT id, last_name, first_name, birth FROM t
    -> ORDER BY birth;
+------+-----------+------------+------------+
| id   | last_name | first_name | birth      |
+------+-----------+------------+------------+
|    2 | Larsson   | Sven       | 1965-01-03 |
|    4 | Larsson   | Selma      | 1968-05-29 |
|    3 | Brown     | Betty      | 1971-07-12 |
```

```
|    1 | Brown     | Bill       | 1972-10-14 |
+------+-----------+------------+------------+
```

If there are additional sort columns, rows with the same value in the first sort column are sorted together, and are then further sorted using the values in the second and remaining sort columns. The following query sorts the Browns before the Larssons, and then within each group of rows with the same last name, sorts them by first name:

```
mysql> SELECT id, last_name, first_name, birth FROM t
    -> ORDER BY last_name, first_name;
+------+-----------+------------+------------+
| id   | last_name | first_name | birth      |
+------+-----------+------------+------------+
|    3 | Brown     | Betty      | 1971-07-12 |
|    1 | Brown     | Bill       | 1972-10-14 |
|    4 | Larsson   | Selma      | 1968-05-29 |
|    2 | Larsson   | Sven       | 1965-01-03 |
+------+-----------+------------+------------+
```

- By default, ORDER BY sorts values in ascending order (smallest to largest). Any sort column may be followed with ASC if you want to specify ascending order explicitly. These ORDER BY clauses are equivalent:

```
ORDER BY last_name, first_name
ORDER BY last_name ASC, first_name ASC
```

To sort values in descending order (largest to smallest), follow the sort column name with DESC:

```
mysql> SELECT id, last_name, first_name, birth FROM t
    -> ORDER BY id DESC;
+------+-----------+------------+------------+
| id   | last_name | first_name | birth      |
+------+-----------+------------+------------+
|    4 | Larsson   | Selma      | 1968-05-29 |
|    3 | Brown     | Betty      | 1971-07-12 |
|    2 | Larsson   | Sven       | 1965-01-03 |
|    1 | Brown     | Bill       | 1972-10-14 |
+------+-----------+------------+------------+
```

When you name a column followed by ASC or DESC, the sort direction specifier applies only to that column. It doesn't affect sort direction for any other columns listed in the ORDER BY clause.

- ORDER BY typically refers to table columns by name:

```
SELECT last_name, first_name FROM t ORDER BY last_name, first_name;
```

However, it's possible to refer to columns in other ways. If a column is given an alias in the output column list, you should refer to that column in the ORDER BY column by its alias:

```
SELECT last_name AS last, first_name AS first FROM t ORDER BY last, first;
```

Or you can specify a number corresponding to the column's position in the column output list (1 for the first output column, 2 for the second, and so forth) :

```
SELECT last_name, first_name FROM t ORDER BY 1, 2;
```

However, the syntax for specifying columns by position has been removed from the SQL Standard (in SQL:1999) and is obsolete. Application developers should consider using one of the other column specification methods.

- It's possible to perform a sort using an expression result. If the expression appears in the output column list, you can use it for sorting by repeating it in the ORDER BY clause. Alternatively, you can refer to the expression by an alias given to it. The following queries each sort the output rows by month of the year:

```
SELECT id, last_name, first_name, MONTH(birth)
    FROM t ORDER BY MONTH(birth);
SELECT id, last_name, first_name, MONTH(birth) AS m
    FROM t ORDER BY m;
```

You can also refer to the expression by its column position, although this is not recommended.

- Output sorting can be based on values that don't appear in the output at all. The following statement displays month names in the output, but sorts the rows using the numeric month value:

```
mysql> SELECT id, last_name, first_name, MONTHNAME(birth) FROM t
    -> ORDER BY MONTH(birth);
+------+-----------+------------+------------------+
| id   | last_name | first_name | MONTHNAME(birth) |
+------+-----------+------------+------------------+
|    2 | Larsson   | Sven       | January          |
|    4 | Larsson   | Selma      | May              |
|    3 | Brown     | Betty      | July             |
|    1 | Brown     | Bill       | October          |
+------+-----------+------------+------------------+
```

- ORDER BY doesn't require the sorted columns to be indexed, although a query might run faster if such an index does exist.

- ORDER BY is useful together with LIMIT for selecting a particular section of a set of sorted rows. (See Section 9.3.3, "Limiting a Selection Using LIMIT.")

- ORDER BY can be used with DELETE or UPDATE to force rows to be deleted or updated in a certain order. (These uses of ORDER BY are covered in Chapter 11, "Updating Data.")

9.3.2 The Natural Sort Order of Data Types

Each type of data managed by MySQL has its own natural sort order. For the most part, these orders are fairly intuitive. The rules for string sorting are the most complex because they depend on whether the strings are non-binary, binary, or come from ENUM or SET columns.

- A numeric column sorts in ascending numeric order by default, or descending order if DESC is specified.

- A temporal column sorts in ascending time order by default, with oldest values first and most recent values last. The order is reversed if DESC is specified.

- The sort order for a string column that has a data type other than ENUM or SET depends on whether the column contains non-binary or binary values. Non-binary strings sort in the order defined by their collation. This order can be case sensitive or not, depending on the collation. Binary strings sort based on the numeric values of the bytes contained in the strings. For example, assume that a table t has a CHAR column c that has the latin1 character set and that contains the following values:

```
mysql> SELECT c FROM t;
+------+
| c    |
+------+
| a    |
| A    |
| B    |
| A    |
| b    |
| a    |
+------+
```

A CHAR column is non-binary, so its contents sort according to the column's collation. If the collation is not case sensitive, values sort lexically without regard to lettercase:

```
mysql> SELECT c FROM t ORDER BY c;
+------+
| c    |
+------+
| a    |
| A    |
| A    |
| a    |
| B    |
| b    |
+------+
```

Notice that the results come out in letter order, but the rows for a given letter are not further sorted by lettercase.

If the collation is case sensitive, lettercase becomes significant. You can force a string column sort to be case sensitive by using the COLLATE operator with a case-sensitive collation:

```
mysql> SELECT c FROM t ORDER BY c COLLATE latin1_general_cs;
+------+
| c    |
+------+
| A    |
| A    |
| a    |
| a    |
| B    |
| b    |
+------+
```

If the collation is binary, numeric character values are the determining factor:

```
mysql> SELECT c FROM t ORDER BY c COLLATE latin1_bin;
+------+
| c    |
+------+
| A    |
| A    |
| B    |
| a    |
| a    |
| b    |
+------+
```

- The sort order for members of an ENUM or SET column is based on their internal numeric values. These values correspond to the order in which the enumeration or set members are listed in the column definition. Suppose that a table t contains a column mon that is an ENUM listing abbreviations for months of the year:

```
CREATE TABLE t
(
    mon ENUM('Jan','Feb','Mar','Apr','May','Jun',
             'Jul','Aug','Sep','Oct','Nov','Dec')
);
```

Assume that table t has 12 rows, one for each of the possible enumeration values. When you sort this column, the values come out in month-of-year order:

```
mysql> SELECT mon FROM t ORDER BY mon;
+------+
| mon  |
+------+
| Jan  |
```

```
| Feb  |
| Mar  |
| Apr  |
| May  |
| Jun  |
| Jul  |
| Aug  |
| Sep  |
| Oct  |
| Nov  |
| Dec  |
+------+
```

This occurs because 'Jan' through 'Dec' are assigned internal values 1 through 12 based on their order in the column definition, and those values determine the sort order. To produce a lexical string sort instead, use CAST() to convert the enumeration values to CHAR values:

```
mysql> SELECT mon FROM t ORDER BY CAST(mon AS CHAR);
+------+
| mon  |
+------+
| Apr  |
| Aug  |
| Dec  |
| Feb  |
| Jan  |
| Jul  |
| Jun  |
| Mar  |
| May  |
| Nov  |
| Oct  |
| Sep  |
+------+
```

SET columns also sort using the internal values of the set's legal members. The ordering is more complex than with ENUM because values may consist of multiple SET members. For example, the following SET column contains three members:

```
CREATE TABLE t (hue SET('red','green','blue'));
```

Assume that t contains the following rows:

```
mysql> SELECT hue FROM t;
+----------------+
| hue            |
+----------------+
```

```
| red,green      |
| red,green,blue |
| red,blue       |
| green,blue     |
+----------------+
```

The SET members 'red', 'green', and 'blue' have internal values of 1, 2, and 4, respectively. Thus, the rows of the table have internal numeric values of 1+2 = 3, 1+2+4 = 7, 1+4 = 5, and 2+4 = 6. An ORDER BY on the column sorts using those numeric values:

```
mysql> SELECT hue FROM t ORDER BY hue;
+----------------+
| hue            |
+----------------+
| red,green      |
| red,blue       |
| green,blue     |
| red,green,blue |
+----------------+
```

As with ENUM, SET values can be sorted lexically by using CAST() to convert them to strings:

```
mysql> SELECT hue FROM t ORDER BY CAST(hue AS CHAR);
+----------------+
| hue            |
+----------------+
| green,blue     |
| red,blue       |
| red,green      |
| red,green,blue |
+----------------+
```

- NULL values in a column sort together at the beginning for ascending sorts and at the end for descending sorts.

9.3.3 Limiting a Selection Using LIMIT

MySQL supports a LIMIT clause in SELECT statements, which tells the server to return only some of the rows selected by the statement. This is useful for retrieving records based on their position within the set of selected rows.

LIMIT may be given with either one or two arguments:

```
LIMIT row_count
LIMIT skip_count, row_count
```

Each argument must be given as an integer constant. You cannot use expressions, user variables, and so forth.

When followed by a single integer, *row_count*, LIMIT returns the first *row_count* rows from the beginning of the result set. To select just the first 10 rows of a result set, use LIMIT 10:

```
SELECT * FROM Country LIMIT 10;
```

When followed by two integers, *skip_count* and *row_count*, LIMIT skips the first *skip_count* rows from the beginning of the result set, and then returns the next *row_count* rows. To skip the first 20 rows and then return the next 10 rows, do this:

```
SELECT * FROM Country LIMIT 20,10;
```

The single-argument form of LIMIT is applicable only when the rows you want to retrieve appear at the beginning of the result set. The two-argument form is more general and can be used to select an arbitrary section of rows from anywhere in the result set.

When you need only some of the rows selected by a query, LIMIT is an efficient way to obtain them. For a client application that fetches rows from the server, you get better performance by adding LIMIT to the query than by having the client fetch all the rows and discard all but the ones of interest. By using LIMIT, the unwanted rows never cross the network at all.

It's often helpful to include an ORDER BY clause to put the rows in a particular order when you use LIMIT. When ORDER BY and LIMIT are used together, MySQL applies ORDER BY first and then LIMIT. One common use for this is to find the row containing the smallest or largest values in a particular column. For example, to find the row in a table t containing the smallest id value, use this statement:

```
SELECT * FROM t ORDER BY id LIMIT 1;
```

To find the largest value instead, use DESC to sort the rows in reverse:

```
SELECT * FROM t ORDER BY id DESC LIMIT 1;
```

The two-argument form of LIMIT is useful in conjunction with ORDER BY for situations in which you want to process successive sections of a result set. For example, in Web applications, it's common to display the result of a large search across a series of pages that each present one section of the result. To retrieve sections of the search result this way, issue a series of statements that all specify the same number of rows to return in the LIMIT clause, but vary the number of initial rows to skip:

```
SELECT * FROM t ORDER BY id LIMIT  0, 20;
SELECT * FROM t ORDER BY id LIMIT 20, 20;
SELECT * FROM t ORDER BY id LIMIT 40, 20;
SELECT * FROM t ORDER BY id LIMIT 60, 20;
...
```

It's possible to abuse the LIMIT feature. For example, it isn't a good idea to use a clause such as LIMIT 1000000, 10 to return 10 rows from a query that normally would return more than a million rows. The server must still process the query to determine the first million rows before returning the 10 rows. It's better to use a WHERE clause to reduce the query result to a more manageable size, and then use LIMIT to pull rows from that reduced result. This also makes the use of ORDER BY with LIMIT more efficient because the server need not sort as large a row set before applying the limit.

The UPDATE and DELETE statements also support the use of LIMIT, which causes only a certain number of rows to be updated or deleted. See Chapter 11, "Updating Data."

9.3.4 Using DISTINCT to Eliminate Duplicates

If a query returns a result that contains duplicate rows, you can remove duplicates to produce a result set in which every row is unique. To do this, include the keyword DISTINCT after SELECT and before the output column list.

Suppose that a query returns a result set that contains duplicated rows:

```
mysql> SELECT last_name FROM t;
+-----------+
| last_name |
+-----------+
| Brown     |
| Larsson   |
| Brown     |
| Larsson   |
+-----------+
```

Adding DISTINCT removes the duplicates and returns only unique rows:

```
mysql> SELECT DISTINCT last_name FROM t;
+-----------+
| last_name |
+-----------+
| Brown     |
| Larsson   |
+-----------+
```

Duplicate elimination for string values happens differently for non-binary and binary strings. The strings 'ABC', 'Abc', and 'abc' are considered distinct if they're binary strings. If they are non-binary strings, they are considered distinct if they have different values based on their collation.

DISTINCT treats all NULL values within a given column as having the same value. Suppose that a table t contains the following rows:

```
mysql> SELECT i, j FROM t;
+------+------+
| i    | j    |
+------+------+
|    1 |    2 |
```

```
|    1 | NULL |
|    1 | NULL |
+------+------+
```

For purposes of DISTINCT, the NULL values in the second column are the same, so the second and third rows are identical. Adding DISTINCT to the query eliminates one of them as a duplicate:

```
mysql> SELECT DISTINCT i, j FROM t;
+------+------+
| i    | j    |
+------+------+
|    1 |    2 |
|    1 | NULL |
+------+------+
```

Using DISTINCT is logically equivalent to using GROUP BY on all selected columns with no aggregate function. For such a query, GROUP BY just produces a list of distinct grouping values. If you display and group by a single column, the query produces the distinct values in that column. If you display and group by multiple columns, the query produces the distinct combinations of values in the column. For example, the following two queries produce the same set of rows:

```
SELECT DISTINCT id FROM t;
SELECT id FROM t GROUP BY id;
```

As do these:

```
SELECT DISTINCT id, name FROM t;
SELECT id, name FROM t GROUP BY id, name;
```

Another correspondence between the behavior of DISTINCT and GROUP BY is that for purposes of assessing distinctness, DISTINCT considers all NULL values the same. This is analogous to the way that GROUP BY groups NULL values.

A difference between DISTINCT and GROUP BY is that DISTINCT doesn't cause row sorting. In MySQL, GROUP BY does cause sorting.

DISTINCT can be used with the COUNT() function to count how many distinct values a column contains. In this case, NULL values are ignored:

```
mysql> SELECT j FROM t;
+------+
| j    |
+------+
|    2 |
| NULL |
| NULL |
+------+
```

```
mysql> SELECT COUNT(DISTINCT j) FROM t;
+-------------------+
| COUNT(DISTINCT j) |
+-------------------+
|                 1 |
+-------------------+
```

COUNT(DISTINCT) is discussed further in Section 9.4.3, "The COUNT() Aggregate Function."

9.4 Aggregating Results

A SELECT statement can produce a list of rows that match a given set of conditions. The list provides the details about the selected rows, but if you want to know about the overall characteristics of the rows, you'll be more interested in getting a summary instead. When that's your goal, use aggregate functions to calculate summary values, possibly combined with a GROUP BY clause to arrange the selected rows into groups so that you can get summaries for each group.

Grouping can be based on the values in one or more columns of the selected rows. For example, the Country table indicates which continent each country is part of, so you can group the records by continent and calculate the average population of countries in each continent:

```
SELECT Continent, AVG(Population) FROM Country GROUP BY Continent;
```

Functions such as AVG() that calculate summary values for groups are known as "aggregate" functions because they're based on aggregates or groups of values. There are several types of aggregate functions. Those discussed here are as follows:

- MIN() and MAX() find smallest and largest values.
- SUM() and AVG() summarize numeric values to produce sums (totals) and averages.
- COUNT() counts rows, values, or the number of distinct values.
- GROUP_CONCAT() concatenates a set of strings to produce a single string value.

Aggregate functions may be used with or without a GROUP BY clause that places rows into groups. Without a GROUP BY clause, an aggregate function calculates a summary value based on the entire set of selected rows. (That is, MySQL treats all the rows as a single group.) With a GROUP BY clause, an aggregate function calculates a summary value for each group. For example, if a WHERE clause selects 20 rows and the GROUP BY clause arranges them into four groups of five rows each, a summary function produces a value for each of the four groups.

This section describes the aggregate functions available to you. Section 9.5, "Grouping Results," shows how to use GROUP BY to group rows appropriately for the type of summary you want to produce.

9.4.1 The `MIN()` and `MAX()` Aggregate Functions

`MIN()` and `MAX()` are comparison functions. They return smallest or largest numeric values, lexically first or last string values, and earliest or latest temporal values. The following queries determine the smallest and largest country populations and the lexically first and last country names:

```
mysql> SELECT MIN(Population), MAX(Population) FROM Country;
+-----------------+-----------------+
| MIN(Population) | MAX(Population) |
+-----------------+-----------------+
|               0 |      1277558000 |
+-----------------+-----------------+
mysql> SELECT MIN(Name), MAX(Name) FROM Country;
+-------------+-----------+
| MIN(Name)   | MAX(Name) |
+-------------+-----------+
| Afghanistan | Zimbabwe  |
+-------------+-----------+
```

For string values, the behavior of `MIN()` and `MAX()` depends on whether the strings are non-binary or binary. Consider a table t that contains the following string values:

```
mysql> SELECT name FROM t;
+--------+
| name   |
+--------+
| Calvin |
| alex   |
+--------+
```

If the name column has a non-binary string data type such as CHAR or TEXT, MAX(name) determines which value is greatest based on the string collation. For the default case-insensitive collation of `latin1_swedish_ci`, `MAX()` returns `'Calvin'` because 'c' is greater than 'a':

```
mysql> SELECT MAX(name) FROM t;
+-----------+
| MAX(name) |
+-----------+
| Calvin    |
+-----------+
```

If the name column has a binary string data type such as BINARY or BLOB, its values are compared using the numeric values of the bytes in the strings. If 'c' has a smaller numeric value 'a' (as is true if characters are stored using ASCII codes), MAX(name) returns `'alex'`:

```
mysql> ALTER TABLE t MODIFY name BINARY(20);
mysql> SELECT MAX(name) FROM t;
```

```
+-----------+
| MAX(name) |
+-----------+
| alex      |
+-----------+
```

MIN() and MAX() ignore NULL values.

9.4.2 The SUM() and AVG() Aggregate Functions

The SUM() and AVG() functions calculate sums and averages. For example, the Country table in the world database contains a Population column, so you can calculate the total world population and the average population per country like this:

```
mysql> SELECT SUM(Population), AVG(Population) FROM Country;
+-----------------+-----------------+
| SUM(Population) | AVG(Population) |
+-----------------+-----------------+
|      6078749450 |   25434098.1172 |
+-----------------+-----------------+
```

SUM() and AVG() are most commonly used with numeric values. If you use them with other types of values, those values are subject to numeric conversion, which might not produce a sensible result.

SUM() and AVG() ignore NULL values.

9.4.3 The COUNT() Aggregate Function

The COUNT() function can be used in several ways to count either rows or values. To illustrate, the examples here use the following table that has several rows containing various combinations of NULL and non-NULL values:

```
mysql> SELECT i, j FROM t;
+------+------+
| i    | j    |
+------+------+
|    1 | NULL |
| NULL |    2 |
|    1 |    1 |
|    1 |    1 |
|    1 |    3 |
| NULL | NULL |
|    1 | NULL |
+------+------+
```

COUNT() may be used as follows:

- COUNT(*) counts the total number of rows:

```
mysql> SELECT COUNT(*) FROM t;
+----------+
| COUNT(*) |
+----------+
|        7 |
+----------+
```

- COUNT(*expression*) counts the number of non-NULL values of the given expression. It's common for *expression* to be a column name, in which case COUNT() counts the number of non-NULL values in the column:

```
mysql> SELECT COUNT(i), COUNT(j) FROM t;
+----------+----------+
| COUNT(i) | COUNT(j) |
+----------+----------+
|        5 |        4 |
+----------+----------+
```

- COUNT(DISTINCT *expression*) counts the number of distinct (unique) non-NULL values of the given expression. *expression* can be a column name to count the number of distinct non-NULL values in the column:

```
mysql> SELECT COUNT(DISTINCT i), COUNT(DISTINCT j) FROM t;
+-------------------+-------------------+
| COUNT(DISTINCT i) | COUNT(DISTINCT j) |
+-------------------+-------------------+
|                 1 |                 3 |
+-------------------+-------------------+
```

It's also possible to give a list of expressions separated by commas. In this case, COUNT() returns the number of distinct combinations of values that contain no NULL values. The following query counts the number of distinct rows for which neither i nor j is NULL:

```
mysql> SELECT COUNT(DISTINCT i, j) FROM t;
+----------------------+
| COUNT(DISTINCT i, j) |
+----------------------+
|                    2 |
+----------------------+
```

9.4.4 The GROUP_CONCAT() Function

The purpose of the GROUP_CONCAT() function is to concatenate column values into a single string. This is useful if you would otherwise perform a lookup of many rows and then concatenate them on the client end. For example, the following query displays the languages spoken in Thailand, one per line:

```
mysql> SELECT Language
    -> FROM CountryLanguage WHERE CountryCode = 'THA';
+----------+
| Language |
+----------+
| Chinese  |
| Khmer    |
| Kuy      |
| Lao      |
| Malay    |
| Thai     |
+----------+
```

To concatenate the values into a single string, use GROUP_CONCAT():

```
mysql> SELECT GROUP_CONCAT(Language)
    -> AS Languages
    -> FROM CountryLanguage WHERE CountryCode = 'THA';
+---------------------------------+
| Languages                       |
+---------------------------------+
| Chinese,Khmer,Kuy,Lao,Malay,Thai |
+---------------------------------+
```

GROUP_CONCAT() supports several modifiers:

- The default string separator used by GROUP_CONCAT() is ',' (comma). To change the separator, use a SEPARATOR clause:

```
mysql> SELECT GROUP_CONCAT(Language SEPARATOR ' - ')
    -> AS Languages
    -> FROM CountryLanguage WHERE CountryCode = 'THA';
+------------------------------------------+
| Languages                                |
+------------------------------------------+
| Chinese - Khmer - Kuy - Lao - Malay - Thai |
+------------------------------------------+
```

- GROUP_CONCAT() adds strings to the result in the order in which the database server reads them. To change the concatenation order, add an ORDER BY clause. You can specify ASC or DESC to control the direction of sorting, just as when you use ORDER BY in other contexts:

```
mysql> SELECT
    -> GROUP_CONCAT(Language ORDER BY Language DESC)
    -> AS Languages
    -> FROM CountryLanguage WHERE CountryCode = 'THA';
+---------------------------------+
| Languages                       |
```

```
+----------------------------------+
| Thai,Malay,Lao,Kuy,Khmer,Chinese |
+----------------------------------+
```

- DISTINCT removes duplicates from the set of concatenated strings. The following two statements both select the languages spoken in North and South Korea, but the second statement eliminates duplicates:

```
mysql> SELECT
    -> GROUP_CONCAT(Language)
    -> AS Languages
    -> FROM CountryLanguage WHERE CountryCode IN('PRK','KOR');
+------------------------------+
| Languages                    |
+------------------------------+
| Chinese,Korean,Chinese,Korean |
+------------------------------+

mysql> SELECT
    -> GROUP_CONCAT(DISTINCT Language)
    -> AS Languages
    -> FROM CountryLanguage WHERE CountryCode IN('PRK','KOR');
+----------------+
| Languages      |
+----------------+
| Chinese,Korean |
+----------------+
```

GROUP_CONCAT() ignores NULL values.

9.4.5 Aggregation for NULL Values or Empty Sets

In general, aggregate functions ignore NULL values. The exception is COUNT(), which behaves as follows:

- COUNT(*) does not ignore NULL values because it counts rows, even those that contain NULL values.

- COUNT(*expression*) and COUNT(DISTINCT) do ignore NULL values.

A SELECT statement might produce an empty result set if the table is empty or the WHERE clause selects no rows from it. If the set of values passed to an aggregate function is empty, the function computes the most sensible value. For COUNT(), the result is zero. But functions such as MIN(), MAX(), SUM(), AVG(), and GROUP_CONCAT() return NULL. They also return NULL if a non-empty result contains only NULL values. These behaviors occur because there is no way for such functions to compute results without at least one non-NULL input value.

9.5 Grouping Results

If a query does not contain a GROUP BY clause to place rows of the result set into groups, an aggregate function produces a result that is based on all the selected rows. A GROUP BY clause may be added to generate a more fine-grained summary that produces values for subgroups within a set of selected rows.

Suppose that a table named personnel contains the following information about company employees:

```
mysql> SELECT * FROM personnel;
+---------+--------+---------+-------------+----------+
| pers_id | name   | dept_id | title       | salary   |
+---------+--------+---------+-------------+----------+
|       1 | Wendy  |      14 | Supervisor  | 38000.00 |
|       2 | Wally  |       7 | Stock clerk | 28000.00 |
|       3 | Ray    |       7 | Programmer  | 41000.00 |
|       4 | Burton |      14 | Secretary   | 32000.00 |
|       5 | Gordon |      14 | President   | 78000.00 |
|       6 | Jeff   |       7 | Stock clerk | 29000.00 |
|       7 | Doris  |       7 | Programmer  | 48000.00 |
|       8 | Daisy  |       7 | Secretary   | 33000.00 |
|       9 | Bea    |       7 | Accountant  | 40000.00 |
+---------+--------+---------+-------------+----------+
```

Use of COUNT(*) to count rows when there is no GROUP BY produces a single value for the entire set of rows:

```
mysql> SELECT COUNT(*) FROM personnel;
+----------+
| COUNT(*) |
+----------+
|        9 |
+----------+
```

Adding a GROUP BY clause arranges rows using the values in the grouping column or columns. The result is that COUNT(*) produces a count for each group. To find out how many times each title occurs, do this:

```
mysql> SELECT title, COUNT(*) FROM personnel
    -> GROUP BY title;
+-------------+----------+
| title       | COUNT(*) |
+-------------+----------+
| Accountant  |        1 |
| President   |        1 |
| Programmer  |        2 |
| Secretary   |        2 |
```

```
| Stock clerk |        2 |
| Supervisor  |        1 |
+-------------+----------+
```

To count the number of people in each department, group by department number:

```
mysql> SELECT dept_id, COUNT(*) FROM personnel
    -> GROUP BY dept_id;
+---------+----------+
| dept_id | COUNT(*) |
+---------+----------+
|       7 |        6 |
|      14 |        3 |
+---------+----------+
```

A GROUP BY that names multiple columns arranges rows according to the combinations of values in those columns. For example, to find out how many times each job title occurs in each department, group by both department and title:

```
mysql> SELECT dept_id, title, COUNT(*) FROM personnel
    -> GROUP BY dept_id, title;
+---------+-------------+----------+
| dept_id | title       | COUNT(*) |
+---------+-------------+----------+
|       7 | Accountant  |        1 |
|       7 | Programmer  |        2 |
|       7 | Secretary   |        1 |
|       7 | Stock clerk |        2 |
|      14 | President   |        1 |
|      14 | Secretary   |        1 |
|      14 | Supervisor  |        1 |
+---------+-------------+----------+
```

The preceding queries use COUNT(*) to count rows, but you can also use summary functions to compute results based on values in specific columns of the rows in each group. For example, numeric functions can tell you about the salary characteristics of each title or department:

```
mysql> SELECT title, MIN(salary), MAX(salary), AVG(salary)
    -> FROM personnel
    -> GROUP BY title;
+-------------+-------------+-------------+--------------+
| title       | MIN(salary) | MAX(salary) | AVG(salary)  |
+-------------+-------------+-------------+--------------+
| Accountant  |    40000.00 |    40000.00 | 40000.000000 |
| President   |    78000.00 |    78000.00 | 78000.000000 |
| Programmer  |    41000.00 |    48000.00 | 44500.000000 |
| Secretary   |    32000.00 |    33000.00 | 32500.000000 |
```

```
| Stock clerk |    28000.00 |     29000.00 | 28500.000000 |
| Supervisor  |    38000.00 |     38000.00 | 38000.000000 |
+-------------+-------------+-------------+--------------+
mysql> SELECT dept_id, MIN(salary), MAX(salary), AVG(salary)
    -> FROM personnel
    -> GROUP BY dept_id;
+---------+-------------+-------------+--------------+
| dept_id | MIN(salary) | MAX(salary) | AVG(salary)  |
+---------+-------------+-------------+--------------+
|       7 |    28000.00 |    48000.00 | 36500.000000 |
|      14 |    32000.00 |    78000.00 | 49333.333333 |
+---------+-------------+-------------+--------------+
```

If you want the results from AVG() to be displayed to two decimals, use
ROUND(AVG(salary),2).

If you combine the GROUP_CONCAT() function with GROUP BY, GROUP_CONCAT() produces a
concatenated result from each group of strings. The following example creates lists of the
countries that have a particular form of government on the South American continent:

```
mysql> SELECT GovernmentForm, GROUP_CONCAT(Name) AS Countries
    -> FROM Country
    -> WHERE Continent = 'South America'
    -> GROUP BY GovernmentForm\G
*************************** 1. row ***************************
GovernmentForm: Dependent Territory of the UK
     Countries: Falkland Islands
*************************** 2. row ***************************
GovernmentForm: Federal Republic
     Countries: Argentina,Venezuela,Brazil
*************************** 3. row ***************************
GovernmentForm: Overseas Department of France
     Countries: French Guiana
*************************** 4. row ***************************
GovernmentForm: Republic
     Countries: Chile,Uruguay,Suriname,Peru,Paraguay,Bolivia,
                Guyana,Ecuador,Colombia
```

The default string separator used by GROUP_CONCAT() is ',' (comma). Records are added to
the resulting string in the order in which the database server reads them. To change the separator and the concatenation order, add SEPARATOR and ORDER BY clauses, respectively, within
the parentheses. For ORDER BY, you can specify ASC or DESC, just as when you use it in other
contexts:

```
mysql> SELECT GovernmentForm,
    ->         GROUP_CONCAT(Name ORDER BY Name ASC SEPARATOR ' - ')
    ->         AS Countries
    -> FROM Country
```

```
     -> WHERE Continent = 'South America'
     -> GROUP BY GovernmentForm\G
*************************** 1. row ***************************
GovernmentForm: Dependent Territory of the UK
     Countries: Falkland Islands
*************************** 2. row ***************************
GovernmentForm: Federal Republic
     Countries: Argentina - Brazil - Venezuela
*************************** 3. row ***************************
GovernmentForm: Overseas Department of France
     Countries: French Guiana
*************************** 4. row ***************************
GovernmentForm: Republic
     Countries: Bolivia - Chile - Colombia - Ecuador - Guyana -
                Paraguay - Peru - Suriname - Uruguay
```

The next example for this function returns the continents that contain countries that have a name beginning with 'I', as well as the form of government for those countries. The example demonstrates that GROUP_CONCAT() accepts a DISTINCT clause to remove duplicates from the concatenated list. The first query shows what the result looks like without DISTINCT, and the second uses DISTINCT to display each form of government only once:

```
mysql> SELECT Continent,
    ->        GROUP_CONCAT(GovernmentForm ORDER BY GovernmentForm ASC)
    ->            AS 'Government Form'
    -> FROM Country
    -> WHERE Name LIKE 'I%'
    -> GROUP BY Continent;
+-----------+----------------------------------------------------------------+
| Continent | Government Form                                                 |
+-----------+----------------------------------------------------------------+
| Asia      | Federal Republic,Islamic Republic,Republic,Republic,Republic   |
| Europe    | Republic,Republic,Republic                                     |
+-----------+----------------------------------------------------------------+
mysql> SELECT Continent,
    ->        GROUP_CONCAT(DISTINCT GovernmentForm
    ->                    ORDER BY GovernmentForm ASC)
    ->            AS 'Government Form'
    -> FROM Country
    -> WHERE Name LIKE 'I%'
    -> GROUP BY Continent;
+-----------+-------------------------------------------+
| Continent | Government Form                           |
+-----------+-------------------------------------------+
| Asia      | Federal Republic,Islamic Republic,Republic |
| Europe    | Republic                                  |
+-----------+-------------------------------------------+
```

Note that in each of the preceding queries, the output columns consist only of the columns listed in the GROUP BY clause, and values produced by summary functions. If you try to retrieve table columns other than those listed in the GROUP BY clause, the values displayed for the extra columns are unpredictable.

9.5.1 GROUP BY and Sorting

In MySQL, a GROUP BY clause has the side effect of sorting rows. If you already have a GROUP BY clause in your query that produces the desired sort order, there's no need for an ORDER BY. Use of ORDER BY is necessary with GROUP BY only to produce a different sort order than that resulting from the GROUP BY. However, this isn't a portable behavior. For database engines other than MySQL, GROUP BY might not sort rows. To write more portable queries, add an ORDER BY even if MySQL does not require it.

9.5.2 Selecting Groups with HAVING

It could be when you use GROUP BY that you're interested only in groups that have particular summary characteristics. To retrieve just those groups and eliminate the rest, use a HAVING clause that identifies the required group characteristics. HAVING acts in a manner somewhat similar to WHERE, but occurs at a different stage of query processing:

1. WHERE, if present, identifies the initial set of records to select from a table.

2. GROUP BY arranges the selected records into groups.

3. Aggregate functions compute summary values for each group.

4. HAVING identifies which groups to retrieve for the final result set.

The following example shows how this progression works, using the personnel table shown earlier in the chapter:

1. A query with no GROUP BY clause or aggregate functions selects a list of records. This list provides details, not overall characteristics:

```
mysql> SELECT title, salary
    -> FROM personnel WHERE dept_id = 7;
+-------------+----------+
| title       | salary   |
+-------------+----------+
| Stock clerk | 28000.00 |
| Programmer  | 41000.00 |
| Stock clerk | 29000.00 |
| Programmer  | 48000.00 |
| Secretary   | 33000.00 |
| Accountant  | 40000.00 |
+-------------+----------+
```

2. Adding GROUP BY and aggregate functions arranges rows into groups and computes summary values for each.

```
mysql> SELECT title, COUNT(*), AVG(salary)
    -> FROM personnel WHERE dept_id = 7
    -> GROUP BY title;
+-------------+----------+--------------+
| title       | COUNT(*) | AVG(salary)  |
+-------------+----------+--------------+
| Accountant  |        1 | 40000.000000 |
| Programmer  |        2 | 44500.000000 |
| Secretary   |        1 | 33000.000000 |
| Stock clerk |        2 | 28500.000000 |
+-------------+----------+--------------+
```

3. Finally, adding HAVING places an additional constraint on the output rows. In the following query, only those groups consisting of two or more people are displayed:

```
mysql> SELECT title, salary, COUNT(*), AVG(salary)
    -> FROM personnel WHERE dept_id = 7
    -> GROUP BY title
    -> HAVING COUNT(*) > 1;
+-------------+----------+----------+--------------+
| title       | salary   | COUNT(*) | AVG(salary)  |
+-------------+----------+----------+--------------+
| Programmer  | 41000.00 |        2 | 44500.000000 |
| Stock clerk | 28000.00 |        2 | 28500.000000 |
+-------------+----------+----------+--------------+
```

Sometimes it's possible to place selection criteria in either the WHERE clause or the HAVING clause. In such cases, it's better to do so in the WHERE clause because that eliminates rows from consideration sooner and allows the query to be processed more efficiently. Choosing values in the HAVING clause might cause the query to perform group calculations on groups in which you have no interest.

9.5.3 Using GROUP BY and WITH ROLLUP

The WITH ROLLUP modifier can be used in the GROUP BY clause to produce multiple levels of summary values. Suppose that you need to generate a listing of the population of each continent, as well as the total of the population on all continents. One way to do this is by running one query to get the per-continent totals and another to get the total for all continents:

```
mysql> SELECT Continent, SUM(Population) AS pop
    -> FROM Country
    -> GROUP BY Continent;
+---------------+-----------+
| Continent     | pop       |
```

```
+---------------+------------+
| Asia          | 3705025700 |
| Europe        | 730074600  |
| North America | 482993000  |
| Africa        | 784475000  |
| Oceania       | 30401150   |
| Antarctica    | 0          |
| South America | 345780000  |
+---------------+------------+
mysql> SELECT SUM(Population) AS pop
    -> FROM Country;
+------------+
| pop        |
+------------+
| 6078749450 |
+------------+
```

Another way to get the results requires some application programming: The application can retrieve the per-continent values and sum those to calculate the total population value.

To avoid either of those approaches, use WITH ROLLUP. This enables you to use a single query to get both the detailed results as well as the total sum of all rows, eliminating the need for multiple queries or extra processing on the client side:

```
mysql> SELECT Continent, SUM(Population) AS pop
    -> FROM Country
    -> GROUP BY Continent WITH ROLLUP;
+---------------+------------+
| Continent     | pop        |
+---------------+------------+
| Asia          | 3705025700 |
| Europe        | 730074600  |
| North America | 482993000  |
| Africa        | 784475000  |
| Oceania       | 30401150   |
| Antarctica    | 0          |
| South America | 345780000  |
| NULL          | 6078749450 |
+---------------+------------+
```

The difference in the output from this statement compared to one without WITH ROLLUP occurs on the last line, where the Continent value contains NULL and the pop value contains the total sum of all populations.

WITH ROLLUP performs a "super-aggregate" operation. It does not simply generate a sum of the numbers that appear in the pop column. Instead, the final line comprises applications of the given aggregate function, as it is written in the SELECT clause, on *every single row selected*.

To illustrate this, consider the following example in which we calculate columns using the AVG() function rather than SUM(). The final rollup line contains the overall average, not the sum of averages:

```
mysql> SELECT Continent, AVG(Population) AS avg_pop
    -> FROM Country
    -> GROUP BY Continent WITH ROLLUP;
+---------------+---------------+
| Continent     | avg_pop       |
+---------------+---------------+
| Asia          | 72647562.7451 |
| Europe        | 15871186.9565 |
| North America | 13053864.8649 |
| Africa        | 13525431.0345 |
| Oceania       |  1085755.3571 |
| Antarctica    |        0.0000 |
| South America | 24698571.4286 |
| NULL          | 25434098.1172 |
+---------------+---------------+
```

In other words, the rollup line contains the numbers that would appear had there been no grouping columns for the query:

```
mysql> SELECT AVG(Population) AS avg_pop
    -> FROM Country;
+---------------+
| avg_pop       |
+---------------+
| 25434098.1172 |
+---------------+
```

Without WITH ROLLUP, getting the per-continent and overall AVG() results produced would require two separate statements: one to get the per-continent data and one to get the overall totals. For large data sets, WITH ROLLUP is more efficient because the data need be scanned only once.

The use of WITH ROLLUP gets more interesting when several columns are grouped at once. The results include a summary for each column named in the GROUP BY clause, as well as a final summary row:

```
mysql> SELECT Continent, Region,
    ->        SUM(Population) AS pop,
    ->        AVG(Population) AS avg_pop
    -> FROM Country
    -> GROUP BY Continent, Region WITH ROLLUP;
+---------------+--------------------------+------------+---------------+
| Continent     | Region                   | pop        | avg_pop       |
+---------------+--------------------------+------------+---------------+
```

```
| Asia          | Eastern Asia            | 1507328000 | 188416000.0000 |
| Asia          | Middle East             |  188380700 |  10465594.4444 |
| Asia          | Southeast Asia          |  518541000 |  47140090.9091 |
| Asia          | Southern and Central Asia | 1490776000 | 106484000.0000 |
| Asia          | NULL                    | 3705025700 |  72647562.7451 |
| Europe        | Baltic Countries        |    7561900 |   2520633.3333 |
| Europe        | British Islands         |   63398500 |  31699250.0000 |
...
| Europe        | Eastern Europe          |  307026000 |  30702600.0000 |
| Europe        | Nordic Countries        |   24166400 |   3452342.8571 |
| Europe        | Southern Europe         |  144674200 |   9644946.6667 |
...
| Europe        | Western Europe          |  183247600 |  20360844.4444 |
| Europe        | NULL                    |  730074600 |  15871186.9565 |
| North America | Caribbean               |   38140000 |   1589166.6667 |
| North America | Central America         |  135221000 |  16902625.0000 |
| North America | North America           |  309632000 |  61926400.0000 |
| North America | NULL                    |  482993000 |  13053864.8649 |
| Africa        | Central Africa          |   95652000 |  10628000.0000 |
...
| Africa        | Eastern Africa          |  246999000 |  12349950.0000 |
| Africa        | Northern Africa         |  173266000 |  24752285.7143 |
| Africa        | Southern Africa         |   46886000 |   9377200.0000 |
...
| Africa        | Western Africa          |  221672000 |  13039529.4118 |
| Africa        | NULL                    |  784475000 |  13525431.0345 |
| Oceania       | Australia and New Zealand |  22753100 |   4550620.0000 |
...
| Oceania       | Melanesia               |    6472000 |   1294400.0000 |
| Oceania       | Micronesia              |     543000 |     77571.4286 |
| Oceania       | Micronesia/Caribbean    |          0 |         0.0000 |
...
| Oceania       | Polynesia               |     633050 |     63305.0000 |
| Oceania       | NULL                    |   30401150 |   1085755.3571 |
| Antarctica    | Antarctica              |          0 |         0.0000 |
| Antarctica    | NULL                    |          0 |         0.0000 |
| South America | South America           |  345780000 |  24698571.4286 |
| South America | NULL                    |  345780000 |  24698571.4286 |
| NULL          | NULL                    | 6078749450 |  25434098.1172 |
+---------------+-------------------------+------------+----------------+
```

Note how the groupwise summaries are presented in the result: In addition to the final summary line, the output includes an intermediate summary of the rows for a given continent whenever the Continent value changes. In these intermediate summary lines, Region is set to NULL.

9.6 Using UNION

The UNION keyword enables you to concatenate the results from two or more SELECT statements. The syntax for using it is as follows:

```
SELECT ... UNION SELECT ... UNION SELECT ...
```

The result of such a statement consists of the rows retrieved by the first SELECT, followed by the rows retrieved by the second SELECT, and so on. Each SELECT must produce the same number of columns.

By default, UNION eliminates duplicate rows from the result set. To retain all rows, replace each instance of UNION with UNION ALL. (UNION ALL is more efficient for the server to process because it need not perform duplicate removal. However, returning the result set to the client involves more network traffic.)

UNION is useful under the following circumstances:

- You have similar information in multiple tables and you want to retrieve rows from all of them at once.
- You want to select several sets of rows from the same table, but the conditions that characterize each set aren't easy to write as a single WHERE clause. UNION allows retrieval of each set with a simpler WHERE clause in its own SELECT statement; the rows retrieved by each are combined and produced as the final query result.

Suppose that you run three mailing lists, each of which is managed using a different MySQL-based software package. Each package uses its own table to store names and email addresses, but they have slightly different conventions about how the tables are set up. The tables used by the list manager packages look like this:

```
CREATE TABLE list1
(
    subscriber  CHAR(60),
    email       CHAR(60)
);

CREATE TABLE list2
(
    name        CHAR(96),
    address     CHAR(128)
);

CREATE TABLE list3
(
    email       CHAR(50),
    real_name   CHAR(30)
);
```

Note that each table contains similar types of information (names and email addresses), but they don't use the same column names or types, and they don't store the columns in the same order. To write a query that produces the combined subscriber list, use UNION. It doesn't matter that the tables don't have exactly the same structure. To select their combined contents, name the columns from each table in the order you want to see them. A query to retrieve names and addresses from the tables looks like this:

```
SELECT subscriber, email FROM list1
UNION SELECT name, address FROM list2
UNION SELECT real_name, email FROM list3;
```

The first column of the result contains names and the second column contains email addresses. The names of the columns resulting from a UNION are taken from the names of the columns in the first SELECT statement. This means that the result set column names are subscriber and email. If you provide aliases for columns in the first SELECT, the aliases are used as the output column names.

The data types of the output columns are determined by considering the values retrieved by all of the SELECT statements. For the query shown, the data types will be CHAR(96) and CHAR(128) because those are the smallest types that are guaranteed to be large enough to hold values from all three tables.

ORDER BY and LIMIT clauses can be used to sort or limit a UNION result set as a whole. To do this, surround each SELECT with parentheses and then add ORDER BY or LIMIT after the last parenthesis. Columns named in such an ORDER BY should refer to columns in the first SELECT of the statement. (This is a consequence of the fact that the first SELECT determines the result set column names.) The following statement sorts the result of the UNION by email address and returns the first 10 rows of the combined result:

```
(SELECT subscriber, email FROM list1)
UNION (SELECT name, address FROM list2)
UNION (SELECT real_name, email FROM list3)
ORDER BY email LIMIT 10;
```

ORDER BY and LIMIT clauses also can be applied to individual SELECT statements within a UNION. Surround each SELECT with parentheses and add ORDER BY or LIMIT to the end of the appropriate SELECT. In this case, an ORDER BY should refer to columns of the particular SELECT with which it's associated. (Also, although LIMIT may be used by itself in this context, ORDER BY has no effect unless combined with LIMIT. The optimizer ignores it otherwise.) The following query sorts the result of each SELECT by email address and returns the first five rows from each one:

```
(SELECT subscriber, email FROM list1 ORDER BY email LIMIT 5)
UNION (SELECT name, address FROM list2 ORDER BY address LIMIT 5)
UNION (SELECT real_name, email FROM list3 ORDER BY email LIMIT 5);
```

SQL Expressions

This chapter discusses how to use expressions in SQL statements. It covers the following exam topics:

- Components of expressions
- Using numeric, string, and temporal values in expressions
- Properties of NULL values
- Types of functions that can be used in expressions
- Writing comments in SQL statements

10.1 Components of SQL Expressions

Expressions are a common element of SQL statements, and they occur in many contexts. For example, expressions often occur in the WHERE clause of SELECT, DELETE, or UPDATE statements to identify which records to retrieve, delete, or update. But expressions may be used in many other places; for example, in the output column list of a SELECT statement, or in ORDER BY or GROUP BY clauses.

Terms of expressions consist of constants (literal numbers, strings, dates, and times), NULL values, references to table columns, and function calls. Terms may be combined using operators into more complex expressions. Many types of operators are available, such as those for arithmetic, comparison, logical, and pattern-matching operations.

Here are some examples of expressions:

- The following statement refers to table columns to select country names and populations from the Country table:

```
SELECT Name, Population FROM Country;
```

- You can work directly with literal data values that aren't stored in a table. The following statement refers to several literal values: an integer, an exact-value decimal value, an approximate-value floating-point value in scientific notation, and a string value:

```
SELECT 14, -312.82, 4.32E-03, 'I am a string';
```

- Another way to produce data values is by invoking functions. This statement calls functions that return the current date and a server version string:

```
SELECT CURDATE(), VERSION();
```

All these types of values can be combined into more complex expressions to produce other values of interest. The following statement demonstrates this:

```
mysql> SELECT Name,
    -> TRUNCATE(Population/SurfaceArea,2) AS 'people/sq. km',
    -> IF(GNP > GNPOld,'Increasing','Not increasing') AS 'GNP Trend'
    -> FROM Country ORDER BY Name LIMIT 10;
+---------------------+---------------+----------------+
| Name                | people/sq. km | GNP Trend      |
+---------------------+---------------+----------------+
| Afghanistan         |         34.84 | Not increasing |
| Albania             |        118.31 | Increasing     |
| Algeria             |         13.21 | Increasing     |
| American Samoa      |        341.70 | Not increasing |
| Andorra             |        166.66 | Not increasing |
| Angola              |         10.32 | Not increasing |
| Anguilla            |         83.33 | Not increasing |
| Antarctica          |          0.00 | Not increasing |
| Antigua and Barbuda |        153.84 | Increasing     |
| Argentina           |         13.31 | Increasing     |
+---------------------+---------------+----------------+
```

The expressions in the preceding statement use these types of values:

- Table columns: Name, Population, SurfaceArea, GNP, and GNPOld. ("GNP" means "gross national product.")

- Literal values: 'Increasing', 'Not increasing', and the column aliases are all string constants.

- Functions: The numeric function TRUNCATE() formats the population/area ratio to two decimal places, and the logical function IF() tests the expression in its first argument and returns its second or third argument depending on whether the expression is true or false.

10.2 Numeric Expressions

Numbers can be exact-value literals or approximate-value literals. Exact-value literals are used just as given in SQL statements when possible and thus are not subject to the inexactness produced by rounding error. On the other hand, approximate-value literals are subject to rounding error and may not necessarily be used exactly as given.

Exact-value literals are written with no exponent. Approximate-value literals are written in scientific notation with an exponent. For example, the numeric values -43, 368.93, and .00214 are exact values, whereas -4.3E1, 3.6893E2, and 2.14E-3 are approximate values. Even though the two sets of numbers look like they have the same values, internally they are represented in different ways:

- Exact-value numbers are integer values with no fractional part after the decimal point or decimal values with a fractional part. They're represented internally like an integer or `DECIMAL` data type. Operations on integers are performed with the precision of `BIGINT` values (that is, 64 bits). Operations on decimal values have a precision of up to 64 decimal digits. Currently, the scale for decimal values allows up to 30 decimal digits after the decimal point.

- Approximate-value literals are represented as floating-point numbers (like the `DOUBLE` data type) and have a mantissa and exponent. The mantissa allows up to 53 bits of precision, which is about 15 decimal digits.

When numbers are used in an arithmetic or comparison operation, the result of the operation may depend on whether it involves exact or approximate values. Consider the following two comparisons:

```
mysql> SELECT 1.1 + 2.2 = 3.3, 1.1E0 + 2.2E0 = 3.3E0;
+-----------------+-----------------------+
| 1.1 + 2.2 = 3.3 | 1.1E0 + 2.2E0 = 3.3E0 |
+-----------------+-----------------------+
|               1 |                     0 |
+-----------------+-----------------------+
```

In the first expression, exact values are used, so the comparison involves exact calculations. In the second expression, approximate values are used and rounding error is possible. This illustrates that if you use approximate values in comparisons, you cannot expect exact-value precision. The internal representation of floating-point numbers inherently allows for the possibility of rounding error.

If you mix numbers with strings in numeric context, MySQL converts the strings to numbers and performs a numeric operation:

```
mysql> SELECT 1 + '1', 1 = '1';
+---------+---------+
| 1 + '1' | 1 = '1' |
```

```
+---------+---------+
|    2 |      1 |
+---------+---------+
```

Several functions take numeric arguments or return numeric values. Section 10.6, "Functions in SQL Expressions," presents some representative examples, including a description of how rounding works for the ROUND() function.

10.3 String Expressions

Literal strings in expressions are written as quoted values. By default, either single quotes or double quotes can be used, although single quotes are more standard. Also, if the ANSI_QUOTES SQL mode is enabled, double quotes are interpreted as identifier-quoting characters, so literal strings can be quoted only with single quotes.

The data types for representing strings in tables include CHAR, VARCHAR, BINARY, VARBINARY, and the TEXT and BLOB types. You choose which type to use depending on factors such as the maximum length of values, whether you require fixed-length or variable-length values, and whether the strings to be stored are non-binary or binary.

Direct use of strings in expressions occurs primarily in comparison operations. Otherwise, most string operations are performed by using functions.

The usual comparison operators apply to string values (=, <>, <, BETWEEN, and so forth). The result of a comparison depends on whether strings are non-binary or binary and, for non-binary strings that have the same character set, on their collation. (A comparison between strings that have different character sets typically results in an error.) String comparisons are dealt with further in Section 10.3.1, "Case Sensitivity in String Comparisons." Pattern matching is another form of comparison; it's covered in Section 10.3.2, "Using LIKE for Pattern Matching."

String concatenation is done with the CONCAT() function:

```
mysql> SELECT CONCAT('abc','def',REPEAT('X',3));
+----------------------------------+
| CONCAT('abc','def',REPEAT('X',3)) |
+----------------------------------+
| abcdefXXX                        |
+----------------------------------+
```

The || operator is treated as the logical OR operator by default, but can be used for string concatenation if you enable the PIPES_AS_CONCAT SQL mode:

```
mysql> SELECT 'abc' || 'def';
+----------------+
| 'abc' || 'def' |
+----------------+
```

```
|              0 |
+---------------+
1 row in set, 2 warnings (0.00 sec)

mysql> SET sql_mode = 'PIPES_AS_CONCAT';
Query OK, 0 rows affected (0.00 sec)

mysql> SELECT 'abc' || 'def';
+---------------+
| 'abc' || 'def' |
+---------------+
| abcdef        |
+---------------+
1 row in set (0.00 sec)
```

In the first SELECT statement, || performs a logical OR operation. This is a numeric operation, so MySQL converts the strings in the expression to numbers first. Neither looks like a number, so MySQL converts them to zero, which is why there is a warning count of two. The resulting operands for the operation are zero, so the result also is zero. After PIPES_AS_CONCAT is enabled, || produces a string concatenation instead.

Several functions take string arguments or return string values. Some types of operations these functions can perform are to convert lettercase, calculate string lengths, or search for, insert, or replace substrings. Section 10.6, "Functions in SQL Expressions," presents some representative examples.

10.3.1 Case Sensitivity in String Comparisons

String comparisons are somewhat more complex than numeric or temporal comparisons. Numbers sort in numeric order and dates and times sort in temporal order, but string comparisons depend not only on the specific content of the strings, but on whether they are non-binary or binary. A letter in uppercase may compare as the same or different than the same letter in lowercase, and a letter with one type of accent may be considered the same or different than that letter with another type of accent.

The earlier discussion in Chapter 5, "Data Types," describes how strings may be non-binary or binary, and how the properties of these two types of strings differ. To summarize:

- A non-binary string contains characters from a particular character set, and is associated with one of the collations (sorting orders) available for the character set. Characters may consist of single or multiple bytes. A collation can be case insensitive (lettercase is not significant), case sensitive (lettercase is significant), or binary (comparisons are based on numeric character values).

- A binary string is treated as raw bytes. It has no character set and no collation. Comparisons between binary strings are based on numeric byte values.

The rules that govern string comparison apply in several ways. They determine the result of comparisons performed explicitly with operators such as = and <, and comparisons performed implicitly by ORDER BY, GROUP BY, and DISTINCT operations.

The default character set and collation for literal strings depend on the values of the character_set_connection and collation_connection system variables. The default character set is latin1. The default collation is latin1_swedish_ci, which is case insensitive as indicated by the "_ci" at the end of the collation name. Assuming these connection settings, literal strings are not case sensitive by default. You can see this by comparing strings that differ only in lettercase:

```
mysql> SELECT 'Hello' = 'hello';
+-------------------+
| 'Hello' = 'hello' |
+-------------------+
|                 1 |
+-------------------+
```

A given collation might cause certain accented characters to compare the same as other characters. For example, 'ü' and 'ue' are different in the default latin1_swedish_ci collation, but with the latin1_german2_ci collation ("German phone-book" collation), they have the same sort value and thus compare as equal:

```
mysql> SELECT 'Müller' = 'Mueller';
+---------------------+
| 'Müller' = 'Mueller' |
+---------------------+
|                   0 |
+---------------------+
mysql> SET collation_connection = latin1_german2_ci;
mysql> SELECT 'Müller' = 'Mueller';
+---------------------+
| 'Müller' = 'Mueller' |
+---------------------+
|                   1 |
+---------------------+
```

For binary strings, lettercase is significant. However, this is not because binary strings are case sensitive *per se*, because binary strings have no character set. Rather, it is because uppercase and lowercase versions of a character have different numeric values.

A non-binary string can be treated as a binary string by preceding it with the BINARY keyword. If either string in a comparison is binary, both strings are treated as binary:

```
mysql> SELECT BINARY 'Hello' = 'hello';
+--------------------------+
| BINARY 'Hello' = 'hello' |
+--------------------------+
```

```
|                        0 |
+------------------------+
mysql> SELECT 'Hello' = BINARY 'hello';
+------------------------+
| 'Hello' = BINARY 'hello' |
+------------------------+
|                        0 |
+------------------------+
```

The sorting principles just described were demonstrated using literal strings, but the same principles apply to string-valued table columns. Suppose that a table t contains a column c and has the following rows:

```
mysql> SELECT c FROM t;
+-----------+
| c         |
+-----------+
| Hello     |
| goodbye   |
| Bonjour   |
| au revoir |
+-----------+
```

If c is a CHAR column that has the latin1_swedish_ci collation, it is a non-binary column with a case-insensitive collation. Uppercase and lowercase letters are treated as identical and a sort operation that uses ORDER BY produces results like this:

```
mysql> SELECT c FROM t ORDER BY c;
+-----------+
| c         |
+-----------+
| au revoir |
| Bonjour   |
| goodbye   |
| Hello     |
+-----------+
```

If c is declared as a BINARY column instead, it has no character set or collation. ORDER BY sorts using raw byte codes and produces a different result. Assuming that the values are stored on a machine that uses ASCII codes, the numeric values for uppercase letters precede those for lowercase letters and the result looks like this:

```
mysql> SELECT c FROM t ORDER BY c;
+-----------+
| c         |
+-----------+
| Bonjour   |
| Hello     |
```

```
| au revoir |
| goodbye   |
+-----------+
```

String comparison rules also apply to GROUP BY and DISTINCT operations. Suppose that t has a column c with the following contents:

```
mysql> SELECT c FROM t;
+---------+
| c       |
+---------+
| Hello   |
| hello   |
| Goodbye |
| goodbye |
+---------+
```

If c is a non-binary, case-insensitive column, GROUP BY and DISTINCT do not make lettercase distinctions:

```
mysql> SELECT c, COUNT(*) FROM t GROUP BY c;
+---------+----------+
| c       | COUNT(*) |
+---------+----------+
| Goodbye |        2 |
| Hello   |        2 |
+---------+----------+
mysql> SELECT DISTINCT c FROM t;
+---------+
| c       |
+---------+
| Hello   |
| Goodbye |
+---------+
```

On the other hand, if c is a BINARY column, those operations use byte values for sorting:

```
mysql> SELECT c, COUNT(*) FROM t GROUP BY c;
+---------+----------+
| c       | COUNT(*) |
+---------+----------+
| Goodbye |        1 |
| Hello   |        1 |
| goodbye |        1 |
| hello   |        1 |
+---------+----------+
mysql> SELECT DISTINCT c FROM t;
+---------+
```

```
| c       |
+---------+
| Hello   |
| hello   |
| Goodbye |
| goodbye |
+---------+
```

The preceding discussion shows that to understand sorting and comparison behavior for strings, it's important to know whether they are non-binary or binary. This is important when using string functions as well. String functions may treat their arguments as non-binary or binary strings, or return binary or non-binary results. It depends on the function. Here are some examples:

- LENGTH() returns the length of a string in bytes, whereas CHAR_LENGTH() returns the length in characters. For strings that contain only single-byte characters, the two functions return identical results. For strings that contain multi-byte characters, you should choose the function that is appropriate for the type of result you want. For example, the sjis character set includes characters that require two bytes to represent. The value of LENGTH() for any string containing such characters will be greater than the value of CHAR_LENGTH().

- The UPPER() and LOWER() functions perform case conversion only if the argument is a non-binary string. Suppose that 'AbCd' is non-binary. In that case, the two functions return a value in the requested lettercase:

```
mysql> SELECT UPPER('AbCd'), LOWER('AbCd');
+---------------+---------------+
| UPPER('AbCd') | LOWER('AbCd') |
+---------------+---------------+
| ABCD          | abcd          |
+---------------+---------------+
```

However, if 'AbCd' is a binary string, it has no character set. In that case, the concept of lettercase does not apply, and UPPER() and LOWER() do nothing:

```
mysql> SELECT UPPER(BINARY 'AbCd'), LOWER(BINARY 'AbCd');
+----------------------+----------------------+
| UPPER(BINARY 'AbCd') | LOWER(BINARY 'AbCd') |
+----------------------+----------------------+
| AbCd                 | AbCd                 |
+----------------------+----------------------+
```

To make the two functions perform case conversion for a binary string, convert it to a non-binary string. For example:

```
mysql> SELECT UPPER(CONVERT(BINARY 'AbCd' USING latin1));
+--------------------------------------------+
| UPPER(CONVERT(BINARY 'AbCd' USING latin1)) |
```

```
+------------------------------------------------+
| ABCD                                           |
+------------------------------------------------+
```

- MD5() takes a string argument and produces a 32-byte checksum represented as a string of hexadecimal digits. It treats its argument as a binary string:

```
mysql> SELECT MD5('a');
+----------------------------------+
| MD5('a')                         |
+----------------------------------+
| 0cc175b9c0f1b6a831c399e269772661 |
+----------------------------------+
mysql> SELECT MD5('A');
+----------------------------------+
| MD5('A')                         |
+----------------------------------+
| 7fc56270e7a70fa81a5935b72eacbe29 |
+----------------------------------+
```

These examples demonstrate that you must take into account the properties of the particular function you want to use. If you don't, you might be surprised at the results you get. See the *MySQL Reference Manual* for details on individual functions.

10.3.2 Using LIKE for Pattern Matching

Operators such as = and != are useful for finding values that are equal to or not equal to a specific exact comparison value. When it's necessary to find values based on similarity instead, a pattern match is useful. To perform a pattern match, use *value* LIKE '*pattern*', where *value* is the value you want to test and '*pattern*' is a pattern string that describes the general form of values that you want to match.

Patterns used with the LIKE pattern-matching operator can contain two special characters (called "metacharacters" or "wildcards") that stand for something other than themselves:

- The '%' character matches any sequence of zero or more characters. For example, the pattern 'a%' matches any string that begins with 'a', '%b' matches any string that ends with 'b', and '%c%' matches any string that contains a 'c'. The pattern '%' matches any string, including empty strings.

- The '_' (underscore) character matches any single character. 'd_g' matches strings such as 'dig', 'dog', and 'd@g'. Because '_' matches any single character, it matches itself and the pattern 'd_g' also matches the string 'd_g'.

A pattern can use these metacharacters in combination. For example, '_%' matches any string containing at least one character.

LIKE evaluates to NULL if either operand is NULL, but any non-NULL literal value matches itself. Likewise, a function call that produces a non-NULL value matches itself (with one exception). Thus, the following expressions evaluate as true:

```
'ABC' LIKE 'ABC'
column_name LIKE column_name
VERSION() LIKE VERSION()
```

The exception is that different invocations of the RAND() random-number function might return different values, even within the same query:

```
mysql> SELECT RAND(), RAND();
+------------------+------------------+
| RAND()           | RAND()           |
+------------------+------------------+
| 0.15430032289987 | 0.30666533979277 |
+------------------+------------------+
```

As a result, the expression RAND() LIKE RAND() normally will be false.

LIKE performs a non-binary comparison if both operands are non-binary strings; otherwise, the comparison is binary:

```
mysql> SELECT 'ABC' LIKE 'abc', 'ABC' LIKE BINARY 'abc';
+------------------+-------------------------+
| 'ABC' LIKE 'abc' | 'ABC' LIKE BINARY 'abc' |
+------------------+-------------------------+
|                1 |                       0 |
+------------------+-------------------------+
```

To invert a pattern match, use NOT LIKE rather than LIKE:

```
mysql> SELECT 'ABC' LIKE 'A%', 'ABC' NOT LIKE 'A%';
+-----------------+---------------------+
| 'ABC' LIKE 'A%' | 'ABC' NOT LIKE 'A%' |
+-----------------+---------------------+
|               1 |                   0 |
+-----------------+---------------------+
```

MySQL, unlike some other database systems, allows use of LIKE with non-string values. This can be useful in some cases. For example, the expression d LIKE '19%' is true for date values d that occur during the 1900s. MySQL evaluates such comparisons by converting non-string values to strings before performing the pattern match.

It's possible to specify the pattern in a LIKE expression using a table column. In this case, the actual pattern that a value is compared to can vary for every row of a result set. The following table has one column containing patterns and another column that characterizes the type of string each pattern matches:

```
mysql> SELECT pattern, description FROM patlist;
+---------+------------------------------+
| pattern | description                  |
+---------+------------------------------+
|         | empty string                 |
| _%      | non-empty string             |
| ___     | string of exactly 3 characters |
+---------+------------------------------+
```

The patterns in the table can be applied to specific values to characterize them:

```
mysql> SELECT description, IF('' LIKE pattern,'YES','NO')
    -> FROM patlist;
+-----------------------------+--------------------------------+
| description                 | IF('' LIKE pattern,'YES','NO') |
+-----------------------------+--------------------------------+
| empty string                | YES                            |
| non-empty string            | NO                             |
| string of exactly 3 characters | NO                          |
+-----------------------------+--------------------------------+
mysql> SELECT description, IF('abc' LIKE pattern,'YES','NO')
    -> FROM patlist;
+-----------------------------+-----------------------------------+
| description                 | IF('abc' LIKE pattern,'YES','NO') |
+-----------------------------+-----------------------------------+
| empty string                | NO                                |
| non-empty string            | YES                               |
| string of exactly 3 characters | YES                            |
+-----------------------------+-----------------------------------+
mysql> SELECT description, IF('hello' LIKE pattern,'YES','NO')
    -> FROM patlist;
+-----------------------------+-------------------------------------+
| description                 | IF('hello' LIKE pattern,'YES','NO') |
+-----------------------------+-------------------------------------+
| empty string                | NO                                  |
| non-empty string            | YES                                 |
| string of exactly 3 characters | NO                               |
+-----------------------------+-------------------------------------+
```

To match a pattern metacharacter literally, escape it by preceding it by a backslash:

```
mysql> SELECT 'AA' LIKE 'A%', 'AA' LIKE 'A\%', 'A%' LIKE 'A\%';
+----------------+-----------------+-----------------+
| 'AA' LIKE 'A%' | 'AA' LIKE 'A\%' | 'A%' LIKE 'A\%' |
+----------------+-----------------+-----------------+
|              1 |               0 |               1 |
+----------------+-----------------+-----------------+
mysql> SELECT 'AA' LIKE 'A_', 'AA' LIKE 'A\_', 'A_' LIKE 'A\_';
```

```
+----------------+-----------------+-----------------+
| 'AA' LIKE 'A_' | 'AA' LIKE 'A\_' | 'A_' LIKE 'A\_' |
+----------------+-----------------+-----------------+
|              1 |               0 |               1 |
+----------------+-----------------+-----------------+
```

To specify a given character as the escape character, use an ESCAPE clause:

```
mysql> SELECT 'AA' LIKE 'A@%' ESCAPE '@', 'A%' LIKE 'A@%' ESCAPE '@';
+---------------------------+---------------------------+
| 'AA' LIKE 'A@%' ESCAPE '@' | 'A%' LIKE 'A@%' ESCAPE '@' |
+---------------------------+---------------------------+
|                         0 |                         1 |
+---------------------------+---------------------------+
```

10.4 Temporal Expressions

Temporal values include dates, times, and datetime values that have both a date and time. More specialized temporal types are timestamp (commonly used for recording "current date and time") and year (for temporal values that require a resolution only to year units).

Direct use of temporal values in expressions occurs primarily in comparison operations, or in arithmetic operations that add an interval to or subtract an interval from a temporal value. Otherwise, most temporal value operations are performed by using functions.

The usual comparison operators apply to temporal values (=, <>, <, BETWEEN, and so forth).

To perform interval arithmetic, use the INTERVAL keyword and a unit value:

```
mysql> SELECT '2010-01-01' + INTERVAL 10 DAY, INTERVAL 10 DAY + '2010-01-01';
+-----------------------------+-----------------------------+
| '2010-01-01' + INTERVAL 10 DAY | INTERVAL 10 DAY + '2010-01-01' |
+-----------------------------+-----------------------------+
| 2010-01-11                  | 2010-01-11                  |
+-----------------------------+-----------------------------+
```

For addition of temporal and interval values, you can write the operands in either order, as just shown. To subtract an interval from a temporal value, the interval value must be second (it doesn't make sense to subtract a temporal value from an interval):

```
mysql> SELECT '2010-01-01' - INTERVAL 10 DAY;
+-------------------------------+
| '2010-01-01' - INTERVAL 10 DAY |
+-------------------------------+
| 2009-12-22                    |
+-------------------------------+
```

Intervals can be specified in units such as SECOND, MINUTE, HOUR, DAY, MONTH, or YEAR. Consult the *MySQL Reference Manual* for the full list.

Several functions take temporal arguments or return temporal values. Some types of operations these functions can perform are to extract parts of a value, convert a value to seconds or days, or reformat values. Section 10.6, "Functions in SQL Expressions," presents some representative examples.

10.5 NULL **Values**

NULL is unusual because it doesn't represent a specific value the way that numeric, string, or temporal values do. Instead, NULL stands for the absence of a known value. The special nature of NULL means that it often is handled differently than other values. This section describes how MySQL processes NULL values in various contexts.

Syntactically, NULL values are written in SQL statements without quotes. Writing NULL is different from writing 'NULL' or "NULL". The latter two values are actually strings that contain the word "NULL". Also, because it is an SQL keyword, NULL is not case sensitive. NULL and null both mean "a NULL value," whereas the string values 'NULL' and 'null' may be different or the same depending on whether they are non-binary or binary strings.

Note that some database systems treat the empty string and NULL as the same value. In MySQL, the two values are different.

Use of NULL values in arithmetic or comparison operations normally produces NULL results:

```
mysql> SELECT NULL + 1, NULL < 1;
+----------+----------+
| NULL + 1 | NULL < 1 |
+----------+----------+
|     NULL |     NULL |
+----------+----------+
```

Even comparing NULL to itself results in NULL, because you cannot tell whether one unknown value is the same as another:

```
mysql> SELECT NULL = 1, NULL != NULL;
+----------+--------------+
| NULL = 1 | NULL != NULL |
+----------+--------------+
|     NULL |         NULL |
+----------+--------------+
```

LIKE evaluates to NULL if either operand is NULL:

```
mysql> SELECT NULL LIKE '%', 'abc' LIKE NULL;
+---------------+-----------------+
| NULL LIKE '%' | 'abc' LIKE NULL |
```

```
+---------------+-----------------+
|         NULL  |          NULL  |
+---------------+-----------------+
```

The proper way to determine whether a value is NULL is to use the IS NULL or IS NOT NULL operators, which produce a true (non-zero) or false (zero) result:

```
mysql> SELECT NULL IS NULL, NULL IS NOT NULL;
+--------------+------------------+
| NULL IS NULL | NULL IS NOT NULL |
+--------------+------------------+
|            1 |                0 |
+--------------+------------------+
```

You can also use the MySQL-specific <=> operator, which is like = except that it works with NULL operands by treating them as any other value:

```
mysql> SELECT 1 <=> NULL, 0 <=> NULL, NULL <=> NULL;
+------------+------------+---------------+
| 1 <=> NULL | 0 <=> NULL | NULL <=> NULL |
+------------+------------+---------------+
|          0 |          0 |             1 |
+------------+------------+---------------+
```

ORDER BY, GROUP BY, and DISTINCT all perform comparisons implicitly. For purposes of these operations, NULL values are considered identical. That is, NULL values sort together, group together, and are not distinct.

Expressions that cannot be evaluated (such as 1/0) produce NULL as a result. However, in the context of inserting data into tables, division by zero can be treated as an error to prevent invalid data from being entered. This behavior is controlled by setting the SQL mode to enable strict mode in conjunction with the ERROR_FOR_DIVISION_BY_ZERO mode. For additional details about data handling and the SQL mode, see Section 5.8, "Handling Missing or Invalid Data Values."

Section 10.6.7, "NULL-Related Functions," discusses functions intended for use with NULL values.

10.6 Functions in SQL Expressions

This section describes the categories of functions that are available in MySQL and provides examples that show how to use several of them. (Some of the constructs mentioned here really are operators, even though the section titles all say "functions.")

> **Note**
> *Many functions are available in MySQL. The following sections demonstrate some representative examples, but those shown make up only a fraction of the number available. Consult the functions chapter in the* MySQL Reference Manual *for a complete list of functions and how to use them. In studying for the exam, you should familiarize yourself with all the SQL functions listed in that chapter. You're not expected to know every little detail about each one, but you'll be expected to know their general behavior.*

Functions can be invoked within expressions and return a value that is used in place of the function call when the expression is evaluated. When you invoke a function, there must be no space after the function name and before the opening parenthesis. It's possible to change this default behavior by enabling the IGNORE_SPACE SQL mode to cause spaces after the function name to be ignored:

```
mysql> SELECT PI ();
ERROR 1305 (42000): FUNCTION world.PI does not exist
mysql> SET sql_mode = 'IGNORE_SPACE';
Query OK, 0 rows affected (0.00 sec)

mysql> SELECT PI ();
+----------+
| PI ()    |
+----------+
| 3.141593 |
+----------+
1 row in set (0.00 sec)
```

10.6.1 Comparison Functions

Comparison functions enable you to test relative values or membership of one value within a set of values.

LEAST() and GREATEST() take a set of values as arguments and return the one that is smallest or largest, respectively:

```
mysql> SELECT LEAST(4,3,8,-1,5), LEAST('cdef','ab','ghi');
+-------------------+--------------------------+
| LEAST(4,3,8,-1,5) | LEAST('cdef','ab','ghi') |
+-------------------+--------------------------+
|                -1 | ab                       |
+-------------------+--------------------------+
mysql> SELECT GREATEST(4,3,8,-1,5), GREATEST('cdef','ab','ghi');
+----------------------+-----------------------------+
| GREATEST(4,3,8,-1,5) | GREATEST('cdef','ab','ghi') |
```

```
+--------------------+----------------------------+
|                  8 | ghi                        |
+--------------------+----------------------------+
```

INTERVAL() takes a comparison value as its first argument. The remaining arguments should be a set of values in sorted order. INTERVAL() compares the first argument to the others and returns a value to indicate how many of them are less than or equal to it.

```
mysql> SELECT INTERVAL(2,1,2,3,4);
+--------------------+
| INTERVAL(2,1,2,3,4) |
+--------------------+
|                  2 |
+--------------------+
mysql> SELECT INTERVAL(0,1,2,3,4);
+--------------------+
| INTERVAL(0,1,2,3,4) |
+--------------------+
|                  0 |
+--------------------+
mysql> SELECT INTERVAL(6.3,2,4,6,8,10);
+------------------------+
| INTERVAL(6.3,2,4,6,8,10) |
+------------------------+
|                      3 |
+------------------------+
```

It's sometimes necessary to determine whether a value is equal to any of several specific values. One way to accomplish this is to combine several equality tests into a single expression with the OR logical operator:

```
... WHERE id = 13 OR id = 45 OR id = 97 OR id = 142
... WHERE name = 'Tom' OR name = 'Dick' OR name = 'Harry'
```

However, MySQL provides an IN() operator that performs the same kind of comparison and that is more concise and easier to read. To use it, provide the comparison values as a comma-separated list of arguments to IN():

```
... WHERE id IN(13,45,97,142)
... WHERE name IN('Tom','Dick','Harry')
```

Using IN() is equivalent to writing a list of comparisons with OR, but IN() is much more efficient.

Arguments to IN() may be of any type (numeric, string, or temporal), although generally all values given within a list should all have the same type.

Elements in a list may be given as expressions that are evaluated to produce a value. If the expression references a column name, the column is evaluated for each row.

IN() always returns NULL when used to test NULL. That is, NULL IN(*list*) is NULL for any list of values, even if NULL is included in the list. This occurs because NULL IN(NULL) is equivalent to NULL = NULL, which evaluates to NULL.

IN() tests membership within a set of individual values. If you're searching for a range of values, a range test might be more suitable. The BETWEEN operator takes the two endpoint values of the range and returns true if a comparison value lies between them:

```
... WHERE id BETWEEN 5 AND 10
```

The comparison is inclusive, so the preceding expression is equivalent to this one:

```
... WHERE id >= 5 AND id <= 10
```

10.6.2 Control Flow Functions

Control flow functions enable you to choose between different values based on the result of an expression. IF() tests the expression in its first argument and returns its second or third argument depending on whether the expression is true or false:

```
mysql> SELECT IF(1 > 0, 'yes','no');
+----------------------+
| IF(1 > 0, 'yes','no') |
+----------------------+
| yes                  |
+----------------------+
```

The CASE construct is not a function, but it too provides flow control. It has two forms of syntax. The first looks like this:

```
CASE case_expr
  WHEN when_expr THEN result
  [WHEN when_expr THEN result] ...
  [ELSE result]
END
```

The expression *case_expr* is evaluated and used to determine which of the following clauses in the rest of the CASE to execute. The *when_expr* in the initial WHEN clause is evaluated and compared to *case_expr*. If the two are equal, the expression following THEN is the result of the CASE. If *when_expr* is not equal to *case_expr*, and there are any following WHEN clauses, they are handled similarly in turn. If no WHEN clause has a *when_expr* equal to *case_expr*, and there is an ELSE clause, the expression in the ELSE clause becomes the CASE result. If there is no ELSE clause the result is NULL.

The following CASE expression returns a string that indicates whether the value of the @val user variable is 0, 1, or something else:

```
mysql> SET @val = 1;
mysql> SELECT CASE @val
```

```
    ->    WHEN 0 THEN '@val is 0'
    ->    WHEN 1 THEN '@val is 1'
    ->    ELSE '@val is not 0 or 1'
    -> END AS result;
+-----------+
| result    |
+-----------+
| @val is 1 |
+-----------+
```

The second CASE syntax looks like this:

```
CASE
  WHEN when_expr THEN result
  [WHEN when_expr THEN result] ...
  [ELSE result]
END
```

For this syntax, the conditional expression in each WHEN clause is executed until one is found to be true, and then its corresponding THEN expression becomes the result of the CASE. If none of them are true and there is an ELSE clause, its expression becomes the CASE result. If there is no ELSE clause the result is NULL.

The following CASE expression tests whether the value of the @val user variable is NULL or less than, greater than, or equal to 0:

```
mysql> SET @val = NULL;
mysql> SELECT CASE
    ->    WHEN @val IS NULL THEN '@val is NULL'
    ->    WHEN @val < 0 THEN '@val is less than 0'
    ->    WHEN @val > 0 THEN '@val is greater than 0'
    ->    ELSE '@val is 0'
    -> END AS result;
+--------------+
| result       |
+--------------+
| @val is NULL |
+--------------+
```

Note that IF() and CASE as used in expressions have somewhat different syntax than the IF and CASE statements that can be used within compound statements (the statements end with END CASE, not just END). For the syntax of the latter, see Section 18.5.8, "Flow Control." That section also contains some discussion about the kinds of test for which each type of CASE statement syntax are appropriate; the same remarks apply to CASE expressions.

10.6.3 Aggregate Functions

Aggregate functions perform summary operations on a set of values, such as counting, averaging, or finding minimum or maximum values. Aggregate functions often are used in conjunction with a GROUP BY clause to arrange values from a result set into groups. In this case, the aggregate function produces a summary value for each group. The use of aggregate functions in MySQL is covered in Section 9.4, "Aggregating Results."

10.6.4 Mathematical Functions

Numeric functions perform several types of operations, such as rounding, truncation, trigonometric calculations, or generating random numbers.

The ROUND() function performs rounding of its argument. The rounding method applied to the fractional part of a number depends on whether the number is an exact or approximate value:

- For positive exact values, ROUND() rounds up to the next integer if the fractional part is .5 or greater, and down to the next integer otherwise. For negative exact values, ROUND() rounds down to the next integer if the fractional part is .5 or greater, and up to the next integer otherwise. Another way to state this is that a fraction of .5 or greater rounds away from zero and a fraction less than .5 rounds toward zero:

```
mysql> SELECT ROUND(28.5), ROUND(-28.5);
+-------------+--------------+
| ROUND(28.5) | ROUND(-28.5) |
+-------------+--------------+
| 29          | -29          |
+-------------+--------------+
```

- For approximate values, ROUND() uses the rounding method provided in the C library used by the MySQL server. This can vary from system to system, but typically rounds to the nearest even integer:

```
mysql> SELECT ROUND(2.85E1), ROUND(-2.85E1);
+---------------+----------------+
| ROUND(2.85E1) | ROUND(-2.85E1) |
+---------------+----------------+
|            28 |            -28 |
+---------------+----------------+
```

FLOOR() returns the largest integer not greater than its argument, and CEILING() returns the smallest integer not less than its argument:

```
mysql> SELECT FLOOR(-14.7), FLOOR(14.7);
+--------------+-------------+
| FLOOR(-14.7) | FLOOR(14.7) |
+--------------+-------------+
|          -15 |          14 |
+--------------+-------------+
```

```
mysql> SELECT CEILING(-14.7), CEILING(14.7);
+----------------+---------------+
| CEILING(-14.7) | CEILING(14.7) |
+----------------+---------------+
|            -14 |            15 |
+----------------+---------------+
```

ABS() and SIGN() extract the absolute value and sign of numeric values:

```
mysql> SELECT ABS(-14.7), ABS(14.7);
+------------+-----------+
| ABS(-14.7) | ABS(14.7) |
+------------+-----------+
| 14.7       | 14.7      |
+------------+-----------+
mysql> SELECT SIGN(-14.7), SIGN(14.7), SIGN(0);
+-------------+------------+---------+
| SIGN(-14.7) | SIGN(14.7) | SIGN(0) |
+-------------+------------+---------+
|          -1 |          1 |       0 |
+-------------+------------+---------+
```

A family of functions performs trigonometric calculations, including conversions between degrees and radians:

```
mysql> SELECT SIN(0), COS(0), TAN(0);
+--------+--------+--------+
| SIN(0) | COS(0) | TAN(0) |
+--------+--------+--------+
|      0 |      1 |      0 |
+--------+--------+--------+
mysql> SELECT PI(), DEGREES(PI()), RADIANS(180);
+----------+---------------+-----------------+
| PI()     | DEGREES(PI()) | RADIANS(180)    |
+----------+---------------+-----------------+
| 3.141593 |           180 | 3.1415926535898 |
+----------+---------------+-----------------+
```

To generate random numbers, invoke the RAND() function:

```
mysql> SELECT RAND(), RAND(), RAND();
+-----------------+-----------------+-----------------+
| RAND()          | RAND()          | RAND()          |
+-----------------+-----------------+-----------------+
| 0.55239934711941 | 0.16831658330589 | 0.18438490590489 |
+-----------------+-----------------+-----------------+
```

10.6.5 String Functions

String functions calculate string lengths, extract pieces of strings, search for substrings or replace them, perform lettercase conversion, and more.

The LENGTH() and CHAR_LENGTH() functions determine string lengths in byte and character units, respectively. The values returned by the two functions will differ for strings that contain multi-byte characters. The following example shows this, using the latin1 single-byte character set and the ucs2 double-byte character set:

```
mysql> SET @s = CONVERT('MySQL' USING latin1);
mysql> SELECT LENGTH(@s), CHAR_LENGTH(@s);
+------------+-----------------+
| LENGTH(@s) | CHAR_LENGTH(@s) |
+------------+-----------------+
|          5 |               5 |
+------------+-----------------+

mysql> SET @s = CONVERT('MySQL' USING ucs2);
mysql> SELECT LENGTH(@s), CHAR_LENGTH(@s);
+------------+-----------------+
| LENGTH(@s) | CHAR_LENGTH(@s) |
+------------+-----------------+
|         10 |               5 |
+------------+-----------------+
```

CONCAT() and CONCAT_WS() concatenate strings. CONCAT() concatenates all of its arguments, whereas CONCAT_WS() interprets its first argument as a separator to place between the following arguments:

```
mysql> SELECT CONCAT('aa','bb','cc','dd');
+----------------------------+
| CONCAT('aa','bb','cc','dd') |
+----------------------------+
| aabbccdd                   |
+----------------------------+
mysql> SELECT CONCAT_WS('aa','bb','cc','dd');
+-------------------------------+
| CONCAT_WS('aa','bb','cc','dd') |
+-------------------------------+
| bbaaccaadd                    |
+-------------------------------+
```

The two functions also differ in their handling of NULL values. CONCAT() returns NULL if any of its arguments are null. CONCAT_WS() ignores NULL values:

```
mysql> SELECT CONCAT('/','a',NULL,'b'), CONCAT_WS('/','a',NULL,'b');
+--------------------------+-----------------------------+
```

```
| CONCAT('/','a',NULL,'b') | CONCAT_WS('/','a',NULL,'b') |
+--------------------------+-----------------------------+
| NULL                     | a/b                         |
+--------------------------+-----------------------------+
```

The STRCMP() function compares two strings and returns –1, 0, or 1 if the first string is less than, equal to, or greater than the second string, respectively:

```
mysql> SELECT STRCMP('abc','def'), STRCMP('def','def'), STRCMP('def','abc');
+---------------------+---------------------+---------------------+
| STRCMP('abc','def') | STRCMP('def','def') | STRCMP('def','abc') |
+---------------------+---------------------+---------------------+
|                  -1 |                   0 |                   1 |
+---------------------+---------------------+---------------------+
```

MySQL encrypts passwords in the grant tables using the PASSWORD() function. This function should be considered for use only for managing MySQL accounts, not for general user applications. One reason for this is that applications often require reversible (two-way) encryption, and PASSWORD() performs irreversible (one-way) encryption. Another reason that applications should avoid reliance on PASSWORD() is that its implementation may change. (In fact, it did change in MySQL 4.1.0 and again in 4.1.1.)

For applications that work with data that must not be stored in unencrypted form, MySQL provides several pairs of functions that perform two-way encryption and decryption:

- ENCODE() and DECODE()
- DES_ENCRYPT() and DES_DECRYPT()
- AES_ENCRYPT() and AES_DECRYPT()

Cryptographically, AES_ENCRYPT() and AES_DECRYPT() can be considered the most secure of the pairs. DES_ENCRYPT() and DES_DECRYPT() can be used if SSL support is enabled. Other details can be found in the *MySQL Reference Manual*.

10.6.6 Temporal Functions

Temporal functions perform operations such as extracting parts of dates and times, reformatting values, or converting values to seconds or days. In many cases, a temporal function that takes a date or time argument also can be given a datetype argument and will ignore the irrelevant part of the datetime value.

There are functions for extracting parts of date or time values:

```
mysql> SET @d = '2010-04-15', @t = '09:23:57';
mysql> SELECT YEAR(@d), MONTH(@d), DAYOFMONTH(@d);
+----------+-----------+----------------+
| YEAR(@d) | MONTH(@d) | DAYOFMONTH(@d) |
+----------+-----------+----------------+
```

```
|    2010 |         4 |              15 |
+----------+----------+----------------+
mysql> SELECT DAYOFYEAR(@d);
+---------------+
| DAYOFYEAR(@d) |
+---------------+
|           105 |
+---------------+
mysql> SELECT HOUR(@t), MINUTE(@t), SECOND(@t);
+----------+------------+------------+
| HOUR(@t) | MINUTE(@t) | SECOND(@t) |
+----------+------------+------------+
|        9 |         23 |         57 |
+----------+------------+------------+
```

MAKEDATE() and MAKETIME() compose dates and times from component values. MAKEDATE() produces a date from year and day of year arguments:

```
mysql> SELECT MAKEDATE(2010,105);
+--------------------+
| MAKEDATE(2010,105) |
+--------------------+
| 2010-04-15         |
+--------------------+
```

MAKETIME() produces a time from hour, minute, and second arguments.

```
mysql> SELECT MAKETIME(9,23,57);
+-------------------+
| MAKETIME(9,23,57) |
+-------------------+
| 09:23:57          |
+-------------------+
```

If you need to determine the current date or time, use CURRENT_DATE or CURRENT_TIME. To get the current date and time as a single value, use CURRENT_TIMESTAMP or NOW():

```
mysql> SELECT CURRENT_DATE, CURRENT_TIME, CURRENT_TIMESTAMP;
+--------------+--------------+---------------------+
| CURRENT_DATE | CURRENT_TIME | CURRENT_TIMESTAMP   |
+--------------+--------------+---------------------+
| 2005-05-31   | 21:40:18     | 2005-05-31 21:40:18 |
+--------------+--------------+---------------------+
```

The three functions in the preceding statement are unlike most functions in that they can be invoked with or without parentheses following the function name.

10.6.7 NULL-Related Functions

Functions intended specifically for use with NULL values include ISNULL() and IFNULL().
ISNULL() is true if its argument is NULL and false otherwise:

```
mysql> SELECT ISNULL(NULL), ISNULL(0), ISNULL(1);
+--------------+-----------+-----------+
| ISNULL(NULL) | ISNULL(0) | ISNULL(1) |
+--------------+-----------+-----------+
|            1 |         0 |         0 |
+--------------+-----------+-----------+
```

IFNULL() takes two arguments. If the first argument is not NULL, that argument is returned;
otherwise, the function returns its second argument:

```
mysql> SELECT IFNULL(NULL,'a'), IFNULL(0,'b');
+-----------------+---------------+
| IFNULL(NULL,'a') | IFNULL(0,'b') |
+-----------------+---------------+
| a               | 0             |
+-----------------+---------------+
```

Other functions handle NULL values in various ways, so you have to know how a given function behaves. In many cases, passing a NULL value to a function results in a NULL return value.
For example, any NULL argument passed to CONCAT() causes it to return NULL:

```
mysql> SELECT CONCAT('a','b'), CONCAT('a',NULL,'b');
+----------------+----------------------+
| CONCAT('a','b') | CONCAT('a',NULL,'b') |
+----------------+----------------------+
| ab             | NULL                 |
+----------------+----------------------+
```

But not all functions behave that way. CONCAT_WS() (concatenate with separator) simply
ignores NULL arguments entirely:

```
mysql> SELECT CONCAT_WS('/','a','b'), CONCAT_WS('/','a',NULL,'b');
+-----------------------+-----------------------------+
| CONCAT_WS('/','a','b') | CONCAT_WS('/','a',NULL,'b') |
+-----------------------+-----------------------------+
| a/b                   | a/b                         |
+-----------------------+-----------------------------+
```

For information about the behavior of specific functions with respect to NULL, consult the
MySQL Reference Manual.

10.7 Comments in SQL Statements

MySQL supports three forms of comment syntax. One of those forms has variants that allow special instructions to be passed through to the MySQL server.

- A '#' character begins a comment that extends to the end of the line. This commenting style is like that used by several other programs, such as Perl, Awk, and several Unix shells.

- A /* sequence begins a comment that ends with a */ sequence. This style is the same as that used for writing comments in the C programming language. A C-style comment may occur on a single line or span multiple lines:

```
/* this is a comment */
/*
  this
  is a
  comment,
  too
*/
```

- A -- (double dash) sequence followed by a space (or control character) begins a comment that extends to the end of the line. This syntax requires a space and thus differs from standard SQL syntax, which allows comments to be introduced by -- without the space. MySQL disallows a double dash without a space as a comment because it's ambiguous. (For example, does 1--3 mean "one minus negative three" or "one followed by a comment"?)

C-style comments can contain embedded SQL text that's treated specially by the MySQL server, but ignored by other database engines. This is an aid to writing more portable SQL because it enables you to write comments that are treated as part of the surrounding statement if executed by MySQL and ignored if executed by other database servers. There are two ways to write embedded SQL in a C-style comment:

- If the comment begins with /*! rather than with /*, MySQL executes the body of the comment as part of the surrounding query. The following statement creates a table named t, but for MySQL creates it specifically as a MEMORY table:

```
CREATE TABLE t (i INT) /*! ENGINE = MEMORY */;
```

- If the comment begins with /*! followed by a version number, the embedded SQL is version specific. The server executes the body of the comment as part of the surrounding query if its version is at least as recent as that specified in the query. Otherwise, it ignores the comment. For example, the FULL keyword for SHOW TABLES was added in MySQL 5.0.2. To write a comment that's understood only by servers from MySQL 5.0.2 and up and ignored by older servers, write it as follows:

```
SHOW /*!50002 FULL */ TABLES;
```

11

Updating Data

This chapter discusses SQL statements that modify the contents of database tables. It covers the following exam topics:

- Using the INSERT and REPLACE statements to add new records to a table
- Using the UPDATE statement to modify existing table records
- Using the DELETE and TRUNCATE statements to remove records from a table
- Handling duplicate key values
- Privileges required for statements that modify tables

11.1 Update Operations

The statements covered in this chapter modify the contents of database tables. Another statement that modifies table contents is LOAD DATA INFILE, which reads records from a data file and loads them into a table. It's discussed in Chapter 15, "Importing and Exporting Data."

For purposes of discussion here, the term "update statement" is used in a collective sense to refer to various kinds of statements that modify tables. "UPDATE statement" refers specifically to statements that begin with the UPDATE keyword. Also, keep in mind the following terminology with regard to indexes:

- The term "unique-valued index" is a generic term meaning any index that contains only unique values.
- The term "primary key" is a generic term meaning a unique-valued index that cannot contain NULL values.
- "UNIQUE index" means specifically a unique-valued index created using the keyword UNIQUE.
- "PRIMARY KEY" means specifically a unique-valued index created using the keywords PRIMARY KEY.

See Section 8.6, "Indexes," for further information about types of indexes.

Much of the discussion in this chapter uses the following table as a source of examples:

```
CREATE TABLE people
(
    id      INT UNSIGNED NOT NULL AUTO_INCREMENT,
    name    CHAR(40) NOT NULL DEFAULT '',
    age     INT NOT NULL DEFAULT 0,
    PRIMARY KEY (id)
);
```

11.2 The INSERT Statement

The INSERT statement adds new records to a table. It has two basic formats, one of which allows for insertion of multiple rows using a single statement:

```
INSERT INTO table_name (column_list) VALUES (value_list);

INSERT INTO table_name
    SET column_name = value [, column_name = value] ... ;
```

The first syntax for INSERT uses separate column and value lists following the name of the table into which you want to add the record. The number of columns and values must be the same. The following statement uses this syntax to create a new record in the people table with id set to 12, name set to 'William', and age set to 25:

```
INSERT INTO people (id,name,age) VALUES(12,'William',25);
```

The second INSERT syntax follows the table name by a SET clause that lists individual column assignments separated by commas:

```
INSERT INTO people SET id = 12, name = 'William', age = 25;
```

The SET clause must assign a value to at least one column.

For any column not assigned an explicit value by an INSERT statement, MySQL sets it to its default value if it has one. For example, to have MySQL set the id column to its default, you can simply omit it from the statement. The following example shows statements using each INSERT syntax that assign no explicit id value:

```
INSERT INTO people (name,age) VALUES('William',25);
INSERT INTO people SET name = 'William', age = 25;
```

In both statements, the effect for the people table is the same: The id column is set to its default value. id is an AUTO_INCREMENT column, so its default is the next sequence number.

In general, if a column has no default value, the effect of omitting it from the INSERT statement depends on whether it can take NULL values and on the SQL mode:

- If the column can take NULL values, it is set to NULL.
- If the column cannot take NULL values, it is set to the implicit default for the column data type if strict SQL mode is not enabled. If strict mode is enabled, an error occurs.

MySQL can be configured to allow or reject attempts to insert invalid data into a row. For details about handling of such values, see Section 5.8, "Handling Missing or Invalid Data Values."

The VALUES form of INSERT has some variations:

- If both the column list and the VALUES list are empty, MySQL creates a new record with each column set to its default:

```
INSERT INTO people () VALUES();
```

The preceding statement creates a record with id, name, and age set to their defaults (the next sequence number, the empty string, and 0, respectively).

- It's allowable to omit the list of column names and provide only the VALUES list. In this case, the list must contain one value for every column in the table. Furthermore, the values must be listed in the same order in which the columns are named in the table's definition. (This is the order in which the columns appear in the output from DESCRIBE table_name.) The following INSERT statement satisfies these conditions because it provides three column values in id, name, and age order:

```
INSERT INTO people VALUES(12,'William',25);
```

On the other hand, this statement is illegal because it provides only two values for a three-column table:

```
INSERT INTO people VALUES('William',25);
```

The following INSERT statement is syntactically legal because it provides a value for every column, but it assigns 25 to name and 'William' to age, which is not likely to serve any useful purpose:

```
INSERT INTO people VALUES(12,25,'William');
```

The statement also will cause an error in strict SQL mode because the age column requires a number and 'William' cannot be converted to a number.

- You can insert multiple records with a single statement by providing several values lists after the VALUES keyword. This is discussed in Section 11.2.1, "Adding Multiple Records with a Single INSERT Statement."

As noted, for an INSERT statement that provides data values in the VALUES list, it's permissible to omit the list of column names if the statement contains a data value for every column. However, it isn't necessarily advisable to do so. When you don't include the list of column names, the VALUES list must not only be complete, the data values must be in the same order as the columns in the table. If it's possible that you'll alter the structure of the table by adding, removing, or rearranging columns, such alterations might require any application that inserts records into the table to be modified. This is much more likely if the INSERT statements don't include a list of column names because they're more sensitive to the structure of the table. When you use an INSERT statement that names the columns, rearranging the table's columns has no effect. Adding columns has no effect, either, if it's appropriate to set the new columns to their default values.

11.2.1 Adding Multiple Records with a Single INSERT Statement

A single INSERT ... VALUES statement can add multiple records to a table if you provide multiple VALUES lists. To do this, provide a parenthesized list of values for each record and separate the lists by commas. For example:

```
INSERT INTO people (name,age)
VALUES('William',25),('Bart',15),('Mary',12);
```

The statement shown creates three new people records, assigning the name and age columns in each record to the values listed. The id column is not listed explicitly, so MySQL assigns its default value (the next sequence value) in each record.

Note that a multiple-row INSERT statement requires a *separate* parenthesized list for each row. Suppose that you have a table t with a single integer column i:

```
CREATE TABLE t (i INT);
```

To insert into the table five records with values of 1 through 5, the following statement does *not* work:

```
mysql> INSERT INTO t (i) VALUES(1,2,3,4,5);
ERROR 1136 (21S01): Column count doesn't match value count at row 1
```

The error occurs because the number of values between parentheses in the VALUES list isn't the same as the number of columns in the column list. To write the statement properly, provide five separate parenthesized lists:

```
mysql> INSERT INTO t (i) VALUES(1),(2),(3),(4),(5);
Query OK, 5 rows affected (0.00 sec)
Records: 5  Duplicates: 0  Warnings: 0
```

It's allowable to omit the list of column names in multiple-row INSERT statements. In this case, each parenthesized list of values must contain a value for every table column.

The preceding example illustrates something about multiple-row INSERT statements that isn't true for single-row statements: MySQL returns an extra information string containing several counts. The counts in each field of this string have the following meanings:

- `Records` indicates the number of records inserted.

- `Duplicates` indicates how many records were ignored because they contained duplicate unique key values. This value can be non-zero if the statement includes the `IGNORE` keyword. The action of this keyword is described in Section 11.2.2, "Handling Duplicate Key Values."

- `Warnings` indicates the number of problems found in the data values. These can occur if values are converted. For example, the warning count is incremented if an empty string is converted to 0 before being in a numeric column. To see what caused the warnings, issue a `SHOW WARNINGS` statement following the `INSERT`.

A multiple-row `INSERT` statement is logically equivalent to a set of individual single-row statements. However, the multiple-row statement is more efficient because the server can process all the rows at once rather than as separate operations. When you have many records to add, multiple-row statements provide better performance and reduce the load on the server. On the other hand, such statements are more likely to reach the maximum size of the communication buffer used to transmit information to the server. (This size is controlled by the `max_allowed_packet` variable, which has a default value of 1MB.)

MySQL treats single-row and multiple-row `INSERT` statements somewhat differently for purposes of error-handling. These differences are described in Section 5.8, "Handling Missing or Invalid Data Values."

11.2.2 Handling Duplicate Key Values

If a table has a unique-valued index, it might not be possible to use `INSERT` to add a given record to the table. This happens when the new record contains a key value for the index that's already present in the table. Suppose that every person in the `people` table has a unique value in the `id` column. If an existing record has an `id` value of 347 and you attempt to insert a new record that also has an `id` of 347, it duplicates an existing key value. MySQL provides three ways to deal with duplicate values in a unique-valued index when adding new records to a table with `INSERT`:

- If you don't indicate explicitly how to handle a duplicate, MySQL aborts the statement with an error and discards the new record. This is the default behavior. (For multiple-record `INSERT` statements, treatment of records inserted before a record that causes a duplicate-key violation is dependent on the storage engine. For `MyISAM`, the records are inserted. For `InnoDB`, the entire statement fails and no records are inserted.)

- You can tell MySQL to ignore the new record without producing an error. To do this, modify the statement so that it begins with `INSERT IGNORE` rather than with `INSERT`. If the record does not duplicate a unique key value, MySQL inserts it as usual. If the record does contain a duplicate key, MySQL ignores it. Client programs that terminate on statement errors will abort with `INSERT` but not with `INSERT IGNORE`.

- You can use the `ON DUPLICATE KEY UPDATE` clause to update specific columns of the existing record.

If you want to replace the old record with the new one when a duplicate key occurs, use the REPLACE statement instead of INSERT. (See Section 11.3, "The REPLACE Statement.")

Note that for a unique-valued index that can contain NULL values, inserting NULL into an indexed column that already contains NULL doesn't cause a duplicate-key violation. This is because such an index can contain multiple NULL values.

11.2.3 Using INSERT ... ON DUPLICATE KEY UPDATE

Normally, if you attempt to insert a row into a table that would result in a duplicate-key error for a unique-valued index, the insertion fails. In some cases, you can use the REPLACE statement instead, which deletes the old row and inserts the new one in its place. (See Section 11.3, "The REPLACE Statement.") However, REPLACE is not suitable if you wish to change only some columns of the old row. By using the ON DUPLICATE KEY UPDATE clause with INSERT, you have the option of choosing to update one or more columns of the existing row, rather than letting the INSERT statement fail or using REPLACE to replace the entire row.

The ON DUPLICATE KEY UPDATE clause allows you to do in one statement what otherwise requires two (INSERT and UPDATE). Also, for non-transactional tables, it saves you from having to explicitly lock the table to prevent UPDATE errors when the referenced row may have been deleted in between the INSERT and UPDATE.

One case where this new behavior is especially useful is when you have a table with counters that are tied to key values. When it's time to increment a counter in the record for a given key, you want to create a new record if none exists for the key, but just increment the counter if the key does exist. For example, suppose that we are tracking elephants in the wild and want to count the number of times each elephant has been spotted at a given location. In this case, we can create a log table to log elephant sightings based on the unique key of elephant name and location:

```
mysql> CREATE TABLE log (
    ->     name     CHAR(30) NOT NULL,
    ->     location CHAR(30) NOT NULL,
    ->     counter  INT UNSIGNED NOT NULL,
    ->     PRIMARY KEY (name, location));
Query OK, 0 rows affected (0.07 sec)
```

Then, every time we wish to log a sighting, we can use INSERT without first checking whether the record exists. This simplifies application logic by reducing the number of conditions that must be tested. For example, if we have just created the table, and the first two sightings that occur are for the elephant "Tantor" over by the waterhole, we would use the same INSERT statement each time. The first instance of the statement inserts a record and the second causes it to be updated:

```
mysql> INSERT INTO log (name, location, counter)
    -> VALUES ('Tantor', 'Waterhole', 1)
    -> ON DUPLICATE KEY UPDATE counter=counter+1;
Query OK, 1 row affected (0.00 sec)
```

```
mysql> SELECT * FROM log;
+--------+-----------+---------+
| name   | location  | counter |
+--------+-----------+---------+
| Tantor | Waterhole |       1 |
+--------+-----------+---------+
1 row in set (0.00 sec)

mysql> INSERT INTO log (name, location, counter)
    -> VALUES ('Tantor', 'Waterhole', 1)
    -> ON DUPLICATE KEY UPDATE counter=counter+1;
Query OK, 2 rows affected (0.00 sec)

mysql> SELECT * FROM log;
+--------+-----------+---------+
| name   | location  | counter |
+--------+-----------+---------+
| Tantor | Waterhole |       2 |
+--------+-----------+---------+
1 row in set (0.00 sec)
```

Notice the difference in the "rows affected" value returned by the server for each INSERT statement: If a new record is inserted, the value is 1; if an already existing record is updated, the value is 2.

11.3 The REPLACE Statement

The REPLACE statement, like INSERT, add new records to a table. The two statements have very similar syntax. The primary difference between them lies in how they handle duplicate records. Also, REPLACE does not support the ON DUPLICATE KEY UPDATE clause.

If a table contains a unique-valued index and you attempt to insert a record containing a key value that already exists in the index, a duplicate-key violation occurs and the row is not inserted. What if you want the new record to take priority over the existing one? You could remove the existing record with DELETE and then use INSERT to add the new record. However, MySQL provides REPLACE as an alternative that is easier to use and is more efficient because it performs both actions with a single statement. REPLACE is like INSERT except that it deletes old records as necessary when a duplicate unique key value is present in a new record. Suppose that you're inserting a record into the people table, which has id as a PRIMARY KEY:

- If the new record doesn't duplicate an existing id value, MySQL just inserts it.
- If the new record does duplicate an existing id value, MySQL first deletes any old records containing that value before inserting the new record.

An advantage of using REPLACE instead of an equivalent DELETE (if needed) and INSERT is that REPLACE is performed as a single atomic operation. There's no need to do any explicit table locking as there might be were you to issue separate DELETE and INSERT statements.

For a comparison of REPLACE with UPDATE, see Section 11.4, "The UPDATE Statement."

The action of REPLACE in replacing rows with duplicate keys depends on the table having a unique-valued index:

- In the absence of any such indexes, REPLACE is equivalent to INSERT because no duplicates will ever be detected.

- Even in the presence of a unique-valued index, if an indexed column allows NULL values, it allows multiple NULL values. A new record with a NULL value in that column does not cause a duplicate-key violation and no replacement occurs.

REPLACE returns an information string that indicates how many rows it affected. If the count is one, the row was inserted without replacing an existing row. If the count is two, a row was deleted before the new row was inserted. If the count is greater than two, it means the table has multiple unique-valued indexes and the new record matched key values in multiple rows, resulting in multiple duplicate-key violations. This causes multiple rows to be deleted, a situation that's described in more detail later in this section.

REPLACE statement syntax is similar to that for INSERT. The following are each valid forms of REPLACE. They're analogous to examples shown earlier in the chapter for INSERT:

- A single-record REPLACE with separate column and value lists:

  ```
  REPLACE INTO people (id,name,age) VALUES(12,'William',25);
  ```

- A multiple-record REPLACE that inserts several rows:

  ```
  REPLACE INTO people (id,name,age)
  VALUES(12,'William',25),(13,'Bart',15),(14,'Mary',12);
  ```

  The rows-affected count for a multiple-row REPLACE often is greater than two because the statement may insert (and delete) several records in a single operation.

- A single-record REPLACE with a SET clause that lists column assignments:

  ```
  REPLACE INTO people SET id = 12, name = 'William', age = 25;
  ```

If a table contains multiple unique-valued indexes, a new record added with REPLACE might cause duplicate-key violations for multiple existing records. In this case, REPLACE replaces each of those records. The following table has three columns, each of which has a UNIQUE index:

```
CREATE TABLE multikey
(
    i INT NOT NULL UNIQUE,
    j INT NOT NULL UNIQUE,
    k INT NOT NULL UNIQUE
);
```

Suppose that the table has these contents:

```
mysql> SELECT * FROM multikey;
+---+---+---+
| i | j | k |
+---+---+---+
| 1 | 1 | 1 |
| 2 | 2 | 2 |
| 3 | 3 | 3 |
| 4 | 4 | 4 |
+---+---+---+
```

Using REPLACE to add a record that duplicates a row in each column causes several records to be replaced with the new row:

```
mysql> REPLACE INTO multikey (i,j,k) VALUES(1,2,3);
Query OK, 4 rows affected (0.00 sec)

mysql> SELECT * FROM multikey;
+---+---+---+
| i | j | k |
+---+---+---+
| 1 | 2 | 3 |
| 4 | 4 | 4 |
+---+---+---+
```

The REPLACE statement reports a row count of four because it deletes three records and inserts one.

11.4 The UPDATE Statement

The UPDATE statement modifies the contents of existing records. To use it, name the table you want to update, provide a SET clause that lists one or more column value assignments, and optionally specify a WHERE clause that identifies which records to update:

```
UPDATE table_name
    SET column_name = value [, column_name = value] ...
    WHERE ... ;
```

For example, to set the age column to 30 for the people table record that has an id value of 12, use this statement:

```
UPDATE people SET age = 30 WHERE id = 12;
```

To update multiple columns, separate the column value assignments in the SET clause by commas:

```
UPDATE people SET age = 30, name = 'Wilhelm' WHERE id = 12;
```

The WHERE clause specifies the conditions that records must satisfy to be selected for updating. If you omit the WHERE clause, MySQL updates every row in the table.

The effects of column assignments made by an UPDATE are subject to column type constraints, just as they are for an INSERT or REPLACE. By default, if you attempt to update a column to a value that doesn't match the column definition, MySQL converts or truncates the value. If you enable strict SQL mode, the server will be more restrictive about allowing invalid values. See Section 5.8, "Handling Missing or Invalid Data Values."

It's possible for an UPDATE statement to have no effect. This can occur under the following conditions:

- When the statement matches no records for updating. This always occurs if the table is empty, of course. It might also occur if no records match the conditions specified in the WHERE clause.

- When the statement does not actually change any column values. For example, if you set a date-valued column to '2000-01-01' and the column already has that date as its value, MySQL ignores the assignment.

UPDATE reports a rows-affected count to indicate how many rows actually were changed. This count doesn't include rows that were selected for updating but for which the update didn't change any columns from their current values. The following statement produces a row count of zero because it doesn't actually change any values, even if there is a record with an id value of 12:

```
mysql> UPDATE people SET age = age WHERE id = 12;
Query OK, 0 rows affected (0.00 sec)
```

If a table contains a TIMESTAMP column that has ON UPDATE CURRENT_TIMESTAMP in its definition, that column is updated automatically only if another column changes value. An UPDATE that sets columns to their current values does not change the TIMESTAMP. If you need the TIMESTAMP to be updated for every UPDATE, you can set it explicitly to the value of the CURRENT_TIMESTAMP function.

Some client programs or APIs enable you to ask the MySQL server to return a rows-matched count rather than a rows-affected count. This causes the row count to include all rows selected for updating, even if their columns weren't changed from their present values. The C API provides an option for selecting the type of count you want when you establish a connection to the server. The MySQL Connector/J Java driver tells the server to operate in rows-matched mode because that behavior is mandated by the JDBC specification.

With respect to handling of records with unique key values, UPDATE is similar to REPLACE in some ways, but the two aren't equivalent:

- UPDATE does nothing if there's no existing record in the table that contains the specified key values. REPLACE doesn't require an existing record with the key values and adds one if none exists.

- UPDATE can be used to change some columns in an existing record while leaving others unchanged. REPLACE entirely discards the existing record. To achieve the effect of leaving some columns unchanged with REPLACE, the new record must specify the same values in those columns that the existing record has. (Another way to update only some columns for an insert operation is to use INSERT with the ON DUPLICATE KEY UPDATE clause.)

11.4.1 Using UPDATE with ORDER BY and LIMIT

UPDATE by default makes no guarantee about the order in which rows are updated. This can sometimes result in problems. Suppose that the people table contains two rows, where id is a PRIMARY KEY:

```
mysql> SELECT * FROM people;
+----+--------+------+
| id | name   | age  |
+----+--------+------+
|  2 | Victor |   21 |
|  3 | Susan  |   15 |
+----+--------+------+
```

If you want to renumber the id values to begin at 1, you might issue this UPDATE statement:

```
UPDATE people SET id = id - 1;
```

The statement succeeds if it updates id values first by setting 2 to 1 and then 3 to 2. However, it fails if it first tries to set 3 to 2. That would result in two records having an id value of 2, so a duplicate-key violation occurs. To solve this problem, add an ORDER BY clause to cause the row updates to occur in a particular order:

```
UPDATE people SET id = id - 1 ORDER BY id;
```

UPDATE also allows a LIMIT clause, which places a limit on the number of records updated. For example, if you have two identical people records with a name value of 'Nicolas' and you want to change just one of them to 'Nick', use this statement:

```
UPDATE people SET name = 'Nick' WHERE name = 'Nicolas' LIMIT 1;
```

ORDER BY and LIMIT may be used together in the same UPDATE statement.

11.4.2 Preventing Dangerous UPDATE Statements

As mentioned earlier, an UPDATE statement that includes no WHERE clause updates every row in the table. Normally, this isn't what you want. It's much more common to update only a specific record or small set of records. An UPDATE with no WHERE is likely to be accidental, and the results can be catastrophic.

It's possible to prevent UPDATE statements from executing unless the records to be updated are identified by key values or a LIMIT clause is present. This might be helpful in preventing accidental overly broad table updates. The mysql client supports this feature if you invoke it with the --safe-updates option. See Section 2.9, "Using the --safe-updates Option," for more information.

11.4.3 Multiple-Table UPDATE Statements

UPDATE supports a multiple-table syntax that enables you to update a table using the contents of another table. This syntax also allows multiple tables to be updated simultaneously. The syntax has much in common with that used for writing multiple-table SELECT statements, so it's discussed in Section 12.5, "Multiple-Table UPDATE and DELETE Statements."

11.5 The DELETE and TRUNCATE TABLE Statements

To remove records from tables, use a DELETE statement or a TRUNCATE TABLE statement. The DELETE statement allows a WHERE clause that identifies which records to remove, whereas TRUNCATE TABLE always removes all records. DELETE therefore can be more precise in its effect.

To empty a table entirely by deleting all its records, you can use either of the following statements:

```
DELETE FROM table_name;
TRUNCATE TABLE table_name;
```

The word TABLE in TRUNCATE TABLE is optional.

To remove only specific records in a table, TRUNCATE TABLE cannot be used. You must issue a DELETE statement that includes a WHERE clause that identifies which records to remove:

```
DELETE FROM table_name WHERE ... ;
```

When you omit the WHERE clause from a DELETE statement, it's logically equivalent to a TRUNCATE TABLE statement in its effect, but there is an operational difference: If you need to know how many records were deleted, DELETE returns a true row count, but TRUNCATE TABLE returns 0.

If a table contains an AUTO_INCREMENT column, emptying it completely with TRUNCATE TABLE might have the side effect of resetting the sequence. This may also happen for a DELETE statement that includes no WHERE clause. Resetting the sequence causes the next record inserted into the table to be assigned an AUTO_INCREMENT value of 1. If this side effect is undesirable when emptying the table, use a WHERE clause that always evaluates to true:

```
DELETE FROM table_name WHERE 1;
```

The presence of the WHERE clause in this statement causes MySQL to evaluate it for each row. The expression 1 is always true, so the effect of the WHERE clause is to produce a row-by-row table-emptying operation. Note that although this form of DELETE avoids the side effect of resetting the AUTO_INCREMENT sequence when performing a complete-table deletion, the disadvantage is that the statement executes much more slowly than a DELETE with no WHERE.

The following comparison summarizes the differences between DELETE and TRUNCATE TABLE:

DELETE:

- Can delete specific rows from a table if a WHERE clause is included
- Usually executes more slowly
- Returns a true row count indicating the number of records deleted

TRUNCATE TABLE:

- Cannot delete just certain rows from a table; always completely empties it
- Usually executes more quickly
- Returns a row count of zero rather than the actual number of records deleted

11.5.1 Using DELETE with ORDER BY and LIMIT

DELETE supports ORDER BY and LIMIT clauses, which provides finer control over the way records are deleted. For example, LIMIT can be useful if you want to remove only some instances of a given set of records. Suppose that the people table contains five records where the name column equals 'Emily'. If you want only one such record, use the following statement to remove four of the duplicated records:

```
DELETE FROM people WHERE name = 'Emily' LIMIT 4;
```

Normally, MySQL makes no guarantees about which four of the five records selected by the WHERE clause it will delete. An ORDER BY clause in conjunction with LIMIT provides better control. For example, to delete four of the records containing 'Emily' but leave the one with the lowest id value, use ORDER BY and LIMIT together as follows:

```
DELETE FROM people WHERE name = 'Emily' ORDER BY id DESC LIMIT 4;
```

11.5.2 Multiple-Table DELETE Statements

DELETE supports a multiple-table syntax that enables you to delete records from a table based on the contents of another table. This syntax also allows records to be deleted from multiple tables simultaneously. The syntax has much in common with that used for writing multiple-table SELECT statements, so it's discussed in Section 12.5, "Multiple-Table UPDATE and DELETE Statements."

11.6 Privileges Required for Update Statements

The privileges required for statements that modify tables are straightforward:

- INSERT, UPDATE, and DELETE require the INSERT, UPDATE, and DELETE privileges, respectively.
- REPLACE inserts records, possibly after deleting old records, so it requires the INSERT and DELETE privileges.
- TRUNCATE TABLE is like DELETE in that it deletes records, so it requires the DELETE privilege.

MySQL Developer II Exam

12

Joins

This chapter covers the following exam topics:

- Writing inner joins using the comma (',') operator and INNER JOIN
- Writing outer joins using LEFT JOIN and RIGHT JOIN
- Resolving name clashes using qualifiers and aliases
- Writing self-joins
- Multiple-table UPDATE and DELETE statements

12.1 Overview

The SELECT queries shown thus far in this study guide retrieve information from a single table at a time. However, not all questions can be answered using just one table. When it's necessary to draw on information that is stored in multiple tables, use a join—an operation that produces a result by combining (joining) information in one table with information in another.

A join between tables is an extension of a single-table SELECT statement, but involves the following additional complexities:

- The FROM clause names all the tables needed to produce the query result, not just one table. The examples in this chapter focus on two-table joins, although in MySQL 5 a join can be extended up to 61 tables as necessary.
- A join that matches records in one table with records in another must specify how to match up the records. These conditions often are given in the WHERE clause, but the particular syntax depends on the type of join.
- The list of columns to display can include columns from any or all of the tables involved in the join.
- If a join refers to a column name that appears in more than one table, the name is ambiguous and you must indicate which table you mean each time you refer to the column.

These complications are addressed in this chapter, which covers the following join-related topics:

- Writing inner joins, which find matches between tables. Inner joins are written using either the comma operator or the INNER JOIN keywords.

- Writing outer joins, which can find matches between tables, but also can identify mismatches (rows in one table not matched by any rows in the other). Outer joins include left and right joins, written using the LEFT JOIN and RIGHT JOIN keywords.

- Using qualifiers and aliases to resolve ambiguity between identifiers that have the same name. Some queries involve tables or columns that have identical names (for example, if two tables each have an id column). Under these circumstances, it's necessary to provide the appropriate database or table name to specify the query more precisely. Aliasing can also be useful in some cases to resolve ambiguities.

- Writing self-joins that join a table to itself.

- Multiple-table UPDATE and DELETE statements. These involve some of the same join concepts as multiple-table SELECT statements.

The material in this chapter builds directly on the single-table SELECT concepts described earlier in this study guide, and it's assumed that you're familiar with those concepts. See Chapter 9, "Querying for Data."

The examples in this chapter are based primarily on the tables in the world database. These tables contain information that can be combined using joins to answer questions that cannot be answered using a single table. For example, you might ask, "What are the names of the countries where people speak Swedish?" The CountryLanguage table lists languages per country, but it contains three-letter country codes, not full names. The Country table lists three-letter codes and full names, so you can use the codes to match up records in the tables and associate a country name with each language.

12.2 Writing Inner Joins

A join that identifies combinations of matching rows from two tables is called an inner join. Inner joins may be written using two different syntaxes. One syntax lists the tables to be joined separated by a comma. The other uses the INNER JOIN keywords.

12.2.1 Writing Inner Joins with the Comma Operator

A simple question you might ask about the information in the world database is, "What languages are spoken in each country?" That question has a trivial answer if you don't mind listing countries by code. Just select the information from the CountryLanguage table. Two of its columns list three-letter country codes and language names:

```
mysql> SELECT CountryCode, Language FROM CountryLanguage;
```

```
+-------------+------------------+
| CountryCode | Language         |
+-------------+------------------+
| ABW         | Dutch            |
| ABW         | English          |
| ABW         | Papiamento       |
| ABW         | Spanish          |
| AFG         | Balochi          |
| AFG         | Dari             |
| AFG         | Pashto           |
| AFG         | Turkmenian       |
| AFG         | Uzbek            |
| AGO         | Ambo             |
| AGO         | Chokwe           |
| AGO         | Kongo            |
| AGO         | Luchazi          |
| AGO         | Luimbe-nganguela |
| AGO         | Luvale           |
...
```

That result would be more meaningful and easier to understand if it displayed countries identified by full name. However, that cannot be done using just the `CountryLanguage` table, which contains country codes and not names. Country names are available in the `world` database, but they're stored in a different table (the `Country` table that contains both the three-letter codes and the names):

```
mysql> SELECT Code, Name FROM Country;
+------+----------------------+
| Code | Name                 |
+------+----------------------+
| AFG  | Afghanistan          |
| NLD  | Netherlands          |
| ANT  | Netherlands Antilles |
| ALB  | Albania              |
| DZA  | Algeria              |
| ASM  | American Samoa       |
| AND  | Andorra              |
| AGO  | Angola               |
| AIA  | Anguilla             |
| ATG  | Antigua and Barbuda  |
| ARE  | United Arab Emirates |
| ARG  | Argentina            |
| ARM  | Armenia              |
| ABW  | Aruba                |
| AUS  | Australia            |
...
```

A query to display languages and full country names can be written as a join that matches the country codes in the CountryLanguage table with those in the Country table. To do that, modify the CountryLanguage query in the following ways:

- Change the FROM clause to name both the CountryLanguage and Country tables, separated by a comma. This tells MySQL that it must consult multiple tables to process the query.

- Add a WHERE clause that indicates how to match records in the two tables. A join has the potential to generate all combinations of rows from the two tables, which generally is more information than is desirable or of interest. A WHERE clause restricts the output by telling MySQL which of these combinations you want to see. To choose the proper matches for the query in question, use the country code values that are common to the two tables. That is, match CountryCode values in the CountryLanguage table with Code values in the Country table.

- Change the output column list to display the Name column from the Country table rather than the CountryCode column from the CountryLanguage table.

The statement that results from these changes is as follows:

```
mysql> SELECT Name, Language FROM CountryLanguage, Country
    -> WHERE CountryCode = Code;
+----------------------+------------+
| Name                 | Language   |
+----------------------+------------+
| Afghanistan          | Balochi    |
| Afghanistan          | Dari       |
| Afghanistan          | Pashto     |
| Afghanistan          | Turkmenian |
| Afghanistan          | Uzbek      |
| Netherlands          | Arabic     |
| Netherlands          | Dutch      |
| Netherlands          | Fries      |
| Netherlands          | Turkish    |
| Netherlands Antilles | Dutch      |
| Netherlands Antilles | English    |
| Netherlands Antilles | Papiamento |
| Albania              | Albaniana  |
| Albania              | Greek      |
| Albania              | Macedonian |
...
```

Essentially what this query does is treat Country as a lookup table. For any given country code in the CountryLanguage table, the query uses that code to find the corresponding row in the Country table and retrieves the country name from that row.

Note several things about this query and the result that it produces:

- For an inner join, the order in which the FROM clause names the tables doesn't matter. Both of these FROM clauses would work:

```
FROM CountryLanguage, Country
FROM Country, CountryLanguage
```

- The output column list of the join displays one column from each table: Name from Country and Language from CountryLanguage. However, that is not a necessary characteristic of joins. The list can name any columns that are appropriate for your purposes, from any of the joined tables. Suppose that you want to show both country code and name, as well as the continent in which each country is located. The following statement does that by adding two columns to the output column list:

```
mysql> SELECT Code, Name, Continent, Language
    -> FROM CountryLanguage, Country
    -> WHERE CountryCode = Code;
+------+---------------------+---------------+-----------+
| Code | Name                | Continent     | Language  |
+------+---------------------+---------------+-----------+
| AFG  | Afghanistan         | Asia          | Balochi   |
| AFG  | Afghanistan         | Asia          | Dari      |
| AFG  | Afghanistan         | Asia          | Pashto    |
| AFG  | Afghanistan         | Asia          | Turkmenian |
| AFG  | Afghanistan         | Asia          | Uzbek     |
| NLD  | Netherlands         | Europe        | Arabic    |
| NLD  | Netherlands         | Europe        | Dutch     |
| NLD  | Netherlands         | Europe        | Fries     |
| NLD  | Netherlands         | Europe        | Turkish   |
| ANT  | Netherlands Antilles | North America | Dutch     |
| ANT  | Netherlands Antilles | North America | English   |
| ANT  | Netherlands Antilles | North America | Papiamento |
| ALB  | Albania             | Europe        | Albaniana |
| ALB  | Albania             | Europe        | Greek     |
| ALB  | Albania             | Europe        | Macedonian |
+------+---------------------+---------------+-----------+
...
```

Or suppose that you want to display each language together with the percentage of people who speak it. Select the Percentage column from the CountryLanguage table:

```
mysql> SELECT Name, Language, Percentage FROM CountryLanguage, Country
    -> WHERE CountryCode = Code;
+---------------------+------------+------------+
| Name                | Language   | Percentage |
+---------------------+------------+------------+
| Afghanistan         | Pashto     |       52.4 |
| Netherlands         | Dutch      |       95.6 |
| Netherlands Antilles | Papiamento |       86.2 |
```

```
| Albania             | Albaniana     |   97.9 |
| Algeria             | Arabic        |   86.0 |
| American Samoa      | Samoan        |   90.6 |
| Andorra             | Spanish       |   44.6 |
| Angola              | Ovimbundu     |   37.2 |
| Anguilla            | English       |    0.0 |
| Antigua and Barbuda | Creole English |   95.7 |
| United Arab Emirates | Arabic       |   42.0 |
| Argentina           | Spanish       |   96.8 |
| Armenia             | Armenian      |   93.4 |
| Aruba               | Papiamento    |   76.7 |
| Australia           | English       |   81.2 |
...
```

- As with any other SELECT, the output rows from a join do not appear in any particular order by default. To sort the results, add an ORDER BY clause. Output from the preceding query would be more easily understood with the rows sorted by country name and language percentage. That enables you to see which languages are most prevalent for countries in which multiple languages are spoken.

```
mysql> SELECT Name, Language, Percentage FROM CountryLanguage, Country
    -> WHERE CountryCode = Code ORDER BY Name, Percentage;
+-----------------+------------+------------+
| Name            | Language   | Percentage |
+-----------------+------------+------------+
| Afghanistan     | Balochi    |        0.9 |
| Afghanistan     | Turkmenian |        1.9 |
| Afghanistan     | Uzbek      |        8.8 |
| Afghanistan     | Dari       |       32.1 |
| Afghanistan     | Pashto     |       52.4 |
| Albania         | Macedonian |        0.1 |
| Albania         | Greek      |        1.8 |
| Albania         | Albaniana  |       97.9 |
| Algeria         | Berberi    |       14.0 |
| Algeria         | Arabic     |       86.0 |
| American Samoa  | English    |        3.1 |
| American Samoa  | Tongan     |        3.1 |
| American Samoa  | Samoan     |       90.6 |
| Andorra         | French     |        6.2 |
| Andorra         | Portuguese |       10.8 |
...
```

The joins shown thus far each have included a WHERE clause. Syntactically, the WHERE clause in a join is optional. However, it's usually necessary in practice to include a WHERE clause to keep the join from producing output far in excess of what you really want to see and to make sure that the output contains only information that's meaningful for the question you're asking.

A join can produce every combination of rows from the two tables, which is in fact what you'll get from an unrestricted join that includes no WHERE clause. This is called a Cartesian product, and the number of rows in the result is the product of the number of rows in the individual tables. For example, the Country and CountryLanguage tables contain approximately 240 and 1,000 rows, respectively, so a Cartesian product between them produces about 240,000 rows. But much of such output is irrelevant because most of the combinations aren't meaningful.

The following query shows what happens if you join records in the CountryLanguage and Country tables without a WHERE clause. The query displays the code from both tables to show that even non-matching combinations are produced by an unrestricted join:

```
mysql> SELECT Code, Name, CountryCode, Language
    -> FROM CountryLanguage, Country;
+------+-------------+-------------+------------------+
| Code | Name        | CountryCode | Language         |
+------+-------------+-------------+------------------+
| AFG  | Afghanistan | ABW         | Dutch            |
| AFG  | Afghanistan | ABW         | English          |
| AFG  | Afghanistan | ABW         | Papiamento       |
| AFG  | Afghanistan | ABW         | Spanish          |
| AFG  | Afghanistan | AFG         | Balochi          |
| AFG  | Afghanistan | AFG         | Dari             |
| AFG  | Afghanistan | AFG         | Pashto           |
| AFG  | Afghanistan | AFG         | Turkmenian       |
| AFG  | Afghanistan | AFG         | Uzbek            |
| AFG  | Afghanistan | AGO         | Ambo             |
| AFG  | Afghanistan | AGO         | Chokwe           |
| AFG  | Afghanistan | AGO         | Kongo            |
| AFG  | Afghanistan | AGO         | Luchazi          |
| AFG  | Afghanistan | AGO         | Luimbe-nganguela |
| AFG  | Afghanistan | AGO         | Luvale           |
...
```

If you're using the mysql client program and want to guard against the possibility of generating huge result sets due to forgetting a WHERE clause, invoke the program with the --safe-updates option (which, despite its name, also affects output from joins). See Section 2.9, "Using the --safe-updates Option," for more information.

The WHERE clause for a join specifies how to match records in the joined tables and eliminates non-corresponding combinations of rows from the output. The WHERE clause also can include additional conditions to further restrict the output and answer more specific questions. Here are some examples:

- *In which countries is the Swedish language spoken?* To answer this, include a condition that identifies the language in which you are interested:

```
mysql> SELECT Name, Language FROM CountryLanguage, Country
    -> WHERE CountryCode = Code AND Language = 'Swedish';
+---------+----------+
| Name    | Language |
+---------+----------+
| Norway  | Swedish  |
| Sweden  | Swedish  |
| Finland | Swedish  |
| Denmark | Swedish  |
+---------+----------+
```

- *What languages are spoken in the country of Sweden?* This question is the complement of the previous one, and can be answered by using a condition that identifies the country of interest rather than the language:

```
mysql> SELECT Name, Language FROM CountryLanguage, Country
    -> WHERE CountryCode = Code AND Name = 'Sweden';
+--------+--------------------------+
| Name   | Language                 |
+--------+--------------------------+
| Sweden | Arabic                   |
| Sweden | Finnish                  |
| Sweden | Norwegian                |
| Sweden | Southern Slavic Languages |
| Sweden | Spanish                  |
| Sweden | Swedish                  |
+--------+--------------------------+
```

Joins can use any of the constructs allowed for single-table SELECT statements. The following join uses the COUNT() function and a GROUP BY clause to summarize the number of languages spoken per country, and a HAVING clause to restrict the output to include only those countries where more than 10 languages are spoken:

```
mysql> SELECT COUNT(*), Name
    -> FROM CountryLanguage, Country
    -> WHERE CountryCode = Code
    -> GROUP BY Name
    -> HAVING COUNT(*) > 10;
+----------+--------------------+
| COUNT(*) | Name               |
+----------+--------------------+
|       12 | Canada             |
|       12 | China              |
|       12 | India              |
|       12 | Russian Federation |
|       11 | South Africa       |
|       11 | Tanzania           |
```

```
|      12 | United States      |
+---------+--------------------+
```

12.2.2 Writing Inner Joins with INNER JOIN

The form of inner join syntax just discussed uses the comma operator in the FROM clause to name the joined tables. Another inner join syntax uses the INNER JOIN keywords. With this syntax, those keywords replace the comma operator between table names in the FROM clause. Also, with INNER JOIN, the conditions that indicate how to perform record matching for the tables move from the WHERE clause to become part of the FROM clause.

There are two syntaxes for specifying matching conditions with INNER JOIN queries:

- Add ON and an expression that states the required relationship between tables. Suppose that a join performs a country code match between the CountryLanguage and Country tables. With the comma operator, you write the join as follows:

```
SELECT Name, Language
FROM CountryLanguage, Country WHERE CountryCode = Code;
```

  With INNER JOIN and ON, write the query like this instead:

```
SELECT Name, Language
FROM CountryLanguage INNER JOIN Country ON CountryCode = Code;
```

- If the name of the joined column is the same in both tables, you can add USING() rather than ON after the table names, and list the name within the parentheses. For example, if the country code column happened to be named Code in both tables, you could write the query like this:

```
SELECT Name, Language
FROM CountryLanguage INNER JOIN Country USING(Code);
```

  If you're joining the tables using more than one pair of like-named columns, list the column names within the parentheses of the USING() clause separated by commas.

JOIN and CROSS JOIN are synonymous with INNER JOIN.

12.3 Writing Outer Joins

As described in the preceding sections, an inner join produces results by selecting combinations of matching rows from the joined tables. However, it cannot find non-matches; that is, instances where a row in one table has no match in another table. For example, an inner join can associate country names listed in the Country table with the languages spoken in those countries through a join based on country codes with the CountryLanguage table. But it cannot tell you which countries aren't associated with any language in the CountryLanguage table. Answering the latter question is a matter of identifying which country codes present in the Country table are *not* present in the CountryLanguage table.

To write a join that provides information about mismatches or missing records, use an outer join. An outer join finds matches (just like an inner join), but also identifies mismatches. Furthermore, with an appropriate WHERE clause, an outer join can filter out matches to display only the mismatches.

Two common forms of outer joins are left joins and right joins. These are written using the LEFT JOIN or RIGHT JOIN keywords rather than the comma operator or the INNER JOIN keywords.

Left and right joins can answer the same kinds of questions and differ only slightly in their syntax. That is, a left join can always be rewritten into an equivalent right join.

In the following sections, the terms "left table" and "right table" refer to the tables named first and second in the FROM clause, respectively.

12.3.1 Writing LEFT JOIN Queries

A left join is a type of outer join, written using the LEFT JOIN keywords. A left join treats the left table (the first one named) as a reference table and produces output for each row selected from it, whether or not the row is matched by rows in the right table. Like a join written with the INNER JOIN keywords, a LEFT JOIN is written using either ON or USING() after the table names in the FROM clause. The examples here use the ON syntax. See Section 12.2.2, "Writing Inner Joins with INNER JOIN," for details on USING() syntax.

To see the difference between an inner join and a left join, begin with the former. An inner join between the CountryLanguage and Country tables might be written like this:

```
mysql> SELECT Name, Language
    -> FROM Country INNER JOIN CountryLanguage ON Code = CountryCode;
+-------------------------------------+--------------------------+
| Name                                | Language                 |
+-------------------------------------+--------------------------+
| Afghanistan                         | Balochi                  |
| Afghanistan                         | Dari                     |
| Afghanistan                         | Pashto                   |
| Afghanistan                         | Turkmenian               |
| Afghanistan                         | Uzbek                    |
| Netherlands                         | Arabic                   |
| Netherlands                         | Dutch                    |
| Netherlands                         | Fries                    |
| Netherlands                         | Turkish                  |
...
| Palestine                           | Arabic                   |
| Palestine                           | Hebrew                   |
| United States Minor Outlying Islands | English                 |
+-------------------------------------+--------------------------+
```

That query displays information from table row combinations that have matching country code values. A LEFT JOIN has a similar syntax (replace INNER JOIN with LEFT JOIN), but produces a different result:

```
mysql> SELECT Name, Language
    -> FROM Country LEFT JOIN CountryLanguage ON Code = CountryCode;
+-----------------------------------------------+-------------------------+
| Name                                          | Language                |
+-----------------------------------------------+-------------------------+
| Afghanistan                                   | Balochi                 |
| Afghanistan                                   | Dari                    |
| Afghanistan                                   | Pashto                  |
| Afghanistan                                   | Turkmenian              |
| Afghanistan                                   | Uzbek                   |
| Netherlands                                   | Arabic                  |
| Netherlands                                   | Dutch                   |
| Netherlands                                   | Fries                   |
| Netherlands                                   | Turkish                 |
| ...                                           |                         |
| Palestine                                     | Arabic                  |
| Palestine                                     | Hebrew                  |
| Antarctica                                    | NULL                    |
| Bouvet Island                                 | NULL                    |
| British Indian Ocean Territory                | NULL                    |
| South Georgia and the South Sandwich Islands  | NULL                    |
| Heard Island and McDonald Islands             | NULL                    |
| French Southern territories                   | NULL                    |
| United States Minor Outlying Islands          | English                 |
+-----------------------------------------------+-------------------------+
```

In this query, the left table is the one named first (Country) and the right table is the one named second (CountryLanguage).

Notice that the LEFT JOIN finds both matches and non-matches. That is, it displays all the rows produced by the inner join, plus a few more besides:

- If a row from the left table matches any right table rows, the result includes for each match a row containing the left table columns and the right table columns. These are rows that an inner join also will produce.

- If the left table row doesn't match any right table rows, the result includes a row containing the left table column values and NULL for any columns from the right table. These are rows that an outer join will produce but an inner join will not.

For the LEFT JOIN just shown, rows in Country not matched by any CountryLanguage rows correspond to countries for which no language is listed. These are the extra rows not produced by an inner join. Any columns that come from CountryLanguage are set to NULL. The NULL values serve two purposes:

- For a query such as the preceding one that displays both matches and non-matches, the NULL values identify which output rows represent non-matches.

- If you're interested *only* in non-matches, you can add a condition that restricts the output to only those rows that contain these NULL values.

For example, the question "Which countries have no languages listed?" is equivalent to asking which country codes in the Country table aren't matched by codes in the CountryLanguage table. To answer the question, write a LEFT JOIN and require row combinations to have NULL in the right table column:

```
mysql> SELECT Name, Language
    -> FROM Country LEFT JOIN CountryLanguage ON Code = CountryCode
    -> WHERE CountryCode IS NULL;
+-----------------------------------------------+----------+
| Name                                          | Language |
+-----------------------------------------------+----------+
| Antarctica                                    | NULL     |
| Bouvet Island                                 | NULL     |
| British Indian Ocean Territory                | NULL     |
| South Georgia and the South Sandwich Islands  | NULL     |
| Heard Island and McDonald Islands             | NULL     |
| French Southern territories                   | NULL     |
+-----------------------------------------------+----------+
```

Because Language is always NULL in the output, you probably would not bother displaying it:

```
mysql> SELECT Name
    -> FROM Country LEFT JOIN CountryLanguage ON Code = CountryCode
    -> WHERE CountryCode IS NULL;
+-----------------------------------------------+
| Name                                          |
+-----------------------------------------------+
| Antarctica                                    |
| Bouvet Island                                 |
| British Indian Ocean Territory                |
| South Georgia and the South Sandwich Islands  |
| Heard Island and McDonald Islands             |
| French Southern territories                   |
+-----------------------------------------------+
```

As mentioned earlier, the order in which you name the tables in the FROM clause doesn't matter for an inner join. The query results are the same regardless of which table you name first. That is not true for an outer join; the output depends very much on the order in which the tables are named. With a LEFT JOIN, the reference table should be listed on the left and the table from which rows might be missing should be listed on the right.

If you're looking only for matches between tables, you can do so with either an inner or outer join. In such cases, it's better to use an inner join because that allows the MySQL optimizer to choose the most efficient order for processing the tables. Outer joins require that the reference table be processed first, which might not be the most efficient order.

12.3.2 Writing RIGHT JOIN Queries

A right join is another type of outer join, written using the RIGHT JOIN keywords. Every right join corresponds to an equivalent left join. The only difference is that the roles of the tables in a right join are reversed relative to the roles in a left join. That is, the right table is the reference table, so a RIGHT JOIN produces a result for each row in the right table, whether or not it has any match in the left table. Thus, if you write a LEFT JOIN as follows:

```
SELECT ... FROM t1 LEFT JOIN t2 ON t1_column = t2_column ...
```

You can convert it to a RIGHT JOIN like this:

```
SELECT ... FROM t2 RIGHT JOIN t1 ON t2_column = t1_column ...
```

For example, a LEFT JOIN query to display countries in the Country table that have no languages listed in the CountryLanguage table can be written this way:

```
mysql> SELECT Name
    -> FROM Country LEFT JOIN CountryLanguage ON Code = CountryCode
    -> WHERE CountryCode IS NULL;
+-----------------------------------------------+
| Name                                          |
+-----------------------------------------------+
| Antarctica                                    |
| Bouvet Island                                 |
| British Indian Ocean Territory                |
| South Georgia and the South Sandwich Islands  |
| Heard Island and McDonald Islands             |
| French Southern territories                   |
+-----------------------------------------------+
```

The corresponding RIGHT JOIN looks like this:

```
mysql> SELECT Name
    -> FROM CountryLanguage RIGHT JOIN Country ON CountryCode = Code
    -> WHERE CountryCode IS NULL;
+-----------------------------------------------+
| Name                                          |
+-----------------------------------------------+
| Antarctica                                    |
| Bouvet Island                                 |
| British Indian Ocean Territory                |
| South Georgia and the South Sandwich Islands  |
```

```
| Heard Island and McDonald Islands              |
| French Southern territories                    |
+------------------------------------------------+
```

Syntactically, converting a left join to a right join requires only that you reverse the order in which you name the tables. It isn't necessary to also reverse the order in which you name the columns in the ON clause, but it can help make the query clearer to name the columns in the same order as the tables in which they appear.

12.4 Resolving Name Clashes Using Qualifiers and Aliases

When you join tables, it's often the case that the tables contain columns with the same names. If you refer to such a column in the query, it's ambiguous which table the column reference applies to. This ambiguity usually can be addressed by qualifying column names with table names. However, if you join a table to itself, even the table name is ambiguous and it's necessary to use aliases to disambiguate table references. This section describes how to address naming issues in queries by qualifying column and table names and by using aliases.

12.4.1 Qualifying Column Names

In each of the joins shown earlier in this chapter, the column names are unambiguous because no query refers to a column that appears in more than one of the joined tables. But it will often be the case that a join involves tables that have similarly named columns. If a column name used in the query appears in more than one table, the name is ambiguous and it's necessary to provide information that identifies which table you mean. To do this, qualify the column name with the appropriate table name.

Suppose that you want to list, for each country named in the Country table, all of its cities named in the City table. In principle, this is a simple query that associates country names and city names based on the country codes that are common to the two tables. In practice, there is a small complication:

```
mysql> SELECT Name, Name FROM Country, City
    -> WHERE Code = CountryCode;
ERROR 1052 (23000): Column: 'Name' in field list is ambiguous
```

The problem here is that the country name column in the Country table and the city name column in the City table both are called Name. MySQL has no way to know which instance of Name in the query goes with which table.

To resolve this ambiguity, qualify the references to Name with the appropriate table name so that MySQL can tell which table to use for each reference:

```
mysql> SELECT Country.Name, City.Name FROM Country, City
    -> WHERE Code = CountryCode;
+-------------+----------------+
| Name        | Name           |
+-------------+----------------+
| Afghanistan | Kabul          |
| Afghanistan | Qandahar       |
| Afghanistan | Herat          |
| Afghanistan | Mazar-e-Sharif |
| Netherlands | Amsterdam      |
| Netherlands | Rotterdam      |
| Netherlands | Haag           |
| Netherlands | Utrecht        |
| Netherlands | Eindhoven      |
| Netherlands | Tilburg        |
| Netherlands | Groningen      |
| Netherlands | Breda          |
| Netherlands | Apeldoorn      |
| Netherlands | Nijmegen       |
| Netherlands | Enschede       |
...
```

Although it might not always be necessary to provide table qualifiers in a join, it's always allowable to do so. Thus, Code and CountryCode in the preceding example are unambiguous because each appears in only one table, but you can qualify them explicitly if you want to do so:

```
mysql> SELECT Country.Name, City.Name FROM Country, City
    -> WHERE Country.Code = City.CountryCode;
+-------------+----------------+
| Name        | Name           |
+-------------+----------------+
| Afghanistan | Kabul          |
| Afghanistan | Qandahar       |
| Afghanistan | Herat          |
| Afghanistan | Mazar-e-Sharif |
| Netherlands | Amsterdam      |
| Netherlands | Rotterdam      |
| Netherlands | Haag           |
| Netherlands | Utrecht        |
| Netherlands | Eindhoven      |
| Netherlands | Tilburg        |
| Netherlands | Groningen      |
| Netherlands | Breda          |
| Netherlands | Apeldoorn      |
| Netherlands | Nijmegen       |
| Netherlands | Enschede       |
...
```

Adding qualifiers even when they aren't necessary to enable MySQL to understand a query often can make the query easier for people to understand, particularly those who are unfamiliar with the tables. Without the qualifiers, it might not be evident which table each column comes from.

More complex queries might involve multiple ambiguous columns. For example, the Country and City tables each have a Population column, and you can compare them to identify cities that contain more than 75% of their country's population:

```
mysql> SELECT Country.Name, Country.Population, City.Name, City.Population
    -> FROM City, Country
    -> WHERE City.CountryCode = Country.Code
    -> AND (Country.Population * .75) < City.Population;
+---------------------------+------------+--------------+------------+
| Name                      | Population | Name         | Population |
+---------------------------+------------+--------------+------------+
| Falkland Islands          |       2000 | Stanley      |       1636 |
| Gibraltar                 |      25000 | Gibraltar    |      27025 |
| Cocos (Keeling) Islands   |        600 | Bantam       |        503 |
| Macao                     |     473000 | Macao        |     437500 |
| Pitcairn                  |         50 | Adamstown    |         42 |
| Saint Pierre and Miquelon |       7000 | Saint-Pierre |       5808 |
| Singapore                 |    3567000 | Singapore    |    4017733 |
+---------------------------+------------+--------------+------------+
```

Both Name and Population require table qualifiers in this query because each is ambiguous.

12.4.2 Qualifying and Aliasing Table Names

Qualifying column names with table names resolves many column name ambiguities, but sometimes even the table name is ambiguous. This happens in two ways.

First, you might perform a join between tables that have the same name but come from different databases. In this case, you provide not only table names as qualifiers, but database names as well. Suppose that two databases world1 and world2 both have a table named Country and that you want to determine which names are present in both tables. The query can be written like this:

```
SELECT world1.Country.Name
FROM world1.Country, world2.Country
WHERE world1.Country.Name = world2.Country.Name;
```

Second, a table name is always ambiguous when you join the table to itself using a self-join. For example, the Country table in the world database contains an IndepYear column indicating the year in which each country achieved independence. To find all countries that have the same year of independence as some given country, you can use a self-join. However, you cannot write the query like this:

```
mysql> SELECT IndepYear, Name, Name
    -> FROM Country, Country
    -> WHERE IndepYear = IndepYear AND Name = 'Qatar';
ERROR 1066 (42000): Not unique table/alias: 'Country'
```

Furthermore, you cannot remove the ambiguity from column references by preceding them with table name qualifiers because the names remain identical:

```
mysql> SELECT Country.IndepYear, Country.Name, Country.Name
    -> FROM Country, Country
    -> WHERE Country.IndepYear = Country.IndepYear
    -> AND Country.Name = 'Qatar';
ERROR 1066 (42000): Not unique table/alias: 'Country'
```

It doesn't even help to add a database name qualifier because the database is the same for both tables. To address this naming issue, create an alias for one or both table references and refer to the aliases elsewhere in the query. The aliases give you alternative unambiguous names by which to refer to each instance of the table in the query. Here is one solution that aliases both tables:

```
mysql> SELECT t1.IndepYear, t1.Name, t2.Name
    -> FROM Country AS t1, Country AS t2
    -> WHERE t1.IndepYear = t2.IndepYear AND t1.Name = 'Qatar';
+-----------+-------+----------------------+
| IndepYear | Name  | Name                 |
+-----------+-------+----------------------+
|      1971 | Qatar | United Arab Emirates |
|      1971 | Qatar | Bahrain              |
|      1971 | Qatar | Bangladesh           |
|      1971 | Qatar | Qatar                |
+-----------+-------+----------------------+
```

12.5 Multiple-Table UPDATE and DELETE Statements

MySQL allows the use of join syntax in UPDATE and DELETE statements to enable updates or deletes that involve multiple tables. Such statements can be used to perform the following operations:

- Update rows in one table by transferring information from another table
- Update rows in one table, determining which rows to update by referring to another table
- Update rows in multiple tables with a single statement

- Delete rows from one table, determining which rows to delete by referring to another table
- Delete rows from multiple tables with a single statement

Some of the principles involved in writing joins in SELECT statements also apply to multiple-table UPDATE and DELETE statements. This section provides a brief overview of their syntax.

A multiple-table UPDATE is an extension of a single-table statement:

- Following the UPDATE keyword, name the tables involved in the operation, separated by commas. (You must name all the tables used in the query, even if you aren't updating all of them.)
- In the WHERE clause, describe the conditions that determine how to match records in the tables.
- In the SET clause, assign values to the columns to be updated. These assignments can refer to columns from any of the joined tables.

For example, this statement identifies matching records in two tables based on id values, and then copies the name column from t2 to t1:

```
UPDATE t1, t2 SET t1.name = t2.name WHERE t1.id = t2.id;
```

Multiple-table DELETE statements can be written in two formats. The following example demonstrates one syntax, for a query that deletes rows from a table t1 where the id values match those in a table t2:

```
DELETE t1 FROM t1, t2 WHERE t1.id = t2.id;
```

The second syntax is slightly different:

```
DELETE FROM t1 USING t1, t2 WHERE t1.id = t2.id;
```

To delete the matching records from both tables, the statements are:

```
DELETE t1, t2 FROM t1, t2 WHERE t1.id = t2.id;
DELETE FROM t1, t2 USING t1, t2 WHERE t1.id = t2.id;
```

The ORDER BY and LIMIT clauses normally supported by UPDATE and DELETE aren't allowed when these statements are used for multiple-table operations.

Subqueries

A subquery is a SELECT statement that is placed within parentheses inside another SQL statement. This chapter discusses how to use subqueries. It covers the following exam topics:

- Type of subqueries
- Using each type of subquery
- Converting subqueries to inner and outer joins
- Using subqueries in statements that modify tables

13.1 Types of Subqueries

In this chapter, we divide subqueries into four general categories, which affect the contexts in which they can be used:

- *Scalar subqueries* return a single value; that is, one row with one column of data.
- *Row subqueries* return a single row with one or more columns of data.
- *Column subqueries* return a single column with one or more rows of data.
- *Table subqueries* return a result with one or more rows containing one or more columns of data.

The following example shows how a simple subquery works. We use the two tables Country and CountryLanguage from the world database to find the languages spoken in Finland:

```
mysql> SELECT Language
    -> FROM CountryLanguage
    -> WHERE CountryCode = (SELECT Code
    ->                      FROM Country
    ->                      WHERE Name='Finland');
+----------+
| Language |
+----------+
| Estonian |
```

```
| Finnish  |
| Russian  |
| Saame    |
| Swedish  |
+----------+
```

The following statement uses a subquery to determine which country has the most populous city in the world:

```
mysql> SELECT  Country.Name
    -> FROM    Country, City
    -> WHERE   Country.Code = City.CountryCode
    ->   AND   City.Population = (SELECT MAX(Population)
    ->                              FROM City);
+-------+
| Name  |
+-------+
| India |
+-------+
```

As you will undoubtedly notice in many of the descriptions and examples in this section, many uses of subqueries can be rewritten to completely equivalent (and often more efficient) queries using joins. Nonetheless, subqueries are preferred by many as an alternative way of specifying relations that otherwise requires complex joins or unions. Some users insist on using subqueries simply because they find them much more readable and easier to maintain than queries involving complex joins. Reasons to convert a subquery to a join are that the join may be more efficient than the equivalent subquery, or you might need to run a query using an older version of MySQL that does not support subqueries. (Subquery support was added in MySQL 4.1.)

13.2 Subqueries as Scalar Expressions

Scalar subqueries can appear almost anywhere that a scalar value is allowed by the SQL syntax. This means that you can use subqueries as function parameters, use mathematical operators on subqueries that contain numeric values, and so forth. The following example shows how to use a scalar subquery as a parameter to the CONCAT() function:

```
mysql> SELECT CONCAT('The country code for Finland is: ',
    ->               (SELECT Code
    ->                FROM Country
    ->                WHERE Name='Finland')) AS s1;
+------------------------------------+
| s1                                 |
+------------------------------------+
| The country code for Finland is: FIN |
+------------------------------------+
```

Notice that the subquery must be enclosed in parentheses here, just as in any other context where a subquery may appear.

The next example shows the use of scalar subqueries in a mathematical expression that calculates the ratio of the people living in cities to that of the world population:

```
mysql> SELECT (SELECT SUM(Population) FROM City) /
    ->        (SELECT SUM(Population) FROM Country) AS ratio;
+-------+
| ratio |
+-------+
|  0.24 |
+-------+
```

A scalar subquery result can be assigned to a user variable for later use. The previous example can be written with user variables as follows:

```
SET @city_pop = (SELECT SUM(Population) FROM City);
SET @country_pop = (SELECT SUM(Population) FROM Country);
SELECT @city_pop / @country_pop;
```

There are some contexts in which scalar subqueries are not allowed. You cannot use a scalar subquery when a literal value is required, such as for an argument in a LIMIT clause.

13.3 Correlated Subqueries

Subqueries can be non-correlated or correlated:

- A non-correlated subquery contains no references to the outer query and is not dependent on it. As a result, a non-correlated subquery could be evaluated as a completely separate statement.
- A correlated subquery contains references to the values in the outer query and cannot be evaluated independently of it.

In the following correlated subquery, we calculate which country on each populated continent has the largest population. The value of the column Continent, which appears in the outer query, is used to limit which rows to consider for the MAX() calculation in the subquery:

```
mysql> SELECT Continent, Name, Population
    -> FROM Country c
    -> WHERE Population = (SELECT MAX(Population)
    ->                     FROM Country c2
    ->                     WHERE c.Continent=c2.Continent
    ->                     AND Population > 0
    ->                     );
+---------------+---------------------+------------+
```

```
| Continent      | Name                | Population |
+----------------+---------------------+------------+
| Oceania        | Australia           |   18886000 |
| South America  | Brazil              |  170115000 |
| Asia           | China               | 1277558000 |
| Africa         | Nigeria             |  111506000 |
| Europe         | Russian Federation  |  146934000 |
| North America  | United States       |  278357000 |
+----------------+---------------------+------------+
```

Note how the table qualifiers c and c2 are used in the example. This is necessary because the columns that are used to correlate values from the inner and outer queries come from different references to the same table and thus have the same name.

13.4 Comparing Subquery Results to Outer Query Columns

The scalar subquery examples shown in previous sections use the = equality operator to compare a single column to the value returned by the subquery. But you are not limited to using the = equality operator. When comparing the values in the outer query with those returned by a scalar subquery, you can use any of the usual comparison operators, such as =, <, >, <>, and >=.

When a comparison requires a scalar subquery, it is an error if the subquery returns more than a single value. Suppose that we wanted to find out whether there is a country that has a city with a population of less than 100, using the following subquery:

```
mysql> SELECT Code c, Name
    -> FROM Country
    -> WHERE 100 > (SELECT Population
    ->                FROM City
    ->                WHERE CountryCode = c);
ERROR 1242 (21000): Subquery returns more than 1 row
```

The subquery returns more than one value, so the statement fails.

Other subquery comparison operations do not require scalar subqueries. The following sections describe operations that allow column subqueries. Section 13.5, "Comparison Using Row Subqueries," discusses how to compare rows.

13.4.1 Using ALL, ANY, and SOME

To perform a comparison between a scalar value and a subquery that returns several rows of data in a single column (a column subquery), we must use a *quantified comparison*. The quantifier keywords ALL, ANY, and SOME allow comparison to multiple-row results.

Using the ALL keyword in a comparison with a column subquery limits the result set to only those records where the comparison is true for *all* values produced by the subquery. Consider the following statement, which tells us the average country population for each of the world's continents:

```
mysql> SELECT Continent, AVG(Population)
    -> FROM Country
    -> GROUP BY Continent;
+---------------+-----------------+
| Continent     | AVG(Population) |
+---------------+-----------------+
| Asia          |   72647562.7451 |
| Europe        |   15871186.9565 |
| North America |   13053864.8649 |
| Africa        |   13525431.0345 |
| Oceania       |    1085755.3571 |
| Antarctica    |          0.0000 |
| South America |   24698571.4286 |
+---------------+-----------------+
```

Now, suppose that we would like to know all the countries in the world where the population is larger than the average country population of all of the world's continents. To get this information, we can use ALL in conjunction with the > operator to compare the value of the country population with every average continent population from the preceding result:

```
mysql> SELECT Name, Population
    -> FROM Country
    -> WHERE Population > ALL (SELECT AVG(Population)
    ->                         FROM Country
    ->                         GROUP BY Continent)
    -> ORDER BY Name;
+--------------------+------------+
| Name               | Population |
+--------------------+------------+
| Bangladesh         |  129155000 |
| Brazil             |  170115000 |
| China              | 1277558000 |
| Germany            |   82164700 |
| India              | 1013662000 |
| Indonesia          |  212107000 |
| Japan              |  126714000 |
| Mexico             |   98881000 |
| Nigeria            |  111506000 |
| Pakistan           |  156483000 |
| Philippines        |   75967000 |
| Russian Federation |  146934000 |
| United States      |  278357000 |
```

```
| Vietnam           |    79832000 |
+-------------------+-------------+
```

Note that Continent has been removed from the subquery's SELECT clause, because a quantified subquery can produce only a single column of values. If the subquery is written to select both the Continent column and the calculated column, MySQL cannot tell which one to use in the comparison and issues a complaint:

```
mysql> SELECT Name
    -> FROM Country
    -> WHERE Population > ALL (SELECT Continent, AVG(Population)
    ->                         FROM Country
    ->                         GROUP BY Continent)
    -> ORDER BY Name;
ERROR 1241 (21000): Operand should contain 1 column(s)
```

The keyword ANY (as well as the other quantified comparison keywords) is not limited to working with the = operator. Any of the standard comparison operators (=, <, >, <>, >=, and so forth) may be used for the comparison.

Comparisons using the word ANY will, as the name implies, succeed for any values in the column of data found by the subquery which succeed in the comparison. The following example finds the countries on the European continent, and, for each one, tests whether the country is among the worldwide list of countries where Spanish is spoken:

```
mysql> SELECT Name
    -> FROM Country
    -> WHERE Continent = 'Europe'
    ->   AND Code = ANY (SELECT CountryCode
    ->                   FROM CountryLanguage
    ->                   WHERE Language = 'Spanish')
    -> ORDER BY Name;
+---------+
| Name    |
+---------+
| Andorra |
| France  |
| Spain   |
| Sweden  |
+---------+
```

Compare that query to the following one using ALL: We run the same query, changing = ANY to = ALL to see if the European continent covers all those countries where Spanish is spoken:

```
mysql> SELECT Name
    -> FROM Country
    -> WHERE Continent = 'Europe'
    ->   AND Code = ALL (SELECT CountryCode
```

```
    ->                        FROM CountryLanguage
    ->                        WHERE Language = 'Spanish')
    -> ORDER BY Name;
Empty set (0.00 sec)
```

Because the result is empty, we can conclude that the European continent is not the only one where Spanish is spoken.

The word SOME is an alias for ANY, and may be used anywhere that ANY is used. The SQL standard defines these two words with the same meaning to overcome a limitation in the English language. Consider the following statement, in which we use <> ANY to negate the sense of the previous ANY example. As you read the example, try to form a sentence in your head to describe the output you would expect from the query (the output has been reduced to enhance readability):

```
mysql> SELECT Name
    -> FROM Country
    -> WHERE Continent = 'Europe'
    ->   AND Code <> ANY (SELECT CountryCode
    ->                    FROM CountryLanguage
    ->                    WHERE Language = 'Spanish')
    -> ORDER BY Name;
+-----------------------------+
| Name                        |
+-----------------------------+
| Albania                     |
| Andorra                     |
| Austria                     |
....
| Finland                     |
| France                      |
| Germany                     |
...
| Svalbard and Jan Mayen      |
| Sweden                      |
| Switzerland                 |
| Ukraine                     |
| United Kingdom              |
| Yugoslavia                  |
+-----------------------------+
```

You probably expected this query to find "all the countries on the European continent where Spanish is not spoken," or something similar. Yet the query actually finds every single country on the European continent.

In the English language, we expect "not any" to mean "none at all." However, in SQL, <> ANY means "one or more do not match." In other words, the statement is really saying "return all the countries, where there are *some* people that do not speak Spanish." In our example, for all of the four countries where there are Spanish speakers, we do in fact also find speakers of other languages.

To alleviate the confusion that might arise from the use of <> ANY, the SQL standard includes the SOME keyword as a synonym for ANY. Using the <> SOME construct makes it easier to understand the expected outcome of the SQL statement:

```
SELECT Name
FROM Country
WHERE Continent = 'Europe'
  AND Code <> SOME (SELECT CountryCode
                    FROM CountryLanguage
                    WHERE Language = 'Spanish')
ORDER BY Name;
```

13.4.2 Using IN

From Section 10.6.1, "Comparison Functions," you are already familiar with the variant of IN that may be used in an expression, as shown in the following example:

```
mysql> SELECT Name
    -> FROM Country
    -> WHERE Code IN ('DEU', 'USA', 'JPN');
+---------------+
| Name          |
+---------------+
| Germany       |
| Japan         |
| United States |
+---------------+
```

In this case, using IN is merely a shorthand for writing WHERE Code='DEU' OR Code='USA' OR Code='JPN'. It has nothing to do with subqueries.

When IN is used with a subquery, it is functionally equivalent to = ANY (note that the = sign is part of the equivalence). Many consider IN to be more readable than = ANY, because what you really want to know is "does this value appear in the subquery?" As an example, consider the equivalent IN version of the = ANY example shown in the previous section:

```
SELECT Name
FROM Country
WHERE Continent = 'Europe'
  AND Code IN (SELECT CountryCode
               FROM CountryLanguage
               WHERE Language = 'Spanish')
ORDER BY Name;
```

IN cannot be combined with any comparison operators such as = or <>.

NOT IN is another "shorthand." However, it is *not* an alias of <> ANY as you might otherwise expect. It is an alias of <> ALL. In other words, NOT IN is only true if none of the records of the subquery can be matched by the outer query. In the example for SOME, we demonstrated that <> ANY would return records of countries where some people didn't speak Spanish. The same query, using NOT IN (that is, <> ALL) will return only those countries where Spanish is not spoken at all. Although it may seem logically flawed that IN and NOT IN are aliases of two very different statements, it fits better with the way that we usually understand the equivalent English terms.

13.4.3 Using EXISTS

The EXISTS predicate performs a simple test: It tells you whether the subquery finds any rows. It does not return the actual values found in any of the rows, it merely returns TRUE if any rows were found. As does one of our previous examples, the following example finds countries on the European continent where Spanish is spoken. But with this query, no actual comparison is made between the data in the outer query and the rows found in the inner query.

```
mysql> SELECT Code c, Name
    -> FROM Country
    -> WHERE Continent = 'Europe'
    ->   AND EXISTS (SELECT *
    ->               FROM CountryLanguage
    ->               WHERE CountryCode = c
    ->                 AND Language = 'Spanish');
+-----+---------+
| c   | Name    |
+-----+---------+
| AND | Andorra |
| ESP | Spain   |
| FRA | France  |
| SWE | Sweden  |
+-----+---------+
```

The use of SELECT * in EXISTS subqueries is purely by tradition. You can use a different column list as long as the subquery is syntactically correct. No column values are ever needed for comparison, so MySQL never actually evaluates the column list given in the subquery SELECT. For example, you could replace the * with a constant value such as 1, 0, or even NULL.

EXISTS can be negated using NOT EXISTS, which, as the name implies, returns TRUE for subquery result sets with no rows. Replacing EXISTS with NOT EXISTS in the previous example shows those 42 countries on the European continent in which Spanish is not spoken at all.

13.5 Comparison Using Row Subqueries

For row subqueries, we can perform an equality comparison for all columns in a row. The subquery must return a single row. This method of comparison is not often used, but can provide some convenience for certain comparison operations. In the following example, we find the name of the capital of Finland. The query makes use of the fact that the city's name is stored in the City table, whereas the ID of a country's capital city is stored in the Country table:

```
mysql> SELECT City.Name
    -> FROM City
    -> WHERE (City.ID, City.CountryCode) =
    ->        (SELECT Capital, Code
    ->         FROM Country
    ->         WHERE Name='Finland');
+-----------------------+
| Name                  |
+-----------------------+
| Helsinki [Helsingfors] |
+-----------------------+
```

Notice the use of the construct (City.ID, City.CountryCode). This creates a tuple of values and is known as a "row constructor." An equivalent method of defining a row is using ROW(), to underscore the fact that the values are used to construct a row of data for comparison. In this case, we would have written ROW(City.ID, City.CountryCode).

Trying to compare a tuple created by the row constructor with a subquery that returns several rows at once produces an error. The following example is similar to the preceding one, but does not work because there is no limit on the number of rows returned by the subquery:

```
mysql> SELECT City.Name
    -> FROM City
    -> WHERE (City.ID, City.CountryCode) =
    ->        (SELECT Capital, Code
    ->         FROM Country);
ERROR 1242 (21000): Subquery returns more than 1 row
```

Row constructors can be used only for equality comparison using the = operator. You may not use other comparison operators such as <, >, or <>; nor may you use special words such as ALL, ANY, IN, or EXISTS.

Row constructors are commonly used with row subqueries, but they can be used in other contexts, and they may contain any type of scalar expression. For example, the following is a legal statement:

```
mysql> SELECT Name, Population
    -> FROM Country
    -> WHERE (Continent, Region) = ('Europe', 'Western Europe');
+---------------+------------+
| Name          | Population |
+---------------+------------+
| Netherlands   |   15864000 |
| Belgium       |   10239000 |
| Austria       |    8091800 |
| Liechtenstein |      32300 |
| Luxembourg    |     435700 |
| Monaco        |      34000 |
| France        |   59225700 |
| Germany       |   82164700 |
| Switzerland   |    7160400 |
+---------------+------------+
```

In practice, row constructors are often inefficient when used like this, so it is more common to write the equivalent expression using AND. The query optimizer performs better if you write the WHERE clause like this:

```
SELECT Name, Population
FROM Country
WHERE Continent = 'Europe' AND Region = 'Western Europe';
```

13.6 Using Subqueries in the FROM Clause

Subqueries may be used in the FROM clause of a SELECT statement. In the following query, we find the average of the sums of the population of each continent:

```
mysql> SELECT AVG(cont_sum)
    -> FROM (SELECT Continent, SUM(Population) AS cont_sum
    ->        FROM Country
    ->        GROUP BY Continent
    ->      ) AS t;
+----------------+
| AVG(cont_sum)  |
+----------------+
| 868392778.5714 |
+----------------+
```

Every table that appears in a FROM clause must have a name, so a subquery in the FROM clause must be followed by a table alias.

The SELECT in the FROM clause can be a table subquery, even if not all of its values are used by the outer query. This is shown by the preceding example, where the Continent column selected by the subquery is not used by the outer query.

Subqueries in FROM clauses cannot be correlated with the outer statement.

13.7 Converting Subqueries to Joins

Standard SQL allows a SELECT statement to contain a nested SELECT, which is known as a subquery. MySQL implements subqueries as of version 4.1. For MySQL 4.0 and earlier, subqueries sometimes can be rewritten as joins, which provides a workaround for lack of subqueries in many cases. Even for MySQL 4.1 and up, a join might be handled by the optimizer more efficiently than an equivalent statement expressed as a subquery.

A subquery that finds matches between tables often can be rewritten as an inner join. A subquery that finds mismatches often can be rewritten as an outer join. The following sections describe how to do this.

13.7.1 Converting Subqueries to Inner Joins

One form of SELECT that uses subqueries finds matches between tables. For example, an IN subquery that identifies countries for which languages are listed in the CountryLanguage table looks like this:

```
mysql> SELECT Name FROM Country
    -> WHERE Code IN (SELECT CountryCode FROM CountryLanguage);
+---------------------------------------+
| Name                                  |
+---------------------------------------+
| Afghanistan                           |
| Netherlands                           |
| Netherlands Antilles                  |
| Albania                               |
| Algeria                               |
| American Samoa                        |
| Andorra                               |
| Angola                                |
| Anguilla                              |
| Antigua and Barbuda                   |
| United Arab Emirates                  |
| Argentina                             |
...
```

To convert this into an inner join, do the following:

1. Move the `CountryLanguage` table named in the subquery to the `FROM` clause.
2. The `WHERE` clause compares the `Code` column to the country codes returned from the subquery. Convert the `IN` expression to an explicit direct comparison between the country code columns of the two tables.

These changes result in the following inner join:

```
mysql> SELECT Name FROM Country, CountryLanguage
    -> WHERE Code = CountryCode;
+--------------------------------------+
| Name                                 |
+--------------------------------------+
| Afghanistan                          |
| Afghanistan                          |
| Afghanistan                          |
| Afghanistan                          |
| Afghanistan                          |
| Netherlands                          |
| Netherlands                          |
| Netherlands                          |
| Netherlands                          |
| Netherlands Antilles                 |
| Netherlands Antilles                 |
| Netherlands Antilles                 |
...
```

Note that this output is not quite the same as that from the subquery, which lists each matched country just once. The output from the join lists each matched country once each time its country code occurs in the `CountryLanguage` table. To list each name just once, as in the subquery, add `DISTINCT` to the join:

```
mysql> SELECT DISTINCT Name FROM Country, CountryLanguage
    -> WHERE Code = CountryCode;
+--------------------------------------+
| Name                                 |
+--------------------------------------+
| Afghanistan                          |
| Netherlands                          |
| Netherlands Antilles                 |
| Albania                              |
| Algeria                              |
| American Samoa                       |
| Andorra                              |
| Angola                               |
| Anguilla                             |
| Antigua and Barbuda                  |
```

```
| United Arab Emirates                      |
| Argentina                                 |
...
```

13.7.2 Converting Subqueries to Outer Joins

Another form of SELECT that uses subqueries finds mismatches between tables. For example, a NOT IN subquery that identifies countries for which no languages are listed in the CountryLanguage table looks like this:

```
mysql> SELECT Name FROM Country
    -> WHERE Code NOT IN (SELECT CountryCode FROM CountryLanguage);
+----------------------------------------------+
| Name                                         |
+----------------------------------------------+
| Antarctica                                   |
| Bouvet Island                                |
| British Indian Ocean Territory               |
| South Georgia and the South Sandwich Islands |
| Heard Island and McDonald Islands            |
| French Southern territories                  |
+----------------------------------------------+
```

This subquery can be rewritten as an outer join. For example, to change the preceding subquery into a left join, modify it as follows:

1. Move the CountryLanguage table named in the subquery to the FROM clause and join it to Country using LEFT JOIN.

2. The WHERE clause compares the Code column to the country codes returned from the subquery. Convert the IN expression to an explicit direct comparison between the country code columns of the two tables in the FROM clause.

3. In the WHERE clause, restrict the output to those rows having NULL in the CountryLanguage table column.

These changes result in the following LEFT JOIN:

```
mysql> SELECT Name
    -> FROM Country LEFT JOIN CountryLanguage ON Code = CountryCode
    -> WHERE CountryCode IS NULL;
+----------------------------------------------+
| Name                                         |
+----------------------------------------------+
| Antarctica                                   |
| Bouvet Island                                |
| British Indian Ocean Territory               |
| South Georgia and the South Sandwich Islands |
```

```
| Heard Island and McDonald Islands      |
| French Southern territories            |
+----------------------------------------+
```

Any left join may be written as an equivalent right join, so the subquery also can be written as a right join:

```
mysql> SELECT Name
    -> FROM CountryLanguage RIGHT JOIN Country ON CountryCode = Code
    -> WHERE CountryCode IS NULL;
+------------------------------------------+
| Name                                     |
+------------------------------------------+
| Antarctica                               |
| Bouvet Island                            |
| British Indian Ocean Territory           |
| South Georgia and the South Sandwich Islands |
| Heard Island and McDonald Islands        |
| French Southern territories              |
+------------------------------------------+
```

13.8 Using Subqueries in Updates

Use of subqueries is not limited to SELECT statements. Any SQL statement that includes a WHERE clause or scalar expression may use subqueries. For example, to create a new table containing every North American city, and then later remove all cities located in countries where the life expectancy is less than 70 years, use these statements:

```
mysql> CREATE TABLE NACities
    -> SELECT * FROM City
    -> WHERE CountryCode IN (SELECT Code
    ->                       FROM Country
    ->                       WHERE Continent='North America');
Query OK, 581 rows affected (0.07 sec)
Records: 581  Duplicates: 0  Warnings: 0

mysql> DELETE FROM NACities
    -> WHERE CountryCode IN (SELECT Code
    ->                       FROM Country
    ->                       WHERE LifeExpectancy < 70.0);
Query OK, 26 rows affected (0.00 sec)
```

Although subqueries can be used to retrieve or aggregate data from other tables for use in statements that modify tables (such as UPDATE, DELETE, INSERT, and REPLACE), MySQL does not allow a table that is being updated in the outer query to be selected from in any subquery of the statement. For example, the following statement yields an error:

```
mysql> DELETE FROM NACities
    -> WHERE ID IN (SELECT ID
    ->                FROM NACities
    ->               WHERE Population < 500);
ERROR 1093 (HY000): You can't specify target table 'NACities'
for update in FROM clause
```

14

Views

A view is a database object that is defined in terms of a SELECT statement that retrieves the data you want the view to produce. Views are sometimes called "virtual tables." A view can be used to select from regular tables (called "base tables") or other views. In some cases, a view is updatable and can be used with statements such as UPDATE, DELETE, or INSERT to modify an underlying base table.

This chapter covers the following exam topics:

- The benefits of using views
- Creating, altering, and dropping views
- Performing validity checks on views
- Obtaining metadata about views
- Privileges required for operations on views

14.1 Reasons to Use Views

Views provide several benefits compared to selecting data directly from base tables:

- Access to data becomes simplified:
  - A view can be used to perform a calculation and display its result. For example, a view definition that invokes aggregate functions can be used to display a summary.
  - A view can be used to select a restricted set of rows by means of an appropriate WHERE clause, or to select only a subset of a table's columns.
  - A view can be used for selecting data from multiple tables by using a join or union.

  A view performs these operations automatically. Users need not specify the expression on which a calculation is based, the conditions that restrict rows in the WHERE clause, or the conditions used to match tables for a join.

- Views can be used to display table contents differently for different users, so that each user sees only the data pertaining to that user's activities. This improves security by hiding information from users that they should not be able to access or modify. It also reduces distraction because irrelevant columns are not displayed.

- If you need to change the structure of your tables to accommodate certain applications, a view can preserve the appearance of the original table structure to minimize disruption to other applications. For example, if you split a table into two new tables, a view can be created with the name of the original table and defined to select data from the new tables such that the view appears to have the original table structure.

14.2 Creating Views

To define a view, use the CREATE VIEW statement, which has this syntax:

```
CREATE [OR REPLACE] [ALGORITHM = algorithm_type]
    VIEW view_name [(column_list)]
    AS select_statement
    [WITH [CASCADED | LOCAL] CHECK OPTION]
```

view_name is the name to give the view. It can be unqualified to create the view in the default database, or qualified as db_name.view_name to create it in a specific database.

select_statement is a SELECT statement that indicates how to retrieve data when the view is used. The statement can select from base tables or other views. References in the SELECT statement to unqualified table or view names refer to objects in your default database. To select from a table or view in a specific database, refer to it using the db_name.table_name or db_name.view_name syntax.

Several parts of the CREATE VIEW statement are optional:

- The OR REPLACE clause causes any existing view with same name as the new one to be dropped prior to creation of the new view.
- The ALGORITHM clause specifies the processing algorithm to use when the view is invoked.
- column_list provides names for the view columns to override the default names.
- When the WITH CHECK OPTION clause is included in a view definition, all data changes made to the view are checked to ensure that the new or updated rows satisfy the view-defining condition. If the condition is not satisfied, the change is not accepted, either in the view or in the underlying base table.

This section discusses most parts of the CREATE VIEW statement. For information about ALGORITHM and WITH CHECK OPTION, see Section 14.2.2, "View Algorithms," and Section 14.2.3, "Updatable Views," respectively.

The following CREATE VIEW statement defines a simple view named CityView that selects the ID and Name columns from the City table. The SELECT statement shows an example of how to retrieve from the view:

```
mysql> CREATE VIEW CityView AS SELECT ID, Name FROM City;
Query OK, 0 rows affected (0.03 sec)

mysql> SELECT * FROM CityView;
+------+---------------------------------+
| ID   | Name                            |
+------+---------------------------------+
|    1 | Kabul                           |
|    2 | Qandahar                        |
|    3 | Herat                           |
|    4 | Mazar-e-Sharif                  |
...
```

Views and base tables share the same namespace, so CREATE VIEW results in an error if a base table or view with the given name already exists. To create the view if it does not exist, or replace a view of the same name if it does exist, use the OR REPLACE clause:

```
mysql> CREATE VIEW CityView AS SELECT ID, Name FROM City;
ERROR 1050 (42S01): Table 'CityView' already exists
mysql> CREATE OR REPLACE VIEW CityView AS SELECT ID, Name FROM City;
Query OK, 0 rows affected (0.00 sec)
```

The OR REPLACE clause works only if the existing object is a view. You cannot use it to replace a base table.

Another way to replace a view is by dropping it with DROP VIEW and re-creating it with CREATE VIEW.

By default, the names of the columns in a view are the same as the names of the columns retrieved by the SELECT statement in the view definition. For the CityView view just defined, the SELECT statement retrieves two columns named ID and Name, which also become the view column names. To select data from CityView, select either or both columns by name, or use * to select all view columns:

```
SELECT ID FROM CityView ... ;
SELECT Name FROM CityView ... ;
SELECT ID, Name FROM CityView ... ;
SELECT * FROM CityView ... ;
```

To override the default view column names and provide explicit names, include a column_list clause following the view name in the CREATE VIEW statement. If present, this list must contain one name per column selected by the view, with multiple names separated by commas. There are some important reasons to name view columns explicitly:

- View column names must be unique within the view. If the columns selected by a view do not satisfy this condition, a list of unique explicit column names resolves name clashes. For example, an attempt to define a view that selects columns with the same name from joined tables fails unless you rename at least one of the columns:

```
mysql> CREATE VIEW v
    -> AS SELECT Country.Name, City.Name
    -> FROM Country, City WHERE Code = CountryCode;
ERROR 1060 (42S21): Duplicate column name 'Name'
mysql> CREATE VIEW v (CountryName, CityName)
    -> AS SELECT Country.Name, City.Name
    -> FROM Country, City WHERE Code = CountryCode;
Query OK, 0 rows affected (0.04 sec)
```

- Explicit view column names make it easier to use columns that are calculated from expressions. (By default, the name for such a column is the expression, which makes it difficult to reference.) The following example creates a view for which the second column is created from an aggregate expression:

```
mysql> CREATE VIEW CountryLangCount AS
    -> SELECT Name, COUNT(Language)
    -> FROM Country, CountryLanguage WHERE Code = CountryCode
    -> GROUP BY Name;
Query OK, 0 rows affected (0.01 sec)


mysql> DESCRIBE CountryLangCount;
+-----------------+------------+------+-----+---------+-------+
| Field           | Type       | Null | Key | Default | Extra |
+-----------------+------------+------+-----+---------+-------+
| Name            | char(52)   | NO   |     |         |       |
| COUNT(Language) | bigint(20) | NO   |     | 0       |       |
+-----------------+------------+------+-----+---------+-------+
2 rows in set (0.00 sec)
```

The name of the second column is COUNT(Language), which must be referred to using a quoted identifier (that is, as `COUNT(Language)`). To avoid this, provide names for the columns by including a column list in the view definition:

```
mysql> CREATE VIEW CountryLangCount (Name, LangCount) AS
    -> SELECT Name, COUNT(Language)
    -> FROM Country, CountryLanguage WHERE Code = CountryCode
    -> GROUP BY Name;
Query OK, 0 rows affected (0.00 sec)


mysql> DESCRIBE CountryLangCount;
+-----------+------------+------+-----+---------+-------+
| Field     | Type       | Null | Key | Default | Extra |
+-----------+------------+------+-----+---------+-------+
| Name      | char(52)   | NO   |     |         |       |
| LangCount | bigint(20) | NO   |     | 0       |       |
+-----------+------------+------+-----+---------+-------+
2 rows in set (0.00 sec)
```

Another way to provide names for view columns is by using column aliases in the SELECT statement. This technique is convenient if only some of the view columns need renaming. For example, CountryLangCount could have been created with a definition that uses an AS clause to provide an alias for the second view column:

```
CREATE VIEW CountryLangCount AS
SELECT Name, COUNT(Language) AS LangCount
FROM Country, CountryLanguage WHERE Code = CountryCode
GROUP BY Name;
```

When you use a SELECT statement that refers to a view, it is possible that the statement will contain clauses that are also present in the view definition. Sometimes the corresponding clauses are both used, sometimes one overrides the other, and sometimes the effect is undefined:

- A view definition can include a WHERE clause. If a statement that refers to the view includes its own WHERE clause, the conditions in both clauses are used. In effect, the conditions are combined with an AND operator.
- If a view definition includes an ORDER BY clause, it is used for sorting view results unless a statement that refers to a view includes its own ORDER BY clause. In that case, the view definition ORDER BY is ignored.
- For some options, such as HIGH_PRIORITY, the effect is undefined if they appear both in the statement that refers to the view and in the view definition. You can avoid ambiguity in such cases by omitting the option from the view definition and specifying it as necessary only when selecting from the view.

14.2.1 Restrictions on Views

A view definition can include most of the constructs that are allowable in SELECT statements, such as WHERE, GROUP BY, and so forth. However, views in MySQL have some restrictions that do not apply to base tables:

- You cannot create a TEMPORARY view.
- You cannot associate a trigger with a view.
- The tables on which a view is to be based must already exist.
- The SELECT statement in a view definition cannot contain any of these constructs:
    - Subqueries in the FROM clause
    - References to TEMPORARY tables
    - References to user variables
    - References to procedure parameters, if the view definition occurs within a stored routine
    - References to prepared statement parameters

14.2.2 View Algorithms

A MySQL-specific extension to the CREATE VIEW statement is the ALGORITHM clause, which specifies the algorithm used to process the view. It has this syntax:

```
ALGORITHM = {UNDEFINED | MERGE | TEMPTABLE}
```

For UNDEFINED, MySQL chooses the algorithm itself. This is the default if no ALGORITHM clause is present.

For MERGE, MySQL processes a statement that refers to the view by merging parts of the view definition into corresponding parts of the statement and executing the resulting merged statement.

For TEMPTABLE, MySQL processes a statement that refers to the view by first retrieving the view contents into an intermediate temporary table, and then using the temporary table to finish executing the statement. If you specify TEMPTABLE, the view becomes non-updatable. That is, the view cannot be used to update the underlying table. (Modifications would be made to the temporary table instead, leaving the base table unchanged.)

The MERGE algorithm requires a one-to-one relationship between the rows in a view and the rows in the base table. Suppose that a view v is defined as follows to display changes in GNP per country:

```
CREATE ALGORITHM = UNDEFINED VIEW v AS
SELECT Name, GNP - GNPOld AS GNPDiff
FROM Country WHERE GNPOld IS NOT NULL;
```

As specified in the CREATE VIEW statement, the algorithm is undefined, so MySQL picks the algorithm. For this view, each row is derived from a single Country table row, so the view can be processed with the MERGE algorithm. Consider the following statement that refers to the view:

```
SELECT Name, GNPDiff FROM v WHERE GNPDiff > 0;
```

The MERGE algorithm merges the view definition into the SELECT statement: MySQL replaces v with Country, replaces the column list by the corresponding view column definitions, and adds the view WHERE conditions to the statement with AND. The resulting transformed SELECT statement that MySQL executes looks something like this:

```
SELECT Name, GNP - GNPOld AS GNPDiff
FROM Country WHERE (GNP - GNPOld > 0) AND (GNPOld IS NOT NULL);
```

The MERGE requirement for a one-to-one relationship is not satisfied if the view definition produces a view row from multiple base table rows, or uses constructs such as DISTINCT, aggregate functions, a subquery in the select list, GROUP BY or HAVING. Suppose that a view v is defined as follows to display the number of languages spoken per country:

```
CREATE VIEW v AS
  SELECT CountryCode, COUNT(*) AS LangCount
  FROM CountryLanguage GROUP BY CountryCode;
```

Each row in the view is not necessarily derived from a single CountryLanguage table row, so the MERGE algorithm cannot be used to process the view. For example, to find the largest number of languages spoken in a single country, we would select from the view like this:

```
SELECT MAX(LangCount) FROM v;
```

But the MERGE algorithm would treat that statement as equivalent to this one, which is illegal due to the nested aggregate functions:

```
SELECT MAX(COUNT(*))
  FROM CountryLanguage GROUP BY CountryCode;
```

Instead, MySQL processes a view such as this by using a temporary table to produce a result that contains the aggregated counts. This is called "materializing" the view (into the temporary table). Then MySQL evaluates SELECT MAX() using the temporary table to get the maximum count. It is as though MySQL does something like this:

```
CREATE TEMPORARY TABLE tmp_table
  SELECT CountryCode, COUNT(*) AS LangCount
  FROM CountryLanguage GROUP BY CountryCode;

SELECT MAX(LangCount) FROM tmp_table;

DROP TABLE tmp_table;
```

When you create a view, should you specify an algorithm explicitly? Generally speaking, it's unnecessary:

- If you specify no algorithm, MySQL picks the algorithm automatically. It uses MERGE if possible because that usually is more efficient than TEMPTABLE and also does not prevent the view from being updatable the way that TEMPTABLE does. MySQL uses a temporary table if MERGE cannot be used.

- If you specify MERGE but the view definition contains any construct that prevents MERGE from being used, MySQL issues a warning and resets the algorithm to UNDEFINED.

For these reasons, there usually is little reason to specify either UNDEFINED or MERGE. On the other hand, you might want to specify TEMPTABLE to influence how MySQL uses locking while it processes the view. Locks used for any underlying tables can be released after the temporary table has been created. This might reduce contention by allowing other clients to access the underlying tables earlier while the temporary table is used to finish processing the view.

14.2.3 Updatable Views

A view is updatable if it can be used with statements such as UPDATE or DELETE to modify the underlying base table. Not all views are updatable. For example, you might be able to update a table, but you cannot update a view on the table if the view is defined in terms of aggregate values calculated from the table. The reason for this is that each view row need not correspond to a unique base table row, in which case MySQL would not be able to determine which table row to update.

The primary conditions for updatability are that there must be a one-to-one relationship between the rows in the view and the rows in the base table, and that the view columns to be updated must be defined as simple table references, not expressions. (There are other conditions as well, but we will not go into them here.)

The following example demonstrates updatability. First, use the following statement to create a CountryPop table containing three columns from the Country table. (By modifying this table, we avoid changing the contents of the original world database tables.)

```
mysql> CREATE TABLE CountryPop
    -> SELECT Name, Population, Continent FROM Country;
Query OK, 239 rows affected (0.01 sec)
Records: 239  Duplicates: 0  Warnings: 0
```

Then create a simple view that contains the rows in CountryPop for countries in Europe:

```
mysql> CREATE VIEW EuropePop AS
    -> SELECT Name, Population FROM CountryPop
    -> WHERE Continent = 'Europe';
Query OK, 0 rows affected (0.02 sec)
```

The EuropePop view satisfies the one-to-one requirement, and its columns are simple column references, not expressions such as col1+1 or col2/col3. EuropePop is updatable, as demonstrated by the following statements. The example also selects from the base table CountryPop to show that the base table is indeed modified by the UPDATE and DELETE statements that use the view.

```
mysql> SELECT * FROM EuropePop WHERE Name = 'San Marino';
+------------+------------+
| Name       | Population |
+------------+------------+
| San Marino |      27000 |
+------------+------------+
1 row in set (0.02 sec)

mysql> UPDATE EuropePop SET Population = Population + 1
    -> WHERE Name = 'San Marino';
Query OK, 1 row affected (0.01 sec)
Rows matched: 1  Changed: 1  Warnings: 0
```

```
mysql> SELECT * FROM EuropePop WHERE Name = 'San Marino';
+------------+------------+
| Name       | Population |
+------------+------------+
| San Marino |      27001 |
+------------+------------+
1 row in set (0.00 sec)

mysql> SELECT * FROM CountryPop WHERE Name = 'San Marino';
+------------+------------+-----------+
| Name       | Population | Continent |
+------------+------------+-----------+
| San Marino |      27001 | Europe    |
+------------+------------+-----------+
1 row in set (0.00 sec)

mysql> DELETE FROM EuropePop WHERE Name = 'San Marino';
Query OK, 1 row affected (0.00 sec)

mysql> SELECT * FROM EuropePop WHERE Name = 'San Marino';
Empty set (0.00 sec)

mysql> SELECT * FROM CountryPop WHERE Name = 'San Marino';
Empty set (0.01 sec)
```

An updatable view might also be insertable (usable with INSERT) if the view columns consist only of simple table column references (not expressions) and if any columns present in the base table but not named in the view or the INSERT have default values. In this case, an INSERT into the view creates a new base table row with each column not named in the INSERT set to its default value.

If a view is updatable, you can use the WITH CHECK OPTION clause to place a constraint on allowable modifications. This clause causes the conditions in the WHERE clause of the view definition to be checked when updates are attempted:

- An UPDATE to an existing row is allowed only if the WHERE clause remains true for the resulting row.
- An INSERT is allowed only if the WHERE clause is true for the new row.

In other words, WITH CHECK OPTION ensures that you cannot update a row in such a way that the view no longer selects it, and that you cannot insert a row that the view will not select.

Using the CountryPop table created earlier in this section, define the following view that selects countries with a population of at least 100 million:

```
mysql> CREATE VIEW LargePop AS
    -> SELECT Name, Population FROM CountryPop
```

```
    -> WHERE Population >= 100000000
    -> WITH CHECK OPTION;
Query OK, 0 rows affected (0.00 sec)

mysql> SELECT * FROM LargePop;
+--------------------+------------+
| Name               | Population |
+--------------------+------------+
| Bangladesh         |  129155000 |
| Brazil             |  170115000 |
| Indonesia          |  212107000 |
| India              | 1013662000 |
| Japan              |  126714000 |
| China              | 1277558000 |
| Nigeria            |  111506000 |
| Pakistan           |  156483000 |
| Russian Federation |  146934000 |
| United States      |  278357000 |
+--------------------+------------+
10 rows in set (0.00 sec)
```

The WITH CHECK OPTION clause in the view definition allows some modifications but disallows others. For example, it's possible to increase the population of any country in the view:

```
mysql> UPDATE LargePop SET Population = Population + 1
    -> WHERE Name = 'Nigeria';
Query OK, 1 row affected (0.00 sec)
Rows matched: 1  Changed: 1  Warnings: 0

mysql> SELECT * FROM LargePop WHERE Name = 'Nigeria';
+---------+------------+
| Name    | Population |
+---------+------------+
| Nigeria |  111506001 |
+---------+------------+
1 row in set (0.01 sec)
```

It is also possible to decrease a population value, but only if it does not drop below the minimum value of 100 million that is required by the view's WHERE clause:

```
mysql> UPDATE LargePop SET Population = 99999999
    -> WHERE Name = 'Nigeria';
ERROR 1369 (HY000): CHECK OPTION failed 'world.LargePop'
```

For inserts, a row can be added unless the Population value is less than 100 million:

```
mysql> INSERT INTO LargePop VALUES('some country',100000000);
Query OK, 1 row affected (0.00 sec)
```

```
mysql> INSERT INTO LargePop VALUES('some country2',99999999);
ERROR 1369 (HY000): CHECK OPTION failed 'world.LargePop'
```

The WITH CHECK OPTION clause takes an optional keyword that controls the extent to which MySQL performs WHERE-checking for updates when a view is defined in terms of other views:

- For WITH LOCAL CHECK OPTION, the check applies only to the view's own WHERE clause.
- For WITH CASCADED CHECK OPTION, the view's WHERE clause is checked, as is the WHERE clause for any underlying views. CASCADED is the default if neither CASCADED nor LOCAL is given.

WITH CHECK OPTION is allowed only for updatable views, and an error occurs if you use it for a non-updatable view. This means that ALGORITHM = TEMPTABLE and WITH CHECK OPTION are mutually exclusive, because TEMPTABLE makes a view non-updatable.

14.3 Altering Views

To change the definition of an existing view, use the ALTER VIEW statement. ALTER VIEW discards the current definition for the view and replaces it with the new definition in the statement. It is an error if the named view does not exist. Syntactically, the only differences from CREATE VIEW are that the initial keyword is ALTER rather than CREATE, and the OR REPLACE option cannot be used.

The following statement redefines the LargePop view created in the previous section so that it no longer includes a WITH CHECK OPTION clause:

```
ALTER VIEW LargePop AS
SELECT Name, Population FROM CountryPop
WHERE Population >= 100000000;
```

14.4 Dropping Views

To destroy one or more views, use the DROP VIEW statement:

```
DROP VIEW [IF EXISTS] view_name [, view_name] ... ;
```

It is an error if a given view does not exist. Include the IF EXISTS clause to generate a warning instead. (The warning can be displayed with SHOW WARNINGS.) IF EXISTS is a MySQL extension to standard SQL. If the view v1 exists but the view v2 does not, the following DROP VIEW statement results in a warning for the attempt to drop v2:

```
mysql> DROP VIEW IF EXISTS v1, v2;
Query OK, 0 rows affected, 1 warning (0.00 sec)
```

```
mysql> SHOW WARNINGS;
+-------+------+-------------------------+
| Level | Code | Message                 |
+-------+------+-------------------------+
| Note  | 1051 | Unknown table 'world.v2' |
+-------+------+-------------------------+
1 row in set (0.00 sec)
```

14.5 Checking Views

When you define a view, any object referenced by the view (such as a table, view, or column) must exist. However, a view can become invalid if a table, view, or column on which it depends is dropped or altered. To check a view for problems of this nature, use the CHECK TABLE statement. The following example shows the output from CHECK TABLE after renaming a table that a view depends on:

```
mysql> CREATE TABLE t1 (i INT);
Query OK, 0 rows affected (0.01 sec)

mysql> CREATE VIEW v AS SELECT i FROM t1;
Query OK, 0 rows affected (0.01 sec)

mysql> RENAME TABLE t1 TO t2;
Query OK, 0 rows affected (0.01 sec)

mysql> CHECK TABLE v\G
*************************** 1. row ***************************
   Table: world.v
      Op: check
Msg_type: error
Msg_text: View 'world.v' references invalid table(s) or column(s)
          or function(s)
1 row in set (0.00 sec)
```

14.6 Obtaining View Metadata

The INFORMATION_SCHEMA database has a VIEWS table that contains view metadata (information about views). For example, to display information about the world.CityView view that was created earlier, use this statement:

```
mysql> SELECT * FROM INFORMATION_SCHEMA.VIEWS
    -> WHERE TABLE_NAME = 'CityView'
    -> AND TABLE_SCHEMA = 'world'\G
*************************** 1. row ***************************
```

```
      TABLE_CATALOG: NULL
       TABLE_SCHEMA: world
         TABLE_NAME: CityView
    VIEW_DEFINITION: select `world`.`City`.`ID` AS `ID`,`world`.`City`.`Name`
                     AS `Name` from `world`.`City`
       CHECK_OPTION: NONE
       IS_UPDATABLE: YES
```

INFORMATION_SCHEMA also has a TABLES table that contains view metadata.

For further information about INFORMATION_SCHEMA, see Chapter 20, "Obtaining Database Metadata."

MySQL also supports a family of SHOW statements that display metadata. To display the definition of a view, use the SHOW CREATE VIEW statement:

```
mysql> SHOW CREATE VIEW CityView\G
*************************** 1. row ***************************
       View: CityView
Create View: CREATE ALGORITHM=UNDEFINED VIEW `world`.`CityView` AS
             select `world`.`City`.`ID` AS `ID`,`world`.`City`.`Name`
             AS `Name` from `world`.`City`
```

Some statements in MySQL that originally were designed to display base table information have been extended so that they also work with views:

- DESCRIBE and SHOW COLUMNS
- SHOW TABLE STATUS
- SHOW TABLES

By default, SHOW TABLES lists only the names of tables and views. MySQL 5 has a SHOW FULL TABLES variant that displays a second column. The values in the column are BASE TABLE or VIEW to indicate what kind of object each name refers to:

```
mysql> SHOW FULL TABLES FROM world;
+------------------+------------+
| Tables_in_world  | Table_type |
+------------------+------------+
| City             | BASE TABLE |
| CityView         | VIEW       |
| Country          | BASE TABLE |
| CountryLangCount | VIEW       |
| CountryLanguage  | BASE TABLE |
| CountryPop       | BASE TABLE |
| EuropePop        | VIEW       |
| LargePop         | VIEW       |
+------------------+------------+
```

14.7 Privileges Required for Views

To create a view, you must have the CREATE VIEW privilege for it, and you must have sufficient privileges for accessing the tables to which the view definition refers:

- For each table column used in the view column list (that is, selected by the view SELECT statement), you must have some privilege for accessing the column, such as SELECT, INSERT, or UPDATE.

- For columns accessed elsewhere in the statement, such as in a WHERE or GROUP BY clause, you must have the SELECT privilege.

For example, to create the following view on the Country table, you must have some privilege for its Code and Name columns, and the SELECT privilege for its Continent column:

```
CREATE VIEW SACountry AS
SELECT Code, Name FROM Country WHERE Continent = 'South America';
```

To use the OR REPLACE clause in a CREATE VIEW statement or to alter a view with ALTER VIEW, you must have the DROP privilege for the view in addition to the privileges required to create the view.

The DROP VIEW statement requires the DROP privilege for the view.

To access existing views, the privileges required are much like those for tables. To select from a view, you must have the SELECT privilege for it. For an updatable view, to use INSERT, DELETE, or UPDATE, you must have the respective INSERT, DELETE, or UPDATE privilege.

Privileges for a view apply to the view, not to the underlying tables. Suppose that you have the UPDATE privilege for an updatable view. That enables you to update the underlying table by using the view, but not to update the table directly. For that, you must have the UPDATE privilege for the table itself.

The SHOW CREATE VIEW statement requires the SELECT privilege for the view. If the view definition refers to tables for which you have no privileges, you must also have the SHOW VIEW privilege in addition to SELECT.

15

Importing and Exporting Data

This chapter discusses how to perform bulk data import and export operations. It covers the following exam topics:

- Using the LOAD DATA INFILE statement to import data from files
- Using SELECT ... INTO OUTFILE to export data to files
- Using mysqlimport and mysqldump for importing and exporting data from the command line

15.1 Import and Export Operations

MySQL includes two SQL statements that can be used to import data from files into your database or export data from your database into files:

- LOAD DATA INFILE reads data records directly from a file and inserts them into a table.
- SELECT ... INTO OUTFILE writes the result of a SELECT operation to a file.

The two statements are related in the sense that they both transfer information between MySQL and data files. Also, both statements use similar syntax for describing the format of data file contents.

Data file import and export also can be performed from the command line. This is done using the mysqlimport and mysqldump client programs. For bulk data transfer operations, these programs act as command-line interfaces to the LOAD DATA INFILE and SELECT ... INTO OUTFILE statements. Each program examines its arguments to determine what you want it to do, and then constructs appropriate SQL statements and sends them to the MySQL server on your behalf.

15.2 Importing and Exporting Using SQL

This section discusses how to perform data import and export operations using SQL statements. LOAD DATA INFILE reads the records from a data file and inserts them into a table. SELECT ... INTO OUTFILE writes the record in a result set to a file.

The two statements are not quite opposites. LOAD DATA INFILE imports a file into a single table, whereas SELECT ... INTO OUTFILE can write a result set that may be produced by selecting from multiple tables.

15.2.1 Importing Data with LOAD DATA INFILE

LOAD DATA INFILE provides an alternative to INSERT for adding new records to a table. INSERT specifies data values directly in the text of the statement. LOAD DATA INFILE reads the values from a separate data file.

The simplest form of the LOAD DATA INFILE statement specifies only the name of the data file and the table into which to load the file:

```
LOAD DATA INFILE 'file_name' INTO TABLE table_name;
```

The filename is given as a quoted string. On Windows, the pathname separator character is '\', but MySQL treats the backslash as the escape character in strings. To deal with this issue, write separators in Windows pathnames either as '/' or as '\\'. To load a file named C:\mydata\data.txt, specify the filename as shown in either of the following statements:

```
LOAD DATA INFILE 'C:/mydata/data.txt' INTO TABLE t;
LOAD DATA INFILE 'C:\\mydata\\data.txt' INTO TABLE t;
```

MySQL assumes, unless told otherwise, that the file is located on the server host, that it has the default file format (columns separated by tab characters and terminated by \n newline characters), and that each input line contains a value for each column in the table. However, LOAD DATA INFILE has clauses that give you control over each of those aspects of data-loading operations and more:

- Which table to load
- The name and location of the data file
- Whether to ignore lines at the beginning of the data file
- Which columns to load
- Whether to skip or transform data values before loading them
- How to handle duplicate records
- The format of the data file

The syntax for LOAD DATA INFILE is as follows, where optional parts of the statement are indicated by square brackets:

```
LOAD DATA [LOCAL] INFILE 'file_name'
    [IGNORE | REPLACE]
    INTO TABLE table_name
    format_specifiers
    [IGNORE n LINES]
    [(column_list)]
    [SET (assignment_list)]
```

15.2.1.1 Specifying the Data File Location

LOAD DATA INFILE can read data files that are located on the server host or on the client host:

- By default, MySQL assumes that the file is located on the server host. The MySQL server reads the file directly.

- If the statement begins with LOAD DATA LOCAL INFILE rather than with LOAD DATA INFILE, the file is read from the client host on which the statement is issued. In other words, LOCAL means local to the client host from which the statement is issued. In this case, the client program reads the data file and sends its contents over the network to the server.

The rules for interpreting the filename are somewhat different for the server host and the client host. Without LOCAL in the LOAD DATA INFILE statement, MySQL looks for the data file located on the server host and interprets the pathname as follows:

- If you refer to the file by its full pathname, the server looks for the file in that exact location.

- If you specify a relative name with a single component, the server looks for the file in the database directory for the default database. (This isn't necessarily the database that contains the table into which you're loading the file.)

- If you specify a relative pathname with more than one component, the server interprets the name relative to its data directory.

Suppose that the server's data directory is /var/mysql/data, the database directory for the test database is /var/mysql/data/test, and the file data.txt is located in that database directory. Using the filename interpretation rules just given, it's possible to refer to the data.txt file three different ways in a LOAD DATA INFILE statement:

- You can refer to the file by its full pathname:
  ```
  LOAD DATA INFILE '/var/mysql/data/test/data.txt' INTO TABLE t;
  ```

- If test is the default database, you can refer to a file in the database directory using just the final component of its pathname:
  ```
  LOAD DATA INFILE 'data.txt' INTO TABLE t;
  ```

- You can refer to any file in or under the server's data directory by its pathname relative to that directory:

```
LOAD DATA INFILE './test/data.txt' INTO TABLE t;
```

If you use LOCAL to read a data file located locally on the client host, pathname interpretation is simpler:

- If you refer to the file by its full pathname, the client program looks for the file in that exact location.

- If you specify a relative pathname, the client program looks for the file relative to its current directory. Normally, this is the directory in which you invoked the program.

Suppose that a data file named data.txt is located in the /var/tmp directory on the client host and you invoke the mysql program while located in that directory. You can load the file into a table t using either of these two statements:

```
LOAD DATA LOCAL INFILE '/var/tmp/data.txt' INTO TABLE t;
LOAD DATA LOCAL INFILE 'data.txt' INTO TABLE t;
```

The first statement names the file using its full pathname. The second names the file relative to the current directory. If you invoke the mysql program in the /var directory instead, you can still load the file using the same full pathname. However, the relative pathname to the file is different than when running the program in the /var/tmp directory:

```
LOAD DATA LOCAL INFILE 'tmp/data.txt' INTO TABLE t;
```

15.2.1.2 Skipping Data File Lines

To ignore the initial part of the data file, use the IGNORE n LINES clause, where n is an integer that indicates the number of input lines to skip. This clause commonly is used when a file begins with a row of column names rather than data values. For example, to skip the first input line, a statement might be written like this:

```
LOAD DATA INFILE '/tmp/data.txt' INTO TABLE t IGNORE 1 LINES;
```

15.2.1.3 Loading Specific Table Columns

By default, LOAD DATA INFILE assumes that data values in input lines are present in the same order as the columns in the table. If the data file contains more columns than the table, MySQL ignores the excess data values. If the data file contains too few columns, each missing column is set to its default value in the table. (This is the same way MySQL handles columns that aren't named in an INSERT statement.)

If input lines don't contain values for every table column, or the data values are not in the same order as table columns, add a comma-separated list of column names within parentheses at the end of the LOAD DATA INFILE statement. This tells MySQL how columns in the table correspond to successive columns in the data file. A list of columns is useful in two ways:

- If the rows of the data file don't contain a value for every column in the table, a column list indicates which columns are present in the file. Suppose that a table named subscriber has the following structure:

```
mysql> DESCRIBE subscriber;
+---------+------------------+------+-----+---------+----------------+
| Field   | Type             | Null | Key | Default | Extra          |
+---------+------------------+------+-----+---------+----------------+
| id      | int(10) unsigned | NO   | PRI | NULL    | auto_increment |
| name    | char(40)         | NO   |     |         |                |
| address | char(40)         | NO   |     |         |                |
+---------+------------------+------+-----+---------+----------------+
```

Here, id is an AUTO_INCREMENT column. If you have a file /tmp/people.txt containing names and addresses and want MySQL to generate ID numbers automatically, load the file like this:

```
LOAD DATA INFILE '/tmp/people.txt' INTO TABLE subscriber (name,address);
```

For any table column that isn't assigned a value from the data file, MySQL sets it to its default value. MySQL thus sets the id column to the next sequence value for each input line.

- If the order of the columns in the data file doesn't correspond to the order of the columns in the table, a column list tells MySQL how to match up columns properly. For example, if the lines in people.txt contain addresses and names rather than names and addresses, the statement to load the file looks like this instead:

```
LOAD DATA INFILE '/tmp/people.txt' INTO TABLE subscriber (address,name);
```

Each item in the column list can be a table column name, as just described, or a user variable. Reasons for specifying user variables in the column list are discussed in Section 15.2.1.4, "Skipping or Transforming Column Values."

15.2.1.4 Skipping or Transforming Column Values

It is possible to skip columns in the data file, or to transform data values read from the file before inserting them into the table. These features are available by specifying user variables in the column list and the optional SET clause.

To assign an input data column to a user variable rather than to a table column, provide the name of a user variable in the column list. If you assign the column to a user variable but do nothing else with the variable, the effect is to ignore the column rather than to insert it into the table. Or, by including a SET clause, you can use expressions that transform the value before inserting it.

Suppose that you have a file named /tmp/people2.txt that was exported from a table similar to the subscriber table, and that it contains four columns for each subscriber: ID number, first name, last name, and address. The file's contents need to be transformed in two ways for loading into the subscriber table. First, the ID values are not compatible with those in the subscriber table and should be ignored. Second, the first name and last name should be concatenated with a space between. These transformations can be achieved as follows:

```
LOAD DATA INFILE '/tmp/people2.txt' INTO TABLE subscriber
(@skip,@first,@last,address)
SET name=CONCAT(@first,' ',@last);
```

15.2.1.5 LOAD DATA INFILE and Duplicate Records

When you add new records to a table with an INSERT or REPLACE statement, you can control how to handle new records containing values that duplicate unique key values already present in the table. You can allow an error to occur, ignore the new records, or replace the old records with the new ones. LOAD DATA INFILE affords the same types of control over duplicate records by means of two modifier keywords. However, its duplicate-handling behavior differs slightly depending on whether the data file is on the server host or the client host, so you must take the data file location into account.

When loading a file that's located on the server host, LOAD DATA INFILE handles records that contain duplicate unique keys as follows:

- By default, an input record that causes a duplicate-key violation results in an error and the rest of the data file isn't loaded. Records processed up to that point are loaded into the table.

- If you specify the IGNORE keyword following the filename, new records that cause duplicate-key violations are ignored and no error occurs. LOAD DATA INFILE processes the entire file, loads all records not containing duplicate keys, and discards the rest.

- If you specify the REPLACE keyword after the filename, new records that cause duplicate-key violations replace any records already in the table that contain the duplicated key values. LOAD DATA INFILE processes the entire file and loads all its records into the table.

IGNORE and REPLACE are mutually exclusive. You can specify one or the other, but not both.

For data files located on the client host, duplicate unique key handling is similar, except that the default is to ignore records that contain duplicate keys rather than to terminate with an error. That is, the default is as though the IGNORE modifier is specified. The reason for this is that the client/server protocol doesn't allow transfer of the data file from the client host to the server to be interrupted after it has started, so there's no convenient way to abort the operation in the middle.

15.2.1.6 Information Provided by LOAD DATA INFILE

As LOAD DATA INFILE executes, it keeps track of the number of records processed and the number of data conversions that occur. Then it returns to the client an information string in the following format (the counts in each field will vary per LOAD DATA INFILE operation):

```
Records: 174  Deleted: 0  Skipped: 3  Warnings: 14
```

The fields have the following meanings:

- Records indicates the number of input records read from the data file. This is not necessarily the number of records added to the table.
- Deleted indicates the number of records in the table that were replaced by input records having the same unique key value as a key already present in the table. The value may be non-zero if you use the REPLACE keyword in the statement.
- Skipped indicates the number of data records that were ignored because they contained a unique key value that duplicated a key already present in the table. The value may be non-zero if you use the IGNORE keyword in the statement.
- Warnings indicates the number of problems found in the input file. These can occur for several reasons, such as missing data values or data conversion (for example, converting an empty string to 0 for a numeric column). The warning count can be larger than the number of input records because warnings can occur for each data value in a record. To see what caused the warnings, issue a SHOW WARNINGS statement after loading the data file.

15.2.1.7 Privileges Required for LOAD DATA INFILE

LOAD DATA INFILE requires that you have the INSERT privilege for the table into which you want to load data, as well as the DELETE privilege if you specify the REPLACE modifier. If the file is located on the client host, you must have read access for the file, but no additional MySQL privileges are required. However, if the data file is located on the server host, the server itself must have read access for the file. In addition, you must have the FILE privilege. FILE is an administrative privilege, so it's likely that to use LOAD DATA INFILE without LOCAL, you'll need to connect to the server as an administrative user such as root.

15.2.1.8 Efficiency of LOAD DATA INFILE

It is more efficient to load data with LOAD DATA INFILE than by using INSERT statements. For a data file that is located on the server host, the MySQL server reads the file directly, so the data values need not cross the network from the client to the server. But even for a data file located locally on the client host, LOAD DATA INFILE is more efficient than INSERT because there's less overhead for parsing data values and because the rows are loaded in a single operation. Some of the efficiency of loading multiple rows at once can be obtained with multiple-row INSERT syntax, but LOAD DATA INFILE still is more efficient.

15.2.2 Exporting Data with SELECT ... INTO OUTFILE

A SELECT statement normally creates a result set that the server returns to the client. For example, when you issue a SELECT using the mysql client, the server returns the result and mysql writes it in tabular format when run interactively or in tab-delimited format when run in batch mode.

A variation on SELECT syntax adds an INTO OUTFILE clause. This form of SELECT writes the result set directly into a file and thus is the complement of LOAD DATA INFILE. To use SELECT in this way, place the INTO OUTFILE clause before the FROM clause. For example, to write the contents of the Country table into a file named Country.txt, issue this statement:

```
SELECT * INTO OUTFILE 'Country.txt' FROM Country;
```

The name of the file indicates the location where you want to write it. MySQL interprets the pathname using the same rules that apply to LOAD DATA INFILE for files located on the server host. For example, given the statement just shown, the server writes the file into the database directory of the default database.

Use of INTO OUTFILE changes the operation of the SELECT statement in several ways:

- The output produced by a SELECT ... INTO OUTFILE statement never leaves the server host. Instead of sending the result over the network to the client, the server writes it to a file on the server host. To prevent files from being overwritten, either accidentally or maliciously, the server requires that the output file not already exist.

- The statement causes the server to write a new file on the server host, so you must connect to the server using an account that has the FILE privilege.

- The file is created with filesystem access permissions that make it owned by the MySQL server but world-readable.

- The output file contains one line per row selected by the statement. By default, column values are delimited by tab characters and lines are terminated with newlines, but you can control the output format by adding format specifiers after the filename, as described in Section 15.2.3, "Data File Format Specifiers."

The location and manner in which SELECT ... INTO OUTFILE creates the file has several implications:

- If you want to access the file directly, you must have a login account on the server host or be otherwise able to access files on that host somehow. For some purposes, this limitation might not be a problem. For example, you don't need to access the file yourself to reload it later with LOAD DATA INFILE because the MySQL server can read it for you.

- The file is world-readable, so anyone who has filesystem access on the server host can read it. You probably don't want to use SELECT ... INTO OUTFILE to create files that contain sensitive information, unless perhaps you're the only person with access to the machine.

- The file is owned by the MySQL server, so you might not be able to remove it after you're done with it. It might be necessary to coordinate with the server administrator to arrange for removal of the file.

Without the OUTFILE keyword, SELECT ... INTO can be used to fetch a single row of data into variables. These can be user variables, stored routine variables, or local variables. See Section 18.5.4.2, "Assigning Variable Values with SELECT ... INTO."

15.2.3 Data File Format Specifiers

LOAD DATA INFILE and SELECT ... INTO OUTFILE assume a default data file format in which column values are separated by tab characters and records are terminated by newlines. If a data file to be read by LOAD DATA INFILE has different column separators or line terminators, you must indicate what the format is so that MySQL can read the file contents correctly. Similarly, if you want SELECT ... INTO OUTFILE to write a file with different separators or terminators, you'll need to indicate the format to use. It's also possible to control data value quoting and escaping behavior.

The format specifiers supported by LOAD DATA INFILE and SELECT ... INTO OUTFILE don't enable you to characterize individual columns in the data file. For example, you cannot indicate that column 3 is numeric or that column 17 contains dates. Instead, you define the general characteristics that apply to all column values: What characters separate column values in data rows, whether values are quoted, and whether there is an escape character that signifies special character sequences.

For LOAD DATA INFILE, format specifiers are listed after the table name. For SELECT ... INTO OUTFILE, they follow the output filename. The syntax for format specifiers is the same for both statements and looks like this:

```
FIELDS
    TERMINATED BY 'string'
    ENCLOSED BY 'char'
    ESCAPED BY 'char'
LINES TERMINATED BY 'string'
```

The FIELDS clause defines the formatting of data values within a line. The LINES clause defines the line-ending sequence. In other words, FIELDS indicates the structure of column values within records and LINES indicates where record boundaries occur.

The TERMINATED BY, ENCLOSED BY, and ESCAPED BY parts of the FIELDS clause may be given in any order. You need not specify all three parts. Defaults are used for any that are missing (or if the FIELDS clause itself is missing) :

- Data values are assumed to be terminated by (that is, separated by) tab characters. To indicate a different value, include a TERMINATED BY option.

- Data values are assumed to be unquoted. To indicate a quote character, include an ENCLOSED BY option. For LOAD DATA INFILE, enclosing quotes are stripped from input values if they're found. For SELECT ... INTO OUTFILE, output values are written enclosed within quote characters.

A variation on ENCLOSED BY is OPTIONALLY ENCLOSED BY. This is the same as ENCLOSED for LOAD DATA INFILE, but different for SELECT ... INTO OUTFILE: The presence of OPTIONALLY causes output value quoting only for string columns, not for all columns.

- The default escape character is backslash ('\'). Any occurrence of this character within a data value modifies interpretation of the character that follows it. To indicate a different escape character, include an ESCAPED BY option. MySQL understands the following special escape sequences:

Sequence	Meaning
\N	NULL value
\0	NUL (zero) byte
\b	Backspace
\n	Newline (linefeed)
\r	Carriage return
\s	Space
\t	Tab
\'	Single quote
\"	Double quote
\\	Backslash

All these sequences except \N are understood whether they appear alone or within a longer data value. \N is understood as NULL only when it appears alone.

The default line terminator is the newline (linefeed) character. To indicate a line-ending sequence explicitly, use a LINES clause. Common line terminators are newline, carriage return, and carriage return/newline pairs. Specify them as follows:

```
LINES TERMINATED BY '\n'
LINES TERMINATED BY '\r'
LINES TERMINATED BY '\r\n'
```

Because newline is the default line terminator, it need be specified only if you want to make the line-ending sequence explicit. Newline terminators are common on Unix systems and carriage return/newline pairs are common on Windows.

The ESCAPED BY option controls only the handling of values in the data file, not how you write the statement itself. If you want to specify a data file escape character of '@', you'd write ESCAPED BY '@'. That doesn't mean you then use '@' to escape special characters elsewhere in the statement. For example, you'd still specify carriage return as the line termination character using LINES TERMINATED BY '\r', not using LINES TERMINATED BY '@r'.

Suppose that a file named `/tmp/data.txt` contains information in comma-separated values (CSV) format, with values quoted by double quote characters and lines terminated by carriage returns. To import the file into a table t, use this LOAD DATA INFILE statement:

```
LOAD DATA INFILE '/tmp/data.txt' INTO TABLE t
FIELDS TERMINATED BY ',' ENCLOSED BY '"'
LINES TERMINATED BY '\r';
```

To export information in that same format, use this SELECT ... INTO OUTFILE statement:

```
SELECT * INTO OUTFILE '/tmp/data-out.txt'
FIELDS TERMINATED BY ',' ENCLOSED BY '"'
LINES TERMINATED BY '\r'
FROM t;
```

15.2.4 Importing and Exporting NULL Values

A NULL value indicates the absence of a value or an unknown value, which is difficult to represent literally in a data file. For import and export purposes, MySQL uses the convention of representing NULL values by \N:

- For LOAD DATA INFILE, a \N appearing unquoted by itself as a column value is interpreted as NULL. MySQL users sometimes assume that an empty value in an input file will be handled as a NULL value, but that isn't true. MySQL converts an empty input value to 0, an empty string, or a "zero" temporal value, depending on the type of the corresponding table column.
- For SELECT ... INTO OUTFILE, MySQL writes NULL values to the output file as \N.

15.3 Importing and Exporting Data from the Command Line

The `mysqlimport` and `mysqldump` client programs provide a command-line interface for importing and exporting data. `mysqlimport` imports data files into tables. `mysqldump` exports tables to data files.

15.3.1 Importing Data with `mysqlimport`

The `mysqlimport` client program loads data files into tables. It provides a command-line interface to the LOAD DATA INFILE statement. That is, `mysqlimport` examines the options given on the command line. It then connects to the server and, for each input file named in the command, issues a LOAD DATA INFILE statement that loads the file into the appropriate table.

Because `mysqlimport` works this way, to use it most effectively, you should be familiar with the LOAD DATA INFILE statement, which is discussed in Section 15.2.1, "Importing Data with

LOAD DATA INFILE." This section describes `mysqlimport` invocation syntax and how its options correspond to various clauses of the LOAD DATA INFILE statement.

Invoke `mysqlimport` from the command line as follows:

```
shell> mysqlimport options db_name input_file ...
```

db_name names the database containing the table to be loaded and *input_file* names the file that contains the data to be loaded. You can name several input files following the database name if you like.

`mysqlimport` uses each filename to determine the name of the corresponding table into which the file's contents should be loaded. The program does this by stripping off any filename extension (the last period and anything following it) and using the result as the table name. For example, `mysqlimport` treats a file named `City.txt` or `City.dat` as input to be loaded into a table named `City`. After determining the table name corresponding to the filename, `mysqlimport` issues a LOAD DATA INFILE statement to load the file into the table.

Each table to be loaded by `mysqlimport` must already exist, and each input file should contain only data values. `mysqlimport` isn't intended for processing dump files that consist of SQL statements. (Such files can be created with the `mysqldump` program; for instructions on processing an SQL-format dump file, see Section 32.8.1, "Reloading `mysqldump` Output.")

The *options* part of the `mysqlimport` command may include any of the standard connection parameter options, such as `--host` or `--user`. You'll need to supply these options if the default connection parameters aren't appropriate. `mysqlimport` also understands options specific to its own operation. Invoke `mysqlimport` with the `--help` option to see a complete list of the options that can be used to tell `mysqlimport` the actions you want it to perform.

By default, input files for `mysqlimport` are assumed to contain lines terminated by newlines, with each line containing tab-separated data values. This is the same default format assumed by the LOAD DATA INFILE statement. For an input file that's in a different format, use the following options to tell `mysqlimport` how to interpret the file:

- `--lines-terminated-by=string`

  string specifies the character sequence that each input line ends with. The default is \n (linefeed, also known as newline); other common line terminators are \r (carriage return) and \r\n (carriage return/linefeed pairs).

- `--fields-terminated-by=string`

  string specifies the delimiter between data values within input lines. The default delimiter is \t (tab) .

- `--fields-enclosed-by=char` or `--fields-optionally-enclosed-by=char`

  char indicates a quote character that surrounds data values in the file. By default, values are assumed to be unquoted. Use one of these options if values are quoted. A common value for *char* is the double quote character ("'). If quote characters enclose a data value, they're removed before the value is loaded into the table.

- `--fields-escaped-by=char`

  By default, '\' within the input is taken as an escape character that signifies a special sequence. For example, if the `\N` sequence occurs alone in a field, it's interpreted as a NULL value. Use this option to specify a different escape character. To turn escaping off (no escape character), specify an empty value for *char*.

The preceding options give you the flexibility to load input files containing data in a variety of formats. Some examples follow; each one loads an input file named `City.txt` into the `City` table in the `world` database. Commands that are shown on multiple lines should be entered on a single line.

The following command loads a file that has lines ending in carriage return/linefeed pairs:

```
shell> mysqlimport --lines-terminated-by="\r\n" world City.txt
```

Note that the `--lines-terminated-by` value is quoted with double quotes. Format option values often contain special characters, such as backslash, that might have special meaning to your command interpreter. It might be necessary to quote such characters to tell your command interpreter to pass them unchanged to `mysqlimport`.

The syntax for specifying a double quote is trickier and depends on which command interpreter you use. The following command loads a data file containing values quoted by double quote characters:

```
shell> mysqlimport --fields-enclosed-by='"' world City.txt
```

This command should work on most Unix shells, which allow the double quote character to be quoted within single quotes. This doesn't work on Windows, where you must specify a double quote within a double-quoted string by escaping it:

```
shell> mysqlimport --fields-enclosed-by="\"" world City.txt
```

The following command loads a file that has data values separated by commas and lines ending with carriage returns:

```
shell> mysqlimport --fields-terminated-by=,
         --lines-terminated-by="\r" world City.txt
```

Other `mysqlimport` options provide additional control over data file loading. The following list discusses some of those you're likely to find useful:

- `--ignore or --replace`

  These options tell `mysqlimport` how to handle input records that contain unique key values that are already present in the table. Such records result in duplicate-key errors and cannot be loaded by default. `--ignore` causes duplicates in the input file to be ignored. `--replace` causes existing records in the table to be replaced by duplicates in the input file. These options correspond to the use of IGNORE or REPLACE with LOAD DATA INFILE.

- --local

  By default, a data file to be loaded into a table is assumed to reside on the server host, allowing the server to read the file directly. This is very efficient, but requires the user running mysqlimport to have the FILE privilege (a powerful privilege normally reserved for administrators). The --local option allows use of a data file that's located locally on the client host where mysqlimport is invoked. With --local, mysqlimport reads the data file and sends it over the network to the server. This allows mysqlimport to read any file on the client host to which the invoker has access, without requiring the invoker to have the FILE privilege. For the --local option to work, the server must be configured to allow local files to be transferred to it. This option corresponds to the use of LOCAL with LOAD DATA INFILE.

15.3.2 Exporting Data with mysqldump

The mysqldump client program dumps table contents to files. It is useful for making database backups or for transferring database contents to another server. mysqldump can export tables as tab-delimited data files or produce SQL-format dump files that contain CREATE TABLE and INSERT statements for re-creating the dumped files. This section discusses how to use mysqldump to export tables as data files. For information on creating SQL-format dump files, see Section 32.4.2, "Making Text Backups with mysqldump."

To use mysqldump to export tables as tab-delimited data files, specify the --tab=dir_name (or -T dir_name) option on the command line. This option causes mysqldump to issue SELECT ... INTO OUTFILE statements to tell the MySQL server to write each dumped table as a tab-delimited text file in the dir_name directory. For each table, mysqldump itself writes a file containing a CREATE TABLE statement that you can use to re-create the table before reloading the data file into it.

Invoke mysqldump from the command line as follows:

```
shell> mysqldump --tab=dir_name options db_name tbl_name ...
```

db_name names the database containing the table to be exported and tbl_name names the table to be exported. To export multiple tables, name all of them following the database name. If you don't provide any table names, mysqldump exports all tables in the database.

The options part of the mysqldump command may include any of the standard connection parameter options, such as --host or --user. You'll need to supply these options if the default connection parameters aren't appropriate. mysqldump also understands options specific to its own operation. Invoke mysqldump with the --help option to see a complete list of the options that can be used to tell mysqldump the actions you want it to perform.

Suppose that you dump the table City from the world database using the /tmp directory as the output directory:

```
shell> mysqldump --tab=/tmp world City
```

The output consists of a `City.sql` file containing the CREATE TABLE statement for the table, and a `City.txt` file containing the table data.

To reload data exported by invoking `mysqldump` with the `--tab` option, change location into the dump directory. Then use `mysql` to process the `.sql` file that contains the CREATE TABLE statement, and use `mysqlimport` to load the `.txt` file that contains the table data:

```
shell> cd /tmp
shell> mysql world < City.sql
shell> mysqlimport world City.txt
```

Using `--tab` to produce tab-delimited dump files is much faster than creating SQL-format files, but you should keep in mind the following points:

- The CREATE TABLE statement for each table *table_name* is sent by the server to `mysqldump`, which writes it to a file named *table_name*.sql in the dump directory on the client host. The `.sql` files are owned by you.

- The table contents are written directly by the server into a file named *table_name*.txt in the dump directory on the server host. The `.txt` files are owned by the server.

- Use of `--tab` can be confusing because some files are created by the client and some by the server, and because the `.sql` files have different ownerships than the `.txt` files. To minimize confusion, run `mysqldump` on the server host, specify the dump directory using its full pathname so that `mysqldump` and the server both interpret it as the same location, and specify a dump directory that is writable both to you and to the server.

- The MySQL account that you use for connecting to the server must have the FILE privilege because the dump operation causes the server to write data files on the server host.

- To create only the data files and not the `.sql` files that contain the CREATE TABLE statements, use the `--no-create-info` option.

The default data file format produced by the `--tab` option consists of tab-delimited lines with newline terminators. This is the same default format assumed by the SELECT ... INTO OUTFILE statement. To control the format of the data files that `mysqldump` generates, use the following options:

- `--lines-terminated-by=`*string*

  string specifies the character sequence that each input line should end with. The default is \n (linefeed, also known as newline). Other common line terminators are \r (carriage return) and \r\n (carriage return/linefeed pairs).

- `--fields-terminated-by=`*string*

  string specifies the delimiter to write between data values within input lines. The default delimiter is \t (tab).

- --fields-enclosed-by=*char* or --fields-optionally-enclosed-by=*char*

  char indicates a quote character that should be written surrounding data values. By default, values are not quoted. A common value for *char* is the double quote character ('"'). With --fields-enclosed-by, all values are quoted. With --fields-optionally-enclosed-by, only values from string columns are quoted.

- --fields-escaped-by=*char*

  By default, special characters in data values are written preceded by '\' as an escape character, and NULL values are written as \N. Use this option to specify a different escape character. To turn escaping off (no escape character), specify an empty value for *char*.

The mysqlimport program has similar options for describing the data file format. See the discussion of that program for information about specifying *char* or *string* values that contain characters that your command interpreter considers special.

If you combine the --tab option with format-control options such as --fields-terminated-by and --fields-enclosed-by, you should specify the same format-control options with mysqlimport so that it knows how to interpret the data files.

The --all-databases and --databases options for mysqldump are used for dumping multiple databases. You cannot use those options together with --tab, which causes mysqldump to write the files for all dumped tables to a single directory. You would have no way to tell which files correspond to tables in each database.

16

User Variables

MySQL allows you to assign values to variables and refer to them later. This is useful when you want to save the results of calculations for use in subsequent statements. This chapter discusses how user variables are defined and used in SQL statements. It covers the following exam topics:

- User variable syntax
- User variable properties

16.1 User Variable Syntax

User variables are written as *@var_name* and may be set to an integer, real, string, or NULL value. In a SET statement, you can assign a value to a variable using either = or := as the assignment operator:

```
mysql> SET @var1 = 'USA';
mysql> SET @var2 := 'GBR';
```

In other contexts, such as in a SELECT statement, use the := assignment operator (not the = operator):

```
mysql> SELECT @var3 := 'CAN';
+----------------+
| @var3 := 'CAN' |
+----------------+
| CAN            |
+----------------+
```

A SET statement can perform multiple variable assignments, separated by commas:

```
mysql> SET @var1 = 'USA', @var2 = 'GBR', @var3 = 'CAN';
```

If you refer to an uninitialized variable that has not been assigned a value explicitly, its value is NULL. In the following statement, @var4 is referenced without having been set previously:

```
mysql> SELECT @var1, @var2, @var3, @var4;
+-------+-------+-------+-------+
| @var1 | @var2 | @var3 | @var4 |
+-------+-------+-------+-------+
| USA   | GBR   | CAN   | NULL  |
+-------+-------+-------+-------+
```

User variables can be used in most contexts where expressions are allowed. However, they cannot be used where a literal value is required. Examples of this restriction include LIMIT, which requires literal integer arguments, and the filename in LOAD DATA INFILE, which must be a literal string.

User variables are specifically required when using EXECUTE to execute a prepared statement. Each data value given as a parameter to EXECUTE must be passed as a user variable. User variables also are used in LOAD DATA INFILE to hold data values read from a file that are to be transformed before being loaded into a table.

User variables are not the same as local variables that you declare in stored routines. The latter are created with a DECLARE statement and are not referred to with a leading '@' character. For more information, see Section 18.5.4, "Variables in Stored Routines."

16.2 User Variable Properties

In MySQL 5, user variable names are not case sensitive. (They are case sensitive before MySQL 5.)

User variables are specific to the client connection within which they are used and exist only for the duration of that connection. A user variable used within a connection cannot be accessed by other connections. When a connection ends, all its user variables are lost.

A user variable that has been assigned a non-binary string value has the same character set and collation as the string. All user variables have an implicit coercibility value.

Prepared Statements

This chapter discusses how to use SQL syntax for prepared statements. It covers the following exam topics:

- Benefits of prepared statements
- Using prepared statements with mysql
- Preparing, executing, and deallocating prepared statements

17.1 Benefits of Prepared Statements

MySQL Server supports prepared statements, which are useful when you want to run several queries that differ only in very small details. For example, you can prepare a statement, and then execute it multiple times, each time with different data values.

Besides offering a convenience, prepared statements also provide enhanced performance because the complete statement is parsed only once by the server. When the parse is complete, the server and client may make use of a new protocol that requires fewer data conversions (and usually makes for less traffic between the server and client) than when sending each statement individually.

17.2 Using Prepared Statements from the mysql Client

In most circumstances, statements are prepared and executed using the programming interface that you normally use for writing applications that use MySQL. However, to aid in testing and debugging, it is possible to define and use prepared statements from within the mysql command-line client. For purposes of certification, prepared statement use with mysql is the context used to explain prepared statements here. It is also the context in which questions on prepared statements appear on the exam.

Here is a short example that illustrates the use of a prepared statement. It prepares a statement that determines how many languages are spoken in a given country, executes it multiple times, and disposes of it:

```
mysql> PREPARE my_stmt FROM
    -> 'SELECT COUNT(*) FROM CountryLanguage WHERE CountryCode = ?';
Query OK, 0 rows affected (0.00 sec)
Statement prepared

mysql> SET @code = 'ESP'; EXECUTE my_stmt USING @code;
Query OK, 0 rows affected (0.00 sec)
+----------+
| COUNT(*) |
+----------+
|        4 |
+----------+
1 row in set (0.00 sec)

mysql> SET @code = 'RUS'; EXECUTE my_stmt USING @code;
Query OK, 0 rows affected (0.00 sec)
+----------+
| COUNT(*) |
+----------+
|       12 |
+----------+
1 row in set (0.00 sec)

mysql> DEALLOCATE PREPARE my_stmt;
Query OK, 0 rows affected (0.00 sec)
```

17.3 Preparing a Statement

The PREPARE statement is used to define an SQL statement that will be executed later. PREPARE takes two arguments: a name to assign to the statement once it has been prepared, and the text of an SQL statement. Prepared statement names are not case sensitive. The text of the statement can be given either as a literal string or as a user variable containing the statement.

The statement may not be complete, because data values that are unknown at preparation time are represented by question mark ('?') characters that serve as parameter markers. At the time the statement is executed, you provide specific data values, one for each parameter in the statement. The server replaces the markers with the data values to complete the statement. Different values can be used each time the statement is executed.

The following example prepares a statement named namepop. When executed later with a country code as a parameter value, the statement will return a result set containing the corresponding country name and population from the world database.

```
mysql> PREPARE namepop FROM '
    '> SELECT Name, Population
    '> FROM Country
    '> WHERE Code = ?
    '> ';
Query OK, 0 rows affected (0.02 sec)
Statement prepared
```

The message Statement prepared indicates that the server is ready to execute the namepop statement. On the other hand, if the server finds a problem as it parses the statement during a PREPARE, it returns an error and does not prepare the statement:

```
mysql> PREPARE error FROM '
    '> SELECT NonExistingColumn
    '> FROM Country
    '> WHERE Code = ?
    '> ';
ERROR 1054 (42S22): Unknown column 'NonExistingColumn' in 'field list'
```

If you PREPARE a statement using a statement name that already exists, the server first discards the prepared statement currently associated with the name, and then prepares the new statement. If the new statement contains an error and cannot be prepared, the result is that no statement with the given name will exist.

MySQL does not allow every type of SQL statement to be prepared. Those that may be prepared are limited to the following:

- SELECT statements
- Statements that modify data: INSERT, REPLACE, UPDATE, and DELETE
- CREATE TABLE statements
- SET, DO, and many SHOW statements

A prepared statement exists only for the duration of the session in which it is created, and is visible only to the session in which it is created. When a session ends, all prepared statements for that session are discarded.

17.4 Executing a Prepared Statement

After a statement has been prepared, it can be executed. If the statement contains any '?' parameter markers, a data value must be supplied for each of them by means of user variables. (General information about user variables is given in Chapter 16, "User Variables.")

To execute a prepared statement, initialize any user variables needed to provide parameter values, and then issue an EXECUTE ... USING statement. The following example prepares a statement and then executes it several times using different data values:

```
mysql> PREPARE namepop FROM '
    '> SELECT Name, Population
    '> FROM Country
    '> WHERE Code = ?
    '> ';
Query OK, 0 rows affected (0.00 sec)
Statement prepared

mysql> SET @var1 = 'USA';
Query OK, 0 rows affected (0.00 sec)

mysql> EXECUTE namepop USING @var1;
+---------------+------------+
| Name          | Population |
+---------------+------------+
| United States |  278357000 |
+---------------+------------+
1 row in set (0.00 sec)

mysql> SET @var2 = 'GBR';
Query OK, 0 rows affected (0.00 sec)

mysql> EXECUTE namepop USING @var2;
+----------------+------------+
| Name           | Population |
+----------------+------------+
| United Kingdom |   59623400 |
+----------------+------------+
1 row in set (0.00 sec)

mysql> SELECT @var3 := 'CAN';
+----------------+
| @var3 := 'CAN' |
+----------------+
| CAN            |
+----------------+
1 row in set (0.00 sec)
```

```
mysql> EXECUTE namepop USING @var3;
+--------+------------+
| Name   | Population |
+--------+------------+
| Canada |   31147000 |
+--------+------------+
1 row in set (0.00 sec)
```

If you refer to a user variable that has not been initialized, its value is NULL:

```
mysql> EXECUTE namepop USING @var4;
Empty set (0.00 sec)
```

17.5 Deallocating Prepared Statements

Prepared statements are dropped automatically when they are redefined or when you close the connection to the server, so there is rarely any reason to drop them explicitly. However, should you wish to do so (for example, to free memory on the server side), use the DEALLOCATE PREPARE statement:

```
mysql> DEALLOCATE PREPARE namepop;
Query OK, 0 rows affected (0.00 sec)
```

MySQL also provides DROP PREPARE as an alias for DEALLOCATE PREPARE.

Stored Procedures and Functions

MySQL provides capabilities for defining and executing stored procedures and functions. A client sends the definition of a procedure or function to the server, which stores it for later use. Clients then invoke it whenever necessary to cause SQL operations to be performed or to produce values.

Stored procedures and functions have a great deal in common and much of the discussion here applies to both. However, to avoid many repetitions of the term "procedures and functions," the following discussion often uses "routine" to indicate material that applies to both. In cases where procedures and functions do have different properties, material that pertains only to one type of routine is indicated by one of the more specific terms "procedure" or "function."

This chapter covers the following exam topics:

- The benefits of using stored routines
- Differences between procedures and functions
- The namespace for stored routines
- Creating, altering, and dropping stored routines
- Invoking stored routines
- Obtaining metadata about stored routines
- Privileges required for operations on stored routines

Stored routine syntax comprises a number of statements, and some of the examples here necessarily use statements that are not discussed until a later section. If you see a statement that has not yet been covered, just keep reading or flip ahead a few pages.

To use stored routines, you must have the access privileges that are described in Section 18.10, "Stored Routine Privileges and Execution Security." However, even with those privileges, the server by default will not let you create stored routines if binary logging is enabled except under certain conditions. This is because use of stored routines introduces certain security issues for replication. Also, routines that modify data may make it problematic to use the binary log for data recovery, particularly if you use routines that have non-deterministic behavior. The details of these issues are not covered here. For purposes of this study guide, it's assumed that if you have binary logging enabled, you have also disabled the restrictions on routine creation so that you can try the examples in this chapter. You can disable the restrictions by starting the server with the `--log-bin-trust-routine-creators` option at server startup, or you can set the `log_bin_trust_routine_creators` system variable at runtime as follows:

```
mysql> SET GLOBAL log_bin_trust_routine_creators = 1;
```

For details about the security and data recovery concerns regarding use of stored routines, and how best to deal with these concerns, see the *MySQL Reference Manual*.

18.1 Benefits of Stored Routines

Stored procedures and functions offer several benefits for application development, deployment, and operation:

- *More flexible SQL syntax.* Stored routines can be written using extensions to SQL syntax, such as compound statements and flow-control constructs, that make it easier to express complex logic.

- *Error handling capabilities.* A stored routine can create error handlers to be used when exceptional conditions arise. The occurrence of an error need not cause termination of the routine but can be handled appropriately.

- *Standards compliance.* The MySQL implementation of stored routines conforms to standard SQL syntax. Routines written for MySQL should be reasonably portable to other database servers that also follow standard SQL syntax.

  Note: Although the implementation is based on standard SQL, it is not yet complete as of this writing and there are limitations. For example, cursors are read-only and cannot be used to modify tables. Cursors also advance through a result set a row at a time; that is, they are not scrollable. Expect these restrictions to be removed over time.

- *Code packaging and encapsulation.* A routine allows the code that performs an operation to be stored once on the server and accessed from multiple applications. The code need not be included within multiple applications. This reduces the potential for variation in how different applications perform the operation.

- *Less "re-invention of the wheel."* A collection of stored routines acts as a library of solutions to problems. Developers can use them "off the shelf" rather than re-implementing the code from scratch themselves. Stored routines also facilitate sharing of knowledge and experience. A skilled SQL developer who solves a difficult problem can implement the solution in a stored routine to be used by developers with less expertise.

- *Separation of logic.* Factoring out the logic of specific application operations into stored routines reduces the complexity of an application's own logic and makes it easier to understand.

- *Ease of maintenance.* A single copy of a routine is easier to maintain than a copy embedded within each application. Upgrading applications is easier if they all use a routine in common, because it is necessary to upgrade only the routine, not every application that uses it.

- *Reduction in network bandwidth requirements.* Consider a multiple-statement operation performed by a client without the use of a stored routine: Each statement and its result crosses the network, even those that calculate intermediate results. If the operation is performed within a stored routine instead, intermediate statements and results are processed entirely on the server side and do not cross the network. This improves performance and results in less contention for resources, particularly for busy or low-bandwidth networks. (The potential benefit of this factor must be weighed against the number of clients and the amount of client processing that is moved onto the server through the use of stored routines.)

- *Server upgrades benefit clients.* Upgrades to the server host improve the performance of stored routines that execute on that host. This improves performance for client applications that use the routines even though the client machines are not upgraded.

- *Better security.* A routine can be written to access sensitive data on the definer's behalf for the invoker, but not return anything that the invoker should not see. A routine can also be used to modify tables in a safe way, without giving users direct access to the tables. This prevents them from making possibly unsafe changes themselves.

18.2 Differences Between Stored Procedures and Functions

The most general difference between procedures and functions is that they are invoked differently and for different purposes:

- A procedure does not return a value. Instead, it is invoked with a CALL statement to perform an operation such as modifying a table or processing retrieved records.

- A function is invoked within an expression and returns a single value directly to the caller to be used in the expression. That is, a function is used in expressions the same way as a constant, a built-in function, or a reference to a table column.

- You cannot invoke a function with a CALL statement, nor can you invoke a procedure in an expression.

Syntax for routine creation differs somewhat for procedures and functions:

- Procedure parameters can be defined as input-only, output-only, or for both input and output. This means that a procedure can pass values back to the caller by using output parameters. These values can be accessed in statements that follow the CALL statement. Functions have only input parameters. As a result, although both procedures and functions can have parameters, procedure parameter declaration syntax differs from that for functions.

- Functions return a value, so there must be a RETURNS clause in a function definition to indicate the data type of the return value. Also, there must be at least one RETURN statement within the function body to return a value to the caller. RETURNS and RETURN do not appear in procedure definitions.

A MySQL extension for stored procedures (but not functions) is that a procedure can generate a result set, or even multiple result sets, which the caller processes the same way as result sets produced by a SELECT statement. However, the contents of such result sets cannot be used directly in expressions.

18.3 The Namespace for Stored Routines

Each stored routine is associated with a particular database, just like a table or a view:

- MySQL interprets an unqualified reference, *routine_name*, as a reference to a procedure or function in the default database. To refer to a routine in a specific database, use a qualified name of the form *db_name.routine_name*.

- When the routine executes, it implicitly changes the default database to the database associated with the routine and restores the previous default database when it terminates. Due to this association of a routine with a database, you must have access to that database to be able to invoke the routine. (The means of access depends on the routine's security characteristic. See Section 18.5, "Creating Stored Routines.")

- When you drop a database, any stored routines in the database are also dropped.

Stored procedures and functions do not share the same namespace. It is not possible to have two procedures or two functions with the same name in a database, but it is possible to have a procedure and a function with the same name in a database.

18.4 Defining Stored Routines

Stored routine definitions can use compound statements. That is, a definition can be given as a BEGIN/END block that contains multiple statements. Each statement within a block must be terminated by a semicolon character (';').

If you are defining a stored routine from within a programming interface that does not use the semicolon as a statement terminator, semicolons within stored routine definitions do not present any special issues. However, if you are using the mysql client program, semicolons are ambiguous within routine definitions because `mysql` itself treats semicolon as a statement terminator. To handle this issue, `mysql` supports a `delimiter` command that enables you to change its statement terminator temporarily while you define a stored routine. By using `delimiter`, you can cause `mysql` to pass semicolons to the server along with the rest of the routine definition. The following example shows how to define a procedure named `world_record_count()` within `mysql` by redefining the terminator as the `//` sequence:

```
mysql> delimiter //
mysql> CREATE PROCEDURE world_record_count ()
    -> BEGIN
    ->   SELECT 'Country', COUNT(*) FROM Country;
    ->   SELECT 'City', COUNT(*) FROM City;
    ->   SELECT 'CountryLanguage', COUNT(*) FROM CountryLanguage;
    -> END;
    -> //
Query OK, 0 rows affected (0.00 sec)

mysql> delimiter ;
```

This study guide generally uses `//` in examples that redefine the statement delimiter, but the choice of delimiter is up to you. Be sure to choose a delimiter that does not contain characters that occur within the definition of the stored routine that you are creating. For example, ')' is a poor choice because it occurs at least once within every stored procedure or function definition.

The `delimiter` command is also useful for creating triggers. (See Chapter 19, "Triggers.") A trigger definition contains a trigger action statement, and the statement can be a compound-statement block that includes multiple statements of its own.

18.5 Creating Stored Routines

This section covers general syntax for stored routine definitions. The sections that follow detail specific statements that are used within routines.

To define a stored procedure or function, use a `CREATE PROCEDURE` or `CREATE FUNCTION` statement, respectively. These statements have the following syntax:

```
CREATE PROCEDURE proc_name ([parameters])
  [characteristics]
  routine_body

CREATE FUNCTION func_name ([parameters])
  RETURNS data_type
  [characteristics]
  routine_body
```

The routine name can be unqualified to create the routine in the default database, or qualified with a database name to create the routine in a specific database.

The database that a routine belongs to is used to interpret unqualified references to tables that occur within the routine definition. To refer to tables in other databases, use qualified names of the form *db_name.table_name*.

The optional parameter list declares the parameters that are to be passed to the routine when it is invoked. For details, see Section 18.5.2, "Declaring Parameters."

The optional *characteristics* clause contains one or more of the following values, which can appear in any order:

- SQL SECURITY {DEFINER | INVOKER}

    A stored routine runs either with the privileges of the user who created it or the user who invoked it. The choice of which set of privileges to use is controlled by the value of the SQL SECURITY characteristic:

    - A value of DEFINER causes the routine to have the privileges of the user who created it. This is the default value.
    - A value of INVOKER causes the routine to run with the privileges of its invoking user. This means the routine has access to database objects only if that user can already access them otherwise.

    SQL SECURITY DEFINER enables you to create routines that access information on behalf of users who otherwise would not be able to do so. For example, a summary of financial data might be generated from tables in a business database. If you want to allow users to generate the summary but not have direct access to the contents of the underlying tables, create a procedure that produces the summary as a result set and define it to have DEFINER security. On the other hand, you must be careful not to create a DEFINER routine if you really do not want other users to have your privileges while the routine executes.

- DETERMINISTIC or NOT DETERMINISTIC

    Indicates whether the routine always produces the same result when invoked with a given set of input parameter values. If it does not, the routine is non-deterministic. For example, a function that returns the country name corresponding to a country code is deterministic, but a function that returns a summary of financial data is non-deterministic because it returns different results as the information changes over time. This characteristic is intended to convey information to the query optimizer, but the optimizer does not use it as of this writing. If neither value is specified, the default is NOT DETERMINISTIC.

- LANGUAGE SQL

    Indicates the language in which the routine is written. Currently, the only supported language is SQL, so SQL is the only allowable value for the LANGUAGE characteristic (and it is also the default value).

- COMMENT '*string*'

    Specifies a descriptive string for the routine. The string is displayed by the statements that return information about routine definitions. See Section 18.9, "Obtaining Stored Routine Metadata."

routine_body specifies the body of the procedure or function. This is the code to be executed when the routine is executed. A routine body consists of a single statement. However, this imposes no limitation on creating complex routines, because you can use a BEGIN ... END block for the routine body, and place multiple statements within the block. See Section 18.5.1, "Compound Statements."

The remarks made thus far about routine syntax are true both for procedures and functions. There are a few ways in which the syntax for creating a function differs from that for procedures:

- Parameter declarations are not quite the same.

- A function must include a RETURNS clause to indicate the data type of the value that the function returns. The type is any valid MySQL data type, such as INT, DECIMAL(10,2), or VARCHAR(40).

- Somewhere in the body of the function there must be a RETURN statement to return a value to the caller.

The following listing shows an example procedure and function:

```
CREATE PROCEDURE rect_area (width INT, height INT)
  SELECT width * height AS area;

CREATE FUNCTION circle_area (radius FLOAT)
  RETURNS FLOAT
  RETURN PI() * radius * radius;
```

RETURNS is not terminated by a semicolon because it is just a clause, not a statement.

When a stored routine executes, its environment is set so that the database that it belongs to becomes its default database for the duration of its execution. Also, the sql_mode system variable value in effect when the routine executes is the value that was current when it was defined. The privileges of the routine are determined by its SQL SECURITY characteristic.

18.5.1 Compound Statements

Stored routine syntax requires that a routine body be a single statement. For a complex routine, you can satisfy this requirement by using a compound statement that contains other statements. A compound statement begins and ends with the BEGIN and END keywords and creates a block. In between BEGIN and END, write the statements that make up the block, each terminated by a semicolon character (';'). The BEGIN/END block itself is terminated by a semicolon, but BEGIN is not.

Here is a simple stored procedure that uses a compound statement containing several SELECT statements. It displays the number of records in tables from the world database:

```
CREATE PROCEDURE world_record_count ()
BEGIN
  SELECT 'Country', COUNT(*) FROM Country;
  SELECT 'City', COUNT(*) FROM City;
  SELECT 'CountryLanguage', COUNT(*) FROM CountryLanguage;
END;
```

The use of semicolon statement terminators in a multiple-statement definition is problematic if the program you are using to define the routine also treats semicolon as special. Section 18.4, "Defining Stored Routines," discusses how to deal with this issue when using the mysql program.

A block can be labeled, which is useful when it's necessary to alter the flow of control. For example, the LEAVE statement can be used to exit a labeled BEGIN/END block. The syntax for labeling a block looks like this:

```
[label:] BEGIN ... END [label]
```

Labels are optional, but the label at the end can be present only if the label at the beginning is also present, and the end label must have the same name as the beginning label. An end label is never required but can make a routine easier to understand because it helps a reader find the end of the labeled construct.

Blocks can be nested. In other words, a BEGIN/END block can contain other BEGIN/END blocks. Here is an example that uses nested blocks where the inner block is labeled. The LEAVE statement transfers control to the end of the labeled block if the expression evaluated by the IF statement is true:

```
BEGIN
  inner_block: BEGIN
    IF DAYNAME(NOW()) = 'Wednesday' THEN
      LEAVE inner_block;
    END IF;
    SELECT 'Today is not Wednesday';
  END inner_block;
END;
```

In an inner block, you cannot use a label that has already been used for an outer block. The label name would be ambiguous for an attempt to transfer control to the label from within the inner block.

Labels can also be given for the LOOP, REPEAT, and WHILE loop-constructor statements; they follow the same labeling rules as for BEGIN/END. These statements are described in Section 18.5.8, "Flow Control."

18.5.2 Declaring Parameters

A stored routine definition can include parameter declarations. Parameters enable you to pass values to the routine when you invoke it. They are useful because you can write routines in a more general fashion, rather than hard-coding specific data values into them. For example, a parameter can identify the employee whose personnel record should be updated or the amount of money to be transferred in a financial transaction. You can invoke the same routine with different parameter values to produce different results. For procedures, parameters also enable you to pass information back from the procedure to the caller.

Here is a simple function that takes two DECIMAL parameters representing the cost for a taxable item and a tax rate, returns the amount of tax to be paid on the item:

```
CREATE FUNCTION tax (cost DECIMAL(10,2), tax_rate DECIMAL(10,2))
  RETURNS DECIMAL(10,4)
  RETURN cost * tax_rate;
```

Parameter declarations occur within the parentheses that follow the routine name in a CREATE PROCEDURE or CREATE FUNCTION statement. If there are multiple parameters, separate them by commas. A parameter declaration includes the parameter name and data type, to identify the name of the parameter within the routine and the kind of value it contains. Each parameter must have a different name. Parameter names are not case sensitive.

For procedures (but not functions), the name in a parameter declaration may be preceded by one of the following keywords to indicate the direction in which information flows through the parameter:

- IN indicates an input parameter. The parameter value is passed in from the caller to the procedure. The procedure can assign a different value to the parameter, but the change is visible only within the procedure, not to the caller.
- OUT indicates an output parameter. The caller passes a variable as the parameter. Any value the parameter has when it is passed is ignored by the procedure, and its initial value within the procedure is NULL. The procedure sets its value, and after the procedure terminates, the parameter value is passed back from the procedure to the caller. The caller sees that value when it accesses the variable.
- INOUT indicates a "two-way" parameter that can be used both for input and for output. The value passed by the caller is the parameter's initial value within the procedure. If the procedure changes the parameter value, that value is seen by the caller after the procedure terminates.

If no keyword is given before a procedure parameter name, it is an IN parameter by default.

Parameters for stored functions are not preceded by IN, OUT, or INOUT. All function parameters are treated as IN parameters.

The following example demonstrates how the different procedure parameter types work. It shows which parameter values passed to a procedure are visible within the procedure, and which of the parameter values changed by the procedure are visible to the caller after the procedure terminates. First, define a procedure with one parameter of each type that displays the initial values of its parameters and then reassigns them before terminating:

```
CREATE PROCEDURE param_test (IN p_in INT,
                             OUT p_out INT,
                             INOUT p_inout INT)
BEGIN
  SELECT p_in, p_out, p_inout;
  SET p_in = 100, p_out = 200, p_inout = 300;
END;
```

Then assign values to three user variables and pass them to the param_test() procedure. The output from param_test() indicates that the original value of the output parameter is not visible within the procedure:

```
mysql> SET @v_in = 0, @v_out = 0, @v_inout = 0;
Query OK, 0 rows affected (0.00 sec)

mysql> CALL param_test(@v_in, @v_out, @v_inout);
+------+-------+---------+
| p_in | p_out | p_inout |
+------+-------+---------+
|    0 | NULL  |       0 |
+------+-------+---------+
1 row in set (0.01 sec)

Query OK, 0 rows affected (0.02 sec)
```

After param_test() terminates, display the variable values. This output indicates that changes to the OUT and INOUT parameters (but not to the IN parameter) have been passed back to and are visible to the caller:

```
mysql> SELECT @v_in, @v_out, @v_inout;
+-------+--------+----------+
| @v_in | @v_out | @v_inout |
+-------+--------+----------+
| 0     | 200    | 300      |
+-------+--------+----------+
1 row in set (0.01 sec)
```

Parameters to stored routines need not be passed as user variables. They can be given as constants or expressions as well. However, for OUT or INOUT procedure parameters, if you do not pass a variable, the value passed back from a procedure will not be accessible.

18.5.3 The DECLARE Statement

The DECLARE statement is used for declaring several types of items in stored routines:

- Local variables
- Conditions, such as warnings or exceptions
- Handlers for conditions
- Cursors for accessing result sets row by row

DECLARE statements can be used only within a BEGIN/END block and must appear in the block before any other statements. If used to declare several types of items within a block, the DECLARE statements must appear in a particular order: You must declare variables and conditions first, then cursors, and finally handlers.

Each variable declared within a block must have a different name. This restriction also applies to declarations for conditions and for cursors. However, items of different types within a block can have the same name. Item names are not case sensitive.

Variables, conditions, handlers, and cursors created by DECLARE statements are local to the block. That is, they are valid only within the block (or any nested blocks). When a block terminates, any cursors still open are closed and all items declared within the block go out of scope and are no longer accessible.

If an inner block contains an item that has the same name as the same kind of item in an outer block, the outer item cannot be accessed within the inner block.

The following sections describe how to use DECLARE for each type of item, although the sections do not appear in the same order in which items must be declared. (Conditions and handlers are related, so they appear in the same section.)

18.5.4 Variables in Stored Routines

To declare local variables for use within a block, use a DECLARE statement that specifies one or more variable names, a data type, and optionally a default value:

```
DECLARE var_name [, var_name] ... data_type [DEFAULT value]
```

Each variable named in the statement has the given data type (and default value, if the DEFAULT clause is present). To declare variables that have different data types or default values, use separate DECLARE statements. The initial value is NULL for variables declared with no DEFAULT clause.

Each variable declared within a block must have a different name.

A variable may be assigned a value using a SET, SELECT ... INTO, or FETCH ... INTO statement. The variable's value can be accessed by using it in an expression. The following sections provide examples.

To avoid name clashes, it is best not to give a local variable the same name as any table columns that you refer to within a routine. For example, if you select the Code column from the Country table, declaring a local variable with a name of Code leads to ambiguity. A naming convention can be helpful here. For example, you could name the variable as code_var. The same principle can be used for routine parameters, by using names such as code_param.

Local routine variable names are not written with a leading '@' character. This differs from the @var_name syntax used for writing user variables.

18.5.4.1 Assigning Variable Values with SET

The SET statement assigns values to variables. These can be system or user variables, just as when you use SET outside the context of stored routines. However, within a stored routine, SET also can refer to local variables that were declared previously with DECLARE.

A SET statement can perform a single assignment or multiple assignments. For example:

```
DECLARE var1, var2, var3 INT;
SET var1 = 1, var2 = 2;
SET var3 = var1 + var2;
```

18.5.4.2 Assigning Variable Values with SELECT ... INTO

The SELECT ... INTO statement assigns the result of a SELECT statement to variables. Outside the context of stored routines, these must be user variables. Within stored routines, the statement also can be used to assign values to local variables that were declared previously with DECLARE. The following statements declare two variables and select into them the country name and population corresponding to a given country code:

```
DECLARE name_var CHAR(52);
DECLARE pop_var INT;
SELECT Name, Population INTO name_var, pop_var
  FROM Country WHERE Code = 'ESP';
```

The SELECT statement must select at most a single row. If it selects more than one row, an error occurs. If the statement selects no rows, the variables following the INTO keyword remain unchanged.

SELECT ... INTO can also assign values to routine parameters. If a parameter is an INOUT or OUT parameter, the value assigned to it is passed back to the caller.

18.5.5 Conditions and Handlers

A handler has a name and a statement to be executed upon occurrence of a given condition such as a warning or an error. Handlers commonly are used for detecting problems and dealing with them in a more appropriate way than simply having the routine terminate with an error.

The following example demonstrates one way to use a handler. It's based on a table, unique_names, that holds unique names, and another table, dup_names, that holds rows that could not be inserted into unique_names. To do this, it's necessary to be able to handle duplicate-key errors when inserting into unique_names and insert into dup_name instead.

The tables are defined as follows, where the only difference is that unique_names has a unique key constraint:

```
CREATE TABLE unique_names
(
    name CHAR(20) NOT NULL PRIMARY KEY
);

CREATE TABLE dup_names
(
    name CHAR(20) NOT NULL
);
```

The following procedure, add_name(), takes a name as its parameter and attempts to insert it into the unique_name table. If that fails because the name is a duplicate, an error with SQLSTATE value 23000 occurs. The routine includes a handler for this condition, and associates it with a block that inserts the name into the dup_key table instead:

```
CREATE PROCEDURE add_name (name_param CHAR(20))
BEGIN
  DECLARE EXIT HANDLER FOR SQLSTATE '23000'
  BEGIN
    INSERT INTO dup_names (name) VALUES(name_param);
    SELECT 'duplicate key found, inserted into dup_names' AS result;
  END;

  INSERT INTO unique_names (, name) VALUES(name_param);
  SELECT 'row inserted successfully into unique_names' AS result;
END;
```

If we invoke the routine with the same name twice, it produces the following result:

```
mysql> CALL add_name ('my name');
+---------------------------------------------+
| result                                      |
+---------------------------------------------+
| row inserted successfully into unique_names |
+---------------------------------------------+

mysql> CALL add_name ('my name');
+---------------------------------------------+
| result                                      |
+---------------------------------------------+
```

```
| duplicate key found, inserted into dup_names |
+----------------------------------------------+
```

It is allowable but not necessary to give a name to a condition by declaring it. You might declare a condition to provide a name for it that is more meaningful than the code that it stands for. For example, the following declaration associates the descriptive name dup_key with the SQLSTATE value '23000', which is returned whenever the MySQL server encounters a duplicate-key error:

```
DECLARE dup_key CONDITION FOR SQLSTATE '23000';
```

Named conditions and handlers are both declared with DECLARE statements. Conditions must be declared along with variables before any cursor or handler declarations. Handler declarations must follow declarations for variables, conditions, and cursors.

To name a condition, use a DECLARE CONDITION statement:

```
DECLARE condition_name CONDITION FOR condition_type
```

Each condition declared within a block must have a different name. After you declare a condition, you can refer to it by name in a DECLARE HANDLER statement.

A condition type can be an SQLSTATE value, specified as SQLSTATE (or SQLSTATE VALUE) followed by a five-character string literal. MySQL extends this to allow numeric MySQL error codes as well. The following declarations are equivalent. Each declares a condition named null_not_allowed for the error that occurs for an attempt to assign NULL when NULL is not allowed:

```
DECLARE null_not_allowed CONDITION FOR SQLSTATE '23000';
DECLARE null_not_allowed CONDITION FOR 1048;
```

The DECLARE HANDLER statement creates a handler for one or more conditions and associates them with an SQL statement that will be executed should any of the conditions occur when the routine is run:

```
DECLARE handler_type HANDLER FOR
  condition_type [, condition_type] ...
  statement
```

The handler type indicates what happens once the handler statement is executed. CONTINUE causes routine execution to continue; the SQL statement that follows the statement in which the condition occurred is the next to be processed. EXIT causes control to transfer to the end of the block in which the handler is declared; the intermediate SQL statements are not processed. Standard SQL defines UNDO handlers as well, but MySQL does not currently support them.

Each condition associated with a handler must be one of the following:

- An SQLSTATE value or MySQL error code, specified the same way as in a DECLARE CONDITION statement

- A condition name declared previously with a DECLARE CONDITION statement

- SQLWARNING, which handles conditions for all SQLSTATE values that begin with 01

- NOT FOUND, which handles conditions for all SQLSTATE values that begin with 02

- SQLEXCEPTION, which handles conditions for all SQLSTATE values not handled by SQLWARNING or NOT FOUND

The statement at the end of DECLARE HANDLER specifies the statement to execute when a handled condition occurs. It can be a simple statement or a compound statement:

```
DECLARE CONTINUE HANDLER FOR SQLSTATE '02000' SET exit_loop = 1;
DECLARE CONTINUE HANDLER FOR SQLSTATE '02000'
  BEGIN
    statement_list
  END;
```

To ignore a condition, declare a CONTINUE handler for it and associate it with an empty block:

```
DECLARE CONTINUE HANDLER FOR SQLWARNING BEGIN END;
```

18.5.6 Cursors

A cursor enables you to access a result set one row at a time. Because of this row orientation, cursors often are used in loops that fetch and process a row within each iteration of the loop.

The cursor implementation in MySQL has the following properties: It provides for read-only cursors; they cannot be used to modify tables. Cursors also only advance through a result row by row; that is, they are not scrollable.

To use a cursor in a stored routine, begin by writing a DECLARE CURSOR statement that names the cursor and associates it with a SELECT statement that produces a result set:

```
DECLARE cursor_name CURSOR FOR select_statement
```

Each cursor declared within a block must have a different name.

To open the cursor, name it in an OPEN statement. This executes the SELECT statement associated with the cursor:

```
OPEN cursor_name
```

The FETCH statement fetches the next row of an open cursor's result set. The statement names the cursor and provides a list of variables into which to fetch row column values. There must be one variable per column in the result set. You can fetch values into local variables or routine parameters:

```
FETCH cursor_name INTO var_name [, var_name] ...
```

FETCH often occurs in a loop so that all rows in the result set can be processed. That raises an issue: What happens when you reach the end of the result? The answer is that a No Data condition occurs (SQLSTATE 02000), which you can detect by declaring a handler for that condition. For example:

```
DECLARE CONTINUE HANDLER FOR SQLSTATE '02000' statement;
```

When you are done with the cursor, close it with a CLOSE statement:

```
CLOSE cursor_name
```

Closing a cursor is optional. Any cursors declared in a block are closed automatically if they are open when the block terminates.

The following example shows how to use each of the cursor-related statements just discussed. The example declares a cursor named c and associates it with a statement that selects rows for African countries in the Country table. It also declares a condition handler that detects the end of the result set. (The handler statement is empty because the only purpose for the handler is to transfer control to the end of its enclosing block.)

```
BEGIN
  DECLARE row_count INT DEFAULT 0;
  DECLARE code_var CHAR(3);
  DECLARE name_var CHAR(52);
  DECLARE c CURSOR FOR
    SELECT Code, Name FROM Country WHERE Continent = 'Africa';
  OPEN c;
  BEGIN
    DECLARE EXIT HANDLER FOR SQLSTATE '02000' BEGIN END;
    LOOP
      FETCH c INTO code_var, name_var;
      SET row_count = row_count + 1;
    END LOOP;
  END;
  CLOSE c;
  SELECT 'number of rows fetched =', row_count;
END;
```

The preceding example uses a nested block because an EXIT handler terminates the block within which it is declared, *not* the loop within which the condition occurs. If no nested block had been used, the handler would transfer control to the end of the main block upon reading the end of the result set, and the CLOSE and SELECT statements following the loop would never execute. An alternative approach does not require a nested block: Use a CONTINUE handler that sets a loop-termination status variable and tests the variable value within the loop. The following example shows one way to do this:

```
BEGIN
  DECLARE exit_flag INT DEFAULT 0;
```

```
    DECLARE row_count INT DEFAULT 0;
    DECLARE code_var CHAR(3);
    DECLARE name_var CHAR(52);
    DECLARE c CURSOR FOR
      SELECT Code, Name FROM Country WHERE Continent = 'Africa';
    DECLARE CONTINUE HANDLER FOR SQLSTATE '02000' SET exit_flag = 1;
    OPEN c;
    fetch_loop: LOOP
      FETCH c INTO code_var, name_var;
      IF exit_flag THEN LEAVE fetch_loop; END IF;
      SET row_count - row_count + 1;
    END LOOP;
    CLOSE c;
    SELECT 'number of rows fetched =', row_count;
END;
```

18.5.7 Retrieving Multiple Result Sets

In standard SQL, a stored procedure that uses SELECT statements to retrieve records processes those records itself (for example, by using a cursor and a row-fetching loop). A MySQL extension to procedures is that SELECT statements can be executed to generate result sets that are returned directly to the client with no intermediate processing. The client retrieves the results as though it had executed the SELECT statements itself. This extension does not apply to stored functions.

An example is the world_record_count() procedure defined in Section 18.4, "Defining Stored Routines." When invoked, it returns three single-record result sets:

```
mysql> CALL world_record_count();
+---------+----------+
| Country | COUNT(*) |
+---------+----------+
| Country |      239 |
+---------+----------+
1 row in set (0.00 sec)

+------+----------+
| City | COUNT(*) |
+------+----------+
| City |     4079 |
+------+----------+
1 row in set (0.00 sec)

+-----------------+----------+
| CountryLanguage | COUNT(*) |
+-----------------+----------+
```

```
| CountryLanguage |        984 |
+-----------------+----------+
1 row in set (0.04 sec)

Query OK, 0 rows affected (0.04 sec)
```

18.5.8 Flow Control

Compound statement syntax includes statements that allow for conditional testing and for creating looping structures:

- IF and CASE perform conditional testing.

- LOOP, REPEAT, and WHILE create loops. LOOP iterates unconditionally, whereas REPEAT and WHILE include a clause that tests whether the loop should continue or terminate.

The following sections describe these statements.

18.5.8.1 Conditional Testing

The IF and CASE statements enable you to perform conditional testing. Note that these statements have different syntax than the IF() function and CASE expression. The latter produce a value and are used in expressions. They are not statements in themselves. Also, they end with END rather than END CASE. Because of the differing syntax, it is possible to use IF() functions and CASE expressions within stored routines without ambiguity, even if they occur within IF or CASE statements.

The IF statement tests a condition and then executes other statements depending on whether the condition is true. It has the following syntax:

```
IF expr
  THEN statement_list
  [ELSEIF expr THEN statement_list] ...
  [ELSE statement_list]
END IF
```

The initial conditional expression is evaluated and, if true, the statement list following THEN is executed. To test additional conditions if the initial expression is not true, include one or more ELSEIF clauses. The expression for each is tested in turn until one is found that is true, and then its statement list is executed. The ELSE clause, if present, contains statements to be executed if none of the tested conditions are true.

The following IF statement performs a simple NULL value test:

```
IF val IS NULL
  THEN SELECT 'val is NULL';
  ELSE SELECT 'val is not NULL';
END IF;
```

CASE is the other statement that performs conditional testing. It has two forms. The first syntax looks like this:

```
CASE case_expr
  WHEN when_expr THEN statement_list
  [WHEN when_expr THEN statement_list] ...
  [ELSE statement_list]
END CASE
```

The expression case_expr is evaluated and used to determine which of the following clauses in the rest of the statement to execute. The when_expr in the initial WHEN clause is evaluated and compared to case_expr. If the two are equal, the statement list following THEN is executed. If when_expr is not equal to case_expr, and there are any following WHEN clauses, they are handled similarly in turn. If no WHEN clause has a when_expr equal to case_expr, and there is an ELSE clause, the ELSE clause's statement list is executed.

Each comparison is of the form case_expr = when_expr. The significance of this is that the comparison is never true if either operand is NULL, no matter the value of the other operand.

The following CASE statement tests whether a given value is 0, 1, or something else:

```
CASE val
  WHEN 0 THEN SELECT 'val is 0';
  WHEN 1 THEN SELECT 'val is 1';
  ELSE SELECT 'val is not 0 or 1';
END CASE;
```

The second CASE syntax looks like this:

```
CASE
  WHEN when_expr THEN statement_list
  [WHEN when_expr THEN statement_list] ...
  [ELSE statement_list]
END CASE
```

For this syntax, the conditional expression in each WHEN clause is executed until one is found to be true, and then its statement list is executed. If none of them are true and there is an ELSE clause, the ELSE clause's statement list is executed. This syntax is preferable to the first syntax for certain types of tests such as those that use IS NULL or IS NOT NULL to test for NULL values, or those that use relative value tests such as val < 0 or val >= 100.

The following CASE statement tests whether a given value is NULL or less than, greater than, or equal to 0:

```
CASE
  WHEN val IS NULL THEN SELECT 'val is NULL';
  WHEN val < 0 THEN SELECT 'val is less than 0';
  WHEN val > 0 THEN SELECT 'val is greater than 0';
  ELSE SELECT 'val is 0';
END CASE;
```

18.5.8.2 Loop Construction

Compound statement syntax in MySQL provides for three kinds of loops:

- LOOP constructs an unconditional loop with no loop-termination syntax. For this reason, it must contain a statement that explicitly exits the loop.

- REPEAT and WHILE, the other two loop constructs, are conditional. They include a clause that determines whether loop execution continues or terminates.

Standard SQL includes a FOR loop as well. MySQL does not currently support FOR loops.

Each of the supported loop-construction statements can be labeled. The rules for labeling loops are the same as for labeling BEGIN/END blocks. (See Section 18.5.1, "Compound Statements.")

The LOOP statement that creates an unconditional loop has this syntax:

```
LOOP
    statement_list
END LOOP
```

The statement list within the loop executes repeatedly. The loop will, in fact, iterate forever unless the statement list contains some statement that exits the loop. An exit can be effected with a LEAVE statement or (in a function) a RETURN statement. The following LOOP iterates as long as the variable i is less than 10:

```
DECLARE i INT DEFAULT 0;
my_loop: LOOP
  SET i = i + 1;
  IF i >= 10 THEN
    LEAVE my_loop;
  END IF;
END LOOP my_loop;
```

The REPEAT statement creates a conditional loop. It has this syntax:

```
REPEAT
    statement_list
UNTIL expr
END REPEAT
```

The statements within the loop execute and then the conditional expression *expr* is evaluated. If the expression is true, the loop terminates. Otherwise, it begins again. Note that there is no semicolon between the expression and END REPEAT. The following REPEAT loop iterates as long as the variable i is less than 10:

```
DECLARE i INT DEFAULT 0;
REPEAT
  SET i = i + 1;
```

```
UNTIL i >= 10
END REPEAT;
```

The WHILE statement creates a conditional loop. It is similar to REPEAT except that the conditional expression appears at the beginning of the loop rather than at the end. Also, a WHILE loop continues as long as the condition is true, whereas a REPEAT loop terminates as soon as the condition becomes true. WHILE syntax is as follows:

```
WHILE expr DO
  statement_list
END WHILE
```

The conditional expression is evaluated and the loop terminates if the condition is not true. Otherwise, the statement list within the loop executes, control transfers back to the beginning, and the expression is tested again. The following WHILE loop iterates as long as the variable i is less than 10:

```
DECLARE i INT DEFAULT 0;
WHILE i < 10 DO
  SET i = i + 1;
END WHILE;
```

Because the test in a REPEAT is at the end of the loop, the statements within the loop always execute at least once. With WHILE, the test is at the beginning, so it is possible for the statements within the loop not to execute even once. For example, the following WHILE loop never executes the SET statement within the loop:

```
WHILE 1 = 0 DO
  SET x = 1;
END WHILE;
```

With any loop construct, be sure that the loop termination condition eventually will become true. Otherwise, the loop will loop forever.

Just as BEGIN/END blocks can be nested, loops can be nested. In such cases, loop labels are useful if it's necessary to exit more than one level of loop at once.

18.5.8.3 Transfer of Control

Two statements provide transfer of control within a routine. Each statement requires a label that indicates which labeled construct it applies to:

```
LEAVE label
ITERATE label
```

LEAVE transfers control to the end of the named construct and can be used with blocks and loops: BEGIN/END, LOOP, REPEAT, or WHILE.

ITERATE transfers control to the beginning of the named construct. It can be used only within loops: LOOP, REPEAT, or WHILE. It cannot be used to restart a BEGIN/END block.

LEAVE and ITERATE must appear within the labeled construct.

The following example includes a labeled loop and shows how to exit the loop or begin it again with LEAVE and ITERATE.

```
DECLARE i INT DEFAULT 0;
my_loop: LOOP
  SET i = i + 1;
  IF i < 10 THEN ITERATE my_loop;
  ELSEIF i > 20 THEN LEAVE my_loop;
  END IF;
  SELECT 'i is between 10 and 20';
END LOOP my_loop;
```

The final way to transfer control is by executing a RETURN statement to return a value to the caller. This applies only to stored functions, not stored procedures. The following example returns the country name associated with a country code:

```
CREATE FUNCTION countryname(code_param CHAR(3))
RETURNS CHAR(52)
BEGIN
  DECLARE name_var CHAR(52);
  SELECT Name INTO name_var FROM Country WHERE Code=code_param;
  RETURN name_var;
END;
```

18.6 Altering Stored Routines

The ALTER PROCEDURE or ALTER FUNCTION statement can be used to alter some of the characteristics of a stored routine:

```
ALTER PROCEDURE proc_name [characteristics]
ALTER FUNCTION func_name [characteristics]
```

The allowable characteristics for these statements are SQL SECURITY and COMMENT. These have the same syntax as for the CREATE PROCEDURE and CREATE FUNCTION statements. For example, if a function currently has DEFINER security, you can change it to INVOKER security and add a comment as follows:

```
ALTER FUNCTION f
  SQL SECURITY INVOKER
  COMMENT 'this function has invoker security';
```

As with the corresponding CREATE statements, the characteristics can be listed in any order if more than one is given.

These statements cannot be used to alter other aspects of routine definitions, such as the parameter declarations or the body. To do that, you must drop the routine first and then create it again with the new definition.

18.7 Dropping Stored Routines

To drop a stored routine, use the DROP PROCEDURE or DROP FUNCTION statement.

```
DROP PROCEDURE [IF EXISTS] proc_name
DROP FUNCTION [IF EXISTS] func_name
```

It is an error if the named routine does not exist. Include the IF EXISTS clause to generate a warning instead. (The warning can be displayed with SHOW WARNINGS.) IF EXISTS is a MySQL extension to standard SQL.

18.8 Invoking Stored Routines

We have already covered the concept of invoking stored routines earlier in the course of this discussion, but just to make it explicit, here are the rules:

- To invoke a procedure, use a CALL statement. This is a separate statement; a procedure cannot be invoked as part of an expression. Suppose that the rect_area() procedure has this definition:

```
CREATE PROCEDURE rect_area (width INT, height INT)
  SELECT width * height AS area;
```

The procedure is invoked with CALL as follows:

```
mysql> CALL rect_area(10,25);
+------+
| area |
+------+
|  250 |
+------+
1 row in set (0.00 sec)
```

If the procedure has OUT or INOUT parameters, the procedure can pass back values to its caller through these parameters.

- To invoke a function, invoke it in an expression. It returns a single value that is used in evaluating the expression, just as for a built-in function. Suppose that the circle_area() function has this definition:

```
CREATE FUNCTION circle_area (radius FLOAT)
  RETURNS FLOAT
  RETURN PI() * radius * radius;
```

The function is invoked in an expression as follows:

```
mysql> SELECT circle_area(10);
+-----------------+
| circle_area(10) |
+-----------------+
| 314.15927124023 |
+-----------------+
1 row in set (0.00 sec)
```

18.9 Obtaining Stored Routine Metadata

The INFORMATION_SCHEMA database has a ROUTINES table that contains information about stored routines. For example, to display information about the world_record_count() procedure defined in Section 18.4, "Defining Stored Routines," use this statement:

```
mysql> SELECT * FROM INFORMATION_SCHEMA.ROUTINES
    -> WHERE ROUTINE_NAME = 'world_record_count'
    -> AND ROUTINE_SCHEMA = 'world'\G
*************************** 1. row ***************************
       SPECIFIC_NAME: world_record_count
      ROUTINE_CATALOG: NULL
      ROUTINE_SCHEMA: world
        ROUTINE_NAME: world_record_count
        ROUTINE_TYPE: PROCEDURE
       DTD_IDENTIFIER: NULL
         ROUTINE_BODY: SQL
   ROUTINE_DEFINITION: BEGIN
      SELECT 'Country', COUNT(*) FROM Country;
      SELECT 'City', COUNT(*) FROM City;
      SELECT 'CountryLanguage', COUNT(*) FROM CountryLanguage;
END
       EXTERNAL_NAME: NULL
    EXTERNAL_LANGUAGE: NULL
      PARAMETER_STYLE: SQL
      IS_DETERMINISTIC: NO
      SQL_DATA_ACCESS: CONTAINS SQL
            SQL_PATH: NULL
        SECURITY_TYPE: DEFINER
             CREATED: 2005-02-24 08:49:36
        LAST_ALTERED: 2005-02-24 08:49:36
            SQL_MODE:
      ROUTINE_COMMENT:
             DEFINER: wuser@localhost
```

For further information about INFORMATION_SCHEMA, see Chapter 20, "Obtaining Database Metadata."

MySQL also supports a family of SHOW statements that display metadata. Some of these display stored routine information:

- SHOW PROCEDURE STATUS and SHOW FUNCTION STATUS display some of the same information that is available in the ROUTINES table. These statements include a LIKE 'pattern' clause. If it is present, the statements display information about the routines that have a name that matches the pattern.

  ```
  SHOW PROCEDURE STATUS LIKE 'w%';
  SHOW FUNCTION STATUS;
  ```

- To display the definition of an individual stored procedure or function, use the SHOW CREATE PROCEDURE or SHOW CREATE FUNCTION statement.

  ```
  SHOW CREATE PROCEDURE world_record_count;
  SHOW CREATE FUNCTION add3;
  ```

18.10 Stored Routine Privileges and Execution Security

Several privileges apply to the use of stored procedures and functions:

- To create a routine, you must have the CREATE ROUTINE privilege for it.
- To execute a routine, you must have the EXECUTE privilege for it.
- To drop a routine or alter its definition, you must have the ALTER ROUTINE privilege for it.
- To grant privileges for a routine, you must have the GRANT OPTION privilege for it.

When you create a stored routine, MySQL automatically grants to you the EXECUTE and ALTER ROUTINE privileges for it. These privileges enable you to invoke the routine or remove it later. (You can verify that you have these privileges by issuing a SHOW GRANTS statement after creating a routine.)

A GRANT statement that grants the ALL privilege specifier at the global or database level includes all stored routine privileges except GRANT OPTION. For example, the following statement grants the given account all privileges for the world database, including privileges to define, use, and drop stored routines:

```
GRANT ALL ON world.* TO 'magellan'@'localhost';
```

To grant the GRANT OPTION privilege as well, include a WITH GRANT OPTION clause at the end of the statement.

The EXECUTE, ALTER ROUTINE, and GRANT OPTION privileges can be granted at the individual routine level, but only for routines that already exist. To grant privileges for an individual routine, name the routine qualified with a database name and preceded with the keyword PROCEDURE or FUNCTION to indicate the routine type. The following statement grants the given account permission to execute or alter the world_record_count() procedure in the world database:

```
GRANT EXECUTE, ALTER ROUTINE ON PROCEDURE world.world_record_count
  TO 'magellan'@'localhost';
```

Triggers

A trigger is a database object that is associated with a table and that is defined to activate (or "trigger") when a particular kind of event occurs for that table. This chapter describes how to define and use triggers in MySQL. It covers the following exam topics:

- Reasons to use triggers
- Trigger concepts
- Creating and dropping triggers
- Privileges required for triggers

The examples in this chapter require a table that can be modified. To avoid changing the original world database tables, we'll use a table named Capital that contains information about the capital city in each country. Create the Capital table by using the following statement:

```
mysql> CREATE TABLE Capital
    -> SELECT Country.Name AS Country, City.Name AS Capital,
    -> City.Population
    -> FROM Country, City
    -> WHERE Country.Capital = City.ID;
Query OK, 232 rows affected (0.13 sec)
Records: 232  Duplicates: 0  Warnings: 0
```

19.1 Reasons to Use Triggers

A trigger provides a means to execute an SQL statement or set of statements when you insert, update, or delete rows in a table. Triggers provide the following benefits:

- A trigger can examine row values to be inserted or updated, and it can determine what values were deleted or what they were updated to.
- A trigger can change values before they are inserted into a table or used to update a table. For example, you can check for out-of-bounds values and modify them to be within bounds. This capability enables the use of triggers as data filters.

- You can modify how INSERT, DELETE, or UPDATE work. For example, during an INSERT, you can provide a default value that is based on the current time for columns with any temporal data type. Normally, only TIMESTAMP columns can be initialized to the current time automatically.

19.2 Trigger Concepts

A trigger is an object that belongs to a database. Each trigger within the database must have a different name. A trigger is defined to activate when a particular kind of event occurs for a given table. (On occasion, you might see it said that a trigger "fires." This study guide uses the term
"activates.") The trigger definition includes a statement to be executed when the trigger activates.

The events for which triggers can be defined are INSERT, DELETE, and UPDATE. A given trigger is defined for only one of these events, but you can define multiple triggers for a table, one trigger per type of event.

Triggers can be defined to activate either before or after the event. This means there can be two triggers per event (for example, one trigger to activate before an UPDATE and one to activate after).

The following example creates a trigger named Capital_bi that activates for inserts into the Capital table:

```
CREATE TRIGGER Capital_bi
  BEFORE INSERT
  ON Capital
  FOR EACH ROW
    SET NEW.Population =
      IF(NEW.Population < 0, 0, TRUNCATE(NEW.Population,-3));
```

The trigger checks the Population value before the insert occurs and "filters" it: Values less than zero are converted to zero, and other values are truncated down to the nearest multiple of 1,000. The result is that the filtered value is inserted, not the value given in the INSERT statement.

When a trigger activates, the triggered statement in the definition executes. The FOR EACH ROW in the syntax means that execution occurs once "for each row inserted, updated, or deleted," not "for each row currently in the table." It also means that a trigger activates multiple times for a statement that affects several rows, such as a multiple-row INSERT statement.

The effect of the `Capital_bi` trigger for inserts into the `Capital` table can be seen as follows:

```
mysql> INSERT INTO Capital VALUES
    -> ('CountryA','CityA',-39),
    -> ('CountryB','CityB',123456);
Query OK, 2 rows affected (0.00 sec)
Records: 2  Duplicates: 0  Warnings: 0

mysql> SELECT * FROM Capital
    -> WHERE Country IN ('CountryA','CountryB');
+----------+---------+------------+
| Country  | Capital | Population |
+----------+---------+------------+
| CountryA | CityA   |          0 |
| CountryB | CityB   |     123000 |
+----------+---------+------------+
2 rows in set (0.00 sec)
```

19.3 Creating a Trigger

To define a trigger for a table, use the CREATE TRIGGER statement, which has the following syntax:

```
CREATE TRIGGER trigger_name
  { BEFORE | AFTER }
  { INSERT | UPDATE | DELETE }
  ON table_name
  FOR EACH ROW
  triggered_statement
```

trigger_name is the name to give the trigger, and *table_name* is the table with which to associate the trigger. BEFORE or AFTER indicates whether the trigger activates before or after the triggering event, and INSERT, UPDATE, or DELETE indicates what that event is.

When creating triggers, you might find it helpful to use a naming convention so that you can easily tell from a trigger name the table that it is associated with and what type of action it is for. In this study guide, trigger names are based on the table name and have a suffix composed of b or a for an activation time of BEFORE or AFTER, and i, u, or d for an activation event of INSERT, UPDATE, or DELETE. Using this convention, a BEFORE trigger for INSERT statements on the `Capital` table is named `Capital_bi`.

triggered_statement is the statement to be executed for each row when the trigger activates. The triggered statement must be a single statement, but if necessary you can use a BEGIN/END compound statement to create a block and include multiple statements within the block. This is similar to the use of compound statements in stored routines. Within a

BEGIN/END block, other compound statement syntax can be used, such as variable definitions, flow of control statements, and conditional statements.

When you define a trigger using a compound statement that consists of multiple statements, individual statements must be terminated by semicolon characters (';'), just as when defining stored procedures and functions. If you are using the mysql client to create such a trigger, you must redefine the statement delimiter. The following example demonstrates this technique. The trigger shown in the example monitors updates to the Capital table. It records the original Country and City values from the updated row and the new value to which the City column is updated:

```
mysql> delimiter //
mysql> CREATE TRIGGER Capital_bu
    ->    BEFORE UPDATE
    ->    ON Capital
    ->    FOR EACH ROW
    ->    BEGIN
    ->      SET @country = OLD.Country;
    ->      SET @capital_old = OLD.Capital;
    ->      SET @capital_new = NEW.Capital;
    ->    END;
    -> //
Query OK, 0 rows affected (0.00 sec)

mysql> delimiter ;
mysql> UPDATE Capital SET Capital = 'Washington D.C.'
    -> WHERE Country = 'United States';
Query OK, 1 row affected (0.00 sec)
Rows matched: 1  Changed: 1  Warnings: 0

mysql> SELECT @country AS Country, @capital_old AS 'Old capital',
    -> @capital_new AS 'New capital';
+---------------+-------------+-----------------+
| Country       | Old capital | New capital     |
+---------------+-------------+-----------------+
| United States | Washington  | Washington D.C. |
+---------------+-------------+-----------------+
1 row in set (0.00 sec)
```

For information about compound statement syntax and statement delimiter redefinition, see Chapter 18, "Stored Procedures and Functions."

A table cannot have two triggers for the same combination of activation time and event. For example, you can have a BEFORE UPDATE and AFTER UPDATE trigger for a table, but not two BEFORE UPDATE or AFTER UPDATE triggers. This property does not pose a limitation. If it's necessary to perform multiple actions with a given type of trigger, they can all be included within a compound statement.

19.4 Restrictions on Triggers

The current trigger implementation in MySQL has some limitations:

- You cannot use the CALL statement.
- You cannot begin or end transactions.
- You cannot create a trigger for a TEMPORARY table or a view.
- Trigger creation is subject to the same binary log-related restriction placed on stored routine creation that is described in the introductory part of Chapter 18, "Stored Procedures and Functions."

19.5 Referring to Old and New Column Values

Within a trigger definition, you can refer to columns of the row being inserted, updated, or deleted. This enables you to examine column values, or to change values before they are used for an insert or update.

To refer to a given column, prefix the column name with a qualifier of OLD to refer to a value from the original row or NEW to refer to a value in the new row. OLD and NEW must be used appropriately, because the triggering event determines which of them are allowable:

- In an INSERT trigger, NEW.col_name indicates a column value to be inserted into a new row. OLD is not allowable.
- In a DELETE trigger, OLD.col_name indicates the value of a column in a row to be deleted. NEW is not allowable.
- In an UPDATE trigger, OLD.col_name and NEW.col_name refer to the value of the column in a row before and after the row is updated, respectively.

OLD must be used in read-only fashion. NEW can be used to read or change column values.

The Capital_bi and Capital_bu triggers shown earlier in the chapter demonstrate the use of OLD and NEW.

19.6 Destroying a Trigger

To destroy a trigger, use the DROP TRIGGER statement. For example, if the Capital table in the world database has a trigger that is named Capital_bi, drop the trigger by using this statement:

```
DROP TRIGGER world.Capital_bi;
```

If you omit the database name, the trigger is assumed to be in the default dastabase. An error occurs if the trigger does not exist.

DROP TRIGGER destroys a trigger explicitly. Triggers also are destroyed implicitly under some circumstances. When you drop a table that has triggers associated with it, MySQL drops the triggers as well. When you drop a database, doing so causes tables in the database to be dropped, and thus also drops any triggers for those tables.

19.7 Privileges Required for Triggers

To create or destroy triggers with CREATE TRIGGER or DROP TRIGGER, you must have the SUPER privilege. This is likely to change MySQL 5.1, such that the required privilege will be CREATE TRIGGER.

If the triggered statement uses OLD or NEW, there are additional privilege requirements:

- To assign the value of a column with SET NEW.col_name = value, you must have the UPDATE privilege for the column.

- To use NEW.col_name in an expression to refer to the new value of a column, you must have the SELECT privilege for the column.

20

Obtaining Database Metadata

Databases contain data, but information about the way databases are structured is metadata. This chapter discusses the various means by which MySQL provides access to metadata for database, tables, and other objects. It covers the following exam topics:

- Metadata access methods
- Using the INFORMATION_SCHEMA database to access metadata
- Using SHOW and DESCRIBE statements to access metadata
- Using the mysqlshow program to access metadata

20.1 Overview of Metadata Access Methods

MySQL produces metadata for several aspects of database structure. To name a few, you can obtain names of databases and tables, information about columns and indexes in tables, or stored routine definitions.

One method by which MySQL makes metadata available is through a family of SHOW statements, each of which displays one kind of information. For example, SHOW DATABASES and SHOW TABLES return lists of database and table names, and SHOW COLUMNS produces information about definitions of columns in a table.

A client program, mysqlshow, acts as a command-line front end to a few of the SHOW statements. When invoked, it examines its arguments to determine what information to display, issues the appropriate SHOW statement, and displays the results that the statement returns.

SHOW and mysqlshow have been available since very early releases of MySQL. As of MySQL 5, metadata access is enhanced through two additions:

- The INFORMATION_SCHEMA database is implemented. This provides better compliance with standard SQL because INFORMATION_SCHEMA is standard, not a MySQL-specific extension like SHOW.

- SHOW statement syntax is extended to support a WHERE clause for describing which rows to display. (Some SHOW statements support a LIKE clause for applying a pattern match to the rows of the result, but WHERE is more flexible.)

The following sections provide more detail about each of the metadata access methods. Chapter 31, "The INFORMATION_SCHEMA Database," provides a comparative breakdown of the advantages and disadvantages of INFORMATION_SCHEMA versus SHOW.

20.2 Using INFORMATION_SCHEMA to Obtain Metadata

The INFORMATION_SCHEMA database serves as a central repository for database metadata. It is a "virtual database" in the sense that it is not stored on disk anywhere, but it contains tables like any other database, and the contents of its tables can be accessed using SELECT like any other tables. Furthermore, you can use SELECT to obtain information about INFORMATION_SCHEMA itself. For example, to list the names of its tables, use the following statement:

```
mysql> SELECT TABLE_NAME FROM INFORMATION_SCHEMA.TABLES
    -> WHERE TABLE_SCHEMA = 'INFORMATION_SCHEMA'
    -> ORDER BY TABLE_NAME;
+---------------------------------------+
| TABLE_NAME                            |
+---------------------------------------+
| CHARACTER_SETS                        |
| COLLATIONS                            |
| COLLATION_CHARACTER_SET_APPLICABILITY |
| COLUMNS                               |
| COLUMN_PRIVILEGES                     |
| KEY_COLUMN_USAGE                      |
| ROUTINES                             |
| SCHEMATA                             |
| SCHEMA_PRIVILEGES                     |
| STATISTICS                           |
| TABLES                               |
| TABLE_CONSTRAINTS                     |
| TABLE_PRIVILEGES                     |
| TRIGGERS                             |
| USER_PRIVILEGES                      |
| VIEWS                                |
+---------------------------------------+
```

The tables shown in that list contain the following types of information:

- CHARACTER_SETS

  Information about available character sets

- COLLATIONS

  Information about collations for each character set

- COLLATION_CHARACTER_SET_APPLICABILITY

  Information about which character set applies to each collation

- COLUMNS

  Information about columns in tables

- COLUMN_PRIVILEGES

  Information about column privileges held by MySQL user accounts

- KEY_COLUMN_USAGE

  Information about constraints on key columns

- ROUTINES

  Information about stored procedures and functions

- SCHEMATA

  Information about databases

- SCHEMA_PRIVILEGES

  Information about database privileges held by MySQL user accounts

- STATISTICS

  Information about table indexes

- TABLES

  Information about tables in databases

- TABLE_CONSTRAINTS

  Information about constraints on tables

- TABLE_PRIVILEGES

  Information about table privileges held by MySQL user accounts

- TRIGGERS

  Information about triggers in databases

- USER_PRIVILEGES

  Information about global privileges held by MySQL user accounts

- VIEWS

  Information about views in databases

To display the names of the columns in a given INFORMATION_SCHEMA table, use a statement of the following form, where the TABLE_NAME comparison value names the table in which you're interested:

```
mysql> SELECT COLUMN_NAME FROM INFORMATION_SCHEMA.COLUMNS
    -> WHERE TABLE_SCHEMA = 'INFORMATION_SCHEMA'
    -> AND TABLE_NAME = 'VIEWS';
+-----------------+
| COLUMN_NAME     |
+-----------------+
| TABLE_CATALOG   |
| TABLE_SCHEMA    |
| TABLE_NAME      |
| VIEW_DEFINITION |
| CHECK_OPTION    |
| IS_UPDATABLE    |
+-----------------+
```

The names of the INFORMATION_SCHEMA database, its tables, and columns are not case sensitive:

```
mysql> SELECT column_name FROM information_schema.columns
    -> WHERE table_schema = 'information_schema'
    -> AND table_name = 'views';
+-----------------+
| column_name     |
+-----------------+
| TABLE_CATALOG   |
| TABLE_SCHEMA    |
| TABLE_NAME      |
| VIEW_DEFINITION |
| CHECK_OPTION    |
| IS_UPDATABLE    |
+-----------------+
```

This study guide does not go into any detail about the columns in INFORMATION_SCHEMA tables. For a more comprehensive description of each table's columns, see the *MySQL Reference Manual*.

When you retrieve metadata from INFORMATION_SCHEMA by using SELECT statements, you have the freedom to use any of the usual SELECT features that you expect:

- You can specify in the select list which columns to retrieve.
- You can restrict which rows to retrieve by specifying conditions in a WHERE clause.
- You can group or sort the results with GROUP BY or ORDER BY.
- You can use joins, unions, and subqueries.
- You can retrieve the result of an INFORMATION_SCHEMA query into another table with CREATE TABLE ... SELECT or INSERT ... SELECT. This enables you to save the result and use it in other statements later.

The following examples demonstrate how to exploit various features of SELECT to pull out information in different ways from INFORMATION_SCHEMA:

- Display the storage engines used for the tables in a given database:

```
SELECT TABLE_NAME, ENGINE FROM INFORMATION_SCHEMA.TABLES
WHERE TABLE_SCHEMA = 'world';
```

- Find all the tables that contain SET columns:

```
SELECT TABLE_SCHEMA, TABLE_NAME, COLUMN_NAME
FROM INFORMATION_SCHEMA.COLUMNS
WHERE DATA_TYPE = 'set';
```

- Display the default collation for each character set:

```
SELECT CHARACTER_SET_NAME, COLLATION_NAME
FROM INFORMATION_SCHEMA.COLLATIONS
WHERE IS_DEFAULT = 'Yes';
```

- Display the number of tables in each database:

```
SELECT TABLE_SCHEMA, COUNT(*)
FROM INFORMATION_SCHEMA.TABLES;
GROUP BY TABLE_SCHEMA;
```

INFORMATION_SCHEMA is read-only. Its tables cannot be modified with statements such as INSERT, DELETE, or UPDATE. If you try, an error occurs:

```
mysql> DELETE FROM INFORMATION_SCHEMA.VIEWS;
ERROR 1288 (HY000): The target table VIEWS of the DELETE is not updatable
```

20.3 Using SHOW and DESCRIBE to Obtain Metadata

MySQL supports a set of SHOW statements that each return one kind of metadata. This section describes a few of them.

- SHOW DATABASES lists the names of the available databases:

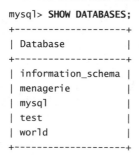

```
mysql> SHOW DATABASES;
+--------------------+
| Database           |
+--------------------+
| information_schema |
| menagerie          |
| mysql              |
| test               |
| world              |
+--------------------+
```

- SHOW TABLES lists the tables in the default database, or in the named database if a FROM clause is present:

```
mysql> SHOW TABLES;
+-----------------+
| Tables_in_world |
+-----------------+
| City            |
| Country         |
| CountryLanguage |
+-----------------+
mysql> SHOW TABLES FROM mysql;
+-------------------------+
| Tables_in_mysql         |
+-------------------------+
| columns_priv            |
| db                      |
| func                    |
| help_category           |
| help_keyword            |
| help_relation           |
| help_topic              |
| host                    |
| proc                    |
| procs_priv              |
| tables_priv             |
| time_zone               |
| time_zone_leap_second   |
| time_zone_name          |
| time_zone_transition    |
| time_zone_transition_type |
| user                    |
+-------------------------+
```

- SHOW COLUMNS displays column structure information for the table named in the FROM clause:

```
mysql> SHOW COLUMNS FROM CountryLanguage;
+-------------+---------------+------+-----+---------+-------+
| Field       | Type          | Null | Key | Default | Extra |
+-------------+---------------+------+-----+---------+-------+
| CountryCode | char(3)       | NO   | PRI |         |       |
| Language    | char(30)      | NO   | PRI |         |       |
| IsOfficial  | enum('T','F') | NO   |     | F       |       |
| Percentage  | float(4,1)    | NO   |     | 0.0     |       |
+-------------+---------------+------+-----+---------+-------+
```

SHOW COLUMNS takes an optional FULL keyword that causes additional information to be displayed (collation, privileges, and comment):

```
mysql> SHOW FULL COLUMNS FROM CountryLanguage\G
*************************** 1. row ***************************
    Field: CountryCode
     Type: char(3)
 Collation: latin1_swedish_ci
     Null: NO
      Key: PRI
  Default:
    Extra:
Privileges: select,insert,update,references
  Comment:
*************************** 2. row ***************************
    Field: Language
     Type: char(30)
 Collation: latin1_swedish_ci
     Null: NO
      Key: PRI
  Default:
    Extra:
Privileges: select,insert,update,references
  Comment:
*************************** 3. row ***************************
    Field: IsOfficial
     Type: enum('T','F')
 Collation: latin1_swedish_ci
     Null: NO
      Key:
  Default: F
    Extra:
Privileges: select,insert,update,references
  Comment:
*************************** 4. row ***************************
    Field: Percentage
     Type: float(4,1)
 Collation: NULL
     Null: NO
      Key:
  Default: 0.0
    Extra:
Privileges: select,insert,update,references
  Comment:
```

SHOW FIELDS is a synonym for SHOW COLUMNS.

- SHOW KEYS displays information about the indexes that a table has:

```
mysql> SHOW KEYS FROM City\G
*************************** 1. row ***************************
        Table: City
   Non_unique: 0
     Key_name: PRIMARY
  Seq_in_index: 1
  Column_name: ID
    Collation: A
  Cardinality: 4079
     Sub_part: NULL
       Packed: NULL
         Null:
   Index_type: BTREE
      Comment:
```

SHOW INDEX is a synonym for SHOW KEYS.

For some SHOW statements, you can give a LIKE clause to perform a pattern-match operation that determines which rows to display. SHOW DATABASES, SHOW TABLES, and SHOW COLUMNS support this feature. For example:

```
mysql> SHOW DATABASES LIKE 'm%';
+---------------+
| Database (m%) |
+---------------+
| menagerie     |
| mysql         |
+---------------+
```

SHOW also supports the use of a WHERE clause. As with the LIKE clause, WHERE determines which rows to display, but WHERE is more flexible because you can use any kind of test, not just a pattern match:

```
mysql> SHOW COLUMNS FROM Country WHERE `Default` IS NULL;
+-----------------+-------------+------+-----+---------+-------+
| Field           | Type        | Null | Key | Default | Extra |
+-----------------+-------------+------+-----+---------+-------+
| IndepYear       | smallint(6) | YES  |     | NULL    |       |
| LifeExpectancy  | float(3,1)  | YES  |     | NULL    |       |
| GNP             | float(10,2) | YES  |     | NULL    |       |
| GNPOld          | float(10,2) | YES  |     | NULL    |       |
| HeadOfState     | char(60)    | YES  |     | NULL    |       |
| Capital         | int(11)     | YES  |     | NULL    |       |
+-----------------+-------------+------+-----+---------+-------+
```

In the preceding statement, the column name (Default) must be given as a quoted identifier because it is a reserved word.

SHOW statements are available for metadata other than for databases, tables, and columns. For example, SHOW CHARACTER SET displays the available character sets and SHOW COLLATION displays the collations for each character set:

```
mysql> SHOW CHARACTER SET;
+----------+---------------------------+----------------------+---------+
| Charset  | Description               | Default collation    | Maxlen  |
+----------+---------------------------+----------------------+---------+
| big5     | Big5 Traditional Chinese  | big5_chinese_ci      |      2  |
| dec8     | DEC West European         | dec8_swedish_ci      |      1  |
| cp850    | DOS West European         | cp850_general_ci     |      1  |
| hp8      | HP West European          | hp8_english_ci       |      1  |
| koi8r    | KOI8-R Relcom Russian     | koi8r_general_ci     |      1  |
| latin1   | ISO 8859-1 West European  | latin1_swedish_ci    |      1  |
| latin2   | ISO 8859-2 Central European | latin2_general_ci  |      1  |
...
```

```
mysql> SHOW COLLATION;
+---------------------+----------+-----+---------+----------+---------+
| Collation           | Charset  | Id  | Default | Compiled | Sortlen |
+---------------------+----------+-----+---------+----------+---------+
| big5_chinese_ci     | big5     |  1  | Yes     | Yes      |      1  |
| big5_bin            | big5     | 84  |         | Yes      |      1  |
| dec8_swedish_ci     | dec8     |  3  | Yes     |          |      0  |
| dec8_bin            | dec8     | 69  |         |          |      0  |
| cp850_general_ci    | cp850    |  4  | Yes     |          |      0  |
| cp850_bin           | cp850    | 80  |         |          |      0  |
| hp8_english_ci      | hp8      |  6  | Yes     |          |      0  |
...
```

DESCRIBE, another metadata-display statement, is equivalent to SHOW COLUMNS. The following two statements display the same information:

```
DESCRIBE table_name;
SHOW COLUMNS FROM table_name;
```

However, whereas SHOW COLUMNS supports the optional FULL keyword, DESCRIBE does not.

Although the contents of INFORMATION_SCHEMA and its tables typically are accessed using SELECT, it's also possible to use SHOW and DESCRIBE with INFORMATION_SCHEMA, just as with any other database. For example, the output from SHOW DATABASES includes INFORMATION_SCHEMA and SHOW TABLES lists its tables:

```
mysql> SHOW DATABASES;
+--------------------+
```

```
| Database           |
+--------------------+
| information_schema |
| menagerie          |
| mysql              |
| test               |
| world              |
+--------------------+
mysql> SHOW TABLES FROM INFORMATION_SCHEMA;
+---------------------------------------+
| Tables_in_information_schema          |
+---------------------------------------+
| SCHEMATA                              |
| TABLES                                |
| COLUMNS                               |
| CHARACTER_SETS                        |
| COLLATIONS                            |
| COLLATION_CHARACTER_SET_APPLICABILITY |
| ROUTINES                              |
| STATISTICS                            |
| VIEWS                                 |
| USER_PRIVILEGES                       |
| SCHEMA_PRIVILEGES                     |
| TABLE_PRIVILEGES                      |
| COLUMN_PRIVILEGES                     |
| TABLE_CONSTRAINTS                     |
| KEY_COLUMN_USAGE                      |
| TRIGGERS                              |
+---------------------------------------+
```

DESCRIBE shows the column definitions for any INFORMATION_SCHEMA table:

```
mysql> DESCRIBE INFORMATION_SCHEMA.CHARACTER_SETS;
+----------------------+-------------+------+-----+---------+-------+
| Field                | Type        | Null | Key | Default | Extra |
+----------------------+-------------+------+-----+---------+-------+
| CHARACTER_SET_NAME   | varchar(64) | NO   |     |         |       |
| DEFAULT_COLLATE_NAME | varchar(64) | NO   |     |         |       |
| DESCRIPTION          | varchar(60) | NO   |     |         |       |
| MAXLEN               | bigint(3)   | NO   |     | 0       |       |
+----------------------+-------------+------+-----+---------+-------+
```

20.4 Using mysqlshow to Obtain Metadata

The mysqlshow client program produces information about the structure of your databases and tables. It provides a command-line interface to various forms of the SHOW statement that list the names of your databases, tables within a database, or information about table columns or indexes. The mysqlshow command has this syntax:

```
mysqlshow [options] [db_name [table_name [column_name]]]
```

The *options* part of the mysqlshow command may include any of the standard connection parameter options, such as --host or --user. You'll need to supply these options if the default connection parameters aren't appropriate. mysqlshow also understands options specific to its own operation. Invoke mysqlshow with the --help option to see a complete list of its options.

The action performed by mysqlshow depends on the number of non-option arguments you provide:

- With no arguments, mysqlshow displays a result similar to that of SHOW DATABASES:

```
shell> mysqlshow
+--------------------+
|      Databases     |
+--------------------+
| information_schema |
| menagerie          |
| mysql              |
| test               |
| world              |
+--------------------+
```

- With a single argument, mysqlshow interprets it as a database name and displays a result similar to that of SHOW TABLES for the database:

```
shell> mysqlshow world
Database: world
+-----------------+
|      Tables     |
+-----------------+
| City            |
| Country         |
| CountryLanguage |
+-----------------+
```

- With two arguments, mysqlshow interprets them as a database and table name and displays a result similar to that of SHOW FULL COLUMNS for the table. With three arguments, the output is the same as for two arguments except that mysqlshow takes the third argument as a column name and displays SHOW FULL COLUMNS output only for that column. The following commands are examples of this invocation syntax. (The output is not shown because it is too wide to fit the page.)

```
shell> mysqlshow world City
shell> mysqlshow world City CountryCode
```

When mysqlshow is used to display table structure, the --keys option may be given to display index structure as well. This information is similar to the output of SHOW INDEX for the table.

If the final argument on the command line contains special characters, mysqlshow interprets the argument as a pattern and displays only the names that match the pattern. The special characters are '%' or '*' to match any sequence of characters, and '_' or '?' to match any single character. For example, the following command shows only those databases with a name that begins with 'w':

```
shell> mysqlshow "w%"
```

The pattern characters might be treated as special by your command interpreter. An argument that contains any such characters should be quoted, as shown in the preceding example. Alternatively, use a character that your command interpreter doesn't treat specially. For example, '*' can be used without quoting on Windows and '%' without quoting on Unix.

Debugging MySQL Applications

MySQL client programs produce diagnostic messages when they encounter problems. These messages help you to determine the causes of these problems so that you can correct them. This chapter discusses how to use diagnostic output produced by MySQL. It covers the following exam topics:

- Interpreting error messages
- Using the SHOW WARNINGS and SHOW ERRORS statements
- Using the perror utility program

Other sources of diagnostic information are the error log and the slow query log. Log files are likely to be available only to database administrators, so use of the logs for diagnostic purposes is covered in the DBA section of this study guide, in Chapter 40, "Interpreting Diagnostic Messages."

21.1 Interpreting Error Messages

If problems occur when you attempt to connect to MySQL Server with a client program or while the server attempts to execute the SQL statements that you send to it, MySQL produces diagnostic messages. Clients can display this information to assist you in troubleshooting and resolving problems.

Diagnostics might be error messages to indicate serious problems or warning messages to indicate less severe problems. MySQL provides diagnostic information in the following ways:

- An error message is returned for statements that fail:

```
mysql> SELECT * FROM no_such_table;
ERROR 1146 (42S02): Table 'test.no_such_table' doesn't exist
```

These messages typically have three components:

- A MySQL-specific error code.
- An SQLSTATE error code. These codes are defined by standard SQL and ODBC.
- A text message that describes the problem.

■ An information string is returned by statements that affect multiple rows. This string provides a summary of the statement outcome:

```
mysql> INSERT INTO integers VALUES ('abc'), (-5), (NULL);
Query OK, 3 rows affected, 3 warnings (0.00 sec)
Records: 3  Duplicates: 0  Warnings: 3
```

■ An operating system-level error might occur:

```
mysql> CREATE TABLE CountryCopy SELECT * FROM Country;
ERROR 1 (HY000): Can't create/write to file './world/CountryCopy.frm'
(Errcode: 13)
```

For cases such as the preceding SELECT from a non-existent table, where all three error values are displayed, you can simply look at the information provided to see what the problem was. In other cases, all information might not be displayed. The information string for multiple-row statements is a summary, not a complete listing of diagnostics. An operating system error includes an Errcode number that might have a system-specific meaning.

You can use the following means to obtain assistance in interpreting diagnostic information:

- The SHOW WARNINGS and SHOW ERRORS statements display warning and error information for statements that produce diagnostic information.
- The perror command-line utility displays the meaning of operating system-related error codes.
- There is a chapter in the *MySQL Reference Manual* that lists error codes and messages.

21.2 The SHOW WARNINGS Statement

MySQL Server generates warnings when it is not able to fully comply with a request or when an action has possibly unintended side effects. These warnings can be displayed with the SHOW WARNINGS statement.

The following example shows how warnings are generated for attempts to insert a character string, a negative integer, and NULL into a column that is defined as INT UNSIGNED NOT NULL:

```
mysql> CREATE TABLE integers (i INT UNSIGNED NOT NULL);
Query OK, 0 rows affected (0.01 sec)
```

```
mysql> INSERT INTO integers VALUES ('abc'), (-5), (NULL);
Query OK, 3 rows affected, 3 warnings (0.00 sec)
Records: 3  Duplicates: 0  Warnings: 3
```

The information returned by the server indicates that there were three instances in which it had to truncate or otherwise change the input to accept the data values that were passed in the INSERT statement. When a statement cannot be executed without some sort of problem occurring, the SHOW WARNINGS statement provides information to help you understand what went wrong. The following example shows the warnings generated by the preceding INSERT statement:

```
mysql> SHOW WARNINGS\G
*************************** 1. row ***************************
  Level: Warning
   Code: 1264
Message: Out of range value adjusted for column 'i' at row 1
*************************** 2. row ***************************
  Level: Warning
   Code: 1264
Message: Out of range value adjusted for column 'i' at row 2
*************************** 3. row ***************************
  Level: Warning
   Code: 1263
Message: Column set to default value; NULL supplied to NOT NULL
         column 'i' at row 3
3 rows in set (0.00 sec)
```

You can combine SHOW WARNINGS with LIMIT, just as you're used to doing with SELECT statements, to "scroll" through the warnings a section at a time:

```
mysql> SHOW WARNINGS LIMIT 1,2\G
*************************** 1. row ***************************
  Level: Warning
   Code: 1264
Message: Out of range value adjusted for column 'i' at row 2
*************************** 2. row ***************************
  Level: Warning
   Code: 1263
Message: Column set to default value; NULL supplied to NOT NULL
         column 'i' at row 3
2 rows in set (0.00 sec)
```

If you want to know only how many warnings there were, use SHOW COUNT(*) WARNINGS.

```
mysql> SHOW COUNT(*) WARNINGS;
+------------------------+
| @@session.warning_count |
```

```
+-------------------------+
|                     3 |
+-------------------------+
```

Warnings generated by one statement are available from the server only for a limited time (until you issue another statement that can generate warnings). If you need to see warnings, you should always fetch them as soon as you detect that they were generated.

"Warnings" actually can occur at several levels of severity:

- Error messages indicate serious problems that prevent the server from completing a request.

- Warning messages indicate problems for which the server can continue processing the request.

- Note messages are informational only.

The following example shows messages that are generated at different levels. An error occurs for the SELECT statement, which cannot be executed successfully because the table does not exist. For the DELETE statement, the message is only a note. The purpose of the statement is to ensure that the table does not exist. That is certainly true when the statement finishes, even though the statement did nothing.

```
mysql> SELECT * FROM no_such_table;
ERROR 1146 (42S02): Table 'test.no_such_table' doesn't exist
mysql> SHOW WARNINGS;
+-------+------+----------------------------------------+
| Level | Code | Message                                |
+-------+------+----------------------------------------+
| Error | 1146 | Table 'test.no_such_table' doesn't exist |
+-------+------+----------------------------------------+
1 row in set (0.01 sec)

mysql> DROP TABLE IF EXISTS no_such_table;
Query OK, 0 rows affected, 1 warning (0.00 sec)

mysql> SHOW WARNINGS;
+-------+------+------------------------------+
| Level | Code | Message                      |
+-------+------+------------------------------+
| Note  | 1051 | Unknown table 'no_such_table' |
+-------+------+------------------------------+
1 row in set (0.00 sec)
```

To suppress generation of Note warnings, you can set the sql_notes system variable to zero:

```
mysql> SET sql_notes = 0;
```

21.3 The SHOW ERRORS Statement

The SHOW ERRORS statement is similar to SHOW WARNINGS, but displays only messages for error conditions. As such, it shows only messages having a higher severity and tends to produce less output than SHOW WARNINGS.

SHOW ERRORS, like SHOW WARNINGS, supports a LIMIT clause to restrict the number of rows to return. It also can be used as SHOW COUNT(*) ERRORS to obtain a count of the error messages.

21.4 The perror Utility

perror is a command-line utility that is included with MySQL distributions. The purpose of the perror program is to show you information about the error codes used by MySQL when operating system-level errors occur. You can use perror in situations when a statement results in a message such as the following being returned to you:

```
mysql> CREATE TABLE CountryCopy SELECT * FROM Country;
ERROR 1 (HY000): Can't create/write to file './world/CountryCopy.frm'
(Errcode: 13)
```

This error message indicates that MySQL cannot write to the file CountryCopy.frm, but does not report the reason. It might be due to a full disk, a filesystem permissions problem, or some other error. To find out, run the perror program with an argument of the number given following Errcode in the preceding error message. perror displays a message indicating that the source of the problem is that someone has incorrectly set the filesystem permissions for the current database:

```
shell> perror 13
Error code  13:  Permission denied
```

22

Basic Optimizations

This chapter discusses general principles that are useful for optimizing queries to run more efficiently. It covers the following exam topics:

- An overview of general optimization principles
- Using indexing and other techniques to optimize query execution
- Choosing storage engines to match application requirements

22.1 Overview of Optimization Principles

There are several optimization strategies that you can take advantage of to make your queries run faster:

- The primary optimization technique for reducing lookup times is to use indexing properly. This is true for retrievals (SELECT statements), and indexing also reduces row lookup time for UPDATE and DELETE statements as well. You should know general principles for creating useful indexes and for avoiding unnecessary ones.

- The way a query is written might prevent indexes from being used even if they are available. Rewriting the query often will allow the optimizer to use an index and process a query faster.

- The EXPLAIN statement provides information about how the MySQL optimizer processes queries. This is of value when you're trying to determine how to make a query run better (for example, if you suspect indexes are not being used as you think they should be).

- In some cases, query processing for a task can be improved by using a different approach to the problem. This includes techniques such as generating summary tables rather than selecting from the raw data repeatedly.

- Queries run more efficiently when you choose a storage engine with properties that best match application requirements.

Why be concerned about optimization? The most obvious reason is to reduce query execution time. Another is that optimizing your queries helps everybody who uses the server, not just you. When the server runs more smoothly and processes more queries with less work, it performs better as a whole:

- A query that takes less time to run doesn't hold locks as long, so other clients that are trying to update a table don't have to wait as long. This reduces the chance of a query backlog building up.

- A query might be slow due to lack of proper indexing. If MySQL cannot find a suitable index to use, it must scan a table in its entirety. For a large table, that involves a lot of processing and disk activity. This extra overhead affects not only your own query, it takes machine resources that could be devoted to processing other queries. Adding effective indexes allows MySQL to read only the relevant parts of the table, which is quicker and less disk intensive.

The optimization strategies covered here are guidelines known to result in generally improved query performance. However, you must test them in specific circumstances and measure the results, particularly if you can choose from more than one technique in a given situation.

The guidelines discussed in this chapter can be used by any client application to improve how the queries it issues are executed by the server. Further discussion of optimization techniques is provided in Chapter 37, "Optimizing Queries." Another approach to performance improvement is to reconfigure the server itself to change its overall operation. Server tuning is addressed in Chapter 39, "Optimizing the Server."

22.2 Using Indexes for Optimization

When you create a table, consider whether it should have indexes, because they have important benefits:

- Indexes contain sorted values. This allows MySQL to find rows containing particular values faster. The effect can be particularly dramatic for joins, which have the potential to require many combinations of rows to be examined.

- Indexes result in less disk I/O. The server can use an index to go directly to the relevant table records, which reduces the number of records it needs to read. Furthermore, if a query displays information only from indexed columns, MySQL might be able to process it by reading only the indexes and without accessing data rows at all.

22.2.1 Types of Indexes

MySQL supports several types of indexes:

- A PRIMARY KEY is a unique-valued index. That is, every key value is required to be different from all others. Every value must be non-NULL.

- A UNIQUE index is unique-valued, like a PRIMARY KEY, but it can be defined to allow NULL values. If so, NULL is an exception to uniqueness because NULL values may occur multiple times.

- A non-unique index is one in which any key value may occur multiple times. This type of index is defined with the keyword INDEX or KEY.

- A FULLTEXT index is specially designed for text searching.

- A SPATIAL index can be used with the spatial data types.

To define indexes when you're initially creating a table, use CREATE TABLE. To add indexes to an already existing table, use ALTER TABLE or CREATE INDEX.

Index creation using the INDEX, UNIQUE, and PRIMARY KEY keywords is discussed in Section 8.6, "Indexes." FULLTEXT indexes provide a means for optimizing text searching in MyISAM tables. They are not covered here, but you can read about them in Section 38.3.3, "FULLTEXT Indexes." Spatial indexes are not covered in this study guide or on the exam.

22.2.2 Principles for Index Creation

An index helps MySQL perform retrievals more quickly than if no index is used, but indexes can be used with varying degrees of success. Keep the following index-related considerations in mind when designing tables:

- Declare an indexed column NOT NULL if possible. Although NULL values can be indexed, NULL is a special value that requires additional decisions by the server when performing comparisons on key values. An index without NULL can be processed more simply and thus faster.

- Avoid over indexing; don't index a column just because you can. If you never refer to a column in comparisons (such as in WHERE, ORDER BY, or GROUP BY clauses), there's no need to index it.

- Another reason to avoid unnecessary indexing is that every index you create slows down table updates. If you insert a row, an entry must be added to each of the table's indexes. Indexes help when looking up values for UPDATE or DELETE statements, but any change to indexed columns require the appropriate indexes to be updated as well.

- One strategy the MySQL optimizer uses is that if it estimates that an index will return a large percentage of the records in the table, it will be just as fast to scan the table as to incur the overhead required to process the index. As a consequence, an index on a column that has very few distinct values is unlikely to do much good. Suppose that a column is declared as ENUM('Y','N') and the values are roughly evenly distributed such that a search for either value returns about half of the records. In this case, an index on the column is unlikely to result in faster queries.

- Choose unique and non-unique indexes appropriately. The choice might be influenced by the data type of a column. If the column is declared as an ENUM, the number of distinct column values that can be stored in it is fixed. This number is equal to the number of enumeration elements, plus one for the ' ' (empty string) element that is used when you attempt to store an illegal value. Should you choose to index an ENUM column, you likely should create a non-unique index. A PRIMARY KEY would allow only as many rows as the number of distinct enumeration values. A UNIQUE index enforces a similar restriction, except that unless the column is declared NOT NULL, the index allows NULL values.

- Index a column prefix rather than the entire column. MySQL caches index information in memory whenever possible to avoid reading it from disk repeatedly. Shortening the length of key values can improve performance by reducing the amount of disk I/O needed to read the index and by increasing the number of key values that fit into the key cache. This technique is discussed in Section 22.2.3, "Indexing Column Prefixes."

- Avoid creating multiple indexes that overlap (have the same initial columns). This is wasteful because MySQL can use a multiple-column index even when a query uses just the initial columns for lookups. For more information, see Section 22.2.4, "Leftmost Index Prefixes."

- The index creation process itself can be optimized if you are creating more than one index for a given table. ALTER TABLE can add several indexes in the same statement, which is faster than processing each one separately. CREATE INDEX allows only one index to be added or dropped at a time.

For indexed MyISAM or InnoDB tables, keeping the internal index statistics up to date helps the query optimizer process queries more efficiently. You can update the statistics with the ANALYZE TABLE statement. See Section 38.3.2, "Keep Optimizer Information Up to Date."

22.2.3 Indexing Column Prefixes

Short index values can be processed more quickly than long ones. Therefore, when you index a column, ask whether it's sufficient to index partial column values rather than complete values. This technique of indexing a column prefix can be applied to string data types.

Suppose that you're considering creating a table using this definition:

```
CREATE TABLE t
(
    name CHAR(255),
    INDEX (name)
);
```

If you index all 255 characters of the values in the name column, index processing will be relatively slow:

- It's necessary to read more information from disk.
- Longer values take longer to compare.
- The index cache is not as effective because fewer key values fit into it at a time.

It's often possible to overcome these problems by indexing only a prefix of the column values. For example, if you expect column values to be distinct most of the time in the first 15 characters, index only that many characters of each value, not all 255 characters.

To specify a prefix length for a column, follow the column name in the index definition by a number in parentheses. The following table definition is the same as the previous one, except that key values in the index use only the first 15 characters of the column values:

```
CREATE TABLE t
(
    name CHAR(255),
    INDEX (name(15))
);
```

Indexing a column prefix can speed up query processing, but works best when the prefix values tend to have about the same amount of uniqueness as the original values. Don't use such a short prefix that you produce a very high frequency of duplicate values in the index. It might require some testing to find the optimal balance between long index values that provide good uniqueness versus shorter values that compare more quickly but have more duplicates. To determine the number of records in the table, the number of distinct values in the column, and the number of duplicates, use this query:

```
SELECT
    COUNT(*) AS 'Total Rows',
    COUNT(DISTINCT name) AS 'Distinct Values',
    COUNT(*) - COUNT(DISTINCT name) AS 'Duplicate Values'
FROM t;
```

The query gives you an estimate of the amount of uniqueness in the name values. Then run a similar query on the prefix values:

```
SELECT
    COUNT(DISTINCT LEFT(name,n)) AS 'Distinct Prefix Values',
    COUNT(*) - COUNT(DISTINCT LEFT(name,n)) AS 'Duplicate Prefix Values'
FROM t;
```

That tells you how the uniqueness characteristics change when you use an n-character prefix of the name values. Run the query with different values of n to determine an acceptable prefix length.

If an index on a full column is a PRIMARY KEY or UNIQUE index, you'll probably have to change the index to be non-unique if you decide to index prefix values instead. When you index partial column values, it's more likely that the prefix values will contain duplicates.

22.2.4 Leftmost Index Prefixes

In a table that has a composite (multiple-column) index, MySQL can use leftmost index prefixes of that index. A leftmost prefix of a composite index consists of one or more of the initial columns of the index. MySQL's capability to use leftmost index prefixes enables you to avoid creating unnecessary (redundant) indexes.

The CountryLanguage table in the world database provides an example of how a leftmost prefix applies. The table has a two-part primary key on the CountryCode and Language columns:

```
mysql> SHOW INDEX FROM CountryLanguage\G
*************************** 1. row ***************************
        Table: CountryLanguage
   Non_unique: 0
     Key_name: PRIMARY
 Seq_in_index: 1
  Column_name: CountryCode
    Collation: A
  Cardinality: NULL
     Sub_part: NULL
       Packed: NULL
         Null:
   Index_type: BTREE
      Comment:
*************************** 2. row ***************************
        Table: CountryLanguage
   Non_unique: 0
     Key_name: PRIMARY
 Seq_in_index: 2
  Column_name: Language
    Collation: A
  Cardinality: 984
     Sub_part: NULL
       Packed: NULL
         Null:
   Index_type: BTREE
      Comment:
```

The index on the CountryCode and Language columns allows records to be looked up quickly based on a given country name and language. However, MySQL also can use the index when given only a country code. Suppose that you want to determine which languages are spoken in France:

```
SELECT * FROM CountryLanguage WHERE CountryCode = 'FRA';
```

MySQL can see that CountryCode is a leftmost prefix of the primary key and use it as though it were a separate index. This means there's no need to define a second index on the CountryCode column alone.

On the other hand, if you want to perform indexed searches using just the Language column of the CountryLanguage table, you do need to create a separate index because Language is not a leftmost prefix of the existing index.

Note that a leftmost prefix of an index and an index on a column prefix are two different things. A leftmost prefix of an index consists of leading columns in a multiple-column index. An index on a column prefix indexes the leading characters of values in the column.

22.3 General Query Enhancement

This section discusses some general techniques that you can apply on a case-by-case basis to individual queries.

22.3.1 Query Rewriting Techniques

The way you write a query often affects how well indexes are used. Use the following principles to make your queries more efficient:

- Don't refer to an indexed column within an expression that must be evaluated for every row in the table. Doing so prevents use of the index. Instead, isolate the column onto one side of a comparison when possible. Suppose that a table t contains a DATE column d that is indexed. One way to select rows containing date values from the year 1994 and up is as follows:

```
SELECT * FROM t WHERE YEAR >= 1994;
```

In this case, the value of YEAR must be evaluated for every row in the table, so the index cannot be used. Instead, write the query like this:

```
SELECT * FROM t WHERE d >= '1994-01-01';
```

In the rewritten expression, the indexed column stands by itself on one side of the comparison and MySQL can apply the index to optimize the query.

For situations like this, the EXPLAIN statement is useful for verifying that one way of writing a query is better than another. Section 22.3.2, "Using EXPLAIN to Obtain Optimizer Information," demonstrates why this is so.

- Indexes are particularly beneficial for joins that compare columns from two tables. Consider the following join:

```
SELECT * FROM Country, CountryLanguage
WHERE Country.Code = CountryLanguage.CountryCode;
```

If neither the Code nor CountryCode column is indexed, every pair of column values must be compared to find those pairs that are equal. For example, for each Code value from the Country table, MySQL would have to compare it with every CountryCode value from the CountryLanguage table. If instead CountryCode is indexed, then for each Code value that MySQL retrieves, it can use the index on CountryCode to quickly look up the rows with matching values. (In practice, you'd normally index both of the joined columns when you use inner joins because the optimizer might process the tables in either order.)

- When comparing an indexed column to a value, use a value that has the same data type as the column. For example, you can look for rows containing a numeric id value of 18 with either of the following WHERE clauses:

```
WHERE id = 18
WHERE id = '18'
```

MySQL will produce the same result either way, even though the value is specified as a number in one case and as a string in the other case. However, for the string value, MySQL must perform a string-to-number conversion, which might cause an index on the id column not to be used.

- In certain cases, MySQL can use an index for pattern-matching operations performed with the LIKE operator. This is true if the pattern begins with a literal prefix value rather than with a wildcard character. An index on a name column can be used for a pattern match like this:

```
WHERE name LIKE 'de%'
```

That's because the pattern match is logically equivalent to a search for a range of values:

```
WHERE name >= 'de' AND name < 'df'
```

On the other hand, the following pattern makes LIKE more difficult for the optimizer:

```
WHERE name LIKE '%de%'
```

When a pattern starts with a wildcard character as just shown, MySQL cannot make efficient use of any indexes associated with that column. (That is, even if an index *is* used, the entire index must be scanned.)

22.3.2 Using EXPLAIN to Obtain Optimizer Information

In the preceding section, an example is shown in which it is stated that of the following two queries, the second can be executed more efficiently because the optimizer can use an index on the column d:

```
SELECT * FROM t WHERE YEAR >= 1994;
SELECT * FROM t WHERE d >= '1994-01-01';
```

To verify whether MySQL actually will use an index to process the second query, use the EXPLAIN statement to get information from the optimizer about the execution plans it would use. For the two date-selection queries just shown, you might find that EXPLAIN tells you something like this:

```
mysql> EXPLAIN SELECT * FROM t WHERE YEAR >= 1994\G
*************************** 1. row ***************************
          id: 1
  select_type: SIMPLE
        table: t
```

```
            type: ALL
    possible_keys: NULL
             key: NULL
         key_len: NULL
             ref: NULL
            rows: 867038
           Extra: Using where
mysql> EXPLAIN SELECT * FROM t WHERE d >= '1994-01-01'\G
*************************** 1. row ***************************
              id: 1
     select_type: SIMPLE
           table: t
            type: range
   possible_keys: d
             key: d
         key_len: 4
             ref: NULL
            rows: 70968
           Extra: Using where
```

These results indicate that the second query is indeed better from the optimizer's point of view. MySQL can perform a range scan using the index for the column d, drastically reducing the number of rows that need to be examined. (The rows value drops from 867,038 to 70,968.)

The use of EXPLAIN is not covered further here. See Section 37.2, "Using EXPLAIN to Analyze Queries," for more information.

22.3.3 Optimizing Queries by Limiting Output

Some optimizations can be done independently of whether indexes are used. A simple but effective technique is to reduce the amount of output a query produces.

One way to eliminate unnecessary output is by using a LIMIT clause. If you don't need the entire result set, specify how many rows the server should return by including LIMIT in your query. This helps in two ways:

- Less information need be returned over the network to the client.
- In many cases, LIMIT allows the server to terminate query processing earlier than it would otherwise. Some row-sorting techniques have the property that the first *n* rows can be known to be in the final order even before the sort has been done completely. This means that when LIMIT *n* is combined with ORDER BY, the server might be able to determine the first *n* rows and then terminate the sort operation early.

Don't use LIMIT as a way to pull out just a few rows from a gigantic result set. For example, if a table has millions of rows, the following statement does not become efficient simply because it uses LIMIT:

```
SELECT * FROM t LIMIT 10;
```

Instead, try to use a WHERE clause that restricts the result so that the server doesn't retrieve as many rows in the first place.

Another way to reduce query output is to limit it "horizontally." Select only the columns you need, rather than using SELECT * to retrieve all columns. Suppose that you want information about countries having names that begin with 'M'. The following query produces that information, but it also produces every other column as well:

```
SELECT * FROM Country WHERE Name LIKE 'M%';
```

If all you really want to know is the country names, don't write the query like that. Most of the information retrieved will be irrelevant to what you want to know, resulting in unnecessary server effort and network traffic. Instead, select specifically just the Name column:

```
SELECT Name FROM Country WHERE Name LIKE 'M%';
```

The second query is faster because MySQL has to return less information when you select just one column rather than all of them.

In addition, if an index on Name exists, you get even more improvement for two reasons:

- The index can be used to determine quickly which Name values satisfy the condition in the WHERE clause. This is faster than scanning the entire table.

- Depending on the storage engine, the server might not read the table rows at all. If the values requested by the query are in the index, then by reading the index MySQL already has the information that the client requested. For example, the MyISAM engine can read the index file to determine which values satisfy the query, and then return them to the client without reading the data file at all. Doing so is faster than reading both the index file and the data file.

22.3.4 Using Summary Tables

Suppose that you run an analysis consisting of a set of retrievals that each perform a complex SELECT of a set of records (perhaps using an expensive join), and that differ only in the way they summarize the records. That's inefficient because it unnecessarily does the work of selecting the records repeatedly. A better technique is to select the records once, and then use them to generate the summaries. In such a situation, consider the following strategy:

1. Select the set of to-be-summarized records into a temporary table. In MySQL, you can do this easily with a CREATE TABLE ... SELECT statement. If the summary table is needed

only for the duration of a single client connection, you can use CREATE TEMPORARY TABLE
... SELECT and the table will be dropped automatically when you disconnect.

2. Create any appropriate indexes on the temporary table.

3. Select the summaries using the temporary table.

The technique of using a summary table has several benefits:

- Calculating the summary information a single time reduces the overall computational burden by eliminating most of the repetition involved in performing the initial record selection.

- If the original table is a type that is subject to table-level locking, such as a MyISAM table, using a summary table leaves the original table available more of the time for updates by other clients by reducing the amount of time that the table remains locked.

- If the summary table is small enough that it's reasonable to hold in memory, you can increase performance even more by making it a MEMORY table. Queries on the table will be especially fast because they require no disk I/O. When the MEMORY table no longer is needed, drop it to free the memory allocated for it.

The following example creates a summary table containing the average GNP value of countries in each continent. Then it compares the summary information to individual countries to find those countries with a GNP much less than the average and much more than the average.

First, create the summary table:

```
mysql> CREATE TABLE ContinentGNP
    -> SELECT Continent, AVG(GNP) AS AvgGNP
    -> FROM Country GROUP BY Continent;
mysql> SELECT * FROM ContinentGNP;
+---------------+---------------+
| Continent     | AvgGNP        |
+---------------+---------------+
| Asia          | 150105.725490 |
| Europe        | 206497.065217 |
| North America | 261854.789189 |
| Africa        |  10006.465517 |
| Oceania       |  14991.953571 |
| Antarctica    |      0.000000 |
| South America | 107991.000000 |
+---------------+---------------+
```

Next, compare the summary table to the original table to find countries that have a GNP less than 1% of the continental average:

```
mysql> SELECT
    ->     Country.Continent, Country.Name,
    ->     Country.GNP AS CountryGNP,
    ->     ContinentGNP.AvgGNP AS ContinentAvgGNP
    -> FROM Country, ContinentGNP
    -> WHERE
    ->     Country.Continent = ContinentGNP.Continent
    ->     AND Country.GNP < ContinentGNP.AvgGNP * .01
    -> ORDER BY Country.Continent, Country.Name;
+-----------+---------------+------------+-----------------+
| Continent | Name          | CountryGNP | ContinentAvgGNP |
+-----------+---------------+------------+-----------------+
| Asia      | Bhutan        |     372.00 |   150105.725490 |
| Asia      | East Timor    |       0.00 |   150105.725490 |
| Asia      | Laos          |    1292.00 |   150105.725490 |
| Asia      | Maldives      |     199.00 |   150105.725490 |
| Asia      | Mongolia      |    1043.00 |   150105.725490 |
| Europe    | Andorra       |    1630.00 |   206497.065217 |
| Europe    | Faroe Islands |       0.00 |   206497.065217 |
| Europe    | Gibraltar     |     258.00 |   206497.065217 |
...
```

Use the summary table again to find countries that have a GNP more than 10 times the continental average:

```
mysql> SELECT
    ->     Country.Continent, Country.Name,
    ->     Country.GNP AS CountryGNP,
    ->     ContinentGNP.AvgGNP AS ContinentAvgGNP
    -> FROM Country, ContinentGNP
    -> WHERE
    ->     Country.Continent = ContinentGNP.Continent
    ->     AND Country.GNP > ContinentGNP.AvgGNP * 10
    -> ORDER BY Country.Continent, Country.Name;
+---------------+---------------+------------+-----------------+
| Continent     | Name          | CountryGNP | ContinentAvgGNP |
+---------------+---------------+------------+-----------------+
| Asia          | Japan         | 3787042.00 |   150105.725490 |
| Europe        | Germany       | 2133367.00 |   206497.065217 |
| North America | United States | 8510700.00 |   261854.789189 |
| Africa        | South Africa  |  116729.00 |    10006.465517 |
| Oceania       | Australia     |  351182.00 |    14991.953571 |
+---------------+---------------+------------+-----------------+
```

Use of summary tables has the disadvantage that the records they contain are up to date only as long as the original values remain unchanged, and thus so are any summaries calculated from them. If the original table rarely or never changes, this might be only a minor concern. For many applications, summaries that are close approximations are sufficiently accurate.

The summary table technique can be applied at multiple levels. Create a summary table that holds the results of an initial summary, and then summarize that table in different ways to produce secondary summaries. This avoids the computational expense of generating the initial summary repeatedly.

When a summary consists of a single value, you need not create a table at all. If you assign the value to a user variable, you can use the variable for comparison purposes in subsequent queries without having to calculate the value again.

22.3.5 Optimizing Updates

The optimizations discussed so far have been shown for SELECT statements, but optimization techniques can be used for statements that update tables, too:

- For a DELETE or UPDATE statement that uses a WHERE clause, try to write it in a way that allows an index to be used for determining which rows to delete or update. The techniques for this that were discussed earlier for SELECT statements apply to DELETE and UPDATE as well.

- EXPLAIN is used with SELECT queries, but you might also find it helpful for analyzing UPDATE and DELETE statements. Write a SELECT that has the same WHERE clause as the UPDATE or DELETE and analyze that.

- Use multiple-row INSERT statements instead of multiple single-row INSERT statements. For example, instead of using three single-row statements like this:

```
mysql> INSERT INTO t (id, name) VALUES(1,'Bea');
mysql> INSERT INTO t (id, name) VALUES(2,'Belle');
mysql> INSERT INTO t (id, name) VALUES(3,'Bernice');
```

You could use a single multiple-row statement that does the same thing:

```
mysql> INSERT INTO t (id, name) VALUES(1,'Bea'),(2,'Belle'),(3,'Bernice');
```

The multiple-row statement is shorter, which is less information to send to the server. More important, it allows the server to perform all the updates at once and flush the index a single time, rather than flushing it after each of the individual inserts. This optimization can be used with any storage engine.

If you're using an InnoDB table, you can get better performance even for single-row statements by grouping them within a transaction rather than by executing them with autocommit mode enabled:

```
mysql> START TRANSACTION;
mysql> INSERT INTO t (id, name) VALUES(1,'Bea');
mysql> INSERT INTO t (id, name) VALUES(2,'Belle');
```

```
mysql> INSERT INTO t (id, name) VALUES(3,'Bernice');
mysql> COMMIT;
```

Using a transaction allows InnoDB to flush all the changes at commit time. In autocommit mode, InnoDB flushes the changes for each INSERT individually.

- For any storage engine, LOAD DATA INFILE is even faster than multiple-row INSERT statements.

- You can disable index updating when loading data into an empty MyISAM table to speed up the operation. LOAD DATA INFILE does this automatically for non-unique indexes if the table is empty; it disables index updating before loading and enables it again after loading.

- To replace existing rows, use REPLACE rather than DELETE plus INSERT.

22.4 Choosing Appropriate Storage Engines

When creating a table, ask yourself what types of queries you'll use it for. Then choose a storage engine that uses a locking level appropriate for the anticipated query mix. MyISAM table-level locking works best for a query mix that is heavily skewed toward retrievals and includes few updates. Use InnoDB if you must process a query mix containing many updates. InnoDB's use of row-level locking and multi-versioning provides good concurrency for a mix of retrievals and updates. One query can update rows while other queries read or update different rows of the table. Additional discussion of locking issues is given in Chapter 28, "Locking."

If you're using MyISAM tables, choose their structure to reflect whether you consider efficiency of processing speed or disk usage to be more important. Different MyISAM storage formats have different performance characteristics. This influences whether you choose fixed-length or variable-length columns to store string data:

- Use fixed-length columns (CHAR, BINARY) for best speed. Fixed-length columns allow MySQL to create the table with fixed-length rows. The advantage is that fixed-length rows all are stored in the table at positions that are a multiple of the row length and can be looked up very quickly. The disadvantage is that fixed-length values are always the same length even for values that do not use the full width of the column, so the column takes more storage space.

- Use variable-length columns (VARCHAR, VARBINARY TEXT, BLOB) for best use of disk space. For example, values in a VARCHAR column take only as much space as necessary to store each value and on average use less storage than a CHAR column. The disadvantage is that variable-length columns result in variable-length rows. These are not stored at fixed positions within the table, so they cannot be retrieved as quickly as fixed-length rows. In addition, the contents of a variable-length row might not even be stored all in one place, another source of processing overhead.

Another option with MyISAM tables is to use compressed read-only tables.

For InnoDB tables, it is also true that CHAR columns take more space on average than VARCHAR. But there is no retrieval speed advantage for InnoDB as there is with MyISAM, because the InnoDB engine implements storage for both CHAR and VARCHAR in a similar way. In fact, retrieval of CHAR values might be slower because on average they require more information to be read from disk.

MERGE tables can use a mix of compressed and uncompressed tables. This can be useful for time-based records. For example, if you log records each year to a different log file, you can use an uncompressed log table for the current year so that you can update it, but compress the tables for past years to save space. If you then create a MERGE table from the collection, you can easily run queries that search all tables together.

More information about storage engine-specific optimizations is given in Chapter 38, "Optimizing Databases."

22.5 Normalization

Normalization refers to the process of restructuring tables to eliminate design problems. Normalizing your tables removes redundant data, makes it possible to access data more flexibly, and eliminates the possibility that inappropriate modifications will take place that make the data inconsistent. Normalization of a complex table often amounts to taking it through a process of decomposition into a set of smaller tables. This process removes repeating groups within rows and then duplicate data within columns.

Although you should understand that normalization is an important part of optimizing your databases to make queries perform efficiently, the normalization process is not covered here. See Section 38.2, "Normalization," for further discussion.

MySQL DBA Exams

MySQL DBA I Exam

MySQL Architecture

A MySQL installation includes a number of programs that work together using a client/server architecture. This chapter discusses the overall characteristics of this architecture, and the general operational characteristics of the MySQL server and the resources that it uses as it runs. The chapter covers the following exam topics:

- The client/server architectural design of MySQL
- Communication protocols that clients can use to connect to the server
- The relationship between the server's storage engines and its SQL parser and optimizer
- How the server uses disk and memory

23.1 Client/Server Overview

The MySQL database system operates using a client/server architecture. The server is the central program that manages database contents, and client programs connect to the server to retrieve or modify data. MySQL also includes non-client utility programs and scripts. Thus, a complete MySQL installation consists of three general categories of programs:

- *MySQL Server.* This is the mysqld program that manages databases and tables. Most users choose a binary (precompiled) MySQL distribution that includes a server ready to run with the capabilities they need, but it's also possible to compile MySQL from source yourself. The types of distributions available are discussed in Chapter 24, "Starting, Stopping, and Configuring MySQL."
- *Client programs.* These are programs that communicate with the server by sending requests to it over a network connection. The server acts on each request and returns a response to the client. For example, you can use the mysql client to send queries to the server, and the server returns the query results.

  The client programs included with MySQL distributions are character-based programs that display output to your terminal. MySQL AB also produces clients that provide a graphical interface. MySQL Query Browser is a general-purpose client for interacting with the server to perform data analysis. MySQL Administrator is oriented more toward managing the server itself. These graphical clients are not included with MySQL distributions but can be obtained from the MySQL AB Web site.

- *Non-client utility programs.* These are programs that generally are used for special purposes and do not act as clients of the server. That is, they do not connect to the server. For example, `mysqld_safe` is a script for starting up and monitoring the server. `myisamchk` is a standalone utility for table checking and repair. It accesses or modifies table files directly. Utilities such as `myisamchk` must be used with care to avoid unintended interaction with the server. If table files are used by two programs at the same time, it's possible to get incorrect results or even to cause table damage.

In addition to the types of programs just described, MySQL AB also makes available several interfaces that can be used by third-party client programs to access the server. These include the API that is provided in the form of a client library written in C that can be linked into other programs, and a family of MySQL Connectors. The connectors are drivers that act as bridges to the MySQL server for client programs that communicate using a particular protocol. Currently, MySQL AB provides MySQL Connector/OBDC, MySQL Connector/J, and MySQL Connector/NET, which are connectors for clients that use the ODBC, JDBC, or .NET protocols. The C client library is available as part of MySQL distributions. The connectors are available as separate packages. (See Chapter 4, "MySQL Connectors.")

The MySQL database system has several important characteristics that enable it to be used in many computing environments:

- MySQL is supported on multiple operating systems, and runs on many varieties of Windows, Unix, and Linux.
- MySQL works in distributed environments. A client program can connect locally to a server running on the same computer or remotely to a server running on a different computer.
- MySQL provides cross-platform interoperability and can be used in heterogeneous networks. Client computers need not run the same operating system as the server computer. For example, a client running on Windows can use a server running on Linux, or vice versa.

Most of the concepts discussed here apply universally to any system on which MySQL runs. Platform-specific information is so indicated. Unless otherwise specified, "Unix" as used here includes Linux and other Unix-like operating systems.

23.2 Communication Protocols

A MySQL client program can connect to a server running on the same machine. This is a local connection. A client can also connect to a server running on another machine, which is a remote connection.

MySQL supports connections between clients and the server using several networking protocols, as shown in the following table.

Protocol	Types of Connections	Supported Operating Systems
TCP/IP	Local, remote	All
Unix socket file	Local only	Unix only
Named pipe	Local only	Windows only
Shared memory	Local only	Windows only

Some protocols are applicable for connecting to either local or remote servers. Others can be used only for local servers. Some protocols are specific to a given operating system.

- TCP/IP connections are supported by any MySQL server unless the server is started with the `--skip-networking` option.

- Unix socket file connections are supported by all Unix servers.

- Named-pipe connections are supported only on Windows and only if you use one of the servers that has -nt in its name (`mysql-nt`, `mysql-max-nt`). However, named pipes are disabled by default. To enable named-pipe connections, you must start the -nt server with the `--enable-named-pipe` option.

- Shared-memory connections are supported by all Windows servers, but are disabled by default. To enable shared-memory connections, you must start the server with the `--shared-memory` option.

From the client perspective, a client run on the same host as the server can use any of the connection protocols that the server supports. If the client is run on a different host, connections always use TCP/IP.

To enable you to indicate which kind of connection to use and which server to connect to, MySQL client programs understand a standard set of command-line options. Section 1.2, "Invoking Client Programs," discusses the syntax for these options and how to use them when invoking client programs.

MySQL communication protocols are implemented by various libraries and program drivers. Client programs included with MySQL distributions (`mysql`, `mysqladmin`, and so forth) establish connections to the server using the native C client library. However, other interfaces are available, such as the MySQL Connectors mentioned in Section 23.1, "Client/Server Overview."

The different connection methods are not all equally efficient:

- In many Windows configurations, communication via named pipes is much slower than using TCP/IP. You should use named pipes only when you choose to disable TCP/IP (using the `--skip-networking` startup parameter) or when you can confirm that named pipes actually are faster for your particular setup.

- On Unix, a Unix socket file connection provides better performance than a TCP/IP connection.

- On any platform, an ODBC connection made via MySQL Connector/ODBC is slower than a connection established directly using the native C client library. This is because ODBC is layered on top of the C library, which adds overhead.

- On any platform, a JDBC connection made via MySQL Connector/J is likely to be roughly about the same speed as a connection established using the native C client library.

23.3 The SQL Parser and Storage Engine Tiers

A client retrieves data from tables or changes data in tables by sending requests to the server in the form of SQL statements such as SELECT, INSERT, or DELETE. The server executes each statement using a two-tier processing model:

- The upper tier includes the SQL parser and optimizer. The server parses each statement to see what kind of request it is, then uses its optimizer to determine how most efficiently to execute the statement. However, this tier does not interact directly with tables named by the statement.

- The lower tier comprises a set of storage engines. The server uses a modular architecture: Each storage engine is a software module to be used for managing tables of a particular type. The storage engine associated with a table directly accesses it to store or retrieve data. MyISAM, MEMORY, and InnoDB are some of the available engines. The use of this modular approach allows storage engines to be easily selected for inclusion in the server at configuration time. New engines also can be added relatively easily.

For the most part, the SQL tier is free of dependencies on which storage engine manages any given table. This means that clients normally need not be concerned about which engines are involved in processing SQL statements, and can access and manipulate tables using statements that are the same no matter which engine manages them. Exceptions to this engine-independence of SQL statements include the following:

- CREATE TABLE has an ENGINE option that enables you to specify which storage engine to use on a per-table basis. ALTER TABLE has an ENGINE option that enables you to convert a table to use a different storage engine.

- Some index types are available only for particular storage engines. For example, only the MyISAM engine supports full-text or spatial indexes.

- COMMIT and ROLLBACK have an effect only for tables managed by transactional storage engines such as InnoDB.

23.4 How MySQL Uses Disk Space

MySQL Server uses disk space in several ways, primarily for directories and files that are found under a single location known as the server's data directory. The server uses its data directory to store all the following:

- Database directories. Each database corresponds to a single directory under the data directory, regardless of what types of tables you create in the database. For example, a given database is represented by one directory whether it contains MyISAM tables, InnoDB tables, or a mix of the two.

- Table format files (.frm files) that contain a description of table structure. Every table has its own .frm file, located in the appropriate database directory. This is true no matter which storage engine manages the table.

- Data and index files are created for each table by some storage engines and placed in the appropriate database directory. For example, the MyISAM storage engine creates a data file and an index file for each table.

- The InnoDB storage engine has its own tablespace and log files. The tablespace contains data and index information for all InnoDB tables, as well as the undo logs that are needed if a transaction must be rolled back. The log files record information about committed transactions and are used to ensure that no data loss occurs. By default, the tablespace and log files are located in the data directory. The default tablespace file is named ibdata1 and the default log files are named ib_logfile0 and ib_logfile1. (It is also possible to configure InnoDB to use one tablespace file per table. In this case, InnoDB creates the tablespace file for a given table in the table's database directory.)

- Server log files and status files. These files contain information about the statements that the server has been processing. Logs are used for replication and data recovery, to obtain information for use in optimizing query performance, and to determine whether operational problems are occurring.

Chapter 24, "Starting, Stopping, and Configuring MySQL," contains additional information about configuration-related aspects of the data directory, such as how to determine its location or set up logging. Chapter 29, "Storage Engines," discusses how storage engines manage table files under the data directory.

23.5 How MySQL Uses Memory

MySQL Server memory use includes data structures that the server sets up to manage communication with clients and to process the contents of databases. The server allocates memory for many kinds of information as it runs:

- Thread handlers. The server is multi-threaded, and a thread is like a small process running inside the server. For each client that connects, the server allocates a thread to it to handle the connection. For performance reasons, the server maintains a small cache of thread handlers. If the cache is not full when a client disconnects, the thread is placed in the cache for later reuse. If the cache is not empty when a client connects, a thread from the cache is reused to handle the connection. Thread handler reuse avoids the overhead of repeated handler setup and teardown.

Threads also may be created for other purposes. Individual storage engines might create their own threads, and replication uses threads.

- The server uses several buffers (caches) to hold information in memory for the purpose of avoiding disk access when possible:

  - Grant table buffers. The grant tables store information about MySQL user accounts and the privileges they have. The server loads a copy of the grant tables into memory for fast access-control checking. Client access is checked for every query, so looking up privilege information in memory rather than from the grant tables on disk results in a significant reduction of disk access overhead.

  - A key buffer holds index blocks for MyISAM tables. By caching index blocks in memory, the server often can avoid reading index contents repeatedly from disk for index-based retrievals and other index-related operations such as sorts.

    In contrast to the handling of MyISAM indexes, there are no buffers specifically for caching MyISAM table data rows because MySQL relies on the operating system to provide efficient caching when reading data from tables.

  - The table cache holds descriptors for open tables. For frequently used tables, keeping the descriptors in the cache avoids having to open the tables again and again.

  - The server supports a query cache that speeds up processing of queries that are issued repeatedly. This feature is discussed in detail in Section 39.4, "Using the Query Cache."

  - The host cache holds the results of hostname resolution lookups. These results are cached to minimize the number of calls to the hostname resolver.

  - The InnoDB storage engine logs information about current transactions in a memory buffer. When a transaction commits, the log buffer is flushed to the InnoDB log files, providing a record on disk that can be used to recommit the transaction if it is lost due to a crash. If the transaction rolls back instead, the flush to disk need not be done at all.

- The MEMORY storage engine creates tables that are held in memory. These tables are very fast because no transfer between disk and memory need be done to access their contents.

- The server might create internal temporary tables in memory during the course of query processing. If the size of such a table exceeds the value of the tmp_table_size system variable, the server converts it to a `MyISAM`-format table on disk and increments its `Created_tmp_disk_tables` status variable.

- The server maintains several buffers for each client connection. One is used as a communications buffer for exchanging information with the client. Other buffers are maintained per client for reading tables and for performing join and sort operations.

Several `SHOW` statements enable you to check the sizes of various memory-related parameters. `SHOW VARIABLES` displays server system variables so that you can see how the server is configured. `SHOW STATUS` displays server status variables. The status indicators enable you to check the runtime state of caches, which can be useful for assessing the effectiveness with which they are being used and for determining whether you would be better off using larger (or in some cases smaller) buffers.

Server memory use can be tuned by setting buffer sizes using command-line options or in an option file that the server reads at startup time. For more information, see Chapter 39, "Optimizing the Server."

Starting, Stopping, and Configuring MySQL

This chapter discusses the issues involved in setting up and configuring MySQL. It covers the following exam topics:

- Types of MySQL distributions available
- Starting and stopping MySQL Server on Windows
- Starting and stopping MySQL Server on Unix and Unix-like systems such as Linux
- Specifying options for server runtime configuration
- Log and status files
- Loading the time zone tables for named time zone support
- Security-related configuration options
- Setting the default SQL mode
- Upgrading an older installation to a newer version of MySQL

This chapter covers general methods for starting and stopping MySQL Server. The material here assumes that MySQL has been installed already and does not go into detail about installation procedures. Those details can be found in the installation chapter of the *MySQL Reference Manual*. If you need to install MySQL, you can get any distribution files you need from the MySQL AB Web site (`http://dev.mysql.com`).

24.1 Types of MySQL Distributions

MySQL is available for several operating systems. Those covered in this chapter are Windows and Unix. Unless otherwise specified, "Unix" as used here includes Linux and other Unix-like operating systems.

You can install MySQL from a binary distribution that contains precompiled programs ready to run, or you can compile MySQL yourself from a source distribution. This section describes the various types of MySQL distributions from which you can choose.

24.1.1 MySQL Binary Distributions

On Windows, you can choose from these types of binary distributions:

- An Essentials distribution contains the minimum set of files needed to install MySQL, as well as the Configuration Wizard. This is the recommended package for most users.

- A Complete distribution contains all files for a MySQL installation, as well as the Configuration Wizard.

- A No-install distribution contains all files for a MySQL installation, but does not have an installer or the Configuration Wizard.

The installer included with Essentials and Complete distributions allows you to choose where to install MySQL. By default, it installs MySQL 5.0 in %ProgramFiles%\MySQL\MySQL Server 5.0, where %ProgramFiles% has a value such as C:\Program Files. The No-install distribution is just a Zip archive. To install it, unpack it and move it to the desired installation location.

On Unix, you can choose from these types of binary distributions:

- RPM files are available for Linux systems. These files are installed by using the rpm program. The installation layout for each RPM is given by a specification file contained within the RPM file itself. (Use rpm -qpl rpm_file to determine where the contents of an RPM file will be installed.)

- tar files are available for many varieties of Unix and Unix-like systems. To install this kind of distribution, unpack it by invoking the tar program in the directory where you want installation to take place.

Post-installation procedures for starting and configuring the server are covered later in this chapter.

24.1.2 MySQL Source Distributions

The preceding section describes the types of precompiled binary distributions containing ready-to-run programs that are available. There are several advantages to using a binary distribution from MySQL AB, aside from the obvious one that you need not go through a possibly somewhat lengthy build process. One significant benefit is that binaries produced by MySQL are likely to provide better performance than those you build yourself:

- MySQL AB has a great deal of experience selecting configuration options such as compiler switches that produce the most highly optimized binaries.

- In many cases, MySQL AB uses commercial compilers that produce superior quality code compared to the compilers typically available for general-purpose use.
- In some cases, MySQL AB produces binaries compiled with libraries that provide capabilities beyond those available in the standard operating system vendor libraries. For example, on Linux systems, a special C library is used that allows a higher maximum number of concurrent connections than can be achieved using the stock C library. Other times, binaries are built using special libraries that work around known bugs in vendor libraries.

It is also possible to build MySQL by compiling it from a source distribution. Despite the advantages of precompiled distributions, there are reasons you might choose to compile MySQL yourself:

- There might be no binary distribution available for your platform. In this case, you have no choice but to build MySQL from source.
- You need to enable a feature that might not be available in a precompiled distribution, such as full debugging support. Or you might want to disable a feature that you don't need, to produce a server that uses less memory when it runs. For example, you can disable optional storage engines, or compile in only those character sets that you really need.
- Binary distributions are available only for released versions, not for the very latest development source code. If you want to run a server built from the current source, you must compile it yourself.

You can configure a source distribution to be installed at a location of your choosing. The default installation location is `/usr/local/mysql`.

Should you decide to build MySQL from source, consult the *MySQL Reference Manual*, which has extensive notes and information on platform-specific issues.

24.2 Starting and Stopping MySQL Server on Windows

This section discusses the prerequisites that you should check before running the server on Windows. It also describes how to run the server manually from the command line or automatically as a Windows service.

24.2.1 Server Startup Prerequisites on Windows

You should know where MySQL is installed because the installation directory contains several important subdirectories. If you install MySQL by using an Essentials or Complete distribution, the installer by default uses an installation location of

`C:\Program Files\MySQL\MySQL Server 5.0` for MySQL 5.0. If you use a No-install archive, the installation location is wherever you happen to place the unpacked archive.

Under the installation location, you'll find a directory named `bin` that contains the MySQL server and client programs, and a directory named `data` where the server stores databases.

For MySQL installations on Windows, the `data` directory is preconfigured and ready to use. For example, it includes a `mysql` directory for the `mysql` database that contains the grant tables, and a `test` directory for a database that can be used for test purposes. After the server has been started, you should set up passwords for the initial accounts listed in the grant tables, as described in Section 35.5.1, "Securing the Initial MySQL Accounts."

Windows MySQL distributions include several servers, which you can find in the `bin` directory under the MySQL installation directory:

- `mysqld` is the standard server. It includes both the `MyISAM` and `InnoDB` storage engines.
- `mysqld-nt` is like `mysqld`, but includes support for named pipes on NT-based systems such as Windows NT, 2000, XP, and 2003.
- `mysqld-max` and `mysql-max-nt` are like `mysqld` and `mysql-nt`, but with extra features such as support for additional storage engines that are not included in the non-max servers.
- `mysqld-debug` contains support for debugging. Normally, you don't choose this server for production use because it has a larger runtime image and uses more memory.

Essentials distributions include only the `mysqld` and `mysqld-nt` servers.

The example commands in the following sections use `mysqld` for the server name. To use a different server, make the appropriate substitutions.

When you start the MySQL server on Windows, it assumes by default that the installation directory is `C:\mysql`. You can install MySQL elsewhere, but if you do, the server must be told what the location is. One way to do this is to set up an option file that specifies the location, using the instructions in Section 24.4, "Runtime MySQL Configuration." The Configuration Wizard included with Essentials and Complete distributions sets up an option file for you using the following procedure:

- The Wizard uses an installation directory of `C:\Program Files\MySQL\MySQL Server 5.0`, and it creates an option file named `my.ini` in that directory. The option file contains a `[mysqld]` group that includes a `basedir` setting that names the installation directory:

```
[mysqld]
basedir="C:/Program Files/MySQL/MySQL Server 5.0"
```

Note that backslashes in Windows pathnames are written using forward slashes in option files.

- The Wizard installs the server to run as a Windows service, using a command that includes a `--defaults-file` option to specify the `my.ini` file pathname:

```
mysqld --install MySQL
    --defaults-file="C:\Program Files\MySQL\MySQL Server 5.0\my.ini"
```

In this way, when the MySQL service starts, the server knows where to find the option file, and that option file specifies where the installation directory is located.

If you use the Configuration Wizard to install MySQL but want to use a server different from `mysqld` for the MySQL service, you'll need to remove the service and install it again using a different server name. Service removal and installation is discussed in Section 24.2.3, "Running MySQL Server as a Windows Service." Substitute a different server name for `mysqld` in the commands shown there.

24.2.2 Running MySQL Server Manually on Windows

To run a Windows MySQL server manually from the command line of a console window, change location into the `bin` directory under the MySQL installation directory. Then invoke the server as follows:

```
shell> mysqld
```

By default, Windows servers write error messages to the file *host_name*.err in the data directory, where *host_name* is the MySQL server hostname. If the server does not start properly, check the error log in the data directory to see why. Alternatively, to display diagnostic output in the console window instead, invoke the server with the `--console` option:

```
shell> mysqld --console
```

Other server options may be specified on the command line or in option files. See Section 24.4, "Runtime MySQL Configuration."

When you invoke the server at the command prompt, the command interpreter might not display another prompt until the server exits. If that happens, open a new console window so that you can invoke other MySQL programs while the server is running.

To stop the server, use `mysqladmin` from the command line:

```
shell> mysqladmin shutdown
```

It's also possible to use the Windows Task Manager, although you should avoid that if you can; the Task Manager terminates the server forcibly without giving it a chance to perform a clean shutdown. The result might be data corruption requiring table repairs.

24.2.3 Running MySQL Server as a Windows Service

The previous section describes how to run the MySQL server by starting it manually. Another way to run MySQL is to install it as a Windows service, so that Windows itself starts and stops the MySQL server when Windows starts and stops.

If you installed MySQL using an Essentials or Complete distribution, you may have used the Configuration Wizard to install the MySQL service and start the server. Otherwise, you'll need to install the server as a Windows service yourself. To do so, change location into the `bin` directory under the MySQL installation directory. Then invoke the server with the `--install` option as follows:

```
shell> mysqld --install
```

If the MySQL installation directory or data directory are not at the built-in default locations assumed by the server (`C:\mysql` and `C:\mysql\data`, respectively), you'll need to specify their locations in the `[mysqld]` group of an option file. This can be done in one of the standard option files. (See Section 24.4, "Runtime MySQL Configuration.") It's necessary to use an option file because a MySQL server that runs as a Windows service reads options only from option files, not from the command line.

It's also possible to put options in a file of your choice and tell the server specifically to read that file. For example, to use `C:\server-opts` for server options, the `--install` command looks like this:

```
shell> mysqld --install MySQL --defaults-file=C:\server-opts
```

When you name a file with the `--defaults-file` option, the server reads options only from the `[mysqld]` option group of the named file when it starts, and ignores the standard option files.

The `--install` command does not actually start the server. It only tells Windows to handle the server as a service, so that when Windows starts up and shuts down, it starts and stops `mysqld` automatically. The service also can be started or stopped manually from the command line. To do so, use these commands:

```
shell> net start MySQL
shell> net stop MySQL
```

`MySQL` is the service name for MySQL. It can be given in any lettercase.

To control the MySQL service using a graphical interface, use the Windows Services Manager. It displays a window that lists all known services and has controls for starting and stopping them.

You can also shut down the server manually from the command line using `mysqladmin shutdown`.

If the server does not start properly when run as a service, check the error log in the data directory or run the server manually with the --console option as described in Section 24.2.2, "Running MySQL Server Manually on Windows." With the --console option, error messages will appear in the console window.

To remove the MySQL service, stop the server if it's running (using any of the means just described), and then issue the following command:

```
shell> mysqld --remove
```

The preceding commands assume the use of the default MySQL service name of MySQL. To use a different service name, use commands that specify the name explicitly:

```
shell> mysqld --install my_service
shell> mysqld --install my_service --defaults-file=C:\server-opts
shell> mysqld --remove my_service
shell> net start my_service
shell> net stop my_service
```

If you install a server using a service name other than MySQL and do not specify a --defaults-file option, the server reads options in the standard option files from the [my_service] group in addition to options from the [mysqld] group.

Another way to install or remove MySQL servers as Windows services, or to start and stop MySQL services is to use MySQL Administrator. See Chapter 26, "MySQL Administrator."

24.3 Starting and Stopping MySQL Server on Unix

MySQL runs on many Unix and Unix-like systems, including those based on BSD Unix, System V Unix, and Linux. This section describes general procedures for running MySQL on them. The topics include the prerequisites to check prior to running the server, and arranging for server startup and shutdown.

On Unix, it's best to use a dedicated login user and group for administering and running MySQL Server so that it can be run with permissions other than those of the root login. In this study guide, it's assumed that the user and group names both are mysql.

24.3.1 Server Startup Prerequisites on Unix

Before attempting to run MySQL Server on Unix, you should make sure that everything has been installed and that there is a login account to use for administering and running the server. You should also initialize the data directory if necessary.

On Unix, precompiled MySQL distributions come in the form of RPM files or as compressed tar files. RPMs are used on Linux systems. tar files are available for many platforms.

RPM installation for MySQL typically requires more than one RPM file because the distribution is split up into different RPMs. The most important RPM files are for the server and for the client programs, so at a minimum, you normally install both of them. If you want to run a Max version of the server, you'll also need a Max server RPM, which must be installed *after* the regular server RPM.

The installation process for RPM files sets up a login account that has user and group names of mysql to use for administering and running the server. It also installs all the files, initializes the data directory and the mysql database that contains the initial MySQL accounts, registers a startup script named mysql in the /etc/init.d directory, and starts the server. The server is installed in /usr/sbin and the data directory is created at /var/lib/mysql.

A tar file distribution is installed simply by unpacking it. For example, if you have a distribution named mysql-max-5.0.10-beta-sun-solaris2.9-sparc.tar.gz on Solaris, you can unpack it in /usr/local to create a subdirectory named mysql-max-5.0.10-beta-sun-solaris2.9-sparc. It's common to create a symbolic link named mysql in /usr/local that points to the installation directory so that it can be referred to more easily as /usr/local/mysql. This study guide assumes the latter pathname of the installation directory for MySQL as installed from a tar file on Unix.

One advantage of setting up a symbolic link (besides that it's shorter than the name created by the tar file) is that when you upgrade to a newer version of MySQL, you can easily retarget the link to the new installation directory. Just delete the link and re-create it to point to the new directory.

With tar file distributions, there is no automatic creation of a login account for running the server, and the data directory is not set up. You must create the login account and initialize the data directory yourself.

The commands to set up a login account for administering and running the server vary for different versions of Unix. For purposes of this guide, it's assumed that you create an account that has user and group names of mysql.

To initialize the data directory, change location into the installation directory and run the mysql_install_db script. For a tar file distribution, this script normally is located in the scripts directory, so you run it like this:

```
shell> cd /usr/local/mysql
shell> scripts/mysql_install_db
```

To make sure that all directories and files that mysql_install_db creates have the proper ownership, run the script as just described while logged in as the mysql user. Alternatively, you can run it as root with the --user=mysql option:

```
shell> cd /usr/local/mysql
shell> scripts/mysql_install_db --user=mysql
```

mysql_install_db creates the data directory and initializes the mysql and test databases. If you do not run this script, the server will complain when you run it later that it cannot find files in the mysql database. For example, the server will issue an error message such as Can't find file: ./host.frm.

With a tar file distribution, you'll also need to install a startup script. That is covered in Section 24.3.2, "Choosing a Server Startup Method on Unix."

Regardless of how you install MySQL on Unix (whether from RPM files or a tar file), the initial MySQL accounts have no passwords. After the server has been started, you should set up passwords as described in Section 35.5.1, "Securing the Initial MySQL Accounts."

24.3.2 Choosing a Server Startup Method on Unix

The server can be started on Unix using any of several different methods:

- You can invoke mysqld manually. This is usually not done except for debugging purposes. If you invoke the server this way, error messages go to the terminal by default rather than to the error log.

- mysqld_safe is a shell script that invokes mysqld. The script sets up the error log, and then launches mysqld and monitors it. If mysqld terminates abnormally, mysqld_safe restarts it.

- mysql.server is a shell script that invokes mysqld_safe. It's used as a wrapper around mysqld_safe for systems such as Linux and Solaris that use System V run-level directories. Typically, this script is renamed to mysql when it is installed in a run-level directory.

- mysqld_multi is a Perl script intended to make it easier to manage multiple servers on a single host. It can start or stop servers, or report on whether servers are running. Use of multiple servers is discussed further in Chapter 42, "Scaling MySQL."

To have the server run automatically at system startup time, a startup script that's appropriate for your system must be installed:

- On BSD-style Unix systems, it's most common to invoke mysqld_safe from one of the system startup scripts, such as the rc.local script in the /etc directory.

- Linux and System V Unix variants that have run-level directories under /etc/init.d use the mysql.server script. If you install the server RPM on Linux, the installation command automatically installs mysql.server under the name mysql for the appropriate run levels. It can be invoked manually with an argument of start or stop to start or stop the server:

```
shell> /etc/init.d/mysql start
shell> /etc/init.d/mysql stop
```

The operating system startup and shutdown procedures issue those commands automatically.

If the server does not start properly, look in the error log. The default error log name on Unix is *host_name*.err in the data directory, where *host_name* is the name of your server host.

To stop the server manually, use one of the following techniques:

- The mysqladmin program has a shutdown command. It connects to the server as a client and can shut down local or remote servers.

- The mysql.server script can shut down the local server when invoked with an argument of stop.

- The mysqld_multi script has a stop command and can shut down any of the servers that it manages. It does so by invoking mysqladmin.

mysqld_safe has no server shutdown capability. You can use mysqladmin shutdown instead. Note that if you forcibly terminate mysqld by using the kill -9 command to send it a signal, mysqld_safe will detect that mysqld terminated abnormally and will restart it. You can work around this by killing mysqld_safe first and then mysqld, but it's better to use mysqladmin shutdown, which initiates a normal (clean) server shutdown.

The mysqld_multi script can be used to manage multiple servers. However, MySQL AB currently is developing another program called MySQL Instance Manager to be used for multiple-server management. This program will offer some significant improvements over mysqld_multi and eventually will replace it:

- mysqld_multi can stop local or remote servers, but can start only local servers. With MySQL Instance Manager, it will be possible to start remote servers as well.

- mysqld_multi runs on Unix systems. MySQL Instance Manager will offer cross-platform compatibility and run on Windows or Unix.

- mysqld_multi requires the Perl DBI module to be installed. MySQL Instance Manager is a standalone binary executable.

24.4 Runtime MySQL Configuration

By default, the server uses built-in values for its configuration variables when it runs. If the default values aren't suitable, you can use runtime options to tell the server to use different values:

- Several options specify the locations of important directories and files. For example, under Windows, the built-in default value for the installation directory (base directory) is C:\mysql. If you install MySQL somewhere else, you must tell the server the correct location by using the --basedir option or the server will not start. Similarly, if you use a data directory other than the directory named data under the installation directory, you must use a --datadir option to tell the server the correct location.

- Options control which log files the server writes.

- Options can be used to override the server's built-in values for performance-related variables, such as those that control the maximum number of simultaneous connections, and the sizes of buffers and caches.

- Some storage engines that are built in can be enabled or disabled at server startup. For example, if the server has been compiled with InnoDB support (which is true by default), the --skip-innodb option can be given to save memory if you are not using InnoDB tables. You can also specify that the default storage engine should be different from the built-in default of MyISAM.

- Several options configure the InnoDB tablespace. If InnoDB is enabled, it creates a default tablespace in the absence of explicit configuration. However, the default tablespace is rather small, so it's better to configure the tablespace yourself.

The examples in this section concentrate on options that relate to general directory and file layout. Section 29.4, "The InnoDB Engine," covers InnoDB-specific configuration. Chapter 39, "Optimizing the Server," concentrates on using performance-related options to tune the server to run more efficiently.

You can specify runtime options when you start the server to change its configuration and behavior. In general, options can be given either on the command line or in option files. (The exception is that if you run the server as a Windows service, you cannot specify options on the command line. You must use a --defaults-file option, as described in Section 24.2.3, "Running MySQL Server as a Windows Service." Keep this in mind for the following discussion.)

For general background on option file syntax, see Section 1.2.3, "Using Option Files." That discussion occurs in the context of running client programs, but the bulk of it also applies to specifying server options.

To find out what options the server supports, invoke it manually as follows:

```
shell> mysqld --verbose --help
```

Any of the server options shown in the help message may be specified on the command line. However, it's more typical to list them in an option file, for several reasons:

- By putting options in a file, you need not specify them on the command line each time you start the server. This is not only more convenient, it's less error-prone for complex options such as those used to configure the InnoDB tablespace.

- If you invoke the server using the mysql.server startup script, you cannot specify server options on the command line of the script. It understands arguments of start or stop only, which makes use of an option file mandatory.

- If you list all server options in a single option file, you can look at this file to see immediately how you've configured the server to run.

The server looks for option files in several standard locations. It uses any that exist, but it is not an error for an option file to be missing. The standard files are different for Windows and Unix.

On Windows, programs look for option files in the following order: my.ini and my.cnf in the Windows directory (for example, the C:\Windows or C:\WinNT directory), and then C:\my.ini and C:\my.cnf.

Note: If you used the Configuration Wizard to install the server as a Windows service, the server does not look in the standard option file locations. Instead, it looks for options only in the my.ini file in the MySQL installation directory. Similarly, if you installed the server as a service yourself and specified a --defaults-file option to name an option file, the server looks for options only in that file. In either case, to make any option changes, you must make them in the single file that the server reads.

On Unix, the search order includes two general option files, /etc/my.cnf and $MYSQL_HOME/my.cnf. The second file is used only if the MYSQL_HOME environment variable is set. Typically, you set it to the MySQL installation directory. (The mysqld_safe script attempts to set MYSQL_HOME if it is not set before starting the server.)

The Unix option file search order also includes ~/.my.cnf, that is, the .my.cnf file located in the home directory of the person running the program. However, because ~/.my.cnf is a user-specific file, it isn't an especially suitable location for server options. (Normally, you invoke the server as mysql, or as root with a --user=mysql option. The user-specific file read by the server would depend on which login account you invoke it from, possibly leading to inconsistent sets of options being used.)

To specify server startup options in an option file, use the [mysqld] option group. If the file does not exist, create it as a plain text file using an editor. To create or modify an option file, you must have write permission for it. The server itself needs only read access; it reads option files but does not create or modify them.

The following examples illustrate some ways to use option files to specify server options:

- If you install MySQL on Windows, the server assumes by default that the installation directory is C:\mysql and the data directory is named data in the installation directory. If you install MySQL somewhere else, such as E:\mysql, you must tell the server that location with a --basedir option. Options in option files are given without the leading dashes, so to indicate the installation directory, specify the option as follows:

```
[mysqld]
basedir=E:/mysql
```

If you use the data directory under E:\mysql as the data directory, the basedir value is sufficient for telling the server the data directory location as well. If you use a different data directory location, you must also specify a --datadir option:

```
[mysqld]
basedir=E:/mysql
datadir=D:/mysql-data
```

Note that in this case you'll also need to copy the data directory from under the installation directory to the new location of D:\mysql-data before starting the server. If the server does not find the data directory in the location that you specify in the option file, it will not start up.

- For any option that specifies a Windows pathname, write any backslashes in the name as slashes or as doubled backslashes. For example, to specify a basedir value of E:\mysql, you can write it using either of the following formats:

```
basedir=E:/mysql
basedir=E:\\mysql
```

- If a pathname contains spaces, quote it. For example:

```
basedir="C:/Program Files/MySQL/MySQL Server 5.0"
```

- On Windows, shared-memory connections are not enabled by default, as discussed in Section 23.2, "Communication Protocols." To use this capability, use the following option:

```
[mysqld]
shared-memory
```

Similarly, the mysqld-nt and mysql-max-nt servers are capable of supporting named-pipe connections but do not enable them by default. To turn on named-pipe support, use this option:

```
[mysqld]
enable-named-pipe
```

- To enable logging, use the options that turn on the types of logs you want. The following options turn on the general query log, the binary log, and the slow query log:

```
[mysqld]
log
log-bin
log-slow-queries
```

Section 24.5, "Log and Status Files," further discusses the contents of these logs.

- To specify a default storage engine different from MyISAM, use the --default-storage-engine option:

```
[mysqld]
default-storage-engine=InnoDB
```

- Option files also can be used to set many server system variable values. For example, to increase the maximum allowed number of client connections from the default of 100 to 200, and to increase the size of the MyISAM key cache from the default of 8MB to 128MB, set the max_connections and key_buffer_size variables, respectively:

```
[mysqld]
max_connections=200
key_buffer_size=128M
```

MySQL distributions contain several sample option files. On Windows, they have names like my-small.ini and my-large.ini and are located in the MySQL installation directory. On Unix, they have names like my-small.cnf and my-large.cnf. Likely locations are in /usr/share/mysql for RPM installations or the share directory under the MySQL installation directory for tar file installations.

You can use a sample option file by copying it to one of the standard option file locations. However, before doing this, be sure to read the file and make sure that you understand the effect that its settings will have on server operation. For example, the file might contain settings that enable certain log files or that change the size of memory buffers.

24.5 Log and Status Files

MySQL Server can write information to several types of log files. The logs record various types of information about the SQL statements processed by the server:

- The general query log records all statements that the server receives from clients.
- The binary log records statements that modify data.
- The slow query log contains a record of queries that take a long time to execute.

These logs can be used to assess the operational state of the server, for data recovery after a crash, for replication purposes, and to help you determine which queries are running slowly. The following sections describe each of these logs briefly and how to enable them. (None of them are enabled by default.) However, it's important to realize that log files, particularly the general query log, can grow to be quite large. Thus, you do not necessarily want to enable them all, especially for a busy server. Here is a recommended logging strategy:

1. Enable the general query log, the binary log, and the slow query log when you set up a server initially.

2. After the server has been configured and you have verified that it is running smoothly, disable the general query log to save disk space.

All logs are written in text format except for the binary log which, as the name implies, is a binary file. Text logs can be viewed using any program capable of displaying text files. For the slow query log, another approach is to use the mysqldumpslow utility; it can summarize the log contents. To view the contents of a binary log file, use the mysqlbinlog utility.

When the server logs statements to the binary log and slow query log, it writes extra information. For example, for the slow query log, the server writes execution times and which user executed each statement. To suppress the extra information, start the server with the --log-short-format option.

The server also produces diagnostic information (which normally is written to an error log), and it creates several status files. Later sections describe these files as well.

24.5.1 The General Query Log

The general query log contains a record of when clients connect and disconnect, and the text of every SQL statement received by the server (whether or not it was processed successfully). The server writes statements to the log in the order that it receives them. This log is useful for determining the frequency of a given type of statement or for troubleshooting queries that are not logged to other log files.

To enable the general query log, use the --log or --log=*file_name* option. If no filename is given, the default name is *host_name*.log, where *host_name* stands for the server hostname. By default, the server creates the general query log file under the data directory unless you specify an absolute pathname.

24.5.2 The Binary Log

The binary log contains a record of statements that modify data. For example, the server logs UPDATE and DELETE statements to the binary log, but not SELECT statements. Statements are written to the binary log only after they execute. Statements that are part of a multiple-statement transaction are written as a group after the transaction has been committed. That is, statements are logged in transactional units.

This log is stored in binary format, but its contents can be viewed using the mysqlbinlog utility. The binary log is used for communication between master and slave replication servers, and also can be used for data recovery.

To enable the binary log, use the --log-bin or --log-bin=*file_name* option. If no filename is given, the default name is *host_name*-bin.*nnnnnn*, where *host_name* stands for the server hostname. *nnnnnn* in the name means that the server writes a numbered series of logs, creating a new log each time the server starts up or the logs are flushed. (This means that "the binary log" actually comprises a set of log files.) By default, the server creates the binary log files under the data directory unless you specify an absolute pathname.

If binary logging is enabled, the server also creates a binary log index file that lists the names of the current set of binary log files. By default, the name of the index file is the same as the binary log basename, with a suffix of .index rather than .nnnnnn. To specify the name explicitly, use a --log-bin-index=file_name option.

24.5.3 The Slow Query Log

The slow query log contains the text of queries that take a long time to execute, as well as information about their execution status. By default, "a long time" is more than 10 seconds. This can be changed by setting the long_query_time server variable. The server writes queries to this log after they finish because execution time is not known until then.

The contents of the slow query log can helpful for identifying queries that should be optimized. For more information, see Section 40.3, "Using The Slow Query Log for Diagnostic Purposes."

To enable the slow query log, use the --log-slow-queries or --log-slow-queries=file_name option. If no filename is given, the default name is host_name-slow.log, where host_name stands for the server hostname. By default, the server creates the slow query log file under the data directory unless you specify an absolute pathname.

To log queries that are not processed with the benefit of indexes, use the --log-queries-not-using-indexes option.

24.5.4 The Error Log

The server produces diagnostic messages about normal startups and shutdowns, as well as about abnormal conditions:

- On Windows, the server opens an error log file, which by default is named host_name.err in the data directory. If you start the server from the command line with the --console option, it writes error information to the console window rather than to the error log.

- On Unix, if you invoke mysqld directly, it sends diagnostics to its standard error output, which normally is your terminal. You can start the server with a --log-error=file_name option to log errors to the given file. However, it's more usual to invoke the mysqld_safe script (or mysql.server, which in turn invokes mysqld_safe). mysqld_safe creates the error log and then starts the server with its output redirected to the error log. (Thus, the server writes to the error log, but does not itself directly create the log file.) The default error log name is host_name.err in the server's data directory. mysqld_safe itself also may write information to the error log. For example, if mysqld_safe detects that the server has died, it automatically restarts the server after writing mysqld restarted to the log.

The contents of the error log can be useful for troubleshooting server operation. For a description of the kinds of information you might find in this log, see Section 40.2, "Using the Error Log for Diagnostic Purposes."

24.5.5 Status Files

The server creates several status files. Some of these are located in the data directory by default, but not all.

The server records its process ID in a PID file, for use by other programs that need to send the server a signal. For example, on Unix, processes send signals to each other using process ID values. mysqld_safe is one program that uses this approach. It looks in the PID file to determine the server process ID, and then tries to send the server a signal to check whether it is running.

The default PID filename is *host_name*.pid in the data directory. The name and location may be changed with the --pid-file=*file_name* option.

Unix servers create a Unix socket file so that local clients can establish socket connections. By default, this file is /tmp/mysql.sock. A different filename can be specified by starting the server with the --socket option. If you change the location, client programs also need to be started with the same --socket option so that they know where the socket file is located.

24.6 Loading Time Zone Tables

The MySQL installation procedure creates a set of time zone tables in the mysql database:

- On Windows, the tables are part of the preinitialized mysql database.
- On Unix, the tables are created when mysql_install_db is executed, either automatically during RPM installation or manually if you install from a tar file.

The server uses the time zone tables to implement support for named time zones such as 'Europe/Warsaw'. However, the time zone tables are created as empty tables, which means that, by default, named time zones cannot be used. To enable this capability, you must load the tables. This is an optional configuration procedure, but unless it is performed, time zone support is limited to the SYSTEM zone and to numeric zone offsets such as '+06:00'.

On operating systems that have their own time zone files, it is best to use them for loading the MySQL time zone tables, to ensure that the system and MySQL time zones are based on the same information. Many Unix systems have these files, often located under /usr/share/zoneinfo. For such systems, use the mysql_tzinfo_to_sql program to convert the file contents into SQL statements that can be loaded into MySQL by the mysql program. If the files are located at /usr/share/zoneinfo, the command looks like this:

```
shell> mysql_tzinfo_to_sql /usr/share/zoneinfo | mysql -u root mysql
```

Some systems have no time zone files, such as Windows and HP-UX. For these cases, MySQL AB provides a distribution at `http://dev.mysql.com/downloads/timezones.html` that contains a set of populated time zone tables (in the form of `MyISAM` table files). You can download the distribution and install the files in your `mysql` database to replace the empty time zone tables. Stop the server, copy the files to the `mysql` database directory, and restart the server.

24.7 Security-Related Configuration

This section discusses some of the server startup options that affect security in various ways. Sections elsewhere in this guide discuss other security topics. Two procedures that you should perform are to set passwords for the initial MySQL accounts that are stored in the grant tables of the `mysql` database, and to make sure that filesystem permissions for the components of your installation do not allow access to anyone but the MySQL administrative login account. These procedures are detailed in Chapter 35, "Securing the MySQL Installation."

If all clients are local clients, you can disable connections from remote clients by starting the server with the `--skip-networking` option to disable TCP/IP connections (the only type of connection that can be made by remote clients). In this case, the server must be able to accept local connections using some other networking protocol. This is not an issue on Unix, because servers always accept connections through a Unix socket file. On Windows, local clients can use shared-memory and (for -nt servers) named-pipe connections, but neither of those protocols is enabled by default. Start the server with the `--shared-memory` and `--enable-named-pipe` options to turn on these connection protocols.

Servers for MySQL 4.1 and up use an authentication mechanism that is more secure and provides better passwords than in older versions. However, client programs from older versions do not understand this mechanism and an error occurs when they attempt to connect to a newer server:

```
ERROR 1251: Client does not support authentication protocol
requested by server; consider upgrading MySQL client
```

The best thing to do, if possible, is to upgrade all older (pre-4.1) clients so that they can use the newer authentication mechanism. If that cannot be done and your MySQL server must support older clients, you must configure it for backward compatibility with the older authentication mechanism. The simplest way to do this and provide support for older clients is to run the server with the `--old-password` option. However, you should start the server with this option *before* setting or changing any passwords. Otherwise, you will have passwords in a mix of old and new formats. (It is possible to have the server support both formats, but this is more complex to configure. For details, see the *MySQL Reference Manual*.)

If you want to take the opposite approach and allow connections only by clients that have new-format passwords, start the server with the --secure-auth option. This causes the server to reject connection attempts for any client that has a password in the old format.

24.8 Setting the Default SQL Mode

MySQL Server has a configurable SQL mode that provides control over aspects of query processing such as how strict or forgiving the server is about accepting input data, and whether to enable or disable behaviors relating to standard SQL conformance.

By default, the SQL mode value is empty, so no special restrictions or conformance behaviors are enabled. Individual clients can configure the SQL mode for their own requirements, but it's also possible to set the default SQL mode at server startup with the --sql-mode option. You might do this to run the server with a mode that is more careful about accepting invalid data or creating MySQL user accounts. For example, if you enable TRADITIONAL mode, the server enforces restrictions on input data values that are like other (more "traditional") database servers, rather than MySQL's more forgiving behavior. It also will not allow new user accounts to be created with the GRANT statement unless a password is specified. You can enable TRADITIONAL SQL mode by placing the following lines in an option file:

```
[mysqld]
sql-mode=TRADITIONAL
```

Further information about the SQL mode can be found in Section 1.3, "Server SQL Modes," and Section 5.8, "Handling Missing or Invalid Data Values."

24.9 Upgrading MySQL

MySQL development is ongoing, and MySQL AB releases new versions frequently. New versions add new features and correct problems found in older versions. Nevertheless, you should not upgrade to a newer version of MySQL without checking the implications and possible difficulties of doing so. Check the *MySQL Reference Manual* before performing any upgrade:

- Always consult the section on upgrading to see whether there are any notes pertaining to the type of upgrade you're performing. If so, follow the recommended procedures described there.

- Check the change note sections for versions more recent than your current version to make sure that you're aware of what has changed since your original install. Note particularly any changes that are not backward compatible with your current version because they may require modifications to your existing applications if you upgrade.

Despite those cautionary remarks, upgrading MySQL usually is straightforward and can be done using the following procedure:

- Back up your databases.
- Stop the server.
- Install the new version of MySQL on top of the existing version.
- Start the new server.

If you install a new version of MySQL on top of an existing one, you might not need to do much reconfiguring. This is common for Windows installations, RPM installations, and installations from source because those types of distributions each tend to use the same installation directory location regardless of MySQL version. However, if you upgrade MySQL using a tar file, the new distribution likely will create a new version-specific base installation directory that differs from your existing installation directory. In this case, some reconfiguration might be necessary. If you have a symbolic link set up that points to the old installation directory, you can delete the link and re-create it to point to the new installation directory. Subsequent references to the new symbolic link will access the new installation.

Upgrading MySQL sometimes gives you access to new security features. See Chapter 36, "Upgrade-Related Security Issues," for information about taking advantage of them.

Client Programs
for DBA Work

This chapter summarizes the functions and capabilities of MySQL client programs that are especially important for database administrators. The chapter discusses the following programs:

- MySQL Administrator
- `mysql`
- `mysqladmin`
- `mysqlimport`
- `mysqldump`

Other programs of administrative interest include `mysqlcheck`, `myisamchk`, and `mysqlhotcopy`. These are covered in Chapter 30, "Table Maintenance," and Chapter 32, "Data Backup and Recovery Methods."

25.1 Overview of Administrative Clients

This section provides an overview of MySQL client programs that are of special interest to database administrators (DBAs). Each program enables you to perform important administrative tasks:

- MySQL Administrator is a graphical client for managing the server.
- `mysql` is a general-purpose command-line client for sending SQL statements to the server, including those of an administrative nature.
- `mysqladmin` is an administrative command-line client that helps you manage the server.
- `mysqlimport` provides a command-line interface to the LOAD DATA INFILE statement. It is used to load data files into tables without having to issue LOAD DATA INFILE statements yourself.

- `mysqldump` is a command-line client for dumping the contents of databases and tables. It's useful for making backups or for copying databases to other machines.

This chapter contains only general summaries of program features and capabilities. The sections that follow include cross-references to other study guide chapters in which you can find additional detail about each program. You can also invoke most of these programs with the `--help` option to obtain a help message that shows the command syntax and the other options that the program supports.

25.2 MySQL Administrator

The MySQL Administrator client is designed specifically for administrative operations. Unlike the other clients discussed in this chapter, MySQL Administrator provides a graphical interface for interacting with the server. Compared to the other clients, which are character-based, MySQL Administrator is more intuitive to use and it is easier to interpret the information about server status that it displays. The tasks that MySQL Administrator enables you to perform include those in the following list:

- Monitor server performance, load, and memory usage information
- Display and set server configuration information
- Start and stop servers
- Set up user accounts, grant and revoke privileges, and set passwords
- Display information about client connections or kill connections
- Create and drop databases
- Check, repair, and optimize tables
- Perform backups and restore data from backups
- Monitor replication servers
- Display the contents of the general query, slow query, and error log files

Some of these capabilities are available for local or remote servers. Others, such as configuring the server or displaying its logs, are available for local servers only.

MySQL Administrator is not included with MySQL distributions but can be obtained from the MySQL AB Web site. It is available in precompiled form for Windows, Linux, and Mac OS X, or it can be compiled from source.

MySQL Administrator requires a graphical environment such as Windows or the X Window System. However, if the MySQL server is running on a host with no graphical environment, you can connect to it remotely by running MySQL Administrator on a client host that does have a graphical environment. Some functionality is available only when MySQL Administrator and the server are run on the same host.

MySQL Administrator is covered further in Chapter 26, "MySQL Administrator."

25.3 mysql

The mysql program is a general-purpose client that sends SQL statements to the server, and thus can perform any administrative operation that can be expressed using SQL. The following list describes some of its administrative capabilities:

- Create and drop databases
- Create, drop, and modify tables and indexes
- Retrieve data from tables
- Modify data in tables
- Set up user accounts, grant and revoke privileges, and set passwords
- Display server configuration and version information
- Display or reset server status variables
- Reload the grant tables
- Flush the log files or various server caches
- Start or stop replication slave servers or display replication status
- Display information about client connections or kill connections

You can use mysql in interactive mode, where you type in queries and see their results. mysql also can operate in batch mode, in which it reads queries stored in a text file. For further information, see Chapter 2, "The mysql Client Program."

25.4 mysqladmin

The mysqladmin command-line client is designed specifically for administrative operations. Its capabilities include those in the following list:

- "Ping" the server to see whether it's running and accepting client connections
- Shut down the server
- Create and drop databases
- Display server configuration and version information
- Display or reset server status variables
- Set passwords
- Reload the grant tables
- Flush the log files or various server caches
- Start or stop replication slave servers
- Display information about client connections or kill connections

For a full list of mysqladmin capabilities, invoke the program with the --help option.

mysqladmin accepts one or more commands on the command line following the program name. For example, the following command displays a brief status message, followed by the list of server system variables:

```
shell> mysqladmin status variables
```

Some mysqladmin commands are available only to MySQL accounts that have administrative privileges. For example, to shut down the server, it's necessary to connect to it using an administrative account such as root that has the SHUTDOWN privilege:

```
shell> mysqladmin -u root -p shutdown
```

25.5 mysqlimport

The mysqlimport client program loads data files into tables. It provides a command-line interface to the LOAD DATA INFILE statement. That is, mysqlimport examines the options given on the command line. It then connects to the server and, for each input file named in the command, issues a LOAD DATA INFILE statement that loads the file into the appropriate table.

By default, mysqlimport expects data files to contain tab-delimited lines terminated by newlines. Files in other formats can be imported by identifying the format using command-line options.

mysqlimport can load files located on the client host or on the server host. It can load tables managed by local or remote servers.

For further information about mysqlimport, see Section 15.3.1, "Importing Data with mysqlimport."

25.6 mysqldump

The mysqldump client program dumps table contents to files. It is useful for making database backups or for transferring database contents to another server. mysqldump can export tables as tab-delimited data files or produce SQL-format dump files that contain CREATE TABLE and INSERT statements for re-creating the dumped files.

When used to dump tables as data files, mysqldump by default writes table records as tab-delimited lines terminated by newlines. Tables can be dumped in other formats by specifying the format using command-line options.

Table contents dumped to data files can be dumped only on the server host, so when using mysqldump this way, it's best to invoke it on the server host.

When using mysqldump to produce SQL-format dump files, the server transfers table contents to mysqldump, which writes the dump file locally on the client host. SQL-format dumps can be generated for tables managed by local or remote servers.

For further information about mysqldump, see Section 15.3.2, "Exporting Data with mysqldump," and Section 32.4.2, "Making Text Backups with mysqldump."

25.7 Client Program Limitations

No administrative client program performs all possible administrative tasks. It's important to understand what a given program can do, but you should also know what it cannot do. For example:

- mysqladmin can create or drop databases, but it has no capabilities for creating or dropping individual tables or indexes. It can change passwords, but cannot create or delete user accounts. The mysql and MySQL Administrator programs can perform all of these operations.

- mysqlimport loads data files, so it can load data files produced by mysqldump. However, mysqldump also can produce SQL-format dump files containing INSERT statements, and mysqlimport cannot load those files. Thus, mysqlimport is only a partial complement to mysqldump. To process dump files containing SQL statements, use mysql instead. Instructions for both types of data-loading operations are given in Section 15.3.2, "Exporting Data with mysqldump," and Section 32.8.1, "Reloading mysqldump Output."

- With one exception, none of the client programs can start the server. Normally, you invoke the server directly or by using a startup script, or you can arrange to have the operating system invoke the server as part of its system startup procedure. Server startup procedures are discussed in Chapter 24, "Starting, Stopping, and Configuring MySQL."

   The exception occurs on Windows if the MySQL server is configured to run as a Windows service. In this case, if you run MySQL Administrator on the same machine, you can use it to start and stop the MySQL service.

- None of the clients discussed in this chapter can shut down the server except mysqladmin and MySQL Administrator. mysqladmin shuts down the server by using a special non-SQL capability of the client/server protocol. If you use an account that has the SHUTDOWN privilege, it can shut down local or remote servers. MySQL Administrator can shut down a local MySQL server on Windows if the server is configured to run as a Windows service.

26

MySQL Administrator

This chapter discusses MySQL Administrator, a client program for performing administrative operations in a graphical environment. The chapter covers the following exam topics:

- An overview of MySQL Administrator features
- Launching MySQL Administrator and selecting an operational mode
- MySQL Administrator server monitoring capabilities
- MySQL Administrator server configuration capabilities
- MySQL Administrator backup and restore capabilities
- The MySQL Administrator System Tray Monitor

26.1 MySQL Administrator Capabilities

MySQL Administrator is a cross-platform GUI client program that's intuitive and easy to use. It is a tool for performing administrative operations in a graphical environment. It's similar in style of use to MySQL Query Browser but is oriented toward server administration rather than accessing database contents.

The following list describes some of the tasks that MySQL Administrator enables you to perform:

- Display and set server configuration information
- Start and stop the server
- Monitor server status and performance
- Set up user accounts, grant and revoke privileges, and set passwords
- Display information about client connections or kill connections
- Check, repair, and optimize tables
- Display the contents of the error log, slow query log, and general query log
- Monitor replication

- Perform database backup and recovery operations
- Create or drop databases and tables, and modify the structure of existing tables

MySQL Administrator supports multiple server connections and opens a separate window for each connection that you establish.

On Windows, MySQL Administrator distributions also include a Windows System Tray monitor that provides quick access to server status information from the tray.

26.2 Using MySQL Administrator

MySQL Administrator is not included with MySQL distributions but can be obtained from the MySQL AB Web site. It's available in precompiled form for Windows, Linux, and Mac OS X, or it can be compiled from source.

MySQL Administrator requires a graphical environment such as Windows or the X Window System. On Linux, MySQL Administrator is designed for Gnome, but can be run under KDE if GTK2 is installed. If a MySQL server is running on a host with no graphical environment, you can connect to it remotely by running MySQL Administrator on a client host that does have a graphical environment. Some functionality is available only when MySQL Administrator and the server are run on the same host.

26.2.1 Starting MySQL Administrator

On Windows, the installer creates a desktop icon and an entry in the Start Menu, so you can start MySQL Administrator using either of those. The program itself is located in the installation directory, `C:\Program Files\MySQL\MySQL Administrator 1.0`, so you can also start MySQL Administrator from the command line by invoking it directly after changing location into that directory:

```
C:\> cd "C:\Program Files\MySQL\MySQL Administrator 1.0"
C:\Program Files\MySQL\MySQL Administrator 1.0> MySQLAdministrator.exe
```

RPM installations on Linux place MySQL Administrator in `/usr/bin`. Assuming that this directory is in your search path, you can invoke the program as follows:

```
shell> mysql-administrator
```

For `tar` file distributions, MySQL Administrator is installed wherever you unpacked the distribution, and the program is located in the `bin` directory under the installation directory. To invoke the program, change location to that `bin` directory. For example, if you installed the distribution at `/opt/mysql-administrator`, start MySQL Administrator like this:

```
shell> cd /opt/mysql-administrator/bin
shell> ./mysql-administrator
```

Mac OS X distributions are disk images that, when mounted, contain a MySQL Administrator program that can be dragged to wherever you want to install it. To launch the program, double-click it in the Finder.

26.2.2 Selecting an Operational Mode

After you start MySQL Administrator, it displays a connection dialog. At that point, you can connect to a server in normal mode or (on Windows) you can enter configure-service mode:

- To connect to a server, fill in the required connection parameters in the dialog or select from among any connection profiles that may already have been defined. MySQL Administrator will connect to the server, enter normal mode, and display its main window, which provides access to the various administrative capabilities that you can use.

- To enter configure-service mode, hold down the Control key to cause the Cancel button in the dialog to change to Skip, and then select this button. MySQL Administrator will display its main window, but only the Service Control, Startup Variables, and Server Logs sections are available. Configure-service mode is described in Section 26.4.1, "Service Control."

The main window has a sidebar along the left edge that displays the available sections from which you can select, and a work area to the right of the sidebar. (See Figure 26.1.) Selecting a section in the sidebar causes the work area to display an interface for that section. The work area for some sections has multiple tabs when there are several types of information available.

The main window also contains several menus from which you can access additional features. For example, to open additional server connections in normal mode, select New Instance Connection … from the File menu.

The rest of this chapter describes the capabilities provided by MySQL Administrator, with the exception of those that are shared with MySQL Query Browser. The following shared capabilities are described in the chapter devoted to MySQL Query Browser:

- The capability for creating tables and modifying their structure is discussed in Section 3.4, "The MySQL Table Editor."

- The Connection dialog is discussed in Section 3.5, "Connection Management."

- The Options dialog is discussed in Section 3.6, "The Options Dialog."

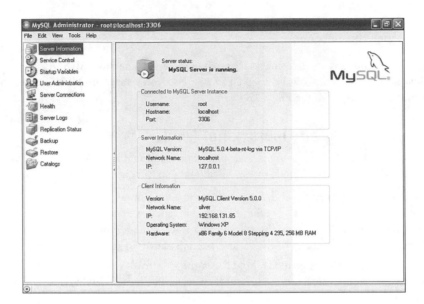

FIGURE 26.1   MySQL Administrator main window.

26.3 Server Monitoring Capabilities

Several sections of the MySQL Administrator main window are devoted exclusively or primarily to monitoring aspects of server operation:

- Server Information provides an overview of the characteristics of your connection to the server.

- Server Connections displays information about the clients connected to the server.

- Health displays performance, load, and memory use information in graphical form, and allows you to examine status variables and to examine and set system variables.

- Server Logs displays the contents of the error log, slow query log, and general query log.

- Replication Status helps you monitor a master server and the slaves that are connected to it.

- Catalogs displays information about databases, tables, columns, and indexes. It also provides access to the MySQL Table Editor and can perform table maintenance operations.

26.3.1 Server Information

The Server Information section provides an overview of server status. It displays information about your connection, the server host and the version of MySQL running on it, and the client host. Information shown by this section can be seen in Figure 26.1.

26.3.2 Server Connections

The Server Connections section displays information about the clients that currently are connected to the server. Connections also are known as "threads," which is the term used by MySQL Administrator. The Server Connections section displays thread information in two formats. One format lists threads by thread ID. The other format lists them grouped by user, which makes it easier to see what a given user is doing when that user has multiple connections open. In either display format, clicking a column heading re-sorts thread information rows by that column.

Clicking a thread line selects it and enables a Kill Thread button that you can use to terminate the connection. Terminating a connection can be useful if, for example, a runaway query has been issued. Clicking a user line selects all threads for that user and enables a Kill User button that you can use to terminate all connections for that user.

In the Server Connections section, the privileges that you have determine the scope of the information that you can see and the connections that you can terminate:

- If you have the PROCESS privilege, you can see all threads. Otherwise, you can see only your own threads.
- If you have the SUPER privilege, you can terminate all threads. Otherwise, you can terminate only your own threads.

26.3.3 Health

The Health section displays server performance and memory use information in graphical form. It displays a predefined set of graphs by default, but is configurable and allows you to define your own graphs for monitoring the server.

The following status-monitoring graphical displays are predefined:

- Connection Usage displays the percentage of the maximum allowed number of connections that are in use. You can use this to see whether the client connection load is approaching the limit imposed by the max_connections system variable. If usage is consistently near the limit, consider increasing the value of this variable.
- Traffic displays a graph showing the number of bytes sent to clients in each measurement interval.
- Number of SQL Queries displays a graph showing how many queries the server receives in each measurement interval.

- Query Cache Hitrate and Key Efficiency show the effectiveness of the query cache and the MyISAM key cache.

You can create your own graphs. Server monitoring graphs are based on formulas that can refer to status and system variables, so you can display whatever information you're interested in monitoring. Formulas can use the cumulative values of variables or the change in value relative to the previous measurement interval. For each graph, you can select characteristics such as the graph type (line or bar), captions, and the minimum and maximum of the graph range. Graphs can be organized into pages and groups.

The Health section also displays the server's status and system variables. These variables are displayed in hierarchical category/subcategory fashion to make it easy to examine related variables together. Categories can be expanded or collapsed to display more or less information.

System variables that are dynamic and can be set at runtime are so marked with a distinctive icon. Double-clicking a settable variable brings up a dialog for changing the value. This allows you to change server configuration easily, although changes made this way persist only until the server stops. Permanent changes can be made via the Server Variables section.

26.3.4 Server Logs

The Server Logs section displays the contents of the error log, slow query log, and general query log, if these logs are enabled. This capability is available for local servers only.

The section has a tab for each kind of log file that is monitored. Each tab contains controls that make it easy to move through the log. A page control selects "pages" of the log and two panels display summary and expanded views of the current page. To make it easier to see how the two views match up, clicking a summary line causes the corresponding expanded view lines to be highlighted.

There is a button to bring up a dialog for opening other log files. You can search for a given string within a log, which is useful when you're looking for a particular log entry. The current page of a log can be saved to a file (for example, to use it in other programs) .

26.3.5 Replication Status

The Replication Status section provides an overview of your replication setup, if the server to which you're connected is acting as a master server. You can see the master's current replication status, and information about each of the master's slaves.

26.3.6 Catalogs

The Catalogs section provides the following capabilities:

- You can browse databases (schemas), tables and indexes within databases, and columns within tables.

- You can access the MySQL Table Editor. The Table Editor allows you to create tables and edit table definitions.
- If you right-click in the database browser, you can create and drop databases.
- If you right-click a table name and select Edit Table Data, MySQL Administrator launches MySQL Query Browser so that you can edit the table's contents.
- You can perform optimization, checking, and repair table-maintenance operations.

26.4 Server Configuration

Several sections of the MySQL Administrator main window are devoted to server configuration:

- Service Control enables you to configure MySQL services on Windows.
- Startup Variables provides an interface to the settings contained in the server's option file. By changing these settings, you can change server configuration.
- User Administration displays MySQL account information and allows you to create, edit, and delete accounts.

There is also an Options ... item in the Tools menu that brings up the Options dialog. This dialog enables you to change general program settings, manage connection profiles, and set MySQL Table Editor preferences. This dialog is largely similar to the Options dialog provided by MySQL Query Browser and is described in Section 3.6, "The Options Dialog."

26.4.1 Service Control

When MySQL Administrator starts, it displays its Connection dialog. Normally, you use this dialog to connect to a server and MySQL Administrator presents its main window in normal mode. If instead you hold down the Control key and select the Skip button in the Connection dialog, MySQL Administrator displays the main window in configure-service mode. This mode is useful for starting a server when no server is running to which you can connect.

MySQL Administrator operation depends on whether you're running in configure-service mode or normal mode:

- In configure-service mode, the main window displays only the Service Control, Startup Variables, and Server Logs sections. In normal mode, those sections are displayed along with all the other sections.
- In configure-service mode, MySQL Administrator displays a panel in the main window that lists all available MySQL services. You can select any of them to indicate which service to configure. In normal mode, you can configure only the first MySQL service and the service-list panel is not displayed.

The capabilities provided by the Service Control section currently work only for local servers, and those provided by the Configure Service tab are designed to control MySQL servers that have been installed to run as Windows services.

The Service Control section has two tabs:

- The Start/Stop Service tab displays status information about the service, such as the service name and whether the server is running. A button enables you to start or stop the service and a display area shows status messages resulting from such actions.

- The Configure Service tab is displayed only on Windows. It allows you to change the configuration of a MySQL Windows service. Changes to most of these settings require a server restart to take effect.

26.4.2 Startup Variables

The Startup Variables section presents an interface to the settings present in the server's option file. This capability is available only for local servers.

If the file is writable, you can change the settings and write the changes back to the file to affect future server operation. For example, you can enable or disable log files, set the default storage engine, and change the size of memory caches. The server must be restarted before changes take effect.

There are many server configuration options, so this section has several tabs that organize the available settings into groups of related options. See Figure 26.2.

26.4.3 User Administration

The User Administration section enables you to manage MySQL user accounts. You can create new accounts, edit accounts, or delete accounts.

An account browser displays a list of existing accounts. Selecting an account allows you to examine and modify its characteristics, such as the username, the password, the privileges held by the account, and its resource limits. Privileges can be granted at the global, database, table, and column levels.

MySQL accounts are defined by a combination of username and hostname, which means that you can have different accounts that have the same username. The account browser in MySQL Administrator provides a hierarchical view that groups accounts by username.

A Clone User feature enables you to create one user from another, which is an easy way to set up new users that differ only slightly from existing users.

The User Administration section has a User Information tab that enables you to associate descriptive information with each user, such as real name, telephone number, email address, and an icon. MySQL Administrator creates a user_info table in the mysql database to store this information. However, the user_info table is not a grant table and does not have anything to do with the privileges held by users.

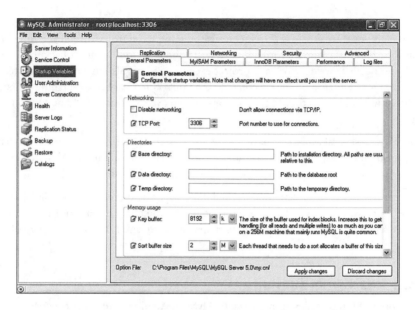

FIGURE 26.2   MySQL Administrator Startup Variables section.

26.5 Backup and Restore Capabilities

The Backup and Restore sections of the MySQL Administrator main window enable you to generate database backups as text files and to perform data recovery operations using those backup files.

26.5.1 Making Backups

The Backup section provides an interface to MySQL Administrator's backup-generation capabilities. MySQL Administrator creates backup files that contain SQL statements such as CREATE TABLE and INSERT that can be reloaded into your MySQL server to re-create databases and tables. These files are similar to the SQL-format backup files generated by mysqldump.

Backups are based on projects. A project is a named set of specifications that you can execute to perform a backup based on those specifications. Projects can be browsed and selecting a project allows you to examine and modify its specifications. The project approach enables you to easily select from among multiple types of backups.

A database browser allows you to specify which databases to use for a project. By default, all tables in a selected database are selected for backup, but you can include or exclude individual tables.

Backup projects include a name to use for the output file. By default, the same name is used every time you execute the project, which causes the file to be overwritten each time. To prevent this, there is an option for adding the date and time to the end of backup files so that a different file is written for each project execution. (This also makes it easy to tell at a glance when a given backup file was created.) The option to enable date-tagging is accessed from the Administrator section of the Options dialog. (See Section 3.6, "The Options Dialog.")

You can control several aspects of backup operation, such as whether to use locking that is more appropriate for MyISAM or InnoDB tables, and the style to use for INSERT statements (single-row versus multiple-row, ANSI-style identifier quoting, and so forth).

Projects can be executed on demand or scheduled for periodic execution at daily, weekly, or monthly intervals. For weekly backups, you can select which day or days of the week on which to execute the project. A monthly backup can be executed on any single day of the month.

26.5.2 Restoring Backups

The Restore section provides an interface to MySQL Administrator's data-recovery capabilities. MySQL Administrator can reload SQL-format dump files containing statements such as CREATE TABLE and INSERT that recreate the dumped tables. The destination where tables are created can be chosen as each table's original database, or you can restore all tables to an existing database or to a new database.

To enable you to restore only part of a dump file, MySQL Administrator provides a dump file analysis feature: Select a dump file, and MySQL Administrator reads it to determine what tables it will restore and presents a dialog showing you what the tables are. You can selectively include or exclude each table to control which ones to reload when MySQL Administrator processes the dump file. This is useful when you want to restore only certain tables from a full-database dump.

26.6 MySQL Administrator System Tray Monitor

On Windows, MySQL Administrator distributions include a Windows System Tray monitor. This monitor is designed to provide quick access to server status information and program-launching capabilities.

When the Tray Monitor is running, its icon in the tray indicates whether the MySQL server is running or stopped. Right-clicking the icon displays a pop-up menu with items that list the status of all installed MySQL Windows services. You can start or stop each service. The menu also provides items that launch MySQL Administrator in configure-service or normal mode or launch MySQL Query Browser.

Character Set Support

This chapter discusses administrative factors in the use of the character sets supported by the MySQL server. It covers the following exam topics:

- Configuring the server to use only character set resources needed for your installation
- Choosing data types for character columns with storage requirements and performance in mind

27.1 Performance Issues

To reduce the amount of disk space required by character sets for your MySQL installation and the amount of memory used by the server as it runs, don't select unneeded character sets when you configure MySQL. This requires that you compile MySQL from source rather than using a precompiled binary distribution.

To see which character sets are available, invoke the `configure` script with the `--help` option and examine the description for the `--with-charset` option.

```
shell> ./configure --help
...
--with-charset=CHARSET
                    Default character set, use one of:
                    binary
                    armscii8 ascii big5 cp1250 cp1251 cp1256 cp1257
                    cp850 cp852 cp866 cp932 dec8 eucjpms euckr gb2312
                    gbk geostd8 greek hebrew hp8 keybcs2 koi8r koi8u
                    latin1 latin2 latin5 latin7 macce macroman
                    sjis swe7 tis620 ucs2 ujis utf8
...
```

To configure MySQL with support for a given set of character sets, invoke `configure` with a `--with-charset` option that specifies the default character set, and a `--with-extra-charsets` option that names any other character sets to include. The value of the latter option should be a comma-separated list of character set names. For example, to make latin1 the default, but include support for the utf8 and ucs2 Unicode character sets, run configure like this:

```
shell> ./configure --with-charset=latin1 \
          --with-extra-charsets=utf8,ucs2
```

To see which character sets your server supports as it's currently configured, use the SHOW CHARACTER SET statement:

```
mysql> SHOW CHARACTER SET;
+----------+----------------------------+---------------------+--------+
| Charset  | Description                | Default collation   | Maxlen |
+----------+----------------------------+---------------------+--------+
| big5     | Big5 Traditional Chinese   | big5_chinese_ci     |      2 |
| dec8     | DEC West European          | dec8_swedish_ci     |      1 |
| cp850    | DOS West European          | cp850_general_ci    |      1 |
| hp8      | HP West European           | hp8_english_ci      |      1 |
| koi8r    | KOI8-R Relcom Russian      | koi8r_general_ci    |      1 |
| latin1   | ISO 8859-1 West European   | latin1_swedish_ci   |      1 |
| latin2   | ISO 8859-2 Central European| latin2_general_ci   |      1 |
...
```

27.2 Choosing Data Types for Character Columns

When you create tables that have string columns for storing character data, consider which data types and character sets will minimize storage, and thus disk I/O.

If stored string values all have the same length, use a fixed-length type rather than a variable-length type. To store values that are always 32 characters long, CHAR(32) requires 32 characters each, whereas VARCHAR(32) requires 32 characters each, plus an extra byte to store the length. In this case, VARCHAR requires one byte more per value than CHAR.

On the other hand, if stored string values vary in length, a variable-length data type takes less space. If values range from 0 to 32 characters with an average of about 16 characters, CHAR(32) values require 32 characters, whereas VARCHAR(32) requires 16 characters plus one byte on average. Here, VARCHAR requires only about half as much storage as CHAR.

For multi-byte character sets that have variable-length encoding, a variable-length data type may be appropriate even if stored values always have the same number of characters. The utf8 character set uses one to three bytes per characters. For fixed-length data types, three bytes per character must always be allocated to allow for the possibility that every character will require the "widest" encoding. Thus, CHAR(32) requires 96 bytes, even if most stored values contain 32 single-byte characters. For variable-length data types, only as much storage is allocated as required. In a VARCHAR(32) column, a 32-character string that consists entirely of three-byte characters requires 96 bytes plus a length byte, whereas it requires only 32 bytes plus a length byte if the string consists entirely of single-byte characters.

If you have a choice between multi-byte character sets, choose the one for which the most commonly used characters take less space. For example, the utf8 and utc2 character sets both can be used for storing Unicode data. In utf8, characters take from one to three bytes, but most non-accented Latin characters take one byte. In ucs2, every character takes two bytes. Therefore, if the majority of your characters are non-accented characters, you'll likely achieve a space savings by using utf8 rather than ucs2. This assumes the use of a variable-length data type such as VARCHAR(n). If you use a fixed-length type such as CHAR(n), stored values require $n \times 3$ bytes for utf8 and only $n \times 2$ bytes for ucs2, regardless of the particular characters in stored values.

28

Locking

This chapter discusses how MySQL uses locking to handle concurrent data access by multiple clients. It covers the following exam topics:

- Locking concepts
- Using explicit table locks
- Using advisory locks

Further discussion of locking issues is presented in Chapter 29, "Storage Engines."

28.1 Locking Concepts

The MySQL server uses a multi-threaded architecture that enables it to service many clients concurrently (simultaneously). For each client that connects, the server allocates a thread as a connection handler. If each client accesses different tables than the others, they do not interfere with each other. However, when multiple clients attempt to access a table at the same time, this creates contention and it's necessary to coordinate the clients. Otherwise, problems could occur, such as one client changing rows while another client is reading them or two clients making changes to the same row concurrently. To avoid these problems and prevent data corruption, MySQL uses locking.

Locking is a mechanism that prevents problems from occurring with simultaneous data access by multiple clients. Locks are managed by the server: It places a lock on data on behalf of one client to restrict access by other clients to the data until the lock has been released. The lock allows access to data by the client that holds the lock, but places limitations on what operations can be done by other clients that are contending for access. The effect of the locking mechanism is to serialize access to data so that when multiple clients want to perform conflicting operations, each must wait its turn.

Not all types of concurrent access produce conflicts, so the type of locking that is necessary to allow a client access to data depends on whether the client wants to read or write:

- If a client wants to read data, other clients that want to read the same data do not produce a conflict, and they all can read at the same time. However, another client that wants to write (modify) data must wait until the read has finished.

- If a client wants to write data, all other clients must wait until the write has finished, regardless of whether those clients want to read or write.

In other words, a reader must block writers, but not other readers. A writer must block both readers and writers. Read locks and write locks allow these restrictions to be enforced. Locking makes clients wait for access until it is safe for them to proceed. In this way, locks prevent data corruption by disallowing concurrent conflicting changes and reading of data that is in the process of being changed.

A lock on data can be acquired implicitly or explicitly:

- For a client that does nothing special to acquire locks, the MySQL server implicitly acquires locks as necessary to process the client's statements safely. For example, the server acquires a read lock when the client issues a SELECT statement and a write lock when the client issues an INSERT statement. Implicit locks are acquired only for the duration of a single statement.

- If implicit locking is insufficient for a client's purposes, it can manage locks explicitly byacquiring them with LOCK TABLES and releasing them with UNLOCK TABLES. Explicit locking may be necessary when a client needs to perform an operation that spans multiple statements and that must not be interrupted by other clients. For example, an application might select a value from one table and then use it to determine which records to update in a set of other tables. With implicit locking, it's possible for another client to perform other, possibly conflicting changes between statements of the first client's operation. To prevent this, the first client can place an explicit lock on the tables that it uses.

Another type of lock is the advisory, or cooperative, lock. Advisory locks do not lock data and they do not prevent access to data by clients except to the extent that they cooperate with each other. Unlike implicit and explicit data locks, advisory locks are not managed by the server. Clients manage advisory locks using a set of function calls to cooperate among themselves.

Data locking in MySQL occurs at different levels. Explicit locks acquired with LOCK TABLES are table locks. For implicit locks, the lock level that MySQL uses depends on the storage engine:

- MyISAM, MEMORY, and MERGE tables are locked at the table level.
- BDB tables are locked at the page level.
- InnoDB tables are locked at the row level.

The different levels of locking "granularity" have different concurrency characteristics:

- Table locking is not as desirable as page or row locking for concurrency in a mixed read/write environment. A table lock prevents other clients from making any changes to the table, even if the client that holds the lock is not accessing the parts of the table that other clients want to modify. With page and row locks, a client that locks a page or row does not prevent changes by other clients to other pages or rows.

- Deadlock cannot occur with table locking as it can with page or row locking. For example, with row-level locking, two clients might each acquire a lock on different rows. If each then tries to modify the row that the other has locked, neither client can proceed. This is called "deadlock." With table locking, the server can determine what locks are needed and acquire them before executing a statement, so deadlock never occurs. (An exception is possible when applications use cursors, because then the server must hold open a lock for a client across multiple statements. Suppose that client 1 opens a cursor for reading table t1 and client 2 opens a cursor for reading table t2. While the cursors are open, if each client tries to update the table being read by the other, deadlock can occur.)

28.2 Explicit Table Locking

Clients manage explicit table locks with two statements. LOCK TABLES acquires table locks and UNLOCK TABLES releases them. Acquisition of explicit locks can be advantageous in certain situations:

- An implicit lock lasts for the duration of a single query only, which is unsuitable should you want to perform a multiple-statement update that requires no interference by other clients. To handle this, you can acquire an explicit lock, which remains in effect until you release it. Other clients cannot modify tables that you have locked.

- Explicit locking can improve performance for multiple statements executed as a group while the lock is in effect. First, less work is required by the server to acquire and release locks because it need not do so for each statement. It simply acquires all needed locks at the beginning of the operation, and releases them at the end. Second, for statements that modify data, index flushing is reduced. For example, if you execute multiple INSERT statements using implicit locking, index flushing occurs following each statement. If you lock the table explicitly and then perform all the inserts, index flushing occurs only once when you release the lock. This results in less disk activity.

The LOCK TABLES statement names each table to be locked and the type of lock to be acquired. The following statement acquires a read lock on the Country table and a write lock on the City table:

```
LOCK TABLES Country READ, City WRITE;
```

To use LOCK TABLES, you must have the LOCK TABLES privilege, and the SELECT privilege for each table to be locked.

If any of the tables to be locked already are in use, LOCK TABLES blocks. It does not return until it has acquired all of the requested locks.

If you need to use multiple tables while holding an explicit lock, you must lock all of them at the same time because you cannot use any unlocked tables while you hold explicit locks. Also, you must lock all the tables with a single LOCK TABLES statement. LOCK TABLES releases any locks that you already hold, so you cannot issue it multiple times to acquire multiple locks.

The following list describes the available lock types and their effects:

- READ

  Locks a table for reading. A READ lock locks a table for read queries such as SELECT that retrieve data from the table. It does not allow write operations such as INSERT, DELETE, or UPDATE that modify the table, even by the client that holds the lock. When a table is locked for reading, other clients can read from the table at the same time, but no client can write to it. A client that wants to write to a table that is read-locked must wait until all clients currently reading from it have finished and released their locks.

- WRITE

  Locks a table for writing. A WRITE lock is an exclusive lock. It can be acquired only when a table is not being used. Once acquired, only the client holding the write lock can read from or write to the table. Other clients can neither read from nor write to it. No other client can lock the table for either reading or writing.

- READ LOCAL

  Locks a table for reading, but allows concurrent inserts. A concurrent insert is an exception to the "readers block writers" principle. It applies only to MyISAM tables. If a MyISAM table has no holes in the middle resulting from deleted or updated records, inserts always take place at the end of the table. In that case, a client that is reading from a table can lock it with a READ LOCAL lock to allow other clients to insert into the table while the client holding the read lock reads from it. If a MyISAM table does have holes, you can remove them by using OPTIMIZE TABLE to defragment the table.

  You can acquire a READ LOCAL lock for a fragmented MyISAM table, or for a non-MyISAM table, but in such cases, concurrent inserts are not allowed. The lock acts like a regular READ lock.

- LOW_PRIORITY WRITE

  Locks a table for writing, but acquires the lock with a lower priority. That is, if the client must wait for the lock, other clients that request read locks during the wait are allowed to get their locks first. A normal write lock request is satisfied when no other clients are using the table. If other clients are using the table when the request is made, it waits until those clients have finished. A LOW_PRIORITY WRITE lock request also waits for any new read requests that arrive while the lock request is pending.

To release explicit locks, issue an UNLOCK TABLES statement. This statement names no tables, because it releases all explicit locks held by the issuing client.

Explicit locks held by a client also are released if the client issues another LOCK TABLES statement. Locks cannot be maintained across connections; if a client has any unreleased locks when its connection to the server terminates, the server implicitly releases its locks. An administrator with the SUPER privilege can terminate a client connection with the KILL statement, which causes release of locks held by the client.

Only the client that holds a lock acquired with LOCK TABLES can release the lock. Another client cannot release it. In other words, if you acquire a lock, it's yours until you give it up. Another client cannot force you to release it.

Table locks may be affected by transactions and vice versa. Beginning a transaction with START TRANSACTION causes an implicit UNLOCK TABLES. Issuing a LOCK TABLES statement will implicitly commit any pending transaction. If you have locked any tables, issuing an UNLOCK TABLES statement will implicitly commit any pending transaction.

28.3 Advisory Locking

An advisory lock is a cooperative lock. That is, an advisory lock has no power to prevent data access by other clients, but instead is based on the concept that all clients will use an agreed-upon convention to cooperate for use of a resource. The convention is the lock name, which is simply a string. While the name is locked, the advisory lock is considered to be in place and every other cooperating client refrains from whatever action it would perform if it held the lock itself.

Advisory locks are implemented using a set of function calls. To acquire a lock, use the GET_LOCK() function:

```
mysql> SELECT GET_LOCK('my lock', 5);
+-----------------------+
| GET_LOCK('my lock', 5) |
+-----------------------+
|                     1 |
+-----------------------+
```

The first argument is a string that specifies the name to be locked, and the second argument is a timeout value in seconds that indicates how long to wait for the lock if it cannot be acquired immediately. GET_LOCK() returns 1 for success, 0 if a timeout occurs and the lock cannot be acquired, or NULL if an error occurs.

A client that has acquired an advisory lock can release it by calling RELEASE_LOCK():

```
mysql> SELECT RELEASE_LOCK('my lock');
+-----------------------+
| RELEASE_LOCK('my lock') |
+-----------------------+
|                     1 |
+-----------------------+
```

RELEASE_LOCK() returns 1 if the lock was released successfully, 0 if the name was locked but not by the client requesting the release, and NULL if the name was not locked.

An advisory lock also is released if the client makes another call to GET_LOCK() or closes its connection to the server.

Two other functions are available for checking the status of advisory locks:

- IS_FREE_LOCK(*lock_name*) returns 1 if the name is not locked, 0 if it is locked, and NULL if an error occurs.
- IS_USED_LOCK(*lock_name*) returns the connection ID of the client that holds the lock on the name, or NULL if the name is not locked.

Storage Engines

MySQL allows you to choose from any of several storage engines when creating a table. Different table types are managed by different storage engines, each of which has specific characteristics. This chapter discusses the features of several storage engines in detail and summarizes others. It covers the following exam topics:

- An overview of the storage engine concept in MySQL
- The MyISAM storage engine
- The MERGE storage engine
- The InnoDB storage engine
- The MEMORY storage engine
- The FEDERATED storage engine
- The Cluster storage engine
- A summary of other storage engines

29.1 MySQL Storage Engines

All tables managed by MySQL Server have certain similarities. For example, every table in a database has a format (.frm) file in the database directory. This file, which stores the definition of the table's structure, is created by the server. Tables have differences as well, which are tied to the storage engines that the server uses to manage table contents. Each storage engine has a particular set of operational characteristics. For example, engines may create additional disk files to accompany the .frm files, but the types of files that they create to manage data and index storage vary per engine. Storage engines differ in other ways as well, such as in the way that they use locking to manage query contention, or in whether the tables that they provide are transactional or non-transactional. These engine properties have implications for query processing performance, concurrency, and deadlock prevention. (Deadlock occurs when multiple queries are blocked and cannot proceed because they are waiting for each other to finish.)

When you create a table, you can choose what storage engine to use. Typically, this choice is made according to which storage engine offers features that best fit the needs of your application. For example, ask yourself what types of queries you'll use the table for. Then choose a storage engine that uses a locking level appropriate for the anticipated query mix. MyISAM table-level locking works best for a query mix that is heavily skewed toward retrievals and includes few updates. Use InnoDB if you must process a query mix containing many updates. InnoDB's use of row-level locking and multi-versioning provides good concurrency for a mix of retrievals and updates. One query can update rows while other queries read or update different rows of the table.

To specify a storage engine explicitly in a CREATE TABLE statement, use an ENGINE option. The following statement creates t as an InnoDB table:

```
CREATE TABLE t (i INT) ENGINE = InnoDB;
```

If you create a table without using an ENGINE option to specify a storage engine explicitly, the MySQL server creates the table using the default engine, which is given by the value of the storage_engine system variable. Section 8.2.2, "Specifying the Storage Engine for a Table," further discusses how to specify storage engines when creating tables and how to change the default storage engine.

To determine which storage engine is used for a given table, you can use the SHOW CREATE TABLE or the SHOW TABLE STATUS statement:

```
mysql> SHOW CREATE TABLE City\G
*************************** 1. row ***************************
       Table: City
Create Table: CREATE TABLE `City` (
  `ID` int(11) NOT NULL auto_increment,
  `Name` char(35) NOT NULL default '',
  `CountryCode` char(3) NOT NULL default '',
  `District` char(20) NOT NULL default '',
  `Population` int(11) NOT NULL default '0',
  PRIMARY KEY  (`ID`)
) ENGINE=MyISAM DEFAULT CHARSET=latin1
1 row in set (0.00 sec)

mysql> SHOW TABLE STATUS LIKE 'CountryLanguage'\G
*************************** 1. row ***************************
          Name: CountryLanguage
        Engine: MyISAM
       Version: 10
    Row_format: Fixed
          Rows: 984
Avg_row_length: 39
   Data_length: 38376
Max_data_length: 167503724543
```

```
    Index_length: 22528
       Data_free: 0
   Auto_increment: NULL
     Create_time: 2005-04-26 22:15:35
     Update_time: 2005-04-26 22:15:43
      Check_time: NULL
        Collation: latin1_swedish_ci
        Checksum: NULL
   Create_options:
         Comment:
1 row in set (0.00 sec)
```

The INFORMATION_SCHEMA TABLES table contains storage engine information as well:

```
mysql> SELECT TABLE_NAME, ENGINE FROM INFORMATION_SCHEMA.TABLES
    -> WHERE TABLE_SCHEMA = 'world';
+-----------------+--------+
| TABLE_NAME      | ENGINE |
+-----------------+--------+
| City            | MyISAM |
| Country         | MyISAM |
| CountryLanguage | MyISAM |
+-----------------+--------+
```

Although you can choose which storage engine to use for a table, in most respects the way that you use the table after creating it is engine independent. Operations on tables of all types are performed using the SQL interface and MySQL manages engine-dependent details for you at a lower level in its architecture. That is, your interface to tables is at the higher SQL tier, and table-management details are at the lower storage-engine tier. There are, nonetheless, times when knowing which storage engine manages a table can enable you to use the table more efficiently. Engine-specific optimizations that you can take advantage of are covered in Chapter 38, "Optimizing Databases."

Before you can use a given storage engine, it must be compiled into the server and enabled. MySQL Server uses a modular architecture: Each storage engine is a software module that is compiled into the server. The use of this modular approach allows storage engines to be easily selected for inclusion in the server at configuration time.

Some storage engines are always available, such as MyISAM, MERGE, and MEMORY. Other engines are optional. Support for optional engines typically can be selected when MySQL is configured and built. Compiled-in optional engines also typically can be enabled or disabled with a server startup option. For example, the InnoDB storage engine is included in all binary distributions. If you build MySQL from source, InnoDB is included by default unless you specify the --without-innodb configuration option. For a server that has the InnoDB storage engine included, support may be disabled at startup with the --skip-innodb option.

To reduce memory use, don't configure unneeded storage engines into the server. This requires that you compile MySQL from source rather than using a precompiled binary distribution. If you are using a binary distribution that includes compiled-in optional engines that you don't need, disable them at runtime.

To see what storage engines are compiled into your server and whether they are available at runtime, use the SHOW ENGINES statement

```
mysql> SHOW ENGINES\G
*************************** 1. row ***************************
 Engine: MyISAM
Support: DEFAULT
Comment: Default engine as of MySQL 3.23 with great performance
*************************** 2. row ***************************
 Engine: MEMORY
Support: YES
Comment: Hash based, stored in memory, useful for temporary tables
*************************** 3. row ***************************
 Engine: HEAP
Support: YES
Comment: Alias for MEMORY
...
```

The following sections examine several of MySQL's storage engines in more detail. Much of the discussion involves locking concepts, so you should be familiar with the material covered in Chapter 28, "Locking." **Note:** When this chapter says that deadlock cannot occur with table locking, that is subject to the exception described in section 28.1 "Locking Concepts."

29.2 The MyISAM Engine

The MyISAM storage engine manages tables that have the following characteristics:

- On disk, MySQL represents each MyISAM table using three files: a format file that stores the definition of the table structure, a data file that stores the contents of table rows, and an index file that stores any indexes on the table. These files are distinguished from one another by their suffixes. For example, the format, data, and index files for a table named mytable are called mytable.frm, mytable.MYD, and mytable.MYI. MySQL normally stores all three files in the database directory for the database that contains the table. On systems that support appropriate symlinking capabilities, MyISAM table data and index files can be placed in a different location than the database directory.

- MyISAM has the most flexible AUTO_INCREMENT column handling of all the storage engines.

- MyISAM tables can be used to set up MERGE tables.

- MyISAM tables can be converted into fast, compressed, read-only tables to save space.

- MyISAM supports FULLTEXT searching and spatial data types.

- MySQL manages contention between queries for MyISAM table access using table-level locking. Query performance is very fast for retrievals. Multiple queries can read the same table simultaneously. For a write query, an exclusive table-level lock is used to prevent use of the table by other read or write queries, leading to reduced performance in environments with a mix of read and write queries. Deadlock cannot occur with table-level locking. (Deadlock occurs when two or more queries are blocked, or stopped from completing, because each is waiting for one of the others to finish.)

- You can influence the scheduling mechanism for queries that use MyISAM tables by using a query modifier such as LOW_PRIORITY or HIGH_PRIORITY. Inserts into a table can be buffered on the server side until the table isn't busy by using INSERT DELAYED; this allows the client to proceed immediately instead of blocking until the insert operation completes.

- The table storage format is portable, so table files can be copied directly to another host and used by a server there. (The conditions for MyISAM portability are given at Section 32.3.4, "Conditions for Binary Portability.")

- You can specify that a MyISAM table must be able to hold at least a certain number of rows, which allows MyISAM to adjust the table's internal row pointer size accordingly. It's also possible to configure the default pointer size that the server uses.

- When loading data into an empty MyISAM table, you can disable updating of non-unique indexes and enable the indexes after loading. This is faster than updating the indexes for each row inserted. In fact, when LOAD DATA INFILE is used for loading an empty MyISAM table, it automatically disables and enables index updating. LOAD DATA INFILE is faster than INSERT anyway, and this optimization speeds it up even more.

- If you run out of disk space while adding rows to a MyISAM table, no error occurs. The server suspends the operation until space becomes available, and then completes the operation.

MyISAM tables use the indexed sequential access method for indexing, as did the older ISAM table format. MyISAM offers better performance and more features than ISAM, so MyISAM is preferred over ISAM, and ISAM is unavailable as of MySQL 5.

MyISAM was introduced in MySQL 3.23.0 and has been the built-in default storage engine since (although you can change the default engine at server startup or while the server runs). Because MyISAM is the built-in default engine, it is always available and cannot be disabled.

29.2.1 MyISAM Locking Characteristics

MyISAM locking occurs at the table level. This is not as desirable as page or row locking for concurrency in a mixed read/write environment. However, deadlock cannot occur with table locking as it can with page or row locking.

When processing queries on MyISAM tables, the server manages contention for the tables by simultaneous clients by implicitly acquiring any locks it needs. You can also lock tables explicitly with the LOCK TABLES and UNLOCK TABLES statements. Explicit table locking has concurrency and performance advantages over implicit locking in certain situations, as discussed in Chapter 28, "Locking."

MyISAM tables support concurrent inserts. If a MyISAM table has no holes in the middle resulting from deleted or updated records, inserts always take place at the end of the table and can be performed while other clients are reading the table. Concurrent inserts can take place even for a table that has been read-locked explicitly if the locking client acquired a READ LOCAL lock rather than a regular READ lock.

If a table does have holes, concurrent inserts cannot be performed. However, you can remove the holes by using OPTIMIZE TABLE to defragment the table. (Note that a record deleted from the end of the table does not create a hole and does not prevent concurrent inserts.)

For applications that use MyISAM tables, you can change the priority of statements that retrieve or modify data. This can be useful in situations where the normal scheduling priorities do not reflect the application's requirements.

By default, the server schedules queries for execution as follows:

- Write requests (such as UPDATE and DELETE statements) take priority over read requests (such as SELECT statements).

- The server tries to perform write requests in the order that it receives them.

However, if a table is being read from when a write request arrives, the write request cannot be processed until all current readers have finished. Any read requests that arrive after the write request must wait until the write request finishes, even if they arrive before the current readers finish. That is, a new read request by default does not jump ahead of a pending write request.

When working with MyISAM tables, certain scheduling modifiers are available to change the priority of requests:

- The LOW_PRIORITY modifier may be applied to statements that update tables (INSERT, DELETE, REPLACE, or UPDATE). A low-priority write request waits not only until all current readers have finished, but for any pending read requests that arrive while the write request itself is waiting. That is, it waits until there are no pending read requests at all. It is therefore possible for a low-priority write request never to be performed, if read requests keep arriving while the write request is waiting.

- HIGH_PRIORITY may be used with a SELECT statement to move it ahead of updates and ahead of other SELECT statements that do not use the HIGH_PRIORITY modifier.

- DELAYED may be used with INSERT (and REPLACE). The server buffers the rows in memory and inserts them when the table is not being used. Delayed inserts increase efficiency because they're done in batches rather than individually. While inserting the rows, the server checks periodically to see whether other requests to use the table have arrived. If so, the server suspends insertion of delayed rows until the table becomes free again. Using DELAYED allows the client to proceed immediately after issuing the INSERT statement rather than waiting until it completes.

Consider an application consisting of a logging process that uses INSERT statements to record information in a log table, and a summary process that periodically issues SELECT queries to generate reports from the log table. Normally, the server will give table updates priority over retrievals, so at times of heavy logging activity, report generation might be delayed. If the application places high importance on having the summary process execute as quickly as possible, it can use scheduling modifiers to alter the usual query priorities. Two approaches are possible:

- To elevate the priority of the summary queries, use SELECT HIGH_PRIORITY rather than SELECT with no modifier. This will move the SELECT ahead of pending INSERT statements that have not yet begin to execute.

- To reduce the priority of record logging statements, use INSERT with either the LOW_PRIORITY or DELAYED modifier.

If you use DELAYED, keep the following points in mind:

- Delayed rows tend to be held for a longer time on a very busy server than on a lightly loaded one.

- If a crash occurs while the server is buffering delayed rows in memory, those rows are lost.

The implication is that DELAYED is more suitable for applications where loss of a few rows is not a problem, rather than applications for which each row is critical. For example, DELAYED can be appropriate for an application that logs activity for informational purposes only and for which it is not important if a small number of rows is lost.

29.2.2 MyISAM Row-Storage Formats

The MyISAM storage engine has the capability of storing rows in three formats: fixed-row, dynamic-row, and compressed. These formats have differing characteristics:

Fixed-row format:

- All rows have the same size.

- Rows are stored within the table at positions that are multiples of the row size, making them easy to look up.

- Fixed-size rows take more space.

Dynamic-row format:

- Rows take varying amounts of space.

- Rows cannot be looked up as efficiently.

- Dynamic-rows tables usually take less space because rows are not padded to a fixed size.
- Fragmentation can occur more easily than for fixed-row tables.

Compressed format:

- Tables are packed to save space.
- Storage is optimized for quick retrieval.
- Tables are read-only.

For more information, see Section 38.3.1, "MyISAM Row-Storage Formats," which also describes how to use the myisampack utility to create compressed MyISAM tables.

29.3 The MERGE Engine

The MERGE storage engine manages tables that have the following characteristics:

- A MERGE table is a collection of identically structured MyISAM tables. Each MERGE table is represented on disk by an .frm format file and an .MRG file that lists the names of the constituent MyISAM files. Both files are located in the database directory.
- Logically, a query on a MERGE table acts as a query on all the MyISAM tables of which it consists.
- A MERGE table creates a logical entity that can exceed the maximum MyISAM table size.
- MySQL manages contention between queries for MERGE table access using table-level locking (including locking of the underlying MyISAM tables). Deadlock cannot occur.
- A MERGE table is portable because the .MRG file is a text file and the MyISAM tables that it names are portable.
- The MERGE engine supports SELECT, DELETE, UPDATE, and INSERT statements. For INSERT, the CREATE TABLE statement can specify whether records should be inserted into the first or last table, or disallowed.

MERGE tables do have some disadvantages:

- They increase the number of file descriptors required because each of the underlying tables must be opened along with the MERGE table.
- It's slower to read indexes because MySQL has to search the indexes of multiple tables.

The following example demonstrates how to create a MERGE table. It creates MyISAM tables that have the same structure, and populates them with information about countries in North America and South America, respectively. From these tables, a MERGE table is created that can be used to access the combined information:

```
mysql> CREATE TABLE NACountry SELECT Code, Name
    -> FROM Country WHERE Continent = 'North America';
```

```
Query OK, 37 rows affected (0.01 sec)
Records: 37  Duplicates: 0  Warnings: 0

mysql> CREATE TABLE SACountry SELECT Code, Name
    -> FROM Country WHERE Continent = 'South America';
Query OK, 14 rows affected (0.01 sec)
Records: 14  Duplicates: 0  Warnings: 0

mysql> DESCRIBE NACountry;
+-------+----------+------+-----+---------+-------+
| Field | Type     | Null | Key | Default | Extra |
+-------+----------+------+-----+---------+-------+
| Code  | char(3)  | NO   |     |         |       |
| Name  | char(52) | NO   |     |         |       |
+-------+----------+------+-----+---------+-------+
2 rows in set (0.00 sec)

mysql> CREATE TABLE NorthAndSouth
    -> (Code CHAR(3) NOT NULL, Name CHAR(52) NOT NULL)
    -> ENGINE = MERGE UNION = (NACountry, SACountry);
Query OK, 0 rows affected (0.01 sec)

mysql> SELECT COUNT(*) FROM NACountry;
+----------+
| COUNT(*) |
+----------+
|       37 |
+----------+
1 row in set (0.00 sec)

mysql> SELECT COUNT(*) FROM SACountry;
+----------+
| COUNT(*) |
+----------+
|       14 |
+----------+
1 row in set (0.00 sec)

mysql> SELECT COUNT(*) FROM NorthAndSouth;
+----------+
| COUNT(*) |
+----------+
|       51 |
+----------+
1 row in set (0.00 sec)
```

29.3.1 MERGE **Locking Characteristics**

The MERGE storage engine uses table-level locking. However, because a MERGE table is defined in terms of other tables, MERGE locking involves locks on those tables as well:

- When the MERGE engine acquires a lock for a MERGE table, it acquires a lock for all the underlying MyISAM tables. Thus, all the tables are locked together.

- The underlying MyISAM tables are read-locked when you issue a SELECT statement for a MERGE table.

- The underlying MyISAM tables are write-locked when you issue a statement that modifies a MERGE table, such as INSERT or DELETE.

- To explicitly lock a MERGE table with LOCK TABLES, it is sufficient to lock just that table. You need not lock the underlying MyISAM tables as well.

29.4 The InnoDB **Engine**

The InnoDB storage engine manages tables that have the following characteristics:

- Each InnoDB table is represented on disk by an .frm format file in the database directory, as well as data and index storage in the InnoDB tablespace. The InnoDB table-space is a logical single storage area that is made up of one or more files or partitions on disk. By default, InnoDB uses a single tablespace that is shared by all InnoDB tables. The tablespace is stored in machine-independent format. It is implemented such that table sizes can exceed the maximum file size allowed by the filesystem. It is also possible to configure InnoDB to create each table with its own tablespace.

- InnoDB supports transactions, with commit and rollback. It provides full ACID (atomicity, consistency, isolation, durability) compliance. Multi-versioning is used to isolate transactions from one another.

- InnoDB provides auto-recovery after a crash of the MySQL server or the host on which the server runs.

- MySQL manages query contention for InnoDB tables using multi-versioning and row-level locking. Multi-versioning gives each transaction its own view of the database. This, combined with row-level locking, keeps contention to a minimum. The result is good query concurrency even if clients are performing a mix of reads and writes. However, it's possible for deadlock to occur.

- InnoDB supports foreign keys and referential integrity, including cascaded deletes and updates.

- The tablespace storage format is portable, so InnoDB files can be copied directly to another host and used by a server there. (The conditions for InnoDB portability are given at Section 32.3.4, "Conditions for Binary Portability.")

Support for the InnoDB storage engine is a standard feature in binary distributions. If you build MySQL from source, InnoDB is included unless you explicitly use the --without-innodb configuration option.

If a given MySQL server has the InnoDB storage engine compiled in, but you're sure that you won't need InnoDB tables, you can disable InnoDB support at runtime by starting the server with the --skip-innodb option. Disabling InnoDB reduces the server's memory requirements because it need not allocate any InnoDB-related data structures. Disabling InnoDB also reduces disk requirements because no InnoDB tablespace or log files need be allocated.

29.4.1 The InnoDB Tablespace and Logs

InnoDB operates using two primary disk-based resources: a tablespace for storing table contents, and a set of log files for recording transaction activity.

Each InnoDB table has a format (.frm) file in the database directory of the database to which the table belongs. This is the same as tables managed by any other MySQL storage engine, such as MyISAM. However, InnoDB manages table contents (data rows and indexes) on disk differently than does the MyISAM engine. By default, InnoDB uses a shared "tablespace," which is one or more files that form a single logical storage area. All InnoDB tables are stored together within the tablespace. There are no table-specific data files or index files for InnoDB the way there are for MyISAM tables. The tablespace also contains a rollback segment. As transactions modify rows, undo log information is stored in the rollback segment. This information is used to roll back failed transactions.

Although InnoDB treats the shared tablespace as a single logical storage area, it can consist of one file or multiple files. Each file can be a regular file or a raw partition. The final file in the shared tablespace can be configured to be auto-extending, in which case InnoDB expands it automatically if the tablespace fills up. Because the shared tablespace is used for InnoDB tables in all databases (and thus is not database specific), tablespace files are stored by default in the server's data directory, not within a particular database directory.

If you do not want to use the shared tablespace for storing table contents, you can start the server with the --innodb_file_per_table option. In this case, for each new table that InnoDB creates, it sets up an .ibd file in the database directory to accompany the table's .frm file. The .ibd file acts as the table's own tablespace file and InnoDB stores table contents in it. (The shared tablespace still is needed because it contains the InnoDB data dictionary and the rollback segment.)

Use of the --innodb_file_per_table option does not affect accessibility of any InnoDB tables that may already have been created in the shared tablespace. Those tables remain accessible.

In addition to its tablespace files, the InnoDB storage engine manages a set of InnoDB-specific log files that contain information about ongoing transactions. As a client performs a transaction, the changes that it makes are held in the InnoDB log. The more recent log contents are cached in memory. Normally, the cached log information is written and flushed to log files on disk at transaction commit time, though that may also occur earlier.

If a crash occurs while the tables are being modified, the log files are used for auto-recovery: When the MySQL server restarts, it reapplies the changes recorded in the logs, to ensure that the tables reflect all committed transactions.

InnoDB tablespace and log setup is discussed in Section 29.4.7, "Configuring and Monitoring InnoDB."

29.4.2 InnoDB and ACID Compliance

The InnoDB storage engine provides transactional capabilities. A transaction is a logical grouping of statements that is handled by the database server as a single unit. Either all the statements execute successfully to completion or all modifications made by the statements are discarded if an error occurs. Transactional systems often are described as being ACID compliant, where "ACID" stands for the following properties:

- *Atomic.* All the statements execute successfully or are canceled as a unit.
- *Consistent.* A database that is in a consistent state when a transaction begins is left in a consistent state by the transaction.
- *Isolated.* One transaction does not affect another.
- *Durable.* All the changes made by a transaction that completes successfully are recorded properly in the database. Changes are not lost.

InnoDB satisfies the conditions for ACID compliance, assuming that its log flushing behavior is set appropriately. InnoDB can be configured for log flushing that provides ACID compliance, or for flushing that gains some in performance at the risk of losing the last few transactions if a crash occurs. By default, InnoDB log flushing is set for ACID compliance. For configuration information, see Section 29.4.7.2, "Configuring InnoDB Buffers and Logs."

29.4.3 The InnoDB Transaction Model

Multiple clients may execute transactions concurrently, but any given client performs transactions serially, one after the other. The client determines when each of its transactions begins and ends by controlling its autocommit mode. MySQL initializes each client to begin with autocommit mode enabled. This causes each statement to be committed immediately. In transactional terms, this means that each statement is a separate transaction. To group multiple statements as a single transaction so that they succeed or fail as a unit, autocommit mode must be disabled. There are two ways to do this:

- The first method is to disable autocommit mode explicitly:

    ```
    SET AUTOCOMMIT = 0;
    ```

    With autocommit disabled, any following statements become part of the current transaction until you end it by issuing a COMMIT statement to accept the transaction and commit its effects to the database, or a ROLLBACK statement to discard the transaction's effects.

When you disable autocommit explicitly, it remains disabled until you enable it again as follows:

```
SET AUTOCOMMIT = 1;
```

- The second method is to suspend the current autocommit mode by beginning a transaction explicitly. Any of the following statements begins a transaction:

```
START TRANSACTION;
BEGIN;
BEGIN WORK;
```

START TRANSACTION is standard SQL syntax. The others are synonyms. (The BEGIN statement that begins a transaction is different from the BEGIN/END syntax that is used to write compound statements in stored routines and triggers. The latter is described in Section 18.5.1, "Compound Statements.")

After beginning a transaction with any of those statements, autocommit remains disabled until you end the transaction by committing it or by rolling it back. The autocommit mode then reverts to the value it had prior to the start of the transaction.

If you disable autocommit explicitly, perform transactions like this:

```
SET AUTOCOMMIT = 0;
... statements for transaction 1 ...
COMMIT;
... statements for transaction 2 ...
COMMIT;
...
```

If you suspend autocommit by using START TRANSACTION, perform transactions like this:

```
START TRANSACTION;
... statements for transaction 1 ...
COMMIT;
START TRANSACTION;
... statements for transaction 2 ...
COMMIT;
...
```

While autocommit mode is enabled, attempts to perform multiple-statement transactions are ineffective. Each statement is committed immediately, so COMMIT is superfluous and ROLLBACK has no effect.

If you want to roll back only part of a transaction, you can set a savepoint by using the SAVEPOINT statement:

```
SAVEPOINT savepoint_name;
```

Multiple savepoints can be set within a transaction. To roll back to a given savepoint, use this statement:

```
ROLLBACK TO SAVEPOINT savepoint_name;
```

The transaction rolls back to the named savepoint and you can continue from there. Any savepoints that were set after the savepoint are deleted.

Under some circumstances, the current transaction may end implicitly:

- If you issue any of the following statements, InnoDB implicitly commits the preceding uncommitted statements of the current transaction and begins a new transaction:

```
ALTER TABLE
BEGIN
CREATE INDEX
DROP DATABASE
DROP INDEX
DROP TABLE
RENAME TABLE
TRUNCATE TABLE
LOCK TABLES
UNLOCK TABLES
SET AUTOCOMMIT = 1
START TRANSACTION
```

  UNLOCK TABLES implicitly commits only if you have explicitly locked tables with LOCK TABLES. SET AUTOCOMMIT = 1 implicitly commits only if autocommit mode wasn't already enabled.

- If a client connection closes while the client has a transaction pending, InnoDB rolls back the transaction implicitly. This occurs regardless of whether the connection closes normally or abnormally.

Because a statement that begins a transaction implicitly commits any current transaction, transactions cannot be nested.

Transaction-control statements can affect explicit table locks. Use of START TRANSACTION or its synonyms causes an implicit UNLOCK TABLES.

The MySQL server initializes each client connection to begin with autocommit enabled. Modifications to the autocommit mode made by a client to its connection persist only to the end of the connection. If a client disconnects and reconnects, the second connection begins with autocommit enabled, regardless of its setting at the end of the first connection.

29.4.4 InnoDB **Locking Characteristics**

This section describes how InnoDB uses locks internally and some query modifiers you can use to affect locking.

InnoDB has the following general locking properties:

- InnoDB does not need to set locks to achieve consistent reads because it uses multi-versioning to make them unnecessary: Transactions that modify rows see their own versions of those rows, and the undo logs allow other transactions to see the original rows. Locking reads may be performed by adding locking modifiers to SELECT statements.

- When locks are necessary, InnoDB uses row-level locking. In conjunction with multi-versioning, this results in good query concurrency because a given table can be read and modified by different clients at the same time. Row-level concurrency properties are as follows:

  - Different clients can read the same rows simultaneously.

  - Different clients can modify different rows simultaneously.

  - Different clients cannot modify the same row at the same time. If one transaction modifies a row, other transactions cannot modify the same row until the first transaction completes. Other transactions cannot read the modified row, either, unless they are using the READ UNCOMMITTED isolation level. That is, they will see the original unmodified row.

- During the course of a transaction, InnoDB may acquire row locks as it discovers them to be necessary. However, it never escalates a lock (for example, by converting it to a page lock or table lock). This keeps lock contention to a minimum and improves concurrency.

- Deadlock can occur. Deadlock is a situation in which each of two transactions is waiting for the release of a lock that the other holds. For example, if two transactions each lock a different row, and then try to modify the row locked by the other, they can deadlock. Deadlock is possible because InnoDB does not acquire locks during a transaction until they are needed. When InnoDB detects a deadlock, it terminates and rolls back one of the deadlocking transactions. It tries to pick the transaction that has modified the smallest number of rows. If InnoDB does not detect deadlock, the deadlocked transactions eventually begin to time out and InnoDB rolls them back as they do.

Isolation levels and multi-versioning are discussed more fully in Section 29.4.5, "InnoDB Isolation Levels, Multi-Versioning, and Concurrency."

InnoDB supports two locking modifiers that may be added to the end of SELECT statements. They acquire shared or exclusive locks and convert non-locking reads into locking reads:

- With LOCK IN SHARE MODE, InnoDB locks each selected row with a shared lock. Other transactions can still read the selected rows, but cannot update or delete them until the first transaction releases the locks, which happens when the transaction finishes. Also, if the SELECT will select rows that have been modified in an uncommitted transaction, IN SHARE MODE will cause the SELECT to block until that transaction commits.

- With FOR UPDATE, InnoDB locks each selected row with an exclusive lock. This is useful if you intend to select and then modify a set of rows, because it prevents other transactions from reading or writing the rows until the first transaction releases the locks, which happens when the transaction finishes.

In the REPEATABLE READ isolation level, you can add LOCK IN SHARE MODE to SELECT operations to force other transactions to wait for your transaction if they want to modify the selected rows. This is similar to operating at the SERIALIZABLE isolation level, for which InnoDB implicitly adds LOCK IN SHARE MODE to SELECT statements that have no explicit locking modifier.

29.4.5 InnoDB Isolation Levels, Multi-Versioning, and Concurrency

As mentioned earlier, multiple transactions may be executing concurrently within the server, one transaction per client. This has the potential to cause problems: If one client's transaction changes data, should transactions for other clients see those changes or should they be isolated from them? The transaction isolation level determines the level of visibility between transactions—that is, the ways in which simultaneous transactions interact when accessing the same data. This section discusses the problems that can occur and how InnoDB implements isolation levels. Note that isolation level definitions vary among database servers, so the levels as implemented by InnoDB might not correspond exactly to levels as implemented in other database systems.

When multiple clients run transactions concurrently, three problems that may result are dirty reads, non-repeatable reads, and phantoms. These occur under the following circumstances:

- A dirty read is a read by one transaction of uncommitted changes made by another. Suppose that transaction T1 modifies a row. If transaction T2 reads the row and sees the modification even though T1 has not committed it, that is a dirty read. One reason this is a problem is that if T1 rolls back, the change is undone but T2 does not know that.

- A non-repeatable read occurs when a transaction performs the same retrieval twice but gets a different result each time. Suppose that T1 reads some rows and that T2 then changes some of those rows and commits the changes. If T1 sees the changes when it reads the rows again, it gets a different result; the initial read is non-repeatable. This is a problem because T1 does not get a consistent result from the same query.

- A phantom is a row that appears where it was not visible before. Suppose that T1 and T2 begin, and T1 reads some rows. If T2 inserts a new row and T1 sees that row when it reads again, the row is a phantom.

InnoDB implements four isolation levels that control the visibility of changes made by one transaction to other concurrently executing transactions:

- READ UNCOMMITTED allows a transaction to see uncommitted changes made by other transactions. This isolation level allows dirty reads, non-repeatable reads, and phantoms to occur.

- READ COMMITTED allows a transaction to see changes made by other transactions only if they've been committed. Uncommitted changes remain invisible. This isolation level allows non-repeatable reads and phantoms to occur.

- REPEATABLE READ ensures that if a transaction issues the same SELECT twice, it gets the same result both times, regardless of committed or uncommitted changes made by other transactions. In other words, it gets a consistent result from different executions of the same query. In some database systems, REPEATABLE READ isolation level allows phantoms, such that if another transaction inserts new rows in the interval between the SELECT statements, the second SELECT will see them. This is not true for InnoDB; phantoms do not occur for the REPEATABLE READ level.

- SERIALIZABLE completely isolates the effects of one transaction from others. It is similar to REPEATABLE READ with the additional restriction that rows selected by one transaction cannot be changed by another until the first transaction finishes.

The essential difference between REPEATABLE READ and SERIALIZABLE is that with REPEATABLE READ, one transaction cannot modify rows another has modified, whereas with SERIALIZABLE, one transaction cannot modify rows if another has merely even read them.

Isolation levels are relevant only within the context of simultaneously executing transactions. After a given transaction has committed, its changes become visible to any transaction that begins after that.

InnoDB operates by default in REPEATABLE READ mode: Each transaction sees a view of the database that consists of all changes that have been committed by the time the transaction issues its first consistent read (such as a SELECT statement), plus any changes that it makes itself. It does not see any uncommitted changes, or committed changes made by transactions that begin later than itself.

InnoDB makes transaction isolation possible by multi-versioning. As transactions modify rows, InnoDB maintains isolation between them by maintaining multiple versions of the rows, and makes available to each transaction the appropriate version of the rows that it should see. Multiple versions of a row that has been changed can be derived from the current version of the row, plus the undo logs.

With multi-versioning, each transaction sees a view of the contents of the database that is appropriate for its isolation level. For example, with a level of REPEATABLE READ, the snapshot of the database that a transaction sees is the state of the database at its first read. One property of this isolation level is that it provides consistent reads: A given SELECT yields the same results when issued at different times during a transaction. The only changes the transaction sees are those it makes itself, not those made by other transactions. For READ COMMITTED, on the other hand, the behavior is slightly different. The view of the database that the transaction sees is updated at each read to take account of commits that have been made by other transactions since the previous read.

To set the server's default transaction isolation level at startup time, use the `--transaction-isolation` option. The option value should be `READ-UNCOMMITTED`, `READ-COMMITTED`, `REPEATABLE-READ`, or `SERIALIZABLE`. For example, to put the server in `READ COMMITTED` mode by default, put these lines in an option file:

```
[mysqld]
transaction-isolation = READ-COMMITTED
```

The isolation level may also be set dynamically for a running server with the `SET TRANSACTION ISOLATION LEVEL` statement. The statement has three forms:

```
SET GLOBAL TRANSACTION ISOLATION LEVEL isolation_level;
SET SESSION TRANSACTION ISOLATION LEVEL isolation_level;
SET TRANSACTION ISOLATION LEVEL isolation_level;
```

The value of `isolation_level` should be `READ UNCOMMITTED`, `READ COMMITTED`, `REPEATABLE READ`, or `SERIALIZABLE`. The first form of the statement sets the server's global isolation level. It applies to all new client connections established from that point on. Existing connections are unaffected. The second form sets the isolation level for the current client connection only and applies to transactions the client performs from that point on. The third form sets the isolation level only for the current client's next transaction.

Only clients that have the `SUPER` privilege may use the first form of the statement. Any client may use the second and third forms of the statement; they affect only its own transactions, so no special privilege is required.

29.4.6 Using Foreign Keys

The `InnoDB` storage engine supports the use of foreign keys. This capability enables you to declare relationships between columns in different tables, and `InnoDB` maintains integrity between the tables by prohibiting operations that violate those relationships. For example, you can specify requirements such as these:

- A table must contain only records with ID values that are known in another reference table.
- If an ID in the referenced table is changed, the ID in all matching records in the referencing table must be changed to match.
- If a record with a given ID in the referenced table is deleted, all records with the matching ID in the referencing table must also be deleted.

The following example demonstrates some of the ways in which `InnoDB` provides referential integrity between tables. It shows how to define a foreign key relationship that enforces the requirements just described. The example is based on the implicit relationship between the `Country` and `City` tables in the `world` database:

- Each Country record has a Code column that specifies a unique country code.
- Each City record has a CountryCode column that matches the code for the country in which the city is located.

The relationship is only implicit because Country and City are MyISAM tables: MyISAM does not have any syntax for specifying the relationship explicitly and provides no means for enforcing it. This means that you could change a Code value in the Country table and any City records with the corresponding country code would not be changed to match. You could delete a Country table row but the corresponding City records would not be deleted. In either case, the City records would become orphaned because there is no longer any corresponding Country table record for them. InnoDB does not allow these types of referential integrity failures to occur.

To define a country-city relationship explicitly, derive a couple of InnoDB tables from the MyISAM tables. We'll call these tables CountryParent and CityChild to illustrate that the country records are the "parent" records and the city records are the "child" records that depend on them:

```
mysql> CREATE TABLE CountryParent
    -> (
    ->     Code CHAR(3) NOT NULL,
    ->     Name CHAR(52) NOT NULL,
    ->     PRIMARY KEY (Code)
    -> ) ENGINE = InnoDB;

mysql> CREATE TABLE CityChild
    -> (
    ->     ID          INT NOT NULL AUTO_INCREMENT,
    ->     Name        CHAR(35) NOT NULL,
    ->     CountryCode CHAR(3) NOT NULL,
    ->     PRIMARY KEY (ID),
    ->     INDEX (CountryCode),
    ->     FOREIGN KEY (CountryCode)
    ->         REFERENCES CountryParent (Code)
    ->         ON UPDATE CASCADE
    ->         ON DELETE CASCADE
    -> ) ENGINE = InnoDB;
```

In these two tables, the column and PRIMARY KEY definitions are the same as in the original Country and City tables. The parts of the syntax that differ from the original tables are the ENGINE table option, which specifies the InnoDB storage engine, and the INDEX and FOREIGN KEY definitions for the CountryCode column in the CityChild table.

It's necessary to use InnoDB because that is the only storage engine that supports foreign keys. (You can specify a FOREIGN KEY clause for other table types, but it would simply be ignored.)

The FOREIGN KEY clause has several parts:

- It names the column in the referring table (CountryCode).

- It names the Code column in the CountryParent table as the referenced column. This column is the "foreign" key.

- It specifies what actions to take if records are modified in the referenced table. The foreign key definition shown specifies the CASCADE action for both UPDATE and DELETE operations. This means that changes in the parent table are cascaded down to the child table. If you change a Code value in the CountryParent table, InnoDB changes any corresponding CityChild records with that value in the CountryCode column to match. If you delete a CountryParent record, InnoDB also deletes any CityChild records with the same country code. (InnoDB supports actions other than CASCADE, but they are not covered here. For details, see the *MySQL Reference Manual*.)

In a foreign key relationship, the referring column and the referenced column should have the same data type, and both must be indexed. (If the referring column has no index, InnoDB creates an index on it automatically.)

The ON UPDATE and ON DELETE parts are optional. If you omit them, InnoDB simply disallows attempts to update or delete Code values in the CountryParent table if there are CityChild records that refer to them.

The preceding CREATE TABLE statements define the foreign key relationship between CountryParent and CityChild. Now let's verify that InnoDB enforces it. Populate the two InnoDB tables with information from the original Country and City tables:

```
mysql> INSERT INTO CountryParent SELECT Code, Name FROM Country;
Query OK, 239 rows affected (0.34 sec)
Records: 239  Duplicates: 0  Warnings: 0

mysql> INSERT INTO CityChild SELECT ID, Name, CountryCode FROM City;
Query OK, 4079 rows affected (2.30 sec)
Records: 4079  Duplicates: 0  Warnings: 0
```

Examine a small set of related records from the two tables so that we can see the effect of updates and deletes on them. The following statement retrieves the country information for Croatia, and the corresponding city records for Croatian cities:

```
mysql> SELECT * FROM CountryParent AS P, CityChild AS C
    -> WHERE P.Code = C.CountryCode AND P.Name = 'Croatia';
+------+---------+------+--------+-------------+
| Code | Name    | ID   | Name   | CountryCode |
+------+---------+------+--------+-------------+
| HRV  | Croatia | 2409 | Zagreb | HRV         |
| HRV  | Croatia | 2410 | Split  | HRV         |
```

```
| HRV  | Croatia | 2411 | Rijeka | HRV         |
| HRV  | Croatia | 2412 | Osijek | HRV         |
+------+---------+------+--------+-------------+
```

Test the effect of ON UPDATE CASCADE by changing the Croatia country code in the CountryParent table, and checking how that affects the CityChild table:

```
mysql> UPDATE CountryParent SET Code = 'xxx' WHERE Name = 'Croatia';
Query OK, 1 row affected (0.21 sec)
Rows matched: 1  Changed: 1  Warnings: 0

mysql> SELECT * FROM CountryParent WHERE Code = 'xxx';
+------+---------+
| Code | Name    |
+------+---------+
| xxx  | Croatia |
+------+---------+
1 row in set (0.00 sec)

mysql> SELECT * FROM CityChild WHERE CountryCode = 'xxx';
+------+--------+-------------+
| ID   | Name   | CountryCode |
+------+--------+-------------+
| 2409 | Zagreb | xxx         |
| 2410 | Split  | xxx         |
| 2411 | Rijeka | xxx         |
| 2412 | Osijek | xxx         |
+------+--------+-------------+
4 rows in set (0.00 sec)
```

InnoDB has changed the country codes in the corresponding CityChild records to match.

Test the effect of ON DELETE CASCADE by deleting the record for Croatia from the CountryParent table (which now has a Code value of 'xxx'), and checking how that affects the CityChild table:

```
mysql> DELETE FROM CountryParent WHERE Name = 'Croatia';
Query OK, 1 row affected (0.25 sec)

mysql> SELECT * FROM CountryParent WHERE Code = 'xxx';
Empty set (0.00 sec)

mysql> SELECT * FROM CityChild WHERE CountryCode = 'xxx';
Empty set (0.00 sec)
```

InnoDB has deleted the corresponding records form the CityChild table.

The example demonstrates that foreign keys help you maintain referential integrity between tables. Because `InnoDB` performs the required changes in the referring table, you don't need to do so. This reduces application programming complexity.

29.4.7 Configuring and Monitoring `InnoDB`

A server that has `InnoDB` enabled uses a default configuration for its tablespace and log files unless you provide configuration options. This section describes how to configure `InnoDB` explicitly, and how to obtain status information from `InnoDB` while the server is running.

29.4.7.1 Configuring the `InnoDB` Tablespace

By default, the `InnoDB` storage engine manages the contents for all `InnoDB` tables in its shared tablespace. The tablespace stores data rows and indexes. It also contains a rollback segment consisting of undo log records for ongoing transactions, in case they need to be rolled back. The shared tablespace has the following general characteristics:

- It can consist of one file or multiple files.
- Each component file of the tablespace can be a regular file or a raw partition (a device file). A given tablespace can include both types of files.
- Tablespace files can be on different filesystems or physical disk drives. One reason to place the files on multiple physical drives is to distribute `InnoDB`-related disk activity among them.
- The tablespace size can exceed the limits that the filesystem places on maximum file size. This is true for two reasons. First, the tablespace can consist of multiple files and thus can be larger than any single file. Second, the tablespace can include raw partitions, which are not bound by filesystem limits on maximum file size. `InnoDB` can use the full extent of partitions, which makes it easy to configure a very large tablespace.
- The last component of the tablespace can be auto-extending, with an optional limit on how large the file can grow.

If you don't specify any tablespace configuration options at all, `InnoDB` creates a shared tablespace consisting of a single 10MB auto-extending regular file named `ibdata1` in the data directory. To control the tablespace configuration explicitly, use the `innodb_data_file_path` and `innodb_data_home_dir` options:

- `innodb_data_file_path` names each of the files in the tablespace, their sizes, and possibly other optional information. The parts of each file specification are delimited by colons. If there are multiple files, separate their specifications by semicolons. The minimum combined size of the files is 10MB.
- `innodb_data_home_dir` specifies a pathname prefix that is prepended to the pathname of each file named by `innodb_data_file_path`. By default, tablespace files are assumed to be located in the data directory. You can set the home directory to the empty value if

you want filenames in `innodb_data_file_path` to be treated as absolute pathnames. This is useful when you want to place tablespace files on different filesystems or if you want to use raw partitions.

Normally, you place the settings for these options in an option file to make sure that the server uses the same tablespace configuration each time it starts. The following examples show various ways to set up an `InnoDB` tablespace:

- A tablespace consisting of a single 100MB file named `innodata1` located in the data directory:

```
[mysqld]
innodb_data_file_path = innodata1:100M
```

  It's unnecessary to specify a value for the `innodb_data_home_dir` option in this case because the data directory is its default value.

- A tablespace like that in the previous example, except that the file is auto-extending:

```
[mysqld]
innodb_data_file_path = innodata1:100M:autoextend
```

- A tablespace like that in the previous example, but with a limit of 500MB on the size to which the auto-extending file may grow:

```
[mysqld]
innodb_data_file_path = innodata1:100M:autoextend:max:500M
```

- A tablespace consisting of two 500MB files named `innodata1` and `innodata2` located in the data directory:

```
[mysqld]
innodb_data_file_path = innodata1:500M;innodata2:500M
```

- A tablespace like that in the previous example, but with the files stored under the `E:\innodb` directory rather than in the data directory.

```
[mysqld]
innodb_data_home_dir = E:/innodb
innodb_data_file_path = innodata1:500M;innodata2:500M
```

  Note that backslashes in Windows pathnames are written as forward slashes in option files.

- A tablespace consisting of two files stored on different filesystems. Here the home directory is set to an empty value so that the file specifications can be given as absolute pathnames on different filesystems:

```
[mysqld]
innodb_data_home_dir =
innodb_data_file_path = E:/innodata1:500M;D:/innodata2:500M
```

When you first configure the tablespace, any regular (non-partition) files named by the configuration options must not exist. InnoDB will create and initialize them when you start the server.

Any raw partitions named in the configuration must exist but must have the modifier newraw listed after the size in the file specification. newraw tells InnoDB to initialize the partition when the server starts up. New partitions are treated as read-only after initialization. After InnoDB initializes the tablespace, stop the server, change newraw to raw in the partition specification, and restart the server. For example, to use a 10GB Unix partition named /dev/hdc6, begin with a configuration like this:

```
[mysqld]
innodb_data_home_dir =
innodb_data_file_path = /dev/hdc6:10Gnewraw
```

Start the server and let InnoDB initialize the tablespace. Then stop the server and change the configuration from newraw to raw:

```
[mysqld]
innodb_data_home_dir =
innodb_data_file_path = /dev/hdc6:10Graw
```

After changing the configuration, restart the server.

If you do not want to use the shared tablespace for storing table contents, you can configure InnoDB with the innodb_file_per_table option. For example:

```
[mysqld]
innodb_data_file_path = innodata1:100M
innodb_file_per_table
```

In this case, for each new table that InnoDB creates, it sets up an .ibd file to accompany the table's .frm file in the database directory. The .ibd file acts as the table's own tablespace file and InnoDB stores table contents in it. (The shared tablespace still is needed because it contains the InnoDB data dictionary and the rollback segment.)

29.4.7.2 Configuring InnoDB Buffers and Logs

InnoDB uses a buffer pool to hold information read from InnoDB tables. The buffer pool serves to reduce disk I/O for information that is frequently accessed, and a larger buffer more effectively achieves this goal. To change the size of the buffer pool, set the innodb_buffer_pool_size option. Its default value is 8MB. If your machine has the memory available, you can set the value much higher.

The InnoDB storage engine logs information about current transactions in a memory buffer. When a transaction commits or rolls back, the log buffer is flushed to disk. If the log buffer is small, it might fill up before the end of the transaction, requiring a flush to the log file before the outcome of the transaction is known. For a committed transaction, this results in multiple disk operations rather than one. For a rolled-back transaction, it results in writes that, with a larger buffer, would not need to have been made at all. To set the size of the log buffer, use the innodb_log_buffer_size option. The default value is 1MB. Typical values range from 1MB to 8MB. Values larger than 8MB are of no benefit.

By default, InnoDB creates two 5MB log files in the data directory named ib_logfile0 and ib_logfile1. To configure the InnoDB log files explicitly, use the innodb_log_files_in_group and innodb_log_file_size options. The first controls how many log files InnoDB uses and the second controls how big each file is. For example, to use two log files of 50MB each, configure the log like this:

```
[mysqld]
innodb_log_files_in_group = 2
innodb_log_file_size = 50M
```

The product of the two values is the total size of the InnoDB log files. Information is logged in circular fashion, with old information at the front of the log being overwritten when the log fills up. However, the log entries cannot be overwritten if the changes they refer to have not yet been recorded in the tablespace. Consequently, a larger log allows InnoDB to run longer without having to force changes recorded in the logs to be applied to the tablespace on disk.

The innodb_flush_log_at_trx_commit setting affects how InnoDB transfers log information from the log buffer in memory to the log files on disk. The buffer contains information about committed transactions, so it is important that it be written properly: It is one thing to perform a write operation, and another to make sure that the operating system actually has written the information to disk. Operating systems typically buffer writes in the filesystem cache briefly and do not actually perform the write to disk immediately. To ensure that buffered information has been recorded on disk, InnoDB must perform a write operation to initiate a disk transfer *and* a flush operation to force the transfer to complete.

InnoDB tries to flush the log approximately once a second in any case, but the innodb_flush_log_at_trx_commit option can be set to determine how log writing and flushing occurs in addition. The setting of this option is directly related to the ACID durability property and to performance as follows:

- If you set innodb_flush_log_at_trx_commit to 1, changes are written from the log buffer to the log file and the log file is flushed to disk for each commit. This guarantees that the changes will not be lost even in the event of a crash. This is the safest setting, and is also the required setting if you need ACID durability. However, this setting also produces slowest performance.

- A setting of 0 causes the log file to be written and flushed to disk approximately once a second, but not after each commit. On a busy system, this can reduce log-related disk activity significantly, but in the event of a crash can result in a loss of about a second's worth of committed changes.

- A setting of 2 causes the log buffer to be written to the log file after each commit, but file writes are flushed to disk approximately once a second. This is somewhat slower than a setting of 0. However, the committed changes will not be lost if it is only the MySQL server that crashes and not the operating system or server host: The machine continues to run, so the changes written to the log file are in the filesystem cache and eventually will be flushed normally.

The tradeoff controlled by the `innodb_flush_log_at_trx_commit` setting therefore is between durability and performance. If ACID durability is required, a setting of 1 is necessary. If a slight risk to durability is acceptable to achieve better performance, a value of 0 or 2 may be used.

29.4.7.3 Viewing InnoDB Status Information

You can ask the InnoDB storage engine to provide information about itself by means of SHOW statements.

SHOW ENGINE INNODB STATUS requires the SUPER privilege and displays extensive information about InnoDB's operation:

```
mysql> SHOW ENGINE INNODB STATUS\G
*************************** 1. row ***************************
Status:
=====================================
030914 17:44:57 INNODB MONITOR OUTPUT
=====================================
Per second averages calculated from the last 35 seconds
----------
SEMAPHORES
----------
OS WAIT ARRAY INFO: reservation count 65, signal count 65
Mutex spin waits 1487, rounds 28720, OS waits 51
RW-shared spins 28, OS waits 13; RW-excl spins 1, OS waits 1
------------
TRANSACTIONS
------------
Trx id counter 0 31923
Purge done for trx's n:o < 0 21287 undo n:o < 0 0
Total number of lock structs in row lock hash table 0
LIST OF TRANSACTIONS FOR EACH SESSION:
--------
FILE I/O
--------
I/O thread 0 state: waiting for i/o request (insert buffer thread)
I/O thread 1 state: waiting for i/o request (log thread)
I/O thread 2 state: waiting for i/o request (read thread)
I/O thread 3 state: waiting for i/o request (write thread)
```

```
Pending normal aio reads: 0, aio writes: 0,
 ibuf aio reads: 0, log i/o's: 0, sync i/o's: 0
Pending flushes (fsync) log: 0; buffer pool: 0
77 OS file reads, 10959 OS file writes, 5620 OS fsyncs
0.00 reads/s, 0 avg bytes/read, 83.20 writes/s, 41.88 fsyncs/s
-------------------------------------
INSERT BUFFER AND ADAPTIVE HASH INDEX
-------------------------------------
Ibuf for space 0: size 1, free list len 0, seg size 2,
0 inserts, 0 merged recs, 0 merges
Hash table size 34679, used cells 1, node heap has 1 buffer(s)
6.06 hash searches/s, 36.68 non-hash searches/s
---
LOG
---
Log sequence number 0 1520665
Log flushed up to   0 1520665
Last checkpoint at  0 1520665
0 pending log writes, 0 pending chkp writes
10892 log i/o's done, 82.80 log i/o's/second
----------------------
BUFFER POOL AND MEMORY
----------------------
Total memory allocated 18373254; in additional pool allocated 725632
Buffer pool size    512
Free buffers        447
Database pages      64
Modified db pages   0
Pending reads 0
Pending writes: LRU 0, flush list 0, single page 0
Pages read 22, created 42, written 141
0.00 reads/s, 0.46 creates/s, 1.49 writes/s
Buffer pool hit rate 1000 / 1000
--------------
ROW OPERATIONS
--------------
0 queries inside InnoDB, 0 queries in queue
Main thread id 10836480, state: waiting for server activity
Number of rows inserted 5305, updated 3, deleted 0, read 10
41.08 inserts/s, 0.00 updates/s, 0.00 deletes/s, 0.00 reads/s
----------------------------
END OF INNODB MONITOR OUTPUT
============================
```

SHOW TABLE STATUS, when used with any InnoDB table, displays in the Comment field of the output the approximate amount of free space available in the InnoDB tablespace:

```
mysql> SHOW TABLE STATUS LIKE 'CountryList'\G
*************************** 1. row ***************************
           Name: CountryList
           Type: InnoDB
     Row_format: Fixed
           Rows: 171
 Avg_row_length: 287
    Data_length: 49152
Max_data_length: NULL
   Index_length: 0
      Data_free: 0
 Auto_increment: NULL
    Create_time: NULL
    Update_time: NULL
     Check_time: NULL
 Create_options:
        Comment: InnoDB free: 13312 kB
```

The free space value applies to the shared tablespace if that is where the table is stored. If the table has its own per-table tablespace (an .ibd file), the value applies to its own tablespace.

The information displayed by SHOW TABLE STATUS also is available in the TABLES table of the INFORMATION_SCHEMA database.

29.5 The MEMORY Engine

The MEMORY storage engine manages tables that have the following characteristics:

- Each MEMORY table is represented on disk by an .frm format file in the database directory. Table data and indexes are stored in memory.

- In-memory storage results in very fast performance.

- MEMORY table contents do not survive a restart of the server. The table structure itself survives, but the table contains zero data rows after a restart.

- MEMORY tables use up memory (obviously), so they should not be used for large tables.

- MySQL manages query contention for MEMORY tables using table-level locking. Deadlock cannot occur.

- MEMORY tables cannot contain TEXT or BLOB columns.

The MEMORY stored engine formerly was called the HEAP engine. You might still see HEAP in older SQL code, and MySQL Server still recognizes HEAP for backward compatibility.

29.5.1 MEMORY **Indexing Options**

The MEMORY storage engine supports two indexing algorithms, HASH and BTREE:

- MEMORY tables use hash indexes by default. This index algorithm provides very fast lookups for all operations that use a unique index. However, hash indexes are usable only for comparisons that use the = or <=> operator.

- The BTREE index algorithm is preferable if the indexed column will be used with comparison operators other than = or <=>. For example, BTREE can be used for range searches such as id < 100 or id BETWEEN 200 AND 300.

The syntax for indicating which algorithm to use when creating a MEMORY table index is given in Section 8.6.3, "Choosing an Indexing Algorithm."

29.6 The FEDERATED **Engine**

The FEDERATED storage engine is new in MySQL 5. It allows a MySQL server to use tables from other MySQL servers and to make them available to its clients as though the tables were its own. The clients need not connect directly to the other servers to access the tables.

One benefit provided by this capability is that you can use a single query to access tables that are managed by different servers. It's not necessary to connect to each server and retrieve data separately for each one. For example, you can perform a join between tables from different servers. FEDERATED is new, so much remains to be done in terms of optimizing such queries, but the fact that they now can be issued is significant.

The FEDERATED storage engine manages tables that have the following characteristics:

- Each FEDERATED table is represented on disk only by an .frm format file in the database directory.

- The FEDERATED storage engine does not support transactions.

- The FEDERATED storage engine supports SELECT, DELETE, UPDATE, and INSERT statements.

- MySQL does not use any locking for FEDERATED tables.

Suppose that there is an instance of the world database located on the remote host world.example.com and that its City table has this definition:

```
CREATE TABLE City
(
    ID          INT NOT NULL AUTO_INCREMENT,
    Name        CHAR(35) NOT NULL,
    CountryCode CHAR(3) NOT NULL,
    District    CHAR(20) NOT NULL,
    Population  INT NOT NULL,
    PRIMARY KEY (ID)
) ENGINE = MyISAM;
```

If the world database on the remote host can be accessed by connecting to the MySQL server there with a username and password of wuser and wpass, a FEDERATED table can be created on the local host that allows the remote City table to be accessed as though it were local. To create a local FEDERATED table, use a definition similar to that of the remote table, but make two changes. First, use an ENGINE = FEDERATED table option. Second, include a COMMENT table option that specifies a connection string. The connection string indicates to the local server where the remote table is located and how to connect to the remote server. Connection string format is as follows, where optional parts are shown in square brackets:

mysql://*user_name*[:*password*]@*host_name*[:*port*]/*db_name*/*table_name*

The username, password, hostname, and port number specify what connection parameters to use for connecting to the remote server. The database and table names indicate which table to access on that server.

With the ENGINE and COMMENT table options, the resulting definition for a FEDERATED table named FedCity looks like this:

```
CREATE TABLE FedCity
(
    ID           INT NOT NULL AUTO_INCREMENT,
    Name         CHAR(35) NOT NULL,
    CountryCode  CHAR(3) NOT NULL,
    District     CHAR(20) NOT NULL,
    Population   INT NOT NULL,
    PRIMARY KEY (ID)
)
ENGINE=FEDERATED
COMMENT='mysql://wuser:wpass@world.example.com/world/City';
```

To access the FedCity table, just refer to it as you would any other table. For example:

```
mysql> SELECT ID, Name, Population FROM FedCity
    -> WHERE CountryCode = 'EGY';
+-----+----------------------+------------+
| ID  | Name                 | Population |
+-----+----------------------+------------+
| 608 | Cairo                |    6789479 |
| 609 | Alexandria           |    3328196 |
| 610 | Giza                 |    2221868 |
| 611 | Shubra al-Khayma     |     870716 |
| 612 | Port Said            |     469533 |
| 613 | Suez                 |     417610 |
| 614 | al-Mahallat al-Kubra |     395402 |
| 615 | Tanta                |     371010 |
| 616 | al-Mansura           |     369621 |
...
```

"Remote" in the preceding discussion actually is not quite accurate: FEDERATED tables can be defined for accessing tables from other servers running on the same host, or even other tables from the same server.

29.7 The Cluster Storage Engine

The NDBCluster storage engine originally appeared in MySQL 4.1. Using the cluster engine is complex, and for the purposes of MySQL 5 certification you are not expected to know the details of how to set up and use NDBCluster. You *are*, however, expected to know the general properties of the cluster engine as compared to other storage engines.

In literature, you will see the two terms "NDB Cluster" (or just "NDB") and "MySQL Cluster." NDB Cluster refers to the cluster technology and is thus specific to the storage engine itself, whereas MySQL Cluster refers to a group of one or more MySQL servers that works as a "front end" to the NDB Cluster engine. That is, a MySQL Cluster consists of a group of one or more server hosts, each of which is usually running multiple processes that include MySQL servers, NDB management processes, and NDB database storage nodes. Cluster processes are also referred to as "cluster nodes" or just "nodes."

The cluster engine does not run internally in MySQL Server, but is, instead, one or more separate processes running outside MySQL Server (perhaps even on different server hosts). In effect, MySQL Server provides the SQL interface to the cluster processes. From the perspective of the server, however, NDBCluster is just another storage engine, like the MyISAM and the InnoDB engines.

NDB Cluster consists of several database processes (nodes) running on one or more physical server hosts. It manages one or more *in-memory* databases in a *shared-nothing system*. In-memory means that all the information in each database is kept in the RAM of the machines making up the cluster. (Updates are written to disk so that they are not lost if problems occur.) Shared-nothing means that the cluster is set up in such a way that no hardware components (such as disks) are shared among two nodes.

The NDB cluster engine is a transactional storage engine, like the InnoDB storage engine.

The following list describes the main reasons to consider using MySQL Cluster:

- *High availability:* All records are available on several nodes. If one node fails (for example, because the server host stops working), the same data can be gotten from another node. Spreading copies of the data across multiple nodes also makes it possible to have replicas of the data in two or more widely distributed locations.

- *Scalability:* If the load becomes too high for the current set of nodes, extra nodes can be added and the system will reconfigure itself to make data available on more nodes, reducing the load on each individual node.

- *High performance:* All records are stored in memory, making data retrieval extremely fast. This does not mean that information is lost if the cluster is shut down (as is the case for tables created with the MEMORY storage engine). All updates are written to disk, and are available when the cluster is restarted.

29.8 Other Storage Engines

MySQL Server supports several other storage engines in addition to those already covered. This section summarizes them briefly, although you are not expected to know about them for the exam.

The BDB storage engine provides transactional tables. Each BDB table is represented on disk by an .frm format file and a .db file that stores data and index information. BDB supports transactions (using the SQL COMMIT and ROLLBACK statements) with full ACID compliance. The BDB engine provides auto-recovery after a crash of the MySQL server or the host where the server runs. BDB uses page-level locking. This locking level provides concurrency performance that is intermediate to that of row-level and table-level locking. It's possible for deadlock to occur.

The ARCHIVE storage engine provides an efficient way to store large amounts of data when you don't need indexes and need to minimize the amount of disk space used. This engine supports only SELECT and INSERT operations. SELECT scans the entire table, and INSERT performs compressed inserts. (Written records are cached until a read occurs, and then they are compressed and flushed to disk. This is done because you get better compression if you compress several rows at a time rather than individually.) To analyze and recompress an ARCHIVE table, use the OPTIMIZE TABLE statement. Each ARCHIVE table is represented on disk by an .frm format file, an .ARZ data file, and an .ARM metadata file.

The CSV storage engine stores records as text in the well-known comma-separated values format. This format is highly portable. The CSV engine does not support indexing. Each CSV table is represented on disk by an .frm format file and a .CSV plain text file that contains data rows.

The BLACKHOLE storage engine creates tables that act as "black holes." That is, what goes in does not come out. Data stored in a BLACKHOLE table disappears because the engine simply discards it. The only disk file associated with a BLACKHOLE table is its .frm format file.

The EXAMPLE storage engine does nothing except create tables. You can't even store any rows in an EXAMPLE table, although this is by design: The purpose of this engine is to provide simple example code in MySQL source distributions that demonstrates how to get started writing a new storage engine. The only disk file associated with an EXAMPLE table is its .frm format file.

The ISAM storage engine is an older engine that has been superceded by MyISAM. It uses an older table format that is obsolete because MyISAM offers better features and performance. ISAM is no longer available as of MySQL 5.

Table Maintenance

MySQL has the capability to check tables for problems and to repair them should problems be found. Other table-maintenance capabilities include table analysis and optimization. This chapter discusses how to perform these types of maintenance operations. It covers the following exam topics:

- Types of table maintenance operations
- SQL statements for table maintenance
- Client and utility programs for table maintenance
- Repairing InnoDB tables
- Enabling auto-repair for MyISAM tables

30.1 Types of Table Maintenance Operations

Table-maintenance operations are useful for identifying and correcting problems with your databases (for example, if a table becomes damaged as a result of a server crash), or for helping MySQL to process queries on your tables more quickly. MySQL enables you to perform several types of maintenance operations:

- A table check performs an integrity check to make sure that the table's structure and content have no problems. This operation can be done for MyISAM and InnoDB tables.
- A table repair corrects integrity problems to restore the table to a known, usable state. This operation can be done for MyISAM tables.
- A table analysis updates statistics about the distribution of index key values. This is information that the optimizer can use to generate better execution plans for queries on the table. This operation can be done for MyISAM and InnoDB tables.
- A table optimization reorganizes a table so that its contents can be accessed more efficiently. This operation can be done for MyISAM and InnoDB tables.

Table analysis and optimization are operations that you might want to perform periodically to keep your tables performing at their best:

- When MySQL analyzes a `MyISAM` or `InnoDB` table, it updates the index statistics. The optimizer uses these statistics when processing queries to make better decisions about how best to look up records in the table and the order in which to read tables in a join.

- When MySQL optimizes a `MyISAM` table, it defragments the data file to reclaim unused space, sorts the indexes, and updates the index statistics. Periodic defragmenting is useful for speeding up table access for tables that contain variable-length columns such as `VARCHAR`, `VARBINARY`, `BLOB`, or `TEXT`. Inserts and deletes can result in many gaps in such tables, particularly those that are modified frequently. Defragmenting eliminates these gaps.

Table analysis and optimization operations are maximally beneficial when performed on a table that is fully populated and that will not change thereafter. The benefits of analysis and optimization diminish if the table continues to be updated, so you might want to repeat these operations periodically.

The tools at your disposal for table maintenance include SQL statements such as `CHECK TABLE` and `REPAIR TABLE`, client programs such as MySQL Administrator and `mysqlcheck`, the `myisamchk` utility, and the server's capabilities for auto-recovery. The following sections describe these tools.

30.2 SQL Statements for Table Maintenance

MySQL has several SQL statements for table maintenance: `CHECK TABLE` for integrity checking, `REPAIR TABLE` for repairs, `ANALYZE TABLE` for analysis, and `OPTIMIZE TABLE` for optimization. This section discusses these SQL statements and describes what they do. Section 30.3, "Client and Utility Programs for Table Maintenance," points out which MySQL client programs can be used to issue the statements.

Each statement, when issued, causes the server to perform the requested operation. The statement takes one or more table names and possibly optional keywords that modify the basic action to be performed. A table name can be unqualified to refer to a table in the current database, or qualified in *db_name.table_name* form to refer to a table in a specific database. For example, if `world` is the current database, the following statements are equivalent and instruct the server to check the `world.City` table:

```
CHECK TABLE City;
CHECK TABLE world.City;
```

After performing the requested operation, the server returns information about the result of the operation to the client. The information takes the form of a result set with four columns. For example:

```
mysql> OPTIMIZE TABLE City, CountryLanguage;
+----------------------+----------+----------+----------+
| Table                | Op       | Msg_type | Msg_text |
+----------------------+----------+----------+----------+
| world.City           | optimize | status   | OK       |
| world.CountryLanguage | optimize | status   | OK       |
+----------------------+----------+----------+----------+
```

Table indicates the table for which the operation was performed. Op names the operation (check, repair, analyze, or optimize). Msg_type provides an indicator of success or failure, and Msg_text provides extra information.

30.2.1 CHECK TABLE

The CHECK TABLE statement performs an integrity check on table structure and contents. It works for MyISAM and InnoDB tables. For MyISAM tables, it also updates the index statistics. If the table is a view, CHECK TABLE verifies the view definition.

If the output from CHECK TABLE indicates that a table has problems, the table should be repaired.

30.2.2 REPAIR TABLE

The REPAIR TABLE statement corrects problems in a table that has become corrupted. It works only for MyISAM tables.

You can tell the server to repair MyISAM tables automatically. See Section 30.5, "Enabling MyISAM Auto-Repair."

30.2.3 ANALYZE TABLE

The ANALYZE TABLE statement updates a table with information about the distribution of key values in the table. This information is used by the optimizer to make better choices about query execution plans. This statement works for MyISAM and InnoDB tables.

30.2.4 OPTIMIZE TABLE

The OPTIMIZE TABLE statement cleans up a MyISAM table by defragmenting it. This involves reclaiming unused space resulting from deletes and updates, and coalescing records that have become split and stored non-contiguously. OPTIMIZE TABLE also sorts the index pages if they are out of order and updates the index statistics.

OPTIMIZE TABLE also works for InnoDB tables, but maps to ALTER TABLE, which rebuilds the table. This updates index statistics and frees space in the clustered index.

30.3 Client and Utility Programs for Table Maintenance

The table-maintenance SQL statements discussed in the preceding sections can be issued from within the mysql client program or from other applications that send statements to the server. By using these statements, you can write your own administrative applications that perform table check and repair operations.

Some MySQL client programs provide a front end for issuing table-maintenance statements:

- MySQL Administrator offers a point-and-click interface for table check, repair, and optimize operations. When you select one of these operations, MySQL Administrator sends the corresponding SQL statement to the server.

- mysqlcheck can check, repair, analyze, and optimize tables. It determines which options were given on the command line, and then sends appropriate SQL statements to the MySQL server to perform the requested operation.

The myisamchk utility for MyISAM tables also performs table maintenance. However, it takes a different approach from MySQL Administrator and mysqlcheck. Rather than sending SQL statements to the server, myisamchk directly reads and modified the table files. For this reason, it's necessary when using myisamchk to ensure that the server does not access the tables at the same time.

30.3.1 The mysqlcheck Client Program

mysqlcheck checks, repairs, analyzes, and optimizes tables. It can perform all these operations on MyISAM tables, and can perform some of them on InnoDB tables. It provides a command-line interface to the various SQL statements that instruct the server to perform table maintenance, such as CHECK TABLE and REPAIR TABLE.

mysqlcheck has properties that in some contexts make it more convenient than issuing SQL statements directly. For example, if you name a database, it determines what tables the database contains and issues statements to process them all. You need not name each table explicitly. Also, because mysqlcheck is a command-line program, it can easily be used in jobs that perform periodic scheduled maintenance.

mysqlcheck has three general modes of operation, depending on the arguments with which you invoke it:

- By default, mysqlcheck interprets its first non-option argument as a database name and checks all the tables in that database. If any other arguments follow the database name, mysqlcheck treats them as table names and checks just those tables. For example, the first of the following commands checks all the tables in the world database; the second checks just the City and Country tables in that database:

```
shell> mysqlcheck world
shell> mysqlcheck world City Country
```

- With the --databases (or -B) option, mysqlcheck interprets its non-option arguments as database names and checks all the tables in each of the named databases. The following command checks the tables in both the world and test databases:

```
shell> mysqlcheck --databases world test
```

- With the --all-databases (or -A) option, mysqlcheck checks all tables in all databases:

```
shell> mysqlcheck --all-databases
```

mysqlcheck also supports options that indicate which operation to perform on the specified tables. --check, --repair, --analyze, and --optimize perform table checking, repair, analysis, and optimization. The default is to check tables if none of these options is given.

For some operations, mysqlcheck supports options that modify the basic action to be performed. A recommended table-checking strategy is to run mysqlcheck with no options. If any errors occur, run mysqlcheck again, first with the --repair and --quick options to attempt a quick repair. If that fails, run mysqlcheck with --repair for a normal repair, and then if necessary with --repair and --force.

30.3.2 The myisamchk Utility

The myisamchk utility performs table maintenance on MyISAM tables. Conceptually, myisamchk is similar in purpose to mysqlcheck, but the two programs do differ in certain ways:

- Both programs can check, repair, and analyze MyISAM tables. mysqlcheck also can optimize MyISAM tables, as well as check InnoDB tables. There are certain operations that myisamchk can perform that mysqlcheck cannot, such as disabling or enabling indexes, although these operations aren't discussed in this study guide.

- The two programs differ significantly in their mode of operation. mysqlcheck is a client program that communicates with the MySQL server over a network connection. This means that mysqlcheck requires the server to be running, but it also means that mysqlcheck can connect to remote servers. In contrast, myisamchk isn't a client program. It's a utility that operates directly on the files that represent MyISAM tables. This means that you must run myisamchk on the server host where those files are located. In addition, you need filesystem read privileges on those files for table check operations, and write privileges for table repair operations.

- The two programs also differ in their relationship with the server while they're running. With mysqlcheck, there's no problem of interaction with the server because mysqlcheck asks the server itself to do the work of checking and repairing the tables. With myisamchk, you need to make sure that the server doesn't have the tables open and isn't using them at the same time. It's possible to get incorrect results or even to cause table damage if table files are used by myisamchk and the server simultaneously. The most certain way to avoid conflict while running myisamchk is to stop the server first. It's also possible to leave the server running and lock the tables while checking or repairing them with myisamchk, but the procedure is not described here. You can find the details in the *MySQL Reference Manual*.

Because you must avoid using tables at the same time the server might be accessing them, the procedure for using myisamchk differs from that for using mysqlcheck. Perform table maintenance with myisamchk as follows:

1. Ensure that the server will not access the tables while you're working with them. One way to guarantee this is to stop the server.

2. From a command prompt, change location into the database directory where the tables are located. This will be the subdirectory of the server's data directory that has the same name as the database containing the tables you would like to check. (The reason for changing location is to make it easier to refer to the table files. You can skip this step if you like, but you'll have to specify to myisamchk the directory where the tables are located.)

3. Invoke myisamchk with options indicating the operation you want performed, followed by arguments that name the tables on which myisamchk should operate. Each of these arguments can be either a table name or the name of the table's index file. An index file-name is the same as the table name, plus an .MYI suffix. Thus, you can refer to a table either as *table_name* or as *table_name*.MYI.

4. Restart the server.

The default myisamchk operation is to check tables. If that's what you want to do, no options are necessary and you need only name the table or tables to be checked. For example, to check a table named City, use either of these commands:

```
shell> myisamchk City
shell> myisamchk City.MYI
```

To repair a table, use the --recover option:

```
shell> myisamchk --recover City
```

If a repair operation performed with --recover encounters problems that it cannot fix, try using the --safe-recover option. --safe-recover can fix some problems that --recover cannot. (--safe-recover is much slower than --recover, which is why you try --recover first.)

30.3.3 Options for mysqlcheck and myisamchk

mysqlcheck and myisamchk both take many options to control the type of table maintenance operation performed. The following list summarizes some of the more commonly used options. For the most part, the list contains options that are understood by both programs.

Where that isn't the case, it's noted in the relevant option description.

- `--analyze` or `-a`

  Analyze the distribution of key values in the table. This can improve performance of queries by speeding up index-based lookups.

- `--auto-repair` (`mysqlcheck` only)

  Repair tables automatically if a check operation discovers problems.

- `--check` or `-c`

  Check tables for problems. This is the default action if no other operation is specified.

- `--check-only-changed` or `-C`

  Skip table checking except for tables that have been changed since they were last checked or tables that haven't been properly closed. The latter condition might occur if the server crashes while a table is open.

- `--fast` or `-F`

  Skip table checking except for tables that haven't been properly closed.

- `--extended` (for `mysqlcheck`), `--extend-check` (for `myisamchk`), or `-e` (for both programs)

  Run an extended table check. For `mysqlcheck`, when this option is given in conjunction with a repair option, a more thorough repair is performed than when the repair option is given alone. That is, the repair operation performed by `mysqlcheck --repair --extended` is more thorough than the operation performed by `mysqlcheck --repair`.

- `--medium-check` or `-m`

  Run a medium table check.

- `--quick` or `-q`

  For `mysqlcheck`, `--quick` without a repair option causes only the index file to be checked, leaving the data file alone. For both programs, `--quick` in conjunction with a repair option causes the program to repair only the index file, leaving the data file alone.

- `--repair` (for `mysqlcheck`), `--recover` (for `myisamchk`), or `-r` (for both programs)

  Run a table repair operation.

30.4 Repairing InnoDB Tables

As mentioned earlier in this chapter, you can check InnoDB tables by using the CHECK TABLE statement or by using a client program that issues the statement for you. However, if an InnoDB table has problems, you cannot fix it by using REPAIR TABLE because that statement applies only to MyISAM.

If a table check indicates that an InnoDB table has problems, you should be able to restore the table to a consistent state by dumping it with mysqldump, dropping it, and re-creating it from the dump file:

```
shell> mysqldump db_name table_name > dump_file
shell> mysql db_name < dump_file
```

In the event of a crash of the MySQL server or the host on which it runs, some InnoDB tables might need repairs. Normally, it suffices simply to restart the server because the InnoDB storage engine performs auto-recovery as part of its startup sequence. In rare cases, the server might not start up due to failure of InnoDB auto-recovery. If that happens, use the following procedure:

- Restart the server with the --innodb_force_recovery option set to a value in the range from 1 to 6. These values indicate increasing levels of caution in avoiding a crash, and increasing levels of tolerance for possible inconsistency in the recovered tables. A good value to start with is 4.

- When you start the server with --innodb_force_recovery set to a non-zero value, InnoDB treats the tablespace as read-only. Consequently, you should dump the InnoDB tables with mysqldump and then drop them while the option is in effect. Then restart the server without the --innodb_force_recovery option. When the server comes up, recover the InnoDB tables from the dump files.

- If the preceding steps fail, it's necessary to restore the InnoDB tables from a previous backup.

30.5 Enabling MyISAM Auto-Repair

The MySQL server can be instructed to check and repair MyISAM tables automatically. With automatic repair enabled, the server checks each MyISAM table when it opens it to see whether the table was closed properly the last time it was used and is not marked as needing repair. If the table is not okay, the server repairs it.

To enable automatic MyISAM table maintenance, start the server with the --myisam-recover option. The option value can consist of a comma-separated list of one or more of the following values:

- DEFAULT for the default checking.
- BACKUP tells the server to make a backup of any table that it must change.
- FORCE causes table recovery to be performed even if it would cause the loss of more than one row of data.
- QUICK performs quick recovery: Tables that have no holes resulting from deletes or updates are skipped.

For example, to tell the server to perform a forced recovery of MyISAM tables found to have problems but make a backup of any table it changes, you can put the following lines in an option file:

```
[mysqld]
myisam-recover=FORCE,BACKUP
```

The INFORMATION_SCHEMA Database

The INFORMATION_SCHEMA database provides access to database metadata. This chapter discusses why you might choose to use (or not use) INFORMATION_SCHEMA in comparison to SHOW statements, which also provide metadata. The chapter covers the following exam topics:

- Syntax for accessing INFORMATION_SCHEMA
- Using INFORMATION_SCHEMA compared to using SHOW statements
- Limitations of INFORMATION_SCHEMA

Chapter 20, "Obtaining Database Metadata," in the Developer section of this study guide contains additional discussion of metadata access methods. That chapter serves as background for the material here.

31.1 INFORMATION_SCHEMA Access Syntax

This section briefly summarizes the syntax for accessing the contents of the INFORMATION_SCHEMA database. See Chapter 20, "Obtaining Database Metadata," for additional detail.

INFORMATION_SCHEMA is a "virtual database" in the sense that it is not stored anywhere on disk. But like any other database, it contains tables, and its tables contain rows and columns that can be accessed by means of SELECT statements.

To retrieve the contents of an INFORMATION_SCHEMA table, you must know what tables are available. This statement displays their names:

```
mysql> SELECT TABLE_NAME FROM INFORMATION_SCHEMA.TABLES
    -> WHERE TABLE_SCHEMA = 'INFORMATION_SCHEMA';
+----------------------------------------+
| TABLE_NAME                             |
+----------------------------------------+
```

```
| SCHEMATA                                |
| TABLES                                  |
| COLUMNS                                 |
| CHARACTER_SETS                          |
| COLLATIONS                              |
| COLLATION_CHARACTER_SET_APPLICABILITY   |
| ROUTINES                                |
| STATISTICS                              |
| VIEWS                                   |
| USER_PRIVILEGES                         |
| SCHEMA_PRIVILEGES                       |
| TABLE_PRIVILEGES                        |
| COLUMN_PRIVILEGES                       |
| TABLE_CONSTRAINTS                       |
| KEY_COLUMN_USAGE                        |
| TRIGGERS                                |
+-----------------------------------------+
```

To see the names of the columns in an INFORMATION_SCHEMA table (for example, the
CHARACTER_SETS table), use a statement like this:

```
mysql> SELECT COLUMN_NAME FROM INFORMATION_SCHEMA.COLUMNS
    -> WHERE TABLE_SCHEMA = 'INFORMATION_SCHEMA'
    -> AND TABLE_NAME = 'CHARACTER_SETS';
+----------------------+
| COLUMN_NAME          |
+----------------------+
| CHARACTER_SET_NAME   |
| DEFAULT_COLLATE_NAME |
| DESCRIPTION          |
| MAXLEN               |
+----------------------+
```

The preceding queries actually provide metadata about the metadata database, because they
describe some of the structure of INFORMATION_SCHEMA itself. Of course, you can select information about other databases as well. The following statement displays a summary of some
of the characteristics of world database tables:

```
mysql> SELECT TABLE_NAME, TABLE_ROWS, TABLE_COLLATION
    -> FROM INFORMATION_SCHEMA.TABLES
    -> WHERE TABLE_SCHEMA = 'world';
+-----------------+------------+-------------------+
| TABLE_NAME      | TABLE_ROWS | TABLE_COLLATION   |
+-----------------+------------+-------------------+
| City            |       4079 | latin1_swedish_ci |
| Country         |        239 | latin1_swedish_ci |
| CountryLanguage |        984 | latin1_swedish_ci |
+-----------------+------------+-------------------+
```

31.2 INFORMATION_SCHEMA **Versus** SHOW

For the most part, the INFORMATION_SCHEMA database and SHOW statements provide access to similar kinds of metadata. However, sometimes one source of information may be preferable to the other. This section compares them for the purpose of highlighting each one's strengths and weaknesses.

Advantages of INFORMATION_SCHEMA over SHOW:

- INFORMATION_SCHEMA is a feature of standard SQL, whereas SHOW is a MySQL-specific statement. This means that INFORMATION_SCHEMA is more portable. You're likely to have an easier time porting applications for use with other database systems if they use INFORMATION_SCHEMA than if they use SHOW statements.

- With INFORMATION_SCHEMA, you always use SELECT syntax to obtain metadata, regardless of the type of information in which you're interested. SHOW involves a different statement for each type of metadata, and they don't all have the same syntax.

- With SELECT and INFORMATION_SCHEMA, you have complete flexibility to choose what to retrieve. You can name which columns to select, apply arbitrary conditions for restricting which rows to retrieve, and sort the result. SHOW is not so versatile. Some forms of SHOW support a LIKE clause to restrict which rows to display, and MySQL 5 adds a WHERE clause as a more flexible way to restrict the rows. But in either case, the rows returned are in a fixed order. They also consist of a fixed set of columns. You cannot omit columns in which you're not interested.

- Because the information in INFORMATION_SCHEMA can be retrieved with all the flexibility of SELECT, you can use joins, unions, and subqueries. You cannot do the same with SHOW statements.

- By using CREATE TABLE ... SELECT or INSERT ... SELECT, the contents of INFORMATION_SCHEMA can be retrieved and stored into another table for use in subsequent statements. The information produced by SHOW can be retrieved for display only. It cannot be stored in another table.

Advantages of SHOW over INFORMATION_SCHEMA:

- SHOW is available for releases of MySQL older than MySQL 5.
- SHOW is often more concise. For example, the following two statements display the names of the tables in the world database, but the one that uses SHOW clearly is shorter:

```
SHOW TABLES FROM world;

SELECT TABLE_NAME FROM INFORMATION_SCHEMA.TABLES
WHERE TABLE_SCHEMA = 'world';
```

The brevity of SHOW can make it an easier statement to issue. This factor often tilts the balance toward SHOW, especially for interactive use when you're entering statements manually. A SHOW statement also can be easier to remember, compared to the corresponding SELECT that uses INFORMATION_SCHEMA.

31.3 Limitations of INFORMATION_SCHEMA

The INFORMATION_SCHEMA implementation is fairly complete, but there are some kinds of information that it does not yet contain. For example, there are no tables for routine parameters or referential constraints for foreign keys. These omissions may be addressed in the future.

INFORMATION_SCHEMA serves solely as a means of access for metadata. SHOW statements also serve this purpose, but the domain of SHOW extends into other areas as well. Certain SHOW statements provide information about the server's configuration or operational state. Some examples:

- SHOW VARIABLES displays system variables that describe server configuration.
- SHOW STATUS displays status variables that provide information about current server operation.
- SHOW ENGINES lists the storage engines that the server knows about.
- SHOW PROCESSLIST provides information about the currently executing server threads.
- SHOW MASTER STATUS and SHOW SLAVE STATUS provide information about replication servers.

32

Data Backup and Recovery Methods

This chapter discusses techniques for making database backups and how to recover databases from your backups if necessary. It covers the following exam topics:

- Types of backups
- Making binary and text backups
- The role of log and status files in backups
- Using a replication slave for backups
- Performing data recovery

32.1 Introduction

A MySQL administrator makes database backups to guard against the possibility of system crashes or hardware failures that may result in data loss or corruption. Backups also are useful when users remove databases or tables by mistake. Another use for backups is to move or copy databases to another server, such as when you migrate a MySQL installation from one machine to another or set up a replication slave server.

Backups can be made by copying database files directly, or by using programs designed for that purpose. Such programs include `mysqldump`, `mysqlhotcopy`, MySQL Administrator, and InnoDB Hot Backup.

It's necessary to make backups, but a backup is only one of the components needed for data recovery after loss or damage. The other is the binary log, which contains a record of data changes. To recover databases, you use the backup to restore them to their state at backup time, and then re-execute statements contained in the binary log that made data changes after the backup was created.

Here are some principles to keep in mind with regard to backups:

- Make backups regularly.
- Enable the binary log so that you have a record of changes made after a given backup.
- Flush the logs when backing up so that the server will begin a new binary log file that corresponds to the time of the backup. (That is, "checkpoint" the log to the backup.)
- Store your data directory and your backups on different physical devices so that a device failure cannot destroy both.
- Include your backups in your normal filesystem backup procedures so that you can recover the backup if necessary.

32.2 Binary Versus Textual Backups

When you back up databases, you have a choice of two backup formats:

- A binary backup is a copy of the files in which database contents are stored. Copying these files preserves the databases in exactly the same format in which MySQL itself stores them on disk. Restoration involves copying the files back to their original locations. Techniques for making binary backups include file copy commands (such as `cp` or `tar`), `mysqlhotcopy`, and InnoDB Hot Backup.
- A text backup is a dump of database contents into text files. Restoration involves loading the file contents back into databases by processing them through the server. Techniques for making text backups include the `SELECT ... INTO OUTFILE` SQL statement, `mysqldump`, and MySQL Administrator.

The two backup formats have different strengths and weaknesses. The general tradeoff is speed versus portability.

It's faster to make a binary backup because it involves only file copy operations that need know nothing about the internal structure of the files. However, if the backup is to be used for transferring databases to another machine that uses a different architecture, the files must be binary portable. Binary portability means that the files are machine independent and that you can directly copy them from one MySQL server to another on a different machine and the second server will be able to access their contents with no problems. (See Section 32.3.4, "Conditions for Binary Portability.") With binary backup methods, it's necessary to make sure that the server does not modify the files while the backup is in progress.

It's slower to make a text backup because the server must read tables (which involves the overhead of interpreting their contents) and then either write the contents out to disk files itself or send the contents to a client program that writes the tables. An example of the latter approach is the `mysqldump` client, which receives table contents from the server and writes them out as `INSERT` statements that can be reloaded to re-create tables. Text backups are portable, so a text backup made on one machine can be reloaded into the MySQL server on another machine, regardless of whether the two machines have the same architecture. With text backup methods, the server must be running because it must read the files that are to be backed up.

The procedure for making binary backups depends on which storage engine created the tables, and generally can be used only for the local MySQL server. Text backup procedures are more general and can be used for tables created by any storage engine. Some methods can be used with either local or remote MySQL servers.

32.3 Making Binary Backups

This section describes methods that you can use to make binary-format database or table backups.

32.3.1 Making Binary MyISAM Backups

To make a binary backup of a MyISAM table, copy the .frm, .MYD, and .MYI files that MySQL uses to represent the table. When you do this, the table must not be in use by other programs (including the server) during the copy operation. If you stop the server while copying the table, there will be no problem of server interaction. If you leave the server running, use an appropriate locking protocol to prevent server access to the table. For example, to copy the Country table in the world database, lock the table and flush any pending changes like this:

```
mysql> USE world;
mysql> LOCK TABLES Country READ;
mysql> FLUSH TABLES Country;
```

Then (with the table still locked) use your operating system's file copy command to copy the table files. After the copy operation completes, release the lock on the table:

```
mysql> UNLOCK TABLES;
```

The preceding strategy works on Unix. On Windows, file-locking behavior is such that you might not be able to copy table files for tables that are locked by the server. In that case, you must stop the server before copying table files.

Another way to make binary MyISAM backups is to use mysqlhotcopy, which does the locking and flushing for you. See Section 32.3.3.1, "mysqlhotcopy."

To recover a MyISAM table from a binary backup, stop the server, copy the backup table files into the appropriate database directory, and restart the server. If you want to use the files with another MySQL server, the requirements that must be satisfied are described in Section 32.3.4, "Conditions for Binary Portability."

32.3.2 Making Binary InnoDB Backups

A binary backup operation that makes a complete InnoDB backup (a backup of all tables in the InnoDB tablespace) is based on making exact copies of all files that InnoDB uses to manage the tablespace.

To make an InnoDB binary backup, use the following procedure:

1. Stop the server for the duration of the copy operation. The tablespace must not be in use when copying the tablespace files.

2. Make sure that the server shut down without error. Binary InnoDB backups require a clean shutdown to be certain that the server has completed any pending transactions.

3. Make a copy of each of the following components:

   - The .frm file for each InnoDB table.
   - The tablespace files. This includes the files for the shared tablespace. It also includes the .ibd files if you have configured InnoDB to use per-table tablespaces.
   - The InnoDB log files.
   - Any InnoDB configuration options, such as those stored in option files. The configuration options are required in case you need to restore the backup from scratch. In that case, you'll need to know how the tablespace and log files were created originally.

4. Restart the server.

Another way to make binary InnoDB backups is to use InnoDB Hot Backup. See Section 32.3.3.2, "InnoDB Hot Backup."

To recover an InnoDB tablespace using a binary backup, stop the server, replace all the components that you made copies of during the backup procedure, and restart the server.

If you want to use a binary InnoDB backup to copy your InnoDB tables to another server, the requirements that must be satisfied are described in Section 32.3.4, "Conditions for Binary Portability." Note that the necessity of copying the tablespace files as a group means that for recovery operations you'll need to *replace* any existing tablespace files on the destination server. You cannot add one tablespace to another using a binary backup.

An alternative to making a binary backup is to dump table contents in text format (for example, with mysqldump). This technique can be useful for copying individual InnoDB tables from one server to another or if the conditions for binary portability are not satisfied. It can also be used to add tables from one tablespace to another: Run mysqldump to dump the tables into a text file, and then load the file into the destination server using mysql.

32.3.3 Other Binary Backup Tools

The programs described in this section, `mysqlhotcopy` and InnoDB Hot Backup, are special-purpose programs that can be used with particular storage engines to help you make binary backups.

32.3.3.1 `mysqlhotcopy`

The `mysqlhotcopy` script copies tables to a backup directory. It is a Perl script and requires the DBI module to be installed. It runs on Unix and NetWare. `mysqlhotcopy` works for `MyISAM` tables but not `InnoDB` tables.

`mysqlhotcopy` connects to the local MySQL server, locks the tables so that the server will not change them, flushes the tables to make sure that any pending changes are written to disk, and then copies the table files. When it has finished the copy operation, it unlocks the tables.

`mysqlhotcopy` must be run on the server host so that it can copy table files while the table locks are in place. It must be run while the server is running so that it can connect to the server to lock and flush the tables.

Operation of `mysqlhotcopy` is fast because it copies table files directly rather than backing them up over the network. It's also more convenient than issuing statements to the server to lock and flush the tables, because it handles those operations for you.

`mysqlhotcopy` has many options, which you can see by invoking it with the `--help` option. The following examples present some simple ways to use `mysqlhotcopy`:

- Back up the `world` database to a directory named `world` in the /var/archive directory:

```
shell> mysqlhotcopy world /var/archive
Locked 3 tables in 0 seconds.
Flushed tables (`world`.`City`, `world`.`Country`,
`world`.`CountryLanguage`) in 0 seconds.
Copying 10 files...
Copying indices for 0 files...
Unlocked tables.
mysqlhotcopy copied 3 tables (10 files) in 0 seconds (0 seconds overall).
```

- Back up only the tables in the `world` database whose name contains `Country`:

```
shell> mysqlhotcopy world./Country/ /var/archive
Locked 2 tables in 0 seconds.
Flushed tables (`world`.`Country`,
`world`.`CountryLanguage`) in 0 seconds.
Copying 6 files...
Copying indices for 0 files...
Unlocked tables.
mysqlhotcopy copied 2 tables (6 files) in 0 seconds (0 seconds overall).
```

32.3.3.2 InnoDB Hot Backup

The InnoDB Hot Backup program (ibbackup) is a commercial product available from Innobase Oy. It can back up InnoDB tables while the server is running without disturbing normal database activity. It's available for Unix and Windows.

32.3.4 Conditions for Binary Portability

Binary portability is important if you want to take a binary backup that was made on one machine and use it on another machine that has a different architecture. For example, using a binary backup is one way to copy databases from one MySQL server to another.

For MyISAM, binary portability means that you can directly copy the files for a MyISAM table from one MySQL server to another on a different machine and the second server will be able to access the table.

For InnoDB, binary portability means that you can directly copy the tablespace files from a MySQL server on one machine to another server on a different machine and the second server will be able to access the tablespace. By default, all InnoDB tables managed by a server are stored together in the tablespace, so portability of the tablespace is a function of whether all individual InnoDB tables are portable. If even one table is not portable, neither is the tablespace.

MyISAM tables and InnoDB tablespaces are binary portable from one host to another if two conditions are met:

- Both machines must use two's-complement integer arithmetic.
- Both machines must use IEEE floating-point format, or else the tables must contain no floating-point columns (FLOAT or DOUBLE).

In practice, those two conditions pose little restriction. Two's-complement integer arithmetic and IEEE floating-point format are the norm on modern hardware.

A third condition for InnoDB binary portability is that you should use lowercase names for databases and tables. This is because InnoDB stores these names internally (in its data dictionary) in lowercase on Windows. Using lowercase names allows binary portability between Windows and Unix. To force the use of lowercase names, you can put the following lines in an option file:

```
[mysqld]
lower_case_table_names=1
```

If you configure InnoDB to use per-table tablespaces, the conditions for binary portability are extended to include the .ibd files for InnoDB tables as well. (The conditions for the shared tablespace still apply because it contains the data dictionary that stores information about all InnoDB tables.)

If the conditions for binary portability are not satisfied, you can copy MyISAM or InnoDB tables from one server to another by dumping them using some text format (for example, with mysqldump) and reloading them into the destination server.

32.4 Making Text Backups

This section describes methods that you can use to make text-format database or table backups.

32.4.1 Making Text Backups via SQL

The SELECT ... INTO OUTFILE statement writes the contents of an arbitrary result set to a disk file on the server host. For backup purposes, it can be used in the following form to write a text dump of an entire table:

```
SELECT * INTO OUTFILE 'file_name' FROM table_name;
```

SELECT ... INTO OUTFILE has the following characteristics:

- The statement can be used with either local or remote servers. The resulting disk file is always created on the server host, however, because the server itself writes the file.
- The output file must not already exist.
- The statement works for any storage engine.
- The statement requires the FILE privilege.
- The output format can be controlled by using statement options that specify column and line delimiters, quote characters, and escape characters.

For more detail on the SELECT ... INTO OUTFILE statement, see Section 15.2.2, "Exporting Data with SELECT ... INTO OUTFILE."

32.4.2 Making Text Backups with mysqldump

The mysqldump client program dumps table contents to files. It has the following characteristics:

- It can dump all databases, specific databases, or specific tables.
- mysqldump can back up local or remote servers, although the destination for the dump files depends on how you invoke it. For tab-delimited data files made using the --tab option, the server writes them on the server host. For SQL-format dump files that contain CREATE TABLE and INSERT statements for re-creating the tables, the server sends table contents to mysqldump, which writes the files on the client host.

- It works for tables created by any storage engine.
- Output files are written in text format and are portable, so they can be used for trans-ferring database contents to another server.

This section concentrates on using mysqldump to produce SQL-format dump files. Instructions for using mysqldump to produce tab-delimited data files are given in Section 15.3.2, "Exporting Data with mysqldump."

When you use mysqldump to make SQL-format dump files, it has three general modes of operation, depending on the arguments with which you invoke it:

- By default, mysqldump interprets its first non-option argument as a database name and dumps all the tables in that database. If any other arguments follow the database name, mysqldump interprets them as table names and dumps just those tables. The following command dumps the contents of all the tables in the world database into a file named world.sql:

```
shell> mysqldump world > world.sql
```

The contents of the world.sql file will begin something like this (statements to create and load the other tables in the database would follow the partial display shown here):

```
-- MySQL dump 10.10
--
-- Host: localhost    Database: world
-- -------------------------------------------------------
-- Server version       5.0.10-beta-log

...


--
-- Table structure for table `City`
--

DROP TABLE IF EXISTS `City`;
CREATE TABLE `City` (
  `ID` int(11) NOT NULL auto_increment,
  `Name` char(35) NOT NULL default '',
  `CountryCode` char(3) NOT NULL default '',
  `District` char(20) NOT NULL default '',
  `Population` int(11) NOT NULL default '0',
  PRIMARY KEY  (`ID`)
) ENGINE=MyISAM DEFAULT CHARSET=latin1;


--
-- Dumping data for table `City`
--
```

```
/*!40000 ALTER TABLE `City` DISABLE KEYS */;
LOCK TABLES `City` WRITE;
INSERT INTO `City` VALUES (1,'Kabul','AFG','Kabol',1780000), ...
UNLOCK TABLES;
...
```

The following command names just the City and Country tables after the database name, so mysqldump dumps just those tables to a file called city_country.sql:

```
shell> mysqldump world City Country > city_country.sql
```

- With the --databases (or -B) option, mysqldump interprets any non-option argument as a database name and dumps all the tables in each of the named databases. For example, the following command dumps both the world and test databases into a single file:

```
shell> mysqldump --databases world test > world_and_test.sql
```

- With the --all-databases (or -A) option, mysqldump dumps all tables in all databases. For example, this command writes a backup for all databases to the file alldb.sql:

```
shell> mysqldump --all-databases > alldb.sql
```

If you manage a lot of data, alldb.sql will be very large. Be sure that you have sufficient free disk space before issuing such a command.

mysqldump understands the standard connection parameter options, such as --host and --user. You'll need to supply these options if the default connection parameters aren't appropriate. mysqldump also understands options that provide more specific control over the dump operation. Invoke mysqldump with the --help option to see a list of available options. The options described in the following list are some of those that you're likely to find most useful:

- --add-drop-table

  Instructs mysqldump to precede the dump output for each table with a DROP TABLE statement that drops the table. This option ensures that when you reload the dump output, the reload operation removes any existing copy of the table before re-creating it.

- --add-locks

  Adds statements around INSERT statements that acquire table locks for the dumped tables.

- --create-options

  Instructs mysqldump to produce CREATE TABLE statements that include all the MySQL-specific options with which each table was created. By default, mysqldump does not include all these options, resulting in dump files that might be more portable for loading with a DBMS other than MySQL. With the --create-options option, tables created during reloading into MySQL will have the same options as the original tables.

- `--disable-keys`

  Includes ALTER TABLE statements in the dump file that disable and enable index updating. For MyISAM tables, this makes reloading faster.

- `--extended-insert` or `-e`

  By default, mysqldump writes each row as a separate INSERT statement. This option produces multiple-row INSERT statements that add several rows to the table at a time. Multiple-row statements can be reloaded more efficiently, although they're less readable than single-row statements if you examine the dump output. They're also less portable and less likely to be understood by other database systems.

- `--flush-logs`

  Tells the server to flush the logs before starting the dump. This causes the next binary log to be synchronized (checkpointed) to the time of the dump, which is useful when performing data recovery operations.

- `--lock-tables`

  Before dumping tables, mysqldump acquires a READ LOCAL lock for all of them. For MyISAM tables, a READ LOCAL lock allows concurrent inserts to proceed while tables are being dumped. (See Section 28.2, "Explicit Table Locking.")

- `--no-create-db` or `-n`

  Normally, when you run mysqldump with the `--all-databases` or `--databases` option, the program precedes the dump output for each database with a CREATE DATABASE statement to ensure that the database is created if it doesn't already exist. The `--no-create-db` option causes CREATE DATABASE statements not to be written. Note that their presence in the file is usually not a problem. They include an IF NOT EXISTS clause, so they're ignored when reloading the dump file for any database that does exist.

- `--no-create-info` or `-t`

  This option suppresses the CREATE TABLE statement that normally precedes the INSERT statements containing a table's data. Use this option when you're interested in dumping only a table's data. The option is useful mostly when you plan to reload the data into tables that already exist.

- `--no-data` or `-d`

  This option suppresses the INSERT statements containing table data. Use this option when you're interested in dumping only the CREATE TABLE statements that describe table structures. The `--no-data` option provides an easy way to get a dump file that can be processed to create empty tables with the same structure as the original tables.

- `--opt`

  This option turns on a set of additional options to make the dump and reload operations more efficient. Specifically, it's equivalent to using the `--add-drop-table`, `--add-locks`, `--create-options`, `--quick`, `--extended-insert`, `--lock-tables`, and `--disable-keys` options together. Note that this option makes the output less portable and less likely to be understood by other database systems. This option has been enabled by default since MySQL 4.1. To disable it, use `--skip-opt`. To leave the option enabled but disable individual options that `--opt` turns on, use their `--skip` forms. For example, to disable `--quick`, use `--skip-quick`.

- `--quick`

  This option tells `mysqldump` to write dump output as it reads each row from the server, which might be useful for large tables. By default, `mysqldump` reads all rows from a table into memory before writing the output; for large tables, this requires large amounts of memory, possibly causing the dump to fail.

- `--single-transaction`

  Dumps tables within a transaction. This is recommended when dumping `InnoDB` tables. It uses a consistent read to allow a dump to be made that reflects `InnoDB` state as of the beginning of the dump, regardless of the activity of other clients.

32.4.3 Making Text Backups with MySQL Administrator

The MySQL Administrator GUI program provides backup and restore capabilities. It generates backup files containing SQL statements that can be reloaded into your MySQL server to re-create databases and tables. These files are similar to the SQL-format backup files generated by `mysqldump`.

MySQL Administrator stores backup configuration options as projects. You can select and execute these projects later to perform a backup operation based on a given set of specifications. The project approach enables you to easily select from among multiple types of backups. You can select backup projects on demand or schedule them for periodic execution.

For more information about these capabilities of MySQL Administrator, see Section 26.5, "Backup and Restore Capabilities."

32.5 Backing Up Log and Status Files

In addition to backing up your databases, you should also back up the following files:

- Your binary log files. This is necessary because if you have to perform a recovery operation, the binary logs store updates that have been made after the backup was made.

- Option files used by the server (`my.cnf` and `my.ini` files). These files contain configuration information that must be restored after a crash.

- Replication slave servers create a `master.info` file that contains information needed for connecting to the master server, and a `relay-log.info` file that indicates the current progress in processing the relay logs.

- Replication slaves create data files for processing `LOAD DATA INFILE` statements. These files are located in the directory named by the `slave_load_tmpdir` system variable, which can be set by starting the server with the `--slave-load-tmpdir` option. If `slave_load_tmpdir` is not set, the value of the `tmpdir` system variable applies. The data files to back up have names beginning with `SQL_LOAD-`.

To back up the preceding files, you can use normal file system operation. Static files such as option files can be backed up with no special precautions. Dynamic files such as logs that the server changes as it runs are best backed up with the server stopped.

32.6 Replication as an Aid to Backup

If your MySQL server acts as a master in a replication setup, you can use a slave server to make your backups instead of backing up the master:

1. Cause the server to stop processing updates received from the master. You can do this by stopping the server, or by issuing a `STOP SLAVE SQL_THREAD` statement. In the latter case, you should also flush the tables to force pending changes to disk.

2. Make a backup of the slave's databases. The allowable methods depend on whether you stop the server or leave it running. For example, if you stop the server, you cannot use any program that must connect to it, such as `mysqldump` or `mysqlhotcopy`.

3. Restart the server if you stopped it. If you left it running, restart the SQL thread by issuing a `START SLAVE SQL_THREAD` statement.

The advantage of making a backup this way is that it doesn't take place on the master server. Thus, the master need not be interrupted at all, and the backup procedure does not impose any extra disk or processing load on it.

32.7 MySQL Cluster as Disaster Prevention

MySQL Cluster uses an architecture in which multiple processes act as cluster nodes that provide multiple copies of table data. This use of multiple processes is not in itself a backup technique, but it does provide data redundancy that lessens the potential for data loss if any given node becomes unavailable. Thus, the likelihood that you'll need to resort to disaster recovery techniques is reduced. Adding more nodes increases redundancy further.

See Section 29.7, "The Cluster Storage Engine," for a general description of MySQL Cluster architecture, and the *MySQL Reference Manual* for detailed discussion.

32.8 Data Recovery

A backup is one component needed for a data recovery operation. It serves as a snapshot of your databases at a given point in time (the time when the backup was made). However, for an active server, data changes will have been made after the most recent backup. The other component of a restore operation is the record that the server has of those changes—that is, the binary log. A recovery operation therefore involves using the backup to restore the databases, and then re-executing the modifications contained in the binary log that were made after the backup.

The general recovery procedure follows these steps:

1. Make a copy of the data directory first, in case something goes wrong during recovery.

2. Recover your databases using your backup files. If you made a binary backup, this step involves stopping the server and replacing the lost or damaged files with the copies. For MyISAM and InnoDB tables, the files that you need to replace are described in Section 32.3, "Making Binary Backups." If you made a text backup, reload the dump file or files as described in Section 32.8.1, "Reloading mysqldump Output," or Section 32.8.2, "Reloading Dumps with MySQL Administrator."

3. Re-execute the changes in the binary log that were recorded after your backup was made. See Section 32.8.3, "Processing Binary Log Contents."

32.8.1 Reloading mysqldump Output

To reload an SQL-format dump file produced by mysqldump, process it with mysql. For example, you might have made a copy of the Country table in the world database with this command:

```
shell> mysqldump world Country > dump.sql
```

To reload the file later, use mysql:

```
shell> mysql world < dump.sql
```

The mysql command for reloading mysqldump output should name the database if the dump file itself does not. It is not necessary to name the database if you are reloading a dump file created by invoking mysqldump with the --database or --all-databases option. In that case, the dump file contains appropriate USE *db_name* statements.

mysqldump output can be used not just to restore tables or databases, but also to copy them. mysql can read from a pipe, so you can combine the use of mysqldump and mysql into a single command that copies tables from one database to another. For example, to copy the Country table from the world database to the test database, use this command:

```
shell> mysqldump world Country | mysql test
```

The pipe technique also can be used to copy databases or tables over the network to another server. The following command uses a pipe to copy the Country table from the world database on the local host to the world database on the remote host other.host.com:

```
shell> mysqldump world Country | mysql -h other.host.com world
```

If a dump file contains very long INSERT statements, they might exceed the default size of the communications buffer (1MB). You can increase the buffer size for both mysqldump and mysql with the --max-allowed-packet option. The option value may be given in bytes or followed by K, M, or G to indicate a size in kilobytes, megabytes, or gigabytes. For example, --max-allowed-packet=32M specifies a size of 32MB. The server also must be run with a --max-allowed-packet value that increases its own communications buffer to be large enough.

If you invoke mysqldump with the --tab option, it produces tab-delimited data files. (See Section 15.3.2, "Exporting Data with mysqldump.") In this case, reloading the files requires a different approach. Suppose that you dump the table City from the world database using the /tmp directory as the output directory:

```
shell> mysqldump --tab=/tmp world City
```

The output will consist of a City.sql file containing the CREATE TABLE statement for the table, and a City.txt file containing the table data. To reload the table, change location into the dump directory, process the .sql file using mysql, and load the .txt file using mysqlimport:

```
shell> cd /tmp
shell> mysql world < City.sql
shell> mysqlimport world City.txt
```

If you combine the --tab option with format-control options such as --fields-terminated-by and --fields-enclosed-by, you should specify the same format-control options with mysqlimport so that it knows how to interpret the data files.

32.8.2 Reloading Dumps with MySQL Administrator

MySQL Administrator can reload SQL-format dump files such as those created by itself or mysqldump. It can also analyze a dump file to see what tables it will restore, and then present a dialog that allows you to exclude tables from the restore operation. This is useful if you want MySQL Administrator to process only part of a dump file (for example, to recover only certain tables from a full-database dump).

For more information about these capabilities of MySQL Administrator, see Section 26.5, "Backup and Restore Capabilities."

32.8.3 Processing Binary Log Contents

After you have restored your binary backup files or reloaded your text backup files, you should finish a recovery operation by reprocessing the data changes that are recorded in the server's binary logs. To do this, determine which logs were written after you made your backup. Then convert their contents to text SQL statements with the mysqlbinlog program and process the resulting statements with mysql.

It's easiest to process the binary logs if each log file was written entirely before or entirely after the time of the backup. For example, if your log files were numbered 1 to 49 before the backup and logs 50 to 52 were written after the backup, you'll need to process logs 50 to 52 after restoring the backup. If your binary logs are named with a prefix of bin, the log processing command looks like this:

```
shell> mysqlbinlog bin.000050 bin.000051 bin.000052 | mysql
```

All the binary log files that you want to process should be handled in a single mysqlbinlog command. There may be inter-file dependencies that will not be satisfied if you process them separately.

If a given binary log file was in the middle of being written during the backup, you must extract from it only the part that was written after the backup, plus all log files written after that. To handle partial-file extraction, mysqlbinlog supports options that enable you to specify the time or log position at which to begin extracting log contents:

- The --start-datetime option specifies the date and time at which to begin extraction, where the option argument is given in DATETIME format.
- The --start-position option can be used to specify extraction beginning at a given log position.
- There are also corresponding --stop-datetime and --stop-position options for specifying the point at which to stop extracting log contents.

For example, to extract the contents of logs 50 to 52 beginning with events recorded at 2005-05-20 17:43:20, modify the previous command as follows:

```
shell> mysqlbinlog --start-datetime="2005-05-20 17:43:20"
          bin.000050 bin.000051 bin.000052 | mysql
```

If you're not sure about the timestamp or position in a log file that corresponds to the point at which you want processing to begin, use mysqlbinlog without mysql to display the log contents for examination. In this case, a pager program can be useful:

```
shell> mysqlbinlog file_name | more
```

MySQL DBA II Exam

Using Stored Routines and Triggers for Administration

This chapter discusses administrative benefits of using stored routines and triggers. It covers the following exam topics:

- Using stored routines and triggers for security purposes
- Using stored routines to enhance performance

33.1 Using Stored Routines and Triggers for Security Purposes

Stored routines provide security benefits for database administrators. You can define routines that safely access protected data on behalf of ordinary (non-administrative) users, but do not return information that these users should not see. To implement this kind of security precaution, use the combination of the DEFINER security characteristic in the routine definition and the EXECUTE access privilege.

Suppose that you have a table containing sales transactions that should not be visible to ordinary users, but for which summary values of total sales volume need no protection. Create a routine that calculates the summary, using an account that has direct access to the table, and use the DEFINER security characteristic in the routine definition so that it executes with that account's privileges and also has access to the table. Then grant the EXECUTE privilege for the routine to those users who should be able to invoke it. In this way, users gain access to the information provided by the routine, but the protected data used to produce that information remains inaccessible to them.

Stored routines also are useful for data protection in operations that modify data. A stored routine can make changes to tables in a safe way, without giving users direct access to the tables. This prevents them from making possibly unsafe changes themselves. To take this approach, use the following strategy:

- For the tables in question, disallow direct access by ordinary users for INSERT, UPDATE, and DELETE statements. (You can do this by granting the appropriate privileges to administrative users only.)

- Implement a procedural interface for modifying each table. That is, using an administrative account that has access to the table, write stored procedures that have DEFINER security and that perform the required modifications to the table, given appropriate data values as parameters. Grant the EXECUTE privilege for these routines to the appropriate users.

- Require users to perform table modifications by calling the stored routines and passing column values for the rows to be modified as parameters. Each procedure examines its arguments and verifies that they satisfy whatever constraints are deemed necessary. If the arguments are suitable, the procedure performs the requested modification. If they are not, the procedure aborts the operation.

The stored procedures thus act as gateways that check incoming data for legality, perform the requested operation only if it is safe to do so, and reject the attempt otherwise.

This procedural approach also can be used if you want to allow or disallow a modification based on factors other than the legality of column value parameters, such as the identity of the client user or the current date and time. For example, you might have a poll that has an expiration date, after which any attempt to insert new records into a vote table should be rejected. A time-based procedure can implement this constraint.

Triggers provide another way to increase database security for data modification operations, by changing the operation of statements with which triggers are associated (INSERT, UPDATE, and DELETE). For this purpose, AFTER triggers are less useful than BEFORE triggers. By the time an AFTER trigger sees an incoming data value, it has already been stored in the database and it is too late to take any corrective action if the value is invalid. A BEFORE trigger, in contrast, can examine an incoming data value and check it to see whether it is reasonable. If not, the trigger can modify the value to be more suitable before it is stored in the database. For example, a value that is out of bounds can be changed to be within bounds. A value that is not in any of a set of allowable categories can be assigned to a default category. In both cases, the trigger prevents an invalid value from entering the database by mapping it to a valid value.

The preceding trigger strategy is useful if you want only to filter incoming data. If the objective is to cancel an operation entirely when data values are unsuitable, you cannot do this in MySQL using a trigger. However, you can do so using the procedural approach outlined earlier in this section: Disallow direct table access to ordinary users and require them to call stored procedures that perform or reject requested modifications.

33.2 Using Stored Routines to Enhance Performance

The use of stored routines can make a significant difference in the performance of an application. The benefits occur in terms of both the amount of network bandwidth consumed by the exchange of information between a client and the server, and the time necessary for those exchanges to occur.

Consider the case of a moderately complex operation that, without the use of stored routines, requires the client to send 10 SQL statements to the server and to process the result of each one before producing a final result. The operation involves 10 statements sent to the server, and 10 results returned to the client. Some of the results might be simple indications of success or failure, but some might be result sets containing many rows to be processed by the client. This can produce a significant amount of network traffic, and it takes time for all of it to be transmitted.

If the operation is implemented as a stored procedure, the performance characteristics change. The procedure is sent to the server once and stored there. To execute the operation later, the client invokes the routine. In this case, the server executes the statements in the routine without them having to be sent again by the client. Also, the server processes the result of each statement as it executes it without the result having to cross the network. The only traffic generated is for the statement that invokes the routine and the final result that it produces.

Moving processing to the server side can be beneficial in environments where clients are not equipped to do much computation, such as is often the case for mobile clients.

34

User Management

This chapter discusses how to manage accounts for clients that connect to the MySQL server to access database contents. It covers the following exam topics:

- The grant tables that store account information
- The SQL statements used for account management
- How the server uses the grant table contents to control client access

34.1 User Account Management

The MySQL access control system enables you to create MySQL accounts and define what each account can do. In MySQL, the concept of "account" is tied to two things: a username and a hostname. That is, when you connect to the server, it checks not only the username that you specify, but also what host you're connecting from. One implication of this concept of an account is that it is possible to set up separate accounts for different users who have the same username but connect from different hosts.

In SQL statements that require account names, the name is given in `'user_name'@'host_name'` format. It is also possible to specify a pattern for the host part so that the account can be used for connecting to the MySQL server from several client hosts. For example, an account name given as `'maria'@'%.example.com'` would apply to a user named maria who connects from any host in the example.com domain.

Several types of privileges can be granted to an account. Privileges should be granted according to how the account is to be used. Some examples:

- An account that needs only read access to a database can be given only the SELECT privilege.
- An account that needs to modify data can be given the DELETE, INSERT, and UPDATE privileges.
- Administrative accounts can be given the PROCESS or SUPER privileges for viewing client process activity or killing connections, or the SHUTDOWN privilege for stopping the server.

The MySQL server bases access control on the contents of the grant tables in the mysql database. These tables define MySQL accounts and the privileges they hold. To manage their contents, use statements such as CREATE USER, GRANT, and REVOKE. These statements provide an interface to the grant tables that enables you to specify account-management operations without having to determine how to modify the tables directly. The MySQL server determines what changes to the grant tables are needed and makes the modifications for you.

The following discussion describes the structure and contents of the grant tables and the various SQL statements that help you manage user accounts. Section 34.2, "Client Access Control," describes how the server uses the grant tables to check access privileges when clients connect.

Note: When you install MySQL, any initial accounts specified in the grant tables should be given passwords. The procedure for doing this is covered in Section 35.5.1, "Securing the Initial MySQL Accounts."

34.1.1 Types of Privileges That MySQL Supports

You can grant several types of privileges to a MySQL account, and you can grant privileges at different levels (globally or just for particular databases, tables, or columns). For example, you can allow a user to select from any table in any database by granting the SELECT privilege at the global level. Or you might grant an account no global privileges, but give it complete control over a specific database. That allows the account to create the database and tables in it, select from the tables, and add new records, delete them, or update them.

The privileges that MySQL supports are shown in the following tables. The first lists the administrative privileges and the second lists the privileges that control access to databases or objects stored in databases.

Administrative Privileges:

Privilege	Operations Allowed by Privilege
CREATE TEMPORARY TABLES	Use TEMPORARY with CREATE TABLE
CREATE USER	Create, drop, rename accounts
FILE	Use statements that read or write files on the server host
LOCK TABLES	Explicitly lock tables with LOCK TABLES
PROCESS	View process (thread) activity
RELOAD	Use FLUSH and RESET
REPLICATION CLIENT	Ask server for information about replication hosts
REPLICATION SLAVE	Act as a replication slave
SHOW DATABASES	See all database names with SHOW DATABASES
SHUTDOWN	Shut down the server
SUPER	Miscellaneous administrative operations

Database-Access Privileges:

Privilege	Operations Allowed by Privilege
ALTER	Modify tables with ALTER TABLE
ALTER ROUTINE	Alter or drop stored routines
CREATE	Create databases and tables
CREATE ROUTINE	Create stored routines
CREATE VIEW	Create views
DELETE	Remove rows from tables
DROP	Drop databases and tables
EXECUTE	Execute stored routines
GRANT OPTION	Grant privileges to other accounts
INDEX	Create and drop indexes
INSERT	Add rows to tables
SELECT	Select records from tables
SHOW VIEW	Use SHOW CREATE VIEW
UPDATE	Modify records in tables

There is also a REFERENCES privilege, but it is unused currently.

There are also some special privilege specifiers:

- ALL and ALL PRIVILEGES are shorthand for "all privileges except GRANT OPTION." That is, they are shorthand for granting all privileges except the ability to give privileges to other accounts.

- USAGE means "no privileges" other than being allowed to connect to the server. Granting this "privilege" causes a record to be created in the user table for the account, but without any privileges. This causes the account to exist, and it can then be used to access the server for limited purposes such as issuing SHOW VARIABLES or SHOW STATUS statements. The account cannot be used to access database contents such as tables (although you could grant such privileges to the account at a later time).

Privileges can exist at different levels:

- Any privilege can be granted globally. An account that possesses a global privilege can exercise it at any time. Global privileges are therefore quite powerful and are normally granted only to administrative accounts. For example, a global DELETE privilege allows the account to remove records from any table in any database.

- Some privileges can be granted for specific databases: ALTER, CREATE, CREATE TEMPORARY TABLES, CREATE VIEW, DELETE, DROP, GRANT OPTION, INDEX, INSERT, LOCK TABLES, SELECT, SHOW VIEW, and UPDATE. A database-level privilege applies to all tables and stored routines in the database.

- Some privileges can be granted for specific tables: ALTER, CREATE, DELETE, DROP, GRANT OPTION, INDEX, INSERT, SELECT, and UPDATE. A table-level privilege applies to all columns in the table.

- Some privileges can be granted for specific table columns: INSERT, SELECT, and UPDATE.

- Some privileges can be granted for specific stored routines: EXECUTE, ALTER ROUTINE, and GRANT OPTION.

34.1.2 The Grant Tables

Several grant tables in the mysql database contain most of the access control information used by the server. They contain information to indicate what the legal accounts are and the privileges held at each access level by each account:

- The user table contains a record for each account known to the server. The user record for an account lists its global privileges. It also indicates other information about the account, such as any resource limits it is subject to, and whether client connections that use the account must be made over a secure connection using the Secure Sockets Layer (SSL). Use of SSL connections is not covered on the exam.

- The db table lists database-specific privileges for accounts.

- The tables_priv table lists table-specific privileges for accounts.

- The columns_priv table lists column-specific privileges for accounts.

- The procs_priv table lists privileges that accounts have for stored procedures and functions.

Every account must have a user table record because the server uses that table's contents when determining whether to accept or reject client connection attempts. An account also will have records in the other grant tables if it has privileges at other than the global level.

Each grant table has columns that identify which accounts its records apply to:

- The server decides whether a client can connect based on the Host, User, and Password columns of the user table. An account is defined by a hostname and username, so for a client to be able to connect, some record in the user table must match the host from which the client connects and the username given by the client. In addition, the client must provide the password listed in the matching record.

- After a client connects, the server determines its access privileges based on the Host and User columns of the user, db, tables_priv, columns_priv, and procs_priv tables. Any privileges enabled in the matching user table record may be used globally by the client. The privileges in the matching records of the other grant tables apply in more limited contexts. For example, privileges in a db table record apply to the database named in the record, but not to other databases.

Use of the grant tables for controlling what clients can do is discussed further in Section 34.2, "Client Access Control."

There is also another grant table named host that exists for historical reasons. It is not affected by the GRANT and REVOKE statements, so it is discussed no further here. For more information about the host table, see the *MySQL Reference Manual.*

If you look in the mysql database, you might also see a user_info table. This table is created by MySQL Administrator, but has nothing to do with access control, so it's not covered here.

The grant tables are created during MySQL installation as MyISAM tables. The MyISAM storage engine is always guaranteed to be enabled, which is not true for optional storage engines such as InnoDB. (InnoDB is enabled by default, but it can be turned off.)

As already mentioned, the server uses the information in the grant tables to determine whether to allow clients to connect, and to determine for every statement that a connected client issues whether it has sufficient privileges to execute it. However, the server does not actually access the on-disk grant tables each time it needs to verify client access because that would result in a great deal of overhead. Instead, the server reads the grant tables into memory during its startup sequence and uses the in-memory copies to check client access.

The server refreshes its in-memory copies of the grant tables under the following conditions:

- You modify a user account in the on-disk tables by issuing a account-management statement such as CREATE USER, GRANT, REVOKE, or SET PASSWORD.
- You tell the server to reload the tables explicitly by issuing a FLUSH PRIVILEGES statement or by executing a mysqladmin flush-privileges or mysqladmin reload command.

34.1.3 Approaches to Account Management

It's possible to manage MySQL accounts by modifying the grant tables directly with SQL statements such as INSERT, DELETE, and UPDATE. The procedure described in Section 35.5.1, "Securing the Initial MySQL Accounts," shows an example of how UPDATE and DELETE can be used in this way. In general, however, the recommended way to set up and modify MySQL accounts is to use statements such as CREATE USER, GRANT, and REVOKE that are intended specifically for account management. These statements offer the following advantages:

- It's easier to use account-management statements than to modify the grant tables directly. Their syntax is more natural and less cumbersome for expressing privilege operations because that's what they're designed for. When you use statements such as CREATE USER and GRANT, the server determines the necessary modifications to the grant tables and makes the changes for you.
- When you issue an account-management statement, the server automatically reloads the in-memory contents of the grant tables. If you modify the tables directly with a

statement such as INSERT or DELETE, you must explicitly tell the server to reload the tables afterward by using a FLUSH PRIVILEGES statement or a mysqladmin flush-privileges command.

34.1.4 Creating and Dropping User Accounts

Three statements create, remove, or rename user accounts:

- CREATE USER creates a new account and optionally assigns it a password. This statement creates a record in the user table. It does not grant any privileges; to do so, use the GRANT statement later. (Alternatively, you can use GRANT to create the account and grant it privileges at the same time.)

  The following statement creates an account for jim@localhost and assigns the account a password of Abc123. That is, a user named jim will be able to connect from the local host, but must specify a password of Abc123:

  ```
  CREATE USER 'jim'@'localhost' IDENTIFIED BY 'Abc123';
  ```

  If the CREATE USER includes no IDENTIFIED BY clause, the account is created with no password. This is insecure and not recommended.

- DROP USER revokes all privileges for an existing account and then removes the account. It deletes all records for the account from any grant table in which they exist. To revoke privileges without removing the account itself, use the REVOKE statement.

  The following statement removes the jim@localhost account:

  ```
  DROP USER 'jim'@'localhost';
  ```

- RENAME USER changes the account name for an existing account. It can change the username or hostname parts of the account name, or both:

  ```
  RENAME USER 'jim'@'localhost' TO 'john'@'localhost';
  ```

For all three statements, accounts are named in 'user_name'@'host_name' format. More detail on account names is given in Section 34.1.5, "Specifying Account Names."

34.1.5 Specifying Account Names

An account name consists of a username and the name of the client host from which the user must connect to the server. The account name is given in SQL statements using 'user_name'@'host_name' format. The user and host parts of account names should be quoted separately. Quotes actually are necessary only for values that contain special characters such as dashes. If a value is legal as an unquoted identifier, the quotes are optional. However, quotes are always acceptable and example SQL statements shown in this study guide use them.

To specify an anonymous-user account (that is, an account that matches any username), specify an empty string for the user part of the account name:

```
CREATE USER ''@'localhost';
```

In general, it is best to avoid creating anonymous accounts, especially ones that have no password. Letting anyone connect to your server opens up your MySQL installation to security risks.

The host part of an account name may be given in any of the following formats:

- The name `localhost`.
- A hostname, such as `myhost.example.com`.
- An IP number, such as `192.168.1.47`.
- A pattern containing the '%' or '_' wildcard characters. Patterns are useful for setting up an account that allows a client to connect from any host in an entire domain or subnet. A host value of `%.example.com` matches any host in the `example.com` domain. A host value of `192.168.%` matches any host in the `192.168` subnet. A host value of `%` matches any host, allowing the client to connect from anywhere.
- An IP number/netmask combination. The value allows a client to connect from any host with an address that matches the IP number for all bits that are 1 in the netmask. For example, a value of `10.0.0.0/255.255.255.0` matches any host with `10.0.0` in the first 24 bits of its IP number. This format is useful for allowing an account with a given username to connect from any host in a subnet.

It's allowable to omit the host part from an account name. A name specified as `'user_name'` in an account-management statement is equivalent to `'user_name'@'%'`.

Keep the proper perspective in mind when specifying the host part of an account name. When you connect to the server using a client program, you specify the host *to which* you want to connect. On the other hand, when the server checks the client against `Host` column values in the grant tables, it uses the host *from which* the client connects. When setting up an account, you should specify the client host from the server's point of view. For example, if the server runs on `server.example.com` and you want to allow `jim` to connect from `client.example.com`, the `CREATE USER` statement should look like this:

```
CREATE USER 'jim'@'client.example.com';
```

Be aware that it is possible to have multiple accounts that could apply to a given client. For example, if you set up accounts for `jim@localhost` and `jim@%`, the server could use either one when `jim` connects from the local host. The rules that the server employs to determine which account to use in such cases are covered in Section 34.2, "Client Access Control."

34.1.6 Granting Privileges

The syntax for the GRANT statement includes several sections. In simplest form, you specify:

- The privileges to be granted
- What the privileges apply to
- The account that should be given the privileges
- A password

As an example, the following statement grants the SELECT privilege for all tables in the world database to a user named jim, who must connect from the local host and use a password of Abc123:

```
GRANT SELECT ON world.* TO 'jim'@'localhost' IDENTIFIED BY 'Abc123';
```

If the account does not already exist, GRANT creates it and assigns the designated privileges. If the account does exist, GRANT modifies it by adding the privileges.

The parts of the statement have the following effects:

- The statement begins with the GRANT keyword and one or more privilege names indicating which privileges are to be granted. Privilege names are not case sensitive. To list multiple privileges, separate them by commas. For example, if you want jim to be able to manipulate records in the world database, not just retrieve them, write the GRANT statement like this:

```
GRANT SELECT, INSERT, DELETE, UPDATE ON world.*
TO 'jim'@'localhost' IDENTIFIED BY 'Abc123';
```

- The ON clause specifies the level of the granted privileges (how broadly they apply). You can grant privileges globally or for a specific database, table, or stored routine. The ON syntax for these levels is as follows:

```
ON *.*
ON db_name.*
ON db_name.table_name
ON db_name.routine_name
```

For the formats that begin with db_name., it's allowable to omit the database name qualifier and specify just *, table_name, or routine_name. In these cases, the privileges are granted to all tables in the current database or to the named table or routine in the current database. Be sure that you know what the current database is, to avoid granting privileges to tables or routines in the incorrect database.

When granting privileges for a table or stored routine, there is an ambiguity if there are multiple objects (table, procedure, or function) with the same name. To indicate the type of object explicitly, use the keyword TABLE, PROCEDURE, or FUNCTION preceding the name:

```
ON TABLE db_name.table_name
ON PROCEDURE db_name.routine_name
ON FUNCTION db_name.routine_name
```

To grant privileges at a column-specific level, use an ON clause that names a particular table, and specify a comma-separated list of column names within parentheses after each privilege to be granted. The following statement indicates that the named account can retrieve three of the columns in the City table of the world database, but can update only two of them:

```
GRANT SELECT (ID, Name, CountryCode), UPDATE (Name, CountryCode)
ON world.City TO 'jim'@'localhost'
IDENTIFIED BY 'Abc123';
```

- The TO clause specifies the account to be granted the privileges. An account name consists of a username and the name of the client host from which the user must connect to the server. The account name is given in 'user_name'@'host_name' format. More detail on this format is given in Section 34.1.5, "Specifying Account Names," but note that the user and host parts of account names should be quoted separately. Quotes actually are necessary only for values that contain special characters such as dashes. If a value is legal as an unquoted identifier, the quotes are optional.

- The IDENTIFIED BY clause is optional. If present, it assigns a password to the account. If the account already exists and IDENTIFIED BY is given, the password replaces any old one. If the account exists but IDENTIFIED BY is omitted from the GRANT statement, the account's current password remains unchanged. If an account has no password, clients can use it to connect to the server without a password!

  As a security measure, you can prevent the GRANT statement from creating new accounts unless an IDENTIFIED BY clause is given. To do this, enable the NO_AUTO_CREATE_USER SQL mode.

If you want to give an account the capability to grant its privileges to other accounts, add a WITH GRANT OPTION clause to the statement. For example, if you want jim to have read access to the world database and to be able to create other users that have read access to that database, use this statement:

```
GRANT SELECT ON world.* TO 'jim'@'localhost'
IDENTIFIED BY 'Abc123'
WITH GRANT OPTION;
```

To find out what privileges a particular account has, use the SHOW GRANTS statement. It displays the GRANT statements that would be required to set up the account.

To see your own privileges, use SHOW GRANTS without an account name or with CURRENT_USER():

```
SHOW GRANTS;
SHOW GRANTS FOR CURRENT_USER();
```

To see the privileges for a specific account, specify that account name in the statement. You cannot see the privileges for other accounts unless you have the SELECT privilege for the mysql database.

Suppose that you've set up an account for a user jen who connects from the host myhost.example.com. To see this account's privileges, use the following statement:

```
mysql> SHOW GRANTS FOR 'jen'@'myhost.example.com';
+----------------------------------------------------------------+
| Grants for jen@myhost.example.com                              |
+----------------------------------------------------------------+
| GRANT FILE ON *.* TO 'jen'@'myhost.example.com'                |
| GRANT SELECT ON `mydb`.* TO 'jen'@'myhost.example.com'         |
| GRANT UPDATE ON `test`.`mytable` TO 'jen'@'myhost.example.com' |
+----------------------------------------------------------------+
```

The output displayed here by SHOW GRANTS consists of three GRANT statements. Their ON clauses indicate that jen has privileges at the global, database, and table levels, respectively.

If the account has a password, SHOW GRANTS displays an IDENTIFIED BY PASSWORD clause, at the end of the GRANT statement which lists the account's global privileges. (The word PASSWORD after IDENTIFIED BY indicates that the password value shown is the encrypted value stored in the user table, not the actual password.) If the account can grant some or all of its privileges to other accounts, SHOW GRANTS displays WITH GRANT OPTION at the end of each GRANT statement to which it applies.

SHOW GRANTS displays privileges only for the exact account specified in the statement. For example, the preceding SHOW GRANTS statement shows privileges only for jen@myhost.example.com, not for jen@%.example.com, jen@%.com, or jen@%.

34.1.7 Revoking Privileges

Use the REVOKE statement to revoke privileges from an account. Its syntax has the following sections:

- The keyword REVOKE followed by the list of privileges to be revoked
- An ON clause indicating the level at which privileges are to be revoked
- A FROM clause that specifies the account name

Suppose that jim on the local host has SELECT, DELETE, INSERT, and UPDATE privileges on the world database, but you want to change the account so that he has SELECT access only. To do this, revoke those privileges that allow him to make changes:

```
REVOKE DELETE, INSERT, UPDATE ON world.* FROM 'jim'@'localhost';
```

To revoke the GRANT OPTION privilege from an account that has it, you must revoke it in a separate statement. For example, if jill has the ability to grant her privileges for the world database to other users, you can revoke that ability as follows:

```
REVOKE GRANT OPTION ON world.* FROM 'jill'@'localhost';
```

To revoke all privileges held by an account at any level, REVOKE supports a special syntax (note that this form of REVOKE has no ON clause):

```
REVOKE ALL PRIVILEGES, GRANT OPTION FROM 'james'@'localhost';
```

To determine what REVOKE statements are needed to revoke an account's privileges, SHOW GRANTS might be helpful. Consider again the output from SHOW GRANTS for the jen@localhost account:

```
mysql> SHOW GRANTS FOR 'jen'@'myhost.example.com';
+----------------------------------------------------------------+
| Grants for jen@myhost.example.com                              |
+----------------------------------------------------------------+
| GRANT FILE ON *.* TO 'jen'@'myhost.example.com'                |
| GRANT SELECT ON `mydb`.* TO 'jen'@'myhost.example.com'         |
| GRANT UPDATE ON `test`.`mytable` TO 'jen'@'myhost.example.com' |
+----------------------------------------------------------------+
```

This output indicates that the account has global, database-level, and table-level privileges. To remove some or all of these privileges, convert the GRANT statements to the corresponding REVOKE statements. The privilege names, privilege levels, and account name must be the same as displayed by SHOW GRANTS. For example, to revoke the global FILE privilege and the table-level privilege for test.mytable, issue these statements:

```
mysql> REVOKE FILE ON *.* FROM 'jen'@'myhost.example.com';
mysql> REVOKE UPDATE ON test.mytable FROM 'jen'@'myhost.example.com';
```

After issuing the REVOKE statements, SHOW GRANTS produces this result:

```
mysql> SHOW GRANTS FOR 'jen'@'myhost.example.com';
+--------------------------------------------------------+
| Grants for jen@myhost.example.com                      |
+--------------------------------------------------------+
| GRANT USAGE ON *.* TO 'jen'@'myhost.example.com'       |
| GRANT SELECT ON `mydb`.* TO 'jen'@'myhost.example.com' |
+--------------------------------------------------------+
```

If you use REVOKE to remove all the privileges enabled by a record in the db, tables_priv, columns_priv, or procs_priv tables, REVOKE removes the record entirely. However, REVOKE does not remove an account's user table record, even if you revoke all privileges for the account. This means that although the account no longer has any privileges, it still exists and thus can be used to connect to the server. If you want to eliminate all traces of an account from the grant tables, you should use the DROP USER statement instead. After that, the account no longer exists and cannot be used to connect to the server.

34.1.8 Changing Account Passwords

As discussed earlier, you can specify a password for an account by including an IDENTIFIED BY clause in a CREATE USER or GRANT statement. For CREATE USER, the clause assigns the initial account password. For GRANT, the clause assigns the initial password or changes the current password, depending on whether the account is new or already exists.

To change an existing account's password without changing any of its privileges, you have two options:

- Use the SET PASSWORD statement, specifying the account name and the new password. For example, to set the password for jim on the local host to NewPass, use this statement:

  ```
  SET PASSWORD FOR 'jim'@'localhost' = PASSWORD('NewPass');
  ```

  Any non-anonymous client can change its own password by omitting the FOR clause:

  ```
  SET PASSWORD = PASSWORD('NewPass');
  ```

- Use GRANT with the USAGE privilege specifier at the global level and an IDENTIFIED BY clause:

  ```
  GRANT USAGE ON *.* TO 'jim'@'localhost' IDENTIFIED BY 'NewPass';
  ```

  USAGE means "no privileges," so the statement changes the password without granting any privileges.

Note that with SET PASSWORD, you use PASSWORD() to encrypt the password, whereas with CREATE USER and GRANT, you do not use it.

To allow a user to connect without specifying a password, change the password to the empty string. However, you cannot "revoke" the password this way with REVOKE. Instead, use either of the following statements:

```
SET PASSWORD FOR 'jim'@'localhost' = '';

GRANT USAGE ON *.* TO 'jim'@'localhost' IDENTIFIED BY '';
```

Be certain that you want to do this, however. Accounts that have no password are insecure.

34.1.9 When Privilege Changes Take Effect

When you change the grant tables with an account-management statement, the effects of changes apply to existing client connections as follows:

- Table and column privilege changes apply to all statements issued after the changes are made.

- Database privilege changes apply with the next USE statement.

- Changes to global privileges and passwords do not apply to a connected client. They apply the next time the client attempts to connect.

34.1.10 Specifying Resource Limits

By default, there is no limit on the number of times a client can connect to the server or the number of queries it can issue. If that is not suitable, GRANT can establish limits on an account's resource consumption for the following characteristics:

- The number of times per hour the account is allowed to connect to the server
- The number of queries per hour the account is allowed to issue
- The number of updates per hour the account is allowed to issue
- The number of times the account can connect simultaneously to the server

Each of these resource limits is specified using an option in a WITH clause. The following example creates an account that can use the test database, but can connect to the server a maximum of only 10 times per hour. The account can issue 50 queries per hour, and at most 20 of those queries can modify data:

```
GRANT ALL ON test.* TO 'quinn'@'localhost' IDENTIFIED BY 'SomePass'
WITH MAX_CONNECTIONS_PER_HOUR 10
MAX_QUERIES_PER_HOUR 50
MAX_UPDATES_PER_HOUR 20;
```

The order in which you name the options in the WITH clause does not matter.

To reset an existing limit for any of the per-hour resources to the default of "no limit," specify a value of zero. For example:

```
GRANT USAGE ON *.* TO 'quinn'@'localhost'
WITH MAX_CONNECTIONS_PER_HOUR 0;
```

The MAX_USER_CONNECTIONS limit also can be set to zero to set it to the default. However, that does not mean "no limit." Instead, when this resource is set to zero, the value that applies to the account is the value of the max_user_connections system variable.

34.1.11 Privileges Needed for Account Management

The statements that are used for account management in MySQL require the following privileges:

- CREATE USER requires the CREATE USER privilege or the INSERT privilege for the mysql database.

- DROP USER requires the CREATE USER privilege or the DELETE privilege for the mysql database.

- RENAME USER requires the CREATE USER privilege or the UPDATE privilege for the mysql database.

- GRANT requires the GRANT OPTION privilege, and you also must have the privileges that you are granting.

- REVOKE without ALL PRIVILEGES requires the GRANT OPTION privilege, and you also must have the privileges that you are revoking. REVOKE ALL PRIVILEGES requires the CREATE USER privilege or the UPDATE privilege for the mysql database.

- Use of SET PASSWORD to change another account's password requires the CREATE USER privilege or the UPDATE privilege for the mysql database. Any non-anonymous client can use SET PASSWORD to change the password for its own account, and no special privileges are required.

- SHOW GRANTS requires the SELECT privilege for the mysql database to see another account's grants. It requires no special privileges to see the grants for your own account.

34.2 Client Access Control

This section describes how the server uses account information in the grant tables to control which clients may connect and what they may do after connecting.

There are two stages of client access control:

- In the first stage, a client attempts to connect and the server either accepts or rejects the connection. For the attempt to succeed, some entry in the user table must match the host from which a client connects, the username, and the password.

- In the second stage (which occurs only if a client has already connected successfully), the server checks every query it receives from the client to see whether the client has sufficient privileges to execute it.

The server matches a client against entries in the grant tables based on the host from which the client connects and the username the client provides. However, it's possible for more than one record to match:

- Host values in grant tables may be specified as patterns containing wildcard values. If a grant table contains entries for myhost.example.com, %.example.com, %.com, and %, all of them match a client who connects from myhost.example.com.

- Patterns are not allowed for User values in grant table entries, but a username may be given as an empty string to specify an anonymous user. The empty string matches any username and thus effectively acts as a wildcard.

When the Host and User values in more than one user table record match a client, the server must decide which one to use. It does this by sorting records with the most specific Host and User column values first, and choosing the matching record that occurs first in the sorted list. Sorting takes place as follows:

- In the Host column, literal values such as localhost, 127.0.0.1, and myhost.example.com sort ahead of values such as %.example.com that have pattern characters in them. Pattern values are sorted according to how specific they are. For example, %.example.com is more specific than %.com, which is more specific than %.

- In the User column, non-blank usernames sort ahead of blank usernames. That is, non-anonymous users sort ahead of anonymous users.

The server performs this sorting when it starts. It reads the grant tables into memory, sorts them, and uses the in-memory copies for access control.

Suppose that the user table contains the following values in the Host and User columns:

```
+--------------------+--------+
| Host               | User   |
+--------------------+--------+
| localhost          |        |
| %                  | james  |
| %.example.com      | jen    |
| %.com              | jobril |
| localhost          | jon    |
| myhost.example.com | james  |
+--------------------+--------+
```

When the server reads the grant tables into memory, it sorts the user table records
as follows:

- localhost and myhost.example.come are literal values, so they sort ahead of the other Host values that contain pattern characters. The Host values that contain pattern characters sort from most specific to least specific.

- The two entries that have localhost in the Host column are ordered based on the User values. The entry with the non-blank username sorts ahead of the one with the blank username.

The sorting rules result in entries that are ordered like this:

```
+--------------------+--------+
| Host               | User   |
+--------------------+--------+
| localhost          | jon    |
| localhost          |        |
| myhost.example.com | james  |
| %.example.com      | jen    |
```

```
| %.com               | jobril |
| %                   | james  |
+---------------------+--------+
```

34.2.1 Connection Request Checking

When a client attempts to connect, the server matches the sorted records to the client using the Host values first and the User values second:

- If jon connects from the local host, the entry with localhost and jon in the Host and User columns matches first.

- If james connects from localhost, the two entries with localhost in the Host column match the host, and the entry with the blank User value matches any username. Therefore, that is the first entry that matches both the client hostname and username. (The entry with % in the Host column matches localhost as well, but the server doesn't consider it in this case because it has already found a matching record.)

- On the other hand, if james connects from pluto.example.com instead, the first entry that matches the hostname has a Host value of %.example.com. That entry's username doesn't match, so the server continues looking. The same thing happens with the entry that has a Host value of %.com: The hostname matches but the username does not. Finally, the entry with a Host value of % matches and the username matches as well.

When you attempt to determine which grant table record the server will find as the best match for a client, remember to take the sort order into account. In particular, the fact that Host matching is done before User matching leads to a property that might be surprising unless you're aware of it. Consider again the case where james connects from the local host. There are two entries with james in the User column, but neither is the first match. Host matching takes place first, so on that basis the entry that matches first is the anonymous-user entry: localhost matches the host from which james connects, and the blank User value matches any username. This means that when james connects from the local host, he will be treated as an anonymous user, not as james.

When you connect successfully to the server, the USER() function returns the username you specified and the client host from which you connected. The CURRENT_USER() function returns the username and hostname values from the User and Host columns of the user table record the server used to authenticate you. The two values may be different. If james connects from the local host, USER() and CURRENT_USER() have these values:

```
mysql> SELECT USER(), CURRENT_USER();
+-----------------+-----------------+
| USER()          | CURRENT_USER()  |
+-----------------+-----------------+
| james@localhost | @localhost      |
+-----------------+-----------------+
```

The username part of CURRENT_USER() is empty. This occurs because the server authenticates james as an anonymous user.

If james connects from pluto.example.com instead, USER() and CURRENT_USER() have these values:

```
mysql> SELECT USER(), CURRENT_USER();
+-----------------------+----------------+
| USER()                | CURRENT_USER() |
+-----------------------+----------------+
| james@pluto.example.com | james@%      |
+-----------------------+----------------+
```

Here the host part of CURRENT_USER() is %, because the server authenticates james using the user table entry that has % as the Host value.

For connection attempts that the server denies, an error message results:

- If the client attempts to connect from a host for which there is no record in the user table with a matching Host value, the error is:

  ```
  Host 'host_name' is not allowed to connect to this MySQL server
  ```

- If connections from the client host are allowed by one or more user table records, but no match can be found for the User and Password values, the error is:

  ```
  "Access denied for user: 'user_name'@'host_name'
  ```

34.2.2 Statement Privilege Checking

Each time the server receives a statement from a client, it checks the client's privileges to see whether it is allowed to execute the statement. For example, if you issue an UPDATE statement, you must possess the UPDATE privilege for each of the columns to be updated.

The server checks privileges in an additive fashion from the global level to the column-specific level. To check a statement, the server determines which privileges the statement requires, and then assesses whether the client possesses them by proceeding successively through the grant tables.

First, the server checks the client's global privileges in the user table. If these are sufficient, the server executes the statement. If the global privileges are not sufficient, the server adds any database-specific privileges indicated for the client in the db table and checks again. If the combined privileges are sufficient, the server executes the statement. Otherwise, it continues as necessary, checking the table-specific and column-specific privileges in the tables_priv and columns_priv tables. (For stored routines, the server checks the procs_priv table.) If, after checking all the grant tables, the client has insufficient privileges, the server refuses to execute the statement.

34.2.3 Resource Limit Checking

For an account that has resource limits, the server applies them to access control as follows:

- If the client has a limit on the number of times per hour it can connect to the server or the number of simultaneous connections it can make, that limit applies in the first stage of access control, when the server determines whether to accept the client connection.

- If the client has a limit on the number of queries or updates per hour it can issue, those limits apply in the second stage of access control. The server checks the limits for each query received before checking whether the client has the proper privileges to execute it.

34.2.4 Disabling Client Access Control

The `--skip-grant-tables` option tells the server not to use the grant tables to control client access. This option has the following effects:

- Anyone can connect from anywhere with no password, and, once connected, has full privileges to do anything. That is convenient if you've forgotten the `root` password and need to reset it, because you can connect without knowing the password. On the other hand, because anyone else can connect, too, running the server in this mode is dangerous. To prevent remote clients from connecting over TCP/IP, you may want to use the `--skip-networking` option as well. Clients then can connect only from the local host using a named pipe or shared memory on Windows, or a socket file on Unix.

- `--skip-grant-tables` disables the account-management statements (CREATE USER, GRANT, REVOKE, SET PASSWORD, and so forth). These statements require the in-memory copies of the grant tables, which aren't set up when you skip use of the tables. To make a change to the grant tables while those statements are inoperative, you can update the tables directly. But that is inconvenient, so it's preferable to issue a FLUSH PRIILEGES statement after you connect to the server. That causes the server to read the table tables, which also enables the account-management statements so that you can use them again. However, FLUSH PRIVILEGES does not affect which network interfaces the server listens to, so if you
started the server with the `--skip-networking` option, you'll still need to restart it without that option to cause it to listen for TCP/IP connections again.

Securing the MySQL Installation

This chapter discusses security risks that MySQL administrators face and what can be done to protect a MySQL installation against them. It covers the following exam topics:

- Operating system security
- Filesystem security
- Log files and security
- Network security
- The FEDERATED storage engine and security

35.1 Security Issues

Information stored in MySQL databases must be kept secure to avoid exposing data that MySQL users expect to be private. Risks to a MySQL installation come in several forms:

- *Operating system security risks.* MySQL usually is administered using a login account dedicated to that purpose. However, the server machine might host other login accounts as well, and those accounts have the potential for being used against the MySQL installation. Minimizing the number of accounts not related to MySQL minimizes this risk.

- *Filesystem security risks.* Database information is stored in directories and files, and the server also maintains log files that contain information about queries that clients execute. Because these directories and files are part of the filesystem, they need to be protected so that other users who have login accounts on the server host cannot access them directly. A MySQL installation also includes the programs and scripts used to manage and access databases. Users need to be able to run some of these (such as the client programs), but should not be able to modify or replace them. This means that MySQL programs need to be protected appropriately as well.

- *Network security risks.* The MySQL server provides access to databases by allowing clients to connect over the network and make requests. Information about client accounts is stored in the mysql database. Each account should be set up with privileges that provide access only to the data the account needs to see or modify. Accounts also should be assigned passwords to make it difficult for people to connect to the server using someone else's account. For example, a MySQL root account has full privileges to perform any database operation, so it's important to assign the account a password that is not easily guessed.

The following sections discuss techniques that an administrator can use to maintain the integrity of a MySQL installation.

The directories and files of a MySQL installation can be protected by changing their ownership and access permissions before running the server, but setting passwords for the MySQL root accounts can be done only while the server is running. Consequently, before starting the server and setting passwords, you should take any actions necessary to protect MySQL-related portions of the filesystem. If you set the passwords first before protecting the files in which the grant tables are stored, it's possible for someone with direct filesystem access on the server host to replace the grant tables. This compromises your MySQL installation and undoes the effect of setting the passwords.

35.2 Operating System Security

Security of a system often is related to the complexity of its configuration. Consequently, you should minimize the number of tasks that the server host is used for that do not directly relate to running MySQL. A host that is configured for fewer tasks can be made secure more easily than a host running a complex configuration that supports many services.

It is best if the MySQL server machine is used primarily or exclusively for MySQL, and not for other purposes such as Web hosting or mail processing, or as a machine that hosts login accounts for general-purpose interactive use.

If other users can log in, there is a potential risk that database information may be exposed that should be kept private to the MySQL installation and its administrative account. For example, improper filesystem privileges may expose data files. Users can run the ps command to view information about processes and their execution environment.

When the machine is used only for MySQL, there is no need to have login accounts except the system administrative accounts and any that might be needed for administering MySQL itself (such as the account for the mysql user). Also, the fewer network services that are run on the server host, the fewer network ports need be kept open. Closing ports minimizes the number of avenues of attack to which the host is exposed.

There is also a performance benefit to minimizing the number of non-MySQL services: More of the system's resources can be devoted to MySQL.

35.3 Filesystem Security

Under multiuser systems such as Unix, all components of a MySQL installation should be owned by a login account with proper administrative privileges, to protect it against unauthorized access by users that are not responsible for database administration. The installation should be accessible to other users only to the extent necessary. To achieve this objective, set up a dedicated login account to use for administering MySQL and give that account ownership of the relevant files. An additional benefit of setting up this account is that you can use it to run the MySQL server, rather than running the server from the Unix root account. A server that has the privileges of the root login account has more filesystem access than necessary and constitutes a security risk.

This section assumes the existence of such an administrative account and that both its username and group name are mysql. However, the details of creating login accounts vary per version of Unix and are outside the scope of the exam, so they are not discussed here. Consult the documentation for your operating system.

To have a secure MySQL installation, the following conditions should be satisfied:

- Every MySQL-related directory and file should have its user and group ownerships set to mysql. This includes the MySQL programs, the database directories and files, and the log, status, and configuration files.

  An allowable alternative to having everything owned by the mysql user is that some program and library directories and files may be owned by root. The principle to follow is that anything the server might need to modify cannot be owned by root.

- Files that only the server should be able to access should be owned by the mysql account and readable only by it. This includes any option files that contain replication passwords, and the master.info replication file on slave servers, which also contains a replication password.

- No files should be set to be readable by any user other than mysql except for those that client programs run by other users need to access. Files that must be accessible to other users include the Unix socket file, global option files, error message files, language files, and character set files.

- In most cases, it's reasonable for client programs and other utilities to be world-executable so that other users with login accounts on the system can run them. Under certain conditions, you might want to restrict access to allow only a subset of the users on the machine to run MySQL programs.

- After you've established the proper filesystem access so that the mysql login account owns the relevant directories and files, the MySQL server should be run using this account. This is important because mysql is a regular login account that has no special filesystem privileges.

  The server should *not* be run as the system root user. There are many reasons for this; one is that there are operations performed by the server that involve reading or writing files in the server host filesystem. (For example, LOAD DATA INFILE and SELECT ... INTO OUTFILE do so.) Running the server as root is a bad idea because doing so gives it root privileges and vastly increases the extent of the filesystem that the server can access or modify.

- The server program need not be executable to anyone other than mysql. Its access privileges can be set accordingly.

The following sample procedure shows how to secure the directories and files of a MySQL installation. Before using this procedure, stop the server if it's running. Also, note that some operations must be done from a privileged login account, so you'll need root login access to perform them. The chown and chgrp commands should be run as the system root user because only root can assign directory and file ownership. After directories and files have been set to be owned by mysql, you can set their access permissions by running chmod as either root or mysql.

The procedure assumes that the MySQL base installation directory is /usr/local/mysql. To protect an installation that has the files located elsewhere, make the appropriate substitutions to the pathnames shown in the commands.

Run the following commands as root to set everything in and under the installation directory to be owned by user mysql and group mysql:

```
shell> chown -R mysql /usr/local/mysql
shell> chgrp -R mysql /usr/local/mysql
```

Then restrict access to the installation directory so that only the mysql user has permission to make changes, and so that its subdirectories are accessible only as necessary by other users. The following commands can be run either as mysql or root:

```
shell> chmod u=rwx,go=rx /usr/local/mysql
shell> chmod u=rwx,go=rx /usr/local/mysql/bin
shell> chmod u=rwx,go-rwx /usr/local/mysql/libexec
shell> chmod -R go-rwx /usr/local/mysql/data
```

These commands give complete access to the mysql user but restrict access by other users. They also make the installation directory and bin directory where the client programs are installed accessible to but not modifiable to other users, and make the libexec directory (where the server is located) and the data directory inaccessible to other users.

You should also protect the global option file, /etc/my.cnf, if it exists. The mysql user should own it and have read/write access to it, but other users need only read access:

```
shell> chown mysql /etc/my.cnf
shell> chgrp mysql /etc/my.cnf
shell> chmod u=rw,go=r /etc/my.cnf
```

Before starting the server, you should arrange to have it execute with the privileges of the mysql login account. This can be done either by starting the server while logged in as mysql, or by starting it as `root` with a `--user=mysql` option to instruct it to change user from `root` to `mysql` during its startup sequence. (It's allowable to *start* the server as `root`, but if you do, you should use a `--user` option to tell the server to change user to the `mysql` account and give up its special `root` privileges. Otherwise, the server continues to execute as `root`, which is dangerous.)

If you have the server set to start automatically during the system boot sequence, the system invokes the server as `root` and does not allow you to specify any options on the command line. To reliably start the server as the `mysql` user, it's best to put the `--user` option in an option file so that the server always uses it whether you start the server manually or automatically. One way to do so is to place the following lines in `/etc/my.cnf`:

```
[mysqld]
user=mysql
```

Each MySQL user on Unix that has a personal option file (`~/.my.cnf`) should be made aware that the file should be inaccessible to other users, to prevent exposure of any MySQL passwords stored in the file. Each user can issue the following command to set the option file access mode properly:

```
shell> chmod u=rw,go-rwx ~/.my.cnf
```

On Windows, the following measures enable you to increase the security of your MySQL installation:

- Use NTFS as the filesystem on the volume where MySQL is installed. NTFS supports access controls and allows data encryption. If you're considering enabling encryption, however, remember that although it increases security, it also lowers performance. Because of this tradeoff, you probably don't want to enable encryption if the server is used for high-volume database processing.
- Create a limited-privilege Windows account to use for running MySQL. Remove permissions on the MySQL installation directory and its contents except for this account.

35.4 Log Files and Security

Filesystem security includes the log files. You should keep the log contents secret. You don't want to expose table data by exposing the log files because they contain statements that include data values. In particular you don't want to expose account passwords that are included in statements such as CREATE USER or SET PASSWORD. To keep your log files secure, follow the data directory protection procedures outlined in Section 35.3, "Filesystem Security."

Log exposure constitutes a security risk that must be addressed by protecting the log files, but logs also play a role in enhancing security. Certain logs, if enabled, provide data security or information that is useful in the event of attack:

- The binary log is needed for data security. It's required for recovery operations should you need to restore your databases (for example, if an attempt to compromise the server does succeed).

- The general query log gives you information about what clients are connecting, which may be helpful in detecting instances of malicious activity and determining their source.

35.5 Network Security

MySQL Server operates in the client/server environment and thus provides an inherently network-oriented service. It's important to make sure that only authorized clients can connect to the server to access its databases. You should make sure that MySQL accounts are protected with passwords and do not have unnecessary privileges. You may also want to consider limiting the network interfaces used by the server.

35.5.1 Securing the Initial MySQL Accounts

MySQL Server controls client access using the `mysql` database, which contains the grant tables. Privileges listed in the grant tables are tied to accounts, each of which is defined by a username and a hostname. That is, a MySQL account depends not only on your username, but the client host from which you connect to the server.

Note: Usernames and passwords for MySQL accounts are unrelated to those for system login accounts. For example, on Unix, your login name need not be the same as the name that you use to identify yourself when connecting to the MySQL server.

The MySQL installation procedure sets up one or more initial accounts in the grant tables. By default, these accounts have no passwords at first. You should assign passwords to these accounts, particularly any that have administrative privileges, so that unauthorized clients cannot connect to the server and gain control over it. This is true no matter what platform you install MySQL Server on, whether Windows or Unix. Any unneeded accounts should be removed.

At a minimum, there will be an account for `root@localhost`. On Unix, there is also an account for `root@`*`host_name`*, where *`host_name`* is the name of the server host. On Windows, depending on your installation method, there may also be a `root@%` account. `root` accounts have full access to the server's capabilities.

The grant tables may also contain anonymous-user accounts that have a blank username and that can be used by anyone.

On Windows, if you install MySQL using a distribution that includes the Configuration Wizard, the wizard presents a dialog containing check boxes that enable you to specify that `root` can connect only from the local host, and that anonymous accounts are to be created. You should check the first box and leave the second unchecked. (The Configuration Wizard also gives you the option of specifying the root password. If you use the wizard to set this password, you don't need to do so using the following instructions.)

The initial MySQL accounts have no password by default. You should assign a password immediately to any root accounts to prevent other people from connecting to the server as root and gaining complete control over it. With regard to anonymous accounts, you could assign passwords to them as well, but the best security is achieved if you remove them. This study guide follows the latter course.

There are various ways to set up MySQL passwords:

- Use the GRANT statement
- Use the SET PASSWORD statement
- Use the mysqladmin password command
- Modify the grant tables directly with the UPDATE statement

Generally, it's preferable to use one of the first three methods, and to avoid modifying the grant tables directly. For example, after installing MySQL, a simple procedure to protect the root accounts by assigning them passwords is to use these two mysqladmin password commands, where *rootpass* represents the password and *host_name* is the hostname of your machine:

```
shell> mysqladmin -u root password 'rootpass'
shell> mysqladmin -u root -h host_name password 'rootpass'
```

However, these commands will not take care of the anonymous accounts. The following procedure secures all the initial accounts by assigning a password to any root accounts and removing any anonymous accounts. The procedure also serves to demonstrate how modifying the grant tables directly can be useful.

1. On the server host, connect to the server as the MySQL root user to access the grant tables in the mysql database. Initially, assuming that the root accounts have no password, you can connect as follows without specifying a password option:

   ```
   shell> mysql -u root mysql
   ```

2. Account names and passwords are stored in the user table of the mysql database. Modify any user table records for root to assign a password. The following statement represents this password as *rootpass*:

   ```
   mysql> UPDATE user SET Password = PASSWORD('rootpass')
       -> WHERE User = 'root';
   ```

3. On Windows, the user table may contain a record for a 'root'@'%' account that allows root connections from any host. To allow only local access by root, remove that account:

   ```
   mysql> DELETE FROM user
   mysql> WHERE User = 'root' AND Host = '%';
   ```

4. To remove any anonymous accounts, use the following statements:

```
mysql> DELETE FROM user WHERE User = '';
mysql> DELETE FROM db WHERE User = '';
```

5. If you want to see what effect the preceding operations have on the user table, issue this statement:

```
mysql> SELECT Host, User, Password FROM user;
```

6. Finally, flush the grant tables:

```
mysql> FLUSH PRIVILEGES;
```

The reason for flushing the grant tables is that the server makes access-control decisions based on in-memory copies of the grant tables. The FLUSH statement tells the server to create new in-memory copies from the on-disk tables that were changed by the previous steps. This is necessary because the procedure changes the grant tables directly using UPDATE and DELETE rather than with account-management statements such as SET PASSWORD. Only the latter statements cause the server to reload the grant statements automatically.

After setting the root password to *rootpass*, you'll need to supply that password whenever you connect to the server with a username of root.

On Unix, MySQL comes with a mysql_secure_installation script that can perform several helpful security-related operations on your installation. This script has the following capabilities:

- Set a password for the root accounts.
- Remove any remotely accessible root accounts. This improves security because it prevents the possibility of anyone connecting to the MySQL server as root from a remote host. The result is that anyone who wants to connect as root must first be able to log in on the server host, which provides an additional barrier against attack.
- Remove the anonymous-user accounts.
- Remove the test database. (If you remove the anonymous accounts, you might also want to remove the test database to which they have access.)

35.5.2 General Privilege Precautions

This section describes general precautions to observe when granting privileges to MySQL accounts.

- Don't grant privileges for the mysql database. Giving a user the ability to modify the grant tables directly is equivalent to granting the user full rights to modify accounts in any manner whatsoever.

- Be selective about granting administrative privileges. The following items describe some of the dangers of giving these privileges to non-administrative users:

    - The FILE privilege allows users to cause the MySQL server to read and write files in the server host filesystem.

    - The PROCESS privilege allows use of SHOW PROCESSLIST to see all client threads. Output from this statement shows the statements that clients are executing, which exposes data.

    - The SUPER privilege allows a client to kill other client connections or to change the runtime configuration of the server.

- To prevent GRANT from creating new accounts unless an IDENTIFIED BY clause is given, enable the NO_AUTO_CREATE_USER SQL mode.

- Make sure that all MySQL accounts have passwords. To find accounts that have no password, connect as the root user to the mysql database and issue this statement:

```
mysql> SELECT Host, User FROM user WHERE Password = '';
```

35.5.2.1 Restricting the Server's Network Interfaces

If your clients all connect to the local server, it's not necessary to allow remotely initiated connections. To prevent remote clients from connecting at all, disable TCP/IP connections by starting the server with the --skip-networking option. With the TCP/IP interface disabled, clients can connect only from the local host, which means that the server must be started with at least one local interface enabled. For Unix servers, this is not an issue, because the Unix socket file is always available. On Windows, the local interfaces are shared memory and named pipes. However, these interfaces are not enabled by default, so you must turn on at least one of them. To enable shared-memory connections, start the server with the --shared-memory option. To enable named-pipe connections, you must use either the mysqld-nt or mysqld-max-nt server and start it with the --enable-named-pipe option.

If clients cannot connect via one of the non-TCP/IP interfaces, you can leave TCP/IP connections enabled, but restrict connections to use only the loopback interface, which has TCP/IP address 127.0.0.1. This is another way to prevent remote clients from connecting. It can be done by using the --bind-address option. For example, place the following lines in an option file:

```
[mysqld]
bind-address=127.0.0.1
```

35.5.3 MySQL Cluster Network Security

If you run MySQL Cluster, all nodes in the cluster should be located on the same local network and protected behind a firewall. Communication between nodes must be fast, so placing them on the same local network allows them to be connected by high-speed media such as 100 Mbps or gigabit ethernet. However, communication is not encrypted because that requires extra processing power and lowers performance. Thus, the cluster nodes should be protected behind a firewall so that internode communication cannot be monitored.

35.6 FEDERATED Table Security

When you create a FEDERATED table, you provide a connection string in the COMMENT option of the CREATE TABLE statement. This string includes the connection parameters to use for connecting to the remote server where the original table actually is located. For example:

```
CREATE TABLE FedCity
(
    ID          INT NOT NULL AUTO_INCREMENT,
    Name        CHAR(35) NOT NULL,
    CountryCode CHAR(3) NOT NULL,
    District    CHAR(20) NOT NULL,
    Population  INT NOT NULL,
    PRIMARY KEY (ID)
)
ENGINE=FEDERATED
COMMENT='mysql://wuser:wpass@world.example.com/world/City';
```

The username and password (wuser and wpass) are visible as plain text in the FedCity table definition, which can present a security risk in several ways:

- A user who can use SHOW CREATE TABLE or SHOW TABLE STATUS for the table can see the COMMENT value. The same is true if the user can select information about the table from the TABLES table of INFORMATION_SCHEMA. To prevent this, don't grant privileges for the FedCity table to other users.

- The FedCity table definition is stored in its .frm format file. A user with read access to the file can see the username and password. To prevent this, follow the data directory protection procedures outlined in Section 35.3, "Filesystem Security."

Upgrade-Related
Security Issues

Whe upgrades to MySQL are released, new distributions sometimes include security enhancements. In some cases, these are simply bug fixes and you need do nothing for them to take effect. In other cases, a security-related change is provided as optional behavior and you can choose whether to enable it. This chapter discusses how these optional behaviors can be enabled should you decide to take advantage of them. It covers the following exam topics:

- Upgrading the grant tables to enable new privileges
- Using new SQL modes to increase data security

36.1 Upgrading the Privilege Tables

MySQL Server controls client access by using the contents of the grant tables in the `mysql` database. The grant tables list accounts for clients that are allowed to connect to the server. They also enumerate the privileges that each account holds and that determine what operations it can perform, such as creating tables or updating records.

As MySQL development proceeds, it sometimes occurs that new privileges are implemented to go along with new features. For example, in MySQL 5, new features include stored routines and views, each of which is accompanied by privileges that enable clients to use them. The `CREATE ROUTINE` and `CREATE VIEW` privileges enable object creation, and other privileges control access to the created objects.

To determine whether a new release of MySQL includes new privileges, check the upgrade notes in the installation chapter of the *MySQL Reference Manual*. When you upgrade MySQL to a version that implements additional privileges compared to your current version, it is not the case that those privileges become part of your existing grant tables automatically. To upgrade your grant tables to the new structure, you should run the `mysql_fix_privilege_tables` program:

1. Make a backup of your `mysql` database:

   ```
   shell> mysqldump mysql > mysql.sql
   ```

   When you run `mysqldump`, you'll need to connect to the MySQL server as `root` or as some other MySQL user that has access to the `mysql` database.

2. The procedure for running `mysql_fix_privilege_tables` differs for Unix and Windows. On Unix, run it like this, where *root_password* is the MySQL root password:

   ```
   shell> mysql_fix_privilege_tables --password=root_password
   ```

   On Windows, change location to the MySQL installation directory and run the following commands, where *root_password* is the MySQL root password:

   ```
   shell> bin\mysql -u root -p mysql
   Enter password: root_password
   mysql> SOURCE scripts/mysql_fix_privilege_tables.sql
   ```

   When you run `mysql_fix_privilege_tables`, `Duplicate column name` errors might occur and can be ignored.

3. After upgrading the grant tables, stop the server and restart it.

4. Consider whether any of your MySQL accounts should be given the new privileges. If so, issue the appropriate `GRANT` statements for those accounts.

36.2 Security-Related SQL Mode Values

Many operational characteristics of MySQL Server can be configured by setting the SQL mode. This mode consists of option values that each control some aspect of query processing or other server behavior. (See Chapter 1, "Client/Server Concepts," for background information on the SQL mode and how to control it.)

New SQL mode values are implemented from time to time. To determine whether a new release of MySQL includes new SQL mode values, check the upgrade notes in the installation chapter of the *MySQL Reference Manual*. By default, new mode values are not enabled by default as part of your server's SQL mode. However, if you decide that a given value should be part of the standard mode used by your server, you can enable that value with the `--sql-mode` startup option. (See Section 24.8, "Setting the Default SQL Mode.") For example, `TRADITIONAL` mode is new in MySQL 5. You can run the server in that mode by putting the following lines in an option file:

```
[mysqld]
sql-mode=TRADITIONAL
```

The following discussion lists examples of security-related SQL mode values that are new in MySQL 5, along with an explanation of why you might want to enable them for your server.

Additional information about these modes can be found in Section 5.8, "Handling Missing or Invalid Data Values."

- Several SQL mode values relate to data security. That is, they protect against data corruption through inadvertent or willful attempts at entering invalid data into tables:

  - Strict mode enables general input value restrictions. In strict mode, the server rejects values that are out of range, that have an incorrect data type, or that are missing for columns that have no default. Strict mode is enabled using the STRICT_ALL_TABLES and STRICT_TRANS_TABLES mode values.

  - Division by zero can be treated as an error for data entry by enabling the ERROR_FOR_DIVISION_BY_ZERO mode value and strict mode. In this case, attempts to enter data via INSERT or UPDATE statements produce an error if an expression includes division by zero. (With ERROR_FOR_DIVISION_BY_ZERO but not strict mode, division by zero results in a value of NULL and a warning, not an error.)

  - Several SQL mode values control how MySQL handles invalid date input. By default, MySQL requires that the month and day values correspond to an actual legal date, except that it allows "zero" dates ('0000-00-00') and dates that have zero parts ('2009-12-00', '2009-00-01'). Zero dates and dates with zero parts are allowed, even in strict mode. To prohibit such dates, enable strict mode and the NO_ZERO_DATE and NO_ZERO_IN_DATE mode values.

  - The TRADITIONAL mode value is a composite mode that enables strict mode as well as the other restrictions just described. If you want your MySQL server to be as restrictive as possible about input data checking (and thus to act like other "traditional" database servers), the simplest way to achieve this is to enable TRADITIONAL mode rather than a list of individual more-specific modes. Specifying TRADITIONAL has the additional advantage that if future versions of MySQL implement other input data restrictions that become part of TRADITIONAL mode, you won't have to change the server configuration to enable those modes to take advantage of them.

- The GRANT statement assigns privileges to an account, and it also creates the account if it does not already exist. However, implicit account creation might be a problem if you neglect to include an IDENTIFIED BY clause: In that case, GRANT creates a new account that has no password and thus is insecure.

  If you want to prevent the GRANT statement from creating new accounts unless an IDENTIFIED BY clause is given, enable the NO_AUTO_CREATE_USER SQL mode. Then, when you issue GRANT statements, you won't accidentally cause new accounts that have no password to spring into existence.

Several SQL mode values control how MySQL handles invalid date input. By default, MySQL requires that the month and day values correspond to an actual legal date, except that it allows "zero" dates ('0000-00-00') and dates that have zero parts ('2009-12-00', '2009-00-01'). Zero dates and dates with zero parts are allowed, even in strict mode. To prohibit such dates, enable strict mode and the NO_ZERO_DATE and NO_ZERO_IN_DATE mode values.

Optimizing Queries

This chapter discusses how to use information provided by the MySQL optimizer to improve query execution times. It also describes how to set up key caches for buffering index information in memory. The chapter covers the following exam topics:

- Identifying candidates for query analysis
- Using EXPLAIN to analyze queries
- Using SHOW WARNINGS for optimization purposes
- Creating key caches for MyISAM tables

37.1 Identifying Candidates for Query Analysis

Much of this chapter is devoted to the use of EXPLAIN as an analysis tool for making queries run faster, but we'll begin with a general discussion of how to identify which queries need optimizing. To this end, you can use several sources of information:

- Use your experience with the performance of individual applications.
- Use the information in the server's log files.
- Use the SHOW PROCESSLIST statement.

The process of identifying which queries to analyze can take into account individual queries and also global information about the query load processed by your MySQL server. At the level of individual queries, you may have some strong suspicions about the need for optimization when a query that you issue (for example, from within a particular application or using the mysql client) clearly takes a long time.

At a more global level, the server's log files can be helpful for getting an overall picture of the types of queries that your server is being used to process:

- The general query log contains a record of all SQL statements received by the server. It is the most representative log in terms of what the server's query mix is. Examining this log can quickly give you an idea of what the server is doing, such as what the typical

SELECT statements are. The perspective provided by this log can be especially useful if you are analyzing the performance of a server that you do not normally use and are unfamiliar with.

- The binary log records all statements that modify data. These don't return rows to clients, but they may be using WHERE clauses to determine which rows to modify. The WHERE clauses provide you with clues about where indexing would be helpful for processing updates more quickly.

- The slow query log records queries that take a log time to execute. A query that appears consistently in this log each time it's issued is likely to warrant some attention. Concentrate on those queries that appear in this log most often because it's not likely to be productive to focus on a query that appears in the log only once.

More information about the logs and how to interpret their contents is given in Chapter 24, "Starting, Stopping, and Configuring MySQL," and Chapter 40, "Interpreting Diagnostic Messages."

Another global tool that provides information about query execution is the SHOW PROCESSLIST statement. Use it periodically to get information about what queries currently are running. If you notice that a particular query often seems to be causing a backlog by making other queries block, see whether you can optimize it. If you're successful, it will alleviate the backlog. To get the most information from SHOW PROCESSLIST, you should have the PROCESS privilege. Then the statement will display queries being run by all clients, not just your own queries.

To some extent, "slow" can be a relative term. You don't want to waste time trying to optimize a query that seems slow but is so only for external reasons and is not inherently slow. Queries in the slow log are determined to be slow using wallclock (elapsed) time. Queries will appear more often in the log when the server host is heavily loaded than when it is not, so you should evaluate query execution time against general system activity on that host. A query might appear slow if the machine is very busy, but otherwise perform acceptably. For example, if filesystem backups are taking place, they'll incur heavy disk activity that impedes the performance of other programs, including the MySQL server. The machine might be processing a heavy load for other reasons, such as if you have a very active Web server running on the same host.

Keeping in mind the preceding considerations, you have a good indicator that a query might be in need of optimization if you find that it is consistently slow in comparison to other queries no matter when you run it, and you know the machine isn't just generally bogged down all the time.

Another factor to recognize is that the mere presence of a query in the slow query log does not necessarily mean that the query is slow. If the server is run with the --log-queries-not-using-indexes option, the slow query log also will contain queries that execute without using any index. In some cases, such a query may indeed be a prime candidate for optimization (for example, by adding an index). But in other cases, MySQL might elect not to use an existing index simply because a table is so small that scanning all of its rows is just as fast as using an index.

37.2 Using EXPLAIN to Analyze Queries

When a SELECT query does not run as quickly as you think it should, use the EXPLAIN statement to ask the MySQL server for information about how the query optimizer processes the query. This information is useful in several ways:

- EXPLAIN can provide information that points out the need to add an index.
- If a table already has indexes, you can use EXPLAIN to find out whether the optimizer is using them.
- If indexes exist but aren't being used, you can try writing a query different ways. EXPLAIN can tell you whether the rewrites are better for helping the server use the available indexes.

When using EXPLAIN to analyze a query, it's helpful to have a good understanding of the tables involved. If you need to determine a table's structure, remember that you can use DESCRIBE to obtain information about a table's columns, and SHOW INDEX for information about its indexes. (See Section 8.8, "Obtaining Table and Index Metadata.")

EXPLAIN works with SELECT queries, but can be used in an indirect way for UPDATE and DELETE statements as well: Write a SELECT statement that has the same WHERE clause as the UPDATE or DELETE and use EXPLAIN to analyze the SELECT.

The following discussion describes how EXPLAIN works. Section 22.3, "General Query Enhancement," discusses some general query-writing principles that help MySQL use indexes more effectively. You can apply those principles in conjunction with EXPLAIN to determine the best way of writing a query.

37.2.1 How EXPLAIN Works

To use EXPLAIN, write your SELECT query as you normally would, but place the keyword EXPLAIN in front of it. As a very simple example, take the following statement:

SELECT 1;

To see what EXPLAIN will do with it, issue the statement like this:

```
mysql> EXPLAIN SELECT 1;
+----------------+
| Comment        |
+----------------+
| No tables used |
+----------------+
```

In practice, it's unlikely that you'd use EXPLAIN very often for a query like that because the output tells you nothing interesting about optimization. Nevertheless, the example illustrates the important principle that EXPLAIN can be applied to any SELECT query. One of the implications of this principle is that you can use EXPLAIN with simple queries while you're learning how to use it and how to interpret its results. You don't have to begin with a complicated multiple-table join.

With that in mind, consider these two simple single-table queries:

```
SELECT * FROM Country WHERE Name = 'France';
SELECT * FROM Country WHERE Code = 'FRA';
```

Both queries produce the same output (information about the country of France), but they are not equally efficient. How do you know that? Because EXPLAIN tells you so. When you use EXPLAIN with each of the two queries, It provides the following information about how the MySQL optimizer views them:

```
mysql> EXPLAIN SELECT * FROM Country WHERE Name = 'France'\G
*************************** 1. row ***************************
           id: 1
  select_type: SIMPLE
        table: Country
         type: ALL
possible_keys: NULL
          key: NULL
      key_len: NULL
          ref: NULL
         rows: 239
        Extra: Using where
mysql> EXPLAIN SELECT * FROM Country WHERE Code = 'FRA'\G
*************************** 1. row ***************************
           id: 1
  select_type: SIMPLE
        table: Country
         type: const
possible_keys: PRIMARY
          key: PRIMARY
      key_len: 3
          ref: const
         rows: 1
        Extra:
```

EXPLAIN produces several columns of information. In the example just shown, NULL in the possible_keys and key columns shows for the first query that no index is considered available or usable for processing the query. For the second query, the table's PRIMARY KEY column (the Code column that contains three-letter country codes) can be used, and is in fact the index that the optimizer would choose. The rows column of the EXPLAIN output shows the effect of this difference. Its value indicates the number of rows that MySQL estimates it will need to examine while processing the query:

- For the first query, the value is 239, which happens to be the number of rows in the Country table. In other words, MySQL would scan all rows of the table, which is inefficient.

- For the second query, only one row need be examined. This is because MySQL can use the table's primary key to go directly to the single relevant row.

This example briefly indicates the kind of useful information that EXPLAIN can provide, even for simple queries. The conclusion to draw is that, if possible, you should use the Code column rather than the Name column to look up Country table records. However, the real power of EXPLAIN lies in what it can tell you about joins—SELECT queries that use multiple tables.

EXPLAIN is especially important for join analysis because joins have such enormous potential to increase the amount of processing the server must do. If you select from a table with a thousand rows, the server might need to scan all one thousand rows in the worst case. But if you perform a join between two tables with a thousand rows each, the server might need to examine every possible combination of rows, which is one million combinations. That's a much worse worst case. EXPLAIN can help you reduce the work the server must do to process such a query, so it's well worth using.

37.2.2 Analyzing a Query

The following example demonstrates how to use EXPLAIN to analyze and optimize a sample query. The purpose of the query is to answer the question, "Which cities have a population of more than 8 million?" and to display for each city its name and population, along with the country name. This question could be answered using only city information, except that to get each country's name rather than its code, city information must be joined to country information.

The example uses tables created from world database information. Initially, these tables will have no indexes, so EXPLAIN will show that the query is not optimal. The example then adds indexes and uses EXPLAIN to determine the effect of indexing on query performance.

Begin by creating the initial tables, CountryList and CityList, as follows. These are derived from the Country and City tables, but need contain only the columns involved in the query:

```
mysql> CREATE TABLE CountryList ENGINE = MyISAM
    -> SELECT Code, Name FROM Country;
Query OK, 239 rows affected (0.06 sec)
Records: 239  Duplicates: 0  Warnings: 0

mysql> CREATE TABLE CityList ENGINE = MyISAM
    -> SELECT CountryCode, Name, Population FROM City;
Query OK, 4079 rows affected (0.10 sec)
Records: 4079  Duplicates: 0  Warnings: 0
```

The query that retrieves the desired information in the required format looks like this:

```
mysql> SELECT CountryList.Name, CityList.Name, CityList.Population
    -> FROM CountryList, CityList
    -> WHERE CountryList.Code = CityList.CountryCode
    -> AND CityList.Population > 8000000;
+--------------------+-------------------+------------+
| Name               | Name              | Population |
+--------------------+-------------------+------------+
| Brazil             | São Paulo         |    9968485 |
| Indonesia          | Jakarta           |    9604900 |
| India              | Mumbai (Bombay)   |   10500000 |
| China              | Shanghai          |    9696300 |
| South Korea        | Seoul             |    9981619 |
| Mexico             | Ciudad de México  |    8591309 |
| Pakistan           | Karachi           |    9269265 |
| Turkey             | Istanbul          |    8787958 |
| Russian Federation | Moscow            |    8389200 |
| United States      | New York          |    8008278 |
+--------------------+-------------------+------------+
10 rows in set (0.03 sec)
```

While the tables are in their initial unindexed state, applying EXPLAIN to the query yields the following result:

```
mysql> EXPLAIN SELECT CountryList.Name, CityList.Name, CityList.Population
    -> FROM CountryList, CityList
    -> WHERE CountryList.Code = CityList.CountryCode
    -> AND CityList.Population > 8000000\G
*************************** 1. row ***************************
           id: 1
  select_type: SIMPLE
        table: CountryList
         type: ALL
possible_keys: NULL
          key: NULL
      key_len: NULL
          ref: NULL
         rows: 239
        Extra:
*************************** 2. row ***************************
           id: 1
  select_type: SIMPLE
        table: CityList
         type: ALL
possible_keys: NULL
          key: NULL
```

```
     key_len: NULL
         ref: NULL
        rows: 4079
       Extra: Using where
```

The information displayed by EXPLAIN shows that no optimizations could be made:

- The type value in each row shows how MySQL will read the corresponding table. For CountryList, the value of ALL indicates a full scan of all rows. For CityList, the value of ALL indicates a scan of all its rows to find a match for each CountryList row. In other words, all combinations of rows will be checked to find country code matches between the two tables.

- The number of row combinations is given by the product of the rows values, where rows represents the optimizer's estimate of how many rows in a table it will need to check at each stage of the join. In this case, the product is 239 × 4,079, or 974,881.

EXPLAIN shows that MySQL would need to check nearly a million row combinations to produce a query result that contains only 10 rows. Clearly, this query would benefit from the creation of indexes that allow the server to look up information faster.

Good columns to index are those that you typically use for searching, grouping, or sorting records. The query does not have any GROUP BY or ORDER BY clauses, but it does use columns for searching:

- The query uses CountryList.Code and CityList.CountryCode to match records between tables.

- The query uses CityList.Population to cull records that do not have a large enough population.

To see the effect of indexing, try creating indexes on the columns used to join the tables. In the CountryList table, Code can be used as a primary key because it uniquely identifies each row. Add the index using ALTER TABLE:

```
mysql> ALTER TABLE CountryList ADD PRIMARY KEY (Code);
```

In the CityList table, CountryCode must be a non-unique index because multiple cities can share the same country code:

```
mysql> ALTER TABLE CityList ADD INDEX (CountryCode);
```

After creating the indexes, EXPLAIN reports a somewhat different result:

```
mysql> EXPLAIN SELECT CountryList.Name, CityList.Name, CityList.Population
    -> FROM CountryList, CityList
    -> WHERE CountryList.Code = CityList.CountryCode
    -> AND CityList.Population > 8000000\G
```

```
*************************** 1. row ***************************
           id: 1
  select_type: SIMPLE
        table: CityList
         type: ALL
possible_keys: CountryCode
          key: NULL
      key_len: NULL
          ref: NULL
         rows: 4079
        Extra: Using where
*************************** 2. row ***************************
           id: 1
  select_type: SIMPLE
        table: CountryList
         type: eq_ref
possible_keys: PRIMARY
          key: PRIMARY
      key_len: 3
          ref: world.CityList.CountryCode
         rows: 1
        Extra:
```

Observe that EXPLAIN now lists the tables in a different order. CityList appears first, which indicates that MySQL will read rows from that table first and use them to search for matches in the second table, CountryList. The change in table processing order reflects the optimizer's use of the index information that is now available for executing the query.

MySQL still will scan all rows of the CityList table (its type value is ALL), but now the server can use each of those rows to directly look up the corresponding CountryList row. This is seen by the information displayed for the CountryList table:

- The type value of eq_ref indicates that an equality test is performed by referring to the column named in the ref field, CityList.CountryCode.

- The possible_keys value of PRIMARY shows that the optimizer sees the primary key as a candidate for optimizing the query, and the key field indicates that it will actually use the primary key when executing the query.

The result from EXPLAIN shows that indexing CountryList.Code as a primary key improves query performance. However, it still indicates a full scan of the CityList table. The optimizer sees that the index on CountryCode is available, but the key value of NULL indicates that it will not be used. Does that mean the index on the CountryCode column is of no value? It depends. For this query, the index is not used. In general, however, it's good to index joined columns, so you likely would find for other queries on the CityList table that the index does help.

The product of the rows now is just 4,079. That's much better than 974,881, but perhaps further improvement is possible. The WHERE clause of the query restricts CityList rows based on their Population values, so try creating an index on that column:

```
mysql> ALTER TABLE CityList ADD INDEX (Population);
```

After creating the index, run EXPLAIN again:

```
mysql> EXPLAIN SELECT CountryList.Name, CityList.Name, CityList.Population
    -> FROM CountryList, CityList
    -> WHERE CountryList.Code = CityList.CountryCode
    -> AND CityList.Population > 8000000\G
*************************** 1. row ***************************
           id: 1
  select_type: SIMPLE
        table: CityList
         type: range
possible_keys: CountryCode,Population
          key: Population
      key_len: 4
          ref: NULL
         rows: 78
        Extra: Using where
*************************** 2. row ***************************
           id: 1
  select_type: SIMPLE
        table: CountryList
         type: eq_ref
possible_keys: PRIMARY
          key: PRIMARY
      key_len: 3
          ref: world.CityList.CountryCode
         rows: 1
        Extra:
```

The output for the CountryList table is unchanged compared to the previous step. That is not a surprise; MySQL already found that it could use a primary key for lookups, which is very efficient. On the other hand, the result for the CityList table is different. The optimizer now sees two indexes in the table as candidates. Furthermore, the key value shows that it will use the index on Population to look up records. This results in an improvement over a full scan, as seen in the change of the rows value from 4,079 to 78.

The query now is optimized. Note that the product of the rows values, 78, still is larger than the actual number of rows produced by the query (10 rows). This is because the rows values are only estimates. The optimizer cannot give an exact count without actually executing the query.

To summarize:

- With unindexed tables, the rows product was 974,881.
- After indexing the join columns, the rows product dropped to 4,079, a 99.6% improvement.
- After indexing the Population column, the rows product dropped to 78, a further improvement of 98.1% over the previous step.

The example shows that using indexes effectively can substantially reduce the work required by the server to execute a query, and that EXPLAIN is a useful tool for assessing the effect of indexing.

37.2.3 EXPLAIN **Output Columns**

The EXPLAIN statement produces one row of output for each table named in each SELECT of the analyzed statement. (A statement can have more than one SELECT if it uses subqueries or UNION.) To use EXPLAIN productively, it's important to know the meaning of the columns in each row of output:

- id indicates which SELECT in the analyzed statement that the EXPLAIN output row refers to.
- select_type categorizes the SELECT referred to by the output row. This column can have any of the values shown in the following table. The word DEPENDENT indicates that a subquery is correlated with the outer query.

select_type Value	Meaning
SIMPLE	Simple SELECT statement (no subqueries or unions)
PRIMARY	The outer SELECT
UNION	Second or later SELECT in a union
DEPENDENT UNION	Second or later SELECT in a union that is dependent on the outer query
UNION RESULT	Result of a union
SUBQUERY	First SELECT in a subquery
DEPENDENT SUBQUERY	First SELECT in a subquery that is dependent on the outer query
DERIVED	Subquery in the FROM clause

- table is the name of the table to which the information in the row applies. The order of the tables indicates the order in which MySQL will read the tables to process the query. This is not necessarily the order in which you name them in the FROM clause, because the optimizer attempts to determine which order will result in the most efficient processing. The example in the preceding section showed this: The table order displayed by successive EXPLAIN statements changed as indexes were added.

- `type` indicates the join type. The value is a measure of how efficiently MySQL can scan the table. The possible `type` values are described later in this section.

- `possible_keys` indicates which of the table's indexes MySQL considers to be candidates for identifying rows that satisfy the query. This value can be a list of one or more index names, or NULL if there are no candidates. The word PRIMARY indicates that MySQL considers the table's primary key to be a candidate.

- `key` indicates the optimizer's decision about which of the candidate indexes listed in `possible_keys` will yield most efficient query execution. If the `key` value is NULL, it means no index was chosen. This might happen either because there were no candidates or because the optimizer believes it will be just as fast to scan the table rows as to use any of the possible indexes. A table scan might be chosen over an index scan if the table is small, or because the index would yield too high a percentage of the rows in the table to be of much use.

- `key_len` indicates how many bytes of index rows are used. From this value, you can derive how many columns from the index are used. For example, if you have an index consisting of three INT columns, each index row contains three 4-byte values. If `key_len` is 12, you know that the optimizer uses the all three columns of the index when processing the query. If `key_len` is 4 or 8, it uses only the first one or two columns (that is, it uses a leftmost prefix of the index).

  If you've indexed partial values of string columns, take that into account when assessing the `key_len` value. Suppose that you have a composite index on two CHAR(8) columns that indexes only the first 4 bytes of each column. In this case, a `key_len` value of 8 means that both columns of the index would be used, not just the first column.

- `ref` indicates which indexed column or columns are used to choose rows from the table. `const` means key values in the index are compared to a constant expression, such as in Code='FRA'. NULL indicates that neither a constant nor another column is being used, indicating selection by an expression or range of values. It might also indicate that the column does not contain the value specified by the constant expression. If neither NULL nor `const` is displayed, a *table_name.column_name* combination will be shown, indicating that the optimizer is looking at *column_name* in the rows returned from *table_name* to identify rows for the current table.

- `rows` is the optimizer's estimate of how many rows from the table it will need to examine. The value is an approximation because, in general, MySQL cannot know the exact number of rows without actually executing the query. For a multiple-table query, the product of the `rows` values is an estimate of the total number of row combinations that need to be read. This product gives you a rough measure of query performance. The smaller the value, the better.

- `Extra` provides other information about the join. The possible values are described later in this section.

The value in the `type` column of `EXPLAIN` output indicates the join type, but joins may be performed with varying degrees of efficiency. The `type` value provides a measure of this efficiency by indicating the basis on which rows are selected from each table. The following list shows the possible values, from the best type to the worst:

- `system`

  The table has exactly one row.

- `const`

  The table has exactly one matching row. This `type` value is similar to `system`, except that the table may have other, non-matching rows. The `EXPLAIN` output from the query with `WHERE Code='FRA'` is an example of this:

```
mysql> EXPLAIN SELECT * FROM Country WHERE Code = 'FRA'\G
*************************** 1. row ***************************
           id: 1
  select_type: SIMPLE
        table: Country
         type: const
possible_keys: PRIMARY
          key: PRIMARY
      key_len: 3
          ref: const
         rows: 1
        Extra:
```

  The query has a `type` value of `const` because only one row out of all its rows need be read. If the table contained *only* the row for France, there would be no non-matching rows and the `type` value would be `system` rather than `const`.

  For both `system` and `const`, because only one row matches, any columns needed from it can be read once and treated as constants while processing the rest of the query.

- `eq_ref`

  Exactly one row is read from the table for each combination of rows from the tables listed earlier by `EXPLAIN`. This is common for joins where MySQL can use a primary key to identify table rows.

- `ref`

  Several rows may be read from the table for each combination of rows from the tables listed earlier by `EXPLAIN`. This is similar to `eq_ref`, but can occur when a non-unique index is used to identify table rows or when only a leftmost prefix of an index is used. For example, the `CountryLanguage` table has a primary key on the `CountryCode` and `Language` columns. If you search using only a `CountryCode` value, MySQL can use that column as a leftmost prefix, but there might be several rows for a country if multiple languages are spoken there.

- `ref_or_null`

  Similar to `ref`, but MySQL also looks for rows that contain NULL.

- `index_merge`

  MySQL uses an index merge algorithm.

- `unique_subquery`

  Similar to `ref`, but used for IN subqueries that select from the primary key column of a single table.

- `index_subquery`

  Similar to `unique_subquery`, but used for IN subqueries that select from an indexed column of a single table.

- `range`

  The index is used to select rows that fall within a given range of index values. This is common for inequality comparisons such as `id < 10`.

- `index`

  MySQL performs a full scan, but it scans the index rather than the data rows. An index scan is preferable: The index is sorted and index rows usually are shorter than data rows, so index rows can be read in order and more of them can be read at a time.

- `ALL`

  A full table scan of all data rows. Typically, this indicates that no optimizations are done and represents the worst case. It is particularly unfortunate when tables listed later in EXPLAIN output have a join type of ALL because that indicates a table scan for every combination of rows selected from the tables processed earlier in the join.

The `Extra` column of EXPLAIN output provides additional information about how a table is processed. Some values indicate that the query is efficient:

- `Using index`

  MySQL can optimize the query by reading values from the index without having to read the corresponding data rows. This optimization is possible when the query selects only columns that are in the index.

- `Where used`

  MySQL uses a WHERE clause to identify rows that satisfy the query. Without a WHERE clause, you get all rows from the table.

- `Distinct`

  MySQL reads a single row from the table for each combination of rows from the tables listed earlier in the EXPLAIN output.

- `Not exists`

  MySQL can perform a LEFT JOIN "missing rows" optimization that quickly eliminates rows from consideration.

By contrast, some `Extra` values indicate that the query is not efficient:

- `Using filesort`

  Rows that satisfy the query must be sorted, which adds an extra processing step.

- `Using temporary`

  A temporary table must be created to process the query.

- `Range checked for each record`

  MySQL cannot determine in advance which index from the table to use. For each combination of rows selected from previous tables, it checks the indexes in the table to see which one will be best. This is not great, but it's better than using no index at all.

`Using filesort` and `Using temporary` generally are the two indicators of worst performance.

To use `EXPLAIN` for query analysis, examine its output for clues to ways the query might be improved. Modify the query, and then run `EXPLAIN` again to see how its output changes. Changes might involve rewriting the query or modifying the structure of your tables.

The following query rewriting techniques can be useful:

- If the keys value is `NULL` even when there are indexes available, you can try adding a `USE INDEX` option as a hint to the optimizer which index is relevant for the query. To force MySQL to use the index, use `FORCE INDEX`. To tell MySQL to ignore an index that it chose and choose a different one instead, use `IGNORE INDEX`. Each of these options is used in the `FROM` clause, following the table name containing the index you want to control. The option is followed by parentheses containing a comma-separated list of one or more index names. `PRIMARY` means the table's primary key.

  ```
  SELECT Name FROM CountryList USE INDEX(PRIMARY) WHERE Code > 'M';

  SELECT Name FROM CountryList IGNORE INDEX(Population)
  WHERE Code < 'B' AND Population > 50000000;
  ```

  The keyword `KEY` may be used instead of `INDEX` in all three options.

- If you want to force MySQL to join tables in a particular order, begin the query with `SELECT STRAIGHT_JOIN` rather than `SELECT`, and then list the tables in the desired order in the `FROM` clause.

- Sometimes a table in a query has an index available, but the query is written in such a way that prevents the index from being used. If you can rewrite the query into an equivalent form that allows use of the index, do so. Rewriting techniques are discussed in Section 22.3, "General Query Enhancement."

Another way to provide the optimizer with better information on which to base its decisions is to change the structure of your tables:

- If the `possible_keys` value is `NULL` in the output from `EXPLAIN`, it means MySQL finds no applicable index for processing the query. See whether an index can be added to the columns that identify which records to retrieve. For example, if you perform a join by matching a column in one table with a column in another, but neither of the columns is indexed, try indexing them.

- Keep table index statistics up to date to help MySQL choose optimal indexes. If the table is a MyISAM or InnoDB table, you can update its statistics with the ANALYZE TABLE statement. As a table's contents change, the statistics go out of date and become less useful to the optimizer in making good decisions about query execution strategies. You should run ANALYZE TABLE more frequently for tables that change often than for those that are updated rarely.

Be careful when using EXPLAIN to analyze a statement that includes a subquery in the FROM clause, if the subquery itself is slow. For such a subquery, MySQL must execute it to determine what it returns so that the optimizer can formulate an execution plan for the outer query.

37.3 Using SHOW WARNINGS for Optimization

The SHOW WARNINGS statement displays diagnostic messages produced by statements that encounter execution abnormalities. (See Section 21.2, "The SHOW WARNINGS Statement.") It's not an analysis tool in the same sense as EXPLAIN because it doesn't provide information about the optimizer. Rather, it can serve to identify statements that may simply be unnecessary. For example, DROP TABLE IF EXISTS produces a warning if the table does not exist. It's true that eliminating a single statement of this kind is likely to provide only a minimal gain in application performance. However, in the case that an application has a bug or is misdesigned, it might indeed be issuing large numbers of unnecessary statements, and use of SHOW WARNINGS can help you diagnose this.

37.4 MyISAM Index Caching

MySQL uses a key cache to buffer index information for MyISAM tables in memory. The key cache improves performance by reducing the need to read index blocks from disk each time they are accessed. By default, there is a single key cache, so all MyISAM tables share it.

MySQL uses the key cache automatically for MyISAM tables, but you can control cache behavior in several ways:

- One way to improve server performance is to make the key cache larger so that the server can hold more index information in memory. Section 39.3.1.3, "The MyISAM Key Cache," discusses key cache configuration in more detail.

- You can create additional key caches and assign specific tables to them. If a table is heavily used and you want to make sure that its index information never is displaced from the cache by indexes from other tables, create a separate cache and dedicate it for use by the table.

- You can preload a table's indexes into the cache to which it is assigned. This causes the server to load the index all at once, which is more efficient than having it read blocks individually as they are needed.

The following example shows how to create a key cache for use by a particular table. The example uses the City table from the world database and assigns it to a key cache named city_cache.

1. Create the key cache. Each cache is associated with a set of system variables that are grouped as components of a structured system variable. Each structured variable has a name, so you refer to a component variable using *cache_name.var_name* syntax. For our purposes here, the only relevant component is the key_buffer_size variable, which determines the size of a key cache. To create a key cache, assign a value to any of its component values. Thus, a cache named city_cache with a size of 4MB is created as follows:

   ```
   mysql> SET GLOBAL city_cache.key_buffer_size = 4194304;
   ```

   Key cache system variables are global, so the GLOBAL keyword is necessary in the SET statement. You must have the SUPER privilege to set global variables.

2. Assign the City table to the city_cache key cache by using a CACHE INDEX statement:

   ```
   mysql> CACHE INDEX world.City IN city_cache;
   +------------+-------------------+----------+----------+
   | Table      | Op                | Msg_type | Msg_text |
   +------------+-------------------+----------+----------+
   | world.City | assign_to_keycache | status   | OK       |
   +------------+-------------------+----------+----------+
   ```

3. Once the table has been assigned to city_cache, MySQL discards any index information for the table that currently is in the default key cache and begins using the new cache for queries that refer to the table. If you want to preload the table's indexes into the cache immediately, use a LOAD INDEX INTO CACHE statement:

   ```
   mysql> LOAD INDEX INTO CACHE world.City;
   +------------+--------------+----------+----------+
   | Table      | Op           | Msg_type | Msg_text |
   +------------+--------------+----------+----------+
   | world.City | preload_keys | status   | OK       |
   +------------+--------------+----------+----------+
   ```

The example demonstrates how to set up a key cache at runtime by issuing the appropriate SQL statements manually. To configure the cache every time the server starts, put the statements in an initialization file and use an --init-file option that names the file. Suppose that the data directory is /usr/local/mysql/data. Create a file named server.init in that directory and place the following statements in the file, one statement per line:

```
SET GLOBAL city_cache.key_buffer_size = 4194304;
CACHE INDEX world.City IN city_cache;
LOAD INDEX INTO CACHE world.City;
```

Then put the following lines in an option file:

```
[mysqld]
init-file=/usr/local/mysql/data/server.init
```

When the server starts, it will read and execute the statements in the file, causing the city_cache key cache to be set up.

The preceding discussion demonstrates how to associate a single table with a key cache, but you need not create a cache for each table. You might create a cache and associate a group of tables with it, such as all the tables used by a particular application.

Optimizing Databases

This chapter discusses how to optimize your databases by designing your tables so that MySQL can process their contents more efficiently. Some of these techniques apply to any storage engine. Others apply to specific engines. The chapter covers the following exam topics:

- General table-design principles that result in faster query processing
- Table normalization principles
- Optimization techniques for particular storage engines: MyISAM, InnoDB, MERGE, and MEMORY

38.1 General Table Optimizations

This section discusses some general table-design principles that apply for any storage engine.

- Use proper indexing for your tables so that MySQL can look up rows faster by value rather than by performing table scans.
- Use columns that are no longer than necessary. For example, don't use BIGINT if MEDIUMINT will do, or CHAR(255) if strings are never more than 100 characters long. Shorter columns require less storage and can be compared faster. If a column is indexed, making the column smaller allows more key values to fit in the index cache, which improves performance of index-based queries.
- Pay special attention to columns that are used to join one table to another. They should be indexed for fast lookup, and shorter columns can be compared to each other more quickly. Use the same data type for joined columns because, in general, like types can be compared faster than unlike types. (CHAR and VARCHAR columns that are declared as the same length are the same for comparison purposes.)
- Define columns as NOT NULL if possible. Allowing NULL values in a column complicates column processing somewhat because the query processor has to treat NULL values specially in some contexts. This results in a slight speed penalty.

- To analyze column contents, use PROCEDURE ANALYSE().
- Normalize your tables.
- Use summary tables.

Normalization is discussed later in this chapter. For further information on indexing techniques and summary tables, see Chapter 22, "Basic Optimizations."

Use of PROCEDURE ANALYSE() can help you determine whether columns can be redefined to smaller data types. It can also determine whether a column contains only a small number of values and could be defined as an ENUM. To tell PROCEDURE ANALYSE() not to suggest long ENUM definitions, pass it two arguments indicating the maximum number of elements and number of characters allowed in the definition. The following example shows the column types that PROCEDURE ANALYSE() suggests for the CountryLanguage table:

```
mysql> SELECT * FROM CountryLanguage PROCEDURE ANALYSE(10,256)\G
*************************** 1. row ***************************
            Field_name: world.CountryLanguage.CountryCode
             Min_value: ABW
             Max_value: ZWE
            Min_length: 3
            Max_length: 3
     Empties_or_zeros: 0
                 Nulls: 0
Avg_value_or_avg_length: 3.0000
                   Std: NULL
     Optimal_fieldtype: CHAR(3) NOT NULL
*************************** 2. row ***************************
            Field_name: world.CountryLanguage.Language
             Min_value: Abhyasi
             Max_value: [South]Mande
            Min_length: 2
            Max_length: 25
     Empties_or_zeros: 0
                 Nulls: 0
Avg_value_or_avg_length: 7.1606
                   Std: NULL
     Optimal_fieldtype: VARCHAR(25) NOT NULL
*************************** 3. row ***************************
            Field_name: world.CountryLanguage.IsOfficial
             Min_value: F
             Max_value: T
            Min_length: 1
            Max_length: 1
     Empties_or_zeros: 0
                 Nulls: 0
Avg_value_or_avg_length: 1.0000
```

```
                 Std: NULL
   Optimal_fieldtype: ENUM('F','T') NOT NULL
*************************** 4. row ***************************
          Field_name: world.CountryLanguage.Percentage
           Min_value: 0.1
           Max_value: 100.0
          Min_length: 3
          Max_length: 5
   Empties_or_zeros: 65
               Nulls: 0
Avg_value_or_avg_length: 20.4
                 Std: 30.8
   Optimal_fieldtype: FLOAT(3,1) NOT NULL
```

The actual types used in the table are shown by DESCRIBE:

```
mysql> DESCRIBE CountryLanguage;
+-------------+---------------+------+-----+---------+-------+
| Field       | Type          | Null | Key | Default | Extra |
+-------------+---------------+------+-----+---------+-------+
| CountryCode | char(3)       | NO   | PRI |         |       |
| Language    | char(30)      | NO   | PRI |         |       |
| IsOfficial  | enum('T','F') | NO   |     | F       |       |
| Percentage  | float(4,1)    | NO   |     | 0.0     |       |
+-------------+---------------+------+-----+---------+-------+
```

Comparing the two results, it appears that CountryLanguage already is defined fairly optimally.

38.2 Normalization

Normalization refers to the process of restructuring tables to eliminate design problems. Normalizing your tables removes redundant data, makes it possible to access data more flexibly, and eliminates the possibility that inappropriate modifications will take place that make the data inconsistent. Normalization of a complex table often amounts to taking it through a process of decomposition into a set of smaller tables. This process removes repeating groups within rows and then removes duplicate data within columns.

Normalization has several levels: First normal form, second normal form, and so forth. Each successive form depends on the preceding form and provides stronger guarantees about the data modification anomalies that are eliminated. This section discusses the first through third normal forms. These are the most common, though higher-level forms are possible.

- A table is in first normal form (1NF) if it contains no repeating groups within rows.
- A table is in second normal form (2NF) if it is in 1NF and every non-key value is fully dependent on the primary key value. The latter constraint means that a non-key value cannot depend only on some columns of the primary key.
- A table is in third normal form (3NF) if it is in 2NF and every non-key value depends directly on the primary key and not on some other non-key value.

The normalization process and the problems that it solves can be illustrated using the parts-and-suppliers scenario of which database designers are so fond. The following example serves as a demonstration that begins with a poorly designed table, and then improves the table design in stages until we reach third normal form. At each stage, the SQL statements are shown that produce the desired table modifications.

Begin with a table that is intended to keep track of a parts inventory. It lists supplier numbers, locations, and ZIP codes. For each supplier, it lists part numbers, names, and quantity-on-hand values: The table definition and some sample data follow:

```
mysql> CREATE TABLE Inventory
    -> (
    ->     sno INT,
    ->     sloc CHAR(20),
    ->     szip CHAR(20),
    ->     pno1 INT,
    ->     pname1 CHAR(20),
    ->     qty1 INT,
    ->     pno2 INT,
    ->     pname2 CHAR(20),
    ->     qty2 INT
    -> );
mysql> INSERT INTO Inventory VALUES
    -> (1,'Chicago','60632', 1,'stool',5,2,'lamp',15),
    -> (2,'Dallas','75206',1,'stool',25,3,'desk',10),
    -> (3,'Chicago','60632',2,'lamp',10,4,'chair',3);
mysql> SELECT * FROM Inventory ORDER BY sno;
+------+---------+-------+------+--------+------+------+--------+------+
| sno  | sloc    | szip  | pno1 | pname1 | qty1 | pno2 | pname2 | qty2 |
+------+---------+-------+------+--------+------+------+--------+------+
|    1 | Chicago | 60632 |    1 | stool  |    5 |    2 | lamp   |   15 |
|    2 | Dallas  | 75206 |    1 | stool  |   25 |    3 | desk   |   10 |
|    3 | Chicago | 60632 |    2 | lamp   |   10 |    4 | chair  |    3 |
+------+---------+-------+------+--------+------+------+--------+------+
```

This table design has several problems:

- The structure uses repeating groups. That is, it has multiple columns for similar types of information (parts for a given supplier). Designing a table this way doesn't allow for more than a fixed number of parts per supplier. The table could be altered to include more part columns, but the number of parts remains fixed and another change would be required should more parts need to be listed for a supplier some day.

- The design wastes space. Rows for suppliers with fewer than two parts have empty columns. Also, the columns for the second part cannot be declared NOT NULL because they might need to be set to NULL to indicate that a second part is not listed in a record.

- It is difficult to formulate efficient queries. To test a condition on part values, you must write an expression that has two terms (one for each part). Such queries are not easy to maintain: If you add more part columns, the query must be rewritten to add terms to conditional expressions.

To put the information in first normal form, the repeating groups must be eliminated. This can be done by creating a table in which rows associate the supplier information with information for only a single part, as follows:

```
mysql> CREATE TABLE Inventory2
    -> (
    ->     sno INT NOT NULL,
    ->     sloc CHAR(20) NOT NULL,
    ->     szip CHAR(20) NOT NULL,
    ->     pno INT NOT NULL,
    ->     pname CHAR(20) NOT NULL,
    ->     qty INT,
    ->     PRIMARY KEY (sno, pno)
    -> );
mysql> INSERT INTO Inventory2 (sno, sloc, szip, pno, pname, qty)
    -> SELECT sno, sloc, szip, pno1, pname1, qty1 FROM Inventory;
mysql> INSERT INTO Inventory2 (sno, sloc, szip, pno, pname, qty)
    -> SELECT sno, sloc, szip, pno2, pname2, qty2 FROM Inventory;
mysql> SELECT * FROM Inventory2 ORDER BY sno, pno;
```

sno	sloc	szip	pno	pname	qty
1	Chicago	60632	1	stool	5
1	Chicago	60632	2	lamp	15
2	Dallas	75206	1	stool	25
2	Dallas	75206	3	desk	10
3	Chicago	60632	2	lamp	10
3	Chicago	60632	4	chair	3

The Inventory2 table has no repeating groups and is in 1NF. However, it has a lot of redundancy. Each row has supplier number, location, and ZIP code, when only the number is needed to associate a part with its supplier.

As a result, inconsistencies can easily result from updates. Deleting a row for a given part also deletes supplier information. If the part was the only one for the supplier, there is no longer any information in the table about the existence of that supplier. If you want to change a supplier's location or ZIP code, you must change multiple rows. There are also constraints on how you add data. You cannot insert a supplier without having a part for it first.

To fix these problems, split apart the `Inventory2` table into separate `Supplier` and `Part` tables, and associate each part only with the supplier number:

```
mysql> CREATE TABLE Supplier
    -> (
    ->     sno INT NOT NULL,
    ->     sloc CHAR(20) NOT NULL,
    ->     szip CHAR(20) NOT NULL,
    ->     PRIMARY KEY (sno)
    -> );
mysql> CREATE TABLE Part
    -> (
    ->     sno INT NOT NULL,
    ->     pno INT NOT NULL,
    ->     pname CHAR(20) NOT NULL,
    ->     qty INT NOT NULL,
    ->     PRIMARY KEY (sno, pno)
    -> );
mysql> INSERT INTO Supplier
    -> SELECT DISTINCT sno, sloc, szip FROM Inventory2;
mysql> INSERT INTO Part (sno, pno, pname, qty)
    -> SELECT sno, pno, pname, qty FROM Inventory2;
mysql> SELECT * FROM Supplier ORDER BY sno;
+-----+---------+-------+
| sno | sloc    | szip  |
+-----+---------+-------+
|   1 | Chicago | 60632 |
|   2 | Dallas  | 75206 |
|   3 | Chicago | 60632 |
+-----+---------+-------+
mysql> SELECT * FROM Part ORDER BY sno, pno;
+-----+-----+-------+-----+
| sno | pno | pname | qty |
+-----+-----+-------+-----+
|   1 |   1 | stool |   5 |
|   1 |   2 | lamp  |  15 |
|   2 |   1 | stool |  25 |
|   2 |   3 | desk  |  10 |
|   3 |   2 | lamp  |  10 |
```

```
|   3 |   4 | chair |   3 |
+-----+-----+-------+-----+
```

The key for the `Supplier` table is the supplier number. The key for the `Part` table is a composite key based on both supplier and part number. (The key for parts must include the supplier number because a given part might be available from more than one supplier.)

The `Supplier` table is 2NF because it is in 1NF and every non-key column depends on the primary key (the supplier number). On the other hand, the `Part` table is not in 2NF. Although the quantity depends on the entire composite primary key (the `sno` and `pno` columns), the part name depends only on the part number. This requires a further modification to split the name information off into another table:

```
mysql> CREATE TABLE PartName
    -> (
    ->     pno INT NOT NULL,
    ->     pname CHAR(20) NOT NULL,
    ->     PRIMARY KEY (pno)
    -> );
mysql> INSERT INTO PartName (pno, pname)
    -> SELECT DISTINCT pno, pname FROM Part;
mysql> ALTER TABLE Part DROP pname;
mysql> SELECT * FROM Part ORDER BY sno, pno;
+-----+-----+-----+
| sno | pno | qty |
+-----+-----+-----+
|   1 |   1 |   5 |
|   1 |   2 |  15 |
|   2 |   1 |  25 |
|   2 |   3 |  10 |
|   3 |   2 |  10 |
|   3 |   4 |   3 |
+-----+-----+-----+
mysql> SELECT * FROM PartName ORDER BY pno;
+-----+-------+
| pno | pname |
+-----+-------+
|   1 | stool |
|   2 | lamp  |
|   3 | desk  |
|   4 | chair |
+-----+-------+
```

At this point, the `Part` and `PartName` are in 3NF because they are in 2NF and each non-key value depends directly on the primary key and not on some other non-key value. However, the `Supplier` table is in 2NF but not 3NF because there is a transitive dependency. The `szip` column depends on the primary key, but not directly: It depends on `sloc`, which depends on the primary key. This allows certain updates to cause problems. For example, you cannot add information about locations and ZIP codes without having a supplier for the given location.

To place the supplier information in 3NF, it's necessary to split out the ZIP code from the Supplier table and create a table that maps supplier location to ZIP code. The resulting Supplier and SupplierZip tables have the following structure.

```
mysql> CREATE TABLE SupplierZip
    -> (
    ->     sloc CHAR(20) NOT NULL,
    ->     szip CHAR(20) NOT NULL,
    ->     PRIMARY KEY (sloc)
    -> );
mysql> INSERT INTO SupplierZip SELECT DISTINCT sloc, szip FROM Supplier;
mysql> ALTER TABLE Supplier DROP szip;
mysql> SELECT * FROM Supplier ORDER BY sno;
+-----+---------+
| sno | sloc    |
+-----+---------+
|   1 | Chicago |
|   2 | Dallas  |
|   3 | Chicago |
+-----+---------+
mysql> SELECT * FROM SupplierZip ORDER BY sloc;
+---------+-------+
| sloc    | szip  |
+---------+-------+
| Chicago | 60632 |
| Dallas  | 75206 |
+---------+-------+
```

Now Supplier and SupplierZip both are in 3NF because no non-key column depends on another non-key column. To modify any non-key value, the row to modify can be identified uniquely by referring to the primary key.

The original non-normal Inventory table has been decomposed into a set of normalized tables. For normalization to be correct, it must result in no loss of data. That is, it must be possible to reconstruct the original data by joining the normalized tables. Let's check that:

```
mysql> SELECT S.sno, S.sloc, SZ.szip, P.pno, PT.pname, P.qty
    -> FROM Supplier S, SupplierZip SZ, Part P, PartName PT
    -> WHERE S.sloc = SZ.sloc AND S.sno = P.sno AND P.pno = PT.pno
    -> ORDER BY S.sno, P.pno;
+-----+---------+-------+-----+-------+-----+
| sno | sloc    | szip  | pno | pname | qty |
+-----+---------+-------+-----+-------+-----+
|   1 | Chicago | 60632 |   1 | stool |   5 |
```

```
|   1 | Chicago | 60632 |   2 | lamp  | 15 |
|   2 | Dallas  | 75206 |   1 | stool | 25 |
|   2 | Dallas  | 75206 |   3 | desk  | 10 |
|   3 | Chicago | 60632 |   2 | lamp  | 10 |
|   3 | Chicago | 60632 |   4 | chair |  3 |
+-----+---------+-------+-----+-------+----+
```

That is indeed the same as the contents of the original Inventory table.

A summary of normalization benefits:

- Tables do not contain redundant data. One result is reduced storage requirements due to elimination of duplicate values. Another result is better data integrity when updates are performed due to the reduced chance of updating one instance of a value but not others when all are to be changed, or updating too many values when only one is to be changed.

- Individual tables become smaller, which improves performance in various ways. For example, index creation is faster, and table locks don't lock as much data so concurrency is better due to reduced contention.

- Normalization makes it easier to identify specific objects uniquely. Breaking data into multiple tables provides the flexibility to combine information in different ways (using joins) more easily.

- Normalized tables make it easier to write better joins, so the optimizer works better. There are fewer indexes per table, so the optimizer doesn't have to consider as many execution plans. This helps both retrievals and updates.

38.3 MyISAM-Specific Optimizations

Several of the structural features of MyISAM tables enable you to optimize how you use them:

- The MyISAM storage engine supports several different table storage formats that have differing characteristics. You can take advantage of these characteristics by choosing the storage format that best matches how you intend to use a table. For example, if you have a table that you'll only read and never update, you can make it a compressed table. It will take less disk space, and internal index optimizations might make retrievals faster. A dynamic-row table for which most queries are made against fixed-length columns can be split into fixed and dynamic tables.

- Perform table maintenance operations to keep optimizer information up to date and eliminate wasted space.

- Create FULLTEXT indexes to enable fast text searching.

- Specify the MAX_ROWS table option to size the internal row pointers appropriately. Increase the pointer size to allow a table to contain more data than the default amount of 256TB. Decrease the pointer size for smaller tables to save on pointer storage.

- To distribute disk activity, use table symlinking to move some of your MyISAM tables to different disks than the one where the data directory is located.

The following discussion covers most of the items in the preceding list. Section 41.2.2, "MyISAM Table Symlinking," describes how to use table symlinking.

38.3.1 MyISAM **Row-Storage Formats**

The MyISAM storage engine supports three row formats for storing table contents. These row-storage formats have an impact on query efficiency. The three allowable formats are fixed-length, dynamic-length, and compressed:

- With fixed-length row format, every row in a table has the same size. Consequently, every row in the table's data file is stored at a position that is a multiple of the row size. This makes it easier to look up rows, with the result that MySQL typically can process fixed-row tables more quickly than dynamic-row tables. However, fixed-row tables on average take more space than dynamic-row tables. Fixed-row tables are not very subject to fragmentation when deletes occur, because the hole left by any deleted row can be exactly filled by any new row.

- With dynamic-length row format, rows in a table use varying amounts of storage. As a result, rows are not stored at fixed positions within data files. Each row has extra information that indicates how long the row is, and it's also possible for a row to be stored non-contiguously with different pieces in different locations. This makes retrievals more complex, and thus slower. Dynamic-row tables generally take less space than fixed-row tables. However, if a table is updated frequently, this storage format can result in fragmentation and wasted space. It can be useful to run OPTIMIZE TABLE from time to time to defragment the table.

- Compressed tables are packed to save space and stored in optimized form that allows quick retrievals. Compressed tables are read-only, so this table format cannot be used for tables that will be updated. To create a compressed table, use the myisampack utility. It can create compressed tables from either fixed-row or dynamic-row MyISAM tables, and can compress columns of any data type.

Before MySQL 5, a MyISAM table could use fixed-row table format only if the table contained no columns with variable-length data types (VARCHAR, VARBINARY, TEXT, or BLOB). If any column had a variable-length type, dynamic-row format was used. Those rules describe the row format you should expect to see for MyISAM tables that were created with an older version of MySQL.

As of MySQL 5, fixed-row format can be used as long as the table does not contain any TEXT or BLOB columns.

To specify a row format explicitly for a new table, include a ROW_FORMAT table option in the CREATE TABLE statement. The value can be FIXED or DYNAMIC. The following statement creates t as a fixed-row table:

```
CREATE TABLE t (c CHAR(50)) ROW_FORMAT = FIXED;
```

To convert a MyISAM table from one format to another, use the ROW_FORMAT option with ALTER TABLE:

```
ALTER TABLE t ROW_FORMAT = DYNAMIC;
```

To determine what storage format a table has, use the SHOW TABLE STATUS statement and examine the value of the Row_format field:

```
mysql> SHOW TABLE STATUS LIKE 'Country'\G
*************************** 1. row ***************************
           Name: Country
         Engine: MyISAM
        Version: 10
     Row_format: Fixed
           Rows: 239
 Avg_row_length: 261
    Data_length: 62379
Max_data_length: 1120986464255
   Index_length: 5120
      Data_free: 0
 Auto_increment: NULL
    Create_time: 2005-05-05 12:30:25
    Update_time: 2005-05-05 12:30:25
     Check_time: NULL
      Collation: latin1_swedish_ci
       Checksum: NULL
 Create_options:
        Comment:
```

The Row_format value will be Fixed, Dynamic, or Compressed. (Only the myisampack utility can set the format to Compressed.)

You can also obtain storage format information from the INFORMATION_SCHEMA database:

```
mysql> SELECT TABLE_NAME, ROW_FORMAT FROM INFORMATION_SCHEMA.TABLES
    -> WHERE TABLE_SCHEMA = 'world';
+-----------------+------------+
| TABLE_NAME      | ROW_FORMAT |
+-----------------+------------+
| City            | Fixed      |
| Country         | Fixed      |
| CountryLanguage | Fixed      |
+-----------------+------------+
```

38.3.1.1 Using Compressed MyISAM Tables

A fixed-row or dynamic-row MyISAM table can be converted to compressed form to save storage space. In many cases, compressing a table improves lookup speed as well because the compression operation optimizes the internal structure of the table to make retrievals faster.

To be a good candidate for compression, a table should contain records that will not be updated in the future, such as archival data or log records. If you log records into different tables by year or month, for example, you can compress all the log tables except the one for the current year or month. To treat the tables as a single logical table, group them by using a MERGE table.

A compressed table is read-only, so a MyISAM table should be compressed only if its content will not change after it has been populated. If you *must* modify a compressed table, you can uncompress it, modify it, and compress it again. But if you have to do this often, the extra processing tends to negate the benefits of using a compressed table, especially because the table is unavailable for querying while it is being uncompressed and recompressed.

To compress a MyISAM table, use the myisampack utility. It's also necessary to use myisamchk afterward to update the indexes. The following example demonstrates how to perform this procedure, using the tables in the world database. **Note:** A table must not be in use by other programs (including the server) while you compress or uncompress it. The easiest thing to do is to stop the server while using myisampack or myisamchk.

1. Back up the tables, just in case:

```
shell> mysqldump world > world.sql
```

2. Stop the server so that it won't use the tables while you're packing them.

3. Change location into the database directory where the world tables are stored, and then use myisampack to compress them:

```
shell> myisampack Country City CountryLanguage
Compressing Country.MYD: (239 records)
- Calculating statistics
- Compressing file
72.95%
Compressing City.MYD: (4079 records)
- Calculating statistics
- Compressing file
70.94%
Compressing CountryLanguage.MYD: (984 records)
- Calculating statistics
- Compressing file
71.42%
Remember to run myisamchk -rq on compressed tables
```

myisampack also understands index filenames as arguments:

```
shell> myisampack *.MYI
```

Using index filenames does not affect the way myisampack works. It simply gives you an easier way to name a group of tables, because you can use filename patterns.

4. After compressing a table, you should run myisamchk to rebuild the indexes (as the final line of myisampack output indicates). Like myisampack, myisamchk understands index filename arguments for naming tables, so you can rebuild the indexes as follows:

```
shell> myisamchk -rq *.MYI
```

The equivalent long-option command is:

```
shell> myisamchk --recover --quick *.MYI
```

5. Restart the server.

If you want to assess how effective a table-packing operation is, use SHOW TABLE STATUS before and after. (The server must be running when you use this statement.) The Data_length and Index_length values should be smaller afterward, and the Row_format value should change from Fixed or Dynamic to Compressed. The following examples show the results for the City table.

Before packing:

```
mysql> SHOW TABLE STATUS FROM world LIKE 'City'\G
*************************** 1. row ***************************
          Name: City
        Engine: MyISAM
       Version: 10
    Row_format: Fixed
          Rows: 4079
Avg_row_length: 67
   Data_length: 273293
Max_data_length: 18858823439613951
  Index_length: 43008
     Data_free: 0
Auto_increment: 4080
   Create_time: 2005-06-09 11:53:30
   Update_time: 2005-06-09 11:53:30
    Check_time: NULL
     Collation: latin1_swedish_ci
      Checksum: NULL
Create_options:
       Comment:
```

After packing:

```
mysql> SHOW TABLE STATUS FROM world LIKE 'City'\G
*************************** 1. row ***************************
          Name: City
        Engine: MyISAM
```

```
        Version: 10
     Row_format: Compressed
           Rows: 4079
 Avg_row_length: 19
    Data_length: 79418
Max_data_length: 281474976710655
   Index_length: 30720
      Data_free: 0
 Auto_increment: 4080
    Create_time: 2005-06-09 11:53:30
    Update_time: 2005-06-09 11:53:30
     Check_time: 2005-06-09 11:54:12
      Collation: latin1_swedish_ci
       Checksum: 2011482258
 Create_options:
        Comment:
```

The results show that compressing the City table compressed the index moderately and that data storage requirements became less than a third of the uncompressed amount.

To uncompress a compressed table, use myisamchk in the database directory where the table files are located:

```
shell> myisamchk --unpack table_name
```

table_name should be either the table name or the name of its index (.MYI) file.

If you do not run myisampack or myisamchk in the database directory where the table files are located, you must specify the pathname to the files, using either absolute pathnames or pathnames relative to your current directory.

Another way to uncompress a table is to dump it, drop it, and re-create it. Do this while the server is running. For example, if the Country table is compressed, you can uncompress it with the following commands:

```
shell> mysqldump world Country > dump.sql
shell> mysql world < dump.sql
```

By default, mysqldump output written to the dump file includes a DROP TABLE statement. When you process the file with mysql, that statement drops the compressed table, and the rest of the dump file re-creates the table in uncompressed form.

38.3.1.2 Splitting Dynamic-Row MyISAM Tables

If a dynamic-row MyISAM table contains a mix of fixed-length and variable-length columns but many of the queries on the table access only its fixed-length columns, it is sometimes possible to gain advantages both of fixed-row tables (faster retrieval) and of dynamic-row tables (lower storage requirements) by splitting the table into two tables. Use a fixed-row table to hold the fixed-length columns and a dynamic-row table to hold the variable-length columns. Use the following procedure to split a table into two tables:

1. Make sure that the table contains a primary key that allows each record to be uniquely identified. (You might use an AUTO_INCREMENT column, for example.)

2. Create a second table that has columns for all the variable-length columns in the original table, plus a column to store values from the primary key of the original table. (This column should be a primary key as well, but should not be an AUTO_INCREMENT column.) Specify the ROW_FORMAT = DYNAMIC option when you create the table.

3. Copy the contents of the primary key column and the variable-length columns from the original table to the second table.

4. Use ALTER TABLE to drop the variable-length columns (but not the primary key) from the original table. Include a ROW_FORMAT = FIXED option as well, to make sure the table is converted to fixed-row format.

After modifying the table structure this way, queries that retrieve only fixed-length columns can use the fixed-row table, and will be quicker. For queries that retrieve both fixed-length and variable-length columns, join the two tables using the primary key values to match up rows.

38.3.2 Keep Optimizer Information Up to Date

You can help the optimizer process queries for a MyISAM table more effectively if you keep the table's internal index statistics up to date. Use the ANALYZE TABLE statement for this:

```
ANALYZE TABLE table_name;
```

Update the index statistics after a table has been has been loaded initially, and periodically thereafter if the table continues to be modified.

If the table contains columns with variable-length data types such as BLOB, TEXT, or VARCHAR, updates and deletes can cause the table to become fragmented. Optimizing the table periodically reorganizes its contents by defragmenting it to eliminate wasted space and coalescing values that might have gotten split into non-contiguous pieces. To optimize a MyISAM table, use OPTIMIZE TABLE:

```
OPTIMIZE TABLE table_name;
```

For MyISAM tables, the OPTIMIZE TABLE statement also updates index statistics; you don't need to use ANALYZE TABLE if you already are using OPTIMIZE TABLE.

38.3.3 FULLTEXT Indexes

FULLTEXT searching is a feature that can be used with MyISAM tables. FULLTEXT indexes are designed to make text searching fast and easy. They have the following characteristics:

- Each column in a FULLTEXT index must have a non-binary string data type (CHAR, VARCHAR, or TEXT). You cannot use binary string data types (BINARY, VARBINARY, or BLOB).

- FULLTEXT indexes can be case sensitive or not, depending on the collation of the indexed columns.

- The syntax for defining a full-text index is much like that for other indexes: an index-type keyword (FULLTEXT), an optional index name, and a parenthesized list of one or more column names to be indexed. A FULLTEXT index may be created with CREATE TABLE, added to a table with ALTER TABLE or CREATE INDEX, and dropped from a table with ALTER TABLE or DROP INDEX. The following are all legal statements for FULLTEXT index manipulation:

```
CREATE TABLE t (name CHAR(40), FULLTEXT (name));
ALTER TABLE t ADD FULLTEXT name_idx (name);
ALTER TABLE t DROP INDEX name_idx;
CREATE FULLTEXT INDEX name_idx ON t (name);
DROP INDEX name_idx ON t;
```

  See Section 8.6, "Indexes," for general information on index-creation syntax.

- Column prefixes are not applicable to FULLTEXT indexes, which always index entire columns. If you specify a prefix length for a column in a FULLTEXT index, MySQL ignores it.

- FULLTEXT index indexes can be constructed on multiple columns, allowing searches to be conducted simultaneously on all the indexed columns. However, leftmost index prefixes are not applicable for FULLTEXT indexes. You must construct one index for every column or combination of columns you want to search. Suppose that you want to search for text sometimes only in column c1 and sometimes in both columns c1 and c2. You must construct two FULLTEXT indexes: one on column c1 and another on columns c1 and c2.

To perform a FULLTEXT search, use MATCH and AGAINST(). For example, to search the table t for records that contain 'Wendell' in the name column, use this query:

```
SELECT * FROM t WHERE MATCH(name) AGAINST('Wendell');
```

The MATCH operator names the column or columns you want to search. As mentioned earlier, there must be a FULLTEXT index on exactly those columns. If you want to search different sets of columns, you'll need one FULLTEXT index for each set. If a table people has name and address columns and you want to search them either separately or together, three FULLTEXT indexes are needed:

```
CREATE TABLE people
(
    name    CHAR(40),
    address CHAR(40),
    FULLTEXT (name),        # index for searching name only
```

```
    FULLTEXT (address),     # index for searching address only
    FULLTEXT (name,address) # index for searching name and address
);
```

The indexes allow queries such as the following to be formulated:

```
SELECT * FROM people WHERE MATCH(name) AGAINST('string');
SELECT * FROM people WHERE MATCH(address) AGAINST('string');
SELECT * FROM people WHERE MATCH(name,address) AGAINST('string');
```

For more information on FULLTEXT indexing and searching, see the *MySQL Reference Manual.*

38.3.4 Specifying MyISAM **Maximum Row Count**

Internally, the MyISAM storage engine represents pointers to rows within a table using values that take from two to seven bytes each. The size for a given table is determined at table-creation time, but can be changed with ALTER TABLE.

Before MySQL 5, the default pointer size was four bytes, which allows for up to 4GB of data in MyISAM tables . In MySQL 5, the default was increased to six bytes to better accommodate the trend toward use of larger tables. The six-byte size allows for up to 256TB of data. You can provide hints to MyISAM about how large the table might become, or set the pointer size directly. With larger pointer sizes, MyISAM tables can contain up to 65,536TB of data.

When you expect a table to contain many rows, MAX_ROWS is useful for telling MyISAM that it needs to use larger internal row pointers so that the amount of table data can be larger than the 256TB allowed by the default six-byte pointer size. Conversely, if you know a table will be small, specifying a small MAX_ROWS value tells MyISAM to use smaller pointers. This saves space and improves table processing efficiency.

To provide the server a hint when you create the table, specify an option in the CREATE TABLE statement that indicates how many rows the table must be able to hold. You can change the option later with ALTER TABLE should the table need to become larger.

To "pre-size" a table when you create it, use a MAX_ROWS option to indicate how many rows the table must be able to hold. The following statement indicates to MySQL that the table must be able to contain at least two million rows:

```
CREATE TABLE t (i INT) MAX_ROWS = 2000000;
```

If a table reaches the row limit allowed by its row pointer size, a data file full error occurs and you cannot add any more rows. This error is unrelated to running of out disk space or reaching the maximum file size allowed by MyISAM or the filesystem. It means that you need to increase the row pointer size. To set or change the MAX_ROWS value for an existing table, use ALTER TABLE:

```
ALTER TABLE t MAX_ROWS = 4000000;
```

MAX_ROWS = *n* does not place an absolute limit of *n* on the number of rows a table can contain. Rather, it means that the table must be able to contain a maximum of at least *n* rows. The table might well be able to hold more than *n* rows.

A related option, AVG_ROW_LENGTH, also gives the server information that it can use to estimate how large the table may become. This option might be helpful for tables with variable-length rows. It is unnecessary for tables with fixed-length rows because the server knows how long each row is.

The MAX_ROWS and AVG_ROW_LENGTH options may be used separately or together. For example, if a table has a BIGINT column (8 bytes each) and a VARCHAR(200) column where you expect the average string length to be 100 bytes, you can specify an AVG_ROW_LENGTH value of 108. If you also want to make sure that the table can hold four million rows, create it like this:

```
CREATE TABLE t (i BIGINT, c VARCHAR(200))
AVG_ROW_LENGTH = 108 MAX_ROWS = 4000000;
```

Note that using MAX_ROWS and AVG_ROW_LENGTH does not allow the size of MyISAM table files to be expanded beyond the limit of what the filesystem allows. For example, if you create a MyISAM table on a filesystem that only allows file sizes up to 2GB, you cannot add more rows once the data file or index file reaches 2GB, no matter what value you set MAX_ROWS to.

To determine the values of MAX_ROWS and AVG_ROW_LENGTH for a table, use SHOW TABLE STATUS and check the Create_options field of the output. If the field is empty, the options have never been set explicitly.

```
mysql> SHOW TABLE STATUS LIKE 't'\G
*************************** 1. row ***************************
           Name: t
         Engine: MyISAM
        Version: 10
     Row_format: Dynamic
           Rows: 0
 Avg_row_length: 0
    Data_length: 0
Max_data_length: 4294967295
   Index_length: 1024
      Data_free: 0
 Auto_increment: NULL
    Create_time: 2005-06-09 12:00:01
    Update_time: 2005-06-09 12:00:01
     Check_time: NULL
      Collation: latin1_swedish_ci
       Checksum: NULL
 Create_options: max_rows=4000000 avg_row_length=108
        Comment:
```

The default row pointer size is determined from the value of the `myisam_data_pointer_size` system variable. This variable has a value of 6 initially, but you can set it to any value from 2 to 7. For example, if you routinely create tables that must be larger than 256TB, make the value larger than 6. You can do this at server startup by setting the value in an option file. The following lines increase the default size to seven bytes:

```
[mysqld]
myisam_data_pointer_size=7
```

38.4 `InnoDB`-Specific Optimizations

Several strategies may be used with `InnoDB` to improve performance. Some of these can be used at the application level. Others are a result of the way that the database administrator configures `InnoDB` itself.

Application-level optimizations may be made in terms of how you design tables or issue queries:

- Take advantage of `InnoDB` indexing structure. Use a primary key in each table, but make the key values as short as possible. `InnoDB` uses the primary key to locate the table rows. Other (secondary) indexes are keyed to the primary key values, which means that there is a level of indirection to find the table rows. Thus, shorter primary key values make for quicker lookups not only for queries that use the primary key, but also for queries that use secondary indexes. Secondary indexes will also take less space because each secondary index record contains a copy of the corresponding primary key value.

- Use `VARCHAR` columns rather than `CHAR` columns in `InnoDB` tables. The average amount of space used will be less, resulting in less disk I/O during query processing. (This behavior differs from that of `MyISAM` tables, which, due to their storage format, generally are faster for fixed-length rows than for dynamic-length rows.)

- Avoid using the `FOR UPDATE` or `LOCK IN SHARE MODE` locking modifiers for queries if there is no index that `InnoDB` can use to look up rows. These modifiers cause `InnoDB` to acquire a row lock for each row examined. In the absence of a usable index, `InnoDB` must perform a complete table scan, which results in a lock being acquired for every row.

- Avoid using `SELECT COUNT(*) FROM` *table_name* queries with `InnoDB` tables. Although this type of query is very efficient for `MyISAM` tables because `MyISAM` stores a row count in the table, `InnoDB` does not store a row count and must perform a table scan to determine how many rows there are.

- Modifications made over the course of multiple statements should be grouped into a transaction whenever it makes sense to do so. This minimizes the number of flush operations that must be performed. For example, if you need to run 100 `UPDATE` statements that each modify a single row based on its primary key value, it's faster to run all the statements within a single transaction than to commit each one as soon as it executes. (A corollary to this principle is that you should avoid making updates with autocommit mode on. That causes the effects of each statement to be flushed individually.)

- Do periodic table rebuilds as necessary. Indexes in an InnoDB table may become fragmented due to deletes and updates if they modify rows at arbitrary positions within the table. This causes index pages to be underfilled and to be spread around on disk in an order that differs from their logical order. Rebuilding an InnoDB table periodically corrects these problems and reclaims index space. There are two ways to perform a rebuild:

  - Use a "null" ALTER TABLE operation:

    ```
    mysql> ALTER TABLE table_name ENGINE = InnoDB;
    ```

  - Dump and reload the table:

    ```
    shell> mysqldump db_name table_name > dump_file
    shell> mysql db_name < dump_file
    ```

- In MySQL 5, InnoDB implements a table format that typically results in a savings of about 20% for disk and memory. If you have InnoDB tables that were created before MySQL 5, you can convert them to use the newer more compact storage format. The table-rebuilding techniques described in the previous item can be used to accomplish this conversion.

It is also possible to make administrative optimizations through the way you configure InnoDB. The following list briefly mentions some of the possibilities:

- To reduce flushing from the in-memory log buffer to disk, configure InnoDB to use a larger buffer.

- Choose a log flushing method that best matches your goals. You can opt to guarantee ACID properties such as durability (no loss of committed changes), or to get faster performance at the possible cost of losing approximately the last second's worth of committed changes in the event of a crash. ACID properties are defined in Section 29.4.2, "InnoDB and ACID Compliance."

- Use raw disk partitions in the tablespace to avoid a level of filesystem-access overhead normally incurred when using regular files.

For information on the options that control these aspects of InnoDB operation, see Section 29.4.7, "Configuring and Monitoring InnoDB."

38.5 MERGE-Specific Optimizations

A MERGE table is a logical collection of MyISAM tables that have the same structure. You can use this property to manage the storage properties of the underlying MyISAM tables:

- MERGE tables provide a workaround when you run up against filesystem file-size limitations for MyISAM tables. If a given MyISAM table is as large as it can be because its data or index files have reached a file-size limit, split the table into multiple smaller MyISAM tables and then create a MERGE table that groups them into a single logical table. The maximum effective size of the MERGE table thus becomes the maximum size of each constituent MyISAM table times the number of tables.

- A MERGE table can contain a mix of compressed and uncompressed MyISAM tables. If some of the MyISAM tables contain archival data that will not be modified, you can compress them to save disk space.

- If you use MyISAM table symlinking, you can place different tables on different physical devices, which allows their contents to be read in parallel.

- If a large MyISAM table is split into smaller tables, you can still access the combined contents by defining a MERGE table. But you also can gain some advantages for certain operations when it is possible to access only particular individual files. A table repair is faster on a smaller table than a larger one. If you happen to have searches where you know all the records needed are contained in a particular table, you can search just that one table rather than the entire collection.

- It's very fast to create or drop MERGE tables, so applications that need to work with dynamically changing sets of tables can easily instantiate MERGE tables on the fly as necessary.

38.6 MEMORY-Specific Optimizations

The MEMORY storage engine keeps table contents in memory, which makes table access very fast. MEMORY thus is a good choice for frequently accessed lookup tables.

The MEMORY engine supports HASH and BTREE indexing methods. Choose the method that is most appropriate to the type of lookups you'll be performing. For information on the characteristics of these methods, see Section 8.6.3, "Choosing an Indexing Algorithm."

Take care not to create MEMORY tables that become very large, or an excessive number of MEMORY tables. The combined size of these tables amounts to memory that is unavailable for other purposes. To prevent runaway memory use, set the max_heap_table_size system variable; an error will occur if you try to make a MEMORY table larger than this size. (However, the limit imposed by this variable is per-table, not global, so it is still possible to use lots of memory by creating many MEMORY tables.)

To free memory used by MEMORY tables, you should drop or truncate them when you no longer need their contents.

Optimizing the Server

This chapter discusses how to gather performance information from MySQL Server and how to change its configuration to improve performance. The chapter covers the following exam topics:

- Obtaining and interpreting information that MySQL Server provides about its configuration and operation
- Assessing server load
- Setting server system variables for performance tuning
- Using the query cache to increase performance of queries that clients issue repeatedly

39.1 Interpreting `mysqld` Server Information

The main purpose of MySQL Server is to perform queries on behalf of clients that need access to databases. However, the server also keeps track of information that is useful to administrators, and you can ask the server to report this information by using various forms of the SHOW statement:

- SHOW VARIABLES displays server system variables. These indicate such things as directory locations, server capabilities, and sizes of caches and buffers. You can set system variables to control how the server operates. They can be set at server startup, and many of them can be changed while the server is running. Also, the built-in values for many system variables can be specified at compile time if you build MySQL from source.

- SHOW STATUS displays server status variables that indicate the extent and types of activities the server is performing. These variables provide information such as how long the server has been running, number of queries processed, amount of network traffic, and statistics about the query cache. You can use status information to assess how much of a load your server is processing and how well it is handling the load. This information provides useful feedback for assessing whether system variables should be changed to improve server performance.

This chapter discusses several representative system and status variables, but many more exist. The *MySQL Reference Manual* provides a full list of variable names and meanings.

39.1.1 Accessing Server System Variables

Many aspects of server operation are controlled by means of a set of system variables that reflect server configuration. To display these variables, use the SHOW VARIABLES statement:

```
mysql> SHOW VARIABLES;
+------------------------+------------------+
| Variable_name          | Value            |
+------------------------+------------------+
| back_log               | 50               |
| basedir                | /usr/local/mysql/ |
| binlog_cache_size      | 32768            |
| bulk_insert_buffer_size | 8388608         |
| character_set          | latin1           |
...
```

To display only those variables with names that match a given pattern, add a LIKE pattern-matching clause. The pattern is not case sensitive and may contain the '%' and '_' wildcard pattern metacharacters. For example, the sizes for many of the server's buffers can be displayed as follows:

```
mysql> SHOW VARIABLES LIKE '%buffer_size';
+------------------------+---------+
| Variable_name          | Value   |
+------------------------+---------+
| bulk_insert_buffer_size | 8388608 |
| innodb_log_buffer_size | 1048576 |
| join_buffer_size       | 131072  |
| key_buffer_size        | 8388600 |
| myisam_sort_buffer_size | 8388608 |
| preload_buffer_size    | 32768   |
| read_buffer_size       | 131072  |
| read_rnd_buffer_size   | 262144  |
| sort_buffer_size       | 2097144 |
+------------------------+---------+
```

If the pattern contains no metacharacters, the statement displays only the named variable:

```
mysql> SHOW VARIABLES LIKE 'datadir';
+--------------+-----------------------+
| Variable_name | Value                |
+--------------+-----------------------+
| datadir      | /usr/local/mysql/data/ |
+--------------+-----------------------+
```

System variables may be displayed in other ways as well. mysqladmin variables provides command-line access to the complete list of system variables. MySQL Administrator has a Health section with a Server Variables tab that displays system variables. Both clients implement this capability by sending a SHOW VARIABLES statement to the server and displaying the results.

System variables can be set at server startup using options on the command line or in option files. For example, on a Unix machine, you can put the following lines in the /etc/my.cnf option file to specify a data directory of /var/mysql/data and a key cache size of 64MB:

```
[mysqld]
datadir = /var/mysql/data
key_buffer_size = 64M
```

Numeric option values can have a suffix letter of K, M, or G to indicate units of kilobytes, megabytes, or gigabytes.

Some server system variables are static and can *only* be set at startup time. (You need not know which for the exam.) For example, you can specify the data directory by means of a datadir startup option, but you cannot tell a server that is running to use a different data directory. Other variables are dynamic and can be changed while the server is running. For example, both of the following statements tell the server to change the size of the key cache to 128MB:

```
mysql> SET GLOBAL key_buffer_size = 128*1024*1024;
mysql> SET @@global.key_buffer_size = 128*1024*1024;
```

With a SET statement, you cannot use a suffix of K, M, or G to indicate units for the value, but you can use an expression.

The key_buffer_size variable is (as the preceding statements indicate) a global server variable. Some variables exist in both global and session forms:

- The global form applies server-wide and is used to initialize the corresponding session variable for new client connections. Each client may subsequently change its own session variable value.

- The session form is session-specific and applies only to a particular client connection.

To set global variables, you must have the SUPER privilege. Any client may set its own session variables.

An example of the type of variable that has both forms is storage_engine, which controls the default storage engine used for CREATE TABLE statements that do not specify a storage engine explicitly. The global storage_engine value is used to set the session storage_engine variable for each client when the client connects, but the client may change its session variable value to use a different default storage engine.

Session variables are set using syntax similar to that for setting global variables. For example, the default storage engine may be set either globally or only for the current connection using the following statements:

```
mysql> SET GLOBAL storage_engine = MyISAM;
mysql> SET @@global.storage_engine = MyISAM;

mysql> SET SESSION storage_engine = InnoDB;
mysql> SET @@session.storage_engine = InnoDB;
```

LOCAL is a synonym for SESSION. Also, if you do not indicate explicitly whether to set the global or session version of a variable, MySQL sets the session variable. Each of these statements sets the session storage_engine variable:

```
mysql> SET LOCAL storage_engine = InnoDB;
mysql> SET @@local.storage_engine = InnoDB;
mysql> SET storage_engine = InnoDB;
mysql> SET @@storage_engine = InnoDB;
```

To explicitly display global or session variable values, use SHOW GLOBAL VARIABLES or SHOW SESSION VARIABLES. Without GLOBAL or SESSION, the SHOW VARIABLES statement displays session values.

It's also possible to use SELECT to display the values of individual global or session values:

```
mysql> SELECT @@global.storage_engine, @@session.storage_engine;
+-------------------------+--------------------------+
| @@global.storage_engine | @@session.storage_engine |
+-------------------------+--------------------------+
| MyISAM                  | InnoDB                   |
+-------------------------+--------------------------+
```

If @@ is not followed by a global or session scope specifier, the server returns the session variable if it exists, and the global variable otherwise:

```
mysql> SELECT @@storage_engine;
+------------------+
| @@storage_engine |
+------------------+
| InnoDB           |
+------------------+
```

The *MySQL Reference Manual* indicates which variables are dynamic and whether they have global or session forms.

39.1.2 Accessing Server Status Variables

The server tracks many aspects of its own operation using a set of status variables. It makes the current values of these variables available through the SHOW STATUS statement, which you use much like SHOW VARIABLES:

```
mysql> SHOW STATUS;
+-------------------------------+------------+
| Variable_name                 | Value      |
+-------------------------------+------------+
| Aborted_clients               | 244        |
| Aborted_connects              | 1          |
| Binlog_cache_disk_use         | 0          |
| Binlog_cache_use              | 1          |
| Bytes_received                | 319102331  |
| Bytes_sent                    | 178928432  |
| Com_admin_commands            | 0          |
...
```

To display only those variables with names that match a given pattern, add a LIKE pattern-matching clause. The pattern is not case sensitive and may contain the '%' and '_' wildcard pattern metacharacters. For example, all query cache status variable names begin with Qcache and may be displayed as follows:

```
mysql> SHOW STATUS LIKE 'qcache%';
+-------------------------+--------+
| Variable_name           | Value  |
+-------------------------+--------+
| Qcache_free_blocks      | 98     |
| Qcache_free_memory      | 231008 |
| Qcache_hits             | 21145  |
| Qcache_inserts          | 12823  |
| Qcache_lowmem_prunes    | 584    |
| Qcache_not_cached       | 10899  |
| Qcache_queries_in_cache | 360    |
| Qcache_total_blocks     | 861    |
+-------------------------+--------+
```

If the pattern contains no metacharacters, the statement displays only the named variable:

```
mysql> SHOW STATUS LIKE 'Uptime';
+---------------+---------+
| Variable_name | Value   |
+---------------+---------+
| Uptime        | 5084640 |
+---------------+---------+
```

Status variables may be obtained in other ways as well. `mysqladmin extended-status` provides command-line access to the complete list of status variables, and `mysqladmin status` displays a brief summary. MySQL Administrator has a Health section with a Status Variables tab that displays status variables.

The following list indicates some of the ways you can use status information:

- Several status variables provide information about how many connections the server is handling, including the number of successful and unsuccessful connection attempts, and also whether successful connections terminate normally or abnormally. From these variables, you can determine the following information:

  - The total number of connection attempts (both successful and unsuccessful):

    `Connections`

  - The number of unsuccessful connection attempts:

    `Aborted_connects`

  - The number of successful connection attempts:

    `Connections - Aborted_connects`

  - The number of successful connections that terminated abnormally (for example, if the client died or the network went down):

    `Aborted_clients`

  - The number of successful connections that terminated normally:

    `Connections - Aborted_connects - Aborted_clients`

  - The number of clients currently connected to the server:

    `Threads_connected`

- The `Com` variables give you a breakdown of the number of statements that the server has executed by statement type. You can see all these variables with the following statement:

  ```
  mysql> SHOW STATUS LIKE 'Com%';
  +-----------------------+-------+
  | Variable_name         | Value |
  +-----------------------+-------+
  | Com_admin_commands    | 0     |
  | Com_alter_db          | 0     |
  | Com_alter_table       | 2     |
  | Com_analyze           | 0     |
  | Com_backup_table      | 0     |
  | Com_begin             | 1     |
  | Com_change_db         | 629   |
  ```

```
| Com_change_master      | 0     |
...
```

Or you can name specific variables:

```
mysql> SHOW STATUS LIKE 'Com_delete';
+---------------+-------+
| Variable_name | Value |
+---------------+-------+
| Com_delete    | 315   |
+---------------+-------+
mysql> SHOW STATUS LIKE 'Com_update';
+---------------+-------+
| Variable_name | Value |
+---------------+-------+
| Com_update    | 19447 |
+---------------+-------+
mysql> SHOW STATUS LIKE 'Com_select';
+---------------+-------+
| Variable_name | Value |
+---------------+-------+
| Com_select    | 46073 |
+---------------+-------+
```

Com_select does not include the number of queries that are processed using the query cache because those queries are not executed in the usual sense. Their results are pulled directly from the query cache without consulting any tables. The number of such queries is given by the Qcache_hits status variable. See Section 39.4, "Using the Query Cache."

- The server caches open file descriptors when possible to avoid repeated file-opening operations, but a cache that's too small will not hold all the file descriptors you need. The Opened_tables variable indicates the number of times the server had to open files to access tables. It provides a measure of whether your table cache is large enough. See Section 39.3, "Tuning Memory Parameters."

- Bytes_received and Bytes_sent show the amount of traffic sent over the network between the server and its clients.

Status information can help you determine how smoothly the server is running or how well it's performing. Section 39.2, "Measuring Server Load," discusses some ways to use status variables to assess server load.

39.2 Measuring Server Load

Status information that the server provides may be used to assess how hard it is working:

- Several status variables displayed by SHOW STATUS provide load information. For example, Questions indicates the number of queries the server has processed and Uptime indicates the number of seconds the server has been running. Combining these, the ratio Questions/Uptime tells you how many queries per second the server has processed.

- Slow_queries indicates the number of queries that take a long time to process. Ideally, its value should increase slowly or not at all. If it increases quickly, you might have a problem with certain queries. The slow query log shows the text of slow queries and provides information about how long they took. Restart the server with the slow query log enabled, let it run for a while, and then take a look at the log to see which queries turn up there. You can use this log to identify queries that might need optimizing. General information about the slow query log and its use in optimization is given in Section 37.1, "Identifying Candidates for Query Analysis."

- SHOW PROCESSLIST displays information about the activity of each currently connected client. For example, the presence of a large number of blocked queries might indicate that another connection is running a query that is inefficient and should be examined to see whether it can be optimized. The SHOW PROCESSLIST statement always shows your own queries. If you have the PROCESS privilege, it also shows queries being run by other accounts.

- To get a concise report of the server's load status from within the mysql client program, use its STATUS (or \s) command to display a general snapshot of the current connection state. The last part of the output provides some information about the server load:

```
mysql> STATUS;
--------------
mysql  Ver 14.12 Distrib 5.0.10-beta, for pc-linux-gnu (i686)

Connection id:          34816
Current database:       world
Current user:           myname@localhost
SSL:                    Not in use
Current pager:          stdout
Using outfile:          ''
Using delimiter:        ;
Server version:         5.0.10-beta-log
Protocol version:       10
Connection:             Localhost via UNIX socket
Server characterset:    latin1
Db     characterset:    latin1
Client characterset:    latin1
Conn.  characterset:    latin1
```

```
UNIX socket:          /tmp/mysql.sock
Uptime:               51 days 3 hours 40 min 37 sec

Threads: 4  Questions: 2910900  Slow queries: 1053  Opens: 3400
Flush tables: 3  Open tables: 64  Queries per second avg: 0.720
--------------
```

The final part of the output also can be obtained by issuing a `mysqladmin status` command.

The preceding items describe how to obtain information that the server provides during the course of its normal operation. The server also provides diagnostic information about exceptional conditions in the form of error messages, which it writes to an error log. Some of these messages pertain to errors that are not fatal but might affect performance, such as aborted connections. (See Section 24.5.4, "The Error Log.")

For a discussion of ways to reduce server load by helping it work more effectively, see Section 39.3, "Tuning Memory Parameters," and Section 39.4, "Using the Query Cache."

39.3 Tuning Memory Parameters

As the server runs, it opens files, reads information from tables to process queries, and sends the results to clients. In many cases, the server processes information that it has accessed earlier. If the server can buffer or cache this information in memory rather than reading it from disk repeatedly, it runs more efficiently and performs better. By tuning server parameters appropriately using system variables, you can control what information the server attempts to keep in memory. Some buffers are used globally and affect server performance as a whole. Others apply to individual clients, although they still are initially set to a default value controlled by the server.

Memory is a finite resource and you should allocate it in ways that make the most sense for your system. For example, if you run lots of complex queries using just a few tables, it doesn't make sense to have a large table cache. You're likely better off increasing the key buffer size. On the other hand, if you run simple queries from many different tables, a large table cache will be of much more value.

Keep in mind that increasing the value of a server parameter increases system resource consumption by the server. You cannot increase parameter values beyond what is available, and you should not allocate so much memory to MySQL that the operating system suffers in its own performance. (Remember that the operating system itself requires system resources.)

In general, the server's default parameter settings are conservative and have small values. This allows the server to run even on modest systems with little memory. If your system has ample memory, you can (and should) allocate more of it to MySQL to tune it to the available resources.

Typically, you set parameter values using options in the [mysqld] section of an option file so that the server uses them consistently each time it starts. For system variables that are dynamic, you can change them while the server runs to test how the changes affect performance. After you determine optimum values this way, set them in the option file for use in subsequent server restarts.

To get an idea of settings that are appropriate for systems of various sizes, look at the sample option files that MySQL distributions include. On Windows, they have names like my-small.ini and my-large.ini and are located in the MySQL installation directory. On Unix, they have names like my-small.cnf and my-large.cnf. Likely locations are in /usr/share/mysql for RPM installations or the share directory under the MySQL installation directory for tar file installations. Each sample file includes comments that indicate the typical kind of system to which it applies. For example, a small system may use options with small values:

```
[mysqld]
key_buffer_size = 16K
table_cache = 4
sort_buffer_size = 64K
```

For a larger system, you can increase the values, and also allocate memory to the query cache:

```
[mysqld]
key_buffer_size = 256M
table_cache = 256
sort_buffer_size = 1M
query_cache_type = ON
query_cache_size = 16M
```

The material in this section is oriented toward server-side tuning. Client-side techniques may be applied to optimize the performance of individual queries, as discussed in Chapter 22, "Basic Optimizations," and Chapter 37, "Optimizing Queries."

39.3.1 Global (Server-Wide) Parameters

This section discusses server parameters for resources that affect server performance as a whole or that are shared among clients. When tuning server parameters, there are three factors to consider:

- The resource that the server manages.
- The system variable that indicates the size of the resource. You can control the size by setting the variable.
- Status variables that relate to the resource. These enable you to determine how well the resource is configured.

For example, the key cache that the server uses to cache MyISAM index blocks is a resource. The size of the key cache is set using the key_buffer_size system variable, and the effectiveness of the key cache can be measured using the Key_reads and Key_read_requests status variables.

This section covers the following memory-related resources:

- The maximum number of simultaneous client connections the server supports.
- The table cache that holds information about tables that storage engines have open.
- The key cache that holds MyISAM index blocks.
- The InnoDB buffer pool that holds InnoDB table data and index information, and the InnoDB log buffer that holds transaction information before it is flushed to the InnoDB log file.

39.3.1.1 Maximum Connections Allowed

The MySQL server uses a multi-threaded architecture that allows it to service multiple clients simultaneously. A thread is like a small process running inside the server. For each client that connects, the server allocates a thread handler to service the connection, so the term "thread" in MySQL is roughly synonymous with "connection."

The max_connections system variable controls the maximum allowable number of simultaneous client connections. The default value is 100, but if your server is very busy and needs to handle many clients at once, the default might be too small. On the other hand, each active connection handler requires some memory, so you don't necessarily want to set the number to the maximum number of threads that your operating system allows.

To see how many clients currently are connected, check the value of the Threads_connected status variable. If its value often is close to the value of max_connections, it might be good to increase the value of the latter to allow more connections. If clients that should be able to connect to the server frequently cannot, that too is an indication that max_connections is too small.

39.3.1.2 The Table Cache

When the server opens a table, it maintains information about that table in the table cache, which is used to avoid reopening tables when possible. The next time a client tries to access the table, the server can use it immediately without opening the table again if it is found in the cache. However, if the cache is full and a client tries to access a table that isn't found there, some open table must be closed to free an entry in the cache for the new table. The table that is closed then must be reopened the next time a client accesses it.

The table_cache system variable controls the number of entries in the table cache. Its default value is 64. The goal when configuring the table cache is to make it large enough that the server need not repeatedly open frequently accessed tables. Against this goal you must balance the fact that with a larger table cache the server requires more file descriptors.

Operating systems place a limit on the number of file descriptors allowed to each process, so the table cache cannot be made arbitrarily large. However, some operating systems do allow the per-process file descriptor limit to be reconfigured.

To determine whether the cache is large enough, check the Open_tables and Opened_tables status variables over time. Open_tables indicates how many tables currently are open, and Opened_tables indicates how many table-opening operations the server has performed since it started. If Open_tables usually is at or near the value of table_cache, and the value of Opened_tables increases steadily, it indicates that the table cache is being used to capacity and that the server often has to close tables in the cache so that it can open other tables. This is a sign that the table cache is too small and that you should increase the value of table_cache.

39.3.1.3 The MyISAM Key Cache

The key cache (key buffer) is a resource in which the server caches index blocks that it reads from MyISAM tables. The key_buffer_size system variable controls the size of the key cache.

Indexes speed up retrievals, so if you can keep index values in memory and reuse them for different queries rather than rereading them from disk, performance is even better. When MySQL needs to read an index block, it checks first whether the block is in the key cache. If so, it can satisfy the read request immediately using a block in the cache. If not, it reads the block from disk first and puts it in the key cache. The frequency of these two actions is reflected by the Key_read_requests and Key_reads status variables. If the key cache is full when a block needs to be read, the server discards a block already in the cache to make room for the new block.

The ideal situation is for MySQL to consistently find the index blocks that it needs in the cache without having to read them from disk. In other words, Key_reads should remain as low as possible relative to Key_read_requests.

You can use the two status variables to assess the effectiveness of the key cache in terms of keys either missing or present in the cache. These values are the key cache miss rate and its efficiency. To calculate the miss rate, use the following formula:

```
Key_reads / Key_read_requests
```

The complementary value, key cache efficiency, is calculated like this:

```
1 - (Key_reads / Key_read_requests)
```

Suppose that the key cache status variables have the following values:

```
mysql> SHOW STATUS LIKE 'Key_read%';
+-------------------+----------+
| Variable_name     | Value    |
+-------------------+----------+
| Key_read_requests | 73137065 |
```

```
| Key_reads         | 2069133  |
+-------------------+----------+
```

From those values, the key cache miss rate and efficiency can be calculated:

```
miss rate = 2069133 / 73137065 = .0283
efficiency = 1 - (2069133 / 73137065) = .9717
```

You want the miss rate to be as close as possible to 0 and the efficiency as close as possible to 1. By that measure, the values just calculated are reasonably good. If the values for your server are not so good and you have memory available, you can improve the key cache's effectiveness by increasing the value of the key_buffer_size system variable. Its default value is 8MB.

MySQL supports the creation of additional MyISAM key caches and enables you to assign tables to specific caches. For details, see Section 37.4, "MyISAM Index Caching."

39.3.1.4 The InnoDB Buffer Pool and Log Buffers

Two memory-related InnoDB resources are the buffer pool and the log buffer:

- The InnoDB buffer pool caches data and index information for InnoDB tables. Making the buffer pool larger reduces disk I/O for frequently accessed InnoDB table contents. The buffer pool size is controlled by the innodb_buffer_pool_size system variable. Its default value is 8MB. On a machine dedicated to MySQL, you can set this variable anywhere from 50% to 80% of the total amount of memory. However, the setting should take into account how large you set the key_buffer_size value.

- The InnoDB log buffer holds information about modifications made during transaction processing. Ideally, you want a transaction's changes to be held in the buffer until the transaction commits, at which point they can be written to the InnoDB log file all at once. If the buffer is too small, changes might need to be written several times before commit time, resulting in additional disk activity. The log buffer size is controlled by the innodb_log_buffer_size system variable. Typical values range from 1MB to 8MB. The default is 1MB.

39.3.1.5 Selecting Storage Engines

If you need to save memory, one way to do so is to disable unneeded storage engines. Some of the compiled-in storage engines can be enabled or disabled at runtime. Disabling an unneeded storage engine reduces the server's memory requirements because it need not allocate buffers and other data structures associated with the engine. You can disable the InnoDB engine this way with the --skip-innodb option at server startup.

It's also possible to disable InnoDB entirely by compiling the server without it. To do this, use the --without-innodb configuration option. Consult the installation chapter of the *MySQL Reference Manual* for further instructions.

The MyISAM storage engine is always compiled in and cannot be disabled at runtime. This ensures that the server always has a reliably available storage engine, no matter how it might otherwise be configured.

39.3.2 Per-Client Parameters

Resources such as the table cache and the MyISAM key cache are shared globally among all clients. The server also allocates a set of buffers for each client that connects. The variables that control their sizes are collectively known as "per-client variables."

Be cautious when increasing the value of a per-client variable. For each per-client buffer, the potential amount of server memory required is the size of the buffer times the maximum allowed number of client connections. Parameters for these buffers normally are set to 1MB or 2MB, at most, to avoid causing exorbitant memory use under conditions when many clients are connected simultaneously.

Per-client buffers include the following:

- MySQL uses a record buffer to perform sequential table scans. Its size is controlled by the read_buffer_size system variable. Increasing the size of this buffer allows larger chunks of the table to be read at one time, which can speed up scanning by reducing the number of disk seeks required. A second record buffer also is allocated for use in reading records after an intermediate sort (such as might be required by an ORDER BY clause) or for non-sequential table reads. Its size is controlled by the read_rnd_buffer_size variable, which defaults to the value of read_buffer_size if you do not set it explicitly. This means that changing read_buffer_size potentially can actually result in double the effective memory increase.

- The sort buffer is used for operations such as ORDER BY and GROUP BY. Its size is controlled by the sort_buffer_size system variable. If clients execute many queries that sort large record sets, increasing the sort buffer size can speed up sorting operations.

- The join buffer is used to process joins. Its size is controlled by the join_buffer_size system variable. Increase the value if clients tend to perform complex joins.

- The server allocates a communication buffer for exchanging information with the client. If clients tend to issue very long queries, the queries will fail if the communication buffer is not large enough to handle them. The buffer size is controlled by the max_allowed_packet parameter. For example, to allow clients to send up to 128MB of information at a time, configure the server like this:

```
[mysqld]
max_allowed_packet = 128M
```

Note that, unlike a parameter such as read_buffer_size, it is generally safe to set the value of max_allowed_packet quite high. The server does not actually allocate a communication buffer that large as soon as a client connects. It begins with a buffer of size net_buffer_length bytes and increases it as necessary, up to a maximum of max_allowed_packet bytes.

Although these buffers are client specific, it isn't necessarily the case that the server actually allocates each one for every client. No sort buffer or join buffer is allocated for a client unless it performs sorts or joins.

One scenario in which very long queries can occur is when you dump tables with mysqldump and reload them with mysql. If you run mysqldump with the --opt option (which is enabled by default) to create a dump file containing long multiple-row INSERT statements, those statements might be too long for the server to handle when you use mysql later to send the contents of the file back to the server to be reloaded. Note that it might be necessary to set the client-side value of max_allowed_packet in both cases as well. mysqldump and mysql both support a --max_allowed_packet option for setting the client-side value.

39.4 Using the Query Cache

MySQL supports a query cache that greatly increases performance under conditions such that the server's query mix includes SELECT statements that are processed repeatedly and return the same results each time. Using the query cache can result in a tremendous performance boost and reduction in server load, especially for disk- or processor-intensive queries.

If you enable the query cache, the server uses it as follows:

- The server compares each SELECT query that it receives to any already present in the cache. If the query is present and none of the tables that it uses have changed since the result was cached, the server returns the result immediately without executing the query again.

- If the query is not present in the cache or if any of the tables that it uses have changed (thus invalidating the saved result), the server executes the query and caches its result.

- The server determines whether a query is in the cache based on exact case-sensitive comparison of query strings. That means the following two queries are not considered the same:

```
SELECT * FROM table_name;
select * from table_name;
```

The server also takes into account any factors that distinguish otherwise-identical queries. Among these are the default database and the character set used by each client. For example, two SELECT * FROM table_name queries may be lexically identical but are semantically different if each applies to a different default database or were sent by clients that are using different default character sets.

The query cache is global, so a query result placed in the cache can be returned to any client that has the necessary privileges for the tables referred to by the query.

39.4.1 Enabling the Query Cache

Several system variables are associated with the query cache:

```
mysql> SHOW VARIABLES LIKE 'query_cache%';
+-----------------------------+---------+
| Variable_name               | Value   |
+-----------------------------+---------+
| query_cache_limit           | 1048576 |
| query_cache_min_res_unit    | 4096    |
| query_cache_size            | 8388608 |
| query_cache_type            | ON      |
| query_cache_wlock_invalidate | OFF     |
+-----------------------------+---------+
```

Three of those variables exert primary control over the query cache:

- query_cache_type specifies the type of caching to perform. The value is OFF if the cache is disabled, ON if it is enabled, and DEMAND if caching is done only for statements that begin with SELECT SQL_CACHE. The default value of query_cache_type is ON (caching allowed). However, the cache is not operational unless its size also is set larger than the default value of zero.

  query_cache_type also controls retrieval of cached results. If the cache contains query results and you disable it, no results are returned from the cache until you enable it again.

- query_cache_size is the size of the query cache in bytes. If the size is 0, the cache is disabled even if query_cache_type is not OFF.

  If you do not intend to use the query cache, you should set the value of query_cache_size to zero. If the value is greater than zero, the server allocates that much memory for the cache even if it is disabled.

- query_cache_limit is the upper bound on how large an individual query result can be and still be eligible for caching. The default limit is 1MB.

  If query results that you want cached are larger than the default query_cache_limit value, increase it. The disadvantage of doing this is that large results leave less room for caching other queries, so you might find it necessary to increase the total cache size (query_cache_size) as well.

The other query cache system variables, query_cache_min_res_unit and query_cache_wlock_invalidate, are of lesser concern than the three primary variables. query_cache_min_res_unit is the allocation block size used when caching results. If you cache many small results, fragmentation can occur. In this case, you may get better allocation behavior by decreasing the variable value. query_cache_wlock_invalidate determines whether a write lock on a table causes other clients to wait for queries that could be served by cached results. Normally, a write lock does not cause a wait for a cached result. Setting this variable to ON causes query results for a table to become invalidated when it is write-locked, which also causes other clients to wait for queries on the table.

Typically you set the query cache variables in an option file where you list the server's startup options. In an option file, the query_cache_type value should be given as a number: 0 for OFF, 1 for ON, and 2 DEMAND. For example, to enable the query cache, allocate 10MB of memory to it, and allow individual query results up to 2MB to be cached, put the following lines in the option file, and restart the server:

```
[mysqld]
query_cache_type = 1
query_cache_size = 10M
query_cache_limit = 2M
```

If you have the SUPER privilege, you can change these variables for a running server without restarting it by using the following statements:

```
SET GLOBAL query_cache_type = ON;
SET GLOBAL query_cache_size = 10485760;
SET GLOBAL query_cache_limit = 2097152;
```

If you set the variables with SET statements, the changes will be lost at the next server restart, so SET is useful primarily for testing cache settings. When you find suitable values, set them in the option file.

query_cache_type also exists as a session variable, which enables clients to set query caching behavior for their own connection (assuming that the cache size is greater than zero). For example, a client can disable caching for its own queries by issuing this statement:

```
SET SESSION query_cache_type = OFF;
```

39.4.2 Measuring Query Cache Utilization

The server provides information about the operation of the query cache by means of a set of status variables. To view these variables, use the following statement:

```
mysql> SHOW STATUS LIKE 'Qcache%';
+-------------------------+--------+
| Variable_name           | Value  |
+-------------------------+--------+
| Qcache_free_blocks      | 98     |
| Qcache_free_memory      | 231008 |
| Qcache_hits             | 21145  |
| Qcache_inserts          | 12823  |
| Qcache_lowmem_prunes    | 584    |
```

```
| Qcache_not_cached      | 10899  |
| Qcache_queries_in_cache | 360   |
| Qcache_total_blocks    | 861    |
+------------------------+--------+
```

Qcache_hits indicates how many times a query did not have to be executed because its result could be served from the cache. Qcache_inserts is the total number of queries that have been put in the cache. Qcache_queries_in_cache indicates the number of queries currently registered in the cache. The difference between the two values indicates how many cached queries were displaced to make room for newer queries, or discarded because they became invalid. Qcache_lowmem_prunes indicates how many query results were displaced due to lack of free memory in the cache.

If your hit count is low and the insert count is high, this might be a symptom of a query cache that is too small. Try increasing its size to see if the ratio of hits to inserts improves. It might also be that the server is attempting to cache query results under conditions when it's really not worth it. Examine the server's query mix to see which tables have both selects and many updates. If a table changes often, it's not likely that results for SELECT statements that retrieve from the table will remain valid very long.

Suppose that an inventory table records stock level values for items in the inventory. This table might be queried frequently to obtain current stock levels, but also modified frequently as items are sold or restocked. With frequent updates, cache results do not remain valid long and are unlikely to provide any real performance benefit. In this situation, you can avoid the overhead of caching the results by including the SQL_NO_CACHE modifier in SELECT statements for the table:

```
SELECT SQL_NO_CACHE ... FROM inventory ... ;
```

Interpreting Diagnostic Messages

This chapter discusses the use of diagnostic information that is available to database administrators. It covers the following exam topics:

- Sources of diagnostic information
- Using the error log
- Using the slow query log

Chapter 21, "Debugging MySQL Applications," in the Developer section of this study guide contains additional discussion of diagnostic information provided by MySQL. That chapter serves as background for the material here.

40.1 Sources of Diagnostic Information

When debugging applications, a database administrator can use the same methods for interpreting diagnostic information that any developer has access to, such as the SHOW WARNINGS and SHOW ERRORS statements, and the perror utility.

However, an administrator also has access to information that may not be available to developers, such as the contents of the error log and the slow query log. These logs normally are located in the data directory, which for security reasons should have restricted access.

This chapter focuses on those sources of information that are available only to administrators. Chapter 21, "Debugging MySQL Applications," covers the use of SHOW WARNINGS, SHOW ERRORS, and perror.

40.2 Using the Error Log for Diagnostic Purposes

MySQL Server writes diagnostic information to an error log as a record of incidents that are not part of normal operation. It also logs messages to indicate when it starts and stops.

Normally, it's desirable for the error log to be as short as possible. Even the presence of start and stop messages might indicate a problem, if the number of them suggests that the server has been restarting unexpectedly and not due to administrative action or system startup and shutdown.

Other messages besides the start and stop indicators provide you with information about problems that the server encounters as it runs:

- Unrecognized startup options. If the server attempts to start up but quits almost immediately, the error log can tell you why. When the server fails to complete its initialization phase, it writes information to the log. A common reason for error messages is that there is a misconfiguration that must be addressed. For example, you might have a bad option listed in an option file.

- Failure of the server to open its network interfaces: the TCP/IP port, the Windows named pipe, Windows shared memory, or the Unix socket file. The server cannot use an interface that already is in use by another server.

- Storage engine initialization failure. This might occur due to incorrect configuration of the storage engine (for example, if a file specified as part of the InnoDB tablespace cannot be opened), or detection of conditions that make it impossible to continue (for example, if a storage engine detects table corruption but cannot correct it automatically).

- Failure to find SSL certificate or key files that are named by startup options.

- Inability of the server to change its user ID on Unix. This can happen if you specify a --user option but do not start the server as root so that it can relinquish root privileges and change to a different user.

- Problems related to replication.

Normally, the error log can be found, if it is enabled, in the server's data directory. Configuration options for enabling it and specifying its name and location are provided in Chapter 24, "Starting, Stopping, and Configuring MySQL."

40.3 Using The Slow Query Log for Diagnostic Purposes

MySQL Server has the capability of writing information about "slow" queries to its slow query log. The value of the long_query_time system variable indicates how long a query can run before being considered slow. Its value is interpreted as number of seconds in wall clock (elapsed) time. The default long_query_time value is 10, so if the slow query log is enabled, queries that run for longer than 10 seconds are logged, along with comments that contain additional information about the queries.

The slow query log does not contain errors, but it is a source of diagnostic information in the sense that the frequent appearance of a query in the log is an indicator that the query should be analyzed to see if any optimizations can be applied to it to make it execute faster. Details about optimizing are beyond the scope of this chapter, but the following list indicates some general types of optimizations that are possible and the chapters where they are discussed further:

- Rewrite the query into more efficient form. (See Chapter 22, "Basic Optimizations.")
- Change the tables that the query uses (for example, by normalizing or adding an index). (See Chapter 37, "Optimizing Queries," and Chapter 38, "Optimizing Databases.")
- Tune server parameters. (See Chapter 39, "Optimizing the Server.")

The server writes queries to the slow query log in plain text format, so you can examine the log using any text display program such as a pager or a text editor. To obtain a summary of the log's contents, use the `mysqldumpslow` utility:

```
shell> mysqldumpslow log_file
```

`mysqldumpslow` tries to determine when queries are similar and can be grouped. For example, the following two queries fit the same pattern because they differ only in the data values:

```
SELECT * FROM t WHERE id = 'H7XQ19' AND age < 10;
SELECT * FROM t WHERE id = 'J8MZ48' AND age < 20;
```

`mysqldumpslow` groups those queries and reports them in its summary output using a "template" that looks like this:

```
SELECT * FROM t WHERE id = 'S' AND age < N;
```

Here, `'S'` and `N` indicate where the query contains string and numeric data values, respectively.

Along with each query, `mysqldumpslow` shows the number of times it appears in the log, the user who issued it, and some execution time information.

Normally, the slow query log can be found, if it is enabled, in the server's data directory. Configuration options for enabling it, specifying its name and location, and changing the value of "slow" are provided in Chapter 24, "Starting, Stopping, and Configuring MySQL."

Optimizing the Environment

This chapter discusses how to configure your hardware and operating system to make MySQL perform better. It covers the following exam topics:

- Choosing hardware for MySQL use
- Network performance factors
- Configuring disks for MySQL use
- Configuring your operating system for MySQL use

41.1 Choosing Hardware for MySQL Use

MySQL can benefit from improvements to several subsystems of your hardware configuration. The following list describes the significant factors, with the most important ones first:

- Add more memory to allow larger buffers to be used. This improves caching so that disk activity can be minimized. The performance effect can be considerable because it's much faster to read information from memory than from disk. Adding memory also can reduce the amount of swapping the operating system needs to do.

- Maximize on-board processing power:
  - Use a 64-bit CPU rather than a 32-bit CPU. A 64-bit CPU allows certain mathematical (and other) functions to complete faster. It also allows MySQL to support larger internal cache sizes.
  - Use a multiprocessor system. If MySQL uses kernel threads, it can take advantage of multiple processors.
  - A faster main logic board (motherboard) improves general system throughput.

- Use a faster network, so that the server can transfer information to clients faster. This lets the server process queries faster, reducing resource contention.

- Choose disks with better performance.

Network and disk issues to consider are discussed in more detail later in the chapter.

41.2 Configuring Disks for MySQL Use

The MySQL server makes heavy use of disk resources. All storage engines except the MEMORY engine store table contents on disk, and log files are recorded on disk. Consequently, the physical characteristics of your disks and disk-related subsystems strongly influence server performance:

- Physical disk characteristics are important because slow disks hinder the server. However, disk "speed" can be measured in various ways, and the most important parameter is seek time, not transfer rate. It's more important for the heads to move quickly from track to track than for the platters to spin more quickly. A RAM disk reduces seek time to near zero, because there is no physical movement at all.

- With a heavy I/O burden, a faster disk controller helps improve disk subsystem throughput. So does installing an additional controller and dividing disk assignments between controllers.

- RAID drives can improve retrieval performance, and some forms of RAID also boost write performance. Other benefits of RAID drives include data redundancy through mirroring and parity checking. Some RAID systems enable you to replace a disk without powering down the server host.

Using disks with better physical characteristics is one way to improve server performance. In addition, the way you employ your disks has a bearing on performance. The following list describes some key strategies for better using your disks:

- Distributing parts of your MySQL installation onto different disks can improve performance by splitting up database-related disk activity to distribute it more evenly. You can do this in several ways:

  - Put log files on one disk and databases on another disk. This can be done using server options; each option that enables a log allows you to specify the log file location. To move the entire data directory, copy it to a different location and specify the new location with the --datadir option.

  - Use a separate disk for temporary file storage. This can be done using the --tmpdir server option.

  - Distribute databases among several disks. To do this for a given database, move it to a different location, and then create a symbolic link in the data directory that points to the new location of the database. Section 41.2.1, "Moving Databases Using Symbolic Links," discusses how to implement this technique.

  - A strategy for distributing disk activity that's possible but not necessarily recommended is to put individual MyISAM tables on different disks by using CREATE TABLE options. This technique is described in Section 41.2.2, "MyISAM Table Symlinking," but it does have some drawbacks. Table symlinking is not universally supported on all systems, and spreading your tables around can make it difficult to keep track of how much table storage you're using on which file systems. In addition, some filesystem commands do not understand symbolic links.

- Use a type of filesystem that is suited for the tables you have. MySQL can run on pretty much any kind of filesystem supported by your operating system, but some types of filesystems might be better for your installation than others. Two factors to consider are the maximum table size you need and the number of tables in your database.

  In general, you can use larger MyISAM tables with filesystems or operating systems that allow larger files. The MyISAM storage engine has an internal file size limit of 65,536TB, but MyISAM tables cannot actually use files that large unless the filesystem allows it. For example, older Linux kernels may impose a size limit of 2GB. If you use a recent Linux kernel instead, the file size limit goes up considerably and the MySQL server can create much larger MyISAM tables.

  The number of tables in a database can have an effect on table-opening time and on the time to check files after a machine crash. For example, because MySQL represents a MyISAM table on disk by three files (the .frm format file, the .MYD data file, and the .MYI index file), that translates into many small files in the database directory if you have many small MyISAM tables in a database. For some filesystem types, this results in significantly increased directory lookup times when opening the files associated with tables. In situations like this, filesystems such as ReiserFS or ext3 can help performance. They're designed to deal well with large numbers of small files and to provide good directory lookup time. Also, the recovery time to check the filesystem after a machine crash is very good, so the MySQL server becomes available again faster.

Table use is subject to the read/write characteristics of the filesystem on which tables are located. It's most common for MySQL installations to store databases and tables on media that are readable and writable, so that both retrieval and update operations can be performed. However, it's possible to initialize a database and then modify the properties of the filesystem on which it is located to disable write access, or to copy a database to read-only media such as CD-ROM. In both cases, the server must only perform retrievals from a disk-based table. Any attempt to issue a query that updates a table fails with an error. MEMORY tables are an exception to this, because table contents reside in memory.

41.2.1 Moving Databases Using Symbolic Links

MySQL represents each database by means of a directory located in the data directory. It is possible to reconfigure the data directory by moving individual databases elsewhere and replacing them with symbolic links in the data directory. Reasons to do this are to achieve redistribution of storage and disk I/O:

- Moving databases to different filesystems can free up disk space on the filesystem that contains the data directory.

- If databases are moved to filesystems that are on different physical devices, database-related disk I/O is distributed among those devices.

The procedure for moving individual databases differs for Windows and Unix. Use the instructions in the following sections. While moving a database, be sure that the MySQL server isn't running.

41.2.1.1 Using Database Symbolic Links on Windows

To relocate a database directory under Windows, use the following procedure:

1. Stop the server if it is running.
2. Move the database directory from the data directory to its new location.
3. In the data directory, create a file that has a basename that's the same as the database name and an extension of .sym. The file should contain the full pathname to the new database location. This .sym file is the symbolic link that enables MySQL Server to find the database in its new location. For example, if you move the world database directory to a new location of D:\world, you must create a world.sym file in the data directory that contains the pathname D:\world.
4. Restart the server.

Use of database symlinking on Windows is subject to the condition that you have not started the server with the --skip-symbolic-links option.

41.2.1.2 Using Database Symbolic Links on Unix

To relocate a database directory under Unix, use the following procedure:

1. Stop the server if it is running.
2. Move the database directory from the data directory to its new location.
3. In the data directory, create a symbolic link that has the same name as the database and that points to the new database location. For example, if you move the world database directory to a new location of /opt/data/world, you must create a symbolic link named world in the data directory that points to /opt/data/world. If the data directory is /usr/local/mysql/data, create the symbolic link like this:

```
shell> cd /usr/local/mysql/data
shell> ln -s /opt/data/world world
```

4. Restart the server.

41.2.2 MyISAM Table Symlinking

By default, a MyISAM table for a given database is created in the database directory under the data directory. This means that the .frm, .MYD, and .MYI files are created in the database directory. It's possible to create the table such that the data file or index file (or both) are located elsewhere. You might do this to distribute storage for the table to a filesystem with more free space, for example. If the filesystem is on a different physical disk, moving the files has the additional effect of distributing database-related disk activity, which might improve performance.

To relocate a table's data file or index file, use the DATA DIRECTORY or INDEX DIRECTORY options in the CREATE TABLE statement. For example, to put both files for a table t in the directory /var/mysql-alt/data/test, use a statement like this:

```
CREATE TABLE t (i INT)
DATA DIRECTORY = '/var/mysql-alt/data/test'
INDEX DIRECTORY = '/var/mysql-alt/data/test';
```

This statement puts the data and index files in the same directory. To put the files in different directories, specify different pathnames for each option. You can also relocate one file only and leave the other in its default location (the database directory) by omitting either the DATA DIRECTORY or the INDEX DIRECTORY option from the CREATE TABLE statement. Directory names for DATA DIRECTORY and INDEX DIRECTORY must be specified as full (absolute) pathnames, not as relative pathnames.

The server implements data file or index file relocation by creating the file in the directory that you specify and placing in the database directory a symbolic link to the file. You can do the same thing manually to relocate an existing MyISAM table's data file or index file, as long as the server does not have the table open and is not using it. For each file to be relocated, use this procedure:

- Move the file to a different directory.
- Create a symlink in the database directory that points to the new location of the moved file.

Table symlinking is subject to the following restrictions:

- It does not work on Windows.
- On Unix, the operating system must have a working realpath() system call, and must have thread-safe symlinks.
- You must not have started the server with the --skip-symbolic-links option.

Relocating MyISAM data files and index files as just described makes it somewhat more difficult to keep track of just where your table files are located or how table storage space is distributed among your filesystems. Thus, although it's possible to relocate MyISAM tables using symlinking, it isn't necessarily recommended as an everyday technique. If you're thinking about relocating several MyISAM tables in a database, consider the simpler alternative of relocating the entire database directory and replacing the original database directory under the data directory with a symbolic link that points to the new location. This is just as effective as moving many tables individually, but requires only a single symlink. For instructions, see Section 41.2.1, "Moving Databases Using Symbolic Links."

41.3 Network Issues

If your MySQL server and its clients all run on the same machine, the clients can connect to the server using local interfaces such as shared memory on Windows or a socket file on Unix. These interfaces require no traffic to cross an external network. In such a configuration, networking performance is a minimal concern.

However, many MySQL installations are more distributed, and the server and its clients do not necessarily run on the same machine. For example, the MySQL server might run on a machine that is dedicated to it, with clients all connecting to the server from other machines. In distributed environments, you should think about factors that affect the performance of your network:

- Network speed is important. With a faster network, the server can transfer information to clients faster. This lets the server process queries faster, reducing resource contention. Consider using gigabit ethernet if your situation allows.

- The speed of your networks, although important, is not the only significant factor. All other things being equal, the network is effectively faster for clients that are near to the server than for those far away. Information need not travel as far for closer clients, so the latency of response is not as great. If possible, keep the network path short. The introduction of routers, switches, and other devices along the way also can increase latency.

41.4 Optimizing the Operating System for MySQL Use

MySQL has many configurable parameters that you can change to optimize server performance. Several of these are related to operating system resources and thus cannot be set higher than what the operating system allows. MySQL operates within the boundaries of the limits set by the OS. For example, you might request enough file descriptors to be able to open 2,000 files at once, but the effective limit is 1,000 if that is how many descriptors the operating system allows to each process. You can sometimes gain more latitude by increasing operating system limits; then the MySQL server can take advantage of the higher limits. Some of the relevant operating system limits include the following:

- The per-process limit on the number of open files. This limits the maximum size of the table cache that holds file descriptors for table files. You can tell MySQL to allocate more file descriptors with the `--open-files-limit` option, but that option cannot be increased beyond the per-process limit allowed by the operating system. If your operating system can be reconfigured, you might be able to increase this limit, which effectively allows a larger maximum table cache size.

- The maximum number of clients that can be connected simultaneously. This limit is controlled by the max_connections server variable. You can increase this variable, but not beyond the number of threads allowed to each process by the operating system. (Thread allocation is the limiting factor because each connection is handled by a separate thread within the server.) To allow more connections than that, you must reconfigure the operating system to allow more threads.

- The number of queued network connections for clients that are waiting to connect. For a busy server with a high rate of client connections, increasing the backlog allowed by the operating system allows you to increase the value of the back_log server variable that governs the size of the server's queue.

42

Scaling MySQL

This chapter discusses how to scale MySQL operations up to include multiple servers. It covers the following exam topics:

- Running multiple servers on a single host
- Replicating databases from one server to another

42.1 Using Multiple Servers

It's common to run a single MySQL server on a given machine, but it's possible to run multiple servers. This is a common scenario when you want to test a new release of MySQL on the same machine where you run your production server. Use of multiple servers also might be desirable for administrative purposes. If clients can be partitioned into groups that use distinct databases, you can run multiple servers, each one serving a single group of clients. Each group can have its own designated root user, and that root user won't be able to see databases that belong to other groups, as would be possible if all clients were to share the same server.

Managing multiple servers is a more complex undertaking than running a single server because you must make sure that the servers do not interfere with each other. None of the servers can share resources that must be used exclusively by a single server. These resources include the following:

- Each server normally manages its own data directory. On Windows, this is a requirement. On Unix, it is possible (though not recommended) for servers to share a data directory under certain circumstances:
  - If the data directory is located on read-only media, there won't be a problem of multiple servers attempting updates of the same data simultaneously. (This precludes use of InnoDB tables because InnoDB currently cannot be used on read-only media.)
  - On read-write media, external locking must be enabled so that servers can cooperate for access to database files. However, external locking does not work on

all systems, is disabled by default, and does not apply to the InnoDB storage engine anyway.

- Each server must have its own network interfaces, including the TCP/IP port, the named pipe or shared memory (on Windows), and the Unix socket file (on Unix). One server cannot use network interfaces that are used by another server; it will not even start up properly if it discovers that its network interfaces are already in use. Note that it isn't necessary to set up multiple hostnames for the server host. All the MySQL servers running on a given host can share the same hostname. They can also share the same IP address as long as they listen on different TCP/IP port numbers.

- Under Windows, each server that is run as a service must use a unique service name.

- Each server must have its own log files. Multiple servers writing to the same log files results in unusable logs. This is also true for status files such as the PID file in which a server records its process ID.

- InnoDB tablespace files cannot be shared by multiple servers. Each server that uses InnoDB must have its own tablespace. The same is true of the InnoDB log files.

To make sure that each server manages a different data directory, start each one with a unique value for the --datadir option. Normally, having distinct data directories is sufficient to ensure distinct sets of log files and InnoDB files as well, because those files are created by default in the data directory if you specify their names using relative pathnames.

On Unix, you can ensure that each server uses its own network interfaces by starting each with a unique value for the --port and --socket options to set up the TCP/IP and Unix socket file interfaces. On Windows, the --port option applies for TCP/IP; for servers that allow named-pipe or shared-memory connections, the options are as follows:

- To enable named-pipe connections, use the mysqld-nt or mysqld-max-nt server and start each instance with the --enable-named-pipe option. Each server must have a distinct pipe name, which you specify using the --socket option.

- To enable shared-memory connections, start each server with the --shared-memory option. Each server must use a different shared-memory name, which you specify using the --shared-memory-base-name option.

To set up Windows servers with distinct service names, follow the --install option of the service installation command with a service name. For example:

```
shell> mysqld --install mysql1
shell> mysqld --install mysql2
```

Installed that way, when the servers start, they will read options from the [mysql1] and [mysql2] groups, respectively, in the standard option files. They'll also read options in the [mysqld] group as usual, which you can use for any options that are common to both services.

Another way to install MySQL as a service is to follow the service name with an option naming the file from which the server should read options when it starts:

```
shell> mysqld --install mysql1 --defaults-file=C:\mysql1.cnf
shell> mysqld --install mysql2 --defaults-file=C:\mysql2.cnf
```

In this case, each server ignores the standard option files when it starts and instead reads options only from the [mysqld] group of the option file named by the --defaults-file option.

Each server installed as a Windows service can read the appropriate options for the data directory location and network interfaces from whichever option file and group is unique to it.

On Windows, management of multiple servers is easiest if they all run as Windows services. Then you can use the native Windows tools such as the Services program that provides a graphical interface for service management. MySQL Administrator also can control MySQL services. If the MySQL servers do not run as services, you must start them manually and stop them using mysqladmin.

On Unix, some administrative assistance is available for controlling multiple servers. mysqld_multi is a Perl script intended to make it easier to manage multiple servers on a single host. It can start or stop servers, or report on whether servers are running. mysqld_multi can either start servers directly, or indirectly by invoking mysqld_safe. (An advantage of using mysqld_safe is that it sets up the error log and monitors the server.) mysqld_multi requires installation of the Perl DBI module.

MySQL AB currently is developing another program called MySQL Instance Manager to be used for multiple-server management. This program will offer some significant improvements over mysqld_multi and eventually will replace it. For example, mysqld_multi can stop local or remote servers, but can start only local servers. With MySQL Instance Manager, it will be possible to start remote servers as well.

MySQL Instance Manager is planned for cross-platform deployment, so it will also be able to control servers on Windows.

42.2 Replication

MySQL supports replication capabilities that allow the databases on one server to be made available on another server. Replication is used for many purposes. For example, by replicating your databases, you have multiple copies available in case a server crashes or goes offline. Clients can use a different server if the one that they normally use becomes unavailable. Replication also can be used to distribute client load. Rather than having a single server to which all clients connect, you can set up multiple servers that each handle a fraction of the client load.

MySQL replication uses a master/slave architecture:

- The server that manages the original databases is the master.

- Any server that manages a copy of the original databases is a slave.

- A given master server can have many slaves, but a slave can have only a single master. (If done with care, it is possible to set up two-way or circular replication, but this study guide does not describe how.)

A replication slave is set up initially by transferring an exact copy of the to-be-replicated databases from the master server to the slave server. Thereafter, each replicated database is kept synchronized to the original database. When the master server makes modifications to its databases, it sends those changes to each slave server, which makes the changes to its copy of the replicated databases.

42.2.1 Setting Up Replication

To set up replication, each slave requires the following:

- A backup copy of the master's databases. This is the replication "baseline" that sets the slave to a known initial state of the master.

- The filename and position within the master's binary log that corresponds to the time of the backup. The values are called the "replication coordinates." They are needed so that the slave can tell the master that it wants all updates made from that point on.

- An account on the master server that the slave can use for connecting to the master and requesting updates. The account must have the global REPLICATION SLAVE privilege. For example, you can set up an account for a slave by issuing these statements on the master server, where *slave_user* and *slave_pass* are the username and password for the account, and *slave_host* is the host from which the slave server will connect:

```
mysql> CREATE USER 'slave_user'@'slave_host' IDENTIFIED BY 'slave_pass';
mysql> GRANT REPLICATION SLAVE ON *.* TO 'slave_user'@'slave_host';
```

Also, you must assign a unique ID value to each server that will participate in your replication setup. ID values are positive integers in the range from 1 to $2^{32} - 1$. The easiest way to assign these ID values is by placing a server-id option in each server's option file:

```
[mysqld]
server-id=id_value
```

It's common, though not required, to use an ID of 1 for the master server and values greater than 1 for the slaves.

The following procedure describes the general process for setting up replication. It is an overview only; for complete details, see the replication chapter of the *MySQL Reference Manual*.

1. Ensure that binary logging is enabled on the master server. If it is not, stop the server, enable logging, and restart the server.

2. On the master server, make a backup of all databases to be replicated. One way to do this is by using mysqldump:

```
shell> mysqldump --all-databases --master-data=2 > dump_file
```

   Assuming that binary logging is enabled, the --master-data=2 option causes the dump file to include a comment containing a CHANGE MASTER statement that indicates the replication coordinates as of the time of the backup. These coordinates can be used later when you tell the slave where to begin replicating in the master's binary log.

   For other backup techniques, see Chapter 32, "Data Backup and Recovery Methods." Whichever technique you use, you must know the exact replication coordinates that correspond to the backup time.

3. Copy the dump file to the replication slave host and load it into the MySQL server on that machine:

```
shell> mysql < dump_file
```

4. Tell the slave what master to connect to and the position in the master's binary log at which to begin replicating. To do this, connect to the slave server and issue a CHANGE MASTER statement:

```
mysql> CHANGE MASTER TO
    -> MASTER_HOST = 'master_host_name',
    -> MASTER_USER = 'slave_user',
    -> MASTER_PASSWORD = 'slave_pass',
    -> MASTER_LOG_FILE = 'master_log_file',
    -> MASTER_LOG_POS = master_log_pos;
```

   The hostname is the host where the master server is running. The username and password are those for the slave account that you set up on the master. The log file and position are the replication coordinates in the master's binary log. (You can get these from the CHANGE MASTER statement near the beginning of the dump file.)

After you perform the preceding procedure, issue a START SLAVE statement. The slave should connect to the master and begin replicating updates that the master sends to it. The slave also creates a master.info file in its data directory and records the values from the CHANGE MASTER statement in the file. As the slave reads updates from the master, it changes the replication coordinates in the master.info file accordingly. Also, when the slave restarts in the future, it looks in this file to determine which master to use.

By default, the master server logs updates for all databases, and the slave server replicates all updates that it receives from the master. For more fine-grained control, it's possible to tell a master which databases to log updates for, and to tell a slave which of those updates that it receives from the master to apply. You can either name databases to be replicated (in which case those not named are ignored), or you can name databases to ignore (in which case those not named are replicated). The master host options are `--binlog-do-db` and `--binlog-ignore-db`. The slave host options are `--replicate-do-db` and `--replicate-ignore-db`.

The following example illustrates how this works, using the options that enable replication for specific databases. Suppose that a master server has three databases named a, b, and c. You can elect to replicate only databases a and b when you start the master server by placing these options in an option file read by that server:

```
[mysqld]
binlog-do-db = a
binlog-do-db = b
```

With those options, the master server will log updates only for the named databases to the binary log. Thus, any slave server that connects to the master will receive information only for databases a and b.

Enabling binary logging only for certain databases has an unfortunate side effect: Data recovery operations require both your backup files and your binary logs, so for any database not logged in the binary log, full recovery cannot be performed. For this reason, you might prefer to have the master log changes for all databases to the binary log, and instead filter updates on the slave side.

A slave that takes no filtering action will replicate all events that it receives. If a slave should replicate events only for certain databases, such as databases a and c, you can start it with these lines in an option file:

```
[mysqld]
replicate-do-db = a
replicate-do-db = c
```

42.2.2 The Binary and Relay Logs

The master server's binary log is the basis for communication between the master and its slaves:

- When the master server makes modifications to its databases, it records the changes in its binary log files. Statements are stored in the log as "events."
- Events recorded in the binary log are sent to each connected slave server, which makes the changes to its copy of the replicated databases. A slave server that isn't connected to the master when an event is recorded will receive the event when it connects later.

When a slave receives an update from the master, it doesn't change its own databases immediately. Instead, it records the event in its relay log. The relay log is stored on disk and processed later, as described in Section 42.2.3, "Replication-Related Threads." The delay normally is minimal for an active slave, but you can defer relay log processing if you want to perform slave maintenance while allowing the slave to continue to receive updates from the master.

42.2.3 Replication-Related Threads

Replication processing involves three threads per master/slave relationship. One thread runs on the master and two on the slave. The slave threads are known as the "I/O thread" and the "SQL thread" because one communicates with the master to receive events and the other processes SQL statements contained in the received events.

Replication threads interact as follows:

1. To begin receiving replication events, an I/O thread starts on the slave server and connects to the master server.
2. The master starts a thread as a connection handler for the slave I/O thread.
3. The master server sends events from its binary log files to the slave I/O thread, which records them in the slave's relay log files. The relay log stores events to be executed later. It has the same storage format as the binary log.
4. The slave SQL thread processes the contents of the relay log files. When it starts, it reads events from the relay logs and executes them. As it finishes processing each relay log file, it deletes it if the I/O thread is writing to a newer relay log. If the SQL thread is reading the same relay log that the I/O thread is writing, the SQL thread pauses until more events are available in the file.

The two slave threads operate asynchronously and it is not necessary for both of them to be running at the same time. You can start or stop them independently with the START SLAVE *thread_type* or STOP SLAVE *thread_type* statements, where *thread_type* is IO_THREAD or SQL_THREAD. This decoupled relationship between slave threads offers certain benefits:

- If a problem occurs while executing events, the SQL thread stops until the problem is resolved. However, the I/O thread can continue to run and receive events from the master server. Events for the slave do not become backlogged on the master.
- A replication slave is, in effect, a copy of its master. This means that you can use the slave for making backups by stopping the SQL thread to prevent changes to databases on the slave (and flushing the logs to force pending changes to disk). Then make the backup on the slave side. The I/O thread can continue to run and record events in the relay log. After making the backup, restart the SQL thread and it processes the pending events received by the I/O thread during the backup. See Section 32.6, "Replication as an Aid to Backup."

You can see whether replication threads are running by using the SHOW PROCESSLIST statement. On the master server, a thread that is serving a slave has a Command value of Binlog Dump:

```
mysql> SHOW PROCESSLIST\G
*************************** 1. row ***************************
     Id: 36693
   User: slaveuser
   Host: localhost:4934
     db: NULL
Command: Binlog Dump
   Time: 2272
  State: Has sent all binlog to slave; waiting for binlog to
         be updated
   Info: NULL
```

The State value in this case shows that the master has no events waiting to be sent to the slave. The value is Sending binlog event to slave while the master is transmitting events.

There will be one Binlog Dump thread on the master for each connected slave. Use SHOW SLAVE HOSTS to see a list of connected slaves.

For a replication slave, SHOW PROCESSLIST displays zero to two replication threads, depending on whether the I/O and SQL threads are running. Both threads have a Command value of Connect, but you can distinguish which is which based on the State value. For example, the following output indicates that thread 9 is the I/O thread because its State value refers to communication with the master. Thread 10 is the SQL thread because it is reading the relay log and because it refers to the other thread as the I/O thread:

```
mysql> SHOW PROCESSLIST\G
*************************** 1. row ***************************
     Id: 9
   User: system user
   Host:
     db: NULL
Command: Connect
   Time: 13
  State: Waiting for master to send event
   Info: NULL
*************************** 2. row ***************************
     Id: 10
   User: system user
   Host:
     db: NULL
Command: Connect
   Time: 50
```

```
    State: Has read all relay log; waiting for the I/O slave
           thread to update it
     Info: NULL
```

Other I/O thread State values usually refer in some way to the master server, the binary log, or the SQL thread. Other SQL thread State values usually refer to reading the relay logs, or, if the thread currently is executing a SQL statement, the State value contains the text of the statement.

42.2.4 Replication Troubleshooting

If replication fails, there are some general strategies you can use to diagnose and resolve the problem. Begin by verifying that replication has gotten started in the first place. If it has, check the current replication status for information about why it stopped.

To see whether replication has gotten started, check the slave's error log for messages that indicate a failure to connect to the master. You can also use the SHOW SLAVE STATUS statement, which indicates whether the slave threads are running. If replication has failed to start, likely causes include the following:

- The master and slave were not configured with the slave-id option, or their ID values are not unique. Check each server's option file and make sure that they contain server-id options that have different values.

- The master server does not have the binary log enabled. Without binary logging, the master has no means of recording events to communicate to slave servers. Enable binary logging if it is not turned on.

- The master server does not allow connections from the slave. Verify that you can connect to the server using the designated replication account. (From the slave host, try connecting to the master server manually using the mysql client.)

If the slave can connect to the master but replication is not proceeding, issue a SHOW SLAVE STATUS statement to check whether the slave threads are running. If not, use START SLAVE to start them. If the SQL thread still does not start, check the error information in the output from SHOW SLAVE STATUS. This often indicates a statement that the slave has trouble processing, which gives a clue to the underlying problem.

Another source of monitoring information is the MySQL Administrator program, which has a Replication Status section that displays replication status information. See Chapter 26, "MySQL Administrator."

42.2.5 Replication Compatibility and Upgrading

As replication capabilities continue to develop, the format of the binary log changes on occasion to accommodate the need to record new kinds of events. For example, log format changes occurred in MySQL 4.0 and again several times in early versions of MySQL 5.0.

The format likely will change again in MySQL 5.1. Because master/slave communication is based on the binary log, these format changes have implications for compatibility and for upgrading:

- The master and its slaves must be able to communicate, so compatibility with a master is possible only for a slave that understands the log format used by the master.

- When you upgrade servers used for replication, take care not to upgrade a master or slave to a version of MySQL that cannot understand the log format used by the other.

Compatibility between replication servers is always best if both servers run the same version of MySQL. As a general rule, for a master and server of dissimilar versions, compatibility often is possible for a newer slave replicating from an older master, but not for an older slave replication from a newer master. In the latter case, the master may sent events in a format that the slave simply cannot interpret.

In addition to the compatibility constraint imposed by the binary log format, incompatibilities may occur at the SQL level. For example, statements executed on the master may use new features that are not available to the older slave server. For example, statements that refer to views cannot be replicated from a MySQL 5 master to a MySQL 4.1 slave because views are not available before MySQL 5. The *MySQL Reference Manual* provides a detailed list of SQL-level constraints on replication compatibility that apply to dissimilar-version master/slave server pairs.

An implication of the preceding remarks is that you should not upgrade a master server before upgrading its slaves. Also, if you're upgrading servers using early (pre-production) versions within a release series for which a binary log format change has been introduced, you should ensure that all the servers are exactly the same version. During early development of a format change, modifications might occur in each release that produces incompatibilities with the previous release. (For example, a MySQL 5.0.3 master cannot replicate to a 5.0.2 slave.)

Appendixes

A

References

Errata for this book are published in the certification section of the MySQL Web site at `http://www.mysql.com/certification/studyguides`.

The *MySQL Certification Candidate Guide* contains the latest details on the certification program, practical details, exam overview, and more. It is available online at `http://www.mysql.com/certification`.

The *MySQL Reference Manual* is the primary source of information on MySQL. It is available in book form and online in several formats and languages from the MySQL AB Web site (`http://dev.mysql.com`). Many other books on MySQL are available in your local bookstore.

The *MySQL Developer's Zone* at `http://dev.mysql.com` is constantly updated with technical articles, many of which refer to subjects covered in this book.

MySQL software may be downloaded from the Developer's Zone of the MySQL Web site, `http://dev.mysql.com`. Other MySQL products may be purchased at `https://shop.mysql.com`.

For many years, the *MySQL mailing lists* have been the primary meeting place for the MySQL community. Archives and signup for the lists are available at `http://lists.mysql.com`. Among the mailing lists is a low-volume list specifically for MySQL certification announcements.

The *MySQL Forums* at `http://forums.mysql.com` cover many different aspects related to MySQL, including certification.

MySQL partners that offer services related to MySQL products and services can be found at `http://solutions.mysql.com`.

B

Other Offers

This study guide serves as an aid to preparing for the MySQL AB Developer and DBA certification exams. MySQL AB also offers training, support, and consulting services. These services can help you use your MySQL installation more effectively, keep it running smoothly, and solve any problems that arise.

- MySQL offers you the most comprehensive set of MySQL training courses that enable you to build database solutions and stay competitive now and into the future. In addition to our open courses, we also offer in-house training. For more information, please see `http://www.mysql.com/training`.

- MySQL AB offers a full range of support options for your specific needs. MySQL Technical Support is designed to save you time and to ensure proper functioning of your MySQL databases. The most complete and economical support is available through MySQL Network. MySQL Network includes technical support services that are designed to ensure that your production database applications are continuously available. For more information, please see `http://www.mysql.com/support`.

- MySQL AB offers a full range of consulting services. Whether you are starting a new project, needing to optimize an existing MySQL application, or migrating from a proprietary database to MySQL, we have an affordable solution for you. Using industry best practices and proven methodologies, your MySQL certified consultant will help you deliver on time and on budget. For more information, please see `http://www.mysql.com/consulting`.

Index

NUMBERS

A

How can we make this index more useful? Email us at indexes@samspublishing.com

metadata, displaying, 106-107

moving via symbolic links, 569-570

performance optimization strategies, 568

removing, warnings, 105

renaming, 105

replication

binary logs, 580

master/slave compatibility, 584

relay logs, 580-581

replication threads, 581-582

server upgrades, 584

troubleshooting, 583

SCHEMA keyword, 104

specific database privileges, 475

stored routines, namespace, 284

table normalization

1NF, 526-528

2NF, 526, 529

3NF, 526, 529

benefits of, 531

table optimization

general design principles, 523-524

InnoDB tables, 541-542

MEMORY tables, 543

MERGE tables, 542-543

MyISAM tables, 531-541

PROCEDURE ANALYSE(), 524-525

tables, performance optimization strategies, 569

--databases option

mysqlcheck client, 441

mysqldump client, 272, 459

DATE_FORMAT() function, 72

DATE temporal data type, 72-73

DATETIME temporal data type, 72-73

deadlocks, 401

DEALLOCATE PREPARE statement, prepared statements, 279

DECIMAL fixed-point data type, 63

DECLARE CURSOR statement, stored routines, 295

DECLARE HANDLER statement, 294-295

DECLARE statement, stored routines, 291

declaring parameters in stored routines, 289-290

DECODE() function, 189

DEFAULT clause, missing data values (input data handling), 92

DEFAULT column attribute, 83

DEFAULT CURRENT_TIMESTAMP attribute, TIMESTAMP temporal data type, 74-78

--defaults-extra-file option, option files, 30

--defaults-file option, option files, 30

DEFINER security characteristic (stored routines), 469-470

defining

indexes at index creation, 123-124

stored routines, 284

compound statements, 287-288, 298

conditions, 294

CREATE FUNCTION statement, 285-287

CREATE PROCEDURE statement, 285-287

cursors, 295-296

DECLARE statement, 291

declaring parameters, 289-290

flow control, 298

handlers, 293-294

SELECT INTO statement, 292

SET statement, 292

variables, 291-292

DELAYED modifier, MyISAM tables, 410-411

DELETE statement

LIMIT clause, 205

optimization, 343

ORDER BY clause, 205

required privileges, 206

tables, emptying, 121

WHERE clause, 204

F

N

S

MySQL Server
  runtime configurations, 370
  startup methods, 367-368
  startup prerequisites, 365-367
UNLOCK TABLES statement, 402
UNSIGNED numeric column attribute, 82, 87
UPDATE privilege
  trigger updates, 312
  user account management, 473
UPDATE statement
  LIMIT clause, 203
  optimization, 343
  ORDER BY clause, 203
  required privileges, 206
  SET clause, 202, 226
  WHERE clause, 202-204, 226
  WITH CHECK OPTION clause, 251-253
updates
  data
    DELETE statement, 204-206, 226
    INSERT statement, 194-198, 206
    REPLACE statement, 199-201, 206
    TRUNCATE TABLE statement, 204-206
    UPDATE statement, 202-206, 226
  indexes, disabling, 344
  MySQL, 377-378
  mysql client, --safe-updates option, 44
  optimization, 343-344
  optimizer, MyISAM table optimization, 537
  subqueries, 241
  tables
    DELETE statement, 205-206, 226
    index effects on performance, 333
    UPDATE statement, 204, 226
  views, 250-253
upgrades
  grant tables, security, 501
  privilege tables, security, 501
  servers, replication, 584

SQL mode values, security, 502-503
UPPER() function, 175
Uptime server status variable, 552
USE statement, selecting/changing databases as default, 30
user accounts
  managing
    administrative privileges list, 474
    applying changes, 484
    changing passwords, 484
    CREATE USER statement, 478, 485
    database-access privileges list, 475
    database-specific privileges, 475
    DROP USER statement, 478, 486
    global privileges, 475
    GRANT statement, 480-481, 485-486
    grant tables, 474-477
    granting privileges, 480-481
    privilege specifiers, 475
    PROCESS privilege, 473
    RENAME USER statement, 478, 486
    required privileges, 485-486
    REVOKE statement, 482-483, 486
    revoking privileges, 482-483
    SELECT privilege, 473
    SET PASSWORD statement, 484-486
    SHOW GRANTS statement, 481-482, 486
    SHUTDOWN privilege, 473
    specifying account names, 478-479
    specifying resource limits, 485
    stored routine-specific privileges, 476
    SUPER privilege, 473
    table column-specific privileges, 476
    table-specific privileges, 476
    UPDATE privilege, 473
    viewing privileges, 481-482
  modifying, 477
  security, 496-498